D0266398

OXFORD EUROPEAN COMMUNITY LAW SERIES

General Editor: F.G. Jacobs
Advocate General, The Court of Justice
of the European Communities

Directives in European Community Law

OXFORD EUROPEAN COMMUNITY LAW SERIES

The aim of this series is to publish important and original studies of the various branches of European Community Law. Each work will provide a clear, concise, and critical exposition of the law in its social, economic, and political context, at a level which will interest the advanced student, the practitioner, the academic, and government and Community officials.

Other Titles in this Series

The European Internal Market and International Trade: A Legal Analysis
P. Eeckhout

The Law of Money and Financial Services in the European Community
J.A. Usher

Legal Aspects of Agriculture in the European Community
J.A. Usher

European Community Sex Equality Law
Evelyn Ellis

European Community Competition Law
Second Edition
Dan Goyder

EC Tax Law
Paul Farmer and Richard Lyal

European Community Company Law
Vanessa Edwards (forthcoming)

Directives in European Community Law

A Study of Directives and Their Enforcement in National Courts

SACHA PRECHAL

Professor of European Community Law, Tilburg University

CLARENDON PRESS · OXFORD
1995

STAFFORDSHIRE UNIVERSITY LIBRARY

Oxford University Press, Walton Street, Oxford OX2 6DP

Oxford New York
Athens Auckland Bangkok Bombay
Calcutta Cape Town Dar es Salaam Delhi
Florence Hong Kong Istanbul Karachi
Kuala Lumpur Madras Madrid Melbourne
Mexico City Nairobi Paris Singapore
Taipei Tokyo Toronto

and associated companies in
Berlin Ibadan

Oxford is a trade mark of Oxford University Press

Published in the United States
by Oxford University Press Inc., New York

© *Sacha Prechal 1995*

All rights reserved. No part of this publication may be reproduced, stored in a retrieval system, or transmitted, in any form or by any means, without the prior permission in writing of Oxford University Press. Within the UK, exceptions are allowed in respect of any fair dealing for the purpose of research or private study, or criticism or review, as permitted under the Copyright, Designs and Patents Act, 1988, or in the case of reprographic reproduction in accordance with the terms of the licences issued by the Copyright Licensing Agency. Enquiries concerning reproduction outside these terms and in other countries should be sent to the Rights Department, Oxford University Press, at the address above.

British Library Cataloguing in Publication Data
Data available

Library of Congress Cataloguing in Publication Data
Data available
ISBN 0-19-826016-4

03354006

1 3 5 7 9 10 8 6 4 2

Typeset by NISER, The Netherlands

Printed in Great Britain
on acid-free paper by
Biddles Ltd., Guildford and King's Lynn

STAFFORDSHIRE
UNIVERSITY
19 MAR 1996
CLASS No.
349. 4
QWK

General Editor's Foreword

In the fifteen Member States of the European Union, a very high proportion of social and economic legislation now has as its essential purpose the implementation of EC directives; this is the case in labour law, in environmental law, in fiscal law, in company law and in a variety of other fields. By far the greater part of the Community's internal market legislation consists of directives. Increasingly, courts and tribunals in all the Member States, and lawyers advising their clients, may have to look beyond their national legislation to the Community directives on which it is based.

Yet the nature of the directive, as a legal instrument, is little understood even today, and it seems to have no true analogue in any other legal system. The distinction drawn by Article 189 of the Treaty between the two principal forms of Community legislation may have seemed reasonably clear at the outset: a regulation has general application, is binding in its entirety and is directly applicable in all Member States, while a directive is binding on Member States as to the result to be achieved, but leaves to the national authorities the choice of form and methods. The fundamental distinction remains that regulations are directly applicable while directives must be transposed into national law. But beyond that, the dichotomy is increasingly uncertain. The Community's legislative practice has been such that directives are not only binding "as to the result to be achieved", but impose very specific obligations on the legislatures of the Member States. Indeed, because of the detailed drafting of directives, the "choice of form and methods" has often proved illusory.

In consequence, issues of great theoretical, practical and even political importance have arisen: by way of example, the extent to which directives are directly enforceable in the courts of Member States in the absence of implementing national measures; the scope of the national courts' obligation to interpret national legislation so as to give effect to directives; and the extent of Member States' liability in damages where individuals are caused loss by non-implementation. On all these issues the case-law of the Court of Justice, which is authoritative for the national courts and tribunals, is still evolving, and many problems remain unresolved.

The author also addresses questions of even wider concern, notably the whole range of substantive and procedural questions raised by the enforcement of Community law in the national courts; here the Court of Justice has sought to balance, on the one hand, the need for effective protection of Community rights and effective enforcement of Community obligations, on the other hand a concern to respect so far as possible the procedural autonomy of the legal systems of the Member States.

STAFFS UNIVERSITY LIBRARY

These issues are fully discussed in this book, the first to address systematically the questions which have surfaced with increasing frequency in recent years. The book draws on an exceptionally wide range of materials, both judicial decisions and scholarly writing; it maintains a lucid and cogent argument throughout; and it certainly achieves its author's aim of writing a book accessible to lawyers from different legal cultures.

This volume is also a particularly appropriate addition to the Oxford European Community Law Series. While all previous books in the Series have dealt with areas of substantive law, the present volume addresses the nature and effect of Community legislation itself. The work will appeal to scholars, practitioners and officials and to all interested in the Community legal system and its relationship with national law. It is also a valuable complement to other books in the Series covering those areas of substantive law, such as company law, tax law and financial services law, which are themselves the subject of directives. In this way the book will illuminate and be of practical value in many areas of substantive Community law.

Francis G. Jacobs
Luxembourg,
February 1995

Preface

Twenty years ago the Court of Justice of the European Communities gave its landmark judgment in the case of Mrs Van Duyn, clearly confirming what was already being argued in the literature: EEC directives may be relied upon by individuals in national courts. Since then the case law relating to directives and their effects in national law has developed into a complex and highly technical area of Community law which is of great interest both to academic lawyers and practitioners. Not surprisingly there is now a considerable volume of material published on this subject.

The purpose of the present book is to define and analyse the European Community law on directives, to draw together the various aspects of the topic and to place it within the broader framework of enforcement of Community law in general.

I have tried to write a book which will be accessible to lawyers from different legal cultures and I have done so in the language of a legal system which is not my own. Although at the European Community level a kind of "Euro (English) legal language" is rapidly developing, this is an important consideration to keep carefully in mind while reading this book.

I have to thank many people for their assistance, either by encouragement or by advice: my former colleagues at the Court of Justice where the idea for this book started to take shape and, next, my colleagues in the Netherlands, in particular those at the Europa Institute (University of Amsterdam), who made it possible for me to complete the study within a reasonable period of time. I am greatly indebted to Professor Richard Lauwaars, former Director of the Europa Institute, who supervised this study which I will also defend as PhD thesis at the University of Amsterdam, in February 1995. Particular thanks must also go to Linda Senden, for her invaluable help in gathering the materials, to Anne Doeve, for her technical assistance, to Janet Taylor, whose unrelenting efforts in reading and re-reading the manuscript have eliminated many mistakes in my English and to Marlon Steine and Carla Groenestein, for their transformation of the manuscript into camera-ready copy.

Finally, I must thank Alex, for his patience and encouragement and his remarkable talent for disturbing me at the right moment.

Sacha Prechal
Amsterdam, December 1994

Table of Contents

STAFFS UNIVERSITY LIBRARY

Abbreviations

Anglo-Am.L.Rev.	Anglo-American Law Review
AA	Ars Aequi
AJDA	Actualité juridique. Droit administratif
Bull.EC	Bulletin of the European Communities
CDE	Cahiers de droit européen
CJEG	Cahiers juridiques de l'electricité et du gaz
CLJ	Cambridge Law Journal
CMLR	Common Market Law Reports
CMLRev.	Common Market Law Review
DöV	Die öffentliche Verwaltung
DVBl	Deutsches Verwaltungsblatt
ECHR	European Convention on Human Rights
ECR	European Court Reports
EELR	Europen Environmental Law Review
EHRR	European Human Rights Reports
ELR	European Law Review
EuGRZ	Europäische Grundrechte-Zeitschrift
EUI	European University Institute
EuR	Europarecht
EuZW	Europäische Zeitschrift für Wirtschaftsrecht
EWS	Europäische Wirtschafts- und Steuerrecht
FED	Fiscaal-Economische Documentatie
ICCRR	International Covenant on Civil and Political Rights
ICLQ	International and Comparative Law Quarterly
ILJ	Industrial Law Journal
JBL	Journal of Business Law
JCMS	Journal of Common Market Studies
JöR	Jahrbuch des öffentlichen Rechts der Gegenwart
JZ	Juristenzeitung
LIEI	Legal Issues of European Integration
LJIL	Leiden Journal of International Law
LQR	Law Quarterly Review
MJ	Maastricht Journal of European and Comparative Law
MLR	Modern Law Review
OJ	Official Journal of the European Communities
NJB	Nederlands Juristenblad
NJCM-Bulletin	Nederlands Juristen Comité voor de Mensenrechten Bulletin
NJW	Neue Juristische Wochenschrift

NTB	Nederlands Tijschrift voor Bestuursrecht
NuR	Natur und Recht
NVwZ	Neue Zeitschrift für Verwaltungsrecht
RabelsZ	Rabels Zeitschrift für ausländisches und internationales Privatrecht
RBDI	Revue belge de droit international
RFDA	Revue française de droit administratif
RIW	Recht der Internationalen Wirtschaft
RMC	Revue du Marché Commun
RTDE	Revue trimestrielle de droit européen
RW	Rechtskundig Weekblad
SEW	Sociaal-Economische Wetgeving
TBP	Tijdschrift voor Bestuurswetenschappen en Publiekrecht
TPR	Tijdschrift voor Privaatrecht
WFR	Weekblad voor Fiscaal Recht
YEL	Yearbook of European Law
ZaoRV	Zeitschrift für ausländisches öffentliches Recht und Völkerrecht
ZGR	Zeitschrift für Unternehmens- und Gesellschaftsrecht
ZRP	Zeitschrift für Rechtspolitik

Table of Cases

European Court of Justice*

Case 3/59 *Germany v. High Authority* [1960] ECR 53 170
Case 6/60 *Humblet v. Belgium* [1960] ECR 559 309, 313
Joined Cases 16 and 17/62 *Producteurs des fruits et légumes v. Council* [1962] ECR 471 15
Case 26/62 *Van Gend en Loos v. Nederlandse Administratie der belastingen* [1963] ECR 1 117, 119, 120, 124, 133, 141, 145, 146, 312, 314
Joined Cases 90-91/63 *Commission v. Luxemburg and Belgium* [1964] ECR 625 56
Case 6/64 *Costa v. ENEL* [1964] ECR 585 119, 121, 135, 147, 312
Case 27/67 *Fink Frucht v. Hauptzollamt München* [1968] ECR 223 283
Case 28/67 *Molkerei-Zentrale Westfalen v. Hauptzollamt Paderborn* [1968] ECR 143 117, 361
Case 34/67 *Lück v. Hauptzollamt Köln-Rheinau* [1968] ECR 254 151
Case 6/68 *Zuckerfabrik Watenstedt v. Council* [1968] ECR 409 15
Case 13/68 *Salgoil v. Italian Ministry of Foreign Trade* [1968] ECR 453 124, 126, 131, 151, 158, 267, 310
Case 26/69 *Commission v. France* [1970] ECR 565 39
Case 77/69 *Commission v. Belgium* [1970] ECR 237 71
Case 8/70 *Commission v. Italy* [1970] ECR 961 30, 71
Case 9/70 *Grad v. Finanzamt Traunstein* [1970] ECR 825 246, 247, 261
Case 11/70 *Internationale Handelsgesellschaft v. Einfur- und Vorratstelle für Getreide und Futtermittel* [1970] ECR 1125 121
Case 33/70 *SACE v. Italy* [1970] ECR 1213 247, 270
Case 5/71 *Zuckerfabrik Schöppenstedt v. Council* [1971] ECR 975 319
Case 7/71 *Commission v. France* [1971] ECR 1003 30
Case 48/71 *Commission v. Italy* [1972] ECR 527 30, 75, 308
Joined Cases 51-54/71 *International Fruit Company v. Produktschap voor Groente en Fruit* [1971] ECR 1107 69
Case 39/72 *Commission v. Italy* [1973] ECR 101 20, 30, 309
Case 70/72 *Commission v. Germany* [1973] ECR 813 309
Case 79/72 *Commission v. Italy* [1973] ECR 667 19, 28
Case 9/73 *Schlüter v. Hauptzollamt Lörrach* [1973] ECR 1135 263
Case 34/73 *Variola v. Italy* [1973] ECR 981 261

* For the period from 2 April [ECR I-2375] to 1 January 1994 references are made to the French version of the ECR in the hope that the missing volumes in English will appear soon.

Case 166/73 *Rheinmühlen Düsseldorf v. Einfuhr und Vorratsstelle für Getreide und Futtermittel* [1974] ECR 33 154
Case 169/73 *Compagnie Continentale v. Council* [1975] ECR 117 332
Case 2/74 *Reyners v. Belgium* [1974] ECR 631 64, 260
Case 31/74 *Galli v. Italy* [1975] ECR 47 262
Case 32/74 *Haaga* [1974] ECR 1201 203
Case 36/74 *Walrave and Koch v. Association Union Cycliste Internationale* [1074] ECR 1405 63
Case 41/74 *Van Duyn v. Home Office* [1974] ECR 1337 9, 18, 124, 167, 247-249, 264, 266, 269, 270, 277, 278, 281, 296
Joined Cases 56-60/74 *Kampffmeyer v. Commission and Council* [1976] ECR 711 334
Case 67/74 *Bonsignore v. Oberstadtdirektor der Stadt Köln* [1975] ECR 297 204, 278
Case 74/74 *CNTA v. Commission* [1975] ECR 533 335
Case 36/75 *Rutili v. Ministre de l'intérieur* [1975] ECR 1219 270, 274, 278
Case 43/75 *Defrenne v. Sabena* [1976] ECR 455 40, 63, 65, 134, 179, 260, 293, 296
Case 48/75 *Procureur du Roi v. Royer* [1976] ECR 497 89, 134, 154
Case 52/75 *Commission v. Italy* [1976] ECR 277 19, 27, 28
Case 60/75 *Russo v. AIMA* [1976] ECR 45 311
Case 111/75 *Mazzalai v. Ferrovia del Renon* [1976] ECR 657 204
Case 118/75 *Watson and Belmann* [1976] ECR 1185 105, 278
Case 10/76 *Commission v. Italy* [1976] ECR 1359 27
Case 33/76 *Rewe Zentral v. Landwirtschaftskammer für das Saarland* [1976] ECR 1989 146, 151, 152, 158, 165, 170, 179
Case 45/76 *Comet v. Produktschap voor Siergewassen* [1976] ECR 2043 146, 151, 152, 158, 165, 170, 179
Case 50/76 *Amsterdam Bulb v. Produktschap voor Siergewassen* [1977] ECR 137 104, 261
Case 51/76 *VNO v. Inspecteur der Invoerrechten en Accijnzen* [1977] ECR 113 49, 248, 275, 278, 284, 285, 288, 295
Joined Cases 64 and 113/76, 167 and 239/78, 27, 28 and 145/79 *Dumortier v. Council* [1979] ECR 3091 332
Case 80/76 *Kerry Milk v. Minister for Agriculture and Fisheries* [1977] ECR 425 233
Case 5/77 *Tedeschi v. Denkavit* [1977] ECR 1555 42
Case 8/77 *Sagulo v. Germany* [1977] ECR 1495 105, 204
Case 38/77 *Enka v. Inspecteur der Invoerrechten en Accijnzen* [1977] ECR 2203 17, 89, 251, 270, 275, 279, 295
Case 95/77 *Commission v. The Netherlands* [1978] ECR 863 27

Cases still pending on 30 August 1994

1
General Introduction

1.1 Controversies about Directives

"... *il [est] difficile d'imaginer acte plus clair que l'article 189*"[1] wrote Boulouis in 1979 in a comment on the notorious *Cohn-Bendit* case[2] which still haunts the corridors of the *Conseil d'Etat* and perhaps even those of the Court of Justice of the EC.[3] If one considers the quantity of publications on Article 189 of the E(E)C Treaty[4] and, in particular, on its third paragraph giving the legal definition of directives, this statement could seem rather bold. All the acts described in Article 189 have received considerable attention in the (Community law) literature; it is, however, the directive in particular which has exercised learned minds. In the past there were three main reasons for this special interest.

Firstly, there is the impossibility of "capturing" the directive in terms of legal acts existing in national and international law. Although it was very quickly recognized that directives have no equivalent under either national or international law,[5] this realization in no way facilitated legal analysis. Some authors attempted to overcome this difficulty somewhat by drawing parallels with framework legislation but this also failed to elucidate the matter.[6]

Secondly, the deficient definition[7] given in Article 189(3) provoked a whole series of questions, leading some authors to propose the abolition of this instrument, which they believed to be rather a failure; others, however, consi-

[1] Boulouis 1979, p. 107.

[2] *Conseil d'Etat* 22 December 1978 [1980] 1 CMLR 543. In this case the *Conseil d'Etat* held that directives cannot be relied upon by individuals in actions for annulment of individual administrative decisions failing general implementing measures by the Government.

[3] Despite some new developments in its case law, the Conseil d'Etat still seems to hold the position that individuals may not rely on a directive where no transposition measures have been enacted. Cf. Louis 1993, p. 513. As to the Court of Justice, in Case C-91/92 *Faccini Dori* [1994] ECR I-3325, it based the absence of horizontal direct effect of directives on an argument relating to the competence of the Community. A comparable argument was also invoked by the Conseil d'Etat; cf. Boulouis 1979, p. 106.

[4] "EC Treaty" refers to the Treaty establishing the European Community, the former "EEC Treaty", as follows from Article G of the Treaty on the European Union. Where appropriate within the specific context and, indeed, if quoted, the terms "EEC Treaty" will be used, or when referring to both, the terms "E(E)C Treaty".

[5] Cf. Ipsen 1965, p. 69 and 71, Boulouis 1975, p. 197, Kapteyn and VerLoren van Themaat 1990, p. 193.

[6] Cf. Louis 1993, p. 503, Ophüls 1966, p. 10.

[7] See below, Introduction Part I.

STAFFS UNIVERSITY LIBRARY

dered the directive to be an "ideal" or "original" instrument, fit to fulfil the functions it was designed to have within the system of the EEC Treaty.[8]

Thirdly, at a relatively early stage a good deal of effort was invested in the consideration of whether directives could produce direct effect.

The controversies and ambiguities surrounding directives as legal instruments of Community action are certainly not things of the past. In a relatively recent document the Commission described directives as an "*instrument hybride, et de statut ambigu*".[9] In particular, the discussion on replacing the directive by a different Community act has on occasions been sparked off again, also in more recent times. In the European Parliament's Draft Treaty for European Union (1984)[10] the directive disappeared as a separate legal act, not least for reasons related to uncertainties as to the effects it could produce within the national legal order. On the other hand, however, because the new "law of the Union",[11] a directly applicable act, should have the character of framework legislation which in principle needs further implementation either by the Union institutions or by the Member States, the nature of this law was to an extent comparable to that of a directive.[12]

During the preparations for the Intergovernmental Conferences on European Union proposals were made which broke with the typology of existing Community acts as defined in Article 189 of the EEC Treaty, the main purpose being to introduce a clear hierarchy of norms.[13] The directive again disappeared but its essence would be retained in a new legal instrument, "the law", establishing the basic principles and leaving the Member States considerable discretion with respect to its implementation. At the end of the day, however, the proposed changes were not adopted. Instead, a *Declaration on the Hierarchy of Community Acts* was annexed to the Maastricht Treaty, providing that

> "the Intergovernmental Conference to be convened in 1996 will examine to what extent it might be possible to review the classification of Community acts with a view to establishing an appropriate hierarchy between the different categories of acts."

[8] See Ipsen 1966, p. 69 for further references. Cf. also Boulouis 1990, p. 167.

[9] See Snyder 1993, p. 41, n. 127. For a less negative, although not enthusiastic appreciation of the directive by the Commission see its Report on European Union, Bull EC Supp. 5/75, p. 13. Cf. also Louis 1976, p. 484-486.

[10] OJ 1984, C 77/41.

[11] Article 34 of the Draft.

[12] Cf. Jacqué 1985, p. 37, Constantinesco 1985, p. 50-53, Capotorti 1988, p. 157.

[13] See e.g. the Resolution of the EP on the nature of Community acts, OJ 1991, C 129/136 and *Intergovernmental Conferences: Contributions by the Commission*, Bull. EC Supp. 2/91, p. 117-123. Cf. also Snyder 1993, p. 41, Curtin 1993, p. 39-41.

In another recent document it was recommended that directives be converted into directly applicable regulations, after a satisfactory degree of approximation of national laws by means of directives had been achieved. The conversion of directives into regulations would constitute an important contribution to the transparency of Community legislation, in particular towards meeting the need on the part of individuals and national enforcement authorities to have a single point of reference throughout the Community as far as the applicable Community legislation is concerned.[14]

The main reasons for this dissatisfaction with directives are arguably no longer of a conceptual nature. More practical considerations undoubtedly also lie behind the proposals to replace them.[15]

Similarly, in more recent legal writing the discussion about directives has certainly not abated. Problems encountered with respect to their implementation and, in particular, their enforcement by national courts have generated an impressive list of publications.

1.2 FUNCTIONS OF DIRECTIVES WITHIN THE EC TREATY

Article 189 alone says nothing about the function of directives within the system of the EC Treaty. From the first paragraph one merely learns that the Council and the Commission shall issue directives in order to carry out their task and they must do this in accordance with the provisions of the Treaty. This implies that an inquiry into the role of directives within the Community law system should primarily focus on the specific Treaty Articles authorizing the Council and the Commission to adopt directives.

In legal writing it was observed at a relatively early stage, on the basis of an analysis of the Articles of the EEC Treaty in which the directive is the only instrument prescribed, that directives will be used in particular in those areas where existing national law is rather complex and voluminous and needs to be adapted for the purposes of the Treaty.[16] From these Treaty provisions alone it already followed that the most important field of activities in which directives will be used as a means of Community intervention will be the harmonization of laws.[17] This view was entirely confirmed in practice, under both provisions

[14] *The Internal Market after 1992*, Report to the EEC Commission by the High Level Group on the Operation of Internal Market (hereafter: *Sutherland Report*), Brussels 1992, p. 33-34.

[15] See below, Section 3. Cf. also Hilf 1993, p. 19-22.

[16] Cf. Kapteyn and VerLoren van Themaat 1990, p. 194-195. For an "early" examination see e.g. Oldenkop 1972, p. 63-71, Fuß 1965, p. 379-380.

[17] See Oldenkop 1972, p. 64.

designating directives as the only instrument of action and provisions leaving the institutions the choice of instrument.[18]

Without entering into the discussion of what "harmonization" exactly means, or whether there is or should be a difference between harmonization, approximation, co-ordination, unification etc. of laws,[19] for the purpose of this Chapter it is sufficient to observe that harmonization represents, at least as it was conceived under the Treaty and in contrast to the introduction of common (uniform) rules, a form of limited intervention. The Member States are required to adapt their laws only to a certain extent, namely as far as necessary for achieving the objectives set out in the relevant Treaty provision which serves as the legal base for the directive.[20] The directive is an instrument which corresponds very well with this idea of limited intervention. Being binding "as to the result to be achieved" but leaving the Member States the choice of "form and methods", it is by its nature very suitable for bringing about the necessary changes in national laws while respecting as far as possible the national legal systems, with their own conceptions and terminology.[21] Not surprisingly, in the *Declaration on Article 100a of the EEC Treaty* annexed to the Single European Act, the Member States expressed their preference for directives as instruments of harmonization of laws above the use of regulations. Similarly, more recently, at the Edinburgh Summit the Member States agreed that the principle of proportionality codified in Article 3B (third paragraph) of the EC Treaty should imply that wherever legislative intervention by the Community is required, preference should be given to directives above regulations and framework directives above detailed measures.[22]

Looking at the directive from a different angle, namely not as a means of limited intervention but rather as a new form of decision making, Boulouis explained the specific function of the directive by referring to the technical difficulty of concentrating the exercise of decision-making power in one single normative act.[23] In his view, a directive aims at restricting and directing the behaviour of a subordinated body according to orientations laid down by a hierarchically higher body. Apart from political considerations,[24] it is notably the

[18] Cf. e.g. Lauwaars and Maarleveld 1987, p. 60-61, Grabitz Kommentar p. 20a, Manin 1990, p. 669.

[19] For a discussion of these concepts see Lauwaars and Maarleveld 1987, p. 7-11 and p. 45-49.

[20] Kapteyn and VerLoren van Themaat (1990, p. 194) point out in this respect that the directive serves to fetter the law-making power of the Member States on certain points.

[21] Cf. Kooijmans 1967, p. 128, Lauwaars and Maarleveld 1987, p. 62, Timmermans 1979, p. 542, Oldenkop 1972, p. 61-62.

[22] *Edinburgh European Council*, Bull. EC 12-1992, p. 15.

[23] Boulouis 1975, p. 197. It should be noted that Boulouis' contribution does not concentrate on the Community directive only but also upon the phenomenon of directives in general.

[24] Namely to respect as far as possible the sovereign powers of the Member States and, in particular, the position of national parliaments. Cf. Bleckmann 1990, p. 84.

need for new organization of decision making, both within the Community and in any other State administration, that has inspired the directive as a specific act of the institutions. The main reasons for this are the diversity, changeability and complexity of the situations to be dealt with, aspects which the central body is unable to oversee. It is therefore better if the more concrete actions are taken at a lower level. However, the coherence of the actions is safeguarded by the orientation laid down in the directive. From this point of view, the directive has a decentralizing function within the decision-making process.[25]

The limited intervention concept and the directive as a means of decentralization have one important feature in common: they should contribute to smooth achievement of the result desired by the directive within the national legal orders. Similarly, by virtue of these characteristics, the directive seems to go hand-in-glove with the principle of subsidiarity.[26]

1.3 THE IMPLEMENTATION PROCESS AND THE TYPES OF NON-COMPLIANCE

Article 189(3) obliges the Member States to achieve the result prescribed by the directive. Consequently, the actual obligations which are imposed upon the Member States will depend on the content of the directive concerned.[27]

The entire process by which obligations under Article 189(3) are fulfilled can be denoted by the term *implementation.* This process can be broken down into a number of separate stages, depending on the obligations imposed.[28]

A prototypical directive must, in the first stage, be *transposed* into national law; this requires the adoption of general measures of a legislative nature. In other words, *transposition of directives* denotes the process of transforming directives into provisions of national law by the competent national legislative body or bodies.[29]

[25] Cf. e.g. Mertens de Wilmars 1991, p. 393, Louis 1993, p. 502, Gaja, Hay, Rotunda 1986, p. 126-128. However, as Capotorti (1988, p. 156-157) has pointed out, practice is often different: especially owing to the detailed description of the result to be achieved, directives attain a considerable degree of centralization.

[26] Cf. Snyder 1993, p. 41, Hilf 1993, p. 2, as well as *Commission's Communication on the principle of subsidiarity*, Bull. EC 10-1992, p. 123-124 and the *Edinburgh Guidelines*, Bull. EC 12-1992, p. 15. Some scholars, however, have argued that these documents, also when dealing with the intensity of legislative action, confuse proportionality with subsidiarity. See Toth 1994, p. 43-46.

[27] For a detailed discussion see Chapter 3.

[28] For a distinction of the different stages see e.g. Krislov, Ehlermann and Weiler 1986, p. 61-62, Capotorti 1988, p. 158, Macrory 1992, p. 348, Snyder 1993, p. 21-27, Curtin and Mortelmans 1994, p. 426-429, Siedentopf and Ziller 1988, p. 27 ff.

[29] In this book the term "legislator" denotes any legislative body of the State enacting primary or delegated legislation, thus comprising the legislature and the executive in its legislative capacity. The term "legislature" refers to bodies enacting primary legislation.

It must be noted, however, that not every (provision of a) directive requires transposition in this sense. Some (provisions of) directives may require some factual conduct. In this connection it is, in my view, not appropriate to use the term transposition: it is better simply to talk about implementation.

The second stage is the *application of directives*, i.e. the administration of directives in a concrete case. Strictly speaking, this expression should in principle refer to the application of the national measures transposing the directive. However, in some situations it is the directive as such which is applied, namely where it is directly effective and there are no appropriate transposition measures. Furthermore, it must be observed that both scholars and Community institutions use the term "application of directives", even in cases where they are actually referring to the application of the national measures transposing them.

In the third stage, directives (or often, again, the measures transposing them) must be enforced. *Enforcement of directives* refers to the process of compelling observance of the directive, either as such or as the national measures transposing it.

Although the implementation process of a directive can thus be divided into several stages, the major problem one encounters in this respect is that neither the EC institutions, including the Court of Justice, nor many scholars follow a coherent terminology (or terminology which they define in advance) to designate the various stages. Furthermore, matters are even more complicated when one compares the terms used in the different languages.[30] In particular, the term "implementation" is often used as equivalent to transposition. In other cases, however, it may denote in general the course of action (to be) adopted by Member States in order to achieve the result prescribed by the directive. It is not my intention to cause a small upheaval in familiar (though unprecise) terminology in this respect. Neither shall I slavishly adhere to the distinction made above between implementation and transposition, in which the former encompasses the latter. Moreover, it is often immaterial, either for the subject under discussion or for proper understanding of the text, to differentiate between the two. I shall therefore frequently use the term implementation (or implementing measures) either as a synonym for transposition (but not *vice versa*) or, where this is irrelevant, in the broader meaning indicated above.

The phased character of the implementation process entails that non-compliance with the obligations under Article 189(3) can take forms which correspond with the different stages: non-transposition/inadequate transposition (or implementation in the the stricter sense), non-application/inadequate application and non-enforcement/inadequate enforcement.

[30] Cf. Curtin and Mortelmans 1994, p. 425-427.

The non-implementation of directives within the time limits set or implementation which is not adequate, like partial and incorrect implementation, is one of the major and by now well-known problems in Community law. The figures produced by the Commission in its annual reports to the European Parliament on monitoring the application of Community law provide some useful indications in this respect. The (latest) Eleventh Report, which covers 1993, reveals that in relation to the approximately 1,150 directives applicable on 31 December 1993 on average 90% of national implementing measures have been notified to the Commission.[31] Nevertheless, in the field of directives the Commission started 1,140 infringement proceedings (987 for failure to notify implementing measures which, as a rule, means non-implementation, 32 for inadequate implementation and 121 for inadequate application). In 300 cases it issued a reasoned opinion (244, 18 and 38 for the various kinds of failure) and 30 cases were referred to the Court of Justice (21, 4 and 5 respectively).[32] When compared with infringement proceedings initiated for failure to comply with Treaty provisions, regulations and decisions (69 proceedings initiated, 52 reasoned opinions and 14 references to the Court),[33] the figures give some indication as to the workload which the control of compliance with directives constitutes for the Commission. Furthermore, a striking detail is the difference between the figures relating to non-notification and the other kinds of failure. Indeed, it is relatively simple to initiate infringement procedures more or less automatically as soon as the period provided for implementation has expired if no national implementing measures have been notified. Yet if they have been notified, nothing is said about either their quality or their application and enforcement in practice. Without much exaggeration it can be said that there is a large area of "hidden failures" by the Member States which the Commission is not able to deal with in the more systematic fashion which a successful strategy for safeguarding compliance would require.[34]

As was stressed in the *Declaration on the implementation of Community law* annexed to the Maastricht Treaty, full and accurate transposition of directives into national law within the period prescribed "is central to the coherence and unity of the process of European construction"; it therefore remains one of the major concerns. Nevertheless, there is also a new development taking shape: the increased focus on application and enforcement at national level. Quite recently a number of documents have appeared which emphasize the importance of these

[31] OJ 1993, C 154/1, p. 7
[32] *Ibid.*, p. 65
[33] *Ibid.*
[34] Cf. Curtin 1990, p. 709-712, Ehlermann 1987, p. 210-212, Timmermans 1994, p. 395-400.

two (last) stages of the implementation process.[35] Similarly, in the above-mentioned Declaration it was considered essential for the proper functioning of the Community that Community law is applied with the same effectiveness and rigour as national law.

One of the important factors causing the shift in emphasis is undoubtedly the completion of the Internal Market. Clearly, after the "legislative stage", comprising the transposition of some 200 directives, had been completed, the next major concern was the actual application and enforcement of the rules.

Another factor is the increasing attention paid to decentralized enforcement of Community law through national courts.[36] As explained above, the control of adequate and timely implementation of directives on Community level is an activity which consumes a good deal of time and (human) resources. Moreover, there still remains a considerable risk that the directives are not complied with fully and correctly, owing not only to the limited enforcement capacity of the Commission but also to the inherent limitations of the infringement proceedings.[37] Not surprisingly, decentralized enforcement through national courts provides a viable alternative, or rather a crucial complement, to the enforcement at Community level.[38] Especially in relation to directives, the case law of the Court of Justice has proved to be a vital source of material for construing a system for their enforcement in national courts.

1.4 Directives in the Court's Case Law: Two Levels, Four Lines and Several Questions

The Court's case law relating to problems of non-implemented or (allegedly) inadequately implemented directives can be situated at two different levels.

The first level is that of infringement proceedings or, to put it differently, the Community level of enforcement. Since the mid-seventies the Commission has been bringing an increasing number of cases for non-implementation or inadequate implementation of directives. Today these types of cases form a

[35] E.g. *Council Resolution of 7 December 1992 on making the Single Market work*, OJ 1992, C 334/1, *Council Conclusions of 21 December 1992 on effective implementation and enforcement of Community legislation in the area of social affairs*, OJ 1993, C 49/6, *Sutherland Report*, p. 14-17 and p. 42-51, *Reinforcing the effectiveness of the Internal Market*, COM (93) 256 final, in particular p. 13-20. Cf. also the Commission's Green Paper on *Access of consumers to justice and the settlement of consumer disputes in the Single Market*, Brussels, 16 November 1993, COM (93) 576 final.

[36] See e.g. Ehlermann 1987, Langenfeld 1991, Curtin 1992, as well as *Fide Reports 1992*. For problems with respect to, in particular, the application and enforcement of environmental directives see Macrory 1992.

[37] Cf. Ehlermann 1987, p. 210-213, Timmermans 1994, p. 379-400.

[38] Cf. Joined Cases C-106/90, C-317/90 and C-129/91 *Emerald Meats* [1993] ECR I-209, para. 40.

considerable part of Article 169 actions brought before the Court.[39] Although cases concerning non-implementation are not very spectacular, they have enabled the Court to rule on several kinds of excuses which the Member States have invoked to justify their failure to implement directives in due time. In cases concerning (alleged) inadequate implementation the Court has developed a set of increasingly strict requirements which adequate implementation must satisfy. On the whole, the case law provides several vital elements concerning the characteristics of the directive and the consequences which the adoption of a directive has for the Member States. Moreover, in some cases the Court has also indicated the (possible) effects of its judgment establishing that a Member State has failed to implement a directive either in due time or adequately.

The second level is that of decentralized enforcement, i.e. enforcement of non-implemented or inadequately implemented directives in national courts. In preliminary proceedings the Court of Justice has elaborated a wealth of case law on the various effects that directives may produce within the national legal order and, particularly, on the role national courts are supposed to play in this context. This case law has developed along four different lines.

The first (and oldest) line is that of direct effect. As from 1974,[40] it became more or less definitively clear that, following the line set out in the case law for Treaty provisions and regulations, directives may have direct effect. This concept is often defined in terms of creation of rights for the benefit of individuals which the national courts must protect, or as the possibility for individuals to rely on directives and the corresponding duty of national courts to apply them. Direct effect has proved to be an important device both for protecting the legal position which individuals derive from directives and for combatting the inertia in implementation on the part of the Member States. Obviously, over the years the doctrine of direct effect of directives has been further refined by the Court of Justice. One of the major setbacks in this development has been the refusal of the Court to recognize horizontal direct effect, i.e. the possibility for an individual to rely on the directive against another private individual.[41] Arguably in order to obviate this setback as far as possible, the Court has expanded considerably the category of bodies against which the directive can be relied upon by giving an extensive interpretation to the concept of "the State". In this way, the relationship at issue could still be dealt with within the scope of vertical direct effect, i.e. the possibility for an individual to rely on the directive as against the State.

[39] Of the 39 infringement proceedings brought by the Commission in 1993, 26 related to non-implementation or inadequate implementation of directives (Source: *système documentaire Minidoc* of the Court of Justice).

[40] Case 41/74 *Van Duyn* [1974] ECR 1337.

[41] Case 152/84 *Marshall I* [1986] ECR 723.

The second line which can be discerned in the Court's case law is that of interpretation of national law in conformity with the directive. In 1984[42] the Court of Justice laid down an obligation for all the authorities of the Member State, and especially for the courts, to proceed to such "consistent interpretation". Although this obligation had been formulated by the Court some two years before the explicit denial of horizontal direct effect of directives and, from this perspective, it would not seem entirely correct to maintain that the obligation to follow this method of interpretation was intentionally designed to palliate the problems caused by the absence of horizontal direct effect of directives, in practice it does actually often function in this way. However, the scope of the obligation of consistent interpretation is more ample than this. It can, for instance, also bring relief in cases where there is no direct effect at all.

Simultaneously with but independently of these two developments, another (third) line in the Court's case law was taking shape: the – what I will call – "effective judicial protection line". This case law, which is in no way limited only to directives, is characterized by increasing interference by the Court with the standards of judicial protection available within the Member States. As from 1986,[43] the Court started to impose increasingly unambigous Community law requirements which national systems of judicial protection must satisfy. These requirements concern a whole range of different issues, such as access to the courts, rules of evidence, time limits for bringing action and, last but not least, the type of redress which must be available for individuals bringing actions with a view to protecting the position accorded to them by Community law.

The fourth (and most recent) line in the developments can be considered as the natural continuation of the "effective judicial protection" case law. Using the necessity of effective judicial protection as one of the two main arguments, the Court decided in 1991[44] that a Member State is in principle liable for harm caused to individuals by breaches of Community law, including the non-implementation of directives. It has been suggested that the Court intentionally denied direct effect of the directive at issue with a view to establishing the liability of the State as a remedy which did not depend on direct effect.[45] In this way, especially the problems arising from the absence of horizontal direct effect of directives can be circumvented.

In the light of these developments it cannot be denied that the enforcement of directives at the decentralized level has become a complex matter. In particular, if one takes into consideration the various conditions and limits governing these different routes to enforcement, it may be asked whether these

[42] Case 14/83 *Von Colson* [1984] ECR 1891.
[43] Case 222/84 *Johnston* [1986] ECR 1651.
[44] Joined Cases C-6/90 and C-9/90 *Francovich and Bonifaci* [1991] ECR I-5357.
[45] Steiner 1993, p. 9. Such a point of view was, however, doubted by e.g. Geiger 1993, p. 470.

developments have not reached such a degree of sophistication that the system – if there is any[46] – has become unworkable for the national courts and entirely opaque for the individual.[47]

The picture becomes even more complicated if the developments at the first level, the case law at the Community level of enforcement, are taken into account. In the past it was to a large extent possible to consider cases decided under Article 169 and the case law developed in preliminary proceedings as two separate matters, particularly since the two types of proceedings serve different purposes. However, on closer consideration, certain links can be discerned between the requirements as to adequate implementation and some elements of the case law developed in preliminary proceedings (and *vice versa*). Furthermore, as regards the characteristics of the directive, the case law as a whole must be taken into consideration.

It will certainly not come as a surprise that directives, and especially their enforcement at both Community and national levels, give rise to complex issues, many of which are as yet far from resolved.

The first and most important group of problems relates to the four different lines of development considered separately: what is the content of the concepts, what are the conditions for their application, what are their limits and effects? Can the developments within the separate lines of case law be considered as consistent? Obviously the answers differ, not least because some concepts, like direct effect, are relatively old and already elaborated, while others, like State liability, have just started to be developed.

The way in which the developments take place could suggest that the Court reacts to individual problems in an *ad hoc* fashion, and thus hardly in a systematic manner. The next question is therefore whether and, if so, to what extent there exists coherence between the distinct lines. Two different aspects can be discerned in this connection. Firstly, there is the question whether and, if so, in what way the four lines elaborated within the decentralized enforcement context are interrelated. Secondly, there is the question as to the relation or interaction of the elements of the case law developed in infringement proceedings and those developed in preliminary proceedings.

Finally, it may be asked: to what extent have the various elements of the Court's case law clarified or perhaps even expanded the definition of directives given in Article 189(3)?

[46] Some have characterized the case law as a "*bateau ivre*": see Emmert and Pereira de Avezedo 1993.

[47] For a critical review of the case law see e.g. Hilf 1993, Manin 1990, and Emmert 1992.

1.5 The Framework of the Analysis

The purpose of this book is to examine in detail the multiple aspects of directives outlined in the previous Section. The analysis will not, however, entirely follow the sequence of the questions formulated above. Moreover, it will primarily be conducted from a particular viewpoint, namely the judicial protection of rights which individuals allegedly derive from Community directives.

The study concentrates on three central themes. Part I deals with the main characteristics of directives. It examines the concept of the directive in a practical rather than a theoretical manner, i.e. drawing heavily upon the relevant case law of the Court and upon the actual texts of several directives. This Part deals primarily, but not exclusively, with the various elements of the "Article 169 case law".

In Part II the directive as an integral part of national legal orders will be considered; in particular, as a source of law valid within the Member States as well as a source of individual rights. The role national courts are supposed to play in protecting these rights will also be addressed in detail. This second component of Part II corresponds mainly with the "effective judicial protection line" mentioned above.

Part III focusses on the three mechanisms available to national courts for enforcement of directives: the concept of consistent interpretation, the doctrine of direct effect and the principle of State liability will be examined in detail.

In Chapter 14, the final Chapter, I shall draw together a number of aspects resulting from the foregoing analysis.

The materials used for this study comprise judgments of the Court of Justice, opinions of Advocates General and legal literature, as well as a number of Community documents. The text, as far as possible, reflects the materials available at the close of August 1994.

The book concentrates primarily on the Community law dimensions of the subject. It is very difficult and, it is submitted, even erroneous, especially with respect to a subject like this, to divorce entirely the Community law and national law sides of the problems. However, within the limited scope of one single book it is unfeasible to integrate both. Nevertheless, in order to illustrate the amplitude of the issues and the interrelationship of Community law and national law, or with a view to clarifying certain contentions, minor excursions into national law of some of the Member States will be made. In my view, there is a fascinating topic challenging "European" legal doctrine: to undertake a comparable study in a comparative perspective.

Part I
Directives: the Main Characteristics

STAFFS UNIVERSITY LIBRARY

Introduction

The distinguishing elements in the definitions of binding Community acts given in Article 189 are the subjects to whom the acts can be addressed, the scope of their binding force, and the effects they may produce in the internal legal orders of the Member States.

With the statement that regulations shall have "general application", the Treaty Article is saying that a regulation applies to abstract categories of persons. It lays down general rules which affect the legal position of general classes of persons. Furthermore, the Court of Justice has emphasized that these terms entail the applicability of the regulation to "objectively determined situations".[1] Decisions on the other hand can be directed to a definite number of addressees, i.e. Member States and private parties, and they only affect specific legal subjects.[2] Both acts are binding in their entirety.

Like a decision, a directive can be addressed to a limited number of subjects, namely one or more Member States, and it too is binding, although in a limited way, namely "as to the result to be achieved".

We also learn from Article 189 that the national authorities have the choice of form and methods for the realization of the result prescribed by a directive.

Finally, Article 189 indicates that regulations are directly applicable *in* all Member States. No comparable indication as to the effect of the acts is given with respect to directives and decisions. The wording of the definition of the two latter acts could indeed suggest that they should not produce legal effects other than between the author and the addressee.[3]

It is not at all surprising that such a rudimentary description[4] of the most important Community instruments and their delimitation has generated an impressive literature in the attempt to fathom the nature of the different acts.

One of the most problematic areas with regard to directives has been their delimitation *vis-à-vis* regulations.[5] This has particularly been caused by a number of practical and jurisprudential developments, namely: the case law of the Court of Justice on direct effect of directives; the facts that, although regulations require no incorporation into national legal order, in practice adoption of national rules is often necessary in order to make them fully operative and that,

[1] See e.g. Case 6/68 *Zuckerfabrik Watenstedt* [1968] ECR 409.

[2] See e.g Joined Cases 16 and 17/62 *Fruit et Légumes* [1962] ECR 471.

[3] Cf. De Ripaisel-Landy and Gérard 1976, p. 44, Ophüls 1966, p. 6.

[4] Cf. Ipsen 1965, p. 70, De Ripaisel-Landy and Gérard 1976, p. 37.

[5] For a discussion of the delimitation of directives and regulations or directives, regulations and decisions see e.g. Kooijmans 1967, p. 130-131 and 136, Capotorti 1988, Galmot 1990, Scherzberg 1991.

in this respect, some discretion may be left to the Member States;[6] the fact that the *content* of directives is largely normative in nature[7] and, finally, the reality that directives have become quite detailed.[8]

The last of these issues in particular has given rise to differences of opinion in legal writing and has also created discord in practice.[9] The problem can be presented under a number of different headings: does the definition of a directive entail a limitation of the competence of the Council or Commission over and above that already contained in the provision constituting the legal base of the directive?[10] Or what is, within the definition, the relationship between the result on the one hand and the form and methods on the other?[11] Or can directives go into detail, and if so to what extent?[12] In German literature a question which is often posed concerns the "*Regelungsintensität*" of directives.[13] Similarly, when attempting to identify the specific nature of the directive the authors could not avoid importing the separation of result and form and methods which together constitute the very essence of the definition.[14]

Whatever the approach may be, from Article 189(3) it appears that the Member States must have a certain amount of freedom in choosing the form and methods. If they do not, the instrument which is adopted loses the character of a directive. In practice, however, the content of a directive may considerably curtail this freedom, being so detailed that in fact the Member States are left with very little latitude.

A prosaic example may be used to illustrate the problem: person A sending person B to buy something for dinner. A could simply say: "Buy something for dinner". On the other hand, A could also say: "Buy some pasta, sauce and wine" or "Buy tagliatelle, pesto and red wine" or "Buy fresh spinach tagliatelle, Buitoni pesto and Chianti". A could also send

[6] Cf. De Ripaisel-Landy and Gérard 1976, p. 46 and 88, Lauwaars 1983.

[7] Cf. Bleckmann 1990, p. 91, De Ripaisel-Landy and Gérard 1976, p. 88.

[8] Cf. Monaco 1987, p. 471, Kooijmans 1967, p. 134, Galmot 1990, p. 74, Capotorti 1988, p. 154.

[9] For instance, an *Aide-mémoire* submitted to the Council in 1966 by the French government stated that "... we cannot escape the fact that in practice the Commission very often proposes directives which set out in detail the rules to be applied. The only freedom then left to the States is to choose the forms in which the content will be clothed and to take the necessary implementing measures. It is evident that such practices constitute an attempt on the part of the Commission to cause the matters dealt with by such directives to slip out of national hands into the Community sphere of competence. Such methods should be avoided in the future". See Bull. EEC 3-1966, p. 6.

[10] Cf. Kapteyn and VerLoren van Themaat 1990, p. 193-194, Smit and Herzog, p. 5-612.

[11] Cf. Kooymans 1967, p. 131, Smit and Herzog, p. 5-611.

[12] Cf. Timmermans 1971, p. 621, Lauwaars 1973, p. 29-32 with references to older literature.

[13] Cf. Oldenkop 1972, p. 74 ff., Bleckmann 1990, p. 85-88.

[14] For an overview of the different positions see De Ripaisel-Landy and Gérard 1976, p. 47-52 and Lauwaars 1973, p. 29-32.

B to the Italian shop on the corner for the tagliatelle and pesto, and to the wine merchant on the other corner for the Chianti etc. Finally, it may happen that B has nothing to do other than to get there. And even in this respect it is conceivable that A says: "Take the car". In other words, one situation may involve a distinction between the result on the one hand and the means to realize it on the other, while in another situation both these facets become the result.[15]

To return to Article 189(3), the crux of the problem is that the definition as such provides little help when determining the extent to which directives may go into detail. Despite some attempts in this direction, doctrine eventually recognized that an abstract analysis of Article 189(3) alone was doomed to failure.[16] A more concrete analysis, however, also reveals that the relationship between "result" and "form and methods" shows fluctuations.[17] If the provision constituting the legal base of the directive is examined in a number of concrete cases, it will become apparent that in some cases detailed rules may be necessary for the accomplishment of the objective pursued, while in others the Community institutions may confine themselves to more general indications. In this respect as well, therefore, no general rule can be given.[18]

Today it is generally accepted, both by doctrine[19] and the Court of Justice,[20] that a directive may give a detailed description of the result to be achieved, provided that it is necessary for effective realization of the objective pursued.[21] Every case must be assessed individually in this respect and the resulting assessments can, if necessary, be submitted to the control of the Court of Justice.[22] It is similarly accepted, however, that Article 189(3) sets a limit: a directive as a whole must leave some latitude to the Member States as far as the form and methods of implementation are concerned. It certainly cannot oblige a Member State simply to introduce an exhaustive set of rules with no consideration of the law existing within the national legal order.[23]

[15] Cf. Louis 1990, p. 500, Bleckmann 1990, p. 85-86.

[16] Cf. Beyerlin 1987, p. 127, Oldenkop 1972, p. 78-92, Bleckmann 1990, p. 85-86.

[17] Kapteyn and VerLoren van Themaat 1990, p. 196.

[18] Cf. Louis 1990, p. 500, Fuß 1965, p. 380-381, Smit and Herzog, p. 5-613.

[19] Cf. e.g. Everling 1984, p. 112, Lauwaars 1973, p. 30, Timmermans 1971, p. 621, Easson 1981, p. 10, Mertens de Wilmars 1991, p. 394.

[20] Case 38/77 *Enka* [1977] ECR 2203.

[21] Cf. Smit and Herzog, p. 5-613, who point out that "the topics concerning which most directives are issued ... require fairly detailed provisions as to how the legislation affected must be modified".

[22] Cf. Kooijmans 1967, p. 134.

[23] Cf. Kapteyn and VerLoren van Themaat 1990, p. 196, Louis 1990, p. 501, Lauwaars 1973, p. 30-31, Hilf 1993, p. 7. Grabitz (Kommentar, p. 22), however, seems to accept that directives may leave no latitude at all, provided that it is necessary for the achievement of the objective pursued.

The essential difference between directives and regulations is "the structural necessity"[24] to enact national transposition measures in order to give them full legal effect. In this respect the terms "two-stage legislation"[25] or "indirect legislation"[26] are often used. In the first -community- stage the intended result of a directive is laid down in an act which is binding for the Member States. In the second -national- stage the Member State effectuates the content of the directive by transposing it into national law and thus turning it into a normative act with an effect *erga omnes*.

Directives as such are addressed to a definite number of subjects, i.e. the Member States, and to this extent they may be seen as decisions. As far as their content is concerned, however, they are usually intended to regulate objectively determined situations and to produce effects with regard to general and abstract categories of persons.[27] In general, directives require further national legislation in order to realize entirely their normative content. Directives therefore, unlike regulations, are not immediately generally applicable. Nevertheless, they are regarded as a piece of legislation. The Court of Justice in particular seems to consider them, without further ado, as legislative acts or as acts of general application.[28] The fact remains, however, that their general applicability is in principle an indirect one.[29]

Although the legal definition of directives given by Article 189(3) may be far from perfect, this certainly does not mean that the separate elements contained therein can be ignored. They provide essential indications for proper understanding of this specific Community instrument. Consequently, the next four Chapters will respectively focus on the binding force, the result to be achieved, the addressees of directives and the freedom to choose the form and methods of implementation. In discussing these issues, however, I shall not restrict myself to abstract speculation on the meaning of the terms. I shall rather consider them within a more concrete context, in particular, within the context of the case law of the Court of Justice, and analyze the consequences resulting therefrom for the characteristics of directives. I shall then wind up the discussion with concluding remarks in Chapter 6.

[24] Capotorti 1988, p. 156.

[25] See e.g. Hilf 1993, p. 4, Capotorti 1988, p. 154.

[26] See e.g Pescatore 1980, p. 171, Capotorti 1988, p. 156, Fuß 1965, p. 379, Lauwaars 1973, p. 29. Cf. also Case C-298/89 *Gibraltar* [1993] ECR I-3605 para. 16.

[27] Cf. e.g. Case 160/88 *Fedesa* [1988] ECR 6399.

[28] As early as Case 41/74 *Van Duyn* [1974] ECR 1337 the Court designated directives as "legislative acts". See further Case 160/88R *Fedesa* [1988] ECR 4121, Case C-298/89 *Gibraltar* [1993] ECR I-3605 and Case C-63/89 *Assurances du Crédit* [1991] ECR I-1799.

[29] Cf. Capotorti 1988, p. 156. See, however, also below, Chapter 11.

2
Binding Force: General Aspects

2.1 ARTICLE 189(3): THE BASIS OF MEMBER STATES' OBLIGATIONS

According to the definition of Article 189(3) a directive is binding in two respects: as to the result to be achieved, and upon each Member State to which it is addressed. In other words, it imposes upon the Member States an obligation to achieve the result required by the directive. The fact that Article 189(3) leaves the Member States free to choose the form and the methods of implementation in no way affects this obligation.[1] The provisions of a directive have no less binding an effect than those of any other rule of Community law.[2]

The obligation to achieve the result envisaged by the directive follows from Article 189(3), since it is by virtue of this provision that directives are binding. The concrete content of the obligation is in turn spelled out in each individual directive. In this respect it must be noted that, in general, when a Member State has not implemented a directive within the time limit or has not implemented it properly, the Court will state in fairly neutral terms that the Member State concerned "has failed to fulfil its obligations under the EEC Treaty",[3] i.e. under Article 189(3).[4] The Court's case law, however, shows little consistency in this respect. In some cases the Court has found that a Member State had not fulfilled its obligations under the directive at issue, while in other cases a similar infringement has amounted to non-fulfilment under the Treaty or under both the Treaty and the directive.[5] In my view, the difference is not relevant, since it is more a matter of formulation.[6] Any failure to comply with a specific (provision of a) directive implies *eo ipso* a violation of Article 189(3).

[1] Cf. Case 14/83 *Von Colson* [1984] ECR 1891.

[2] See Case 79/72 *Commission v. Italy* [1973] ECR 667 and Case 52/75 *Commission v. Italy* [1976] ECR 277.

[3] See e.g. Case 235/84 *Commission v. Italy* [1986] ECR 2291 and Case C-131/88 *Commission v. Germany* [1991] ECR I-825.

[4] Cf. Case 145/82 *Commission v. Italy* [1983] ECR 711.

[5] For reference to a directive only see e.g. Case 235/85 *Commission v. The Netherlands* [1987] ECR 1471 and Case C-45/89 *Commission v. Italy* [1991] ECR I-2053. For reference to the Treaty see e.g. Case 420/85 *Commission v. Italy* [1987] ECR 2983 and Case C-290/89 *Commission v. Belgium* [1991] ECR I-2851. For reference to the Treaty and a directive see e.g. Case 107/84 *Commission v. Germany* [1985] ECR 2655 and Case C-239/91 *Commission v. France* [1993] ECR I-1.

[6] See e.g. Case 415/85 *Commission v. Ireland* [1988] ECR 3097 and Case 416/85 *Commission v. UK* [1988] ECR 3127 in which the Court stated explicitly that the Member States concerned, by having contravened the provisions of the directive at issue, had therefore failed to fulfil their obligations under the Treaty.

Directives usually stipulate explicitly that the Member States shall bring into force the laws, regulations and administrative provisions which are necessary to comply with the directive, or that they shall take the necessary measures and so on. In this way they reiterate the obligation already laid down in Article 189(3).

The obligation to achieve the result prescribed by a directive also follows from the more generally worded Article 5 of the EC Treaty, i.e. the duty of the Member States to take all appropriate measures to ensure fulfilment of the obligations arising out of the Treaty or resulting from an act of an institution.[7] In practice, this cumulation of obligations has no special significance. According to the Court of Justice the mere non-fulfilment of specific obligations arising under a directive makes unnecessary an inquiry into the question whether a Member State has also failed its obligations under Article 5.[8] Only when a breach *distinct* from non-compliance with Article 189(3) or the directive can be established will Article 5 play a part as an independent standard for review.[9] This does not mean, however, that Article 5 is entirely irrelevant for the obligation at issue. As the case law shows, the Court uses Article 5 as an additional argument for a certain interpretation of Article 189(3), and thus to reinforce the obligations arising therefrom.[10]

The binding force of directives further requires not only that directives *are* implemented, but that they are also implemented *in due time* and *correctly*. The underlying reason is the uniform and (thus) simultaneous application of Community law, which is the very essence of the Community legal order. As the Court has explained

"[i]n permitting Member States to profit from the advantages of the Community, the Treaty imposes on them also the obligation to respect its rules. For a State unilaterally to break ... the equilibrium between advantages and obligations flowing from its adherence to the Community brings into question the equality of Member States before Community law and creates discriminations at the expense of their nationals, and above all of the nationals of the State itself which places itself outside the Community rules. This failure in the duty of solidarity accepted by Member States by the fact of their adherence to the Community strikes at the fundamental basis of the Community legal order."[11]

[7] Cf. Ipsen 1965, p. 75.

[8] Case C-48/89 *Commission v. Italy* [1990] ECR I-2425.

[9] Cf. Case C-374/89 *Commission v. Belgium* [1991] ECR I-367 and Case C-382/92 *Commission v. United Kingdom* [1994] ECR I-2435. Cf. also Due 1992, p. 356-357 and Prechal 1992, p. 374-377. Incidentally the Court finds that the directive at issue, Article 189(3) and Article 5 have been violated: Case 239/85 *Commission v. Belgium* [1986] ECR 3645.

[10] Cf. Due 1992, p. 357. In particular, Article 5 reinforces Article 189(3) as a basis for consistent interpretation and direct effect. See below, Chapters 10 and 11.

[11] Case 39/72 *Commission v. Italy* [1973] ECR 101, para. 24-25.

More recently, in a declaration annexed to the Maastricht Treaty, the Member States underlined

"that it is central to the coherence and unity of the process of European construction that each Member State should fully and accurately transpose into national law the Community Directives addressed to it within the deadlines laid down therein."[12]

The duty of implementing directives within the time limits and the duty of implementing them correctly will now be discussed in turn.

2.2 The Obligation to Implement the Directive in Due Time: the Relevance of Deadlines

From Article 191(2) of the EEC Treaty it followed that the obligation to implement started to run as from the day on which the directive was notified to the Member States concerned. Since the entry into force of the Treaty on European Union,[13] directives adopted in accordance with the codecision procedure[14] and those directed to all Member States will enter into force after publication and on the date specified in them. In the absence of such a specification, they will enter into force on the twentieth day following that of their publication.[15] Yet directives do allow the Member States a certain period, varying from a few months to several years, within which the directive must be implemented. The deadline for implementation will usually be uniform for all addressees. However, directives may sometimes fix different deadlines for certain Member States, as with Directive 89/654 (health and safety at the workplace) for Greece and Directive 92/13 (public contracts – excluded sectors) for Greece, Portugal and Spain.[16] According to Article 12(1) of Directive 86/613 (equal treatment of the self-employed) a different deadline applies for those Member States which, in order to comply with it, have to amend their legislation on

[12] *Declaration on the Implementation of Community Law.*

[13] 1 November 1993.

[14] Article 189b EC Treaty.

[15] Publication is now provided for in 191 EC Treaty. Under the EEC Treaty there was no obligation to publish directives in the OJ.

[16] Articles 10(1) and 13(1) respectively; OJ 1989, L 393/1 and OJ, L 76/14.

matrimonial rights and obligations.[17] In some cases the deadline may be postponed[18] or must still be decided upon by the Council.[19]

Although the Treaty is silent on this point, and thus appears not to exclude *eo ipso* the entry into force of the directive coinciding with the date at which the measures necessary for its implementation must be adopted,[20] it has been argued in the legal literature[21] that such a coincidence would not be in accordance with the nature of the directive.

In the first place, the fact that there is choice of form and methods of implementation makes a certain lapse of time necessary.

Secondly, a period for implementation is necessitated by the very purpose of the directive, i.e. to compel the Member States to take measures within their internal legal order.

Whatever the theoretical considerations may be, it is clear that the inclusion of time limits for the implementation of a directive bears witness to a healthy realism. In this respect the time limit can be compared to the transitional periods in the EEC Treaty or in Acts of Accession.

The dissociation of the entry into force of a directive and the required entry into force of the implementing measures raises a number of questions as to the effects produced by the obligation during this interval of time. Obviously, during the period provided for implementation the Member States should consider and prepare the national measures which must be taken to enable them to comply with their obligation in due time.[22] However, it has been argued in the legal literature that the binding force of a directive as from the time it enters into force

[17] OJ 1986, L 359/56.

[18] E.g. Directive 89/104 (trade marks), Article 16 (2), OJ 1989, L 40/1. See for this postponement Council Decision 92/10, OJ 1992, L 6/35. Cf. also Directive 80/778 (drinking water), Article 19, OJ 1980, L 229/11: Commission may grant an additional period. Furthermore it must be noted that Member States may not unilaterally or *de facto* postpone the deadline through, for instance, national transitional measures. See Case C-396/92 *Bund Naturschutz in Bayern* [1994] ECR I-3717.

[19] Directive 80/217 (classical swine fever), Article 19, OJ 1980, L 47/11. Furthermore it must be noted that certain directives provide for different implementation periods: a shorter period for the adoption of legislative etc. measures and a longer one within which the factual situation must be achieved. See e.g. Directive 76/760 (bathing water), OJ 1976, L 31/1: two years for legislative etc. measures and ten years for achievement of the prescribed limit values. Cf. also Directive 86/378 (equal treatment in occupational social security schemes), OJ 1986, L 225/40: three years for legislative etc. measures and three and a half years following thereupon for adjustment of the schemes.

[20] And must, as a rule, also enter into force in national legal order. For the sake of clarity it must be observed that the term "entry into force of the directive" should refer, in my opinion, to the moment that the directive becomes binding upon the Member States and *not* to the entry into force of the implementing measures.

[21] De Ripaisel-Landy and Gérard 1976, p. 54.

[22] Cf. Kooijmans 1967, p. 141 and Lauwaars and Maarleveld 1987, p. 191.

entails more far-reaching effects, even before the expiry of the deadline provided for implementation.

Firstly, some authors read the judgment of the Court in *Kolpinghuis*[23] as implying an obligation for the national courts to interpret national law in conformity with the directive concerned actually before the expiry of the time limit.[24] In other words, in their view, there is an obligation to "anticipatory interpretation" of national law in conformity with the directive at issue. In my opinion, however, the judgment is not as clear as some would claim. In fact, in this judgment the Court only addressed the question of the *limits* which Community law may impose on the obligation or power of the national court to interpret national law in conformity with the directive. In this particular respect it was held to be irrelevant whether or not the period for implementation has expired.[25] In my view, this consideration is in no way conclusive as to the said obligation.[26] Moreover, as the obligation contained in a directive is an obligation to act *within a stated period*, it is difficult to understand why national courts should be bound by an obligation which must be complied with at some point in the future. In this respect it is also useful to refer to the case law of the Court of Justice on the direct effect of directives: a directive provision cannot be relied upon by individuals before the period prescribed for its implementation has expired.[27] Furthermore, no additional argument for the obligation at issue can be drawn from Article 5(1), first phrase, of the Treaty, for reasons comparable to those mentioned above. This provision requires the Member States to take all appropriate measures to ensure the fulfilment of the obligations arising out of the Treaty or resulting from the actions of Community institutions. As stated above, the obligation imposed by Article 189(3), together with a concrete directive, is to act within a stated period. This does not necessarily mean, of course, that the courts are not entitled to proceed to an anticipatory interpretation if the latter is

[23] Case 80/86 [1987] 3969.

[24] E.g. Timmermans 1988, p. 333, Lenz 1990, p. 908, Prechal and Burrows 1990, p. 36. Cf. also, for instance, the opinion of A-G Darmon in Case C-236/92 *Comitato* [1994] ECR I-483, para. 27 and the opinion of A-G Jacobs in Case C-295/90 *European Parliament v. Council* [1992] ECR I-4193, para. 43. A-G Jacobs did, however, take a more balanced position in Case C-156/91 *Mundt* [1992] ECR I-5567, para. 23-27. See below, Chapter 10, Section 10.3.

[25] Para. 15 of the judgment. The limits concerned were the general principles of law, in particular legal certainty and non-retroactivity. For a detailed discussion of the limits see below, Chapter 10, Section 10.7.

[26] Cf. also Dommering-Van Rongen 1991, p. 36, De Burca 1992, p. 218, n. 24, Götz 1992, p. 1854, A-G Jacobs in Case C-156/91 *Mundt* [1992] ECR I-5567, para. 26.

[27] See e.g. Case 148/78 *Ratti* [1979] ECR 1629 and, more recently, Joined Cases C-140/91, C-141/91, C-278/91 and C-279/91 *Suffritti* [1992] ECR I-6337. For a brief discussion of some speculations as to whether a person should perhaps be entitled to rely on a directive which has been implemented before the deadline but the implementation has not been adequate see A-G Jacobs in Case C-156/91 *Mundt* [1992] ECR I-5567, para. 18-22.

possible as a matter of national law. Matters may be different, however, if the Member State implements the directive before the deadline. Arguably, in such a situation the implementing measures, a narrower category than national law in general, must be interpreted in accordance with the directive from the date of the actual implementation.[28]

Secondly, the duty to interpret national law in conformity with the directive concerned does not exist solely for national courts, but for all national authorities of the Member States.[29] Basing their arguments on *Kolpinghuis*, some writers submit that an obligation to this type of anticipatory interpretation exists for other national authorities as well.[30] Yet the same considerations as presented above with respect to such an obligation for national courts also militate, in my opinion, against an obligation of anticipatory interpretation on the part of other national authorities.

Closely related to this problem of the obligation to anticipatory interpretation is the idea expressed by Ipsen,[31] namely that since national authorities, including the courts, are bound by the directive concerned as from its entry into force, they must comply with the directive even before the expiry of the period allowed for implementation, provided that they possess the powers to do so under national law. In the light of the above considerations, it will scarcely be surprising that I fail to see how such an obligation can be based in Community law. The power to do this under national law cannot however be excluded.

In short, in my view and for the reasons stated above, there is no obligation for national authorities and national courts to comply with a directive before the deadline for implementation has expired.

Thirdly, one may wonder whether what is known as the "*Sperrwirkung*" (blocking effect) of directives produces effects after the entry into force of the directive but before the time limit for implementation has expired. Briefly, "blocking effect" means that the enactment of directives entails a change in the division of powers between the Member States and the Community in the sense that it causes a transfer of legislative power from Member States to the Community.[32] *Sperrwirkung* is often discussed when considering the problem of amendments to harmonized national law made for the purpose of adapting it to socio-economic developments, and thus after the deadline for implementation has expired. It is accepted that national legislature lacks competence in this respect,

[28] See also below, Chapter 10, Section 10.3.

[29] See e.g. Case 14/83 *Von Colson* [1984] ECR 1891, para. 26.

[30] Cf. Curtin and Mortelmans 1994, p. 444 and Hilf 1993, p. 7, who, however, points out that the situation is unclear.

[31] Ipsen 1965, p. 77. Cf. also Kooijmans 1967, p. 141.

[32] Cf. Ipsen 1972, p. 267 and p. 701, Timmermans 1979, p. 551-553, Constantinesco 1977, p. 624, Lauwaars and Maarleveld 1987, p. 189.

unless and in so far as the directive concerned provides otherwise. Any necessary changes can be initiated only by a new directive.[33] From the concept of *Sperrwirkung*, however, it also follows that a directive produces the stated effect from the moment of its entry into force.[34] The only legislative competence the Member States retain with respect to the issues covered by the directive is to enact the measures necessary for its implementation.

Fourthly, a question addressed both in legal writing and in practice concerns the problem whether, during the period provided for implementation, Member States may take measures which, when compared with the directive at issue, entail a retrograde step.[35] The answer to this question can be found in the blocking effect of directives discussed above, which also means that once the directive has entered into force, it prohibits the adoption of measures contrary to its provisions, even during the implementation period.[36] Two further arguments may be added in this respect.

First, it follows from Article 5(2) that Member States are not allowed to take any measure which could jeopardize the attainment of the objectives of the Treaty.[37] Directives being instruments for the realization of the objectives of the Treaty, it is a matter of common sense that during a period allowed to the Member States for purposes of implementation they should prepare the appropriate measures. The adoption of retrograde measures following upon the entry into force of a directive may endanger the achievement of the result

[33] Cf. Lauwaars and Maarleveld 1987, p. 188. See also e.g. Scherzberg 1991, p. 38 and Oldenkop 1972, p. 100.

[34] Cf. Timmermans 1979, p. 551, Hilf 1993, p. 7, Bebr 1981, p. 588. According to Schwartz (1991, p. 5816) blocking effect exists even before the adoption of the directive. For further references on this point see Lauwaars and Maarleveld 1987, p. 190. Contra: Hilf 1993, p. 7.

[35] See Lauwaars and Maarleveld 1987, p. 191, referring to Commissioner Richards, who announced that the Commission may start infringement proceedings wherever a Member State makes retrograde steps during the period provided for implementation of Directive 79/7 (equal treatment in statutory schemes of social security), OJ 1979, L 6/24. Cf. also for some explicit safeguards against retrograde steps after notification Directive 64/221 (public policy and public health), Article 4(3), OJ English Spec. Ed. 1963-1964, p. 177. Another form of safeguard against reducing the level of protection existing at the time of adoption of the directive can be found in Article 1(3) of directive 92/85 (pregnant workers), OJ 1992, L 348/1.

[36] Cf. A-G Mancini in Case 30/85 *Teuling* [1987] ECR 2497, para. 7, and Hilf 1993, p. 7.

[37] Ipsen 1965, p. 75; Bebr 1981, p. 588. In this context it must be noted that there is no clear-cut distinction between *Sperrwirkung* and the obligations under Article 5(2). Some authors see as the basis for *Sperrwirkung* the principle of supremacy of Community law, (e.g. Ipsen 1972, p. 267, Pieper 1990, p. 685, Grabitz Kommentar, p. 21a, Lauwaars and Timmermans 1994, p. 37) while according to others the basis lies in Article 5(2) (e.g. Schwartz 1991, p. 5817 and Hilf as referred to by Schwartz 1991, p. 5816. In the same sense also De Ripaisel-Landy and Gérard 1976, p. 53). According to Oldenkop (1972, p. 100) "*Sperrwirkung*" is to be considered as a secondary "negative" obligation resulting from the primary "positive" obligation under Article 189(3). In Case 30/85 *Teuling* [1987] 2497, para. 7, Mancini links blocking effect and Article 5(2).

STAFFS UNIVERSITY LIBRARY

prescribed. Consequently, it will amount – at least – to a violation of the obligation under Article 5(2).[38]

Second, the Court found in *Peskeloglou*[39] that during the transitory period provided for in Article 45(1) of the Act of Accession of Greece the Member States were not allowed to adopt more restrictive measures than those already in force. It has been suggested that, by analogy, the same should apply to the problem under discussion here.[40] Although, as already stated, there is a certain parallel between transitory provisions in an Act of Accession and the period provided for implementation in a directive, in my view a closer reading of the judgment indicates that the proposed application by analogy does not necessarily hold true. In *Peskeloglou* the Court based its finding on a restrictive interpretation of a derogation (i.e. Article 45(1)) from the principle of free movement of workers enshrined in Article 48 of the Treaty, an interpretation within the specific context of the provisions of the Act of Accession. In my opinion, this reasoning cannot simply be transposed to directives in general.

2.3 The Rigour of the Obligation to Implement the Directive in Due Time

The obligation to adopt the measures for implementation of a directive and to do so within the period prescribed by the directive at issue is an extremely rigorous obligation. With respect to the failure to enact the necessary measures within the specified time, various excuses have been offered by the Member States, but they have not been accepted by the Court of Justice. According to established case law a Member State may not plead provisions, practices or circumstances existing in its internal legal system or, more generally, practical, financial and administrative difficulties in order to justify non-compliance with the obligations and time limits.[41] Similarly, the fact that a directive may pose serious

[38] Cf. Lauwaars and Maarleveld 1987, p. 191. According to them, retrograde steps amount to a whole range of violations, such as violation of Article 5, Article 100, Article 189(3) and the directive at issue.

[39] Case 77/82 [1983] ECR 1085.

[40] Cf. Leenen 1986, p. 42, and to an extent also Lauwaars and Maarleveld 1987, p. 190.

[41] See e.g. Case 163/78 *Commision v. Italy* [1979] ECR 771, Case 44/80 *Commission v. Italy* [1981] ECR 343, Case 45/80 *Commission v. Italy* [1981] ECR 353, Case 390/85 *Commission v. Belgium* [1987] ECR 761, Case 419/85 *Commission v. Italy* [1987] ECR 2115, Case 42/80 *Commission v. Italy* [1980] ECR 3635, Case 43/80 *Commission v. Italy* [1980] ECR 3643, Case 100/81 *Commission v. The Netherlands* [1982] ECR 1837, Case C-42/89 *Commission v. Belgium* [1990] ECR I-2821. The arguments put forward relate, for instance, to government crisis, the complexity of national procedures, the dissolution of parliament and the need to hear advisory bodies. In Case C-45/91 *Commission v. Greece* [1992] ECR I-2509 the Greek government invoked opposition of the local

problems of interpretation cannot constitute a valid excuse for failing to implement it within the required time.[42] The view of the Court is that since the governments of the Member States participate in the preparation of a directive, they must be able to draft the necessary measures within the period allowed for implementation.[43] Moreover, if the said period nevertheless proves to be too short, the Member State concerned must take the appropriate initiatives within the Community in order to obtain an extension of the period by either the Council or the Commission.[44]

Apart from these excuses of – what one may call – a predominantly practical nature, other types of justifications have also been put forward by the Member States. These justifications actually all reduce to the argument that implementation was not necessary because, for instance, the directive had direct effect or because the objective of the directive had already been fully realized in the legal order of the Member State concerned.[45] In one case a government even suggested that the directive itself was superfluous, arguing that the failure to implement it had no adverse effect on the functioning of the Common Market.[46] Furthermore, since each Member State is responsible for its own default, it may not justify its failure by stating that another Member State had also not complied with the obligation to implement the directive in due time.[47] Finally, Member States are in principle obliged to implement the directive even when there is doubt about its validity.[48]

The strictness of the Court with respect to implementation of directives within the period provided can be explained by the following arguments. A non-simultaneous implementation may result in discrimination[49] and endangers the uniform application of Community law within all Member States.[50] Indeed, the

population against the implementation of the directive concerned.

[42] Case 301/81 *Commission v. Belgium* [1983] ECR 467.

[43] See e.g. Case 136/81 *Commission v. Italy* [1982] ECR 3547 and Case 361/85 *Commission v. Italy* [1987] ECR 479.

[44] See e.g. Case 52/75 *Commission v. Italy* [1976] ECR 277, Case 301/81 *Commission v. Belgium* [1983] ECR 467. Under certain directives, the Commission may grant an additional period on special request: see e.g. the above-mentioned Article 19 of Directive 80/778 (drinking water), OJ 1980, L 229/11 and Case C-42/89 *Commission v. Belgium* [1990] ECR I-2821.

[45] The argument drawing upon "direct effect" was rejected by the Court in e.g. Case 102/79 *Commission v. Belgium* [1980] ECR 1473. The second argument is related to the question as to what constitutes adequate implementation; this subject will be discussed below in Section 2.5 and also in Chapter 5.

[46] Case 95/77 *Commission v. The Netherlands* [1978] ECR 863.

[47] See e.g. Case 52/75 *Commission v. Italy* [1976] ECR 277. Cf. also Case C-38/89 *Blanguernon* [1990] ECR I-83.

[48] See below, Section 2.6.

[49] Case 52/75 *Commission v. Italy* [1976] ECR 277.

[50] Case 10/76 *Commission v. Italy* [1976] ECR 1359.

harmonizing effect of directives requires entry into force of the implementing measures from the same date, since the very purpose of a directive would otherwise be seriously compromised.[51]

As mentioned above, no excuses for delayed implementation have as yet been accepted by the Court of Justice. In my view, however, one cannot maintain that the obligation is absolute.[52] It is conceivable that in certain situations a Member State could invoke particular circumstances which could free it, at least for a certain period, from the obligation to implement a directive. In this respect at least two types of situations can be distinguished.

The first is a situation of practical difficulties connected with serious internal disturbances, such as a state of emergency, (imminent) war, and so on. After all, it can hardly be expected of a Member State to implement a directive on the marketing of vegetable seed, for instance, while a war is going on. It is uncertain whether Article 224 EC Treaty could be relied on since this Article is limited to *measures taken* by a Member State "in the event of serious internal disturbances affecting the maintenance of law and order" and so on. This problem was touched upon in *Johnston*,[53] albeit in a different context. The circumstances of the case, however, caused the Court to decide that the question whether Article 224 may be relied upon by a Member State in order to avoid compliance with the obligations imposed by Community law and in particular by the directive at issue did not arise. Furthermore, in the same case the Court also decided that the Treaty does not contain a general proviso covering all measures taken for reasons of public safety.[54]

Another, more commonsense argument could be a plea of *force majeure*. In Case *101/84 (statistical returns)*[55] the Court accepted in principle that a bomb attack may constitute a case of *force majeure*.[56] In this case, however, it was of no avail for the Italian government, as the Court found that the government could not rely on this event to justify continuing failure to comply with the directive concerned several years after the bomb attack had occurred.

[51] See e.g. Case 79/72 *Commission v. Italy* [1973] ECR 667 and Case 52/75 *Commission v. Italy* [1976] ECR 277. Cf. also Maresceau 1980b, p. 659.

[52] Cf. Curtin 1990b, p. 714, Morris 1989, p. 238.

[53] Case 222/84 [1986] ECR 1651.

[54] Cf. also Joined Cases C-19/90 and C-20/90 *Karrella and Karrellas* [1991] ECR I-2691. Cf. however also Case C-57/89 (*Commission v. Germany* [1991] ECR I-883), which suggests that, exceptionally, Member States may deviate from a directive for reasons based on general interest which is superior to the interest represented by a directive (para. 21 and 22).

[55] *Commission v. Italy* [1985] ECR 2629.

[56] Which may in this context be defined as "a temporary absolute impossibility to implement due to an unforseeable and irresistible event". Cf. also Case C-56/90 *Commission v. United Kingdom* [1993] ECR I-4109, in particular para. 46.

The second type of situation is concerned with obligations of the Member States under international law: namely, that the implementation of a directive may entail a violation of an obligation resulting from a bilateral or multilateral treaty. This was the background to the *Stoeckel* and *Levy* cases,[57] for instance.

Article L 213-1 of the French Labour Code prohibiting nightwork of women was enacted in order to give effect to ILO Convention no. 89,[58] ratified by France in 1953. Directive 76/207 (equal treatment at work),[59] however, as interpreted by the Court, prohibits discrimination between men and women with respect to working conditions and access to employment, including nightwork. The prohibition of nightwork of women only was therefore contrary to the said directive. Yet as France had not denounced the Convention (which was only possible at intervals of 10 years), a conflict arose between the Community obligations on the one hand and the obligations under the ILO Convention on the other. By virtue of Article 234 of the EEC Treaty, France's obligations under the Convention could not be affected by Community law. Indeed, under the second paragraph of Article 234 France was only obliged to take "all appropriate steps to eliminate the incompatibilities", i.e. to denounce the Convention in due course in order to be able to meet its obligations under the directive. The deadline for implementation of the directive was 14 February 1980, but the Convention could not be denounced before 27 February 1981 at the earliest. In *Stoeckel* the Court did not address this problem. In *Levy*, however, the Court found that national courts are under a duty to ensure that Article 5 of Directive 76/207 is fully complied with by leaving unapplied any contrary provisions of national legislation, unless the application of such a provision is necessary in order to ensure the performance by the Member State concerned, pursuant to Article 234 of the Treaty, of obligations arising from agreements concluded with third countries before the entry into force of the Treaty.[60]

Although the *Levy* case was decided under Article 177, in my view on the basis of the judgment it could be argued that the same reasoning will also apply in an infringement procedure, the obligation under international law being a sufficient argument to excuse temporarily the Member State's failure to comply with its obligation. This case illustrates nicely how an international agreement may block the implementation of a directive within the period prescribed.

There is another important element to be taken into account in the present discussion, namely the nature of the Article 169 procedure. It is generally accepted that this procedure aims at an *objective* finding of a failure to fulfil the obligations under the Treaty, which should clarify the law and enable the

[57] Case C-345/89 [1991] ECR I-4047 and Case C-158/91 [1993] ECR I-4287. Cf. also Case C-13/93 *Minne* [1994] ECR I-371.

[58] Convention concerning Night-work of Women Employed in Industry of 9 July 1948.

[59] OJ 1976, L 39/40.

[60] Case C-158/91 [1993] ECR I-4287, para. 22.

Member States to know the exact scope of their obligations.[61] The procedure is, as expressed by A-G Roemer,

> "intended to establish whether a specified national legislation or administrative practice is in harmony with Community law, that is a procedure which in principle excludes any considerations of fault."[62]

The judgment of the Court is declaratory; it formally establishes the violation, which, with all its legal consequences, existed as from the date it was committed. Moreover, it lacks executory force, no sanctions whatsoever being provided until recently and no national measures being thereby annulled.[63] From this viewpoint it is understandable that the Court accepts no excuses for belated (or incorrect) implementation.

The declaratory nature of the judgment, however, does not imply that it has no consequences.

Firstly, pursuant to Article 171 EC, the Member State concerned is obliged to terminate the violation; all its institutions, including the courts, must draw the necessary inferences from the judgment.[64] The finding that a Member State has not complied with its obligations entails for its authorities a prohibition against applying a national rule recognized as incompatible with the Treaty and, if the circumstances so require, they are obliged to take all appropriate measures to enable Community law to be fully applied.[65] These effects apply *ex tunc*, i.e. from the time the breach occurred.[66]

Secondly, the judgment can form the basis for "responsibility that a Member State can incur as a result of its default, as regards other Member States, the Community or private parties."[67]

Thirdly, the judgment can generate, albeit indirectly and in limited fields, negative financial consequences.[68]

[61] Cf. Kapteyn and VerLoren van Themaat 1990, p. 274-275. See also Case 301/81 *Commission v. Belgium* [1983] ECR 467.

[62] Case 8/70 *Commission v. Italy* [1970] ECR 961, at p. 970. Cf. also his opinion in Case 7/71 *Commission v. France* [1971] ECR 1003, at p. 1034 and, more recently, Case C-73/92 *Commission v. Spain* [1993] ECR I-5997.

[63] Cf. Brown and Jacobs 1989, p. 88.

[64] Joined Cases 314 to 316/81 and 83/82 *Waterkeyn* [1982] ECR 4337.

[65] See e.g. Case 48/71 *Commission v. Italy* [1972] ECR 527 and Case C-101/91 *Commission v. Italy* [1993] ECR I-191.

[66] Cf. Schermers and Waelbroeck 1992, p. 313. Cf. also the opinion of A-G Slynn in C-293/85 *Commission v. Belgium* [1988] ECR 305 where the possibility of limiting the retroactive effects of a judgment given under Article 169 is discussed: p. 342-344.

[67] Case 39/72 *Commission v. Italy* [1973] ECR 101. See also below, Chapter 12, Subsection 12.1.2.

[68] E.g. payments out of the European Guidance and Guarantee Fund for Agriculture or other Structural Funds. Cf. Ehlermann 1987, p. 214-215.

Fourthly, since the entry into force of the Maastricht Treaty, financial sanctions can be directly imposed in cases of failure to comply with Article 171 EC.

In summary, on the one hand, a judgment under Article 169 *as such* has no legal effects; the latter result from the Treaty itself. On the other hand, these effects may be considerable. Since the judgment and the effects are two different matters, a careful distinction should be made between the fact that the Court is in principle not willing to accept excuses in an infringement procedure and the possibility that excuses may play a part when the effects come under consideration. In particular, in my view, certain types of justifications could be relevant once the questions of direct effect and of liability of the State for damages resulting from non-implementation are addressed. The Court's strict attitude in Article 169 proceedings with respect to possible justifications cannot in fact be transposed to these issues when they emerge within the context of procedures of a different nature.[69]

2.4 Delays in Implementation and Retroactive Legislation

Although, as stated above, the obligation to implement directives in due time should not, in my opinion, be considered to be absolute, in principle the Court of Justice vigorously upholds the observation of the time limits for implementation by the Member States. It is however no secret that the deadlines are frequently not respected. The next question is therefore how the national implementing measures can minimize the detrimental effects of belated implementation.

It appears from the judgment in *Dik*[70] that if national implementing measures are adopted after the expiry of the period for implementation "the simultaneous entry into force of [the directive concerned] in all Member States is ensured by giving such measures effect retroactively as from [the date for implementation]."[71] The Court added an important proviso to this: that in such a case the rights which the directive confers on individuals in the Member States must be respected as from the expiry of the said period.[72] From *Dik* it is not entirely clear whether implementation with retroactive effect is an obligation under Community law. The operative part of the judgment states that the Member States *may* fix the date of the entry into force of the implementing measures retroactively to the date of expiry of the prescribed period. It is

[69] Cf. also Chapter 11, Subsection 11.5.1 and Chapter 12, Subsection 12.4.3.

[70] Case 80/87 [1988] ECR 1601.

[71] Strictly speaking it should be "entry into force of the implementing measures". See above, n. 20.

[72] The directive at issue "conferred rights" by virtue of direct effect. Cf. also Case C-343/92 *Roks* [1994] ECR I-571.

submitted that this formulation may be due to the terms of the question posed by the national court, which wanted to know *whether it is compatible with the directive at issue* for a transitional period to be given retroactive effect. The term "may" should therefore not be considered to be decisive.

If it is assumed that a defaulting Member State is in principle under the duty to implement the directive with retroactive effect – and in my view, for the reasons given above, this is the best solution – another problem arises, namely the admissibility of retroactive legislation. In *Dik* Advocate General Mancini remarked that the lawfulness of retroactive laws must be determined on the basis of national law.[73] I feel I cannot entirely agree with this position, since in this respect also, owing to the supremacy of Community law, national law – whether a legislative provision or a general principle of law[74]- should not frustrate full compliance with a Community law obligation. Matters are complicated, however, because there are two possible approaches to the problem. Firstly, there is case law of the Court of Justice which allows the application of *national general principles of law.*

A judgment which may be instructive in this respect is the Court's judgment in Case *C-5/89 (Bug-Alutechnik).*[75] Although the problem of this case occurred in a context different from the one under discussion here, namely the recovery of illegally paid state aid, some considerations are nevertheless relevant. In this case the Court addressed, among other things, the question whether the principles of legitimate expectations and legal certainty may in certain circumstances protect an undertaking which has received illegal aid against such a recovery imposed by Community law.[76] Referring to the judgment in *Deutsche Milchkontor,*[77] the Court recalled that the principle of legitimate expectations is part of the legal order of the Community; the fact that national legislation also provides for the principles of the protection of legitimate expectations and assurance of legal certainty to be observed can therefore not be considered contrary to that same legal order. According to the Court the same solution was applicable in the present case. The application and interpretation of these principles, however, is not entirely a matter for the national courts. Indeed, the Court of Justice considered "that a recipient of illegally granted aid is not precluded from relying on exceptional circumstances on the basis of which it had legitimately assumed the aid to be lawful" but "it is for [a national] court to assess the material circumstances, if necessary after obtaining a preliminary ruling on interpretation from the Court of Justice."[78]

[73] Case 80/87 [1988] 1601, para. 3.

[74] See e.g. Case 309/85 *Barra* [1988] ECR 355 and opinion of A-G Mischo in Case C-377/89 *Cotter and McDermott II* [1991] ECR I-1155, para. 34.

[75] *Commission v. Germany* [1990] ECR I-3437.

[76] Decision 88/174 of the Commission, OJ 1988, L 79/29.

[77] Joined Cases 205-215/82, [1983] ECR 2633.

[78] Case C-5/89 *Commission v. Germany* [1990] ECR I-3437, para. 16.

From this judgment it follows that, in principle, the application of general principles of law in the national legal order cannot be considered contrary to Community law, but, at the same time, their application is not unlimited. The national principles may prevail over the obligations under Community law by virtue of the fact that they also form a part of Community law itself, but their interpretation and application is ultimately submitted to the control of the Court of Justice. In this way their content and scope are in effect partly determined by this Court. The same line of reasoning as in *Bug-Alutechnik* can likewise be found in fields of Community law other than the recovery of illegal state aid.[79]

Conversely, however, other cases suggest that it is rather *general principles of Community law* which apply as the standard for reviewing national measures. In *Zuckerfabrik Franken*[80] the Court considered it necessary to examine whether certain German measures taken in execution of a regulation were compatible with superior rules of Community law, in particular with the principles of legal certainty and proportionality. Similarly, from *Kent Kirk*[81] it follows that national measures imposing criminal sanctions with retroactive effect are incompatible with Community law: the principle of non-retroactivity of criminal provisions is a principle common to all the legal orders of the Member States and is enshrined in Article 7 of the European Convention for the Protection of Human Rights. As such it occupies a place among the general principles of law whose observance is ensured by the Court of Justice.

In general, there is no sharp distinction in the Court's case law between fundamental rights in the strict sense of the term and general principles of law.[82] Furthermore, the Court's case law shows a particular tendency to expand the application of fundamental rights to national measures giving effect to Community law[83] or merely falling within the scope of Community law,[84] which supports the idea that the measures implementing a directive must comply with the general principles of Community law. An additional argument can be drawn from the fact that the implementation of directives is already governed in certain respects by Community law principles, particularly in that it must meet certain requirements imposed by the principle of legal certainty.[85]

[79] Cf. opinion of A-G Darmon in C-5/89 *Commission v. Germany* [1990] ECR I-3437, para. 16-18.
[80] Case 77/81 [1982] ECR 681.
[81] Case 63/83 [1984] ECR 2689.
[82] Cf. e.g. Kapteyn and VerLoren van Themaat 1990, p. 160 and 166 and Temple Lang 1991, p. 23.
[83] See e.g Case 5/88 *Wachauf* [1989] ECR 2609.
[84] See e.g. Case C-260/89 *ERT* [1991] ECR I-2925. See for an overview of the relevant case law Temple Lang 1991.
[85] See below, Chapter 5.

Returning to the problem of implementation of directives with retroactive effect in order to safeguard as far as possible simultaneous entry into force of measures implementing a directive, the foregoing must lead to the conclusion that the lawfulness of such retroactive legislation is not solely a matter of national law. Either national principles of law apply but in their "curtailed" form, or the Community law principles are applicable. Whatever the solution might be, in so far as national provisions and legal principles, such as the *nulla poena sine lege* and legal certainty, should make implementation with retroactive effect impossible, this limitation must be appreciated in the context of Community law: i.e. in the light of the general principles as interpreted by the Court of Justice or, at least, taking into account the limits imposed by the Court upon the application of national principles.

The distinction between the two approaches is important in so far as the contents and modalities of application of the respective principles may differ.[86] It should be noted, however, that in practice the difference is not a fundamental one. The Court of Justice, in order to ascertain the existence and the possible content of a legal principle, often resorts to the general principles common to the laws of the Member States. By using the method of *kritisch-wertende Rechtsvergleichung*[87] (evaluative comparison of laws) the Court chooses "the best and most appropriate solution" for Community law.[88] This process safeguards the basic elements of the principles at issue as they exist within the legal order of the Member States.

Finally, some arguments in favour of reviewing the retroactivity of national implementing measures in the context of Community law can be based on the Court's case law on retroactive effect of Community legislation. In this area the principle laid down by the Court is that retroactivity is allowed in exceptional cases only, since the principle of legal certainty militates against such an effect.[89] If Community legislation, including directives, "must be unequivocal and in its application must be predictable for those who are subject to it"[90] and, moreover, a directive cannot impose on Member States an obligation to adopt measures which conflict with the principle of legitimate expectations and the principle of non-retroactivity of penal provisions,[91] it follows, in my opinion, *a*

[86] Cf. on the differences existing between Dutch law and Community law, also with respect to the principle of legal certainty, Widdershoven and De Lange 1994.

[87] Ipsen 1972, p. 113.

[88] Cf. Kutscher 1976, p. 29.

[89] Cf. e.g. the opinion of A-G VerLoren van Themaat in Case 70/83 *Kloppenburg* [1984] ECR 1075, Section 5 and 6. For a detailed discussion of retroactive legislation see Heukels 1991, in particular Chapters II and III.

[90] Case 70/83 *Kloppenburg* [1984] ECR 1075, para. 11.

[91] See Case C-331/88 *Fedesa* [1990] ECR I-4023.

fortiori that implementing measures adopted by the Member States must satisfy the same requirements, particularly when the result of those measures is to impose obligations on individuals.[92] In this situation, however, there is an apparent tension between the principle of non-retroactivity on the one hand and the imperative that implementing measures should enter into force simultaneously. In my view, it is ultimately up to the Court of Justice to find the balance between the two.

2.5 THE OBLIGATION TO IMPLEMENT THE DIRECTIVE CORRECTLY: A PRELIMINARY INQUIRY

By comparison with the problem of implementation of directives in due time, correct implementation is a considerably more complex matter. It is "intellectually much more demanding", as one author expresses it,[93] since it "requires both understanding of the legal meaning of the provisions of the directive and ability to interpret the meaning of national legislation in the light of the Member State's own legal and administrative practice."[94]

It is obvious that the national implementing measures must correspond to the internal substance of the directive concerned. A directive requiring equal pay for men and women for "work of *equal value*" is not adequately implemented by national provivions providing for equal pay for "the *same* work";[95] if a directive contains exhaustive rules as to the obligation of traders to give notification of the placing on the market of certain new substances, the Member States cannot, in their legislation adopted to implement the directive, widen or restrict the obligation at issue;[96] a provision of a directive exempting from VAT the care administered to persons in the exercise of the medical and paramedical professions may not be implemented as exempting veterinary surgeons from taxation.[97]

In fact, since a directive imposes upon the Member States an obligation of result, the measures taken by the Member States must be such as to ensure that the directive is "fully effective, in accordance with the objective which it

[92] Rights which individuals derive from directives are safeguarded under the "Dik construction", at least for the period between the deadline provided for implementation and the actual (but belated) implementation itself. There is, however, no such guarantee for the future. See Case C-343/92 *Roks* [1994] ECR I-571.

[93] Macrory 1992, p. 354.

[94] *Ibid.* Cf. also Easson 1981, p. 31-32.

[95] Case 143/83 *Commission v. Denmark* [1985] ECR 427.

[96] Case 278/85 *Commission v. Denmark* [1987] ECR 4069.

[97] Case 122/87 *Commission v. Italy* [1988] ECR 2685.

STAFFS UNIVERSITY LIBRARY

pursues".[98] This means that the obligation arising from Article 189(3) goes further than the actual text of the directive at issue and the mere transposition of this text into national law. It imposes certain requirements as to the nature of the implementing measures (i.e. the legal effects they produce) and, moreover, it requires that these measures are applied and enforced in practice in an effective manner.[99]

In other words, the question of correct implementation comprises three closely related but nevertheless distinguishable issues. The first concerns the requirements regarding the *content* of the measures adopted with a view to implementation, the second relates to the requirements regarding the *nature* of the measures, and the third relates to their *effective application and enforcement in practice.* These requirements actually appear to interfere with the freedom ostensibly enjoyed by the Member States with respect to the "form and methods" of implementation under Article 189(3). The scope of these requirements and the reasons for imposing them will be discussed in more detail in Chapter 5.

At this point, I would like to continue by addressing two more general issues related to the proper implementation of directives, which have much in common with some of the problems discussed above in Sections 2.3 and 2.4 on belated implementation. They concern the possible justifications for incorrect implementation and the measures a Member State should take once it has been established that the directive has not been implemented properly.

When enacting the measures necessary to meet their obligations under Article 189(3), the Member States have the choice of different modalities of implementation, lying anywhere between verbatim transposition of the directive's provisions into national law at one end of the spectrum and a "translation" of the directive into the terminology and concepts of their national legal system at the other.[100]

Verbatim reproduction may have the advantage that, at least at first sight, the Member State has complied with its obligation. The obvious disadvantage is then, however, that national legislation may be using unfamiliar terms. Consequently, there is no guarantee that the implementing measures will be understood, interpreted and applied correctly.

Although it may be preferable and may correspond more with the character of the directive, implementation by way of "translation" of the directive into national legal equivalents is also not unproblematic. In the first place, it may be that equivalent national concepts and terms simply do not exist or that their equivalence is only one of appearance. In *CILFIT,*[101] the Court of Justice indicated this danger very clearly when it held that Community law uses

[98] Case 14/83 *Von Colson* [1984] ECR 1891, para. 15.
[99] Cf. Chapter 3, Section 3.3.
[100] Cf. Easson 1981, p. 34-35. See also below, Chapter 5, in particular Subsection 5.2.2.
[101] Case 283/81 [1982] ECR 3415.

terminology which is peculiar to itself: its legal concepts do not necessarily have the same meaning as they have in the law of the various Member States; moreover, every provision of Community law must be placed in its context and interpreted in the light of the provisions of Community law as a whole. Although this case was concerned with, *inter alia*, the application of the doctrine of "*acte clair*" by national courts, the same considerations apply equally with respect to the problem of proper implementation of directives.

Furthermore, directives themselves are often vague and open to a variety of interpretations, since they must accommodate different national legal concepts and constructions. Their vagueness may also be the result of political compromise within the Council. It is also possible that both of these aspects may play a part respectively. Combined with the facts that they may be quite complicated, may have a structure of their own which does not necessarily correspond with the structure of the national law which is to be adapted,[102] and may be internally inconsistent or incompatible with other provisions of Community law,[103] this means that their implementation is often not an easy task.[104]

Although the *COM documents* which usually accompany a draft directive may be of some help for better understanding of its provisions, the final outcome of the Community decision-making process can differ considerably from the original draft. Yet the only explanatory text the implementing authorities can rely on is the directive's preamble, often expressed in non-committal terms. A partial remedy for this unsatisfactory situation could in fact be a detailed explanatory memorandum drafted by the Council, to be released at the time of the adoption of the directive.[105] It is submitted that such a practice would be very much in line with the professed and currently fashionable transparency of the Community decision-making process.

Another suggestion is to involve the Commission more closely in the process of implementation of directives.[106] The problem is, however, that sometimes the

[102] Cf. Kortmann 1991, p. 48.

[103] Cf. *Sutherland Report*, p. 35-36 and e.g. the consequences resulting from Case C-262/88 *Barber* [1990] ECR I-1889 for Directive 86/378 (equal treatment in occupational social security schemes), OJ 1986, L 225/40.

[104] In relation to the unsatisfactory quality of EC legislation see e.g. Barents 1994 and Kellerman 1994. Cf. also *Conclusions of Edinburgh Summit*, Bull. EC 12-1992, p. 19, *Council Resolution of 8 June 1993 on the quality of drafting of Community legislation*, OJ 1993, C 166/1 and *Reinforcing the effectiveness of the Internal Market*, COM (93) 256 final, p. 30-31.

[105] Instead of recording declarations in the Council minutes which, however, are carefully kept secret. Cf. Hilf 1993, p. 8.

[106] Cf. *Sutherland report*, p. 33-34. This view is also endorsed by the Commission. See e.g. the *Eleventh annual report to the European Parliament on monitoring the application of Community law*, OJ 1994, C 154/1, p. 7-8.

Commission itself also does not understand the exact meaning of a directive's provisions and especially their concrete implications.[107]

The fact that the Commission is also far from certain of the exact meaning of a directive's provisions and what should be considered as adequate implementation in a concrete case is perhaps best illustrated by the withdrawal of its complaints during the administrative or judicial stage of Article 169 proceedings. It is well known that the administrative stage in particular often has more the character of negotiations between the Commission and the Member States than that of straightforward control by the Commission or a mutual exchange of views on points of law.[108] If the Commission and the Member State concerned fail to reach an agreement on the divisive issues, and the Commission decides to bring the case before the Court of Justice, even then it is not unusual for the Commission to withdraw some of its complaints or even the entire case. The reasons for such a withdrawal may vary. In some cases the Member State eventually complies with Community law provisions as interpreted by the Commission. In other cases, however, it is the Commission which admits that it was mistaken.[109] Finally, in one case it appeared that the Commission was so utterly confused about the application of a directive in a Member State that it did not even know what the precise complaint should be.[110]

It is against this – roughly sketched – background of frequently complicated questions on the interpretation of both Community and national law, to which neither the Commission nor the Member State concerned will instantly know the answer, that the problem of possible justifications for inadequate implementation must be considered.

The solution to the problem seems to be rather simple: in principle no excuses from the Member States are accepted for incorrect implementation. As in the case of justifications presented for delays in implementation, practical difficulties and serious problems of interpretation cannot constitute valid excuses for deficient implementation. Indeed, difficulties which may be encountered by

[107] Cf. Case 291/84 *Commission v. The Netherlands* [1987] ECR 3483, para. 6, Case C-58/89 *Commission v. Germany* [1991] ECR I-4983, para. 8.

[108] Cf. Snyder 1993, p. 27-31. For a brief description of the administrative stage see also Kapteyn and VerLoren van Themaat 1990, p. 275.

[109] See e.g. Case 274/83 *Commission v. Italy* [1985] ECR 1077, para. 12, C-190/90 *Commission v. The Netherlands* [1991] ECR I-2535, para. 8. As regards the administrative stage of Article 169 proceedings, which is confidential, it is indeed difficult to determine the exact reasons for the Commission's withdrawal of certain complaints.

[110] Case C-52/90 *Commission v. Denmark* [1992] ECR I-2187, in particular para. 21. Cf. also Case C-43/90 *Commission v. Germany* [1992] ECR I-1909, where the Commission argued that Germany had not complied with certain obligations under Directive 79/831 (labelling of dangerous substances) OJ 1979, L 259/10, although, with the best will in the world, these could not be found in the Directive concerned.

the implementing authorities during the implementation phase can be overcome to a large extent by, for instance, proper information from those who participated in the negotiations about the directive or by involving those who will be responsible for the implementation from the very beginning of the decision-making process.[111]

Furthermore, since the Member States themselves participate in the elaboration of a directive, they are, in a way, also at the source of the difficulties which the directive may pose at a later stage. Under these circumstances it is difficult to accept the vagueness and obscurity of its terms as a valid argument.[112] In this context it should also be noted that the Member States cannot rely upon declarations in the Council minutes for the interpretation of a provision of a directive. The true meaning can be derived only from the actual wording and the directive itself.[113]

Ultimately, however, after having submitted the implementing measures to the Commission and after being informed that the Commission is satisfied with the measures at issue, can a Member State believe with reason that it has implemented the directive correctly?

In this respect at least two situations must be distinguished. The very first examination by the Commission after the notification of the implementing measures by the Member States cannot really give rise to such expectations, since this examination is very general in nature and mainly serves the purpose of ascertaining whether implementing measures have been enacted at all.[114]

The situation could be different after the implementing measures have been more closely scrutinized, or when the Commission has given an unequivocal opinion on a particular problem of implementation at the request of the Member State concerned. Depending on the formulation of the views expressed by the Commission or perhaps also in cases of sustained and tacit tolerance of a certain way of implementation, the possibility should not be excluded that a Member State might derive some protection as a result of the Commission's conduct.

This may seem to be a rather arguable submission since, according to the Court, implied or even explicit approval by the Commission of a measure adopted by a Member State cannot justify a breach of an obligation under the Treaty.[115] However, in this respect the distinction made in Section 2.3 above

[111] Thus following the "English model" of implementing directives. Cf. Jeffreys 1991.

[112] See, however, the (rather exceptional) judgment in Case 26/69 *Commission v. France* [1970] ECR 565: "bearing in mind the equivocal nature of the situation thus brought about, the French Republic cannot be accused of any failure to fulfil its obligations" (para. 32).

[113] See e.g. Case 237/84 *Commission v. Belgium* [1986] ECR 1247. Cf. also Case 429/85 *Commission v. Italy* [1988] ECR 843.

[114] Cf. Case 96/81 *Commission v. The Netherlands* [1982] ECR 1791.

[115] Case 288/83 *Commission v. Ireland* [1985] ECR 1761.

between the objective finding that a breach was committed as such and the possible legal effects of such a finding again becomes relevant. While the Member State concerned should not be allowed to rely on justifications or other excuses relating to the absence of fault for the purposes of the declaratory judgment under Article 169, including an unambigous statement by the Commission that the directive has been implemented correctly, as far as the consequences are concerned, the Member State may be protected by the principle of legitimate expectations or other related principles. It has been argued in legal writing that the Commission's laxity in enforcing the law, where it has the duty to enforce it, cannot give rise to any legitimate expectations on the part of the Member States or individuals.[116] I do not believe this position is entirely correct. As the Court's case law shows, the Commission's point of view or its inaction may serve, in exceptional circumstances, as grounds for applying a time limit to the Court's judgments. The ratio behind this démarche by the Court is the principle of legal certainty, including the protection of legitimate expectations.[117]

To summarize, it is my opinion that when the Court finds in a judgment under Article 169 that a Member State has not fulfilled its obligations under the Treaty, the possibility should not be excluded that, as far as the legal consequences resulting from such a finding are concerned, the Court might impose a limitation on the grounds of legitimate expectations on the part of the Member States, raised by the conduct of the Commission.[118]

Once it has been established that a Member State has not implemented a directive properly, how should it remedy the situation? In my view, the same requirements as in the case of belated implementation must apply:[119] i.e. reparation with retroactive effect with possible limitations by general principles of law. Moreover, the rights which individuals might have derived directly from

[116] Schermers and Waelbroeck 1990, p. 66-67.

[117] See in particular Case 43/75 *Defrenne II* [1976] ECR 455 and Case C-163/90 *Legros* [1992] I-4625. Cf. also Report of the hearing in Case C-9/91 *EOC* [1992] ECR I-4297, at p. I-4313: "The Commission has to concede that its silence ... may have reinforced the United Kingdom's view that the difference in contribution requirements as between men and women was permitted by Article 7(1) of directive 79/7."

[118] In this respect, a parallel can perhaps be drawn with Case 223/85 *RSV* [1987] ECR 4617. In this case the Court accepted that the Commission's long-lasting silence in an Article 93(2) procedure established legitimate expectations on the applicant's part and, although this did not render the aid legal, the Commission was therefore prevented from asking for the refund of the aid at issue. Cf. also the opinion of A-G Slynn in Case C-293/85 *Commission v. Belgium* [1988] ECR 305 as regards the possible application of Article 174 within the context of an infringement proceedings (p. 342-344). On the other hand, it must be noted that in Case C-317/92 *Commission v. Germany* [1994] ECR I-2039 the Court did not accept that a silence of 24 years on the part of the Commission in an infringement proceeding gave rise to legitimate expectations. Cf. also Case C-56/90 *Commission v. United Kingdom* [1993] ECR I-4109.

[119] See above, Section 2.4.

the directive at issue must also be observed. From the point of view of Community law there is no difference between delayed and incorrect implementation. In both cases, the legal situation prescribed by the directive has not been achieved, to the detriment of uniform and simultaneous entry into force of the directive's content within the national legal orders of the Member States.

2.6 AN END TO THE OBLIGATIONS?

The obligation to achieve the result prescribed by the directive exists for the Member States as long as the directive is in force.[120] Directives are not however written for eternity. Accordingly, the obligations may change or cease to exist. Essentially, in this respect the following situations may arise:

The directive itself is limited in time, as with the Sixth Directive on summertime arrangements, which concerns only the years 1993 and 1994.[121]

The provisions of a directive are amended by a later directive[122] or by an Act of Accession,[123] which can involve a number of possibilities, such as repealing or replacing (parts of) articles of the old directive, inserting new articles or parts of text, adding or updating (technical) annexes etc. This will consequently change the content of the Member States' obligation.[124]

Similarly, an entire directive may be repealed (and at the same time replaced) by another directive, as happened in the fields of driving licences and public works contracts,[125] for instance.

Another – far less common – way to terminate the existence of the obligation occurs as a rule when the directive is tainted with illegality, i.e. the directive itself

[120] Cf. Case C-310/89 *Commission v. The Netherlands* [1991] ECR I-1381 where the Court pointed out that "the Member States are bound to comply with all their obligations under an existing directive. ... In any event, the binding force of a directive may not be challenged as long as it has not been abrogated or amended." (Summary publication, para. 2 of the summary). Cf. also Case C-137/92P *Commission v. BASF* [1994] ECR I-2555, in particular para. 48.

[121] Directive 92/20, OJ 1992, L 89/28.

[122] E.g. Directive 71/305 (public works contracts), OJ English Spec. Ed. 1971 (II) p. 682 by Directive 89/440, OJ 1989, L 210/1, Directive 82/606 (surveys of earnings of workers in agriculture), OJ 1982, L 247/22, by Directive 91/534, OJ 1991, L 288/36, Directive 69/169 (tax-free allowances for travellers), OJ English Spec. Ed. 1969 (I), p. 232, by Directive 91/191, OJ 1991, L 94/24.

[123] E.g. Directive 71/305 (public works contracts), OJ English Spec. Ed. 1971 (II) p. 682, by the Act of Accession of Spain and Portugal.

[124] Member States are, however, not allowed to invoke the pending amendments in order to justify their failure to implement the directive at issue fully and correctly. Cf. Case 306/84 *Commission v. Belgium* [1987] ECR 675.

[125] Cf. Directive 91/439 (driving licences), OJ 1991, L 237/1, repealing Directive 80/1263 and Directive 89/440 (public works contracts), OJ 1989, L 210/1, repealing Directive 77/277. For a regulation repealing a directive see e.g. Regulation 259/93 (shipments of waste), OJ 1993, L 30/1.

or the way in which it was adopted are in violation of the law. Yet in this respect a further distinction must be made as to the consequences of such a finding. The issue of illegality can be raised in several different types of proceedings; the consequences of the challenge will vary according to the proceedings under which it was brought.

In an action for annulment under Article 173, a directive (or a provision of a directive) will be declared void[126] with an effect *erga omnes* and *ex tunc*, unless the Court decides, by applying Article 174, to uphold (some of) the effects of the directive.[127] In a preliminary procedure the Court may declare the directive to be invalid.[128] Likewise, a judgment in an action for damages may give the necessary indications as to the illegality of the directive at issue, even if the action is not ultimately successful as far as the claim for damages is concerned. While this has not yet been entirely settled, it is conceivable that the illegality of a directive could be raised under Article 184,[129] although this would mean that the directive is merely inapplicable in the concrete case before the Court of Justice.

In theory, in the last three types of actions the directive will be made inoperative only in the particular case. There is thus no effect *erga omnes*. Yet in practice the finding that the directive is invalid or illegal or inapplicable has a much wider scope, as it will *de facto* compel the institutions to replace the act.

According to the Court, a national court should regard an act which has been declared invalid in another preliminary procedure as invalid for the purposes of a judgment to be given by this court.[130] The much broader practical effect of a declaration of invalidity is likewise underlined by the apparent need to limit the effects of such a declaration by applying Article 174 by analogy.[131] A finding under Article 215 and Article 184 does not as such affect the validity of the act. Nevertheless, in order to prevent the illegality being raised repeatedly in the Court of Justice, the best policy is to amend, withdraw or replace the act at issue.

If it results from a judgment of the Court under Articles 173 or 177 that a directive or a provision of a directive is declared void or illegal, the obligation at

[126] See e.g. Case C-202/88 *France v. Commission* [1991] ECR I-1223.

[127] Cf. Case C-295/90 *European Parliament v. Council* [1992] ECR I-4193.

[128] As regards preliminary questions concerning the validity of a directive (provision) see e.g. Case 5/77 *Tedeschi* [1977] ECR 1555, Case 21/78 *Delkvist* [1978] ECR 2327 and Case C-331/88 *Fedesa* [1990] ECR I-4023.

[129] It is, in particular, uncertain whether a Member State in an infringement proceedings may rely on Article 184. Cf. Brown and Jacobs 1989, p. 129-130 and opinion of A-G Darmon in case C-258/89 *Commission v. Spain* [1991] I-3977, para. 13-32.

[130] Case 66/80 *ICC* [1981] ECR 1191.

[131] See e.g. Case 4/79 *Providence agricole* [1980] ECR 2823 and Case 41/84 *Pinna I* [1986] ECR 1.

issue ceases to exist.[132] The condition is, however, that there has been a judgment of the Court, since the latter has made clear that a Community act must be presumed to be valid until it has been held to be invalid (or declared void, as the case may be) by a competent court, i.e. – since *Foto-Frost*[133] – the Court of Justice itself; if there has not been such a judgment, national authorities are obliged to apply the rules of Community law.[134] Clearly it is not for the Member States to decide on the validity of a Community act, in the same way as it is not for the national courts to declare such an act invalid.[135]

On the other hand, illegality established under Article 215 and, in so far as this is conceivable, under Article 184, does not appear to be sufficient to release the Member States from their obligations resulting from Article 189(3). Similarly, in a preliminary judgment the Court of Justice may give an interpretation of a Treaty Article which makes it clear that a directive is (on certain points) incompatible with the Treaty.[136] Formally, the directive is not declared to be invalid or void and the Member States will have to comply with their obligation to implement the directive. However, from a more practical point of view, obliging them to implement a deficient directive shows little common sense.[137] Obviously, in such a situation a prompt intervention of the Community legislature is highly desirable for the sake of legal certainty.

[132] Complex issues may then arise as to the status and effects of national measures implementing the directive concerned.

[133] Case 314/85 [1987] ECR 4199.

[134] See Case 101/78 *Granaria* [1979] ECR 623. Cf. also Case C-310/89 *Commission v. The Netherlands* [1991] ECR I-1381.

[135] Cf. Case 314/85 *Foto-Frost* [1987] ECR 4199 and, for further support, Case C-217/88 *Commission v. Germany* [1990] ECR I-2879.

[136] Cf. the whole line of "pension cases" on interpretation of Article 119, which started with Case C-262/88 *Barber* [1990] ECR I-1889.

[137] Cf. Easson 1981, p. 25. Furthermore it must be noted that the Court is prepared to accept an exception to the presumption of lawfulness of Community acts in case of "acts tainted by an irregularity whose gravity is so obvious that it cannot be tolerated by the Community legal order". Case C-137/92P *Commission v. BASF* [1994] ECR I-2555, para. 49.

3
The Result to be Achieved

3.1 Abstract Speculations

By stating that directives are binding as to the result to be achieved, Article 189(3) may suggest that they lay down in fairly general terms certain objectives which are to be accomplished. In particular the German version of the Treaty, which employs the term "*Ziel*" (objective), has given rise to considerable speculation as to its meaning *and* its implications for the content of a directive. As the term "*Ziel*" gives an idea of overall coherence, something all-embracing and certainly not detailed, which leaves considerable flexibility as to its actual substantiation,[1] it was suggested that a directive should restrict itself to a description of the essential elements of the measures proposed: provisions going beyond this specification should not be binding.[2] However, a terminological comparison of the different linguistic versions of the Treaty led Ipsen to conclude that a more appropriate word to have used in Article 189(3) would have been "*Ergebnis*" (result).[3] Consequently, in his opinion, the term "result" should be understood as the legal effects arising from the content of a directive.[4] In other words, the result to be achieved is determined by the content of the directive at issue. According to Ipsen[5] the term "result" (or "*Ziel*" in the German version) does not entail limitations as to the directive's content, as has been argued by others.[6] As pointed out above, in the Introduction to Part I, it is generally accepted that directives may go into detail. Consequently they may meticulously spell out the result to be achieved.[7] Since, in this way, the result to be achieved depends on and varies according to the content of a directive, any definition of the term "result" must remain abstract and rather general.[8]

Apart from the above-mentioned description given by Ipsen, result is often defined, notably in German literature, as a general legal, economic or social

[1] Cf. Louis 1993, p. 500-501. According to Ipsen (1965, p. 72-73) the term "*Ziel*" gives a "*Vorstellung von Globalität, Gesamtzusammenhang, jedenfalls von Nicht-Detailliertheit, von verbleibenden, flexibelen Gestaltungsmöglichkeiten*".

[2] Cf. Smit and Herzog, p. 5-612, referring to Zuleeg.

[3] Ipsen 1965, p. 74.

[4] *Ibid.*

[5] *Ibid.*

[6] Cf. Smit and Herzog, p. 5-612, referring to Zuleeg. For criticism of Ipsen's views see Oldenkop 1972, p. 83-84.

[7] Cf. e.g. Fuß 1965, p. 380, as well as Daig and Smidt 1991, p. 4962.

[8] Cf. Oldenkop 1972, p. 85.

situation[9] or "*Erfolg der sich zwar im Rahmen der von EWGV als Ziele des Vertrages gekennzeichneten Konzeption hält, gleichzeitig jedoch eine Aufschlüsselung dieser Konzeption enthalten kann und in der Regel auch enthalten wird*".[10] Another definition, although not drastically dissimilar from the previous one as regards the basic elements, is given by Kapteyn and VerLoren van Themaat,[11] namely "a legal or factual situation which does justice to the Community interest which, under the Treaty, the directive is to ensure". In other words, the result may concern both the state of affairs in law and in fact and must be situated within one or more objectives of the Treaty.[12]

From the foregoing it clearly follows that a search for more concrete indications as to the result to be achieved boils down to an analysis of every individual directive.[13] This is quite beyond the scope of this book. Yet some general remarks on the *type* of provisions a directive will usually contain may be helpful in comprehending *what* – in general terms – can be the content of the obligation a directive may impose. On the basis of this inquiry I shall indicate what is to be understood by the term "result" for the purposes of this book.

3.2 Different Types of Provisions which a Directive May Contain

3.2.1 The "Hard Core" Rules

The "hard core" of a directive is its substantive rules spelling out the matters to which the directive relates, thus defining its scope, and often indicating its purpose, thus setting the framework for implementation. The substantive rules also contain provisions which describe, often in a very precise manner, the legal and / or factual situation which the Member States are required to bring about, and which often indicate the ways in which the desired situation must be realized.

Thus, for instance, Member States may be required to protect employees in the case of insolvency of their employer by setting up guarantee funds;[14] to communicate to the Commission certain prices (specified in the directive) of crude oil and petroleum products which they obtain from oil undertakings;[15] to maintain minimum stocks of crude oil and

[9] Cf. Daig and Smidt 1991, p. 4962.
[10] Bleckmann 1990, p. 85, under reference to Oldenkop.
[11] Kapteyn and VerLoren van Themaat 1990, p. 195.
[12] This actually already follows from the structure of the Treaty and the system of "attributed powers" ("*compétences d'attribution*").
[13] Cf. Easson 1981, p. 27.
[14] 80/987 (protection of workers – insolvency of employers), OJ 1980, L 283/23.
[15] 76/491 (information on oil prices), OJ 1976, L 140/4.

petroleum products, the directive specifying, among other things, the way in which the level of minimum stocks must be calculated;[16] to protect birds by *inter alia* prohibiting the killing or catching of birds and by creating biotopes;[17] to control the acquisition and possession of weapons by *inter alia* subjecting dealers to a system of authorization which is further described in the directive, and likewise stating that dealers must be required to keep a register of certain types of information further specified in the directive.[18] According to Directive 91/157 (batteries containing dangerous substances)[19] Member States may, in order to encourage recycling, introduce incentives by means of economic instruments which may not, however, cause distortion of competition (Article 7); or, according to Article 8, they must provide certain information to consumers. Directive 89/48 (mutual recognition of diplomas)[20] aims at establishing a system for mutual recognition of certain types of higher-education diplomas and it lays down rules as to how this recognition system must operate. Pursuant to Directive 76/630 (surveys of pig production)[21] Member States must carry out quarterly surveys of the pig population, which must then be communicated to the Commission; the directive spells out how these surveys must be conducted and the categories of pigs which they must cover. Under Directive 75/34 (retired self-employed)[22] nationals of one Member State have the right to remain in the territory of the host Member State after having pursued therein an activity as a self-employed worker; the exact conditions to be met are quite precisely elaborated in the directive. Directive 74/562 (road passenger transport operators)[23] aims at the introduction of common rules for the admission to the occupation of road passenger transport operator; the Directive specifies, among other things, the requirements which must be satisfied by a person wishing to engage in this occupation.

In some cases it is immediately clear from the directive that it is aiming at the introduction of legal rules, and thus at changing or establishing a legal situation. However, even a directive which at first sight obliges the Member States to establish a factual situation will actually in the majority of cases require national legal provisions to be changed or introduced in order to achieve the situation prescribed. The question whether legal provisions must be adopted or not is, however, a matter concerning the choice of form and methods covered below in Chapter 5, Subsection 5.2.3.

The (hard core) substantive rules may concern both substantive *national* law and procedures, including those before national courts.

[16] 68/414 (crude oil stocks), OJ English Spec. Ed. 1968 (II), p. 586.
[17] 79/409 (conservation of wild birds), OJ 1979, L 103/1.
[18] 91/477 (arms control), OJ 1991, L 256/51.
[19] OJ 1991, L 78/38.
[20] OJ 1989, L 19/16.
[21] OJ 1976, L 223/4.
[22] OJ 1975, L 14/10.
[23] OJ 1974, L 308/38.

An example of the first category is Directive 68/415 (freedom of access to aid for farmers),[24] which provides *inter alia* that access to aid for farmers who are nationals of a Member State other than the host Member State may not be denied or subjected to special conditions; in pursuance of Directive 91/671 (use of safety belts)[25] the driver and passengers travelling in a (certain type of) vehicle on the road must wear safety belts; Directive 92/28 (advertising of medicinal products)[26] prohibits advertising to the general public of medicinal products available only on medical prescription.

Examples of directive provisions relating to procedures are Directive 91/263 (telecommunication terminal equipment)[27] providing for a procedure of conformity assessment; Directive 84/631 (transfrontier shipment of hazardous waste)[28] which gave a procedure to be followed in the case of shipment of hazardous waste crossing one or more borders; Directive 64/221 (public policy and public health)[29] laying down rules for the procedure to be followed in the case of refusal of a residence permit. Some directives also stipulate explicitly that the persons concerned must be enabled to defend their rights as laid down in the directive before a national court;[30] this may in fact entail an adjustment of national procedural rules.

For the purposes of implementation, it makes no difference whether the directive's provisions concern substantive law or are provisions relating to procedures.[31] In both respects the directive must be fully transposed into national law. Furthermore, it is not only procedures involving the direct participation of private individuals which have to be implemented into national law. A transposition of provisions concerning the Member States *inter se*, for instance those imposing a consultation procedure between two or more Member States prior to adoption of certain measures, must also, under certain circumstances, be laid down in national law.[32]

[24] OJ English Spec. Ed. 1968 (III), p. 589.

[25] OJ 1991, L 373/26.

[26] OJ 1992, L 113/13.

[27] OJ 1991, L 128/1.

[28] OJ 1984, L 326/31.

[29] OJ English Spec. Ed. 1963-1964, p. 117.

[30] Cf. e.g. Directive 64/221 (public policy and public health), Article 8, OJ English Spec. Ed. 1963-1964, p. 117, Directive 76/207 (equal treatment at work), Article 6, OJ 1976, L 39/40, Directive 92/59 (product safety), Article 14, OJ 1992, L 228/4, Directive 73/239 (insurance other than life assurance I), Article 12, OJ 1973, L 228/3, Directive 91/533 (conditions of employment relationship – information of employees), Article 8, OJ 1991, L 288/32, Directive 92/28 (advertising of medicinal products), Article 12, OJ 1992, L 113/13, Directive 92/49 (insurance other than life assurance II), Article 56, OJ 1992, L 228/1.

[31] Cf. e.g. Case C-131/88 *Commission v. Germany* [1991] ECR I-825, para. 61.

[32] Cf. Case C-186/91 *Commission v. Belgium* [1993] ECR I-851.

The various obligations can be formulated in a negative way, as prohibitions of particular activities, or in a positive way, prescribing certain conduct.[33]

The obligations formulated *in the substantive provisions of the directive*, i.e. as opposed to the fact that a directive *as a whole* is addressed to the Member States, are addressed either to the Member States or to persons or bodies they will ultimately concern once the directive is implemented. To put it another way, a directive may "double" the obligations for the Member States in the sense that the instrument is addressed to them and so too are the separate substantive provisions; or it may be that the instrument is addressed to them but the separate substantive provisions are formulated in terms of obligations of (some) individuals or bodies. The difference is in fact merely one of drafting technique.

Thus for instance, on the one hand, Article 7 of Directive 83/189 (technical standards)[34] provides that "Member States shall take all appropriate measures to ensure that their standard institutions do not draw up or introduce standards ..."; Article 3 of Directive 91/383 (health and safety of temporary workers)[35] stipulates that "Member States shall take the necessary steps to ensure that ... the worker is informed by the undertaking ... making use of his services of the risks which he faces"; according to Article 3(3) of Directive 91/296 (transit of natural gas through grids)[36] "Member States take the measures necessary to ensure that the entities under their jurisdiction ... open negotiations on the conditions of the natural gas transit requested".

On the other hand, Article 19(2) of Directive 92/46 (milk products)[37] provides that "... the competent authority shall where it is suspected that this Directive is not being complied with carry out any checks it deems appropriate"; Article 22 of Directive 77/388 (Sixth VAT Directive)[38] lays down that "every taxable person shall state when his activity as a taxable person commences, changes or ceases"; according to Article 11 of Directive 92/50 (public service contracts)[39] "in awarding public service contracts, contracting authorities shall apply the procedures defined in Article ..."; Article 10(4) of Directive 92/51 (recognition of professional education and training)[40] requires that "... the [competent] authority shall ensure that an appropriate and equivalent form of oath or declaration is offered to the person concerned"; according to Article 3(2) of Directive

[33] Cf. e.g. Directive 68/415 (freedom of access to aid for farmers), OJ English Spec. Ed. 1968 (II), p. 589, Article 3: "Member States shall abolish the following restrictions ...", Article 4: "No Member State shall grant ...", or Article 6: "Each Member State shall make the taking-up of the business ... subject to an official authorization". According to Article 2 (2) of Directive 64/221 (public policy and public health), OJ English Spec. Ed. 1963-1964, p. 117, "grounds [of public policy, public security or public health] shall not be invoked to service economic ends".

[34] OJ 1983, L 109/8.

[35] OJ 1991, L 206/19.

[36] OJ 1991, L 147/37.

[37] OJ 1992, L 268/1.

[38] OJ 1977, L 145/1.

[39] OJ 1992, L 209/1.

[40] OJ 1992, L 209/25.

92/59 (product safety)[41] "... producers shall ... provide consumers with the relevant information ..." and according to Article 6(1) of Directive 89/391 (health and safety of workers)[42] "... the employer shall take the measures necessary for the safety and health protection of workers ...".

A directive will also often contain provisions which leave it to the discretion of the Member States to derogate from its contents[43] or to give their own interpretation to certain concepts,[44] thus allowing them room for manoeuvre. In some cases, however, the exercise of the discretion which is left to the Member States may be submitted to a special procedure; it may be made conditional upon permission of another body[45] or it may be submitted to periodical assessment by the Member States themselves.[46]

To summarize, the content of the result to be achieved, i.e. the content of the national implementing measures, is determined by the substantive rules of the directive at issue. This does not necessarily mean that no latitude is left to the Member States, since a directive may give them an option for derogations or require them to "fill in" certain concepts. However, if the directive does this, it goes without saying that the measures taken may not go beyond the limits set forth in the directive.[47]

3.2.2 Ancillary Obligations for the Member States

Directives also contain other types of provisions formulating obligations for the Member States. These can be designated as ancillary, as completing the

[41] OJ 1992, L 228/24.

[42] OJ 1989, L 183/1.

[43] Usually by providing that the directive "does not prevent the Member States from" [applying different provisions], or that the directive is "without prejudice to the right of the Member States to ...", or that "the Member States may ...". See e.g. Article 8 (3) of Directive 73/239 (insurance other than life assurance I), OJ 1973, L 228/3, Article 6 of Directive 77/249 (lawyers), OJ 1977, L 278/17, Article 9 of Directive 91/383 (health and safety of temporary workers), OJ 1991, L 206/19, Article 3 of Directive 91/477 (arms control), OJ 1991, L 256/51, Article 2 of Directive 76/207 (equal treatment at work), OJ 1976, L 39/40 and Article 10 of Directive 80/987 (protection of workers – insolvency of employers), OJ 1980, L 283/23.

[44] Cf. e.g. Article 20 (4) of Directive 77/388 (Sixth VAT Directive), OJ 1977, L 145/1, or Article 2 of Directive 74/562 (road passenger transport operators), OJ 1974, L 308/23.

[45] See below, Subsection 3.2.2.

[46] Under the ultimate control of the Commission. See below, Subsection 3.2.2. Cf. also Case 248/83 *Commission v. Germany* [1985] ECR 1459.

[47] Cf. e.g. Case 815/79 *Cremonini* [1980] ECR 3583, in particular para. 6, Case 51/76 *VNO* [1977] ECR 113, and Case 415/85 *Commission v. Ireland* [1981] ECR 3503.

STAFFS UNIVERSITY LIBRARY

substantive provisions. This is certainly not to suggest that they are less binding or less important.[48] Their function however is different.

In the first place, there is the *vital* provision laying down the period allowed for implementation, thus specifying the date from which the substantive content of the directive must be a reality within the Member States.[49]

Secondly, directives require the Member States to adopt laws, regulations and administrative provisions or, in more neutral terms, to take the measures necessary in order to comply with the directive.[50] As argued above,[51] this should be seen as an explicit restatement of the obligation under Article 189(3) and the more general obligation under Article 5 of the Treaty. Moreover, since 1991, directives have required the Member States, when adopting the implementing measures, to include a reference to the directive concerned or to accompany the measures by such a reference on the occasion of their official publication. The methods of making the reference are left to the discretion of the Member States. The purpose of such a reference is to make the Community origin of the implementing measures explicit. This will make transparent the relationship between a piece of national legislation and the underlying directive, which is of particular importance for the judicial protection of individuals and for the control and interpretation of the implementing measures by national courts or national authorities, where appropriate.

Thirdly, directives oblige the Member States to inform the Commission of the measures adopted in order to comply with the directive in question. The Court has explained that this duty must be seen in the light of Article 5 of the Treaty, which obliges the Member States to facilitate the achievement of the Commission's tasks under Aricle 155. According to the latter the Commission must, *inter alia*, ensure that the provisions of the Treaty and the measures adopted by the institutions pursuant thereto are applied.[52] This obligation also extends to cases where, in the opinion of the Member State concerned, no specific implementing measures need to be enacted.[53] The Court has further stated that, in order to be effective for the purposes for which it is required, the information must be

[48] Cf. Case 274/83 *Commission v. Italy* [1985] ECR 1077: in particular from the opinion of A-G Lenz it appears that the Italian government suggested that an obligation to notify the Commission of the implementing measures is of minor importance. The Court found, however, as with respect to any other provision of the directive, that Italy had failed to fulfil its obligations.

[49] As to the vital character of this type of provision see Chapter 2, Sections 2.2 and 2.3.

[50] Exceptionally this may not be so, depending on the substance matter of the directive concerned. See for instance Directive 90/684 (aid to shipbuilding), OJ 1990, L 380/7 and Directive 91/675 (setting up an Insurance Committee), OJ 1991, L 374/32.

[51] Chapter 2, Section 2.1.

[52] Cf. e.g. Case 96/81 *Commission v. The Netherlands* [1982] ECR 1791, Case 97/81 *Commission v. The Netherlands* [1982] ECR 1891 and Case C-33/90 *Commission v. Italy* [1991] ECR I-5987.

[53] Cf. Case C-69/90 *Commission v. Italy* [1991] ECR I-6011.

clear and precise, indicating unequivocally the measures which have been adopted. Failure to provide the information required or providing information of poor quality would mean that the Commission would be unable to ascertain whether the Member State had effectively and completely implemented the directive;[54] even if the Commission becomes aware of the implementing measures through other channels, this does not release the Member State concerned from its duty to notify the Commission officially of the measures adopted.[55]

Fourthly, directives may contain provisions requiring the Member States to submit to the Commission the texts of the main national legal measures which they are planning to adopt in the field governed by the directive. The purpose of this type of obligation is probably to ensure that the Commission is able to monitor the conformity of national measures adopted after the actual implementation of the directive and to intervene wherever the subsequent national measures are incompatible with the directive at issue.

In the fifth place, an obligation of notification, information or consultation may exist with respect to national measures adopted within the margin of discretion left to the Member States or with respect to national draft measures before their final adoption in general.

The implications of the obligation may differ. Sometimes the obligation involves only a simple information or consultation procedure. For instance, notification of national draft measures under Article 3(2) of Directive 75/442 (waste)[56] has no legal consequences. It is merely intended to ensure that the Commission is informed of any plans for national measures. This should enable it, *inter alia,* to consider whether (further) Community harmonization is necessary.[57] In some cases, upon notification of the measures which have been taken, a procedure of consultation will be set in motion resulting in a non-binding recommendation or opinion, which also has no legal consequences.[58] In other cases the exercise of discretion or the adoption of draft measures may be made

[54] Cf. Case 96/81 *Commission v. The Netherlands* [1982] ECR 1791 and Case C-33/90 *Commission v. Italy* [1991] ECR I-5987.

[55] Cf. Case 274/83 *Commission v. Italy* [1985] ECR 1077.

[56] OJ 1975, L 194/47.

[57] Cf. Case 380/87 *Enichem* [1989] ECR 2491. See e.g. also Article 4 (3) of Directive 80/987 (protection of workers – insolvency of employers), OJ 1980, L 283/23 and Article 11 of Directive 85/203 (air quality – nitrogen dioxide), OJ 1985, L 87/1.

[58] Cf. e.g. Article 9 of Directive 73/23 (electrical equipment), OJ 1973, L 77/29. Cf. also Article 7 of Directive 92/59 (product safety), OJ 1992, L 228/24: According to Article 6 of the same Directive Member States may, *inter alia,* withdraw a dangerous product from the market. After the Commission has been informed of the measure, the latter may conclude that the measure is justified or that it is not justified. Although such a conclusion has no immediate legal consequences under the Directive itself, it has implications for the application of Articles 30 and 36 of the Treaty.

conditional upon permission granted by, for instance, the Commission,[59] or they may be subjected to a procedure which may result in an obligation to modify the measures in accordance with a decision of a Community institution;[60] in some cases the measures concerned must be held in abeyance for a certain period of time[61] or they may be applied only temporarily, i.e. until a decision by a Community institution (for instance, the Council) has been taken.[62]

In summary, the adoption of the measures concerned may be submitted to some specific procedure or requirement laid down in the directive, non-observance of which may have legal effects.[63]

In the sixth place, different types of collaboration, mutual consultation and exchange of information between the Member States (or their "competent authorities"[64]) and / or between the Member States (or the "competent authorities") and the Commission are provided for under various directives.[65] The information to be exchanged may concern a variety of matters, such as the national authorities designated to act in pursuance of the directive,[66] or installations, undertakings etc. which have a specific task under the directive,[67] or the experiences acquired concerning the application of the directive at issue.[68] A directive may likewise oblige Member States to set up information networks.[69]

In the seventh place, some directives request the Member States to make certain assessments or studies. For instance, Directive 76/207 (equal treatment at work) and Directive 79/7 (equal treatment in statutory schemes of social security)[70] require the Member States to make periodic assessment of whether

[59] Cf. e.g. Article 10 (2) of Directive 89/48 (mutual recognition of diplomas), OJ 1989, L 19/16 and Article 14(2) of Directive 92/51 (recognition of professional education and training), OJ 1992, L 209/25.

[60] Cf. e.g. Article 6 of Directive 80/271 (classical swine fever), OJ 1980, L 447/11.

[61] Cf. Article 15 of Directive 85/374 (product liability), OJ 1985, L 210/29.

[62] Cf. Article 7 of Directive 70/524 (additions in feedingstuffs), OJ English Spec. Ed. 1970 (III), p. 840, as amended by Directive 73/103, OJ 1973, L 124/17.

[63] Cf. Case 380/87 *Enichem* [1989] ECR 2491, in particular the opinion of A-G Jacobs, para. 14 and para. 22 of the judgment.

[64] Often to be entrusted by the Member States with specific tasks under the directive concerned.

[65] Cf. e.g. Article 13 and Article 33 of Directive 73/239 (insurance other than life assurance I), OJ 1973, L 228/3, Article 6 of Directive 77/489 (transport of animals), OJ 1977, L 200/10, Article 9 (1) of Directive 89/48 (mutual recognition of diplomas), OJ 1989, L 19/16 and Article 12 of Directive 80/217 (classical swine fever), OJ 1980, L 47/11.

[66] Cf. e.g. Article 9 of Directive 89/48 (mutual recognition of diplomas), OJ 1989, L 19/16.

[67] Cf. e.g. Article 12 of Directive 84/631 (transfrontier shipment of hazardous waste), OJ 1984, L 326/31.

[68] Cf. e.g. Article 11 of Directive 85/337 (environmental impact assessment), OJ 1985, L 175/40.

[69] Cf. e.g. Article 13(3) of Directive 91/477 (arms control), OJ 1991, L 256/51.

[70] OJ 1976, L 39/40 and OJ 1979, L 6/24.

certain exclusions allowed for under the respective Directives remain justified; they must inform the Commission of the results of these assessments. As the Court pointed out in Case *248/83 (equal treatment in public service)*[71] these provisions provide for supervision in two stages: firstly by the Member States themselves and secondly by the Commission, enabling it to exercise effective supervision of the application of the Directive, in pursuance of Article 155 of the Treaty.

As regards studies, Article 8 of Directive 86/613 (equal treatment of the self-employed)[72] provides that the Member States shall examine whether and under what conditions female self-employed workers and the wives of male self-employed workers have access, during an interruption in their occupational activity owing to pregnancy or motherhood, to – among other things – services supplying temporary replacements. Another example can be drawn from Article 22(1) of Directive 92/43 (natural habitats),[73] which provides that the Member States shall study the desirability of re-introducing certain species that are native to their territory where this might contribute to their conservation.

Finally, Member States may be obliged to draft and submit regular reports on the application of the directive at issue.[74] The directive concerned will normally specify the type of information which must especially be included in the reports.

3.2.3 Provisions Regarding the Institutions

Although according to Article 189(3) directives are addressed to the Member States, they often also contain provisions directed to Community institutions, usually the Council and the Commission.

Directives may provide for further decision making which is necessary for their implementation[75] and which may concern a considerable variety of issues. In the majority of cases it is the Commission which is empowered by the Council to adopt measures for this purpose.[76] The Commission's power in this respect is often delineated by procedures for consultation with the Member States,

[71] *Commission v. Germany* [1985] ECR 1459.

[72] OJ 1986, L 359/56.

[73] OJ 1992, L 206/7.

[74] Cf. e.g. Article 13 of Directive 84/631 (transfrontier shipment of hazardous waste), OJ 1984, L 326/31, Article 11 of Directive 89/48 (mutual recognition of diplomas), OJ 1989, L 19/16, Article 10 of Directive 91/383 (health and safety of temporary workers), OJ 1991, L 206/19, Article 8 of Directive 91/689 (hazardous waste), OJ 1991, L 377/20 and Article 39 of Directive 92/50 (public service contracts), OJ 1992, L 209/1.

[75] Cf. e.g. Article 7 of Directive 76/491 (information on oil prices), OJ 1976, L 140/4.

[76] Cf. Article 145 and 155 of the EC Treaty.

various committees or the Council;[77] not infrequently, a management committee type of procedure must be followed.[78]

Adjustments of the provisions of a directive, particularly with respect to technical progress, are also often left to the Commission.[79]

Some directives include a provision stating that the Council will in the future adopt other directives or measures related to the subject matter of the directive at issue,[80] or that it will re-examine or review the directive in question within a certain period.[81]

Directives quite often request the Commission to draw up a report on the application of the directive and submit it to the Council,[82] to the Council and the European Parliament[83] or to both of these and the Economic and Social Committee.[84] Similarly, the Commission may be requested on this occasion to submit proposals for improvement.[85]

[77] Cf. e.g. Article 6(3) of Directive 77/489 (transport of animals), OJ 1977, L 200/10, Article 13 of Directive 91/263 (telecommunications terminal equipment), OJ 1991, L 128/1, and Article 3 of Directive 92/85 (pregnant workers), OJ 1992, L 348/1.

[78] Cf. e.g. Article 11 of Directive 76/630 (surveys of pig production), OJ 1976, L 223/4 (reference to Standing Committee for Agricultural Statistics), Article 16 of Directive 80/217 (classical swine fever), OJ 1980, L 47/11 (reference to Standing Veterinary Committee), Article 17 of Directive 79/409 (conservation of wild birds), OJ 1979, L 103/1, Article 17 of Directive 89/391 (health and safety of workers), OJ 1989, L 183/1, Article 18 of Directive 91/271 (urban waste-water), OJ 1991, L 135/40, Article 15 of Directive 92/51 (recognition of professional education and training), OJ 1992, L 209/25 (all referring to Committees set up under the respective directives). On conditions governing the exercise of powers delegated to the Commission in general, see Council decision of 13 July 1987 (commitology), OJ 1987, L 197/33.

[79] Cf. e.g. Article 10 of Directive 91/157 (batteries containing dangerous substances), OJ 1991, L 78/38, Article 13(1) of Directive 92/85 (pregnant workers), OJ 1992, L 348/1; a "management committee type" procedure may be provided for in this respect as well: see Article 17 of Directive 89/391 (health and safety of workers), OJ 1989, L 183/1. In other cases it will be for the Council to adjust the directives. See e.g. Article 21 of Directive 92/46 (milk products), OJ 1992, L 268/1 and Article 4 of Directive 91/441 (emissions from motor vehicles), OJ 1991, L 242/1.

[80] Cf. e.g. Article 16 of Directive 89/391 (health and safety of workers), OJ 1989, L 183/1, and Article 1 (2) of Directive 76/207 (equal treatment at work), OJ 1976, L 39/40.

[81] Cf. e.g. Article 11 of Directive 86/613 (equal treatment of the self-employed), OJ 1986, L 359/56, Article 18 of Directive 80/217 (classical swine fever), OJ 1980, L 47/11, and Article 14 (6) of Directive 92/85 (pregnant workers), OJ 1992, L 348/1.

[82] Cf. e.g. Article 12(2) of Directive 86/378 (equal treatment in occupational social security schemes), OJ 1986, L 225/40.

[83] Cf. e.g. Article 4 of Directive 90/364 (right of residence), OJ 1990, L 180/26.

[84] Cf. e.g. Article 10 of Directive 89/654 (health and safety at work), OJ 1989, L 393/1.

[85] Cf. e.g. Article 7 of Directive 91/671 (use of safety belts), OJ 1991, L 373/26, Article 9 of Directive 79/7 (equal treatment in statutory schemes of social security), OJ 1979, L 6/24, Article 13 of Directive 89/48 (mutual recognition of diplomas), OJ 1989, L 19/16, Article 5 of Directive 90/366 (right of residence for students), OJ 1990, L 180/30.

Finally, to give just a few examples of the other types of provisions which directives may contain, the Commission may be requested to examine information submitted by the Member States,[86] or to communicate certain information to the Member States,[87] or the directive may set up a body entrusted with specific tasks.[88]

3.2.4 Conclusions Concerning the Different Types of Provisions

What lessons can be learned from this brief anthology of the various types of provisions which may be contained by a directive, as regards the subject under discussion here?

It would seem that directives comprise *more* binding elements than simply the "hard core provisions", as I have termed them, which describe (in a more or less detailed way) the content of the adjustment of national law or of the factual situation to be brought about by the Member States and which are the primary purpose of a directive.

To a large extent directives impose ancillary obligations upon the Member States which by their very nature do not lend themselves to transposition into national law. This applies particularly for provisions laying down obligations of the Member States *vis-à-vis* the Commission (or other Community institution, as the case may be) or for certain obligations for the Member States *inter se.*[89]

It would also seem, from the foregoing paragraphs, that these provisions serve several purposes.

Some of them curtail (with different degrees of intensity of Community interference[90]) the discretion left to the Member States under the directive in question, thus providing for different forms of supervision of the exercice of discretion.

Other provisions are to enable the Commission to supervise effectively, according to its duty under Article 155 of the Treaty, the transposition of the directive into national law or to monitor the actual application of the rules laid down in the directive: depending on the experience gained with the application of the rules, the Commission may consider whether further Community interference in the matter concerned is necessary.

[86] Cf. e.g. Article 9 of Directive 76/630 (surveys of pig production), OJ 1976, L 223/4.
[87] Cf. e.g. Article 4 of Directive 76/491 (information on oil prices), OJ 1976, L 140/4.
[88] Cf. e.g. Article 9(2) of Directive 89/48 (mutual recognition of diplomas), OJ 1989, L 19/16.
[89] However, as case C-186/91 (*Commission v. Belgium* [1993] ECR I-851) shows, mutual consultation between the Member States prior to introduction of certain measures has to have been provided for in national legislation. A careful approach is therefore necessary in this respect. The same holds true for obligations relating to notification: Case C-237/90 *Commission v. Germany* [1992] ECR I-5973.
[90] And, in particular, with different legal consequences.

Provisions on collaboration, mutual exchange of information or various types of consultation between the Member States or the Member States and the Commission are often indispensable for effective operation of the system provided for.

Studies and ostensibly non-comittal examinations by the Member States usually relate to issues which are relevant as such for the subject matter of the directive but which, for a number of reasons (not uncommonly political) are not yet suitable for being governed by Community rules.

Together the substantive and ancillary provisions constitute the inseparable entity of the system of rules laid down by a directive. They must therefore be seen as the result the Member States are required to achieve and, consequently, they are equally binding upon the Member States. Non-observance of ancillary obligations, such as failing to provide the Commission with information or a unilateral derogation from the directive, which in fact required a particular procedure to be followed, amounts to infringement of Article 189(3) with possible implications for the judicial protection of individual citizens.[91]

As regards the provisions concerning Community institutions, at first sight they may appear rather peculiar. According to Article 189(3) directives are addressed to the Member States and by virtue of this Article they are binding upon them. Provisions which are directed to the Commission or the Council or which concern some committee that is to be established or which operate at Community level therefore look rather inappropriate and cannot be considered as binding upon the institutions in pursuance of Article 189(3). In fact, these provisions raise a number of intricate questions as to their legal nature. One of these questions is whether they should be considered as decisions *sui generis*[92] which are binding for the institutions concerned. Or are they merely the expression of (political) intentions with no binding effect whatsoever?[93] The discussion of these problems is actually beyond the scope of this book. It should

[91] Although not every violation of Article 189(3) and, in particular, a violation consisting of non-observance of ancillary provisions, will be equally relevant for individuals who may try to invoke this fact in national courts. Cf. Case 380/87 *Enichem* [1989] ECR 2491. See, however, also Case 5/84 *Direct Cosmetics* [1985] ECR 617 and Case C-97/90 *Lennartz* [1991] ECR I-3795, which show that national provisions derogating from the Sixth VAT Directive cannot be relied upon by national tax authorities to the detriment of taxable persons if the procedure provided for in Article 27 (notification and authorization) has not been followed. Cf. also opinion of A-G Warner in Case 815/79 *Cremonini* [1980] ECR 3583, at p. 3629 and opinion of A-G Reischl in Joined Cases 181 and 229/78 *Van Paassen* [1979] ECR 2063, para. 4.

[92] I.e. *not* decisions in the sense of Article 189(4); as to the terminological confusion see Lasok and Bridge 1991, p. 151-153. Cf. also Louis 1993, p. 518-520.

[93] Cf. Joined cases 90 and 91/63 *Commission v. Luxemburg and Belgium* [1964] ECR 625: Resolution to set up a common organization of markets for dairy products by a certain date was not binding and therefore could not constitute an obligation for the Council.

be noted, however, that the legal literature does not exclude the possibility of the provisions at issue, or at least some of them, being obligatory for the institutions.[94]

As far as their function is concerned, it becomes clear from a closer consideration of the directive as an instrument of Community intervention, laying down a system of rules aimed at regulating a certain subject matter, that this type of provisions is also intimately linked with the objective a directive seeks to achieve, which is not necessarily a static situation.

To make the rules work effectively in practice and to ensure that they remain up-to-date, it may be necessary to delegate powers to (usually) the Commission enabling it to lay down further implementing rules; adjustments or amendments are indispensable if Community rules are not to become outdated, which would potentially frustrate rather than promote the achievement of the objective. Permanent monitoring at Community level of the operation of the rules in practice should ensure surveillance of their effectiveness and may give rise to their improvement or to further Community action.

A review or examination of directives should be seen in the same perspective. Another factor which may play a part in this respect will often be that a directive may be the result of a highly political compromise at a particular point in time; provisions for review or re-examination will make it possible to reconsider certain issues governed by the directive when the political climate has changed.

In summary, directives lay down a frequently complex system of different rights and duties for different legal subjects of Community law, not only for the Member States and their national authorities, but also, where appropriate, for Community institutions and, particularly through transposition into national law, for individuals.[95] Although the primary purpose of most directives is the obligation for the Member States to transpose the content of the directive into national law, in so far as the directive provisions concerned lend themselves to such a transposition, for an actual and effective achievement of the objective pursued a directive may often require that the obligations imposed go far beyond a "simple" transposition by the Member States.[96]

[94] Cf. Daig and Smidt 1991, p. 4948, according to whom regulations, directives and decisions "*werden zwar häufig, wenn nicht stets, auch Befugnisse und Verpflichtungen ihrer Urheber oder anderer Gemeinschaftsorgane und -hilfsorgane normieren*". Much will of course depend on the content and purpose of the provisions concerned. Delegation of powers, for instance, is not only a matter of the legal relationship between the Commission and the Council; it also has external effects: lack of competence can be invoked by third parties. Cf. also Case C-212/91 *Angelopharm* [1994] ECR I-171. Furthermore it should not be ruled out that in some cases the institutions might be bound on the basis of "*patere legem quam ipse fecisti*".

[95] See below, Chapter 7, Section 7.2.

[96] Cf. De Ripaisel-Landy and Gérard 1976, p. 52-53. See also below, Section 3.3.

In the light of these many considerations it is submitted that *the result to be achieved under a directive is both a legal and factual situation as determined by the substantive and ancillary provisions* of the directive at issue. Provisions directed at the institutions are obviously not a part of the "result" in the sense of Article 189(3). For the correct operation of the entire system envisaged by a directive, however, they are of great importance.

It is striking that the "factual component" of the obligation has been given relatively little attention, both in the literature and the case law of the Court. This issue will therefore be discussed in more detail in the following Section.

3.3 The Result to be Achieved: in Law and in Fact

As indicated in Subsection 3.2.1 above, in the vast majority of cases the Member States have to enact national legal measures in order to comply with the obligations resulting from the substantive rules of a directive. The Court of Justice has repeatedly held that the Member States must secure full implementation of directives in law and not only in fact.[97] However, the opposite is equally true. In principle, the ultimate purpose of the rules laid down in a directive is, just like the purpose of *any* legal rule,[98] to influence the behaviour of legal subjects.[99] The transposition of the terms of a directive is therefore not an end in itself but rather a means to bring about a certain situation. Consequently, the obligations imposed by a directive are not fulfilled merely by the fact that national rules have been enacted. The rules must then be applied and enforced in practice. Thus even after the adoption of national rules a continous obligation is incumbent upon the Member States. As Mertens de Wilmars put it:

"La directive implique ... l'obligation, puisque L'Etat membre a assumé une obligation de résultat, de veiller à l'application efficace de la législation nationale à l'objectif communautaire."[100]

Although the problem of non-application or insufficient enforcement of Community law, including directives,[101] is certainly not new,[102] it is only in recent times that particular attention has been paid to it.[103] Similarly, the majority of

[97] Cf. e.g. Case C-361/88 *Commission v. Germany* [1991] ECR I-2567, para. 24.
[98] Unless the legislation is merely "symbolic".
[99] Cf. Capotorti 1988, p. 157.
[100] Mertens de Wilmars 1991, p. 393; cf. also Capotorti 1988, p. 160.
[101] More properly expressed: the national measures transposing the directive. See above, Chapter 1, Section 3.
[102] Cf. Krislov, Ehlermann, Weiler 1986, p. 59 ff.
[103] Cf. above, Chapter 1, Section 3.

cases brought by the Commission before the Court of Justice in infringement proceedings has until recently concerned the absence or the inadequacy of national rules transposing a directive, and not the issue of effective application and enforcement. Nevertheless, there is case law from which it can be deduced that application and enforcement *in practice* are just as important as the enactment of the rules. On the one hand, in several preliminary rulings the Court has held that that the third paragraph of Article 189 requires the Member States to adopt in their national legal systems all the measures necessary to ensure that the provisions of the directive at issue are fully effective.[104] This is, according to the Court, a general obligation of the Member States.[105] From the context of the cases it appears that the main concern of the Court is that provisions of directives will not remain a dead letter but will be given practical effect. On the other hand, as will be shown in Chapter 5, in infringement proceedings the same concern lies behind the requirements imposed by the Court upon the Member States with respect to the implementing measures they adopt.[106] In Case *29/84 (nurses)*, for instance, the Court stressed that the principles of constitutional and administrative law relied on by the German government as a means of implementation "must guarantee that the national authorities will in fact apply the directive".[107] That these two jurisprudential lines are two sides of the same coin was made patently obvious in *Emmott*,[108] where they were brought together.

In a number of more recent cases the Court addressed the issue of practical application more explicitly, i.e. without focussing on the adequacy of the rules enacted pursuant to a directive. For instance, in two cases brought by the Commission against Italy the Italian government was found to be in breach of Directive 71/305 (public work contracts)[109] because two bodies awarding a public work contract failed to publish a notice in the Official Journal.[110] In

[104] Cf. Case 14/83 *Von Colson* [1984] ECR 1891 and Case C-271/91 *Marshall II* [1993] ECR I-4367.

[105] Cf. Case C-143/91 *Van der Tas* [1992] ECR I-5045.

[106] A clear example in this respect is case C-361/88 *Commission v. Germany* [1991] ECR I-2567 concerning the proper implementation of Directive 80/779 (air quality), OJ 1980, L 29/30, which requires, among other things, the Member States to take appropriate measures so that the concentration of sulphur dioxide in the air does not exceed certain limit values. The Court held that mandatory rules are necessary under which the administrative authorities are required to adopt measures in all the cases where the limit values of the Directive are likely to be exceeded. In other words, putting the values into a piece of legislation is not sufficient. The authorities must be obliged to take action where necessary.

[107] *Commission v. Germany* [1985] ECR 1661, para. 23.

[108] Case C-208/90 [1991] ECR I-4269.

[109] OJ English Spec. Ed. 1971 (II), p. 682.

[110] Case 199/85 *Commission v. Italy* [1987] ECR 1039 and Case 194/88R *Commission v. Italy* [1988] ECR 5647.

Case *C-42/89 (water supply Verviers)* the Belgian government failed to fulfil its obligations under the Treaty because the Verviers water supply did not accord with the parameters of Directive 80/778 relating to the quality of water intended for human consumption.[111] This failure was not caused by inadequate (regional) legislation but rather the costs and complexity of the construction work at the water treatment station which was necessary for providing Verviers with "good water". The most obvious example in this respect, however, is the judgment of the Court in Case *C-287/91 (reimbursement of VAT)*:[112] Italy in fact correctly transposed the Eighth VAT Directive[113] concerning the relevant point but in practice the fiscal authorities did not observe the 6-month period within which VAT has to be reimbursed to certain categories of persons. The Court recalled its established case law according to which the Member States must guarantee that directive provisions are fully applied, and it found that Italy was in breach of the said directive as it allowed the Ministry of Finance to disregard the time limits for refunds of VAT, without intervening from the outset to remove the consequent prejudice to Community law.[114]

To sum up, a new tendency can be discerned in the Court's case law. It would appear that the Court and, in particular, the Commission, which is responsible for bringing cases under Article 169 against the Member States for their failure to comply with the obligations under Article 189(3), no longer concentrate almost exclusively on the extent to which there is conformity between the directive and the national legal texts which transpose it. There has been a discernable shift in attention towards situations concerning the non-application of the directive which has, as such, been correctly transposed. This tendency fits in with the new concerns of the Community relating to the application and enforcement of Community law mentioned in Chapter 1.

[111] OJ 1980, L 229/11; *Commission v. Belgium* [1990] ECR I-2821.

[112] *Commission v. Italy* [1992] ECR I-3515.

[113] Directive 79/1072, OJ 1979, L 331/11.

[114] Cf. also case C-337/89 *Commission v. UK* [1992] ECR I-6103, which concerned (partly) the non-achievement of a factual situation, namely an excessively high concentration of nitrates in drinking water and Case C-56/90 *Commission v. UK* [1993] ECR I- 4109 on quality of bathing water.

4
The Addressees of a Directive

4.1 INTRODUCTION

From Article 189(3) it follows that a directive can be addressed to and is binding upon Member States alone. Unlike ECSC recommendations,[1] an EC directive cannot be addressed to subjects of Community law other than the Member States. Although directives may be directed to one Member State or to a certain number of Member States,[2] in practice they are usually addressed to all of them.[3] Furthermore, the fact that according to the terms of Article 189(3) the binding force of a directive exists only in relation to the Member State to which it is addressed has led the Court of Justice to decide that a directive cannot impose obligations on an individual.[4] This finding of the Court merits particular attention, notably because it forms the basis for denying horizontal direct effect of directives, i.e. that a provision of a directive may not be relied upon as such against an individual.[5] I will deal with the ruling that directives cannot impose obligations on individuals in more detail in Section 4.2.

The statement that a directive is binding upon the Member State concerned does not however put an end to the matter. The first point is that the Court has gone beyond the abstraction, in itself not very revealing, that directives are binding upon the Member States, by considering explicitly that

"the Member States' obligation arising from a directive to achieve the result envisaged by the directive and their duty under Article 5 of the Treaty to take all appropriate measures ... to ensure the fulfilment of that obligation, is binding on all the authorities of Member States including, for matters within their jurisdiction, the courts."[6]

The Court's finding gives rise to two questions. Firstly, in a concrete case, which authorities are bound by the obligation laid down in a directive? In other words, who are the *actual* addressees within the Member State of a particular directive?

[1] Article 14 of the ECSC Treaty.

[2] Cf. Ipsen 1965, p. 75, Lauwaars 1973, p. 28, Daig and Smidt 1991, p. 4961.

[3] Cf. Capotorti 1988, p. 153.

[4] Cf. Case 152/84 *Marshall I* [1986] ECR 723 and Case 80/86 *Kolpinghuis* [1987] ECR 3969.

[5] For a detailed discussion of horizontal direct effect of directives see Chapter 11, Subsections 11.5.2 and 11.5.3.

[6] Case 14/83 *Von Colson* [1984] ECR 1891. Since then it has become established case law. Cf. also Grabitz 1971, p. 5, who already argued that the "*Zurechnungsendpunkte*" of directives are not Member States as such but their organs.

Secondly, what are the implications of the fact that the obligation is binding upon *all* national authorities?

A second point, as will be explained in more detail in Chapter 11, Section 11.2, is that the binding force of a directive upon the Member States, again together with Article 5 of the Treaty, is the basis of the possibility for an individual to rely, under certain conditions, within the national legal order on the provisions of a directive against the Member State.[7] However, since in legal relationships within this order an individual does not usually deal with the Member State as such but rather with one of its organs, bodies, agents etc., the question arises as to how far the concept of "the State" reaches.

In Sections 4.3, 4.4 and 4.5 I shall address the above three questions in turn.

4.2 No Obligations for Individuals

4.2.1 Combination of a Directive and Another Provision

In *Marshall I*[8] the Court stated that a directive may not *of itself* impose obligations upon individuals and, therefore, it may not be relied upon *as such* against such a person.

It is generally assumed that the Court was referring here to the fact that only national law can directly create obligations for individuals.[9] If a directive is properly implemented the national implementing measures will impose these obligations. However, as the case law of the Court shows, provisions of national law which have *not* been specifically enacted in order to implement the directive may under certain circumstances create an obligation which the directive desired, although the latter was not in fact properly implemented. By the technique of interpretation of national law in conformity with the directive, an obligation is imposed upon the individual by national law read together with the directive. This was what occurred in *Dekker*,[10] for instance. In this case the national court

[7] Cf. Case 190/87 *Moormann* [1988] ECR 4689.

[8] Case 152/84 [1986] ECR 723, most recently confirmed in Case C-91/92 *Faccini Dori* [1994] ECR I-3325. In The Netherlands, the question as to whether VAT Directives can be relied upon by the tax authorities against an individual was answered in the negative before *Marshall I* by the Hoge Raad (20 Februari 1985, BNB 1985 nr. 128) without the case being referred to the Court of Justice. See for discussion of the case Bijl 1986 and Kortenaar 1985. Cf. also the opinion of A-G VerLoren van Themaat in Case 89/81 *Hong Kong Trade* [1982] ECR 1277, Section 4.

[9] Cf. Arnull 1986, p. 945 and Lauwaars 1993, p. 707. This, of course, does not preclude the individual from complying with the obligations laid down in a directive if he desires to do so for whatever reason. Cf. Case 148/78 *Ratti* [1979] ECR 1629.

[10] Case C-177/88 [1990] ECR I-3941.

was induced to interpret a pre-existing[11] provision of national law in a way which was in conformity with the objective sought by the directive at issue, and this resulted in an obligation for the (potential) employer concerned. Without the directive (and the associated obligation to interpret national law in accordance with the directive) the outcome of the case, resolved on the basis of national law alone, would have been entirely different. The same applies *a fortiori* to national implementing measures which are, however, as such not entirely adequate. Interpreting them in conformity with the underlying directive may result in imposing an obligation on the individual.[12]

Another form of "reading together", as opposed to "directive of itself", should also be mentioned briefly here. In his opinion in *Barber*, A-G Van Gerven suggested that a provision of international law, in this particular case the prohibition of (sex) discrimination in the UN Covenants,[13] could possibly of its own accord take effect between individuals in the Community legal order. A directive should then be seen as rendering a provision of international law more precise and thus removing a possible obstacle to horizontal direct effect of the provision. In the past I have called this "a tempting solution", arguing that the combination of a directive and a provision of international law having horizontal direct effect may create an obligation for individuals under Community law.[14] Unfortunately, two crucial problems arise with this: firstly the not undisputed question of horizontal direct effect of provisions of international law,[15] and secondly the effects of international law and internationally guaranteed fundamental rights within the Community legal order.[16] While I am still convinced that this is an interesting approach, certainly since the more recent developments in the Court's case law on the protection of fundamental rights in the Community,[17] I feel that this subject is beyond the scope of the present study.

A third alternative is to read a directive together with a directly effective provision of the Treaty which a directive merely implements but does not expand.[18] It is generally accepted that certain Treaty provisions may impose obligations upon individuals.[19] If a provision of a directive implements a provision of the Treaty which imposes an obligation on individuals, the former

[11] I.e. anterior to the directive.
[12] For further discussion see Chapter 10, in particular Section 10.9.
[13] Case C-262/88 [1990] ECR I-1889, para. 53 of the opinion.
[14] Prechal 1990, p. 463.
[15] Cf. Van Gerven in his opinion, para. 53 and Prechal 1990, p. 465.
[16] Cf. the opinion of A-G Van Gerven in *Barber*, para. 53 and also his opinion in *Grogan*, Case C-159/90 [1991] I-4685, para. 30-31. Cf. also Prechal 1990, p. 463-465.
[17] Cf. Case C-260/89 *ERT* [1991] ECR I-2925.
[18] Cf. Wyatt 1983, p. 245-246, Easson 1979b, p. 78 and Easson 1981, p. 40-41.
[19] Cf. Case 43/75 *Defrenne II* [1976] ECR 455 and Case 36/74 *Walrave and Koch* [1974] ECR 1405.

should also be capable of imposing an obligation. This approach however has limited effect. Only in cases where the relevant Treaty provision and the provision of a directive converge does it appear to be acceptable to impose an obligation on an individual under the *Marshall I* judgment. In other words, only in so far as the obligation formulated in the provision of the directive is (implicitly) contained in the Treaty provision[20] can such an obligation actually be imposed upon individuals. As has been observed by Easson, an approach of this kind poses "the difficulty in determining whether the directive merely defines the Treaty provision or augments it: in effect, one must ask if the Court could have reached the particular result without the assistance of the directive".[21] In such a case, however, the obligation already exists by virtue of the Treaty provision itself and it can therefore be imposed on this basis alone; in this case, it is submitted, there is no need to answer the question whether the directive in combination with the relevant Treaty provision can impose an obligation upon the individual. Moreover, the purpose of directives is often to go beyond the well-defined obligations of the Treaty provisions (which are thus directly effective and can *as such* also be binding on individuals), such as the national treatment clause in Article 52(2) of the EC Treaty. Directives often aim at positive measures to be taken in order to achieve the objectives of the Treaty, like, for instance, facilitating the effective exercise of the right of freedom of establishment by introducing a system of mutual recognition of diplomas, professional qualifications, and so on. In this respect, they "implement" provisions of the Treaty which in any case are as such insufficiently complete to impose obligations on individuals.[22] This does not, however, prevent the Court from drawing inspiration from directives when interpreting provisions of the Treaty which are directly effective and can thus impose obligations upon individuals.[23]

On the other hand, directives may contain provisions designed to facilitate the practical application of a Treaty Article while in no way altering its content or

[20] Or can be "*hineininterpretiert*" (literally: interpreted into).

[21] Easson 1981, p. 40.

[22] Cf. Case 2/74 *Reyners* [1974] ECR 648, where the Court held that the priniciple of equal treatment has direct effect and directives have become superfluous with regard to implementing the rule on nationality. Cf. however also Case 136/78 *Auer I* [1979] ECR 437, where the Court found that prior to the date on which the Member States were required to have taken the measures necessary to implement Directives Nos. 78/1026 and 78/1027 (veterinary surgeons), the nationals of a Member State could not rely on Article 52 with a view to practising the profession of veterinary surgeon in that Member State on any conditions other than those laid down by national legislation. After the required implementation Auer was however entitled to rely on the Directives and not on Article 52. See Case 271/82 *Auer II* [1983] ECR 2727.

[23] Cf. Case C-340/89 *Vlassopoulou* [1991] ECR I-2357 in which the Court's interpretation of the national treatment clause of Article 52 was clearly inspired by Directive 89/48 (mutual recognition of diplomas), OJ 1989, L 19/16.

scope. This is particularly the case in relation to Article 119 and Article 1 of Directive 75/117 (equal pay for men and women).[24]

In *Defrenne II*[25] the Court denied direct effect (and thus the possibility of being binding on individuals) of Article 119 if the discrimination cannot be identified using the criteria "equal work" and "equal pay". In such cases more explicit implementing provisions of a Community or national character would first have to be adopted for the purposes of such an identification. Now, Article 1 of Directive 75/117 undoubtedly contains a "more explicit implementing provision" of this kind, providing that job classification systems must be based on the same criteria for both men and women and must be drawn up in such a way as to exclude any discrimination on grounds of sex. In cases of discrimination in job classification systems Article 119 is directly applicable since Article 1 of the Directive now provides sufficient guidance for the identification of discrimination.[26] From the point of view of a private employer, this result could be considered as imposing an obligation. However, since Article 1 of Directive 75/117 is considered not to alter the content or scope of Article 119, it must be assumed that the employer concerned is bound by the obligation which results from Article 119 but is made explicit in the Directive.

4.2.2 Multi-Angular Relationships

Another aspect deserving of attention here is the question of the scope of the term "impose obligations". Several obligations may devolve upon individuals from the text of a directive,[27] but these individuals are in principle bound by the obligation only from the time that the directive is implemented in national law. For instance, a café owner cannot be prevented from selling water as mineral water because it does not meet the requirements laid down in a directive which has not yet been implemented in national law.[28] This type of obligation can certainly not be imposed on individuals by the directive itself.

However, directives do impose obligations on the Member States and their authorities which are binding upon them without an intercession of national implementing rules. Provided that the relevant provisions of the directive meet the requirements of direct effect, an individual may compel the State or competent authorities to comply with the provision, although compliance by the authorities with this obligation may entail consequences to the detriment of

[24] OJ 1975, L 45/19. On the relationship see e.g. Case 96/80 *Jenkins* [1981] ECR 911.

[25] Case 43/75 [1976] ECR 455.

[26] Cf. Case 109/88 *Danfoss* [1989] ECR 3199 concerning the interpretation of equal pay directive and Case C-184/89 *Nimz* [991] ECR I-2097, which refined *Danfoss* but was decided under Article 119.

[27] Cf. also above, Chapter 3, Subsection 3.2.1.

[28] Cf. Case 80/86 *Kolpinghuis* [1987] ECR 3969.

another individual. This state of affairs will particularly occur in triangular (or multi-angular) relationships.[29]

The most obvious examples of such relationships occur under the public works and environmental directives.[30] For instance, a public authority may award a contract of work to a private undertaking in accordance with national rules which are, however, incompatible with the directive. A subsequent claim by another undertaking which argues that the authority has violated the provisions of the directive may result in the work being given to the claimant, to the detriment of the first undertaking. Similarly, an environmental interest group or another person with standing under national law may rely on the provisions of a directive against a national authority, resulting in the withdrawal of a permit given to an undertaking in accordance with national rules but in violation of the rules laid down in the directive at issue.

The possibility for an individual to press claims based directly on the directive against a public authority may detrimentally affect another individual. Nevertheless, negative consequences of this kind did not prevent the Court from acknowledging the right of the claimant to rely on the directive, and the obligation of the national authorities to apply the directive and disapply national rules which were in conflict with it.[31] The position of the Court may be explained by two types of reasons.

According to the first, which is associated with the relationship within which the directive is relied on, the acceptance of the claims against the authorities should not be considered as an application of the directive against the individuals who are detrimentally affected. After all, strictly speaking, the claimant (Costanzo) relied on the directive against the State authorities (Commune di Milano) and not against another undertaking (Logiani).[32] The negative consequences for third parties are simply a part of the total deal.[33]

Another explanation could be given by the particular setting of the *Costanzo* case. Article 29(5) of Directive 71/305 (public works contracts), which Costanzo relied on against the municipality, is intended to protect tenderers against

[29] Another type of detrimental consequences for third (private) parties was under discussion in *Becker* (Case 8/81 [1982] ECR 53) and *Weissgerber* (Case 207/87 [1988] ECR 4433), namely the possible adverse effects on other traders of a claim for exemption from VAT made *a posteriori* by the person claiming exemption on the basis of direct effect of the Sixth VAT Directive. In *Becker* and particularly in *Weissgerber* the Court aimed at preventing such an adverse effect on third parties by requiring that the person claiming exemption had not passed the tax on to the recipient of the service at issue.

[30] Cf. Jans 1992, p. 10-11. In German literature this problem is often discussed under the heading "*Doppelwirkung*" of directives. Cf. e.g. Classen 1993, p. 84-85, Langenfeld 1992, p. 960-961, Jarass 1991, p. 2667-2668.

[31] Cf. Case 103/88 *Costanzo* [1989] ECR 1839.

[32] Cf. A-G Mischo in Case C-221/88 *Busseni* [1990] ECR I-495, para. 57-58.

[33] Cf. Jans 1992, p. 11 and Prechal 1990, p. 454-455.

arbitrariness on the part of the awarding authority.[34] It lays down procedural guarantees for the tenderers providing for a precise and detailed procedure to be followed. In the case under consideration the application of this procedure in no way imposed an obligation upon the undertaking to which the contract was originally awarded.

However, this may not be so in other situations. For instance, a directive may make the granting of an authorization to undertake certain activities dependent upon certain substantive requirements which must be met by the applicant. A claim by a third party against the competent national authorities which have, in the opinion of the former, granted the authorization to an undertaking which meets requirements under national law but not the (stricter) requirements of the directive concerned will lead to a withdrawal of the authorization by virtue of the application of the directive. Does this amount to anything other than imposing an obligation upon an individual, or, at least, affecting the position an undertaking has under national law?

A situation like this can be distinguished from the one at issue in *Costanzo*, which concerned primarily procedural guarantees. It is conceivable that such "negative effects" for an individual will not be accepted by the Court.[35] Indications in this direction can be found in *Busseni*.[36]

In this case, the ECSC sought to recover a sum of money owed to it by a bankrupt Italian steel company. The Commission lodged a claim in respect of a preferential debt with the *"giudice delegato"* (official receiver) relying on certain provisions of ECSC recommendation 86/198,[37] according to which the ECSC should have the same privileged creditor status as national tax authorities. The recommendation had not been implemented in Italian law within the time limit. The official receiver refused to accept the claim. One of the questions the Court of Justice had to answer in this case was whether the ECSC could in fact rely on the provisions concerned. The Court's answer, based on its judgment in *Marshall I*,[38] was carefully balanced. First, it recalled that a directive can be relied on only against the State and that it cannot, of itself, impose obligations on an individual. Next the Court considered that, in the present setting, the ECSC's claims could be in competition not only with those of the Member State concerned but also with those of other creditors of the undertaking. The application of the recommendation, far from operating solely against the Member State to which it is addressed, may also reduce the prospects of payment for some of the other creditors. The rights of all the other creditors would be

[34] OJ English Spec. Ed. 1971 (II), p. 682. Cf. Case 76/81 *Transporoute* [1982] ECR 417.

[35] As to this "dilemma" see in particular the German literature mentioned above in n. 30 and also Winter 1991b, p. 663. In general, there is no clear-cut answer available. Nevertheless, some authors decide in favour of direct effect. Cf. Jarass 1991, p. 2668 and Jans 1992, p. 11.

[36] Case C-221/88 [1990] ECR I-495.

[37] OJ 1986, L 144/40. The Court treated the recommendation in the same way as an EEC directive. Cf. para. 21-22 of the judgment.

[38] Case 152/84 [1986] ECR 723.

directly affected if the preferential status were conferred on certain debts owed to the ECSC. The ECSC could therefore rely on the recommendation as against the State, but the grant of preferential status to debts owed to it could be effective only as against that State. The preferential status could not prejudice the rights of creditors other than the State under national legislation on the rights of creditors in the absence of the recommendation.

The outcome of the *Busseni* case is the more interesting since the Commission argued that it asserted the "ECSC's rights" against the Italian State rather than against private individuals by applying to the official receiver, a person entrusted by the State with a particular public task. In the Commission's logic the official receiver was, by virtue of the recommendation, obliged to give the ECSC's debts a preferential status. However, the Court looked beyond this construction by taking into consideration two questions: against whom would the application of the recommendation operate; and whose rights would be directly affected? Although it admitted that the ECSC may rely on the recommendation against the receiver, as the Commission argued,[39] the consequences of the application of the recommendation by the latter were limited.

The lesson that can be learned from *Busseni* for the subject under discussion here is that a directive can neither impose obligations on individuals nor prejudice a person's rights under national law, at least not *directly*. However, the exact meaning of this last term as used by the Court is not entirely clear. Perhaps it had in mind a *Costanzo*-like situation, where the possible negative effects were fairly remote from the application of the provision concerned. Another hypothesis could be that *Costanzo* is overruled by *Busseni*. In any case, it follows from *Busseni* that the terms "impose obligations" do not merely refer to the situation whereby a directive as such cannot oblige a person to do or refrain from doing something. It would also seem that tolerating an interference with a person's rights might under certain circumstances be prevented by the prohibition of imposing obligations on the basis of the directive alone, as laid down in *Marshall I*.

[39] The judgment can also be understood as stating that the recommendation can be relied on against the State in *its quality of one of the creditors*, as I have argued (Prechal 1990, p. 455, n. 21). The use of the term "Member State" gives a decisive answer in this respect. However, the relationship within which the recommendation was invoked was one between the ECSC and the receiver who refused to grant the debts preferential status; the Commission appealed against his decision. Only indirectly did it assert its rights against the entirety of creditors.

4.3 The Actual Addressees of a Directive

In principle, it is assumed that Community law is not concerned with the question of which authorities take the necessary measures in order to fulfil the Member State's obligation under Community law. In this respect Community law maintains the traditional rule of international law that the State as such and not its individual organs bears responsibility in international relations, and that it is up to the Member State concerned to decide on the way it will realize its international obligations within its own legal order.[40] In *International Fruit Company II* the Court of Justice stated in unequivocal terms that

"when provisions of the Treaty or of regulations confer power or impose obligations upon the States for the purposes of the implementation of Community law the question of how the exercise of such powers and the fulfilment of such obligations may be entrusted by Member States to specific national bodies is solely a matter of the constitutional system of each State."[41]

In a number of cases this principle of institutional autonomy has also been explicitly confirmed with respect to directives. The Court held that each Member State is free to delegate such powers to its authorities as it considers fit, and to implement directives by means of measures adopted by regional or local authorities.[42] Likewise, in the legal literature it is generally accepted that a directive does not interfere with the institutional structure of the Member States. It therefore does not authorize an organ of the state to take the necessary measures if this organ is not competent to do so under national law. In other words, it does not constitute an independent source of power for the authorities concerned.[43] The Court's finding, quoted in Section 4.1, that the obligations imposed on Member States by Article 189(3) and Article 5(1) are equally binding

[40] Cf. Bleckmann 1984, p. 776 and Hessel and Mortelmans 1993, p. 929.

[41] Joined Cases 51-54/71 [1971] ECR 1107, para. 4. Confirmed in Case 240/78 *Atalanta* [1979] ECR 2137. More recently the Court found in Case C-8/88 *Germany v. Commission* [1990] ECR 2321, that "... it is not for the Commission to rule on the division of competences by the institutional rules proper to each Member State, or on the obligations which may be imposed on federal and Länder authorities respectively" (para. 13).

[42] Cf. Case 96/81 *Commission v. The Netherlands* [1982] ECR 1791, Case 97/81 *Commission v. The Netherlands* [1982] ECR 1819, Joined Cases 227-230/85 *Commission v. Belgium* [1988] ECR 1, Case C-156/91 *Mundt* [1992] ECR I-5567 and Case C-435/92 *Association pour protection des animaux sauvages* [1994] ECR I-67. Cf. also Hessel and Mortelmans 1993, p. 916.

[43] Cf. Ipsen 1965, p. 76, Kooijmans 1967, p. 137, Lauwaars 1973, p. 28, Monaco 1987, p. 466-468, Kortmann 1991, p. 47, Grabitz Kommentar, p. 21a, Everling 1992b, p. 378. For another view, i.e. that a directive as such can serve as a direct source of powers enabling national authorities to act even if they do not have the necessary powers under national law, see Emde Boas in Droit Communautaire et Droit National, p. 148-149.

STAFFS UNIVERSITY LIBRARY

on all the authorities of the Member States, does not seem to change the matter, on the face of it at least. The proviso added with respect to the obligations for the courts, namely "for matters within their jurisdiction", can be understood as indicating that the obligations are binding for those authorities which already possess the necessary powers by virtue of national law.[44]

From the above it follows that the answer to the question of which organ or authority of a Member State is actually bound by a directive will, depending on the subject matter of the directive at issue, vary from Member State to Member State, according to the internal distribution of tasks and competences.[45]

Similarly, the foregoing suggests that the Member States are free to decide which organ or authority will be entrusted with the actual implementation of a particular directive.[46] This is however true only to a certain extent. As pointed out above (and discussed in more detail below),[47] Community law imposes certain requirements as to the nature of the implementing measures. This limitation of the freedom to choose the measures will also entail a limitation as to the choice of the organ or authority.[48] Thus, for instance, where a proper implementation of a directive requires transposition by primary legislation, collaboration of the Parliament will be necessary. In other cases implementation by secondary legislation may suffice and consequently, other bodies with appropriate legislative competences will be involved.

Another factor with implications for the principle of institutional autonomy and the internal structure of a Member State is the *indifference* of Community institutions, and the Court of Justice in particular, with regard to the internal state order. Although, on the one hand, the Court demonstrates that it is willing to look beyond the abstraction of the "Member State" when it says that all national authorities are bound by the obligation to achieve the result prescribed by a directive, on the other hand, it is the Member State as such that is

[44] Cf. Everling 1992b, p. 380, Daig and Smidt 1991, p. 4965, Jarass 1991, p. 216. Cf. also the opinion of A-G Mancini in Joined Cases 227-230/85 *Commission v. Belgium* [1988] ECR 1, para. 2 and Case C-8/88 *Germany v. Commission* [1990] ECR 2321, para. 13: "it is for all the authorities of the Member States, whether it be central authorities of the State or the authorities of a federated State, or other territorial authorities, to ensure observance of the rules of Community law *within the sphere of their competence*" (emphasis added – SP). See however below, Section 4.2 and Chapter 10, Subsection 10.8.4.

[45] Or, as Pescatore put it (1971, p. 91): "*dire que la directive s'adresse aux Etats Membres cela signifie concrètement qu'elle engage les organes des Etats Membres dont l'action peut être requise pour la mise en application de la directive. Quels sont ces organes? Ceci dépend des circonstances de chaque cas: tantôt ce sera le pouvoir législatif; tantôt le gouvernement en tant qu'il est investi du pouvoir réglementaire et de la haute direction de l'administration nationale.*"

[46] Cf. the term national authorities in Article 189(3).

[47] See Chapter 2, Section 2.5 and Chapter 5.

[48] Cf. Kortmann 1991, p. 47.

responsible for the transposition and application of Community law in the national legal order.[49]

The most obvious example of this can be found in the case law of the Court in infringement proceedings: a Member State is liable under Article 169 of the Treaty, irrespective of which State authority has occasioned the infringement through its act or its omission, even if it is a constitutionally independent body.[50] The same principle also applies in full with respect to directives. According to the Court's established case law "a Member State may not plead provisions, practices or circumstances in its internal legal system to justify failure to comply with obligations under Community directives".[51] These internal provisions, practices or circumstances include the division of powers, the different competences of Member State's organs, their mutual relationships etc. Whatever they might be, these factors cannot release the Member States from their obligation to ensure that the provisions of a directive are properly implemented in the national legal order. Arguments based on the fact that a government does not have the necessary powers at its disposal to compel other organs to implement a directive are of no avail.[52] Consequently, the Member States may be obliged to provide for a mechanism by means of which national authorities, whatever their place in the institutional structure might be, are induced to comply with the obligations arising from a directive.[53] Similarly, if *ratione materiae* competent organs do not have the appropriate powers at their disposal to adopt the measures necessary for full compliance with the obligations, or where there is no competent organ at all, it is up to the Member State, i.e. usually the legislature, to create the powers or organs respectively. In this regard a directive will in fact have consequences for the institutional structure of the State.

[49] Thus not the government; the latter only represents the State *vis-à-vis* the Community institutions and *vis-à-vis* other Member States.

[50] Cf. Case 77/69 *Commission v. Belgium* [1970] ECR 243 and Case 8/70 *Commission v. Italy* [1970] ECR 961. Cf. also Arts 199., p. 508.

[51] Cf. Case 68/81 *Commission v. Belgium* [1982] ECR 153, para. 5; cf. also above, Chapter 2, Section 2.3.

[52] Cf. e.g. Joined Cases 227-230/85 *Commission v. Belgium* [1988] ECR 1 and Case 1/86 *Commission v. Belgium* [1987] ECR 2797. See also Case C-237/90 *Commission v. Germany* [1992] ECR I-5973, where the German government argued that it was not necessary to compel the Länder by an explicit provision since the principle of "*Bundestreue*" constituted sufficient guarantee.

[53] Cf. Winter 1991a, p. 54. On possible sanctions against decentralized authorities which do not comply with Community law in general see Fide Reports 1992.

4.4 The Implications of Binding Force upon "All National Authorities"

4.4.1 Introduction

What inferences must be drawn from the fact that, according to the Court, the obligations imposed on Member States by Article 189(3) and Article 5(1) are binding on *all* the national authorities?

It appears that when considered from the point of view of different functions, the obligation concerns legislative,[54] executive and judicial authorities. Likewise, when considered from a geographical angle, it concerns both central and decentralized bodies.[55] As far as legislative authorities are concerned, the Court's finding does not entail a significant change. Proper implementation of directives will usually require the enactment of binding rules of general application.[56] It is therefore generally assumed that the organ which is *primarily* concerned by a directive is the legislator.[57] In other words, it is first and foremost the responsibility of the respective authorities which exercise legislative power to draw, within the field of their competence, the inferences from a directive, i.e. to adopt the necessary rules.

However, the Court's statement has some rather less expected implications for the judiciary and, in particular, for the administration (acting as the executive), which are responsible for the application and enforcement of the rules of the directive in their respective areas of competence.

The binding effect which Article 189(3) ascribes to directives, together with Article 5(1), is – as mentioned above[58] – the basis for the obligation to interpret national law in conformity with the directive at issue and it is the basis for direct effect of directives. As this binding effect exists in relation to the courts and the administration, as well as to the legislator, they are both obliged to proceed to

[54] Both legislature and the executive in its rule-making capacity. Depending on the subject matter of the directive at issue, the competence of the respective bodies and the state of national law of which the provisions of the directive will be a part, the organ actually adressed will not necessarily be the one responsible for primary legislation. As to the tendency to transpose directives by means of secondary legislation see Siedentopf and Ziller 1988, p. 44. Cf. also Case C-339/87 *Commission v. The Netherlands* [1990] ECR I-851, in which the Court of Justice accepted as proper means of implementation a combination of a Law and ministerial regulations (generally binding instruments under Dutch law).

[55] Cf. Case 103/88 *Costanzo* [1989] ECR 1839. See also Daig and Smidt 1991, p. 4965 and Hessel and Mortelmans 1993, in particular p. 916.

[56] Cf. Chapter 5, Subsection 5.2.3.

[57] Cf. e.g. Pescatore 1971, p. 90, Wyatt 1983, p. 247, Lutter 1992, p. 594 and the opinion of A-G Cruz Vilaça in Case 412/85 *Commission v. Germany* [1987] ECR 3503, para. 19.

[58] Section 4.1.

the interpretation described above and to ensure the full application of directly effective provisions, i.e. to apply them and to refrain from applying national provisions which conflict with them.[59]

It is not the purpose of this Section to anticipate the subsequent Chapters which will cover in detail interpretation in accordance with the directive, direct effect of directives and the particular role played by national courts in the enforcement of Community directives.[60] However, with respect to the administration, which will not be the focal point of the analysis in the following Chapters, a number of consequences should be discussed here.

4.4.2 Application of Directives by the Executive

In Section 3.3 it was explained that it is not sufficient to transpose directives into national law. The directives, or more precisely, the national implementing provisions, must be applied and enforced by the competent administrative bodies. When carrying out this task the administration is bound, by virtue of the obligation to interpret national law in conformity with the directive, to interpret and apply this law in the way which corresponds most with the provisions of the underlying directive.[61] The more discretion is left to the administration, the more important is this obligation. Moreover, as will be explained in Chapter 10, the obligation is not limited to national rules actually implementing the directive. It exists with respect to *all* national law suitable to achieve the objective pursued by the directive. In the same Chapter the limits of the obligation at issue will likewise be explored. One of the limits arguably lies in the competence of the authorities concerned. This means that they cannot proceed to an interpretation of national law such that it amounts to exceeding the various powers given to them by national law.[62]

Thus, for instance, it is highly questionable whether a (quasi-judicial) administrative body, hearing and examining complaints about sex discrimination in pay may broaden, by interpretation, its own competence to the field of occupational pensions for the simple reason that according to the Court of Justice the Community concept of pay includes occupational pensions as well.[63]

[59] Cf. Case 103/88 *Costanzo* [1989] ECR 1839.

[60] Chapters 10, 11 and 8 respectively.

[61] See e.g. Case 14/83 *Von Colson* [1984] ECR 1891. Cf. also Steyger 1991. Although it may be argued that the interpretative obligation is particularly addressed to the courts, this of course does not imply that the executive should not be bound in the same way.

[62] Cf. e.g. Everling 1992a, p. 380 and Jarass 1991, p. 216.

[63] Commissie gelijke behandeling van mannen en vrouwen bij de arbeid 3 April 1991, no. 143-91-15 and 27 April 1993, no. 340-93-15.

However, it must be pointed out that it is far from clear what the Court means by the term "for matters within their jurisdiction",[64] which is relevant in this context.

Interpretation of national law in conformity with a directive may often help to overcome inconsistencies between national law and the directive at issue. Whenever this method does not work for some reason, national administrative authorities will be required to apply directly the provisions of the directive wherever the provisions lend themselves to such an application.

Traditionally, obligations resulting from directly effective provisions of directives were approached both in the literature and the Court's case law from the point of view of the judiciary: what must the national court do if an individual relies in a case before it on directly effective provisions? In the past only a few authors have explicitly addressed the question whether, in cases of belated or incorrect implementation, the administration must apply directly effective provisions of a directive and whether, where appropriate, they must disapply national provisions which are incompatible with it. The question was answered in the affirmative by Grabitz[65] and – although with some hesitation – by Everling.[66] Other authors have denied such an obligation on the part of national administration.[67]

The line of reasoning of the latter was partly followed by A-G Lenz in *Costanzo*.[68] In his view only proper implementation by the legislature can create the obligation for the administration to give effect to a legal situation consistent with the directive. National administrative authorities cannot be obliged to make a decision in conformity with Community law by directly applying a provision, because they do not have the possibility of obtaining a ruling from the Court of Justice on the direct effect of the provision at issue. In this respect they would lack the necessary endorsement of the Court, which the Advocate General sees as a form of requisite legal protection of the authorities concerned.

On the other hand however, according to the Advocate General, national administrative authorities are entitled to apply a provision of a directive if its direct effect is beyond doubt. This will particularly be the case if a prior ruling on the issue already exists: the conflict of rules being resolved *in abstracto*, the administration cannot be prevented from applying the directly effective provision *in concreto*.

By accepting that administrative authorities are entitled to apply a directly effective provision of a directive, the Advocate General rejects another argument against the obligation of administrative authorities to apply these provisions, namely that the

[64] See for a detailed discussion Chapter 10, Subsection 10.8.4.

[65] Grabitz 1971, p.21. Cf. also Klein 1988, p. 29 and Oldenbourg 1984, p. 30. For Community law in general see Bebr 1981, p. 559.

[66] Everling 1983, p. 108 and, with even more hesitations, Everling 1993, p. 215.

[67] Cf. Seidel 1983, p. 19 and further references by Oldenbourg 1984, p. 30.

[68] Case 103/88 [1989] ECR 1839, para. 28-36.

subordination of the executive power to the legislative power should prevent the administration from refusing to apply the law.[69]

The Court's solution of the problem was uncompromising. In *Costanzo* it held that administrative authorities are under the same obligation as a national court to apply provisions which have direct effect and to refrain from applying provisions of national law which conflict with them.[70]

The Court gave two arguments for this finding. Firstly, it recalled that an individual may rely against the State on directly effective provisions of a directive in proceedings before the national courts *because* the obligations arising under the provisions are binding upon all the authorities of the Member States. Furthermore, it would be contradictory to rule, on the one hand, that an individual may rely upon directly effective provisions in national proceedings seeking an order against administrative authorities and, on the other hand, to hold that these authorities are under no obligation to apply the provisions concerned and refrain from applying provisions of national law which conflict with them.

The consequence of *Costanzo* seems to be that where a provision of a directive has direct effect the administrative authorities, by virtue of Article 189(3) and Article 5(1), must – if necessary – disregard their respective competences[71] and apply the provision of the directive regardless of the fact that there is no legal basis in national law for such an application. As Curtin and Mortelmans have observed, in this respect Community law confers new competences upon national authorities.[72] Accordingly, in contrast to that stated in Section 4.3 and also above concerning the interpretative obligation, it is possible that a directive may interfere with the internal division of powers within a Member State.

This approach, however, is not very revolutionary when compared with the Court's case law on the effects of a judgment under Article 169 of the E(E)C Treaty. In 1972 the Court explained that a judgment of this kind entails

"a prohibition having the full force of law on the competent national authorities against applying a national rule recognized as incompatible with the Treaty and, if the circumstances so require, an obligation on them to take all appropriate measures to enable Community law to be fully applied."[73]

[69] See the observations of *Comune di Milano* in *Costanzo*, p. 1849-1850. Cf. also Seidel 1983, p. 19 and Winter 1991b, p. 660.

[70] Para. 33.

[71] Cf. Winter 1991b, p. 666 and Everling 1992a, p. 380.

[72] Curtin and Mortelmans 1994, p. 457.

[73] Case 48/71 *Commission v. Italy* [1972] ECR 527, para. 7.

More recently the Court reaffirmed this principle, under reference to the case just quoted and also to *Costanzo*, in Case *C-101/91 (exemption fom VAT)*.[74] The principle may indeed involve direct application of the rules of the directive when they are suitable for such an application.

The binding force of the judgment upon all the national authorities results in these cases from the authority attaching to the judgment (*res judicata*).[75] Arguably, there is no fundamental difference between a judgment having the authority of *res judicata* and the binding force by virtue of Article 189(3) coupled with Article 5(1). Neither may the fact that in the former case there is an intervention by the Court of Justice while in the latter there is not, at least not necessarily, be considered as decisive for the administration's obligation to apply a provision of a directive. It is defensible that the risk of applying such a provision or disapplying national law erroneously should lie with the authorities rather than with the individual, for at least two reasons. Firstly, the problems are caused by the authorities of a Member State which has not implemented the directive within the time limit or not correctly. Secondly, if matters were otherwise, the individual would be forced to start proceedings in a national court *in every single case* in order to enforce his rights under Community law, for as long as the Member State concerned did not adapt national law and the administration was unwilling to disapply it or to apply the provision of the directive, as the case may be.

On the other hand, it must be observed that an unqualified obligation for national authorities to apply a directive and disapply national law, certainly *before* the Court of Justice or at least a national court has clarified the matter, may seriously compromise legal certainty.[76] It is submitted, that there is a need to develop a more balanced approach to the "Costanzo obligation".

[74] *Commission v. Italy* [1993] ECR I-191.

[75] Cf. Joined Cases 314-316/81 and 83/82 *Waterkeyn* [1982] ECR 4337. Furthermore it must be observed that in this Case the Court held that "all institutions of the Member State concerned must ... ensure *within the fields covered by their powers* that the judgments of the Court are complied with" (emphasis added – SP). It is again not entirely clear what the Court has exactly in mind by making this reference. The most plausible interpretation seems to be that the competence *ratione materiae* is at issue.

[76] As to a number of mainly practical difficulties occasioned by the *Costanzo* judgment see Pieper 1990, p. 688.

4.5 THE CONCEPT OF "THE STATE"

4.5.1 The Court's Approach in General

The answer to the question whether, in a specific setting, a certain entity or person is *directly* bound by an obligation laid down in a directive,[77] with all the consequences resulting therefrom, will depend on the definition of the term "State" given for this particular purpose.

As mentioned above, this problem arose in relation to the question concerning the parties against which an individual may rely on a provision of a directive, i.e. within the context of direct effect.[78] In this respect it must be pointed out that the terminology used by the Court is rather loose. It uses the terms "State", "organ of the State", "emanation of the State", "State authority" and "public authority" interchangeably.

The problem of designating an entity as a part of the State, a public authority or any other synonym is certainly not new, the notions being involved in several areas of Community law.[79]

For instance, Article 30 of the Treaty relates to measures adopted by the Member States. A campaign promoting the sale of Irish goods conducted by a company limited was considered by the Court to be a measure in the sense of Article 30, since the Irish Government defined the aims and the broad outline of the campaign, appointed the members of the Management Committee of the company and granted the company considerable public subsidies covering the greater part of the expenses.[80] Likewise, measures adopted by a professional body which lays down rules of ethics applicable to the members of the profession and has a committee upon which national legislation has conferred disciplinary powers that could involve removal from the register of persons authorized to exercise the profession, may constitute "measures" within the meaning of Article 30.[81]

Under Article 90 the problem may arise whether a certain undertaking should be regarded as "public". Although no specific cases dealing with this question have as yet been rendered by the Court, in Joined Cases *188-190/80 (transparency)*[82] there is an indication of the elements which will be important in this respect. The Court held that the reason for the inclusion of this Article in the Treaty is the influence which the public authorities are able to exert over the commercial decisions of public undertakings. This

[77] I.e. whether the directive imposes an obligation without the intercession of national rules.
[78] See above, Section 4.1.
[79] The issue of "public authority" may also arise in the context of the Brussels Convention on Jurisdiction and Enforcement of Judgements in Civil and Commercial Matters: see Case 814/79 *Rüffer* [1980] ECR 3807.
[80] Case 249/81 *Commission v. Ireland* [1982] ECR 4005.
[81] Joined Cases 266 and 267/87 *Royal Pharmaceutical Society* [1989] ECR 1295.
[82] *France, Italy, United Kingdom v. Commission* [1982] ECR 2545.

influence may be exerted on the basis of financial participation or of rules governing the management of the undertaking.[83]

For the purposes of Article 92 it is immaterial whether aid is granted directly by the State or by public or private bodies established or appointed by the State to administer the aid. A company incorporated under private law in which the State holds directly or indirectly 50% of the shares, where the State appoints half of the members of the supervisory board and whose decisions have to be approved by the competent Minister, must be regarded as acting under the control and on the instructions of public authorities.[84]

As far as the "public service" exception of Article 48(4) of the Treaty is concerned, the Court has explained that the posts covered by this provision are those directly relating to the specific activities of the public service, i.e. those involving the exercise of powers conferred by public law and responsibility for safeguarding the general interest of the State.[85]

In *Broekmeulen*[86] the Court had to decide whether the Appeals Committee established by the Royal Netherlands Society for the Promotion of Medicine should be considered as a "court or tribunal" of a Member State within the meaning of Article 177. In its reasoning the Court stressed two aspects which are relevant for the present discussion: firstly, there was a significant degree of involvement of the Dutch public authorities in the composition of the Committee; and secondly, where a Member State assigns the task of implementing Community law provisions to a professional body acting under a degree of governmental supervision and where that body, together with the public authorities concerned, creates appeal procedures, the Court should have an opportunity to rule on questions of interpretation and validity arising out of such proceedings.[87]

Under several directives it might equally be necessary to decide whether a certain entity acts as or must be considered as a "public authority".

Article 1 of Directive 71/305 concerning the co-ordination of procedures for the award of public works contracts[88] describes the bodies to be considered as "contracting authorities" for the purposes of the Directive. In *Beentjes*[89] the Court found that a body which is not a part of the State administration in formal terms must nevertheless be regarded as falling within the notion of State for the purpose of Article 1, since its composition and functions are laid down by legislation, the Provincial Executive appoints its members, the body is obliged to apply rules laid down by a committee established by a royal decree whose members are appointed by the Crown, the State ensures the observance of the obligations arising for the body out of the measures of the committee and the State finances the public works contracts which the body awards.

[83] Cf. also the definition given in Directive 80/723 (transparency), OJ 1980, L 195/35, also discussed briefly below.

[84] Joined Cases 67, 68 and 70/85 *Gebroeders van der Kooy* [1988] ECR 219.

[85] Case 149/79 *Commission v. Belgium* [1980] ECR 3881.

[86] Case 246/80 [1981] ECR 2311.

[87] Cf. also Case 271/82 *Auer II* [1983] ECR 2727.

[88] OJ English Spec. Ed. 1971 (II), p. 682.

[89] Case 31/87 [1988] ECR 4635.

Under Article 4(5) of the Sixth VAT Directive[90] activities or transactions in which the State, regional and local authorities and other bodies governed by public law engage "as public authorities" are exempt from VAT. According to the Court, this provision draws a distinction between the activities in which the bodies concerned engage under the special regime applicable to them and activities pursued under the same legal conditions as those which apply to private traders. The latter cannot be regarded as activities of "public authorities" within the meaning of the Diretive.[91]

Another distinction is made under Directive 80/723 on the transparency of financial relations between Member States and public undertakings,[92] namely one between "public authorities", defined as the state and regional or local authorities, and "public undertakings", defined in the terms of the Directive as undertakings over which the public authorities may exercise directly or indirectly a dominant influence by virtue of their ownership of such a undertaking, their financial participation therein or the rules which govern it. When confronted with the question whether a certain body with no legal personality separate from that of the State should neverthless be regarded as a "public undertaking" within the terms of the Directive, the Court stressed that it is not the legal form but rather the activities exercised which are decisive.[93]

From this case law we learn that the Court interprets the concept of "the State" in the way which best achieves the objectives of the measure at issue.[94] For those familiar with the Court's methods of interpretation, this will hardly come as a surprise. At the same time, however, it means that there is no generic definition at Community level of the types of entities which should be assimilated to the State. The approach of the Court is highly functional, i.e. the interpretation is related to the objective pursued by the rules within which the concept figures and, moreover, the interpretation is more or less tailored to the factual situation of the entity in question.[95]

For the purposes of deciding whether a particular body is directly bound by a directive, unlike in the cases discussed above, a *specific* frame of reference is lacking. If the obligations upon the Member States result from the binding nature which Article 189(3) confers on the directive *in general*, the objective of a particular directive is irrelevant and, therefore, it is arguable that the directive as such will be of no avail in this respect.

[90] Directive 77/388, OJ 1977, L 145/1.
[91] Joined Cases 231/87 and 129/88 *Carpaneto I* [1989] ECR 3233.
[92] OJ 1980, L 195/35.
[93] Case 118/85 *Commission v. Italy* [1987] ECR 2599.
[94] Cf. also the opinion of A-G Van Gerven in Case C-188/89 *Foster* [1990] ECR I-3313, para. 11.
[95] Cf. on this subject in general Hecquard-Theron 1990 and as regards direct effect of directives in particular Curtin 1990a.

4.5.2 Foster versus British Gas

Arguments Before the Court and the Opinion of the Advocate General
The problem of the criteria to be applied in order to find out whether a directive imposes obligations upon a certain body or, in other words, whether the body concerned should be regarded as falling within the concept of "the State", was submitted to the Court of Justice in *Foster.*[96] Briefly, in this case the House of Lords wished to know whether a female employee, who was dismissed on discriminatory terms, might rely on Article 5(1) of Directive 76/207 (equal treatment at work)[97] against the British Gas Corporation (hereafter the BGC) which was, at the material time, a nationalized gas undertaking.

In *Foster*, basically two types of tests were discussed in the written observations and, subsequently, at the hearing.

The first of these was a *functional test*, involving consideration of the activities in which the body is engaged. A body carrying out a public function on behalf of the State or a body entrusted with a public duty by the State, should be considered as a part of the State.

The second was an approach based on the existence of *control* on the part of the State in relation to the entity concerned. Within this test, two forms of possible control were identified. The first form was regulation by the State by means of binding directions or specific legislation. The second form of possible control was based on "economic reality", that is to say on the possibility of controlling a body by means of ownership of shares in the body or through financial means, such as funding by the State. There was, however, a disagreement about which test should apply. Furthermore, problems arose with respect to the functional test in that there was uncertainty as to the kind of activities which should be considered as public functions; and with respect to the control test in that it was not clear how far the control should go and what kind of control should be required.[98]

In his opinion, A-G Van Gerven found that, as in the Court's case law on the interpretation of the term State / public authority in other Community law contexts, the starting point should be to give the concept of State the meaning which corresponds most closely to the underlying reasoning. As in the case of direct effect of directives, the rationale is that a Member State may under no circumstances benefit from its failure to implement the relevant provision of a directive, so obviously the term State must be given a broad scope.

[96] Case C-188/89 [1990] ECR I-3313.
[97] OJ 1976, L 39/40.
[98] For a discussion of the separate criteria see A-G Van Gerven in Case C-188/89 [1990] ECR I-3313, para. 17-20 and Prechal 1990, p. 457-459.

According to the Advocate General, this means firstly, that all bodies which can exercise any authority over individuals pursuant to the constitutional structure of a Member State fall within the concept of "the State", irrespective of how that authority is organized and irrespective of the duties it performs.[99]

Secondly, when the "authority test" becomes questionable or unworkable, as in the case of public undertakings, an alternative test must be available. In this respect the Advocate General pointed out that, whenever the concept of "the State" is interpreted broadly, a number of common criteria emerge from the Court's case law, namely: the public authorities must have actual control, dominating influence or the possibility of giving binding directions. The manner in which the control is exercised seems to be immaterial, whether through specific legislative provisions, by means of dependence for purposes of management or finance, through financial participation or in the capacity of proprietor.

On the basis of these considerations *and* the rationale behind the direct effect of directives the Advocate General found that the concept of "the State" may extend to persons or bodies

> "... in respect of which the State ... has assumed responsibilities which put it in a position to decisively influence the conduct of that person or body in any manner whatsoever ... with regard to the matter in respect of which the relevant provision of the directive imposes an obligation which the Member State has failed to implement in national law."[100]

The Advocate General further specified that the nature (public or private) of the bodies, their sphere of activity and the manner in which the State can influence their conduct (*de jure* or *de facto*) are irrelevant. Only one proviso should apply as far as the last of these aspects is concerned: the possibility of exercising influence must stem from something other than a general legislative power, since the State can compel everyone to do or not do something by means of general legislative measures.

In fact, the Advocate General has streamlined the control test by linking it to the subject matter of the directive in question. On the one hand, this approach is tempting since by linking the sphere of influence to the subject matter of the directive concerned a framework is created which might be helpful for the examination of whether a body should be considered as being a part of the State or not. On the other hand, however, it entails a limitation which, although it fits entirely within the logic of the approach, is nevertheless questionable. It means that even in cases of very substantive State involvement the body will not be bound by the directive in question if the subject matter of the directive is outside

[99] See the opinion of A-G Van Gerven, para. 21.
[100] *Ibid.* para 22.

the State's scope of influence. The Advocate General argued in this respect that as the competent Secretary of State had the power to give the BGC binding directions with regard to both the most efficient management of its activities and the exercise and performance of its functions in general if the national interest so required, binding instructions *could* be given to the BGC to comply with Directive 76/207 since compliance with Community law is certainly an objective of national interest. Yet it seems to me that the control by the Secretary of State concerned gas distribution in the UK and related matters and not the undertaking's dismissal policy. In other words, the link laid down by the Advocate General is very tenuous; and after all, as Curtin has pointed out:

"... how realistic is it to expect a State which has failed to implement a directive in time to seek to influence any organ of authority with regard to the subject matter of the same directive?"[101]

The judgment of the Court

In *Foster*, the Court did not define the concept of "the State" in the abstract but gave guidelines which seem to be written for the particular situation of the BGC; this is highlighted by the fact that the judgment starts with an analysis of the Gas Act 1972 which governed the BGC at the material time, focussing in particular on the relationship between the BGC and the competent Secretary of State. Subsequently, the Court referred to its case law on direct effect of directives, stressing that "it is necessary to prevent the State from taking advantage of its own failure to comply with Community law". As to the question concerning the entities against which a directive can be relied on, the Court summarized its position as follows: a provision of a directive meeting the requirements of direct effect

"could be relied on against organizations or bodies which were subject to the authority or control of the State or had special powers beyond those which result from the normal rules applicable to relations between individuals."[102]

The bodies in question were tax authorities,[103] local or regional authorities,[104] constitutionally independent authorities responsible for the maintenance of public

[101] Curtin 1990a, p. 220.
[102] Case C-188/89 *Foster* [1990] ECR I-3313, para. 18.
[103] Case 8/81 *Becker* [1982] ECR 52 and Case C-221/88 *Busseni* [1990] ECR I-495.
[104] Case 103/88 *Costanzo* [1989] ECR 1839.

order and safety[105] and public authorities providing public health services.[106] Consequently the Court held that

"a body, whatever its legal form, which has been made responsible, pursuant to a measure adopted by the State, for providing a public service under the control of the State and has for that purpose special powers beyond those which result from the normal rules applicable in relations between individuals is included in any event among the bodies against which the provision of a directive capable of having direct effect may be relied upon."[107]

The four criteria laid down in *Foster* seem to relate both to the possibility of control and the functions performed, in their broadest senses; or, to put it another way, both the control test and the functional test seem to apply. The constitutive elements of the respective tests are the separate criteria. On the one hand, the performance of the activities of the body concerned was subject to the control of the State and, moreover, this performance derived from the authority of the State (BGC was made responsible "pursuant to a measure adopted by the State"). On the other hand, the Court emphasized both the nature of the activities (providing a public service) and the conditions under which the activities were pursued (special powers possessed by the BGC).

The separate criteria leave many questions unanswered. In the first place it is not entirely clear whether they are cumulative or not. While in the reasoning the Court mentions "authority or control of the State" and "special powers" as two alternative elements, in the *dictum* "control" and "special powers" are presented as cumulative criteria. However, since the Court found that a body fulfilling these two criteria is *in any event* a body against which the directive may be relied upon, it is submitted that they must be considered to be alternatives.[108]

Secondly, while it can be argued that "authority" – in so far as this is relevant at all in *Foster*[109] – presupposes a form of hierarchical relationship, as far as the much broader concept of "control" is concerned, the question of what constitutes "control" is left entirely open. Unlike the Advocate General, the Court abstained from giving any indication of its views in this respect.[110]

[105] Case 222/84 *Johnston* [1986] ECR 1631.

[106] Case 152/84 *Marshall I* [1986] ECR 723.

[107] Para. 20. There is a striking resemblance with the description given by A-G Darmon of the Royal Pharmaceutical Society in his opinion in Joined Cases 266 and 267/87 [1989] ECR 1295, para. 14, in particular the French version.

[108] Cf. also on this issue Gilliams 1990-1991, p. 1358.

[109] Authority is explicitly mentioned in para. 18 but is at the utmost only implicitly present in the *dictum* of the judgment.

[110] As to possible forms of control cf. Prechal 1990, p. 458-459.

Thirdly, the Court's reasoning seems to suggest that having special powers is sufficient. However, in the *dictum* the special powers are linked to the element of "providing a public service". From this one could assume that the existence of special powers entails by implication that the body does provide a public service. In my view this is not necessarily true. Special powers merely refer to the fact that the body is not acting under the same terms as private individuals.[111] Similarly, it may be questioned whether "public service" is a "hard" requirement. In my opinion, it should be regarded more as a pointer. Moreover, that which constitutes a "public service" may differ considerably from one Member State to another, within each Member State from one time to another and arguably also within the context of Community law.[112]

Fourthly, the importance of the element that the basis of the body's activity is a measure adopted by the State is uncertain, since it might not necessarily apply to 100% state owned companies, although these are by implication entirely controlled by the State.

One thing so far is straightforward, however: the activities in which the body concerned is engaged comprise a much broader category than the so-called "classical duties" of the State, i.e. the exercise of legislative, judicial and executive functions in "Montesquian" terms. The mere fact that the State has assumed the responsibility for the activity at issue may suffice to bring it within the scope of the functional test.

To summarize, *Foster* made clear that both the control test and the functional test are not mutually exclusive. They rather apply cumulatively or, as has been submitted, alternatively. For the rest, the judgment gives some possible indications as to how the tests can be given substance, but the scope of the separate elements and their relative importance is far from clear. On the other hand, the judgment certainly testifies that the Court is willing to apply a broadbrush approach which could cover the whole panoply of bodies through which the State pursues its policies, whether in its regulatory capacity or in its interventionist capacity, where it operates as a market participant, irrespective of the legal form of the bodies or their status under national law. Accordingly, the approach will likewise cut through the existing dividing lines between the different kinds of bodies applicable within the Member States.[113] Yet given the immense variety of entities which operate within the Member States outside the traditional structures of administration on the one hand and the indicative nature of the Court's guidelines on the other, it is to be expected that the "labelling" of the various bodies will pose considerable problems, the more so since the authorities which must decide this, in particular the courts, will be inclined to stick to the common and familiar

[111] That will occur, for instance, in the case of State monopolies or undertakings with exclusive rights granted by the State. Cf. Gilliams 1991-1992, p. 1358.

[112] See the overview given above, in Subsection 4.5.1. Cf. also Prechal 1990, p. 457-462.

[113] Dividing lines which are often far from clear in national law itself. For a discussion of some national case law dealing with the classification of different bodies see Curtin 1990a.

concepts when applying the guidelines. Perhaps paradoxically, however, it is precisely this immense variety of bodies which makes it more or less impossible for the Court to give more specific criteria covering all possible situations. Consequently, a case-to-case approach seems unavoidable.

Finally, mention should be made of one possibly far-reaching consequence of *Foster.* The judgment seems to suggest that the application of the guidelines should take place independently of the directive at issue. More *in concreto*, this will mean that once the body in question has satisfied the control test and/or the functional test it must be regarded as being bound by the obligations laid down in the directive – if this is relevant for its conduct – even in those areas which are beyond the control or which fall outside the scope of the activities causing the body to be considered a part of the State.[114] This development actually started to take shape in *Marshall I*,[115] where the Court held that the capacity, i.e. as public authority or as employer, in which a body (characterized by the national court as a public authority) acted was irrelevant. Although the Health Authority in question was, in functional terms, operating at arm's length from the government in the field of national health care and it is at least arguable whether its employment policy was under the control of the State, the Authority had to comply with the obligations resulting from Directive 76/207 (equal treatment at work).[116]

If this interpretation of *Foster* is correct, the category of entities which must comply with the terms of a directive and which might, where appropriate, be called upon to apply the directive[117] greatly expands, far beyond the bodies which are, under national law, primarily responsible for the implementation. This would only be otherwise if one were to assume that the *Foster* approach is relevant solely for the question whether an individual may rely on the directive against such a body.

[114] Thus since in Case 271/82 *Auer II* [1983] ECR 2727 the National Society of Veterinary Surgeons of France was bound by Directive 78/1026 (veterinary surgeons – recognition of qualifications) because it was exercising public powers conferred on it by national law and consequently the Society was to be considered as an "emanation of the State", the Society shall also have to observe other directives, relating to areas in which no public powers had been conferred to it, like employment of its own staff.

[115] Case 152/84 [1986] ECR 723.

[116] OJ 1976, L 39/40. This approach clearly entails that the distinction proposed by Dashwood (1978, p. 243), namely that the State acting in the exercise of its imperium is bound as addressee of the directive, while the State acting as market participant should have the same position in relation to the directive as any other undertaking, is not to be followed.

[117] See above Section 4.4. Cf. also Fischer 1992b, p. 636.

STAFFS UNIVERSITY LIBRARY

5
Form and Methods of Implementation

5.1 The Meaning of and the Freedom with Respect to Form and Methods

By making the distinction between that which is imperative, i.e. the result to be achieved, and that which is left to the discretion of the Member States, i.e. the choice of form and methods, Article 189(3) indicates what is within the competence of the Community and what remains within the competence of the Member States.[1] It also follows from this Article that the choice is limited to the *kind* of measures to be taken; their *content* is entirely determined by the directive at issue.[2] Thus the discretion as far as the form and methods are concerned does not mean that Member States necessarily have a margin in terms of policy making.

The reasons for leaving the Member States the freedom to choose the form and the methods are twofold. On the one hand the need for the discretion was inspired by the concern to respect as far as possible the sovereignty and the law-making power of the Member States and, in particular, the position of national parliaments. On the other hand, the freedom to choose the form and methods gives the Member States a certain latitude and consequently enables them to take into account national (legal) peculiarities and economic, social and other circumstances when implementing a directive.[3] This allows the Member States to insert the content of a directive into their national legal order, particularly into pre-existing national legislation related to the same matter, and to do so by means of the most appropriate and familiar legislative techniques. This latter aspect in particular is now considered to constitute the very essence of a directive.[4]

If, however, one tries to discover the exact meaning of the term "form and methods", in general neither the literature nor the case law of the Court of Justice is very helpful in this respect. Fuß suggests that form concerns primarily the *type* of rules a Member State enacts, while method refers to the political,

[1] Cf. Kovar 1987, p. 365, De Ripaisel-Landy and Gérard 1976, 47. Although, as was pointed out by, for instance, Capotorti (1988, p. 153), the boundary between the mandatory results and the means implying a margin of appreciation is far from clear.

[2] Cf. above, Chapter 3, Subsection 3.2.4. See also Ipsen 1965, p. 74.

[3] Cf. Fuß 1965, p. 379 and 381, Green 1984, p. 302, Bleckmann 1990, p. 84. What measures will be taken also depends on the "state of the law" within the Member State concerned. Cf. Capotorti 1988, p. 160 and Pescatore (1971, p. 92), who points out that in some cases national law will require a "*réforme profonde*" while in others a "*retouche à la législation*" will suffice.

[4] Cf. Everling 1992a, p. 380.

economic, financial or social measures to be taken.[5] According to Easson, form means the legal instrument selected; method relates to the contents.[6] Lasok and Bridge[7] disagree with Easson, pointing out that choice of methods implies a procedural discretion, i.e. the choice of the type of instrument or machinery of implementation. As far as the content is concerned (or substance, as they put it), this depends upon the particularity or the degree of detail of the directive in question as well as the state of the existing national law involved. However, in so far as Easson under the heading "contents of the instrument" addresses questions such as whether the directive should literally be transposed into national law or rather "translated" into national legal terminology, or whether it can be implemented within the framework of a general consolidation or reform,[8] the criticism is in my view not justified. Another author[9] defines methods as the measures taken by the Member States or the subjects they deal with. Form is the mode and way in which the measures come about, as well as their external appearance, the institutionalized forms of exercise of the State's powers (statutes, regulations etc.) or an institutionalized method. Bleckmann,[10] who relies on Oldenkop's interpretation, explains that the form concerns the questions of which organ of the state adopts the necessary instruments and in what kind of procedure and, moreover, which requirements (as to publication, written form etc.) these instruments must satisfy. In other words, in general there is a tendency to distinguish between the formal aspects of the implementing measures and the *technique* which is followed. In my view, it is less appropriate in this respect to speak of "content", as this might cause confusion between the substantive provisions of a directive,[11] which are – as a rule – to be transposed into national law and which are not necessarily left to the discretion of the Member States, and the means, which should, according to Article 189(3), be left to the Member States.

However, Oldenkop[12] has quite correctly observed that a clear distinction between form and methods cannot always be made. According to Ipsen the terms are an "unsuccessful alliteration".[13] In his view, the term "method" ("*Mittel*" in the German version of the Treaty, i.e. "means") is broader than the term "form", and in fact the former embraces the latter, since once the measures are

[5] Fuß 1965, p. 380. Cf. also Daig and Smidt 1991, p. 4963.

[6] Easson 1981, p. 33. Similarly, Capotorti (1988, p. 154) equates method with content, because the formal aspect is covered by the reference to "form".

[7] Lasok and Bridge 1991, p. 139.

[8] Easson 1981, p. 34.

[9] Oldenkop 1972, p. 85.

[10] Bleckmann 1990, p. 85.

[11] Cf. Chapter 3, Subsection 3.2.1.

[12] Oldenkop 1972, p. 85-86.

[13] Ipsen 1965, p. 80 ("*missglückte Alliteration*").

chosen the form is often predetermined by the rules of national (constitutional) law.

Seen against this background it is not surprising that several authors restrict themselves, when discussing the freedom to choose form and methods, to simply pointing out that it is the ways, or the different legal constructions,[14] that are left to the discretion of the Member States. The Court of Justice apparently also does not see the two terms as problematic, usually confining itself to their simple restatement or sometimes using slightly different words, like "ways and means".[15]

The choice of form and methods is left to the Member States, or more precisely, according to the terms of Article 189(3), to the national authorities. As explained above, in Chapter 4, Section 4.3, Community law is in principle not concerned with the question of which authorities enact the necessary measures, and it does not interfere with the internal structure of the Member States. Thus the choice of the measures, like the choice of the competent authority, is made within the framework of national constitutional law.[16] This is the purpose *and* consequence of the discretion which is left by Article 189(3) and the division of powers between the Community and the Member States which is entailed in it.

From the point of view of Community law, however, the Member States as such remain responsible for the action or inaction of all their organs and they cannot rely on provisions of national law or internal difficulties in order to justify non-compliance with their obligations under Community law.[17]

5.2 Curtailing the Freedom

5.2.1 Introduction

Although, as indicated in the previous Section, the directive was designed as a relatively "mild" instrument of Community intervention, leaving the Member States considerable leeway with respect to the measures to be taken for implementation, this freedom of the Member States is far from absolute. Firstly, as mentioned above in the Introduction to Part I, directives can be extremely detailed. It is fairly obvious that the more precise and detailed the content of a directive, the less room for manoeuvre is left for the implementing authorities,

[14] Cf. Kooymans 1967, p. 135 and Mertens de Wilmars 1991, p. 393.

[15] Cf. Case 14/83 *Von Colson* [1984] ECR 1891, also in other languages (*voies et moyens*; *Mittel und Wege*).

[16] Cf. Smit and Herzog, p. 5-611, Capotorti 1988, p. 160.

[17] See above, Chapter 4, Section 4.3.

with respect not only to the substance of the measures but also to the mode of implementation.[18]

Secondly, the scope of the Member States' discretion has been considerably curtailed by the Court of Justice. Following a somewhat hesitant start[19] the Court's case law began to develop rapidly after 1980. In Case *102/79 (tractors)*[20] it held that a particular mode of implementation, depending on the content of the directive, may be necessary. In this particular case the directives at issue had to be converted into provisions of national law with the same legal force as those applicable in the Member State in regard to the subject matter of the directives.[21] Likewise, later amendments of national implementing measures pursuant to a directive amending a preceding directive must be transposed by provisions of domestic law with the same legal force as the national provisions to be amended.[22] The Court also stressed that each Member State "should implement the directives in question in a way which fully meets the requirements of clarity and certainty in legal situations which the directives seek ...".[23]

As the case law now stands, the way in which a directive is implemented must

> "guarantee that the national authorities will in fact apply the directive fully and that, where the directive is intended to create rights for individuals, [their] legal position ... is sufficiently precise and clear and the persons concerned are made fully aware of their rights and, where appropriate, afforded the possibility of relying on them before the national courts."[24]

The same applies *a fortiori* where a directive aims at creating obligations for individuals: the persons concerned must also be able to ascertain the full extent of their obligations.[25]

[18] Cf. Capotorti 1988, p. 154 and Pescatore (1971, p. 92), who points out that a directive may restrict itself to the simple formulation of the objective to be achieved but equally it may impose upon the Member States a sort of "*loi modèle*".

[19] Cf. Case 48/75 *Royer* [1976] ECR 497 and Case 38/77 *Enka* [1977] ECR 2203.

[20] *Commission v. Belgium* [1980] ECR 1473.

[21] Though in later case law the "same legal force" requirement is less emphasized. Cf. Kovar 1987, p. 370.

[22] Cf. Case 116/86 *Commission v. Italy* [1988] ECR 1323.

[23] Case 102/79 *Commission v. Belgium* [1980] ECR 1473, para. 11. For a critical comment of this early case law see Green 1984, p. 298-300.

[24] Case 29/84 *Commission v. Germany* [1985] ECR 1661, para. 18. Reiterated in a whole line of subsequent cases. See e.g. C-131/88 *Commission v. Germany* [1991] ECR I-825, Case C-58/89 *Commission v. Germany* [1991] ECR I-4983, Case 363/85 *Commission v. Italy* [1987] ECR 1733.

[25] Cf. Case C-58/89 *Commission v. Germany* [1991] ECR I-4983, Case C-13/90 *Commission v. France* [1991] ECR I-4327, Case C-59/89 *Commission v. Germany* [1991] ECR I-2607, Case 257/86 *Commission v. Italy* [1988] ECR 3249, Case C-366/89 *Commission v. Italy* [1993] ECR I-4201.

The central notions of this case law are the two intertwined principles of full effect[26] and legal certainty. On the basis of these two principles the Court has formulated a number of more specific requirements which the implementing measures must satisfy, namely the binding nature of these measures, specificity, precision and clarity.[27] The requirements are, for their part, crucial for the opportunity of affected individuals to enforce their rights in national courts. This principle of effective judicial protection is another central *Leitmotif* of the Court's case law.[28]

The concrete application of these principles may differ from case to case. Indeed, the approach of the Court is casuistic and cannot be otherwise. The evaluation of whether the requirements are met depends, on the one hand, on the provisions of the directive at issue and, on the other hand, on the implementing measures adopted by the Member States concerned; in every single case these two aspects must be compared with each other. Nevertheless some general lessons can also be drawn from this case law.

As pointed out above in Chapter 2, Section 2.5, three different problem areas can be distinguished with respect to the proper implementation of directives. These are the content of the measures, the nature of the measures, and the application and enforcement of the measures in practice. The principles described above have implications for all three of these areas.

Following this trichotomy, the next three Subsections aim to give a general overview of the requirements of adequate implementation as laid down in the case law of the Court of Justice.[29] They will not address the implementation policy and the problems related thereto within the Member States.

In the majority of cases the Court's case law concerns directives which, pursuant to their content, had to be *transposed* into national law. However, for the sake of comprehensiveness, I will in principle use the "umbrella" term *implementation/implementing measures*.[30]

[26] In particular in the sense of producing effects in practice. Cf. above, Chapter 3, Section 3.3.

[27] Cf. Case C-361/88 *Commision v. Germany* [1991] ECR I-2567, Case C-58/89 *Commission v. Germany* [1991] ECR I-4983, Case 291/84 *Commission v. The Netherlands* [1987] ECR 3483.

[28] Cf. Case 29/84 *Commission v. Germany* [1985] ECR 1661, Case C-131/88 *Commission v. Germany* [1991] ECR I-825, Case C-360/87 *Commission v. Italy* [1991] ECR I-791, Case C-58/89 *Commission v. Germany* [1991] ECR I-4983, Case C-13/90 *Commisson v. France* [1991] ECR I-4327. Cf. also Everling 1992a, p. 382, Kovar 1987, p. 367 and Curtin 1990b, p. 716.

[29] For overviews of the Court's case law see e.g. Heukels 1993, p. 63-70, Curtin 1990b, p. 714-718, Beyerlin 1987, p. 127-135, Everling 1992a, p. 380-381 and Kovar 1987, p. 365-372. Cf. also the opinion of A-G Van Gerven in Case C-131/88 *Commission v. Germany* [1991] ECR I-825, para. 6-11.

[30] For the distinction see above, Chapter 1, Section 3.

5.2.2 The Content of the Measures Implementing the Directive

As regards the content of the measures, it was mentioned above that this must correspond with the directive to be implemented.[31] It was also noted that the Member States have in principle the choice between verbatim transposition on the one hand, and "translation" of the directive into national legal concepts and terminology on the other (plus all the possible variations lying between these two extremes).[32]

According to the Court, the implementation of a directive does not in fact necessarily require that its provisions be transposed literally.[33] Neither is there a requirement that the implementing measures must follow the structure of the directive.[34] However, the content of the implementing measures must be clear and precise, particularly when the directive is intended to create rights and duties for individuals.[35] Ambiguous provisions or provisions which are too generally worded[36] would leave the individuals uncertain both as to their rights and duties and as to the possibility of enforcing them in a court. Similarly, even when the directive is not intended to create such rights and duties, if the implementing measures are unclear and vague, the mere risk of their misapplication by domestic authorities may justify the requirements of clarity and precision being imposed.[37] Depending on the subject matter of the directive in question, a particularly precise and detailed transposition may be required for specific reasons, such as the absence of economic incentive for respecting the rules and

[31] See above, Chapter 2, Section 2.5. Cf. also Case C-9/92 *Commission v. Greece* [1993] ECR I-4467.

[32] *Ibid.* Cf. also Capotorti 1988, p. 161, who gives a brief overview of "implementation techniques".

[33] Cf. Case C-131/88 *Commission v. Germany* [1991] ECR I-825, Case 363/85 *Commission v. Italy* [1987] ECR 1733. However, the national terminology must correspond with the terms employed by the directive; cf. Case 412/85 *Commission v. Germany* [1987] ECR 3503, Case 247/85 *Commission v. Belgium* [1987] ECR 3029, Case 363/85 *Commission v. Italy* [1987] ECR 1733.

[34] Thus the transposition of one single directive may be effectuated by amending several different national statutes and other pieces of (secondary) legislation. Cf. Case C-190/90 *Commission v. The Netherlands* [1992] ECR I-3265.

[35] Cf. Case C-131/88 *Commission v. Germany* [1991] ECR I-825, Case C-59/89 *Commission v. Germany* [1991] ECR I-2607, Case C-306/91 *Commission v. Italy* [1993] ECR I-2133.

[36] Cf. Case 116/86 *Commission v. Italy* [1988] ECR 1323, Case C-360/87 *Commission v. Italy* [1991] ECR I-791.

[37] Cf. Case C-339/87 *Commission v. The Netherlands* [1990] ECR I-851, Case 247/85 *Commission v. Belgium* [1987] ECR 3029, Case 262/85 *Commission v. Italy* [1987] ECR 3073. In the last case the Italian law implementing the directive at issue did not guarantee that regions, in their regulations, will fully comply with the obligations resulting from the directive, as the law itself was not sufficiently clear. Consequently, the regions were left in a state of uncertainty as to the scope of their obligations.

the difficulties which effective monitoring of compliance with the rules in practice may pose.[38]

Usually, in order to satisfy these criteria, enactment of *specific* legislation will be necessary, since it is not very likely that pre-existing legislation will correspond with the (terminology of) the directive to be implemented. Yet according to the Court, a *general* legal context may be sufficient in certain circumstances, namely if it ensures the full application of the directive in a sufficiently clear and precise manner.[39] Thus the combination of existing (general) rules of national law, including general principles of constitutional or administrative law,[40] and their application and interpretation, or the combination of general provisions and specific provisions enacted for the purposes of transposition of the directive[41] may suffice, provided that the necessary clarity and precision is guaranteed and that there is no practical or theoretical risk of misapplying the rules.[42] A combination of (pre-existing) imprecise provisions and administrative practice does not however satisfy these criteria.[43] Since administrative practices are often not given adequate publicity (e.g. administrative circulars that are not available), and do not allow individuals to become acquainted with their legal position, they cannot meet the requirement of legal clarity.[44]

An integral part of the general legal context is the interpretation and application of national law by the national courts. As the Court of Justice has pointed out, the scope of national legal provisions must be assessed in the light

[38] Cf. the opinion of A-G Van Gerven in Case C-131/88 *Commission v. Germany* [1991] ECR I-825, Para. 9. In Case 252/85 *Commission v. France* [1988] ECR 2243 and Case 236/85 *Commission v. The Netherlands* [1987] ECR 3989, for instance, the Court emphasized the need for faithful implementation because the directive concerned "entrusted the management of a common heritage" to the Member States in their respective territories.

[39] Cf. Case C-131/88 *Commission v. Germany* [1991] ECR I-825, Case C-360/87 *Commission v. Italy* [1991] ECR I-791, Case 252/85 *Commission v. France* [1988] ECR 2243 and especially Case C-190/90 *Commission v. The Netherlands* [1992] ECR I-3265, in which the Court accepted that a whole complex of rules (in particular a combination of legislative provisions and a system of permits) satisfied the requirements for adequate implementation.

[40] Cf. Case 29/84 *Commission v. Germany* [1985] ECR 1661, Case 248/83 *Commission v. Germany* [1985] ECR 1459.

[41] Cf. Case 163/82 *Commission v. Italy* [1983] ECR 3273. Cf. also Case C-339/87 *Commission v. The Netherlands* [1990] ECR I-851 relating to a combination of a statute and ministerial regulation.

[42] Cf. 363/85 *Commission v. Italy* [1987] ECR 1733.

[43] Cf. Case 29/84 *Commission v. Germany* [1985] ECR 1661, Case 116/86 *Commission v. Italy* [1988] ECR 1323, Case 429/85 *Commission V. Italy* [1988] ECR 843.

[44] Cf. Case 29/84 *Commission v. Germany* [1985] ECR 1661, Case C-131/88 *Commission v. Germany* [1991] ECR I-825; on administrative practices and their non-binding nature see below, Subsection 5.2.3.

of the interpretation given to them by the courts.[45] It is also significant in this respect that in Case *C-361/88 (TA-Luft)*[46] the Court did not accept the *"technical circular 'air'"* as an appropriate means of implementation *because* the German government had not produced any *national cases* establishing that the circular had external effects *vis-à-vis* third parties instead of being binding only for the administration.[47] Conversely, in Case *235/84 (transfers of undertakings)*[48] the Commission did not establish that Italian law failed to provide the protection required by Directive 77/187 (transfers of undertakings – protection of employees' rights),[49] in particular by not refuting the Italian government's argument that the protection was safeguarded by established case law of the *Corte Suprema di Cassazione*. In other words, the question whether the general legal context can be considered as ensuring appropriate implementation of a directive will also depend on national case law. This actually raises a more general problem: to what extent can case law be considered as a proper means of implementation?[50] As far as the subject matter of this Subsection is concerned, the concrete question is whether a combination of an imprecise provision and its construction by national courts will satisfy the requirement of precision and clarity; provided, that is, that the construction itself is compatible with the directive at issue. It is difficult to give a general answer to this question. On the one hand, construction of national law is an inevitable everyday business of the courts. On the other hand, vaguely formulated national provisions which must first be substantiated by case law will as such scarcely meet the requirements. The matter will thus first of all depend on the degree of imprecision. Secondly, a combination of a vague provision and its interpretation by the courts could possibly be accepted if the case law is adequately publicized and sufficiently predictable.[51] The first element may indeed pose problems, as the "culture" of

[45] Joined Cases C-132/91, C-138/91 and C-139/91 *Katsikas* [1992] ECR I-6577, para. 39: "*la portée des dispositions législatives ... doit s'apprécier compte tenu de l'interprétation qu'en donnent les juridictions nationales.*"

[46] *Commission v. Germany* [1991] ECR I-2567.

[47] On external effects see below, Subsection 5.2.3.

[48] *Commission v. Italy* [1986] ECR 2291. Cf. also Case C-382/92 *Commission v. United Kingdom* [1994] ECR I-2435.

[49] OJ 1977, L 61/26.

[50] Cf. Easson (1981, p. 29) who, thinking of the common law system, raised the problem of the subject matter of a directive being governed by case law rather than by statute. He wondered whether such a situation meets the requirement of maximum clarity.

[51] Cf. in this respect the case law of the ECHR on judge-made rules of common law which may restrict certain rights and freedoms under the European Convention. In the *Sunday Times* case the European Court accepted that judge-made law may restrict Article 10(1) of the Convention. However, the law must be adequately accessible (the citizen must be able to have an indication that is adequate in the circumstances of the legal rules applicable in a given case) and it must be formulated with sufficient precision to enable the citizen to regulate his conduct. This case law is inspired by concerns

publishing courts' decisions differs from Member State to Member State. Moreover, an objection comparable to the one raised by the Court of Justice in Case *29/84 (nurses)*,[52] namely that nationals from a different Member State are normally not aware of principles of constitutional or administrative law applicable within the host Member State, applies mutatis mutandis to case law. The second condition will probably be satisfied once there exists established case law of a supreme national court.[53] Another relevant factor could also be the authority possessed by judicial decisions within the national legal system.[54] However, the risk that a (supreme) court will depart from its case law will remain.[55]

Unfortunately, the matter is even more complicated because the Court of Justice does not accept that interpretation of national law in conformity with a directive, in accordance with the obligation laid down in *Von Colson*,[56] can expunge incorrect implementation.[57] This raises the question of the delimitation of two concepts. On the one hand there is what I shall call "*interpretation within the context of judicial implementation*", denoting the interpretation by the courts of national law which, as such, constitutes correct implementation of the directive, although for the purposes of application of the rules in the concrete case further interpretation of the – by their very nature – abstract terms is necessary. On the other hand there is "*remedial interpretation*", i.e. interpretation of national law with a view to temporarily palliating the Member State's failure to implement the directive at all or to implement it correctly. I shall address these issues in more detail in Chapter 10. Nevertheless, it should be pointed out here that interpretation *contra legem* by the courts, or national case law consistently disapplying a national legal provision can certainly not result in national law being considered to be in conformity with the directive concerned.[58] The basic requirement of the Court's case law on proper implementation of directives is that individuals must be able to ascertain their rights and duties *from the legislative text itself*. It seems to

of legal certainty comparable to those inspiting as the case law of the ECJ. (Judgment of 26 April 1979, 2 EHRR 245, p. 271).

[52] *Commission v. Germany* [1985] ECR 1661.

[53] Cf. the opinion of A-G Van Gerven in Joined Cases C-132/91, C-138/91 and C-139/91 *Katsikas* [1992] ECR I-6577, para. 20.

[54] In particular whether it constitutes a "binding precedent" or not.

[55] Cf. the opinion of A-G Darmon in Case C-338/91 *Steenhorst-Neerings* [1993] ECR I-5475, para. 48.

[56] Case 14/83 [1984] ECR 1891.

[57] Cf. Everling 1992a, p. 380, Jans 1994, p. 252 and the opinion of A-G Cruz Vilaça in Case 412/85 *Commission v. Germany* [1987] ECR 3503, para. 19.

[58] Cf. the opinion of A-G Darmon in Case C-338/91 *Steenhorst-Neerings* [1993] ECR I-5475, para.47 concerning an application *contra legem* of a national social security provision in pursuance of Article 26 of the ICCPR by the *Centrale Raad van Beroep*. The Court's judgment in this case also makes plain that the judicial practice at issue did not amount to correct implementation. See in particular para. 33 and 34. Cf. also Jans 1994, p. 253.

me that the situation just described, of interpretation of national law *contra legem* or consistent dissapplication by the courts of national legal provisions, will draw too heavily on an individual's knowledge of the law.[59]

This point brings me to the final, more general remark, namely that the requirement of clear and unambiguous legal situations also entails that all conflicting legislation must be repealed.[60]

5.2.3 The Nature of the Implementing Measures

The principles of full effectiveness, legal certainty and effective judicial protection are also normative for the nature of the implementing measures.

On several occasions the Court has stressed that full implementation of directives must be secured not only in fact but also in law.[61] Absence of incompatible practice or the fact that a practice is consistent with the directive in question does not discharge the Member State concerned from the obligation of actually and fully implementing the directive.[62] The basic requirement is that the measures giving effect to a directive must be *legally binding*.[63]

According to the Court's case law the choice of form and methods, which is left to the Member States, depends upon the result intended by the directive, and thus on the content of the directive.[64] The content should therefore be examined first. The central question to be answered seems to be whether the directive is intended to create rights and duties for individuals,[65] not only between national authorities and those directly concerned but also with respect to third parties.[66] As will be argued below,[67] the Court is quite readily disposed to

[59] Cf. also case law which makes clear that direct effect of the provisions at issue does not expunge inadequate implementation or non-implementation: Case 102/79 *Commission v. Belgium* [1980] ECR 1473. See also Case C-208/90 *Emmott* [1991] ECR I-4269.

[60] Cf. Case 169/87 *Commission v. France* [1988] ECR 4093 and Case 74/86 *Commission v. Germany* [1988] ECR 2139. See also Easson 1981, p. 30 and the opinion of A-G Darmon in Case C-338/91 *Steenhorst-Neerings* [1993] ECR I-5457, para. 49-50.

[61] Cf. Case C-339/87 *Commission v. The Netherlands* [1990] ECR I-851.

[62] Cf. Case C-131/88 *Commission v. Germany* [1991] ECR I-825 and Case C-366/89 *Commission v. Italy* [1993] ECR I-4201.

[63] Cf. Mertens de Wilmars 1991, p. 397, Heukels 1993, p. 64, Capotorti 1988, p. 160.

[64] Cf. Case 102/79 *Commission v. Belgium* [1980] ECR 1473; more recently, see e.g Case C-59/89 *Commission v. Germany* [1991] I-2607. According to Case C-190/90 *Commission v. The Netherlands* [1992] ECR I-3265, consistent case law.

[65] Cf. Case 29/84 *Commission v. Germany* [1985] ECR 1661; more recently e.g. Case C-131/88 *Commission v. Germany* [1991] ECR I-825. According to Case C-306/89 *Commission v. Greece* [1991] ECR I-5863 and Case C-190/90 *Commission v. The Netherlands* [1992] I-3265, consistent case law.

[66] Cf. the opinion of A-G Van Gerven in Case C-131/88 *Commission v. Germany* [1991] ECR I-825, para. 7: environmental groups or neighbouring residents, for instance.

[67] Cf. Chapter 7, Section 7.3.

accept that they do. However, in a number of cases the Court has held that directives must be implemented by national provisions of a binding nature, without addressing explicitly the issue of an individual's rights and duties or without adressing it at all.

In Case *C-186/91 (consultations on nitrogen dioxide)*[68] the Court found that in order to ensure complete and effective protection of the atmosphere against excessive concentrations of nitrogen dioxide it was indispensable that the Member State concerned should lay down explicitly in its legislation that consultations with the neighbouring Member State, provided for in directive 85/203 (air quality – nitrogen dioxide),[69] must take place before certain limit values of nitrogen dioxide can be fixed in a border region. Although the Commission argued that Article 11 of the directive created rights and duties with regard to individuals, the Court disregarded this argument. Apparently the very purpose of the directive (and indeed the fact that concentrations of nitrogen dioxide do not observe borderlines) was sufficient grounds for the obligation at issue.[70]

Furthermore, the Court categorically and particularly rejects administrative practices and circulars as a means of adequate implementation.[71] While some older cases[72] suggest that administrative practices could not be accepted as valid implementation *in the particular circumstances*, more recent case law seems to imply that administrative practices can *never* constitute proper implementation. In Case *C-131/88 (German groundwater)*, after having considered that the provisions in question had to be transposed with the precision and clarity necessary to satisfy fully the requirement of legal certainty because they were intended to create rights and obligations for individuals, the Court added:

[68] *Commission v. Belgium* [1993] ECR I-851.

[69] OJ 1985, L 87/1.

[70] In this case explicit provision obliging the regions to consult neighbouring Member States was probably the more necessary since the subject matter was within their legislative competence. For a requirement to impose a duty of notification explicitly upon a decentralized body see Case C-237/90 *Commission v. Germany* [1992] ECR I-5973.

[71] Cf. Case 116/86 *Commission v. Italy* [1988] ECR 1323, Case 236/85 *Commission v. The Netherlands* [1987] ECR 3989, Case 239/85 *Commission v. Belgium* 1986] ECR 3645, Case 160/82 *Commission v. The Netherlands* [1982] ECR 4637, Case C-13/90 *Commission v. France* [1991] ECR I-4327, Case C-339/87 *Commission v. the Netherlands* [1990] ECR I-851, Case C-381/92 *Commission v. Ireland* [1994] ECR I-215.

[72] Cf. Case 96/81 *Commission v. The Netherlands* [1982] ECR 1791 and Case 97/81 *Commission v. The Netherlands* [1982] ECR 1891. In both cases the Court stressed the fact that the directives at issue were adopted *inter alia* pursuant to Article 100 of the Treaty and were intended to approximate the applicable laws, regulations and administrative provisions. For this reason, the judgment suggests, implementation by administrative practices cannot be accepted. Cf. also Case 300/81 *Commission v. Italy* [1983] ECR 449.

"Moreover, the Court has consistently held that mere administrative practices, which are alterable at the will of the administration and are not given adequate publicity, cannot be regarded as constituting adequate compliance with the obligation imposed on Member States to whom a directive is addressed by Article 189 of the EEC Treaty."[73]

This consideration can be understood as reinforcing the foregoing argument or it may imply that in *any case* administrative practices cannot transpose a directive properly. However this may be, as soon as a directive has been enacted in order to harmonize the laws of the respective Member States, and this is generally the case,[74] it will usually have implications for the legal position of individuals. Moreover, harmonization of laws, i.e. legally binding acts, cannot be properly assured by an instrument which does not have the same legal nature as the one to be harmonized. Consequently, it is not surprising that *in principle* the Court requires that provisions of directives are turned into binding rules of national law[75] or that the Member States establish a precise legal framework.[76]

The binding nature of provisions implementing a directive is of crucial importance in several respects. In the first place, administrative practices which may be changed as and when the administration pleases cannot guarantee the necessary legal certainty and will jeopardize the continuity of full application of the rules laid down in the directive. However, even if, by virtue of general principles of national (constitutional or administrative) law or specific instruments such as circulars, the rules are binding for the administration as such,[77] this is in principle not sufficient. Since the ratio for demanding implementation by binding measures is often the rights and obligations a directive is intended to

[73] *Commission v. Germany* [1991] ECR I-825, para. 61.

[74] Cf. above, Chapter 3, Subsection 3.2.1.

[75] Cf. Case 102/79 *Commission v. Belgium* [1980] ECR 1473, Case 96/81 *Commission v. The Netherlands* [1982] ECR 1791, Case 97/81 *Commission v. The Netherlands* [1982] ECR 1819, Case C-361/88 *Commission v. Germany* [1991] ECR I-2567.

[76] Cf. Case C-131/88 *Commission v. Germany* [1991] ECR I-825, Case C-339/87 *Commission v. The Netherlands* [1990] ECR I-851, Case C-13/90 *Commission v. France* [1990] ECR I-4327, Case C-64/90 *Commission v. France* [1991] ECR I-4335.

[77] For instance by virtue of the doctrine of "self-binding of the administration" as it exists in German law or because it results from the hierarchic structure of the administration. Cf. Case C-13/90 *Commission v. France* [1991] ECR I-4327: according to the full text of the judgment (summary publication only in ECR) the circular at issue "*contient des instructions et recommandations qui s'imposent, en vertu du pouvoir hiérarchique, aux commissaires de la République*" (para. 10). Cf. also the opinion of A-G Slynn in Case 29/84 *Commission v. Germany* [1985] ECR 1661, at p. 1666, who pointed out that in the case of binding force by virtue of general principles of law a change is possible without intervention of the legislator.

create for individuals, the binding force must produce *external* effects,[78] i.e. the measures must bind the administration *vis-à-vis* private individuals (and *vice versa* in the case of obligations).[79] It is also important in this respect that legally binding measures are given appropriate publicity.

For individuals, the binding nature of the implementing measures is significant from two points of view: from the point of view of legal certainty, since it enables them to ascertain in a sufficiently predictable manner the extent of their rights and duties, and from the point of view of effective judicial protection, since it gives them a defined legal position.

Thus *full* (i.e. internally and externally) binding force of implementing measures is essential for both the application of the rules by the administration and the position of those subjected to them. It is for these reasons that the Court requires *inter alia* that prohibitions and possible derogations from them, or conditions for granting, refusing or withdrawing of permits, must expressly be laid down in national legal provisions.[80]

The requirement of being binding in nature must, in the first place, be satisfied by the measures specifically enacted for the purpose of implementation. Secondly, if the Member State concerned argues that the rules of the directive are guaranteed by the general legal context, this combination of rules and their application must similarly produce the desired legal effects. In Case *C-339/87 (wild birds)* the Court accepted that implementation can be effected by a legislative provision serving as the basis for the adoption of administrative measures, provided that the latter are officially published, general in scope and capable of creating rights and obligations for individuals.[81] In Case *248/83 (equal treatment in public service)* the Court found that since the relevant provisions of the German Basic Law are intended to be directly applicable and there is an existing system of judicial remedies, including the possibility of instituting proceedings before the Constitutional Court, the legal context constitutes an adequate guarantee of implementation, in the field of public administration, of the principle of equal treatment laid down in Directive 76/207 (equal treatment at work).[82]

[78] According to Everling (1992, p. 383) the lack of external effects was decisive in the *TA-Luft case* (Case C-361/88 *Commission v. Germany* [1991] ECR I-2567). There was hardly any doubt about the binding force upon the administration as such. Cf. also Case C-9/92 *Commission v. Greece* [1993] ECR I-4467.

[79] Cf. Case C-361/88 *Commission v. Germany* [1991] ECR I-2567, Case C-131/88 *Commission v. Germany* [1991] ECR I-825, Case C-190/90 *Commission v. The Netherlands* [1992] ECR I-3265.

[80] Cf. Case 252/85 *Commission v. France* [1988] ECR 2243, Case C-339/87 *Commission v. The Netherlands* [1990] ECR I-851, Case 300/81 *Commission v. Italy* [1983] ECR 449, Case 291/84 *Commission v. The Netherlands* [1987] EC 3483.

[81] Case C-339/87 *Commission v. The Netherlands* [1990] ECR I-851. Cf. also Case C-435/92 *Association pour la protection des animaux sauvages* [1994] ECR I-67.

[82] OJ 1976, L 39/40, *Commission v. Germany* [1985] ECR 1459.

In general, however, the Court is not easily satisfied in this respect.[83] In particular, binding force through the application of general principles of constitutional or administrative law is closely scrutinized and is not readily accepted, since the effects of these are often not undisputed.[84]

So far, the discussion has focussed on the implementation of directives dealing with – what can be called – "vertical relationships", i.e. directives concerning primarily the relationship between national authorities and individuals. However, a considerable number of directives purport to regulate legal relationships between natural or legal persons. In other words, they are intended to create rights and obligations for individuals *inter se*. The need to implement this type of directives by binding rules of national law is quite evident. Yet comparable problems concerning the binding nature of the measures may occur in this area as well. Particularly in the field of labour law, the question has been raised whether directives can be implemented by means of collective agreements instead of being transposed into national legislation.[85] Although the Court considered that the implementation of certain issues of labour law may in the first instance be left to the representatives of management and labour,[86] it does not however release the Member States from their obligation of ensuring, by appropriate legislative and administrative provisions, that the rules of the directive are fully transposed and applied. This means firstly that, in terms of their content, collective agreements must fully correspond with the directive at issue. The Member States must be able to intervene by appropriate measures against inadequacies resulting from collective negotiations.[87]

However, in so far as relevant for the purpose of this Subsection, the major problem with collective agreements is that – even when taken as a whole – they do not necessarily cover all the persons protected by the directive in question, as they are only binding for the members of the trade unions and the employers

[83] Cf. Case C-361/88 *Commission v. Germany* [1991] ECR I-2567, in particular para. 20.

[84] Cf. Case 29/84 *Commission v. Germany* [1985] ECR 1661, in particular para. 28-32. Cf. also observations made on judicial construction as a part of the general legal context made above in Subsection 5.2.1.

[85] Cf. Adinolfi 1988 and Heukels 1993, p. 65.

[86] Sometimes this is explicitly provided in certain directives. See e.g. Directive 91/533 (conditions of employment relationship – information of employees), OJ 1991 L 288/32, Article 9, Directive 92/56 (collective redundancies), OJ 1992 L 245/3, Article 2, Directive 92/85 (pregnant workers), OJ 1992 L 348/1, Article 14. Cf. further Case 235/84 *Commission v. Italy* [1986] ECR 2291, Case 91/81 *Commission v. Italy* [1982] ECR 2133 and Case 143/83 *Commission v. Denmark* [1985] ECR 427.

[87] Cf. Case 312/86 *Commission v. France* [1988] ECR 6315, Case 165/82 *Commission v. UK* [1983] ECR 3431.

who are party to the agreement; if, indeed, they are legally binding at all.[88] In such a case the Member States are obliged to secure the application of the agreement(s) to all the persons falling within the personal scope of the directive, for instance by extending them *erga omnes*,[89] or they must "fill the gaps" by appropriate additional binding measures.[90]

More recently, the approach of the Court of Justice has been confirmed by Article 4 of the Agreement on Social Policy annexed to the Treaty of Maastricht. This Article provides that management and labour may be entrusted with the implementation of certain directives, but the Member States must ensure that the social partners have introduced the necessary measures no later than the date on which the directive in question had to be transposed. Moreover, the Member States are required to take any necessary measures enabling them at any time to be in a position to guarantee the results imposed by the directive.[91]

Finally, the requirement of implementing measures being binding and properly published entails another important feature: it involves a degree of transparency which enables the Commission to control whether and how a directive has been transposed in national law.[92]

5.2.4 The Application and Enforcement of Directives and the Requirements Resulting Therefrom for Implementing Measures

As explained in Chapter 3, Section 3.3, the obligations imposed upon Member States are not fulfilled by the mere enactment of national rules. The rules must also be applied and enforced in practice.

As regards their application, it is up to the Member States to decide – where appropriate – upon the national body which will be responsible. It goes without saying that the competent national authority must act in conformity with the

[88] In the UK, for instance, the legal status of collective agreements is controversial and, in particular, they are not enforceable in the courts. Cf. Adinolfi, 1988, p. 310. Cf. also Case 165/82 *Commission v. UK* [1983] ECR 3431.

[89] That may however be difficult in some Member States. Adinolfi (1988, p. 305), for instance, reports a judgment of the Italian Constitutional Court which found such an extension to be unconstitutional. A *de facto* extension, on the other hand, is questionable from the point of view of legal certainty.

[90] Cf. Case 143/83 *Commission v. Denmark* [1985] ECR 427, Case 235/84 *Commission v. Italy* [1986] ECR 2291.

[91] Cf. also Commission's Communication concerning the application of the agreement on social policy, COM (93) 600 final.

[92] Cf. the opinion of A-G Slynn in Case 29/84 *Commission v. Germany* [1985] ECR 1661, at p. 1666.

rules laid down in the directive.[93] In this respect, the requirements, discussed above, of clarity and precision of the implementing measures and their legally binding nature are crucial for avoiding their misapplication and ensuring that the administration *will* apply them. Likewise, with regard to directives (primarily) concerning relationships between private individuals or intended to impose obligations upon individuals, the same requirements are a prerequisite for securing compliance with the terms of the directives which underlie the national implementing measures. Briefly, the requirements imposed by the Court as to the content of the measures and their nature must guarantee the correct application of the directive in practice as well. This will hardly come as a surprise, since the principle of full effect, including actual application of the rules,[94] together with the principle of legal certainty, forms the very basis of these requirements.

As in the case of national rules, in order to compel observance of the provisions of the directive (as transposed in national law) the State will often be obliged to provide for an appropriate system of sanctions,[95] since otherwise effective enforcement will be unrealistic.

Before turning to the Community law requirements relating to sanctions, a preliminary remark should be made. As I have just pointed out, national authorities and the like are under an obligation to apply the national implementing measures. It would however be naive to assume that in everyday practice they always do so. This raises the question of what measures are available *within* the administration to ensure the observance of the rules at issue. The problem may be particularly serious if the body responsible for the application has autonomous status. However, Community law is in principle not concerned with this problem. In Chapter 4, Section 4.3, it was stated that it does not interfere with the internal structure of the Member States; the failure of the responsible authorities to apply the implementing measures is regarded as a failure of the Member State as a whole. Excuses of a practical nature, the lack of power of the central government to influence or compel other bodies, are not accepted.[96]

With respect to sanctions which should ensure observance of the terms of the directive by individuals, i.e. natural or legal persons, three different situations can be distinguished.[97]

Firstly, in some cases, which up to the present have been relatively rare, a directive may give specific indications as to the sanctions which should be imposed for non-compliance with the norm resulting from the directive. Under

[93] Cf. above, Chapter 4, Section 4.4.
[94] Cf. above, Chapter 3, Section 3.3.
[95] Sanctions are understood here broadly, namely as legal consequences laid down in a secondary norm for non-compliance with a primary norm of conduct.
[96] Cf. Joined Cases 227-230/85 *Commission v. Belgium* [1988] ECR 1.
[97] Cf. Timmermans (Rapport communautaire) in Fide Reports 1992, p. 36-42.

STAFFS UNIVERSITY LIBRARY

Directive 79/207 (equal treatment at work), for instance, provisions contrary to the principle of equal treatment which are included in individual contracts shall be, or may be declared, null and void.[98] Another form of specific sanction is exemplified by the possible withdrawal of authorization provided for in Directive 73/293 (insurance other than life assurance I),[99] or different measures spelled out in Directive 92/28 (advertising of medicinal products) in the case of misleading advertising.[100]

Secondly, some directives stipulate in fairly general terms that the Member States shall introduce penalties for failure to comply with the provisions adopted pursuant to the directive and that the penalties must be suitable or sufficient to promote compliance with the provisions concerned.[101]

So far, the requirements relating to sanctions have been a part of the content of a directive and, depending on the terms of the relevant provisions, they entail different margins of discretion for the Member States when transposing them. However, it is the third and largest category of directives which is the most interesting; namely those in which no indications whatsoever are given as to the sanctions to be imposed. The Member States consequently appear to enjoy a considerable margin of discretion in two respects: firstly as to whether they will provide for sanctions at all and secondly, if they do, as to the form and content the sanctions will have. In both of these respects, however, the discretion is becoming less and less unfettered.

As to the question *whether* Member States must provide for sanctions, from their obligation "to adopt in their national legal systems all the measures necessary to ensure that the directive is fully effective, in accordance with the objective which it pursues"[102] it follows that the answer will depend on the objective of the directive at issue. Until recently the case law of the Court has only concerned directive 76/207 (equal treatment at work).[103] With respect to this directive, the Court held that both from its actual purpose, i.e. to establish real equality of opportunity, and from Article 6, which requires that (alleged)

[98] OJ 1976, L 39/40, Article 5(2)b.

[99] OJ 1973, L 228/3, Article 22(1)c.

[100] OJ 1992, L 113/13; e.g. courts or administrative authorities must be able to order the cessation or the prohibition of misleading advertising (Article 12(2)).

[101] Cf. Article 16 of Directive 91/477 (arms control), OJ 1991, L 256/51, Article 5 of Directive 92/59 (product safety), OJ 1992, L 228/24, Article 14 of Directive 91/308 (money laundering), OJ 1991, L 166/77, Article 13 of Directive 89/592 (insider dealing), OJ 1989, L 334/30, Article 19 of Directive 92/46 (milk products), OJ 1992, L 268/1.

[102] Case 14/83 *Von Colson* [1984] ECR 1891, para. 15. This requirement also implies that the Member States are allowed to adopt provisions other than sanctions for which the directive does not provide at all but which are nevertheless useful for ensuring the full effect of the directive: cf. Case C-143/91 *Van der Tas* [1992] ECR I-5045.

[103] OJ 1976, L 39/40.

victims of discrimination must be able to pursue their claims by judicial process, it follows that the Member States must provide for *an* appropriate system of sanctions.

If the directive is totally silent on the issue, the Member States are actually free to choose among the possible solutions, i.e. from sanctions under civil law, administrative law or criminal law, plus the further options which are possible within these branches of law.[104] In this respect too, however, the Court poses certain requirements as to the content of the sanction chosen. In other words, it specifies the conditions under which the sanction can be considered to be appropriate, in the light of the objective of the directive at issue.

In *Von Colson*[105] the Court stipulated that the sanction chosen must be such as to guarantee real and effective judicial protection and it must have a real deterrent effect. In *Marshall II*[106] it further specified that when looking into the question whether these requirements are satisfied the particular circumstances of each case must be taken into account. According to *Von Colson*, if the Member State chooses the award of compensation, the latter must be adequate in relation to the damage sustained. Although one might think that at this point the Court would stop giving indications, the opposite is true. Even the question whether or not the compensation is adequate is not a matter for national law alone. In *Von Colson* the Court already made clear that compensation consisting of a purely nominal amount could not be considered to be adequate. Subsequently, further refinement of the standards to be met was given in *Marshall II.* In this case adequate financial compensation meant that the loss and damage actually sustained had to be made good in full, including the award of interest, which in the Court's view is an essential component of compensation.[107]

To summarize, the Court is apparently willing to go into detail when the content of the sanctions is at issue. The result of this approach is that the Member States' discretion is considerably limited in this respect.

Furthermore, as appears from the judgment in the *Dekker* case,[108] the requirement that the sanction must be effective not only concerns the sanction itself and its content, but also has consequences for the substantive conditions which must be fulfilled before the sanction can be imposed. According to the judgment in *Dekker*, the requirements of fault and absence of grounds of exemption applicable under the Dutch rules on civil liability had to be disregarded.

[104] E.g. compensation or reinstatement, imprisonment or penalties etc.

[105] Case 14/83 [1984] ECR 1891.

[106] Case C-271/91 [1993] ECR I-4367.

[107] For a detailed discussion of the different components of compensation see the opinion of A-G Van Gerven in Case C-271/91 *Marshall II* [1993] ECR I-4367, para. 18-19.

[108] Case C-177/88 [1990] ECR I-3941.

As mentioned above, until recently the Court's case law on sanctions, as far as directives are concerned, has focussed on the interpretation of Directive 76/207. Yet a very similar approach seems to apply in the case of any other directive. From two recent cases[109] it appears that certain requirements formulated by the Court with respect to the enforcement of regulations apply equally in the field of directives. The requirements have been laid down in Case *68/88 (Greek maize).*[110]

This case concerned the insufficient enforcement of a regulation by Greek authorities and, more particularly, it related to Greek criminal penalties. In very broadly worded terms the Court held that where Community legislation does not specifically provide any penalty for an infringement or refers for that purpose to national law, by virtue of Article 5 of the Treaty the Member States are required to take all measures to guarantee the application and the effectiveness of Community law.[111]

This requirement entails in particular that, firstly, breaches of Community law are penalized under conditions, both procedural and substantive, which are analogous to those applicable to infringements of national law of a similar nature, secondly, that penalties and the procedures which result in imposing them are in any event effective, proportionate and dissuasive, and, thirdly, that national authoritites must proceed with respect to infringements of Community law with the same diligence as that which they bring to bear in implementing corresponding national laws.[112]

A number of issues merit attention here. Firstly, the difference between the reasoning in *Von Colson* and the "Greek maize approach" lies in the fact that the requirement of sanctions and their contents in *Von Colson* is based on the interpretation of Article 189(3) and the terms of the directive, while in Case *68/88 (Greek maize)* and the two cases brought against the United Kingdom it is Article 5 of the Treaty which forms the basis of the obligation. To a large extent the difference is, in my opinion, immaterial. As argued above in Chapter 2, Section 2.1, Article 5 is a more general provision and in this respect contains an obligation which in any case is imposed upon the Member States by Article 189(3); the obligation to achieve the result prescribed by the directive may *as such* already entail the necessity to provide for an appropriate system of sanctions.

[109] Case C-382/92 *Commission v. United Kingdom* [1994] ECR I-2435 and Case C-383/92 *Commission v. United Kingdom* [1994] ECR I-2479.

[110] *Commission v. Greece* [1989] ECR 2965.

[111] Cf. also Case 50/76 *Amsterdam Bulb* [1977] ECR 137 in which, however, the Court merely stated that the Member States are competent to adopt such sanctions as appear to them to be appropriate (para. 32).

[112] Confirmed also in Case C-326/88 *Hansen* [1990] ECR I-2911 and Case C-7/90 *Vandevenne* [1991] ECR I-4371. The requirement that the national authorities must act with the same care and attention as they exercise in applying national law was already laid down in older case law. See e.g. Joined Cases 119 and 126/79 *Lippische Hauptgenossenschaft* [1980] ECR 1863.

Secondly, unlike the case law on directive 76/207, the judgments in the cases under discussion here lay down two types of requirements; namely the "comparability" with sanctions for breaches of "purely" national law and the requirements as to the effectiveness, proportionality and dissuasive effect.[113] As the second must be satisfied *in any event*, the two types obviously apply in a cumulative way.[114] Accordingly, even if the sanctions are comparable but, from the point of view of Community law, they are ineffective, disproportionate or not dissuasive, they do not meet the standard resulting from Article 5. The sanction must apparently be *at least* comparable to the sanctions imposed for infringements of national law. This is however as such no guarantee that they will be effective as well. Furthermore, the comparability issue is relevant in another type of cases, decided in a different context and forming in a way a mirror image of the problems at issue here; namely those in which the sanctions for infringement of rules originating in Community law or falling within the scope of Community law are more severe than those for breaches of similar provisions of national law. As long as the two types of provisions and their respective infringements can be compared,[115] the comparability principle, which is often applied together with the principle of proportionality, may function as an *upper* limit to the sanctions.[116]

Thirdly, the requirements laid down by the Court apparently not only concern the content of the sanctions but also relate to the procedures which result in their imposition. In this respect it should be noted that if national authorities proceed with respect to infringements of Community law with the same *negligence* as with respect to national laws, rather than diligence, Community

[113] What those terms imply in a particular set of circumstances is certainly not clear yet. However, by way of a preliminary orientation, it is submitted that *effective* should be understood in this context as producing the desired result, which is to compel observance of the terms and spirit of Community law, *proportionate* as referring to the relation between the nature of the offence committed and the sanction imposed laying down both a lower limit and an upper limit, and *dissuasive* as preventing disobedience of the Community law rules. Indeed, there seems to be hardly any difference between an effective and a dissuasive sanction. This is clearly illustrated by *Von Colson*, where compensation, in order to be both effective and deterrent, had to be adequate in relation to the damage sustained. Futhermore, an effective sanction under civil law might have a different meaning from an effective sanction under criminal law, the former usually having the function of restoring the respective breach as well. Compare in this respect the judgement in *Marshall II*, in particular para. 24, 25 and 26. For a slightly different definition of the terms effective, proportionate and dissuasive see the opinion of A-G Van Gerven in Case C-326/88 *Hansen* [1990] ECR I-2911, para. 8.

[114] Cf. the opinion of A-G Van Gerven in Case C-271/91 *Marshall II* [1993] ECR I-4367, para. 15.

[115] Cf. Case 8/77 *Sagulo* [1977] ECR 1495 and, although in a slightly different context, Case 299/86 *Drexl* [1988] ECR 1213.

[116] Cf. Case 118/75 *Watson and Belmann* [1976] ECR 1185, Case 299/86 *Drexl* [1988] ECR 1213, and Case C-276/91 *Commission v. France* [1993] ECR I-4413.

law may require a higher standard of control and enforcement than that which is common practice in the Member State concerned.

To conclude this Subsection, a remark should be made regarding judicial protection. Obviously, a system of effective judicial protection is vital for the enforcement of norms resulting from a directive,[117] and it is, as pointed out above, one of the principles underlying the requirements posed by the Court concerning the implementing measures. This principle therefore curtails the freedom of the Member States with respect to form and methods of implementation. This principle will be discussed at greater length in Chapter 8.

[117] Cf. also Timmermans (Rapport communautaire) in Fide Reports 1992, p. 21-25 and Mertens de Wilmars 1991, p. 395-396.

6
Conclusions Part I

Behind the austere terms of Article 189(3) there hides a complex reality which the drafters of the Treaty probably never dreamed of. Instead of merely giving general instructions for action, as its name would at first sight suggest, the directive has developed into a fully-fledged legislative instrument of the Community. The most essential characteristic distinguishing it from a regulation is the fact that a directive is never self-sufficient. In order to be fully effective, implementing measures have to be enacted at the national level. As a rule, the implementation of a directive requires its transposition into national law.

The directive is binding by virtue of Article 189(3), which entails that every instance of incorrect or belated implementation will amount to a breach of this Article. The requirement that directives must be implemented in due time and correctly is based on the fundamental necessity of uniform and simultaneous application of Community law.

The fact that directives allow the Member States a certain period of time for their implementation and the gap resulting therefrom between the entry into force of the directive and the prescribed entry into force of the national implementing measures give rise to some problems as to the obligations of the Member States during this intervening period.

The first of these relates to the question whether national authorities and, in particular, national courts are under an obligation to interpret national law in conformity with the directive concerned or otherwise to comply with its terms if they possess, as a matter of national law, the necessary powers to do so. I have argued that – in principle – no such obligation exists, as it would be incompatible with the very purpose of the period allowed for implementation. This does not however mean that they are not allowed to proceed in accordance with the directive.

The second issue concerns the effects produced by the "blocking effect" or the "*Sperrwirkung*" of directives, where appropriate coupled with the Member States' obligation under Article 5(2) E(E)C, during the period for implementation. It was submitted that the Member States are not allowed to adopt measures contrary to the directive or to take other retrograde steps. Their obligation in fact is to prepare adequate implementing measures, since this is precisely the reason why a period for implementation exists.

The deadlines for implementation are very strict. In principle, the Court of Justice does not accept any excuses whatsoever for belated implementation. Yet, in my view, it is not correct to state that the obligation to implement a directive in due time is an absolute obligation. It should not be ruled out in advance that, for instance, in a state of emergency, owing to *force majeure* or as a result of obligations existing under international law the Member States will not be obliged to implement the directive. The Court's case law actually contains important indications in this respect. It should also be pointed out that the Court's unrelenting position with respect to the excuses presented is prompted by the nature of the infringement procedure, i.e. the objective finding that a Member State has not complied with its obligations under the Treaty. It does not, however, go without saying that the same strictness should be transposed to other situations, for instance, where the consequences of a judgment given in an infringement proceedings are under consideration, or that it should apply to other types of procedure as well, such as an action for damages resulting from the Member State's failure.

Likewise regarding the question of correct implementation, although the Court is very severe in this respect as well, there are some considerations which could mitigate the Member States' liability for inadequate implementing measures. Given the frequently poor quality of Community directives, the problems resulting therefrom for their implementation, the uncertain conduct of the Commission with respect to the question whether in a concrete case a directive has been implemented adequately, or its silence on what constitutes correct implementation, it is not inconceivable that, exceptionally, the Member States may enjoy, like any other subject of Community law, the protection provided by the principles of legal certainty and legitimate expectations. This possible protection will be particularly important when – again – the consequences of a finding that a Member State has failed to meet its obligations under Article 189(3) are under consideration.

Once it has been established that a directive has not been implemented in due time or has been implemented inadequately, the proper remedy is implementation with retroactive effect. However, two conditions must be satisfied in such a situation, namely that the rights the individuals might have derived from the directive in the meantime are respected and that the principle of legal certainty is observed. At the moment it is not entirely clear whether the principle of legal certainty applicable in this context is the Community principle or the national principle, although the latter is, regarding its application, circumscribed by the Court of Justice.

From the time when the directive enters into force and for as long as it remains in force, the Member States must fulfil their obligations arising from it. Only if the directive or some of its provisions are declared invalid by the Court of Justice are the Member States released from their obligations. There is as yet uncertainty with respect to the situation where a judgment of the Court implicitly states that a directive or certain of its provisions should not be regarded as valid.

The result the Member States are required to achieve is determined by the content of each individual directive, which may be extremely detailed in this respect. The content of a directive may relate to a legal situation which is to be brought about, to a factual situation or to both.

Within the content of a directive three different types of provisions can be distinguished. Firstly, there are the substantive provisions, which I have called the "hard core" provisions, describing the primary content of the directive to be realized by the Member States. The content of these substantive provisions will often relate to rights to be given to or obligations to be imposed upon private individuals by means of the implementing measures. Secondly, directives impose other obligations upon the Member States, such as those of notification, information and consultation, which may be considered as ancillary. This does not mean, however, that they are less binding than the first category. Non-compliance with either of these types of provisions will amount to a breach of Article 189(3) by the Member State concerned. The substantive and ancillary provisions together form the result to be achieved by the Member States. The third type of provisions is directed towards the Community institutions. They relate to matters such as revision or adjustment of the directive in question, the enactment of further Community measures in pursuance of the directive and so on. The legal nature of these provisions is not clear, but at least some of them form binding rules for the institutions.

All the provisions contained in a directive constitute an entity that should work properly in practice; it must be possible to monitor permanently the operation of the directive and where necessary to adjust the directive to the developments within the Member States, in accordance with the objectives pursued by the Community. Considered in its entirety, a directive may lay down a complex system of rights and duties for a variety of subjects of Community law.

The enactment of measures in pursuance of a directive is not, however, an end in itself. The Member States are required to achieve the result not merely in law but also in fact. The measures enacted must therefore be subsequently applied and enforced in practice. This requirement may entail obligations for the Member States which go beyond the actual text of the directive concerned, particularly in the sphere of the sanctions which are to be provided for.

At first sight, according to the terms of Article 189(3), the directive leaves the Member States a far-reaching degree of latitude as to the form and methods of implementation, including the choice of the body actually responsible for the implementation. It also suggests that the obligations exist solely with respect to the Member States. Yet the Court of Justice has expanded the obligations arising from a directive with respect to both the subjects actually bound and the form and methods of implementation, while at the same time trying to maintain the textual limitation of Article 189(3).

As regards the subjects bound by the directive, the Court has deduced from the fact that a directive may impose obligations only on Member States that it cannot *as such* impose obligations upon individuals. Indirectly, however, a directive may result in such an obligation; namely when read together with national law or, arguably, together with a provision of international law or, potentially, together with a provision of the Treaty which has horizontal direct effect. This last construction will however be extremely limited in effect. Furthermore, the term "impose obligations" should be understood as having a narrow meaning in this context. The mere fact that the vertical direct effect of a directive provision might result in negative consequences for individuals does not prevent the application of such a provision. Nevertheless, a directive may not directly affect the rights of private individuals. The borderline between negative effects which are allowed on the one hand and the direct prejudice to the rights of individuals on the other is, however, not entirely clear.

Although the Court has repeatedly stressed that Community law does not interfere with the institutional structure of the Member States, with the consequence that the Member States are free to choose the bodies responsible for implementation, in reality the scope of the principle of institutional autonomy is somewhat limited.

Firstly, since the nature of the implementing measures is largely determined by certain requirements of Community law, the choice of the implementing authority will accordingly be limited. If, for instance, these requirements necessitate implementation by primary legislation, involvement of the Parliament is, by implication, the consequence.

Secondly, there will be interference with the institutional structure of a Member State when, pursuant to Community law requirements, a mechanism is required to compel compliance with the terms of a directive by, in national constitutional terms, an independent body. For instance, if the subject matter of a directive is within the autonomous legislative powers of the regions, the central government must nevertheless be able, by some means, to induce the regions to implement the directive and to do so correctly.

Thirdly, the Court has stipulated that the directive is binding upon all national authorities. This means that it is binding not only upon the legislator, which is often the national authority primarily responsible for implementation, but also upon other bodies of the judiciary and the executive. They are obliged to comply with the directive to the extent that it is within the sphere of their respective functions: thus, broadly speaking, in the administration of justice and the application of the directive in a concrete case.

For the executive, the binding force of the directive may have certain implications for the powers attributed to the various authorities. In particular circumstances, namely where the directive has not been implemented in time or adequately and the relevant provisions meet the requirements of direct effect, they are obliged, irrespective of their powers under national law, to apply the provisions in question. Where, for instance, a local authority is, in pursuance of national law, empowered to grant authorizations for certain industrial activities under conditions laid down in national law and, by virtue of direct effect of a directive, the authority grants the authorization required under different conditions, namely those of the directive, the authority is clearly doing something which it is not allowed to do under national law. Moreover, disregarding the national provisions and instead applying those of the directive is at odds with the principle of subordination of the executive power to the legislative power.

The possibility should also not be excluded that the obligation for national authorities to interpret national law in conformity with the directive could lead to similar results. In this respect, however, it is uncertain whether or not the limits of this obligation are formed by the powers given to the authorities concerned.

Furthermore, the category of bodies actually bound by the directive has been expanded by the Court of Justice through extensive interpretation of the concept of "the State". Consequently, even bodies which as a matter of national law were not in any way considered as addressees of the directive, are also under the obligation to apply directly effective provisions of directives and to proceed to interpretation of national law in conformity with the directive concerned.

The Court has not given an abstract definition of "the State". It has made clear that two tests can be applied in this respect, namely the "control test" and the "functional test". It is not yet entirely clear whether these tests apply cumulatively or alternatively; neither is there clarity regarding their content, since the indications given in *Foster*,[1] as yet the only relevant judgment, are tailored to the specific circumstances of the case. Furthermore, the extension of the category of bodies which are bound, through the interpretation of the concept of "the State", is reinforced by the fact that the control test and the functional test are not linked to the directive at issue in the concrete case. This means that as soon as a body is considered to be a part of the State under (one of) the two tests, it has to comply with the terms of the directive even if the directive has nothing in common with the activities which caused the body to fall within the limits of the functional test, or the directive relates to activities which are not the subject of the specific control which the State exercises *vis-à-vis* the body at issue. Thus while the "public service" entrusted to the BGC which caused the undertaking to fall within the terms of the functional test related to the distribution of gas, the BGC was nevertheless bound to observe the Equal Treatment Directive. Similarly, the control exercised by the State with respect to the activities of the BGC concerned the distribution of gas rather than the employment policy of the undertaking. Nevertheless, this control was sufficient to bring the BGC under the control test.

[1] Case C-188/89 [1990] ECR I-3331.

The freedom to choose the form and methods of implementation is likewise much less unfettered than might be assumed upon reading Article 189(3). In the first place, the freedom relates to the kind of measures to be adopted and not to the content of the measures, the latter being determined by the directive concerned. Moreover, since directives may go into detail, the other side of this coin is that the choice among the measures available will be rather limited.

The most remarkable development which has significantly curtailed the discretion left to the Member States, has taken place in the case law of the Court of Justice. In the majority of cases it follows from the content of the directive that it is aiming, in the first stage, at the achievement of a certain legal situation. This situation is, however, not an end in itself. In the second stage, after appropriate transposition into national law, the legal rules must operate fully in practice as well. On the basis of the combination of the content of the directive in question on the one hand and the principles of full effectiveness, legal certainty and effective judicial protection on the other, the Court has laid down strict requirements which must be satisfied by the implementing measures.

These three principles produce effects on three different levels, namely as regards the content of the implementing measures, their legal nature and the rules to be provided for in order to safeguard adequate enforcement of the directive.

On the first two levels the application of the principles brings about a number of more specific requirements which can be summarized as follows: The content of the measures must of course correspond to the content of the directive and, furthermore, it must be clear and precise in order to guarantee an unambigous legal situation. Although in the majority of cases specific implementing measures must be enacted, under certain circumstances a general legal context may suffice as a way of implementation, with the proviso, however, that the above requirements are fully satisfied.

As far as their legal nature is concerned, the implementing measures must in principle be legally binding, particularly but not exclusively where the directive aims at creating rights and duties for individuals.

The requirements concerning the content and the legal nature of the measure are relevant in two respects. Firstly, they have to guarantee the full and correct application of the measures in question. Secondly, they are essential for the judicial protection of individuals and for allowing individuals to know the full extent of their rights and duties resulting from the directive. In the Court's view, administrative practices cannot, in principle, satisfy these requirements and are therefore not accepted as a proper means of implementation.

Specific problems arise when one considers the role played by national courts in the process of implementation. On the one hand, there is no doubt that the interpretation and application of the relevant provisions of national law by the courts is a vital element of the implementation of the directive. It is often within the light of this interpretation and application that the question as to whether the content of the directive has been correctly implemented must be examined. On the other hand, when it is argued that the obligations of the directive are fulfilled through the case law of the national courts, this case law must be sufficiently accessible and predictable to satisfy the principle of legal certainty. Established case law of the highest courts will probably meet these conditions, but where the courts interpret and apply national law in a certain manner with the purpose of palliating their Member State's failure to implement the directive properly, this technique will not amount to correct implementation and the Member State will not be released from its obligation to take the necessary implementing measures.

Since directives must be fully effective in everyday practice, the implementing measures must often be accompanied by an appropriate system of sanctions in order to compel obedience. In this respect it is the principle of full effectiveness and, where appropriate, the principle of effective judicial protection which produce effects at the third level, namely that of national rules aiming at enforcement of the directive, particularly the sanctions to be provided for.

Three types of situations can be distinguished in this regard: the directive itself provides for a specific sanction, the directive gives only general indications or the directive is silent on the issue.

Especially in the last – and most common – situation two questions arise: whether a sanction must be provided at all and, if so, what the content of the sanction should be. Although the initial position is discretion of the Member States, in this respect too the Member States are not entirely free. The answer to the first question depends on the content of the directive and the objective it pursues or, alternatively or cumulatively, it follows from the Member States' obligation under Article 5 to take all the measures to guarantee the application and the effectiveness of Community law. As regards the second question, the Court shows by its case law that it is inclined to impose some minimum requirements which must be met by the sanctions, and in some cases it may specify in detail what the content of the sanctions must be. The two central principles applicable in this context are the "assimilation principle" and the principle of effectiveness. The former requires that breaches of Community law are penalized under conditions which are analogous to those applicable to infringements of national law of a similar nature. The latter stipulates that the sanctions are effective, proportionate and dissuasive. The mere fulfilment of the principle of assimilation as such is not sufficient. The principle of effectiveness must be satisfied as well.

Furthermore, not only is the content of the sanction determined by Community law requirements: the substantive conditions to be fulfilled before the sanction can be imposed and the procedures which result in the imposition of the sanction are also governed by the minimum Community law requirements.

Part II

Directives as a Part of the National Legal Order and the Role of National Courts

Introduction

Although in the early years of the Community it seemed inconceivable that directives could be of any direct relevance to private individuals,[1] the reality has proved to be different. Today, directives are invoked by individuals for several purposes and they are frequently applied or, at least, taken into account as legal rules by national courts. The focus of this Part is the role which national courts (are supposed to) play in this respect. It does not, however, deal with the actual application itself or the ways in which the courts take directives into account. The starting point of the analysis is rather one of the most crucial elements of Community law, namely the requirement that national courts must protect the rights which individuals derive from Community law, including directives.

The Court of Justice stated as early as 1963[2] that Community law may create rights for the benefit of individuals and that it is a duty of national courts to protect these rights, irrespective of other procedures for enforcement of Community law available at the Community level. Some five years later the autonomous role assigned to national courts was re-emphasized in the *Molkerei-Zentrale* case.[3] In this case the Court made clear that actions brought by private individuals in national courts on the one hand and actions brought by Community institutions in the Court of Justice on the other were two distinct issues, and the respective actions were in no way mutually exclusive. While proceedings by an individual aim at protecting individual rights in a specific case, intervention by Community institutions "has as its object the general and uniform observance of Community law". Although the national courts were thus entrusted with an important mission of their own, for a long time the Court was not forthcoming on the question of how the courts should realize this protection. It was not until the mid-eighties that the principle of effective judicial protection was introduced into the Court's case law and given substance in a number of subsequent cases.

Protection of rights implies that there is indeed a right to be protected. Rights which individuals derive from Community law, often called "Community law rights", are now a widespread legal phenomenon and it might perhaps seem unnecessary to devote a lengthy discussion to the subject. However, as will become apparent during Chapter 7, the matter is quite complicated, not least as a result of a fairly indiscriminate right-talk of the Court of Justice.

[1] For a brief overview of the different positions see e.g. Lauwaars 1973, p.33-35 and Louis 1993, p. 501-505.

[2] Case 26/62 *Van Gend en Loos* [1963] ECR 1.

[3] Case 28/67 [1968] ECR 143.

STAFFS UNIVERSITY LIBRARY

Furthermore, protection of Community law rights by the national courts equally implies that the courts have on some basis been made responsible for the protection required and, moreover, that the law provides for appropriate procedures in which this protection can be effectuated. In Chapter 8 I shall firstly consider the juristic construction underlying the role of the national courts. The requirements imposed by the Court with respect to the national systems of judicial protection and their development will then be discussed in detail.

The majority of issues under consideration in this Part are not specific to directives alone. The discussion will therefore often relate to the enforcement in the courts of Community law in general.

7
Directives in the National Legal Order

7.1 THE PLACE OF DIRECTIVES WITHIN THE NATIONAL LEGAL SYSTEM

The fundamental choice made by the Court of Justice in *Van Gend en Loos* and *Costa v. ENEL*[1] as to the relationship between Community law and national law in general also determines the place of directives within the legal orders of the Member States. The Community's own legal system is an integral part of the legal systems of the Member States.[2] This means that the whole body of Community law (including directives, which are a component of this law) is as such incorporated within the national legal orders, without measures of transformation, incorporation – or whatever else the terminology might be – being necessary.[3] This *automatic* incorporation was in the past not always readily accepted. While regulations engendered the least discussion in legal writing, since the Treaty provides that they are "directly applicable" in the Member States,[4] the status of other provisions of Community law, and directives in particular, was regarded as uncertain, to say the least. The different views covered a whole gamut of possibilities. Some authors considered that directives, being binding upon Member States only, were as such irrelevant within the national legal order.[5] Others were of the opinion that in so far as directives were directly effective they were integrated in the national legal order.[6] Yet another group considered them, without reservations, to be a part of the law of the Member States, although the effects which directives could produce within the internal legal order could vary considerably according to the circumstances.[7] In the view of this last group, the requirement of further implementation of directives did not imply that they had to be treated as a "*non-être juridique*"[8] in national law; the requirement of implementation provided for in Article 189(3) should not be equated to a necessity to be incorporated.[9]

[1] Case 26/62 [1963] ECR 1 and Case 6/64 [1964] ECR 585.

[2] Confirmed recently in Joined Cases C-6/90 and C-9/90 *Francovich* [1991] ECR I-5357.

[3] For terminology and analysis see e.g. Kovar 1987, p. 351-362 and Kovar 1983, p. 130-137.

[4] On the concept of "direct applicability", which I do not use in the technical sense often attributed to it, namely as not necessitating incorporation, see Chapter 11, Subsection 11.3.2.

[5] Cf. Kovar 1987, p. 360, Everling 1984, p. 97, Louis 1993, p. 501-502.

[6] Cf. Kovar 1987, p. 362.

[7] Cf. Grabitz 1971, p. 5, Timmermans 1979, p. 534, Everling 1984, p. 106, Daig and Smidt 1991, p. 4945.

[8] Pescatore 1980, p. 176.

[9] Cf. Timmermans 1979, p. 534-535.

Today this discussion seems to be outdated and there can be little doubt that in the view of the Court of Justice directives *are* integrated in the national legal systems as from the date of their entry into force.[10] If this were otherwise, there would be no explanation for the fact that individuals can rely on provisions of Community directives before national courts and that the latter must take them into consideration as elements of Community law which they are bound to apply. Indeed, the concept of direct effect of directive provisions is based on the very theory that directives are a part of the national legal order.[11] Similarly, the Court's case law obliging national authorities and, in particular, national courts to interpret national law in conformity with a directive can more readily be understood if one accepts that directives are an integral part of the legal systems of the Member States.[12] Once a directive has entered into force and become a part of the law in the Member States, it should as a rule produce effects since, as is generally assumed, any legal rule is in principle intended to operate effectively.[13] In the vast majority of cases legal rules are designed to be applied in practice. A different question is whether such an application is possible in a concrete case and, if it is, how this application will take shape.[14] The answer depends on several other factors, such as the purpose for which an individual is relying on a provision and whether this can be satisfied by a court, having regard to the terms and content of the relevant provision.

A difference with respect to directives is that they are devised to become fully operative in national law through implementation, and the Member States are given a certain period of time for the purpose of accomplishing this. This is an additional factor to be taken into account when the question of possible modalities of application of directives is addressed.[15] This does not, however,

[10] For entry into force of directives see above, Chapter 2, Section 2.1, in particular n. 20. Cf., in addition to authors mentioned in n. 4, Klein 1988, p. 9-10, Langefeld 1992, p. 955-956, Hartley 1994, p. 197. Cf. also the first edition of this last work, Hartley 1981, p. 215.

[11] Declaring that Community law is a part of the national legal order is the quintessence of Case 26/62 *Van Gend en Loos* [1963] ECR 1. On this basis the Court was able to develop the doctrine of direct effect. Cf. Kapteyn an VerLoren van Themaat 1990, p. 40-51. See also Mertens de Wilmars 1969, p. 69 and Everling 1984, p. 107.

[12] Cf. Everling 1984, p. 107.

[13] Pescatore 1983, p. 155. Although, as was observed by Emmert (1992, p. 66), the stepmotherly way in which, in this perspective, Pescatore treats directives is striking. Cf. also Mertens de Wilmars 1991, p. 398.

[14] Very illuminating in this respect is the four-step approach made by Klein (1988, p. 8-9) who distinguishes 1) the *Existenz* and *Gültigkeit* of the norm (existence and validity), 2) *Geltung* (its force as law to be applied within the State), 3) *Anwendbarkeit* (its applicability or its suitability to be applied) and 4) *Anwendung* (its actual application in a concrete case). Cf. for a similar approach Langenfeld 1992, p. 955-957, Bach 1990, p. 1110-1111.

[15] Cf. Klein 1988, p. 12, Pescatore 1980, p. 171.

alter the fact that directives *are* a part of the body of law which is valid within the national legal order[16] and may as such produce various kinds of effects.[17]

The theory that directives are, as a part of Community law, integrated into the legal systems of the Member States says nothing as such about their position *vis-à-vis* other national rules. However, from the case law of the Court of Justice it follows unambiguously that directives take precedence over the law of the Member States. Ever since *Costa v. ENEL*[18] the Court has constantly affirmed the supremacy of Community law over national law. This principle holds true for both primary and secondary Community law and, in my opinion, irrespective of whether the provisions at issue are directly effective or not. Although direct effect and supremacy often go hand in hand, they are two separate concepts.[19] The reason why they are often coupled[20] is that, as a rule, national courts encounter supremacy each time an individual relies on a directly effective provision of Community law in order to have contrary provisions of national law set aside and to have the Community provision applied instead, where necessary. However, the principle of supremacy also means that a national court may not review the validity of Community acts in the light of national provisions of (constitutional) law.[21] In such a case the individual does not rely on the provisions of Community law in the sense indicated above. On the contrary, he argues that the Community act is invalid, for instance, for reasons of incompatibility with his constitutionally guaranteed rights. Similarly, it is submitted, the national courts may not construe the Community law provision in accordance with national legal rules.

From the point of view of the courts and, arguably, also from the point of view of national administration,[22] supremacy can be conceived as a rule of conflict. For the legislator, the principle of supremacy has more the effect of blocking the enactment of unilateral and contrary national measures.[23]

If the theoretical underpinning of the principle of supremacy is the conception of an autonomous Community legal order involving a transfer of powers to the Community and consequent limitation of Member States' sovereign rights, as is

[16] Cf. Everling 1984, p. 106-107, Kovar 1987, p. 365.

[17] Cf. Langefeld 1992, p. 957, Timmermans 1979, p. 534-535.

[18] Case 6/64 [1964] ECR 585.

[19] Cf. Kovar 1983, p. 114, Mertens de Wilmars 1969, p. 71, Lauwaars and Timmermans 1994, p. 38, Louis 1993, p. 547, Maresceau 1978, p. 26-27, Langenfeld 1991, p. 174.

[20] Cf. Louis 1993, p. 546 ff., Maresceau 1978, p. 26-27. See also for a discussion as to the relationship between the two concepts De Witte 1984, p. 440.

[21] Cf. Case 11/70 *Internationale Handelsgesellschaft* [1970] ECR 1125.

[22] Cf. Case 103/88 *Costanzo* [1989] ECR 1839.

[23] Cf. Case 106/77 *Simmenthal* [1978] ECR 629. See also above, Chapter 2, Section 2.2.; national provisions which are not in conflict with Community law are however allowed. Cf. Case C-143/91 *Van der Tas* [1992] I-5045.

frequently contended,[24] national legal rules which are contrary to a directive cannot apply or cannot validly be adopted, as they are *ultra vires.*[25] Thus although the principle of supremacy was not initially conceived as differentiating between legal rules of a lower order (national rules) and higher order (Community rules),[26] in practice the construction often amounts to giving directives and Community law in general a higher ranking in the hierarchy of norms which are valid within a national legal system.[27]

7.2 Directives as (Indirect) Sources of Rights and Duties of Individuals

7.2.1 Indirect versus Direct Source

As an instrument of Community intervention, the directive imposes upon the Member States the obligation to implement it. This obligation exists primarily *vis-à-vis* the Community and other Member States. However, as was argued in Section 7.1, from their entry into force directives form part of the law in the Member States and thus constitute a source of law within the national legal system. Furthermore, as explained in Chapter 3, particularly Section 3.2, the actual content of a directive may aim at establishing different types of legal relationships. In principle, it is designed to result in the creation of a whole conglomerate of rights and obligations between Community institutions and Member States, Member States *inter se*, Member States and individuals and individuals amongst themselves. For every single case, depending on the terms of the provision concerned or the combination of provisions, an answer must be established to the question of who is obliged or entitled to what or, at least, *will be* obliged or entitled at the end of the day, i.e. once the directive has been transposed.

For the purpose of this Chapter, the focal point is the relationship between the Member State and individuals and individuals *inter se.* With respect to the question of who will be party to the relationship(s) which the directive intends to establish, it should be recalled[28] that the substantive provisions of a directive may formulate obligations for either the Member States or for individuals and,

[24] Cf. Lasok and Bridge 1991, p. 176, Kapteyn and VerLoren van Themaat 1990, p. 44-45. For a critique of this position see De Witte 1984, p. 437-438.

[25] Cf. Kapteyn and VerLoren van Themaat 1990, p. 45.

[26] Cf. Kapteyn and VerLoren van Themaat 1990, p. 45, Lasok and Bridge 1991, p. 176, Mertens de Wilmars 1969, p. 70.

[27] Cf. Case 106/77 *Simmenthal* [1978] ECR 629, para. 17.

[28] Cf. also above, Chapter 3, Subsection 3.2.1.

similarly, they may formulate "rights" for either Member States[29] or for individuals.

For the sake of clarity: the rights and obligations formulated for the respective subjects by the substantive provisions must be distinguished from the obligation of a Member State to implement a directive and from the fact that directives as such cannot impose obligations upon individuals.

The specific nature of the directive as an instrument of two-stage legislation means that a Member State is under two distinct types of obligations. Firstly, it has the obligation to implement the directive and, secondly, it has certain obligations which are imposed on it by the *actual* text of a directive, such as to allow the sale of products when these products satisfy the conditions of the directive, grant exemption from VAT, award public works contracts in accordance with the procedure laid down in the relevant directive and give social security benefits to men and women on a non-discriminatory basis.

In Chapter 4 I discussed in detail the problem that a directive as such cannot *impose* obligations upon individuals and, consequently, neither the State nor another individual can base a claim against an individual directly on a directive. This in no way precludes that directives may *formulate* the obligations: it is, however, only upon transposition that the obligations become enforceable.

In summary, the substantive provisions may formulate both the persons who will be the beneficiaries and the persons who will be under obligation after the transposition into national law of the directive at issue. The fact that the directive as a whole is binding upon the Member State only is in this respect immaterial.

As regards the content of the relationship, in some cases the obligations and rights may be laid down in the provisions of the directive very precisely and in concrete terms.[30] In other cases the content and scope must subsequently be defined with more precision by national or – less usually – Community measures. However, even in the latter cases, it should be possible, as a rule, to establish whether a directive or particular provisions are aiming to confer rights or impose obligations on individuals, or whether they are rather intended to regulate, for instance, the relations between administrative bodies. The answer to the question will only be facilitated by precision and (consequently) more concrete wording.

Considered from these two points of view, a directive will often be a source of rights and duties of individuals. In principle, however, it is an *indirect* source in the sense that it is the origin of rights and obligations laid down in national legislation. In other words, it reaches the individuals through implementing

[29] The somewhat unusual term "rights" denotes in this context the right as the correlative of an individual's obligation. E.g. Member State authorities are entitled to claim certain conduct from the individual, like the payment of VAT. Cf. also Joined Cases 66, 127 and 129/79 *Salumi* [1980] ECR 1237, where the Court talks about the rights of public authorities.

[30] Cf. above, Introduction to Part I and Chapter 3, Subsection 3.2.1.

measures adopted by the Member States.[31] Yet in some cases it could be considered as a *direct* source of rights (but not obligations), namely where the provisions apply by virtue of "direct effect", i.e. in cases where provisions of directives can apply and actually are applied without the intercession of national measures implementing the directive at issue.

7.2.2 Direct Effect and the Creation of Rights

Direct effect of Community law provisions and the creation of rights or obligations[32] with respect to individuals are often regarded as synonyms which can be used interchangeably. The situation is, however, rather more complicated.

The root of the problem lies in the terminology of the Court of Justice.[33] In *Van Gend en Loos* the Court held that "Article 12 must be interpreted as producing direct effects and creating individual rights which national courts must protect".[34] The implicit suggestion of this phrase, that rights come into being by virtue of direct effect, seems to be affirmed in cases like *Salgoil* where the Court found that "Article 31 ... lends itself perfectly to producing direct effect ... *Thus* Article 31 creates rights which national courts must protect."[35] Another example is *Van Duyn*. In this case, after an examination of the conditions to be satisfied by a provision in order to be directly effective, the Court held that "Article 3(1) of Council Directive No. 64/221 ... confers on individuals rights which are enforceable by them in the courts of a Member State and which the national courts must protect".[36] In numerous other cases the Court has used the same or comparable terms to indicate the meaning of the fact that a provision has direct effect.[37] Even more recently, in *Dansk Denkavit*, the Court held with respect to Article 33 of the Sixth VAT Directive, which prohibits the introduction of taxes which can be characterized as turnover taxes, that this provision can be relied upon by individuals since it meets the requirements for direct effect.

[31] Cf. Case 270/81 *Rickmers* [1982] ECR 2771, Case 8/81 *Becker* [1982] ECR 53.

[32] Where appropriate. As was explained in Chapter 4, Section 4.2, directives as such cannot impose obligations upon individuals, but only by virtue of implementing legislation.

[33] Cf. Maresceau 1978, p.45-47, Mertens de Wilmars 1969, p. 67. For a more general discussion see also Kovar 1981, p. 161 and Timmermans 1979, p. 538-539.

[34] Case 26/62 [1963] ECR 1, at p. 13.

[35] Case 13/68 [1968] ECR 453, at p. 461 (emphasis added – SP).

[36] Case 41/74 [1974] ECR 1337, para. 15.

[37] Cf. for older case law Mertens de Wilmars 1969, p. 62-64, Maresceau 1978, p. 45-49 and also Case 265/78 *Ferwerda* [1980] ECR 617, para. 10, where the Court talks about "the rights which subjects obtain through the direct effect of Community law".

According to the Court, this Article "creates rights for the benefit of individuals which the national courts are obliged to protect."[38]

However, in the first place, as has been pointed out by several authors,[39] "direct effect" is a broader concept, in the sense that a directly effective provision of Community law may be relied upon for several purposes. Defining direct effect in terms of the creation of individual or subjective[40] rights as understood in national law will often be, if not impossible, then rather artificial and, moreover, unnecessary.[41]

For instance, in the case of discriminatory dismissal the person concerned may base her or his claim to compensation on the right to equal treatment as laid down in Directive 76/207 (equal treatment at work).[42] On the other hand an employer may raise the provisions of the same directive in his defence in criminal proceedings brought against him for reasons of employing women at night, which is prohibited under national law, while no such prohibition exists with respect to male employees.[43] While in the first situation it is plausible to speak of a right to equal treatment of men and women, in the latter case it is difficult to maintain that the directive creates a substantive right for the employer.

The essential point with respect to direct effect is *the possibility for an individual to invoke provisions of Community law in order to protect his interests.*[44] If direct effect must be classified as a right, then this right will be, at the most, *a right to invoke Community law,*[45] thus a kind of "procedural" right, with a corresponding obligation for the national courts to apply it.

[38] Case C-200/90 [1992] ECR 2217, para. 18. Cf. also Case C-236/92 *Comitato* [1994] ECR I-483 where the Court found, after having applied the usual test for direct effect, that the provision in question "does not confer on individuals rights which the national courts must safeguard" (para. 15).

[39] Cf. Mertens de Wilmars 1969, p. 67, Maresceau 1978, p. 49-50, Timmermans 1979, p. 538-539, Bleckmann 1984, p. 775 and Bleckmann 1978, p. 89, Barents 1982, p. 98, Kovar 1981, p. 161, Klein 1988, p. 15.

[40] Or personal rights; the adjectives added vary in legal writing. According to David 1984, p. 6, the English term "individual rights" can be used as the equivalent of "subjective rights" commonly employed in the civil law tradition. The latter term stems from the need to distinguish between "law" and "rights" as these two notions have been fused into one single word, e.g. "droit" in French or "Recht" in German. Hence the distinction between "droit objectif" and "droit subjectif" or "objektives" and "subjektives Recht."

[41] Cf. Barents 1982, p. 98. However, some scholars hold a different view. Cf. Kovar 1978, p. 250-251.

[42] OJ 1976, L 39/40; cf. Case 152/84 *Marshall I* [1986] ECR 723 and Case C-271/91 *Marshall II* [1993] ECR I-4367.

[43] Cf. Case C-345/89 *Stoeckel* [1991] ECR I-4047.

[44] Barents (1982, p. 98) quoting Mertens de Wilmars. Cf. also Mertens de Wilmars 1991, p. 398.

[45] Cf. Bebr 1981, p. 559, Steiner p. 1986, p. 109, Kapteyn and VerLoren van Themaat 1990, p. 332, Lauwaars 1976, p. 77, Easson 1981, p. 35, Everling 1984, p. 101.

Since Community law provisions are relied upon within the context of national proceedings and for various purposes, it is a matter of national law to define the individual's position.

Thus, for instance, in Italy the modality of protection depends on the notoriously difficult distinction between "subjective right" and "legitimate interest".[46] When this distinction came before the Court of Justice in the *Salgoil* case, the latter found that it was for the national court to classify the position as one of having a subjective right or a legitimate interest or perhaps even a "diminished right" under national law, provided however that the protection granted was direct and immediate.[47]

In France the classification of the individual's position as having a subjective right will be irrelevant for the purposes of, for instance, a "*recours pour excès de pouvoir*", which aims at controlling the legality of an administrative act. The question of classification will, however, be relevant within the context of, for instance, a "*recours en responsabilité*", where the central issue is whether the challenged act constitutes an encroachment upon a subjective right.[48]

In German administrative law, where the fundamental principle is the "*Individual Rechtsschutz*" and the basic requirement is that the individual is "*in seinen Rechten verletzt*,"[49] the classification of an individual's position as a right plays a crucial role.[50] From this point of view it is no surprise that German legal literature contains a number of attempts to classify the protection of an individual's position by Community law using, for an outsider, rather sophisticated categories of rights.[51] An illustration of this approach is the opinion of A-G Lenz in the *Costanzo* case.[52] In his view, the nature of Article 29(5) of Directive 71/305 (public works contracts)[53] was such as to create rights for individuals. He recalled the *Transporoute* judgment,[54] in which the Court held that "the aim of the provision ... is to protect tenderers against arbitrariness on the part of the authority awarding contracts". The Advocate General continued by saying that "the obligation to examine the tender, which has the effect of a procedural guarantee, may be construed as a right vesting in the tenderer who submits an obviously abnormally low tender". To a Dutch lawyer, for instance, it may not be clear why it should be necessary to translate a procedural guarantee into a right.[55]

[46] Cf. Clarich in Bell and Bradley 1991, p. 239-241.

[47] Case 13/68 [1968] ECR 661.

[48] Cf. Bok 1992, p. 59-60.

[49] See Article 42 II of the *Verwaltungsgerichtsordnung* (code of administrative procedure) and Article 19 IV of the Basic Law.

[50] What is meant by "Recht" for these purposes was the subject of a long and complicated development. See e.g. Bok 1992, p. 136-138. Here it suffices to remark that nowadays protection is offered not only to subjective rights but also to interests protected by the law.

[51] Cf. Winter 1991b, p. 659 ff.; cf. on this issue also Grabitz 1971, p. 22.

[52] Case 103/88 [1989] ECR 1839, para. 27.

[53] OJ English Spec. Ed. 1971 (II), p. 682.

[54] Case 76/81 [1982] ECR 417.

[55] Cf. however Winter (1991b, p. 662) who criticizes the Court for not having dealt with this issue more carefully and for not giving reasons.

Similarly, the English approach may also appear strange to some continental lawyers. For instance, it has been argued that in the case of the exercise of statutory powers by public authorities in a way that contravenes a directly effective provision of Community law, the "Community law right is akin to a right in English law not to be subjected to an *ultra vires* act."[56] Moreover, in the United Kingdom another type of classification is crucial for individual protection, namely whether the "right" at issue can be considered as a public law right or a private law right, since the remedies available differ accordingly.[57]

From the foregoing it follows that the classification will differ not only from Member State to Member State but also from procedure to procedure. The classification of an individual's position depends on the character and the subject matter of the national proceedings. In a non-contractual liability proceedings as a rule one has to invoke an infringement of a (subjective) right, while for the purposes of a more objective control of the legality of an administrative decision the protection of a mere interest will often suffice.[58] In criminal proceedings where the Community law provision is raised in defence, the classification of the individual's position will be immaterial.[59]

Seen against this background, the Court's usual definition of direct effect, i.e. as conferring rights upon individuals or equivalent formulations, must be employed with a good deal of caution. In this respect the more *objective* definitions, given in particular by the doctrine, are to be preferred.[60] As regards provisions of directives, the Court's definition of direct effect seems to take into account the various roles this concept may play in national procedures when it holds that

"... wherever the provisions of a directive appear ... to be unconditional and sufficiently precise, those provisions may ... be relied upon as against any national provision which is incompatible with the directive or in so far as the provisions define rights which individuals are able to assert against the state."[61]

Equating direct effect with the creation of rights for individuals is also deceptive from another point of view. It is not only incorrect to maintain that only

[56] Lewis 1992, p. 457.

[57] For difficulties occasioned by this distinction in relation to the enforcement of Community law see e.g. Steiner 1986 and Ward 1990, p. 25 ff.

[58] Cf. Mertens de Wilmars 1969, p. 74.

[59] Cf. the opinion of A-G Reischl in Case 269/80 *Tijmen* [1981] ECR 3079, at 3103.

[60] Cf. Mertens de Wilmars as referred to by Barents 1982, p. 98, Timmermans 1979, p. 538, Kovar 1981, in particular p. 160. For further discussion of this subject see also below, Chapter 11, Section 11.3.

[61] Case C-221/88 *Busseni* [1990] ECR I-495, para. 22. Since Case 8/81 *Becker* [1982] ECR 53 this has been consistent case law.

Community law provisions which (are intended to) grant rights to individuals are able to produce direct effect:[62] it is similarly erroneous to argue that *only* directly effective provisions may confer rights upon individuals. In *Waterkeyn*[63] the Court held that the rights accruing to individuals derive from the actual provisions of Community law *having direct effect*. This is, however, certainly in the light of more recent developments, an outdated point of view. The question whether a provision creates individual rights is, in my opinion, *a matter of its content*; the question whether a provision has direct effect relates to *the quality ascribed to it*, namely whether it can be invoked by those concerned within the national legal system.[64] Moreover, the basis of the two is entirely different. While the "procedural right" of an individual to rely on a provision of a directive is based on Article 189(3) combined with Article 5 EC,[65] the substantive right which the individual seeks to enforce stems from a particular (provision of a) directive.[66]

Direct effect and creation of rights may and will often coincide. It appears that provisions of directives may define rights which, provided that the provisions are unconditional and sufficiently precise and the directive has not been implemented correctly, can be asserted against the State.[67] The provision can thus both have direct effect and define rights, although this is not always necessarily the case. The most obvious example in this respect is the *Francovich* case.[68] In this case the directive was regarded as being designed to create rights for the benefit of individuals but the direct effect doctrine was of no avail for the individuals concerned, since the provisions on the identity of the debtor were not sufficiently clear and unconditional. In other words, they did not meet the

[62] Cf. the opinion of A-G Warner in Case 152/79 *Lee* [1980] ECR 1495, at p. 1514: "a provision in a directive cannot have direct effect unless it is to be inferred from "the nature, general scheme and wording of the provision" that it required Member States to confer, by their own law, rights on private persons". Cf. also his opinion in Case 131/79 *Santillo* [1980] ECR 1585.

[63] Joined Cases 314 to 316/81 and 83/82 [1982] ECR 4337.

[64] Provided that it meets certain conditions for this purpose; see below, Chapter 11, Sections 11.3 and 11.4. For a comparable distinction see Grabitz 1971, p. 22.

[65] Case 190/87 *Moormann* [1988] ECR 4689.

[66] Cf. also Case C-208/90 *Emmott* [1991] ECR I-4269. On the one hand the Court found (para. 19) that where directives are intended to create rights for individuals clear and precise transposition is necessary since only then can they ascertain the full extent of those rights. On the other hand the Court reiterated in para. 20 that where a Member State has failed to take the implementing measures required "the Court has recognized the right of a person affected thereby to rely ... on a directive as against a defaulting State". Cf. also Case C-338/91 *Steenhorst-Neerings* [1993] ECR I-5475, where the Court refers on the one hand to the rights stemming from the directive at issue and on the other hand to the right to rely on the directive. Furthermore it must be observed that the substantive right may, in turn, be procedural in character: e.g. the right to be heard versus the right to an exemption from taxes, social security benefit etc.

[67] Cf. Case 8/81 *Becker* [1982] ECR 53.

[68] Joined Cases C-6/90 and C-9/90 [1991] ECR I-5357.

classical conditions for direct effect. Consequently, for this reason *and* in the absence of implementing measures, the individuals could not "enforce the right granted to them by Community law before national courts", as the Court put it.[69]

Another example to indicate that the creation of rights and the possible direct effect must be considered separately can be drawn from cases concerning rights of individuals which are to be asserted against other individuals. The content of the relevant provisions may very well confer rights upon a person but since directives do not have horizontal direct effect the person concerned cannot assert them against another individual.[70] This does not mean, however, that no right has been created. It is "only" not enforceable against the other individual. In principle, of course, there is no point in having a right if a person has no opportunity to enforce it in practice. However, the existence of a right and the ways in which it is protected are two separate issues.[71]

In summary, direct effect and the creation of rights should not be equated. Direct effect refers to the ability to rely on a provision of Community law for a variety of purposes, even where the provision does not confer substantive rights. On the other hand, Community law provisions may confer rights upon individuals, or order Member States to do this, without being directly effective.

7.2.3 The Conception of Rights: the Pitfalls

In the Court's case law the creation of rights appears to have a crucial function both within the context of proper implementation of directives[72] and for the role assigned by the Court to national courts. The latter are required to protect the rights which individuals derive from Community law, including directives. Consequently, the next question to be addressed is that of the circumstances in which provisions of directives confer rights upon individuals, or at least, are intended to confer rights.[73]

[69] Cf. also the opinion of A-G Mischo in Joined Cases C-6/90 and C-9/90 *Francovich* [1991] ECR I-5357, para. 60, where he observes that "the lack of direct effect does not mean that the effect sought by the directive is not to confer rights on individuals but solely that those rights are not sufficiently precise and unconditional to be relied upon and applied as they stand without any action on the part of the Member States to which the directive is addressed".

[70] Cf. Schockweiler 1992, p. 38 and Case C-91/92 *Faccini Dori* [1994] ECR I-3325.

[71] This might seem peculiar from the point of view of common law where, it is understood, the existence of a remedy at common law or under statute enables the English lawyer to deduce the existence of a right. EC law operates the other way round: it confers rights and national law must supply remedy. Cf. Durand 1987, p. 43, Van Gerven 1994, p. 341. See also on this approach in general MacCormick 1977, p. 195-199.

[72] Cf. above, Chapter 5.

[73] Namely through implementation. Cf. above, Subsection 7.2.1.

Finding the answer is far from simple, for a number of reasons. The Court of Justice frequently uses the term "rights" but its "language of rights" as such seems to be particularly unhelpful in the search for parameters to enable us to identify occasions when a provision gives rise to rights.

As mentioned above with respect to direct effect, in so far as the Court defines direct effect in terms of "conferring rights", the legal literature has featured two arguments. Firstly, the definition suggests that the rights thus created are "subjective rights" but, as explained in the last Subsection, directly effective provisions produce wider effects than merely granting subjective or individual rights. Secondly, it has quite correctly been submitted that this definition raises the problem of what constitutes a subjective right in Community law.[74] *For the purposes of direct effect*, understood as the possibility for an individual to rely on Community law provisions in various situations and the corresponding obligation of the courts to apply the provisions, I have argued that the classification is a matter of national law and therefore the question of what is a (subjective) right under Community law[75] is immaterial. In this context to say that the obligation of the courts is to protect the rights which individuals derive from Community law is only another way of saying that the courts must protect the individual's position, whatever the classification of the effects of Community law for this position might be under national law. Nevertheless, this does not mean that the issue of *what is a right in Community law* can entirely be side-stepped. In particular, the problem emerges more concretely with respect to the liability of the State as laid down in *Francovich*[76] and wherever an individual relies on the *Emmott rule*.[77] As will be discussed in more detail in Chapter 12, one of the conditions giving rise to liability of the State in the case of non-implementation of a directive is that the directive should entail the granting of rights to individuals. The application of the *Emmott rule*, i.e. that national time limits for bringing proceedings do not apply as long as the directive has not been properly transposed, is equally related to the question whether or not the directive concerned is intended to create rights for individuals. Furthermore, as I observed above, the issue is relevant for the modalities of implementation of the directive in question.

Whatever the classification of the effects of a Community law provision might be, once it has been applied in the national legal order, either as a directly

[74] Cf. Barents 1982, p. 98.

[75] For the sake of clarity it must be observed that wherever I use the term "Community right" or similar expression this does not correspond to the term "enforceable Community right" as employed in the European Communities Act 1972, Section 2(1) which, it is understood, relates to directly effective Community law provisions.

[76] Joined Cases C-6/90 and C-9/90 [1991] ECR I-5357.

[77] Case C-208/90 [1991] ECR I-4269.

effective provision or as a national provision after implementation, this should (in principle) not influence the fact that, from the Community law point of view, it must be considered as granting rights. In other words, as explained above with respect to direct effect, the provision concerned can be relied on as safeguarding (subjective) rights, protecting interests or providing grounds for illegality, depending on the context within which it is invoked. Similarly, after the provision has been implemented it will be considered as granting (subjective) rights or merely as a rule protecting certain interests or, more generally, it will be a part of national law valid within the Member State concerned and will be applied accordingly. The way in which the provisions granting rights under Community law will be treated in the national context depends on the notions used within the various national legal systems and the branch of law – for instance criminal, civil, administrative – in which the provisions will be applied or implemented.

Thus, for instance, while in Germany the entitlement to social security benefits under Directive 79/7 (equal treatment in statutory schemes of social security)[78] will be classified as a "*subjektives öffentliches Recht*" (a public law subjective right),[79] in Dutch law, where the notion of "subjective right" is often reserved for rights under private law, such a classification will be unusual.[80] This "reclassification" of legal concepts of Community law into national legal concepts is a consequence of the very fact that the transition from Community law level to national law level entails a certain alteration of the provision at issue.[81]

The inevitable translation of Community law rights into national legal notions is presumably also the reason why the Court of Justice uses the rather neutral term "rights" and why it is reticent in indicating the nature of the right at issue.[82] The various and often subtle (dogmatic) distinctions and contructions which exist within the national law of the Member States are determined by tradition, the purposes they serve and the particular structures and organization of the respective legal systems. From this point of view it is understandable and even inevitable that the Court should adopt a somewhat aloof attitude.

On the other hand, as mentioned above, the question whether a provision, a group of provisions or a directive as a whole confers or intends to confer rights upon individuals plays a vital role in the Court's case law. It would therefore seem that at least some minimum guidelines would be indispensable. The notion

[78] OJ 1976, L 6/24.

[79] More precisely a "*Leistungsrecht*"; cf. Winter 1991b, p. 661.

[80] Some efforts have been made however to construe a subjective right also in the public law sphere. Cf. Bergamin 1991, Holtmaat 1992, p. 263 ff.

[81] Mertens de Wilmars 1969, p. 79. Cf. also Mertens de Wilmars 1981, p. 391.

[82] Cf. Case 13/68 *Salgoil* [1968] ECR 661. The issue of classification was recently raised again in Case C-236/92 *Comitato* [1994] ECR I-483, but the Court answered the preliminary question by reasoning purely along the line of direct effect.

of rights, in this context, is a Community law notion: obviously one cannot simply use, for this purpose, the national criteria of what consitutes a right.[83] It has been suggested in this respect that useful criteria could be derived from a comparative legal study.[84] Without excluding the usefulness of such an excercise *a priori*, one may nevertheless wonder whether, given the national differences, this method would be feasible or whether it would lead to satisfactory results. Another possibility is to fall back on legal theory which should, in principle, be less hampered by the peculiarities, technicalities and vicissitudes of the various national legal systems. However, in this respect one encounters another problem: the impressive quantity of treatises on the concept of (subjective) rights but which diverge on the definitive interpretation.[85]

It is certainly not my intention to undertake a comparative study in this respect or to plunge into legal theory: both of these would be quite beyond the scope of this book. However, despite the doubt expressed above, it may be that to a certain extent, in combination with some very basic notions about rights, some useful lessons can be drawn from the case law of the Court of Justice.

7.3 RIGHTS FOR INDIVIDUALS: PARAMETERS IN THE COURT'S CASE LAW

7.3.1 Introduction

It has already been noted that when searching for the answer to the question as to the conditions under which a certain provision of Community law should be considered as conferring rights upon individuals or, at least, as being intended to do so, the Court's case law is not especially helpful. The main reason is probably that under Community law until now *this specific question* has scarcely been an issue.

For the sake of clarity it must first be pointed out that many of the preliminary questions submitted to the Court of Justice have been and continue to be worded in terms of whether a provision creates rights, and the Court's answers are couched in the same terms. What the national courts are anxious to know, however, relates to *direct effect* and thus to the questions whether the individual can rely on the provision in question and whether the courts have to apply it.

Nonetheless, the lack of cases dealing explicitly with the problem at issue here certainly does not mean that the case law contains no indications in this respect.

[83] Cf. Langenfeld 1992, p. 962, Winter 1991c, p.455. Cf. also Caranta 1993, p. 286 ff.
[84] Cf. Langefeld 1992, p. 962.
[85] Cf. Alexy 1985, p. 159. Exemplary for the disagreement are e.g. White 1984 and MacCormick 1982.

In fact three points were made clear in *Van Gend en Loos*:[86] firstly, Community law may grant rights to individuals *expressis verbis*; secondly, obligations imposed on individuals, on the Member States and on the Community institutions may also give rise to rights in favour of (other) individuals, provided, however, that the obligations are clearly defined; and thirdly, it appears that the addressee of the relevant provisions, whether Member State, Community institution or individual, is not important – the obligation of one subject of Community law is correlative to the right of another. There is, in fact, nothing revolutionary in this approach. The most common attempts to explain the conception of right utilize the notion of a duty or obligation and many jurisprudents assume that one person's duty implies another person's right.[87] With respect to directives, it may seem that matters are complicated in so far as a directive cannot, as such, impose obligations upon individuals. This is, however, as stated above, a problem of enforceability. From the terms of a provision it may very well follow that its purpose is to impose an obligation on an individual, and it is from these terms that another person may derive rights.

7.3.2 Terms of the Provisions

In many situations it appears to be easy to see that the terms of the Community law provisions concerned, combined – where necessary – with the purpose of the rules, confer rights; so easy, in fact, that it must be accepted without further ado. The most obvious examples in this respect can be found in the field of free movement of workers or persons in general, freedom of establishment and freedom to provide services. In the opinion of the Court, both Treaty provisions and secondary legislation enacted in order to facilitate the exercise of these freedoms confer rights upon individuals.

For instance in *Royer*, after having quoted Articles 48(3), 52 and 59, the Court held that "these provisions, which may be construed as prohibiting Member States from setting up

[86] Case 26/62 [1963] ECR 1. It must be noted that, although the relevant consideration in *Van Gend en Loos* was "preparing the ground" for the finding that Article 12 EEC was directly effective, in my view, the granting of rights on the one hand and direct effect on the other, as laid down in this judgment, must be distinguished. This is particularly confirmed by *Francovich* (Joined Cases C-6/90 and C-9/90 [1991] ECR I-5357), where the Court reiterated its consideration about the conferment of rights which must be protected while the protection by means of direct effect did not work in this case. Cf. also (already) Bleckmann 1978, p. 116.

[87] The system of correlatives has been elaborated in detail by Hohfeld (Fundamental legal conceptions). His jurisprudential analysis made him conclude that there are in fact four kinds of rights with, similarly, four kinds of correlatives. Although his conceptual framework is still used by some, e.g. Alexy 1985, p. 187 ff., Salmond 1966, p. 224-233, it has been equally criticized to an extent by others; see e.g. Waldron 1984, p. 7 ff. and *passim* MacCormick 1977, MacCormick 1982, White 1984.

STAFFS UNIVERSITY LIBRARY

restrictions or obstacles to the entry into and residence in their territory of nationals of other Member States, have the effect of conferring rights directly on all persons falling within the ambit of the above-mentioned provisions ...".[88] The same holds true with respect to equal treatment of men and women[89] and most probably with respect to any other rules of Community law in the field of social policy intended to protect the individual, such as directive 80/987 on the approximation of laws relating to the protection of employees in the event of the insolvency of the employer, at issue in *Francovich*.[90] The right granted by this directive was the employees' entitlement to a guarantee of payment of their unpaid wage claims. Undoubtedly in many other fields of Community law, on the basis of the terms of the provisions alone, it can be said that they confer rights in the broad sense of the term.[91]

Terms are not however always unequivocal and conversely, of course, even if a provision is couched in clear terms, it does not necessarily imply that rights are granted to individuals. It may therefore be necessary to apply other parameters as well.

7.3.3 Parties to the Legal Relationship

In the first place, if rights may come into being by virtue of an obligation imposed on another, the relevant question to be considered in this respect relates to the legal relationship laid down in the provision concerned; or, more precisely,

[88] Case 48/75 [1976] ECR 497, para. 24. It must be observed that here the Court was answering the question whether the provisions were a direct "source of rights" and that the passage did *not* relate to the question of direct effect. Cf. further also Case 222/86 *Heylens* [1987] ECR 4097, Case 29/84 *Commission v. Germany* [1985] ECR 1661, Case C-306/89 *Commission v. Greece* [1991] ECR I-5863.

[89] Cf. Case 43/75 *Defrenne II* [1976] ECR 455, Case C-208/90 *Emmott* [1991] ECR I-4269.

[90] OJ 1980, L 283/23. Cf. also with respect to Directive 77/187 (safeguarding employees' rights in the event of transfer of undertakings), OJ 1977, L 61/26, Case C-362/89 *D'Urso* [1991] ECR I-4105. With respect to Directive 85/577 (contracts negotiated away from business premises), OJ 1985, L 372/31, Case C-91/92 *Faccini Dori* [1994] ECR I-3325.

[91] By this latter term I refer to the theory developed by Hohfeld. According to him (and many others) the term "right" as used in legal language has at least four different meanings, according to the relationship at issue. Namely: *claim* (or *right strictly speaking*) which says something about the existence of duties of others, *privilege*, which says something about the existence of the duties of the person having the "right", *power*, which says something about the possible alteration of the duties of the persons involved in the relationship and *immunity*, which says something about the freedom from possible alteration in the duties of the person in which the "right" is vested. Cf. Perrot 1973, p. 3-4. Thus, for instance, Ms Becker's right to exemption from VAT is in this approach rather a privilege: she has no duty to pay VAT.

It is not my intention to carry on these distinctions throughout the text. It is however important to note that behind the term "right" are hidden different types of legal relationships. Cf. also Van Gerven in C-70/88 *European Parliament v. Council* [1990] ECR I-2041, para. 6, who pointed out the necessity to conceive "rights" in the widest sense of the term, namely as right, power and prerogative.

it relates to the issue of *who* are the parties to the relationship in the concrete case: *vis-à-vis* whom does the obligation exist?

In *Costa v. ENEL*[92] the Court held that by virtue of Article 102 EEC the Member States have bound themselves to prior consultation with the Commission and have thus undertaken an obligation to the Community. For its part, the Commission is bound to ensure respect for the provisions of the Article. However, according to the Court, these obligations did not create rights in favour of individuals. More recently, in *Enichem*[93] the Court found that Article 3(2) of Directive 75/442 (waste),[94] obliging the Member States to inform the Commission in good time of any draft rules within the scope of that provision, had to be construed as concerning relations between the Member States and the Commission only. It therefore did not give rise to any rights for individuals.

The judgment in *Costa v. ENEL* suggests that if the individual is not a party to the relationship at issue, the provision cannot create rights in his favour.

However, proper regard must be given in this respect to the fact that a provision may give rise to multiple relationships. It is a matter of interpretation whether a particular person in a concrete case is party to one of these or not. In particular, the purpose of the provision concerned is highly relevant in this respect.

In *Enichem* the relevant article was intended, according to the Court, to ensure that the Commission is informed of any plans for national measures in the area of waste disposal. The information should enable the Commission to consider whether Community harmonizing legislation is called for and whether the draft rules are compatible with Community law. The Commission could subsequently consider taking appropriate measures. These aspects are apparently not considered as being of immediate concern to private individuals. It has been suggested that this would be otherwise if the draft measures had to be submitted to the Commission, for instance, for approval, and pending the approval procedure the Member States were precluded from adopting them in a legally valid manner.[95] Yet although the measures thus adopted would be rendered unlawful, this mere fact does not *eo ipso* imply that a right of an individual would have been equally violated. Whether this is the case or not depends, it is

[92] Case 6/64 [1964] ECR 585.
[93] Case 380/87 [1989] ECR 2491.
[94] OJ 1975, L 194/39.
[95] Opinion of A-G Jacobs in Case 380/87 *Enichem* [1989] ECR 2491, para. 14.

submitted, on the question whether or not the approval procedure also served the protection of the individual interest of the person concerned.[96]

Thus, in summary, a provision may at first sight appear to only concern the relationship between the Member State and the Commission. If, however, the purpose of the provision is to protect the interest of the individual, the individual becomes party to a different relationship under the provision at issue, namely the relationship between him and the Member State, with as subject matter the obligation of the Member State to refrain from enacting the rules which must be subjected to approval and the obligation preceding thereto to notify the draft measures to the Commission.

7.3.4 Protection of Individual Interest

At the end of the last Subsection, I came to the second relevant element for the problem under discussion here, namely that the legal rules which are at the source of the alleged right must exist to protect the individual interest and not merely to protect the general (or public) interest.

This view, which is still generally accepted, linking a right to interest,[97] dates back in particular to Jhering, according to whom

"Zwei Momente sind es, die den Begriff des Rechts konstituieren, ein substantielles, in dem der praktische Zweck desselben liegt, nämlich der Nutzen, Vorteil, Gewinn, der durch das Recht gewährleistet werden soll, und ein formales, welches sich zu jenem Zweck bloss als Mittel verhält, nämlich der Rechtsschutz, die Klage."[98]

For Jhering it is primarily the substantive criterion which is important. This view has strongly marked the general thinking about rights and explains the common thesis that rights are considered to serve the protection of individual interests.[99]

The problem is that the distinction between general and individual interest is not black and white but rather a matter of degree. Every legal rule and its correct application can be considered as protecting general interest and as being the concern – in principle – of everybody, or at least, of very large and general

[96] In the same line it can be argued that where the State is obliged not to effectuate State aid measures until they have been approved by the Commission, this obligation exists not only *vis-à-vis* the Community but apparently also *vis-à-vis* private undertakings. The latter can rely in national courts on the "blocking provision" of Article 93(3), last sentence. The explanation for this is that the procedure to be followed by the Commission also serves the protection of their individual interests.

[97] Cf. White 1984, p. 79 and 102. See also the opinion of A-G Capotorti in Case 158/80 *Butter-buying cruises* [1981] ECR 1805, para. 6. However, for Community law a requirement of interest was denied by Bleckmann 1978, p. 94.

[98] Jhering, *Geist des Römischen Rechts*, Vol. 3, p. 339, quoted by Alexy 1985, p. 165.

[99] Cf. White 1984, p. 79, Salmond 1966, p. 217-221, MacCormick 1977, p. 192.

groups of persons. Whether over and above this the rule protects the special interest which some individuals might have is a problem of interpretation of the provision at issue.[100] Environmental law directives are often mentioned in this connection as examples of Community law rules intended to protect the general interest.[101] For instance, in his discussion of the conditions for State liability as formulated in the *Francovich* judgement[102] Judge Schockweiler explained that the first condition, i.e. that the result prescribed by the directive should entail *the grant of rights to individuals*, must be understood in the sense that the Court wanted to exclude State liability for violation of "*simple intérêts*" which the relevant directive intended to protect. To give examples of directives which most probably do not intend to grant rights to individuals he refers to directives in the field of environmental law.[103] This position is rather surprising, as in the same year that the *Francovich* judgment was rendered the Court found in a number of cases brought under Article 169 and relating to environmental directives that these directives *are* intended to create rights and obligations for individuals.[104] More recently, A-G Jacobs found, following from one of these judgments, that Directive 80/778 (drinking water) does confer rights on individuals and its incorrect implementation could therefore give rise to liability under *Francovich*.[105] Judge Zuleeg, on the other hand, fails to see how a subjective right can be construed on the basis of the mere fact that the directives concerned aim at protecting human health.[106]

Several explanations can be given for this difference in opinion. It is arguable that Judge Schockweiler and Judge Zuleeg use the term "*droit subjectif*" in a more limited sense than the term "right" employed by the Court and A-G Jacobs respectively. Likewise it is conceivable that the rights to which the Court refers

[100] Cf. also what has been said about the provisions on State aids above, in n. 96. Undoubtedly, the rules of the Treaty are general rules against distortion. However, at the same time they protect the individual interests of the undertakings affected. Cf. also Temple Lang 1992-1993, p. 33-35.

[101] Cf. Temple Lang 1992-1993, p. 28. See also Case 240/83 *ADBHU* [1985] ECR 531, in particular para. 15.

[102] Joined Cases C-6/90 and C-9/90 [1991] ECR I-5357.

[103] Schockweiler 1992, p. 44. More specifically he mentions as examples Directive 75/440 (surface water I), OJ 1975, L 194/56, Directive 79/869 (surface water II), OJ 1979, L 271/44 and Directive 80/68 (groundwater), OJ 1980, L 20/43. Cf. also Gilliams 1991-1992, p. 19. Cf. however also Schockweiler 1993b, p. 114.

[104] Case C-59/89 *Commission v. Germany* [1991] ECR I-2607, Case C-58/89 *Commission v. Germany* [1991] ECR I-4983, Case C-361/88 *Commission v. Germany* [1991] ECR I-2567 and Case C-131/88 *Commission v. Germany* [1991] ECR I-825. In particular the last Case relates to a directive which Schockweiler has given as an example of a "non rights granting" directive. Cf. also Van Gerven 1993, p. 19.

[105] OJ 1980, L 229/11. Opinion in Case C-237/90 *Commission v. Germany* [1992] ECR I-5973, para. 15.

[106] Zuleeg 1993, p. 214. Cf. also Everling 1992a, p. 384-385 and Everling 1993, p. 214-215.

STAFFS UNIVERSITY LIBRARY

in *Francovich* are different from the rights referred to in the above-mentioned infringement procèedings. However, I do not see – presently – any reason why these concepts should differ. Moreover, such a differentiation does not seem to be beneficial to the coherence of Community law. Finally, the difference in opinion could be due to a blurring of the overall objective of a directive and the intentions behind the actual terms of its specific provisions.[107]

It is undoubtedly true that some directives *as a whole* protect the general or public interest more than other directives. An example can be drawn – again – from environmental directives protecting the general interest in a less polluted environment on the one hand, and directives like Directive 77/187 safeguarding the rights of employees in the case of transfer of an undertaking on the other.[108] However, with a view to realizing the general interest objective pursued by a directive, the directive will often contain (more) detailed and concrete provisions. These may as such grant rights to (or have the purpose of imposing obligations upon[109]) individuals. This was stated in unambiguous terms by the Court of Justice in Case *C-131/88 (groundwater)*, where it held that the directive at issue

"seeks to protect the Community's groundwater ... by laying down specific and detailed provisions requiring the Member States to adopt a series of prohibitions, authorization schemes and monitoring procedures in order to prevent or limit discharges of certain substances. The purpose of those provisions of the directive is thus to create rights and obligations for individuals."[110]

In brief, it seems that it is not the kind of interest which a directive as a whole intends to protect but the protection sought by its separate provisions that is decisive.

A number of relatively recent judgments suggest that the Court is rather easily satisfied that a directive provision also intends to protect individual interests. Two cases concerning Germany related to directives laying down air-quality limit values for sulphur dioxide (80/779) and lead respectively (82/884).[111] The relevant articles of the respective directives obliged the Member States to prescribe limit values which must not be exceeded within specified periods and specified circumstances. It likewise appeared from the

[107] A directive may have the objective of creating rights for individuals but it is up to the Member States to give substance to the rights to be created. Conversely, directives which are as such and taken in their entirety not aiming at the creation of rights may nevertheless contain provisions which entail rights for the benefit of individuals. See on this issue also Chapter 12, Subsection 12.4.3.

[108] OJ 1977, L 61/26.

[109] With rights resulting therefrom as "correlatives".

[110] *Commission v. Germany* [1991] ECR I-825, para. 7.

[111] OJ 1980, L 229/30 and OJ 1982, L 378/15.

directives that this obligation is imposed on the Member States "in order to protect human health in particular"[112] or "specifically in order to help protect human beings against the effects of lead in the environment."[113] These objectives implied, in the opinion of the Court, that "whenever the exceeding of the limit values could endanger human health, the persons concerned must be in a position to rely on mandatory rules in order to be able to assert their rights."[114]

In Case *C-58/89 (drinking water from surface water),*[115] the Court considered that from the preamble of Directive 75/440 (surface water I)[116] it appeared that the Directive (and Directive 79/869 (surface water II)[117] which complements it) are intended to protect public health and to that end to ensure the exercise of surveillance over surface water and over the purification treatment of the water. According to the Court this implies that whenever non-compliance with the measures required by the directives in question might endanger the health of persons, those concerned should be able to rely on manadatory rules in order to enforce their rights.

This very complex reasoning of the Court suggests, among other things, that the mere fact of the directives at issue being enacted – inter alia – with a view to protecting human health is sufficient to assume that there is an individual (health) interest of those who are exposed to higher values than the ones provided for in the directives or of those whose health is endangered because the measures required have not been observed. In other words, a phrase expressed in terms of protection of general (public) interest is relied upon in order to assert that the directives' provisions protect individual interest as well or even "in particular". It may tentatively be concluded that the "individual interest requirement" can hardly be considered as a serious restriction.[118]

[112] Case C-361/88 *Commission v. Germany* [1991] ECR I-2567, para. 16. Other objectives of the Directive are the elimination or prevention of unequal conditions of competition and the protection of the quality of the environment.

[113] Case C-59/89 *Commission v. Germany* [1991] ECR I-2607, para. 19.

[114] Case C-361/88 *Commission v. Germany* [1991] ECR I-2567, para. 16 and Case C-59/89 *Commission v. Germany* [1991] ECR I-2607, para. 19. These judgments were subsequently confirmed in three judgments brought by the Commission against France: C-13/90 [1991] ECR I-4327, C-14/90 [1991] ECR I-4331 and C-64/90 [1991] ECR I-4335 (summary publications).

[115] *Commission v. Germany* [1991] ECR I-4983.

[116] OJ 1975, L 194/56.

[117] OJ 1979, L 271/44.

[118] This does not come as a surprise when one takes into consideration the application of a similar requirement in cases brought under Article 215 of the Treaty. Cf. Grabitz 1988, p. 6-7.

7.3.5 Enforceability: Two Different Aspects

In general it is assumed that a right must be enforceable by some form of legal process by the person concerned;[119] or as White puts it, the "common jurisprudential definition of a right is that it is a legally enforceable claim".[120] Indeed, this characteristic can be found in the quotation from Jhering given above ("*der Rechtschutz, die Klage*") and it has been considered by some as the decisive element for the existence of a right.[121] However, not everyone agrees with this latter requirement, pointing out that in every legal system there are classes of legal rights which are not enforceable by any legal process. Those who contend that rights which are not enforceable are in reality not legal rights at all are, in this view, confusing obligatoriness with enforceability.[122]

With respect to the "enforceability", two different aspects must be distinguished. First, the ascertainability of the content of the right and second, the availability of judicial protection of the right.

Ascertainability

The subject matter, the content of the right, must be ascertainable, i.e. sufficiently concrete or delineated. Or, in other – everyday – words, one must know *what* one is claiming *in concreto* and, accordingly, the other party must know *to what* it is obliged *in concreto*. Thus in the case of directives, the content of the right must be circumscribed in the provisions of the directive.[123] If this were otherwise, the matter would not be justiciable.

In public law this aspect of ascertainability will often pose problems. Public law rules may impose obligations on public authorities or on the State as a whole, while leaving them a considerable degree of discretion with respect to the concrete fulfilment or realization of those obligations. As the (corresponding) right of an individual must be ascertainable with sufficient precision, it can only exist

[119] Cf. Bergamin 1991, p. 96.

[120] White 1984, p. 129.

[121] In fact Jhering's quote reflects the old and still not satisfactorily resolved (Cf. Alexy 1985, p.166-165) discussion between the adherents of the "will theory" and "interest theory". Jhering himself was an adherent of the latter and defined rights as "*rechtlich geschützte Interessen*". For those advocating the "will theory" the second, formal element was decisive. In this respect it was similarly argued that in cases where the formal criterion, the possibility of enforcement, was lacking but nevertheless the legal rule did protect an interest, there existed the so-called "reflex right" (*Reflex Recht*). Cf. also MacCormick 1977.

[122] Cf. Salmond 1966, p. 234, MacCormick 1977 *passim*.

[123] Cf. the opinion of A-G Darmon in Case C-236/92 *Comitato* [1994] ECR I-483, para. 40: from the fact that the directive in question did not impose on the Member States an obligation to give preference to the treatment of waste by recycling (thus a concrete obligation), the Advocate General deduced that no right was vested in individuals.

as a correlative of the obligation when the latter is sufficiently defined. Whether this is the case will depend on the extent to which the public authority is bound. Thus while some provisions do not as such give rise to an individual right, they may define the conditions in which rights come to be created. The less discretion is left to the authorities concerned, the more probable it is that the requirement of ascertainability will be satisfied.[124]

In Community law, the prerequisite that (the subject matter of) the right is defined in sufficiently concrete terms is a familiar feature. It is very similar to the requirement for a Community law provision to have direct effect and is therefore frequently encountered in the Court's case law.[125] In this respect, it is submitted that an affirmative answer to the question whether the test for direct effect is satisfied will usually also indicate that there is a right conferred upon individuals, provided that the other conditions are fulfilled as well.

As explained above,[126] direct effect should not be equated without qualification to the creation of rights. In *Enichem*,[127] for instance, the relevant provision was undoubtedly sufficiently precise and unconditional and could, from that perspective, be relied upon before the court. Nevertheless, no right was created for the applicant, as he was not a party to the relationship governed by the provision.

Conversely, as has also been pointed out,[128] Community law provisions may grant rights without being directly effective, for instance, because of the lack of *horizontal* direct effect of directives or because the *concrete identity* of the person at the other end of the relationship is not yet entirely certain, as was the case in *Francovich*.

In brief, the ascertainability (or identifiability) of the subject matter of the right and the test for direct effect will often coincide, but one should bear in mind that the concepts are not interchangeable. A good example of such a coincidence is – again – the *Van Gend en Loos* case. The Court held in this case, *inter alia*, that rights for individuals also arise by virtue of obligations which the Treaty imposes in a clearly defined manner on others. The subsequent examination undertaken by the Court with respect to Article 12 of the Treaty led the Court to decide that this Article is – to put it briefly – sufficiently precise as to be directly effective *and* to create individual rights.[129]

As regards the connection between the ascertainability of rights, or, more precisely, of their subject matter and the discretion left to the administration or

[124] Cf. Bergamin 1991, p. 106-107 and Holtmaat 1992, p. 281 and p. 283-284.
[125] See Chapter 11, Section 11.4.
[126] Subsection 7.2.2.
[127] Case 380/87 [1989] ECR 2491.
[128] Subsection 7.2.2.
[129] Case 26/62 [1963] ECR 1, at p. 12-13.

the legislature – as the case may be[130] – it has been noted that the (potential) creation of rights depends in particular on the degree of discretion left to the administration and the legislature respectively. It is obvious that in Community law, and in particular with respect to directives, this problem is extremely real. The very nature and purpose of directives is to be transposed into national law. The question as to the choice left to the implementing authorities will therefore be decisive for the problem of whether the subject matter of the (alleged) right is defined with sufficient precision. When the test for direct effect – which ultimately also concerns the issue of discretion[131] – is satisfied, the provision must be considered as being sufficiently precise with respect to the subject matter of the right. However the question could be raised whether a provision which leaves some choice to the authorities transposing it, and therefore cannot be considered as directly effective, but which, nevertheless, gives *grosso modo* sufficient indications as to the subject matter concerned, could in fact be considered as creating rights. The problem boils down, for the moment, to the meaning of the second condition laid down in the *Francovich* judgement for the purposes of State liability in the case of non-implementation of a directive; namely the requirement that "it should be possible to identify the content of (the) rights (at issue) on the basis of the provisions of the directive".[132] In legal writing it has been suggested that the Court intentionally did not use the orthodox terms of direct effect conditions "unconditional and sufficiently precise".[133] In my view, it is quite conceivable that this "identification of the content" and the requirements for direct effect are intimately linked. Moreover, even if the identification were to refer to less rigorous conditions, the tendency in the Court's case law to apply a less strict test with respect to direct effect will cause the two approaches to converge.

Finally, it should be pointed out that even when Member States are left with some discretion as to the exact scope and modalities of the content of the measures to be enacted at national level in pursuance of the directive, this may not lead to the conclusion that a directive is *not intended* to create rights in favour of individuals, with all the consequences for the requirements posed with respect

[130] For instance the discretion left to the legislature to substantiate the content in implementing legislation.

[131] See below, Chapter 11, Subsection 11.4.2.

[132] Joined Cases C-6/90 and C-9/90 [1991] ECR I-5357, para. 40. Cf. also Case C-91/92 *Faccini Dori* [1994] ECR I-3325. See also Schockweiler (1992, p. 44) who observed with respect to the second condition: "*cette deuxième condition est intimement liée à la première qu'elle ne semble vouloir que préciser et développer*".

[133] Cf. Gilliams 1991-1992, p. 879. See also below, Chapter 12, Subsection 12.4.3.

to its implementation.[134] This situation is then different from the former in that the *actual* rights will result from the national measures, which must, for this very reason, be sufficiently precise.[135]

Judicial protection

The second aspect relates to the question whether the (sufficiently precisely defined) right at issue can actually be enforced; i.e. whether appropriate judicial protection exists for the right concerned.

In some directives specific provisions are laid down as to the enforceability of the rights which they grant. These types of provisions could – if necessary – be used as an argument for the thesis that the directive intends to create rights. In the majority of cases, however, such provisions are lacking.

In general, in Community law the problem of judicial remedies available for the protection of the rights which this law confers or intends to confer stands out in particularly sharp relief. The main reason for this is that Communty law relies heavily on national legal orders for its enforcement. Thus where Community law confers rights it is left to national law to supply the remedy. This system of articulation may operate in an imperfect manner with, as a possible consequence the existence of a Community law right without an appropriate remedy at the national level. As far as directives are concerned, the most obvious example of the difficulties which may occur is the poor record of their implementation. Even if there are rights which should be conferred upon individuals by a certain directive, in the absence of proper implementation they would not be enforceable in national courts. The fact that the situation is otherwise is the consequence of several jurisprudential developments at Community law level which concentrate on the possibilities for individuals to assert their rights and on the obligation in the national courts to protect them. These developments will be addressed in detail in the next Chapters.

Considered against this background, it may be clear that the element of "judicial protection" (which is necessarily protection through national courts) as an indication for the existence of a right does not work. Where the approach is that enforcement and judicial protection are consequential on the recognition or conferment of rights, and for the reasons just explained this must be the only approach in Community law, one cannot turn things upside down and make the existence of the right depend on whether or not the right is protected in the courts. In other words, in Community law it is not "*ubi remedium ibi ius*" but "*ubi ius ibi remedium*".

[134] See above, Chapter 5. The two conditions laid down in *Francovich*, namely 1) entail the grant of rights, and 2) identify the content of those rights on the basis of the provisions, suggest that condition 1 may exist without condition 2.

[135] See above, Chapter 5, Subsection 5.2.2.

7.3.6 The Parameters: a Summary

Where do all these reflections lead? Certainly not to an unequivocal answer to the question regarding the circumstances in which a directive confers or is intended to confer rights upon individuals. Nevertheless, some general points can be made. Apart from cases where the answer can be given simply because the terms of the directive are clear, the following issues at least must be taken into consideration. Firstly, there is the question whether an individual can be party to the relationships to which the directive in question gives rise. Secondly, the directive as a whole or one or more of its provisions must be such that it protects individual interest, along with other things, like general interest. I have contended that the Court is apparently willing to accept readily that this is the case. Thirdly, there is the issue of "concreteness". Here the following distinction must be made: if the content of the alleged right is defined in sufficiently precise and concrete terms, then the directive will be a direct source of the right at issue; however if this is not the case, the directive may still be intended to confer rights, but the actual creation will take place at a later (implementing) stage. Whether a directive is intended to do this must be decided on the basis of its text and purpose, using the other parameters as well. Finally, the fact that a directive requires appropriate judicial protection will be a useful indication that it creates or is intended to create rights. This is not, however, a condition which must be satisfied.

8
The Role of National Courts

8.1 NATIONAL JUDGE MADE ACCOMPLICE

The very purpose of directives is their implementation in national law. As a rule, therefore, their provisions should apply within the national legal order in their "converted" form, i.e. as provisions of national law. Whenever the question of effects of directives is addressed, this should be the point of departure. This normal state of affairs was described by the Court of Justice in very clear terms in *Becker*, where it held that

"wherever a directive is correctly implemented, its effects extend to individuals through the medium of the implementing measures adopted by the Member State concerned."[1]

Directives are, however, notorious for not being implemented correctly or not being implemented in due time. In the same judgment the Court expressed this as follows:

"... special problems arise where a Member State has failed to implement a directive correctly and, more particularly, where the provisions of the directive have not been implemented by the end of the period prescribed for that purpose."[2]

The special problems referred to by the Court in the context of Becker related primarily to the questions whether and, if so, to what extent the effect of directives can also reach individuals *without* the mediation of national implementing measures. Directives may and often do create rights for individuals (or, at least, may be of direct concern for them),[3] but in the absence of implementing measures the individual would be deprived of the possibility of asserting those rights and having them protected.[4] The problem is, however, more extensive. It relates to the more *objective* necessity of implementation of directives in a correct way and within the period prescribed as discussed in Chapter 5. In order to counteract, as far as possible, the detrimental effects of inappropriate (i.e. incorrect, belated or both) implementation of directives, the Court of Justice,

[1] Case 8/81 [1982] ECR 53, para. 19.
[2] *Ibid.*, para. 20.
[3] Cf. above, Chapter 7.
[4] As early as 1963 the Court recognized that procedures provided for in Articles 169 and 170 of the Treaty do not guarantee sufficient and direct legal protection of individuals. See Case 26/62 *Van Gend en Loos* [1963] ECR 1.

assisted by "vigilant individuals",[5] resorts to its natural allies, namely the national courts. These courts are entrusted with the task of protecting the rights which individuals derive from directives and of ensuring the full effect of the latter.

The two intimately linked concerns of the Court, namely the protection of the individual and the full force and effect of Community law, are of course not peculiar to directives but concern Community law in general. Ever since *Van Gend en Loos*[6] the Court has maintained that it is the task of the national court to protect the rights of individuals under Community law without, however, indicating the precise basis of this obligation in the Treaty.

For a long time it was assumed that this task of the national court stemmed from or was a corollary of supremacy of Community law and, in particular, the doctrine of direct effect.[7] This point of view was confirmed by a sequence of consistent case law where the task of the national courts was always coupled with direct effect of the provisions at issue.[8] In 1976, the Court made explicit the basis of the national court's duty in the *Comet* and *Rewe* judgments, where it held that

"... in application of the principle of cooperation laid down in Article 5 of the Treaty, the national courts are entrusted with ensuring the legal protection conferred on individuals by the direct effect of the provisions of Community law."[9]

Again in these cases, the protection by the courts was related to direct effect.

The approach of the Court is, viewed from the historical perspective, entirely understandable. For a long time the issue of direct effect was raised only in judicial procedures and the sole interlocutors of the Court of Justice in Article 177 proceedings are the national courts. Likewise, the coupling of direct effect and the task of the national courts can be considered as a way of expressing that the counterpart of the individual's right to rely on directly effective Community law provisions is the courts' duty to apply them. However, in the light of more recent developments, the point of view that the task of national courts derives from direct effect of Community law provisions or relates only to those provisions is too limited. Moreover, as explained above in Chapter 7, Subsection 7.2.2, the creation of rights which had to be protected was generally seen as a consequence of direct effect. In the same Subsection I argued that the creation of rights and

[5] *Ibid.*, at p. 13.

[6] Case 26/62 [1963] ECR 1.

[7] Cf. Barav 1991, p. 2, Kapteyn 1993, p. 39, Kovar 1981, p. 164.

[8] Cf. Case 106/77 *Simmenthal* [1978] ECR 629 and, more recently, Case C-213/89 *Factortame* [1990] ECR I-2433.

[9] Case 45/76 *Comet* [1976] ECR 2043 and Case 33/76 *Rewe* [1976] ECR 1989; quotation is from *Comet*, para. 12. Cf. also Due 1992, p. 360-361.

direct effect are not identical. Nevertheless, the need for protection remains. It is therefore not surprising that in *Francovich* the Court modified its position slightly and stated that

"the national courts whose task it is to apply the provisions of Community law in cases within their jurisdiction must ensure that those rules have full effect and protect the rights which they confer on individuals."[10]

By deleting the reference to direct effect (and the Court could hardly do otherwise in this case) a more satisfactory solution has been reached, in my view. Apart from a national court's obligation under Article 5 of the Treaty, the protection of individuals by national courts and, generally, their duty to take Community law into consideration and ensure its full effect, follow from the very fact that Community law is an integral part of the legal systems of the Member States, "which their Courts are bound to apply"[11] in principle in exactly the same way as they are bound to apply any other rule of national law, irrespective of its "external" origin.

Another, in my view more cogent, argument than that based on direct effect can be drawn from the fundamental principle of the "*Rechtsstaat*", the rule of law. The Court, albeit in a different context, has stressed several times that the Community is a community based upon the rule of law. This entails, *inter alia*, that neither the Member States nor the national authorities can avoid a review of whether the measures they adopt are in conformity with the law, including Community law.[12] Under the Community law system this control lies partly with the Court of Justice and partly with the national courts. Thus the control required by the rule of law necessarily involves the application of Community law by the national courts. Similarly, the principle of the "*Rechtsstaat*" requires that rights of individuals are effectively protected, and this task, in the absence of protection provided directly by the Court of Justice, must be assumed by the national courts.[13]

Thus, anxious both to ensure effective operation of Community law and to safeguard the judicial protection of individuals, the Court entrusted the national courts with an important mission. However, this was not the end of the matter. In *Becker*, to palliate the effects of the non-implementation of the directive concerned, the Court had recourse to the principle of direct effect, stating that

[10] Joined Cases C-6/90 and C-9/90 [1991] ECR I-5357, para. 32.

[11] Case 6/64 *Costa v. ENEL* [1964] ECR 585, at. p. 593.

[12] Cf. Case 294/83 *Les Verts* [1986] ECR 1339, Case C-2/88Imm. *Zwartveld I* [1990] ECR I-3365, Opinion 1/91 *EEA* [1991] ECR I-6079.

[13] Cf. Klein 1988, p. 17.

"... wherever the provisions of a directive appear ... to be unconditional and sufficiently precise, those provisions may ... be relied upon as against any national provision which is incompatible with the directive or in so far as the provisions define rights which individuals are able to assert against the State."[14]

Direct effect proved to be a powerful device, placed at the disposal of national courts to enable them to accomplish their task under Community law. In the meantime, however, it has become clear that direct effect has its limits. Nevertheless, the need for judicial protection remains. In order to complete the system of effective operation of Community law and the judicial protection of individuals, the Court has designed two other tools for national courts, namely the interpretation of national law in conformity with Community law and the principle of liability of the State for harm caused to individuals by breaches of Community law.

These mechanisms do not operate in a vacuum, but within the framework of the national systems of judicial protection. To put this another way, whether Community law can be put into effect by the courts and, accordingly, whether the legal position of individuals under Community law can be protected by means of the three mechanisms depend on the availability and organization of national procedures leading to some form of legal relief. This "environment" within which the mechanisms can be deployed determines to a large extent the outcome of their operation and, consequently, the extent of the protection afforded. In the following Sections it will become apparent that the articulation between Community law and the national systems of judicial protection poses several problems which often call for a Community law solution.

8.2 Judicial Protection under National Law and Community Law Requirements

8.2.1 Principles Laid Down in Early Case Law

According to the system laid down in the E(E)C Treaty the actual application and enforcement of Community law is, in general, dependent upon the legal systems of the Member States. This dichotomy between the law-making power of the Community institutions and the power of the Member States to apply and enforce Community law entails that the task assigned to the national courts to protect rights which individuals derive from Community law is accomplished

[14] Case 8/81 [1982] ECR 53, para. 25.

within the framework of national procedures.[15] In other words, an individual with a right under Community law or, more generally, an interest in its application, makes use of national procedures and remedies in order to enforce it. It is within the context of proceedings brought in national courts that the need for interpretation of national law in accordance with Community law may arise, directly effective provisions are relied upon and the liability of the Member State for a breach of Community law must be established. The degree of judicial protection afforded therefore depends in the final analysis on national courts, national procedures and national remedies.

On the one hand, an important merit of this construction is that Community law is enforced in familiar national courts, in accordance with familiar national rules of procedure, and in this way it promotes the actual integration of Community law into the national legal order.[16] Moreover, the construction involves a minimum degree of Community intervention in matters such as the organization of the administration of justice, paying due regard to what is known as "procedural autonomy".[17]

On the other hand, there are also several disadvantages. Since Community law rules must, in view of their application and enforcement, pass through the national systems, the effect of Community rules may be affected by the particularities of these systems of judicial protection. National rules of procedure relating, for instance, to delays in bringing action or to prescription of action, to *locus standi* or to burden of proof are unlikely to be uniform within the various Member States. This obviously leads to unequal protection of individuals within the Community. Similarly, the effectiveness of remedies available for enforcement of Community law provisions may differ considerably, as may the powers of the courts. The problems which stem from disparities of this kind could actually be tempered by harmonization. Until now, however, very few measures have been adopted in this respect and the Community has to live with the "regrettable absence of Community provisions harmonizing procedure ... [which] entails differences in treatment on a Community scale", as the Court put it in *Express Dairy Foods*.[18]

[15] For this clear assumption compare the definition of regulations in Article 189 and the system of judicial co-operation provided for in Article 177 of the Treaty. Cf. also Bridge 1984, p. 31 and Barav 1989, p. 369 with further references.

[16] Cf. Bridge 1984, p. 28-29.

[17] Cf. Kovar (1978, p. 248), who considers procedural autonomy as a specific form of institutional autonomy. For the latter see above, Chapter 4, Section 4.3. The term "procedural" must not be understood too strictly in this context. It relates not only to procedural rules *stricto sensu*, but also to "any rules and principles of organizational or substantive nature which concern actions in law aiming at judicial protection" (See Kapteyn and VerLoren van Themaat 1995, Chapter VI, Subsection 2.3.2; translation is mine). Cf. in the same sense also Mertens de Wilmars 1981, p. 390.

[18] Case 130/79 [1980] ECR 1887, para. 12. Cf. also Langenfeld 1991, p. 185.

To describe the problems encountered at this stage, i.e. when addressing the question of how judicial protection of an individual's position under Community law is safeguarded at the national level, Mertens de Wilmars has used the imaginative expression "problems of the second generation".[19] By now, the Court has found some second generation answers.

Apart from some rather isolated instances of harmonization of different procedural aspects, such as Regulation 2913/92 (Community Custom Code)[20] and Directives 89/665 (public contracts – review procedures) and 92/13 (*ibid.* for excluded sectors),[21] two kinds of situations occur in Community law: either no provisions on procedures and remedies are laid down or the Member States are obliged, by some in principle very generally worded provisions, to provide for judicial protection in the area concerned.

As examples of this last kind of provisions can be mentioned the directives in the field of equal treatment of men and women,[22] all of which contain a provision whereby Member States must introduce into their national legal systems such measures as are necessary to enable all persons who consider themselves to be victims of discrimination to pursue their claims by judicial process. Similarly, Directive 64/221 (public policy and public health)[23] prescribes that the person concerned shall have the same legal remedies in respect of any decision concerning entry, or refusing the issue of a residence permit, as are available to the nationals of the State concerned in respect of acts of administration. Article 8 of Directive 89/48 (mutual recognition of diplomas)[24] provides that a remedy shall be available against a decision on recognition of professional qualifications, or the absence thereof, before a court or tribunal in accordance with the provisions of national law.[25]

[19] Mertens de Wilmars 1981, p. 380.
[20] OJ 1992, L 302/1 (Title VII).
[21] OJ 1989, L 395/33 and OJ 1992, L 76/14.
[22] Directive 75/117, OJ 1975, L 45/19, Directive 76/207, OJ 1976, L 39/40, Directive 79/7, OJ 1979, L 6/24, Directive 86/378, OJ 1986, L 225/40 and Directive 86/613, OJ 1986, L 359/56.
[23] OJ English Spec. Ed. 1963-1964, p. 117.
[24] OJ 1989, L 19/16.
[25] Other examples can be found in Directive 73/239 (insurance other than life assurance I), OJ 1973, L 228/3, Directive 91/533 (conditions applicable to the employment relationship – information of employees), OJ 1991, L 288/32, Directive 92/28 (advertising of medicinal products), OJ 1992, L 113/13, Directive 92/49 (insurance other than life assurance III), OJ 1992, L 228/1, Directive 92/50 (public service contracts), OJ 1992, L 209/1, Directive 92/51 (recognition of professional education and training), OJ 1992, L 209/25, Directive 92/59 (product safety), OJ 1992, L 228/24, Directive 92/85 (pregnant workers), OJ 1992, L 348/1, Directive 90/313 (information on environment), OJ 1990, L 58/56, Directive 93/13 (consumer contracts), OJ 1993, L 95/29, Directive 92/53 (type-approval of motor vehicles), OJ 1992, L 225/1.

In principle, it is not important whether there are some very general provisions or no provisions at all, as the former are usually rather non-committal.[26] In both situations it is left to the Member States to determine the competent courts and to lay down rules for the legal proceedings in which Community law is to be enforced.[27]

A Court with Appropriate Jurisdiction

In the first place, and although, as the Court has stressed, Community law was not intended to create new remedies in the national courts to ensure its observance other than those which already exist,[28] the Member States must make sure that in any case where Community rights are involved there *is a court having jurisdiction.* Furthermore, the Member States are responsible for ensuring that the courts provide "direct and immediate protection"[29] and that the rights are "effectively protected in each case."[30] Yet it was held to be for the national courts to apply the most appropriate of the various measures available under national law in order to protect the individual rights conferred by Community law.[31] In other words, there must be *a* court and *a* procedure available before which and within the context of which an individual can enforce his Community law rights.[32] However the decision as to which court is competent, what kind of procedure can be used and how this procedure is organized is in principle left to the discretion of the Member States. Exceptionally this can be otherwise, namely if from Community law itself, for instance from a directive, it follows that there is an obligation to make a certain type of judicial protection available to the persons concerned.[33]

Requirements of Non-Discrimination and Effectiveness

In the second place, the Court of Justice has curtailed national discretion by formulating two minimum requirements which national procedural law must

[26] See however Subsection 8.3.5: explicit provisions may serve as a written basis for national courts to extend their powers.

[27] Cf. Case 33/76 *Rewe* [1976] ECR 1989, Case 45/76 *Comet* [1976] ECR 2043. The approach is comparable to that with respect to sanctions. See above, Chapter 5, Subsection 5.2.4.

[28] Case 158/80 *Butter-buying cruises* [1981] ECR 1805. It is however doubtful whether this proposition still holds true nowadays. See below, Subsection 8.3.4. Cf. also Schockweiler 1992, p. 39-40 and Barav 1994, p. 269.

[29] Case 13/68 *Salgoil* [1968] ECR 453, at p. 463.

[30] Case 179/84 *Bozzetti* [1985] ECR 2301, para. 17.

[31] Cf. Case 34/67 *Lück* [1968] ECR 245.

[32] Cf. also Case 244/80 *Foglia Novello II* [1984] ECR 3045.

[33] Cf. Case 152/79 *Lee* [1980] ECR 1495. In the absence of specific provisions the obligation to provide judicial protection is based on Article 5 of the Treaty. Cf. above, Section 8.1 and Mertens de Wilmars 1981, p. 392.

satisfy. According to the first requirement, which can be called the principle of non-discrimination,[34] the substantive and procedural conditions governing the respective actions for the enforcement of Community law cannot be less favourable than those relating to similar actions of a domestic nature. The second principle, which can be designated with the term the principle of effectiveness,[35] requires that the conditions are not framed in such a way as to render virtually impossible the exercise of the rights conferred by Community law. Ever since *Rewe* and *Comet* these two principles have been confirmed in a consistent sequence of cases, using the same or similar language. In *San Giorgio*[36] the Court appeared to have added a new proviso, namely when it held that the conditions should not make the exercise of Community law rights not only virtually impossible but also excessively difficult. In my view, there is a difference in degree between "virtually impossible" and "excessively difficult". In the Court's case law, however, there is no indication that it wished to broaden the scope of the second requirement accordingly.

For a considerable period of time these requirements led a fairly subdued existence. On the one hand, it was clear that the two principles applied both where Community law referred explicitly to national law and where it did not.[37] Furthermore, they applied to all actions, regardless of whether they were brought by a private party or by public authorities.[38] On the other hand, the Court gave little guidance as to the meaning of either of these principles. Moreover, they largely evolved in a rather limited area of Community law, namely in cases concerned with (re)payment of sums of money. Bridge[39] classified the cases according to the type of claims: 1) reimbursement of payments which had been made but which had been demanded contrary to Community law;[40] 2) payment of sums which should have, but had not in fact, been paid as required by Community law;[41] and 3) refund of sums erroneously paid out on behalf of the Community.[42] The cases concerned matters like the application of national limitation periods,[43] rules on the payment of interest[44] or on the burden of

[34] Cf. Oliver 1987, p. 883.

[35] *Ibid.*

[36] Case 199/82 [1983] ECR 3595.

[37] Cf. Case 265/78 *Ferwerda* [1980] ECR 617.

[38] Cf. Case 33/76 *Rewe* [1976] ECR 1989 on the one hand and Joined Cases 119 and 126/79 *Lippische Hauptgenossenschaft* [1980] ECR 1863 on the other.

[39] Bridge 1984, p. 32.

[40] E.g. Case 45/76 *Comet* [1976] ECR 2043.

[41] E.g. Joined Cases 66, 127 and 128/79 *Salumi* [1980] ECR 1237.

[42] E.g. Case 265/78 *Ferwerda* [1980] ECR 617.

[43] E.g. Case 45/76 *Comet* [1976] ECR 2043 and, more recently, Case 386/87 *Bessin and Salson* [1989] ECR 3551.

[44] E.g. Case 130/79 *Express Dairy Foods* [1980] ECR 1887.

proof;[45] principles which exist under national law having the effect of limiting the remedial outcomes of full application of Community law rules, such as unjust enrichment[46] and what was called "the principle of innocent error",[47] were also submitted to the Court. This case law concentrated more on the principle of effectiveness than on that of non-discrimination,[48] although the latter requirement is also not unproblematic. It has been pointed out that the decision as to what is a "similar action of domestic nature" is sometimes far from obvious.[49]

Furthermore, the case law made clear that the mere equivalence of the applicable rules was as such not a guarantee that the requirements were satisfied. In *San Giorgio* the Court held in unequivocal terms that

> "the requirements of non-discrimination laid down by the Court cannot be construed as justifying legislative measures intended to render any repayment of charges levied contrary to Community law virtually impossible, even if the treatment is extended to tax payers who have similar claims arising from an infringement of national tax law."[50]

In other words, the requirements are cumulative and not alternative. Even if national procedural rules are applied without distinction, if they render nugatory the exercise of Community law rights the second requirement is clearly not satisfied.[51]

Once it is established that one or both of the requirements are not satisfied, the case law suggested that the national provisions concerned cannot be applied by the national court.[52]

[45] E.g. Case 199/82 *San Giorgio* [1983] ECR 3595 and, more recently, Joined Cases 331, 376 and 378/85 *Bianco* [1988] ECR 1099.

[46] E.g. Case 68/79 *Just* [1980] ECR 501.

[47] Cf. Oliver 1987, p. 887 with respect to Case 265/78 *Ferwerda* [1980] ECR 617.

[48] See however Joined Cases 66, 127 and 128/79 *Salumi* [1980] ECR 1237. Also Case 240/87 *Deville* [1988] ECR 3513 was in fact concerned with the application of the principle of non-discrimination.

[49] Cf. Steiner 1986, p. 103 and the opinion of A-G Jacobs, of 4 May 1994, in Case C-312/93 *Van Peterbroeck*, para. 20-27.

[50] Case 199/82 [1983] ECR 3595, para. 17. Cf. also Case 104/86 *Commission v. Italy* [1988] ECR 1799 and Joined Cases 331, 376 and 378/85 *Bianco* [1988] ECR 1099.

[51] Cf. also the opinion of A-G Van Gerven in Case C-271/91 *Marshall II* [1993] ECR I-4367, para. 15.

[52] Cf. Case 199/82 *San Giorgio* [1983] ECR 3595 where the Court found that "once it is established that the levying of the charge is incompatible with Community law, *the court must be free* to decide whether or not the burden of the charge has been passed on ... to other persons" (para. 14, emphasis added – SP). In Case 309/85 *Barra* [1988] ECR 355 the Court held with respect to a limitation period rendering impossible the exercise of Community law rights that "the national court ... must not apply such a provision of national law" (para. 20).

Parallel to this case law on minimum requirements to be met by national procedural law, which at that stage was rather limited both in scope and in depth of scrutiny, two other developments took place which should be mentioned briefly within the context of this Section.

Protection Prescribed by Directive 64/221

The first relates to case law which evolved around Article 48 (3) of the Treaty and the provisions of Directive 64/221 (public policy and public health),[53] in particular Article 8 of this. In a number of cases relating to the entry into and residence in the territory of Member States of persons covered by Community law, the Court made plain, in very clear terms, not only the pre-eminent importance to be attached to the legal protection of the persons concerned as ensured by the Directive, but also what the implications of the relevant provisions might be.

Thus, for instance, in *Royer*[54] the Court pointed out that immediate expulsion is, in principle,[55] incompatible with the Directive, as it would deprive the person concerned of the opportunity of effectively making use of the remedies guaranteed by Articles 8 and 9 of the Directive.

In *Pecastaing*[56] the Court explained what was meant by the principle of non-discrimination with respect to remedies as laid down in Article 8: the Member States cannot render the right of appeal for those covered by the Directive conditional on particular requirements as to form or procedure which are less favourable than those pertaining to remedies available to nationals in respect of acts of the administration. On the other hand, in the opinion of the Court, this Article did not imply a right to remain in the territory of the Member State for the duration of the proceedings, provided however that the person "is able to obtain a fair hearing and to present his defence in full". Similarly, it found that Article 9 of the Directive[57] cannot be applied in such a way that its practical effect would be to restrict or render ineffective the remedies made available under Article 8.

These cases actually concerned the interpretation of particular provisions laid down in a directive. However, the approach of the Court illustrates nicely its willingness to give the provisions on protection of individuals a substantive meaning and to guarantee their effectiveness as much as possible.

[53] OJ English Spec. Ed. 1963-1964, p. 117.

[54] Case 48/75 [1976] ECR 497.

[55] Save in cases of urgency.

[56] Case 98/79 [1980] ECR 691.

[57] Which is complementary to Article 8 and gives certain minimum safeguards in order to compensate for some of the imperfections resulting from the application of Article 8, such as the absence of suspensory effect.

Rheinmühlen II and Simmenthal

The second development to be discussed concerned national procedural obstacles which, in the ultimate analysis, were also likely to impair the effectiveness of Community law but which were treated in a different way by the Court of Justice compared with those at issue in the *Rewe / Comet* and related cases.

In *Rheinmühlen II*[58] the Court of Justice turned down a procedural rule which fettered the discretion of the lower national court under Article 177 of the Treaty to request a preliminary ruling. According to the Court, a rule whereby a court is bound on a point of law by the rulings of the court superior to it and, consequently, is not able to refer matters to the Court of Justice, would compromise the application of Community law at all levels of the judicial system of the Member States. However, *Rheinmühlen II* was different from *Comet* and *Rewe* and related cases because the power limited by the national rule was a power stemming directly from Article 177. The principles defined in *Comet* and *Rewe* therefore did not apply.

Simmenthal,[59] which is usually considered to be a culmination of the doctrine of supremacy and direct effect making plain their ultimate consequences,[60] also concerned a crucial aspect of procedural law (and even constitutional law). The Court first spelled out that direct applicability means that rules of Community law must be fully and uniformly applied in all Member States, that the provisions are direct sources of rights and duties for all those affected thereby, and that this consequence also concerns any national court in its capacity as an organ of a Member State. Consequently, the Court held, after having also explained the meaning of the principle of supremacy, that the national court must

"in a case within its jurisdiction, apply Community law in its entirety and protect rights which the latter confers on individuals and must accordingly set aside any provision of national law which may conflict with it."[61]

The Court next turned to the national judge-made rule reserving to the Constitutional Court the power to set aside provisions of national law contrary to Community law. In this respect it found that any rule

"which might impair the effectiveness of Community law by withholding from the national court having jurisdiction to apply such law the power to do everything necessary at the moment of its application to set aside national legislative provisions which may prevent

[58] Case 166/73 [1974] ECR 33.
[59] Case 106/77 [1978] ECR 629.
[60] Cf. Pescatore 1983, p. 156, Barav 1991, p. 9.
[61] Case 106/77 *Simmenthal* [1978] ECR 629, para. 21.

Community rules from having full force and effect [is] incompatible with these requirements, which are the very essence of Community law."[62]

Thus in *Simmenthal* the Court stated clearly that for the sake of effectiveness of Community law a national rule relating to the power of the national court had to be disregarded by the national court *a quo*. Remarkably, the reasoning of the Court of Justice did not follow the same line as in *Rewe* and *Comet*, leaving domestic procedural law more or less intact and, where necessary, focussing on the minimum requirement of effectiveness, although there was no doubt that the rule laid down by the Constitutional Court made the exercise of Community law rights virtually impossible.[63] Instead, it approached the problem in terms of consequences for the national judge of direct effect and supremacy of Community law, with a considerably more far-reaching outcome, which resulted in empowering the national court to do something it was unable to do under national law.

The judgment in *Simmenthal* is deceptive in that the Court of Justice refers to the national court "having jurisdiction" or to "the limits of its jurisdiction" in the *dictum*. At first sight this could suggest that there was jurisdiction to apply Community law but the national rule prevented the court from exercising it. Wyatt has very cogently argued, however, that

"the very problem which had arisen in the national court had arisen because national law was withholding jurisdiction from the national court to apply Community law in the case before it."[64]

Therefore the jurisdiction referred to by the Court of Justice is solely subject matter jurisdiction. Jurisdiction, or power, to apply the regulation at issue was lacking.[65] Yet it is difficult to understand how direct effect and supremacy of Community law, or its full effectiveness, or Article 5 of the Treaty to which the Court implicitly refers[66] can *create powers* for the national courts which did not exist before. However this might be, *Simmenthal* remained an isolated case in this respect for the next 12 years until the judgment in *Factortame* was given, which again raised comparable problems.[67]

[62] *Ibid.*, para. 22.

[63] *Ibid.*, Report for the Hearing, p. 633-635, in particular the fact that the "cumbersome and complex" procedure leads to a declaration of unconstitutionality with an only partial retroactive effect.

[64] Wyatt 1989, p. 208. Cf. also Abraham 1989, p. 182-183.

[65] Wyatt 1989, p. 209. For a comparable reference to "areas within their jurisdiction" see also Joined Cases C-6/90 and C-9/90 *Francovich* [1991] ECR I-5357, para. 32.

[66] Case 106/77 *Simmenthal* [1978] ECR 629, para. 16.

[67] Case C-213/89 [1990] ECR I-2433. Cf. also below, Subsections 8.3.4 and 8.3.5.

Contradictions in the Court's Approaches?

Another issue which has not yet been entirely clarified relates to a contradiction, or at least a tension, between cases like *Rewe* and *Comet* on the one hand and *Simmenthal* on the other.[68] In the former type of cases direct effect and supremacy are equally compromised by the application of a rule limiting the power of a domestic court which has to safeguard the full force and effect of Community law.[69] Persons who have not brought action within the period established by national law to seek protection of their Community law rights or who see their action frustrated by the application of the principle of unjust enrichment[70] are *de facto* denied a remedy for breaches of Community law by the Member State or by other individuals, as the case may be. Why in some cases the Court follows the line set out in *Simmenthal*, while in other cases it applies the minimum principles laid down in *Comet* and *Rewe* is somewhat puzzling.[71]

One possible explanation for the difference in approach could lie in the fact that the principles underlying *Rewe / Comet* and related cases, i.e. the principle of legal certainty and the principle of unjust enrichment, are to be considered as legitimate limitations to the applications of the principle of direct effect[72] (or legitimate *vis-à-vis* the Community legal order in general), while there was no such general principle of law at the origin of the rule at issue in *Simmenthal*. Similarly, it can be argued that the national rules under consideration in the *Rewe / Comet* type cases were regarded more as ancillary questions,[73] or rules limiting in certain respects the exercise of the rights. Having merely a "procedural dimension", therefore, they could in principle be left to national law. The limitation of the power of the national court in *Simmenthal*, however, was considered to be incompatible with the Community legal order as such, since it amounted to an almost absolute bar.[74] Its application would go so far as to challenge the very principles of supremacy and direct effect. In other words, it was a matter of concern regarding Community constitutional law.

[68] Cf. also Cases like *Factortame* and *Francovich* where it was pleaded that it was a matter of national law whether and under what conditions a certain type of action can be brought. The Court, however, took a different approach.

[69] Or, in the terms of Mertens de Wilmars (1981, p. 381), they affect the "*effet utile de l'effet direct*".

[70] As was, for instance, the situation in Case 68/79 *Just* [1980] ECR 501 and several subsequent cases. Cf. also Oliver 1987, p. 889.

[71] *Rewe* and *Comet* are still "good" law. See e.g. Joined Cases C-31/91 to C-44/91, *Lageder and Others*, [1993] ECR I-1761.

[72] Cf. also below, Chapter 11, Subsection 11.5.2.

[73] Cf. Case 130/79 *Express Dairy Foods* [1980] ECR 1887, para. 17.

[74] Cf. the opinion of A-G Jacobs, of 4 May 1994, in Case C-312/93 *Peterbroeck*, para. 43.

STAFFS UNIVERSITY LIBRARY

In some cases[75] it seems that the Court of Justice made an attempt to reconcile the *Comet / Rewe* approach and the *Simmenthal* approach. On the one hand it stressed, under reference to *Simmenthal*, that (directly effective) rules of Community law must be fully and uniformly applied in all Member States from the date of their entry into force and for so long as they continue in force. On the other hand it held that the safeguard of the rights conferred upon individuals by those rules does not necessarily require a uniform rule common to the Member States relating to the formal and substantive conditions for the recovery of charges levied in violation of Community law. The Court continued by explaining the immense variety of rules governing the recovery within the Member States and wound up with a reference to the *Comet / Rewe* principles. The result of this approach was in fact the acceptance of the "special features of national laws"[76] which govern the recovery of unduly paid charges. This acceptance can be explained by the fact that the Court found it beyond its jurisdiction to give *positive rules* in this respect, as that would amount to transgressing the boundaries of its own role. Or, as the Court put it in *Express Dairy Foods*:

"It is not for the Court to issue general rules of substance or procedural provisions which only the competent institutions may adopt."[77]

The difference from *Simmenthal* boils down to the distinction between, on the one hand, setting aside a single rule and, on the other, designing a general set of positive rules which should govern the recovery of unduly paid charges or other actions in national courts.

8.2.2 The Principle of Effective Judicial Protection

For some considerable time the Court of Justice did not spell out what is meant by the requirements "not less favourable" or "virtually impossible" laid down in *Comet* and *Rewe*.[78] Neither did it indicate in more concrete terms what constitutes direct, immediate and effective protection as required in *Salgoil* and *Bozetti*.[79] The early case law did not extend deeply in these respects. More

[75] Cf. Case 61/79 *Denkavit* [1980] ECR 1205, Case 826/79 *Mireco* [1980] ECR 2559 and Case 811/79 *Ariette* [1980] ECR 2545.

[76] Case 826/79 *Mireco* [1980] ECR 2559, para. 15.

[77] Case 130/79 [1980] ECR 1887, para. 12.

[78] Case 45/76 [1976] ECR 2043 and Case 33/76 [1976] ECR 1989. For discussion of the principles see above, Subsection 8.2.1.

[79] Case 13/68 [1968] ECR 453 and Case 179/84 [1985] ECR 2301. For discussion of these requirements see above, Subsection 8.2.1.

recently, however, national judicial protection and the function assigned in this context to national courts has become the focus of particular attention on the part of the Court of Justice.

The new leading principle of the Court's case law seems to be the *principle of effective judicial protection* identified *expressis verbis* in the landmark judgment in the case of Mrs. *Johnston,*[80] following a prelude given in *Von Colson.*[81] In *Johnston* the Court objected to an evidential rule in the Sex Discrimination (Northern Ireland) Order 1976 which rendered judicially unreviewable a decision of the Chief Constable of the Royal Ulster Constabulary and, consequently, deprived Mrs. Johnston of any remedy. The central provision of this (part of the) judgment was Article 6 of Directive 76/207.[82] With respect to this Article the Court of Justice held the following:

"The requirement of judicial control stipulated by that article reflects a general principle of law which underlies the constitutional traditions common to the Member States. That principle is also laid down in Articles 6 and 13 of the European Convention for the Protection of Human Rights and Fundamental Freedoms of 4 November 1950. As the European Parliament, Council and Commission recognized in their Joint Declaration of 5 April 1977 (Official Journal, no. C 103, p. 1) and as the Court has recognized in its decisions, the principles on which that Convention is based must be taken into consideration in Communty law.

By virtue of Article 6 of Directive no. 76/207, interpreted in the light of the general principle stated above, all persons have the right to obtain an effective remedy in a competent court against measures which they consider to be contrary to the principle of equal treatment for men and women laid down in the directive. It is for the Member States to ensure effective judicial control as regards compliance with the applicable provisions of Community law and of national legislation intended to give effect to the rights for which the directive provides."[83]

The Court's statement that Article 6 reflects a general principle of law proved to be crucial for the further application of the principle in areas of Community law where no such principle existed in a codified form. Moreover, it is similarly important to note in this context that the principle does not apply solely where a person relies *directly* on provisions of a directive, but also where the national law provisions implementing the directive are invoked and applied. In other words, even if a directive which – in contrast to Directive 76/207 – does not contain a provision relating to judicial protection, is as such correctly implemented in

[80] Case 222/84 [1986] ECR 1651.

[81] Case 14/83 [1984] ECR 1891: sanction chosen by the Member State must be such as to guarantee real and effective judicial protection. Cf. above, Chapter 5, Subsection 5.2.4.

[82] OJ 1976, L 39/40.

[83] Case 222/84 [1986] ECR 1651, para. 18-19.

national law, the Member States must ensure that the rights *under the national implementing measures* can be asserted by judicial process by the individuals concerned. The absence of such a possibility will amount to inadequate implementation.[84]

The principle of effective judicial protection seems to be a *self-standing general principle of law* rather than a corollary to direct effect of Community law provisions.[85] The underlying rationale is the fact that in a Community based on the rule of law everyone must have the opportunity to assert, on his own initiative, his rights before the courts.[86] Moreover, the protection provided must be *effective*. From this point of view the new principle can be considered as an expansion of the principle of effectiveness as laid down earlier in *Rewe* and *Comet*,[87] which in the *Johnston* case was given a specific basis, namely the constitutional traditions of the Member States and the ECHR. On the other hand, there are grounds for not considering the principle of effectiveness and the principle of effective judicial protection as one and the same thing. In *Verholen*,[88] for instance, both principles figure alongside each other in the judgment. Furthermore, it should be noted that the principle of effectiveness has a much broader scope of application. It may also be relevant for the imposition of sanctions upon individuals,[89] for instance, or for the way in which collection of Community charges from the individual is organized.[90]

In accordance with its *general* nature the principle has now been extended to other areas of Community law, even to those where it does not exist in a codified form, as it does in the area of equal treatment of men and women. A few months after *Johnston*, this newly discovered principle appeared in *Heylens* in the field of free movement of workers, where the Court held, under reference to *Johnston*, that

[84] Cf. above, Chapter 5, Subsection 5.2.4.

[85] As it was considered in the past. Cf. above, Section 8.1. However, Bleckmann (1976, p. 486) for instance construed the requirement of effective judicial protection on the basis of Article 5 EEC.

[86] Cf. the opinion of A-G Van Gerven in Case C-70/88 *European Parliament v. Council* [1990] ECR I-2071, para. 6. On the principle of effective judicial protection in general see also Dubouis 1988.

[87] Cf. Kapteyn 1993, p. 43.

[88] Joined Cases C-87/90, C-88/90 and C-89/90 [1991] ECR I-3757.

[89] Cf. above, Chapter 5, Subsection 5.2.4 and, in particular, Case 68/88 *Commission v. Greece* [1989] ECR 2965.

[90] Cf. Joined Cases 66, 127 and 128/79 *Salumi* [1980] ECR 1237, para. 20, Case 54/81 *Fromme* [1982] ECR 1449, para. 6 and, more recently, Case C-290/91 *Peter* [1993] ECR I-2981, para. 8.

"the existence of a remedy of a judicial nature against any decision of a national authority refusing the benefit of that right[91] is essential in order to secure for the individual effective protection of his right."[92]

The absence of appropriate judicial proceedings would amount to a violation of Article 48 of the Treaty.[93] The principle as applied in *Heylens* was subsequently transposed to the area of freedom of establishment.[94]

A similar development can be found in the Court's case law on free movement of goods, although in this area the Court did not explicitly rely on the principle of effective judicial protection. Here the requirement of judicial protection is construed as stemming from Article 30 of the Treaty and the principle of proportionality.[95]

In order to constitute a legitimate exception to the prohibition in Article 30 of the Treaty, national measures at issue must, firstly, aim at the protection of certain valid interests, such as human health under Article 36 or protection of the consumers under the "*Cassis de Dijon rule*".[96] Secondly, they must also meet the principle of proportionality, i.e. they must not go further than necessary for the achievement of the objective pursued. In the cases referred to above the Court found that decisions taken by the national administration under national legislative provisions (for instance, a refusal to grant an authorization for importation) cannot be considered as satisfying the principle of proportionality if the persons concerned have no opportunity to challenge the decision before the courts.

In my opinion, an approach based on *Heylens* is to be preferred. Article 30 grants a right to individuals which must be adequately protected by the courts. The principle of effective judicial protection implies, as it did in *Heylens*, the necessity of a control of legality "*au regard du droit communautaire*" by a competent court of any decision touching upon this right.[97] Although the above-mentioned reasoning of the Court may fit into the logic of the case law on Article 30, at first sight it is rather complex. It is not immediately clear how the requirement of judicial protection can follow from the principle of proportionality. Moreover, from the point of view of a uniform approach to issues relating to judicial protection, one single strategy should be followed.

[91] I.e. free access to employment which is "a fundamental right which the Treaty confers individually on each worker".

[92] Case 222/86 [1987] ECR 4097, para. 14.

[93] *Ibid.*, para. 17.

[94] Cf. Case C-340/89 *Vlassopoulou* [1991] ECR I-2357, Case C-104/91 *Borrell* [1992] ECR I-3003, Case C-19/92, *Kraus* [1993] ECR I-1663.

[95] Case 178/84 *Commision v. Germany* [1987] ECR I-1227, Case C-18/88 *RTT* [1991] ECR I-5941, and Case C-42/90 *Bellon* [1990] ECR I-4863. Cf. also Jans 1993a, p. 200.

[96] Case 120/78 [1979] ECR 649.

[97] Cf. also the opinion of A-G Darmon in Case C-18/88 *RTT* [1991] ECR I-5941, para. 21.

The potential impact of the principle of effective judicial protection and its extension to Community law in general is likewise illustrated by cases concerning the protection of individuals and, where appropriate, even Member States against Community institutions.[98] In this area an approach of this kind can be found, for instance, in the Court's judgments dealing with the question whether a "preparatory" decision constitutes an act which can be challenged under Article 173 of the Treaty. In *AKZO*, for instance, the Court found that the Commission decision at issue in that case[99] did in fact constitute such an act, since

"the opportunity which the applicant has to bring an action against a final decision establishing that the competititon rules have been infringed is not of such a nature as to provide it with an adequate degree of protection of its rights in the matter."[100]

The principle having thus been established in the mid-eighties, it has since been applied by the Court of Justice in different types of cases which illustrate the possible implications of the requirement that the protection should be *effective*. The cases can be divided into three main groups, according to the aspects to which they relate. However, before turning to the discussion of these three categories of cases in the next Section, it should be noted that the principle of effective judicial protection has also strongly influenced the Court's case law on sanctions for breaches of Community law or of rules intended to implement Community law. This subject has already been discussed above, in Chapter 5, Subsection 5.2.4.

8.3 The Shortcomings of the System and the Court's Responses

8.3.1 Introduction

The conception of the Court of Justice of the judicial protection of individuals in the national courts has been quite cogently described by Barav[101] as a kind of obligation of result, leaving the courts the choice of the procedures and means by which this result has to be achieved, fully respecting the institutional and

[98] Or even in cases involving disputes of institutions *inter se*. Cf. the opinion of A-G Van Gerven in Case C-70/88 *European Parliament v. Council* [1990] ECR I-2041, para. 3 and para. 6.

[99] I.e. Commission decision to communicate documents of a confidential nature to a third party who had submitted a complaint.

[100] Case 53/85 [1986] ECR 1965, para. 20. For other direct actions in which the requirement of effective judicial protection played a part see e.g. Case C-312/90 *Spain v. Commission* [1992] ECR I-4117, Case 169/84 *Cofaz* [1986] ECR 391, Case C-152/88 *Sofrimport* [1990] ECR I-2477, Case T-24/90 *Automec* [1992] ECR II-2223.

[101] Barav 1991, p. 9.

procedural autonomy of the Member States. The same author[102] has similarly pointed out that the Court's conception of the task to be assumed by national courts is based upon two presumptions: firstly, the existence of courts having jurisdiction and having the necessary powers to safeguard rights which derive from Community law; and secondly, the availability of appropriate procedures and remedies[103] which offer the individuals concerned access to justice and the opportunity to assert in an effective manner the protection of their rights. It is against this background that one must consider the Court's judgment in the "*Butter-buying cruises*" case, where it held that Community law was not intended to create new remedies, although at the same time it must be possible for every type of action provided for by national law to be available for the purposes of ensuring observance of Community provisions.[104] By now, however, it has appeared on several occasions that the mere reference to national procedures and remedies could be inadequate. The relevant national rules may contain certain lacunas and weaknesses which may preclude the national court from accomplishing the task assigned to it and this may accordingly compromise the effectiveness of the protection of individuals.[105] If this is the case, an adaptation of the existing national rules with a view to giving full and effective protection to the individuals concerned will be indispensable.[106] Moreover, it has been argued that in certain circumstances the ultimate consequence could be the creation of a new remedy.[107]

The shape which this adaptation should take will obviously depend on the concrete circumstances of the case. For this reason, on the basis of cases decided by the Court of Justice up to now, only a number of general indications can be given in this respect. Two features which the cases have in common are the far-reaching intervention by the Court into what was believed to be the province of the Member States' procedural autonomy and the high quality of the solutions

[102] Barav 1991, p. 14.

[103] The dichotomy "procedures and remedies" is made here purposely. The term "remedies" can basically mean two things. Firstly, the means provided by the law to recover rights or to obtain redress, relief etc. In this sense the term "remedies" is usually translated into the French "*voies de recours*". Cf. Case 158/80 *Butter-buying cruises* [1981] ECR 1805, para. 44. Secondly, it may denote the (form of) relief or redress given by a court. I will use the term "remedy" in this latter (narrow) sense.

[104] Case 158/80 [1981] ECR 1805.

[105] Barav 1991, p. 14, Simon 1991, p. 484. For an overview of the development of the Court's case law see also Jacobs 1994.

[106] Cf. (already) Mertens de Wilmars 1969, p. 81. Cf. also the opinion of A-G Mischo in Joined Cases C-6/90 and C-9/90 *Francovich* [1991] ECR I-5337, para. 49.

[107] See below, Subsection 8.3.4.

imposed. By analogy with the "second generation answers",[108] it is very appropriate to call them "third generation solutions".[109]

The Court's case law can be divided into three groups. In the first place there are cases which relate to the initial stage of a procedure. The central issues here are those concerning different aspects of the *access to judicial process*. The second group of cases concerns the rules applicable *during the proceedings* and has up to now concerned evidential rules. More recently, a new problem has been submitted to the Court of Justice which can also be classified within this category: the question as to whether the national court is obliged to apply Community law of its own motion. Thirdly, there are cases in which the *remedial aspects* are the focus of attention. The subdivision of the case law may actually seem somewhat arbitrary. In my view, however, it helps to present matters in a structured way.

8.3.2 Access to Judicial Process

As regards the first group of cases, it has already been noted that Community law requires the existence of *a* court having jurisdiction.[110] It does not, however, interfere with the organization of the courts and the division of the jurisdiction of the judicial bodies within the Member States. Whether the remedy is to be sought from ordinary courts, administrative courts or otherwise specialized courts is left to the national legal system.[111] On the other hand the access to the courts as such and even the stage before the judicial process starts may be governed by certain requirements imposed by Community law. Thus in *Heylens*,[112] the principle of effective judicial protection produced effects in the prelitigation stage, as the Court obliged the competent authorities to give reasons for the decision at issue, either in the decision itself or subsequently, upon request of the individuals affected. According to the Court, the latter must be able to defend their rights under the best possible conditions and to decide with full knowledge of the relevant facts whether there is any point in bringing a case in a court.[113]

[108] See above, Section 8.2.

[109] Cf. Curtin and Mortelmans 1994, p. 433.

[110] See above, Subsection 8.2.1.

[111] Provided, however, that the protection given is effective. As to the Member States' latitude, see e.g. Case 98/79 *Pecastaing* [1980] ECR 691, para. 11.

[112] Case 222/86 [1987] ECR 4097.

[113] The obligation to give reasons is also explicitly laid down in a number of directives. See e.g. Directive 73/239 (insurance other than life assurance I), OJ 1973, L 228/3, Directive 64/221 (public policy and public health), OJ English Spec. Ed. 1963-1964, p. 117, Directive 92/59 (product safety), OJ 1992, L 228/14, Directive 92/50 (public service contracts), OJ 1992, L 209/1, Directive 90/313 (information on environment), OJ 1990, L 158/6, Directive 92/53 (type-approval of motor vehicles), OJ 1992, L 225/1, Directive 84/532 (construction plants), OJ 1984, L 300/111.

Another issue within the sphere of *conditions* under which the right to access to justice is exercised and on which Community law could potentially have an effect is the availability of legal aid. In the literature it has been suggested that the absence of legal aid or the existence of very strict conditions for allowing legal aid, could *de facto* render nugatory the principle of effective judicial protection.[114]

Access to the courts in the stricter sense of the term usually depends on the satisfaction of a number of requirements, such as *locus standi* on the part of the applicant, i.e. the person's right to bring an action or challenge a decision, which is usually described in terms of the individual's interest in the matter.[115] Similarly, the nature of the decision being challenged is relevant, as are the time limits for bringing proceedings. In principle, these matters are, according to the *Rewe / Comet* case law,[116] governed by national law. Yet, as demonstrated by some relatively recent cases, Community law does not leave these matters entirely unaffected either.

Locus Standi

In the *Verholen*[117] case one of the questions referred to the Court of Justice asked whether in proceedings before a national court an individual could rely on Directive 79/7 (equal treatment in statutory schemes of social security)[118] if he suffered the effects of a discriminatory national provision regarding his spouse, although she herself was not, and according to national law could not be, a party to the proceedings. The Court answered the question in the affirmative.

It found that persons other than those falling within the personal scope of the Directive may also have a direct interest in ensuring that the principle of non-discrimination is respected as regards persons who are protected, and therefore the former must be able to rely on the Directive in question. In this respect the Court stressed that it was in principle for national law to determine an individual's standing and legal interest in bringing proceedings. Nevertheless, Community law required that national legislation should not restrict the right to effective judicial protection and its application could not render virtually impossible the exercise of the rights conferred by Community law.

[114] Cf. Herbert 1993, p. 61-63.

[115] Obviously, the interest required and the test applied may vary considerably from Member State to Member State and even between the different types of proceedings within one single Member State.

[116] Case 33/76 [1976] ECR 1989 and Case 45/76 [1976] ECR 2043, discussed above, in Subsection 8.2.1.

[117] Joined Cases C-87/90, C-88/90 and C-89/90 [1991] ECR I-3757, confirmed in Case C-343/92 *Roks* [1994] ECR I-571.

[118] OJ 1979, L 6/24.

The inferences to be drawn from this judgment are that Community law requirements may influence national standing rules and that, in the ultimate analysis, the persons concerned should, under certain circumstances, be given *locus standi*, even in situations where they have no standing under national law, if this is necessary for safeguarding effective judicial protection.

Although until now the question has scarcely been raised,[119] delineating the class of persons who should be allowed to bring an action in pursuance of Community law requirements is not always unproblematic. It will often be possible to establish on the basis of the relevant Community law provisions which persons are to be protected and, consequently, should be able to bring an action. This can be the case because a provision gives an explicit statement in this respect.[120] Similarly, few problems will arise when the personal scope of, for instance, a directive can be deduced from its actual text. As a rule, persons falling within the personal scope of the directive will be sufficiently affected by the misapplication or non-application of the provisions which give them some advantage or right. Since they will then have an interest in the judicial decision which they are striving to obtain, they should be given standing.[121] With respect to some directives, however, it may be quite difficult to establish which (categories of) persons are protected and should accordingly be able to bring an action or challenge a decision. This is for instance *and* in particular the case with respect to environmental law directives, since these directives often aim at protecting the environment as such rather than being concerned with securing advantages to individual members of given classes separately.[122] Furthermore, if it appears

[119] Cf. Oliver 1992, p. 360. Relatively recently, however, attention has been paid to issues related to *locus standi* by some authors. See e.g. Jans 1993a and Jans 1993b, Kraemer, 1992, p. 173/176, Geddes 1992, Ward 1993, p. 232-235, Herbert 1993, p. 36-48. Cf. also the opinion of A-G Capotorti in Case 158/80 *Butter-buying cruises* [1981] ECR 1805, para. 6.

[120] Cf. Article 6 of Directive 76/207 (equal treatment at work), OJ 1976, L 39/40: "all persons who consider themselves wronged by sex discriminaton ..." and Article 12 of Directive 92/28 (advertising of medicinal products), OJ 1992, L 113/13, which provides that persons or organizations regarded under national law as having a legitimate interest in prohibiting any advertisement inconsistent with the Directive must be able to take legal action. A similar provision can also be found in Article 7(2) of Directive 93/13 (consumer contracts), OJ 1993, L 95/29. Cf. also Directive 90/313 (information on environment), OJ 1990, L 158/56, Article 3 (any legal or natural person must obtain information).

[121] As to the identification of persons falling within the scope of a directive see e.g. Case 115/78 *Knoors* [1979] ECR 399, Joined Cases C-6/90 and C-9/90 *Francovich* [1991] ECR I- 5357 and Case C-91/92 *Faccini Dori* [1994] ECR I-3325.

[122] Cf. Jans 1992, p. 6 ff.

that the directive is protecting some interest of the public at large, it is not self-evident that consequently everybody should be given standing.[123]

Be this as it may, the scope of the Court's case law is not limited to those within the personal scope of the directive. In the *Van Duyn*[124] case the Court found in very general terms that *persons concerned* must have the opportunity to rely on (directly effective) provisions of a directive. From *Verholen*[125] we learn that also those having a direct interest in the application of a directive's provision (in this case with respect to persons who *do* fall within its personal scope) must be able to rely on it, which in fact entails that they should be given *locus standi* in a court having jurisdiction. In other words, from *Verholen* it follows that the category of "persons concerned" includes those who have a direct interest in the application of the rules and not merely those who are directly protected by the rules at issue. Furthermore, in my view, the principles which can thus be deduced from Community law do not apply solely where an individual wishes to rely *directly* on the directive in questions but also where the person brings an action under the national law transposing the directive. A different solution would lead to an anomaly, namely, as long as the person was invoking the directive he would have standing, while as soon as he relied on national law (with Community origins) his *locus standi* would potentially be curtailed. When a directive is being implemented, therefore, a part of the implementation process should relate to amendments of national standing rules if this seems necessary from the Community law point of view.

The questions of who should be considered as "persons concerned" by Community law provisions and, thus, what degree of interest is necessary and what the appropriate test for standing should be are to be decided under Community law and ultimately by the Court of Justice. However, according to the principles rehearsed in *Verholen*, the Member States are left discretion as to the question of an individual's standing. The only provisos are that the applicable rules must not render the exercise of the rights virtually impossible and they must observe the requirement of effective judicial protection. It is submitted that when deciding whether these limits have been transgressed in a particular case, the Court of Justice will take into account the entire system of judicial protection under the national law of the Member State concerned in order to ascertain whether the requirement of effective judicial protection remains safeguarded or

[123] Cf. A-G Jacobs who remarked in his opinion in Case C-58/89, [1991] ECR I-4983, para. 34, that "the public at large, as well as ecologists and environmental pressure groups, have a general interest in water quality and indeed in the respect of Community law. It does not however automatically follow that enforceable rights must be made available to them in national courts". Arguably, it also does not follow that those having "general interest" must be given standing.

[124] Case 41/74 [1974] ECR 1337.

[125] Joined Cases C-87/90, C-88/90 and C-89/90 [1991] ECR I-3757.

not.[126] Moreover, proper account should also be taken of the functions of the respective standing rules[127] and they should be weighed against the two requirements.

The final remark regarding *locus standi* relates to the "*air and groundwater*" cases[128] discussed above in Chapter 7, Subsection 7.3.4. In these cases the Court found that whenever the exceeding of the limit values laid down in the directives could endanger human health, the persons concerned must be able to rely on mandatory rules in order to be able to assert their rights. In the literature it has been submitted that,[129] or at least questioned whether,[130] the Court in fact requires an *actio popularis*, i.e. that in principle every person should have the right to bring an action. In my view, this conclusion goes too far. The Court's judgment focussed on the fact that the directives had not been transposed into mandatory rules of national law in the Member States concerned and this fact alone meant there was no guarantee that the implementing measures taken could be relied upon by individuals, since their binding nature and their ability to produce "external" effects was doubtful.[131] As such the judgment says little about the category of persons who should be able to bring an action once the limits have been exceeded. It merely refers to "the persons concerned". The Court has not yet determined who should be considered as the persons concerned and, consequently, should have standing;[132] this will, in turn, depend on the measures enacted.[133]

[126] The absence of standing in a certain type of procedure does not *eo ipso* mean that there is no effective judicial protection: the individual concerned has for instance standing in another type of procedure.

[127] As to the function of standing rules see Cane 1986, p. 165-166. Cf. also the opinion of A-G Capotorti in Case 158/80 *Butter-buying cruises* [1981] ECR 1805, para. 6.

[128] Case C-361/88 *Commission v. Germany* [1991] ECR I-2567, Case C-59/89 *Commission v. Germany* [1991] ECR I-2607, Case C- 58/89 *Commission v. Germany* [1991] ECR I-4983.

[129] Cf. Jans 1993a, p. 205-206 and Jans 1993b, p. 158.

[130] Cf. Everling 1992a, p. 384-385 and Everling 1993; p. 214-215.

[131] On the (alleged) absence of legally binding nature and "external" effects see above, Chapter 5, Subsection 5.2.3.

[132] Langenfeld 1992, p. 962, Zuleeg 1993, p.37, Everling 1993, p. 215.

[133] The cases at issue clearly suggest that the implementing measures should impose obligations upon "all those whose activities are liable to give rise to nuisances" or, respectively, upon "undertakings which abstract surface water for the purposes of supplying drinking water to the public". Therefore, it is submitted, there must be the possibility of some form of action against, for instance, authorizations or an action in the case of violation of the obligations imposed upon the undertakings concerned. However, who will be considered as "a person concerned" in this context is the next issue to be resolved. I do not believe that by stating that "wherever the exceeding of limit values could endanger human health" is to be understood as a right of action for everyone.

The Nature of the Challenged Act

As with the question of the individual's standing, Community law may also have implications for the conditions of admissibility of an action in which a *certain act* is challenged. In other words, the focus of attention in these cases is more the *nature of the act* at issue than the person of the applicant.

In the *Borrelli*[134] case the applicant brought an action for annulment against a decision of the Commission, by which the latter refused to grant the applicant aid from the EAGGF funds. The Commission did this in pursuance of a negative opinion of the Regional Council of Liguria. This negative opinion meant that one of the conditions required under the applicable rules had not been fulfilled: aid can only be granted if the competent national authorities give a favourable opinion. The principal ground of illegality submitted by the applicant was the alleged illegality of the negative opinion of the Regional Council. The applicant argued that if this illegality had no effect on the validity of the Commission's decision he would be deprived of all judicial protection, since the opinion, as a preparatory act, cannot be challenged under Italian law. Obviously the Court held that in Article 173 proceedings it has no jurisdiction as to the legality of an act of a national authority. The mere fact that the "national" opinion was a part of a process resulting in a Community decision could not alter this conclusion. On the other hand, the Commission was bound by the opinion of the national authorities and was also unable to control the legality. It was against this background that the Court considered that it is for the national courts to decide upon the legality of the act in question under the same conditions as those governing any final act which, when adopted by the same authority, is capable of affecting the interests of third parties. The national court had to consider as admissible the action brought for this purpose, even if the national procedural rules do not provide for this. In other words, an act against which no appeal could be made under national law had nevertheless to be considered as an act which could be appealed. The Court based this decision on the requirement of effective judicial protection as expounded in *Johnston* and *Heylens.*[135] Since the national opinion was integrated in a procedure which ultimately led to a decision under Community law, the Member State concerned was obliged to observe the requirement of effective judicial protection.

The more general implications of the judgment in *Borelli* are that under defined circumstances and with a view to safeguarding effective judicial protection a certain type of action must be declared admissible, even if no appeal against a comparable decision is possible under national law alone.[136]

[134] C-97/91 [1992] ECR I-6313.

[135] Case 222/84 [1986] ECR 1651 and Case 222/86 [1987] ECR 4097.

[136] Cf. also Case 53/85 *AKZO* [1986] ECR 1965, discussed above, in Subsection 8.2.2.

Time Limits

The last category of potential obstacles to access to judicial process which up to now have been addressed by the Court of Justice consists of the time limits for bringing action.

In principle, time limits – just as all other conditions governing (national) actions at law in which individuals enforce the rights they derive from Community law – are a matter which is left to national legal systems. The only two conditions to be satisfied are that the time limits are not less favourable than those for similar actions of a domestic nature and that they do not make impossible in practice the exercise of the rights conferred. In *Rewe* and *Comet* the Court found that "a reasonable period of limitation within which an action must be brought" in fact satisfies the latter requirement.[137] The Court pointed out in this respect that fixing a period of this kind is actually an application of the principle of legal certainty, which protects both the national authorities concerned and private individuals.

The finding that time limits serve the need to respect the principle of legal certainty was scarcely a surprise. As early as 1960 the Court found with respect to Article 33 of the ECSC Treaty that

> "the limitation period for bringing an action fulfils a generally recognized need, namely the need to prevent the legality of administrative decisions from being called into question indefinitely, and this means that there is a prohibition on reopening a question after the limitation period has expired."[138]

By accepting the existence of reasonable time limits for instituting proceedings in national courts for reasons of legal certainty the Court also accepted the consequences: in certain circumstances the individual will be deprived of the opportunity to enforce the rights which he derives from Community law. However, the Court apparently gave priority to the principle of legal certainty over the need for judicial protection of the individuals concerned *and* the full force and effect which Community law should have in national legal orders.

This apparently well-established rule was confirmed in several subsequent cases.[139] However, an important exception to it was created by the Court in the *Emmott*[140] case.

[137] Case 33/76 [1976] ECR 1989 and Case 45/76 [1976] ECR 2043. Cf. also Case C-208/90 *Emmott* [1991] ECR I-4269, para. 16.

[138] Case 3/59 *Germany v. High Authority* [1960] ECR 53, at p. 61. Cf. also 156/77 *Commission v. Belgium* [1978] ECR 1881, para. 23.

[139] Cf. Case 826/78 *Mireco* [1980] ECR 2559, Case 811/79 *Ariete* [1980] 2545. Cf. also Case 386/87 *Bessin and Salson* [1989] ECR 3551, which concerned time limits for submission of application for reimbursement with the competent authorities and not time limits for bringing action *stricto sensu*.

[140] Case C-208/90 [1991] ECR I-4269.

In brief, the case concerned the problem that by the time the applicant became aware of the possibility of claiming a certain social security benefit on the basis of Directive 79/7 (equal treatment in statutory schemes of social security)[141] the three-month time limit for bringing an action for judicial review under Irish law had expired. The question submitted to the Court was whether a Member State which has not correctly transposed the Directive at issue may preclude an individual from initiating proceedings on the ground that the above-mentioned time limit has expired. Instead of applying its established case law, the Court focussed on "the particular nature of directives". It referred to the cases on the necessity of proper implementation of directives[142] and stressed three central features of this case law. Firstly, the binding nature of directives as it follows from Article 189(3) of the Treaty. Secondly, the need for implementation of directives in a sufficiently clear and precise manner so that, where directives are intended to create rights for individuals, the latter are able to ascertain the full extent of those rights and, where necessary, to rely on them before the courts. Thirdly, the character of minimum guarantee provided by direct effect: the possibility of relying on the directive against the defaulting Member State does not absolve the Member State from its obligation to implement the directive fully. On the basis of these considerations the Court held that:

"So long as a directive has not been properly transposed into national law, individuals are unable to ascertain the full extent of their rights. That state of uncertainty for individuals subsists even after the Court has delivered a judgment finding that the Member State in question has not fulfilled its obligations under the directive and even if the Court has held that a particular provision or provisions of the directive are sufficiently precise and unconditional to be relied upon before a national court.

Only the proper transposition of the directive will bring that state of uncertainty to an end and it is only upon that transposition that the legal certainty which must exist if individuals are to be required to assert their rights is created."[143]

The Member State may therefore not rely on national time limits for initiating proceedings until the directive has been properly implemented. The period for bringing proceedings also cannot begin to run before that date.

The Court's judgment in *Emmott* was surprising for at least two reasons. In the first place it was prepared to depart from its – what was considered to be – firmly-rooted case law. According to some authors the judgment can hardly be reconciled with the line set out in *Comet*, *Rewe* and subsequent cases.[144] In the second place, it is noteworthy that the Court chose such a "broadbrush approach" covering potentially any instance of inadequate implementation. This

[141] OJ 1979, l 6/24. The eye-opener for Ms Emmott was the Court's judgment in Case 286/85 *McDermott and Cotter I* [1987] ECR 1453.
[142] Cf. above, Chapter 5.
[143] Case C-208/90 [1991] ECR I-4269, para. 21-22.
[144] Cf. Oliver 1992, p. 369.

is the more remarkable as several less far-reaching or less general solutions had been suggested to it.[145] In particular, the facts of the case offered sufficient elements for mitigating the harsh consequences of the *Rewe/Comet* line.[146]

It has been argued that the implicit reasoning of the Court in the *Emmott* case is similar to the principle of estoppel such as that developed in *Ratti*; i.e. a Member State which has not fulfilled its obligations to implement the directive in time or correctly may not rely on national law to deny individual rights in the national courts.[147] This is undoubtedly an important aspect of the case. However, in the Court's decision there is another implicit choice which may, in my view, explain the irreconcilability which at first sight exists between *Emmott* and the more "traditional" case law on limitation periods. The *Emmott* case in fact reveals a conflict of two modalities of the principle of legal certainty. Moreover, there was apparently a conflict between the principle of legal certainty and the principle of effective judicial protection. Firstly, on the one hand, the acceptance by the Court of Justice of the application of national time limits for bringing proceedings is justified by the need to ensure legal certainty in the sense of a certain legal situation not being called into question indefinitely. On the other hand, the Court's case law on implementation of directives is likewise inspired by the concern for legal certainty, namely the possibility for the individuals to ascertain the full extent of their rights.[148] The Court decided this conflict in favour of the second modality of the principle of legal certainty. Secondly, the Court balanced the first modality of legal certainty against the requirement of effective judicial protection which is, as observed in Chapter 5, in particular in Subsection 5.2.3, intimately linked to the principle of legal certainty in the sense of ascertainability of the rights.

To a large extent this point of view was more recently confirmed in the *Steenhorst-Neerings*[149] case. In this case the Court considered that the time-bar which results from the expiration of time limits serves to ensure that the legality of administrative decisions is not called into question indefinitely. However, according to the judgment in *Emmott* this need cannot prevail over the need to protect the rights an individual derives from directly effective provisions of a

[145] By A-G Mischo, para. 30 of the opinion and the Commission in its written observations: Report for the Hearing, p. I-4282-4283.

[146] I.e. dissuasive correspondence and misleading of the applicant by the competent national authorities.

[147] Case 148/78 [1979] ECR 1629. Cf. Szyszczak 1992b, p. 613.

[148] Cf. above, Chapter 5, Subsection 5.2.1.

[149] Case C-338/91 [1993] ECR I-5475.

directive as long as the defaulting Member State has not properly implemented the relevant provisions into national law.[150]

The question could be raised whether comparable considerations should not apply in cases involving Treaty provisions and regulations, which were at issue in cases like *Rewe* and *Comet*. The difference must, in my opinion, be sought in the different nature of regulations or Treaty provisions when compared with directives, which "particular nature" was stressed by the Court itself in *Emmott*. With respect to both categories it could be argued that the general principle "everyone must be assumed to know the law" applies fully. The EEC Treaty was published in the respective Member States upon ratification and regulations must be published in pursuance of Article 191 of the Treaty. Moreover, the Court's acceptance that both can impose obligations upon individuals implicitly presupposes that the persons concerned are also able to know those obligations. As explained above, the situation is different with respect to directives: these are binding only upon the Member States, until the entry into force of the Maastricht Treaty there was no obligation to publish them and they cannot as such impose obligations upon individuals:[151] hence the Court's requirements as to the proper implementation of directives, and its emphasis on the particular nature of directives in the *Emmott* judgment. Seen against this background, it can hardly be maintained that the above-mentioned general "presumption" should also apply with respect to directives. Yet it is this principle which justifies the sometimes harsh consequences of the *Rewe/Comet* case law.

The judgment in *Steenhorst-Neerings* is also important in another respect. This judgment made clear that the "*Emmott rule*" does not apply indiscriminately to all types of limitation periods, as was argued on the basis of the *Emmott* ratio.[152] Given the structure of this Section, I shall deal with *Steenhorst-Neerings* later,[153] since this case did not concern the potential limitation of the access to the courts. Here it suffices to point out that it follows from this judgment that the Court will take into account the purposes of the limitation period at issue and will weigh them against the leading principles expounded in *Emmott*; i.e. legal certainty in the sense of ascertainability and the need for effective judicial protection. As appears from *Steenhorst-Neerings*, other imperative needs may prevail over these two principles.

One issue remains to be addressed briefly here, namely the different kinds of limitation periods. Access to the courts (in the broad sense of the term) in the various Member States and even access to different courts within a single

[150] The question whether the Emmott rule fully applies also in *inter alia* a situation of incorrect (but putatively correct) implementation of a directive has been submitted to the Court in Case C-2/94 *Denkavit*, pending. For some other implications of *Emmott* see also Chapter 12, Subsection 12.5.2.

[151] Cf. above, Chapter 4, Section 4.2.

[152] Cf. Case C-338/91 *Steenhorst-Neerings* [1993] ECR I-5475, para. 17.

[153] See below, Subsection 8.3.4.

Member State is regulated in different ways. Several types of conditions often have to be satisfied before proceedings can be brought before a court. In administrative law, for instance, the requirement will quite often be posed that the individual concerned first makes a complaint to the competent authority. This complaint usually has to be made within a certain period of time. Similarly, where applications (e.g. for reimbursement or for a social security benefit) to an authority first have to be made, a certain time limit will often apply. In other words, in the prelitigation stage there are already time limits to be observed. The rules governing those time limits obviously do not directly concern a deadline for bringing an action before the courts. Indirectly, however, their expiry may have the same effect as the expiry of time limits for bringing proceedings.

Another common distinction relates to the nature of limitation periods. Some time limits, in particular time limits for bringing action in administrative law (*délai de recours*), are considered as procedural time limits in the strict sense of the term and they are relatively short. Other – often longer – limitation periods are periods of prescription (*délai de prescription*) which are more common in civil law. They may relate to the right of action or to the substantive right itself. Their observance will often not be treated as a matter of admissibility but rather as concerning the merits of the case.[154] Whatever their consequences might be under national law, the effect of the expiry of both types of limitation periods, as regards the possibility of asserting one's right in the courts, is similar.

Given all the possible varieties of limitation periods as they exist within the Member States and the differences in their legal classifications and in their application, the question arises as to the scope of application of the rule laid down in the *Emmott* judgment. In my view, all the national differences, which are often historically determined, cannot as such play a part. As soon as a certain type of limitation period constitutes *in its effect* a bar to, or a limitation on, obtaining a remedy in the courts it should be treated as falling within the *Emmott* rule. As long as the directive has not been properly implemented, the individual "is deemed" to be unaware of (the extent of) his right and, accordingly, unable to assert it. Once this has been established, the next question to be addressed is that relating to the purpose of the limitation period at issue. If the purpose is the observance of legal certainty protecting the State authorities, in pursuance of *Emmott* the protection of the individual will prevail. However, if the limitation

[154] Cf. as to the classification of the five-year limitation period of an action for damages under the E(E)C Treaty (Article 43 of the Statute of the Court of Justice) Heukels 1988, p. 97-98.

period serves another objective, it follows from *Steenhorst-Neerings* that balancing the two conflicting needs may lead to a different outcome.[155]

8.3.3 Rules Applicable During the Proceedings

Evidential Rules

On the borderline between the first category of cases and the second category of cases, which have so far been mainly limited to the rules of evidence, one can situate the *Johnston*[156] case. As explained above,[157] *Johnston* concerned an evidential rule according to which a certificate signed by or on behalf of the Secretary of State had to be treated as conclusive evidence. The rule prevented the national court from exercising any judicial control. Thus although Mrs. Johnston was not strictly speaking denied access to the court, her application was aborted at such an early stage and in such a way that it could be considered as tantamount to refusing her access to justice. The rule was found to be incompatible with the principle of effective judicial control as laid down in Article 6 of Directive 76/207 (equal treatment at work).[158]

There are, however, national rules of evidence with less draconian effects; i.e. they do not as such exclude judicial control but, on the other hand, the burden of proof falling upon a party may be extremely difficult to satisfy. In principle, as noted above,[159] in the absence of relevant rules of Community law,[160] the rules of evidence are governed by national law. The only requirements to be met are the requirements of non-discrimination and effectiveness. Likewise in its "early case law", as I have termed it, there are some instances in which the Court disapproved the burden of proof being placed upon the applicant, since it made the exercise of the rights derived from Community law virtually impossible.[161]

In some more recent case law the Court did not reiterate that evidential rules were a matter to be determined by national law, nor did it focus on the question

[155] However, the scope of *Steenhorst-Neerings* and, more importantly, the (alleged) irreconcilability of this case with *Emmott* was under discussion in Case C-410/92 *Johnson*, pending. The main arguments are summarized in the opinion of A-G Gulmann, of 1 June 1994. The A-G himself follows *Steenhorst-Neerings*.

[156] Case 222/84 [1986] ECR 1651.

[157] See above, Subsection 8.2.2.

[158] OJ 1976, L 39/40.

[159] Subsection 8.2.1.

[160] See however, for instance, Directive 85/374 (product liability), OJ 1985, L 210/29, which contains provisions as to the burden of proof and Directive 93/13 (consumer contracts), OJ 1993, L 95/29.

[161] Cf. Case 199/82 *San Giorgio* [1983] ECR 3595, Joined Cases 331, 376 and 378/85 *Bianco* [1988] ECR 1099.

whether the exercise of the rights was virtually impossible. The focal point was rather the principle of effective judicial protection, which in equal pay cases is embodied in Article 6 of Directive 75/117 (equal pay).[162]

In *Danfoss*[163] one of the questions submitted to the Court concerned the appropriate burden of proof for proving pay discrimination. The case related to a pay system which was "characterized by a total lack of transparency". The applicants could only establish that there was a difference between average pay paid to men and women but it was impossible to indicate whether the difference was caused by discrimination or not. The Court found that in such circumstances the applicants "would be deprived of any effective means of enforcing the principle of equal pay before national courts if the effect of adducing such evidence was not to impose upon the employer the burden of proving that his practice in the matter of wages is not, in fact, discriminatory".[164] In the Court's view the concern for effectiveness which underlies Article 6 of the Directive entails that the Directive "must be interpreted as implying adjustments to national rules on the burden of proof in special cases where such adjustments are necessary for the effective implementation of the principle of equal pay".[165]

The approach chosen by the Court in *Danfoss* was subsequently confirmed in *Enderby*.[166] Although in this case the Court's starting point was that "it is normally for the person alleging facts in support of a claim to adduce proof of such facts", it recalled that "the onus may shift when it is necessary to avoid depriving workers who appear to be the victims of discrimination of any effective means of enforcing the principle of equal pay". In *Enderby* the Court itself indicated the conditions for a *prima facie* case of sex discrimination. It continued by stating, relying "by analogy"[167] on *Danfoss*, that where there is a *prima facie* case the onus of proof shifts to the employer who must show that the pay differential is not in fact discriminatory.

Obviously, these cases concerned the interpretation of written provisions of Community law.[168] However, as the principle of effective judicial protection was declared by the Court to be a general principle of Community law, it is of general application. Consequently, it may also have implications for the rules of evidence applicable with respect to other issues arising under Community law.[169]

[162] OJ 1975, L 45/19.
[163] Case 109/88 [1989] ECR 3199.
[164] *Ibid.*, para. 13.
[165] *Ibid.*, para. 14.
[166] C-127/92 [1993] ECR I-5535.
[167] *Ibid.*, para. 18.
[168] Directive 75/117, Article 6 and Article 119 of the Treaty.
[169] For other interferences with evidential rules see e.g. Case 251/78 *Denkavit* [1979] ECR 3369, Case 124/83 *Corman* [1985] ECR 3777 and Case C-42/90 *Bellon* [1990] ECR I-4863. Cf. also Oliver 1992, p. 364.

Application of Community Law by the National Court of its Own Motion

The subject to be discussed here relates to the question whether a national court is obliged to apply Community law or take it into consideration for purposes of interpretation of national law in conformity therewith in a case before it where the parties have not presented any arguments drawing upon Community law provisions.

Some confusion has been caused in this respect by the Court's description of direct effect of directives, i.e. that individuals may rely upon the provisions concerned wherever they appear to be unconditional and sufficiently precise. This was possibly the background to the somewhat curious question[170] of a Dutch court which desired to know whether

"... Community law preclude[s] the national courts from reviewing (of their own motion) a national legal provision in the light of an EEC directive, ... , if an individual (possibly through ignorance) has not relied on the directive."[171]

Similarly, a case was reported from Germany where a *Finanz Gericht* found that the Sixth VAT-Directive could only be applied when the claimant relied on it explicitly.[172]

In *Verholen*[173] the Court of Justice made plain that Community law does not preclude a national court from examining of its own motion whether national rules are in conformity with directly effective provisions of a directive where the individual has not relied upon it in the court. It also follows from this judgment that the same applies *mutatis mutandis* when the court, of its own motion, wishes to proceed to an interpretation of national law in conformity with the directive at issue.

Whether the national court is under the duty to do so is quite another question. In *Verholen* A-G Darmon gave an affirmative answer. Basically he referred to the Community law obligation of national courts to apply directly effective provisions of Community law and the obligation to interpret national law in conformity with the latter. Furthermore, in his view

"The primacy of Community law cannot be left to the discretion of the national courts, without the risk of its *uniform* application being seriously compromised."[174]

[170] Cf. Prechal 1993, p. 168

[171] Joined Cases C-87/90, C-88/90 and C-89/90 *Verholen* [1991] ECR I-3757, at p. I-3786.

[172] See Fischer 1991.

[173] Joined Cases C-87/90, C-88/90 and 89/90 [1991] ECR I-3757.

[174] Joined Cases C-87/90, C-88/90 and C-89/90 [1991] ECR I-3757, para. 19.

In the literature the question has not yet been addressed in much detail. Several authors have suggested that national courts are under the obligation to apply Community law of their own motion, although the basis for such an obligation is scarcely discussed.[175] Apparently, it is common understanding that since Community law, including directives, forms a part of the legal norms valid within the Member State, the courts must apply it accordingly and where necessary of their own motion. Furthermore, the obligation seems to be reinforced by the principle of supremacy and the need for uniform application of Community law, as argued by A-G Darmon.

Another argument has been submitted by Lenaerts, who argues that Community law is "of public policy" (*d'ordre publique*) within the legal orders of the Member States and therefore the courts must apply it of their own motion.[176] Similarly, Bleckmann has pointed out that the parties to a contract cannot exclude the application of Community law provisions.[177] I cannot but agree with this latter point of view. On the other hand, it should be noted that derogation by contract from the rules laid down in a directive may be possible if the directive itself allows for it. This is however a matter of the *content* of the directive concerned.[178]

The question of obligatory application of Community law by national courts of their own motion is however much more complex. There is of course the obligation for the courts to apply directly effective Community law and, furthermore, to interpret national law in conformity with the latter. These obligations have been formulated with respect to cases where at least one of the parties was relying on the Community law provisions. However, the question whether a national court must apply Community law of its own motion is a distinct problem. It does not automatically follow from the obligations which have just been described that there is a duty for national courts to apply Community law provisions of their own motion. An unqualified obligation to apply Community law *ex officio* would, taken to its ultimate conclusion, involve that in every single case before it the national court had to examine whether some rule of Community law was applicable to the case or whether some Community provision had been violated. Indeed, one may dig up the old (and fairly

[175] Cf. Fuß 1981, p. 192, Bleckmann 1976, p. 486, Ress 1993, p. 360, Grabitz 1971, p. 21, Jarass 1991, p. 2669, Winter 1991b, p. 664, Fischer 1991, p. 561. On the other hand, the obligation has been denied by Weymüller 1991, p. 503 or it has been submitted that the case law is not clear in this respect: Classen 1993, p. 84. As to this issue cf. also (already) Kovar 1978, p. 266.

[176] Lenaerts 1993, p. 1105

[177] Bleckmann 1990, p. 184

[178] Cf. Case 324/86, *Daddy's Dance Hall*, [1988] ECR 739, para. 14-15 and, e.g. Article 6 of Directive 85/577 (contracts negotiated away from business premises), OJ 1985, L 372/31.

unrealistic) adage *iura novit curia*,[179] but this amounts to begging the question. In my view, the problem needs a balanced approach. A more appropriate way to deal with the matter is to seek alliance with the rules applicable within the Member States with respect to application of national law by the courts of their own motion. In this respect the principles of non-discrimination and effectiveness as laid down in *Rewe* and *Comet*[180] should apply, as well as, where appropriate, the principle of effective judicial protection. The last two of these principles may indeed mean that Community law must be applied by the courts of their own motion, even in situations where a similar application is not prescribed for rules of national law. Whether such an application must be required should depend, in my opinion, on issues like the nature of the provisions in question and their importance within the system of Community law. For instance, since the Court has labelled Article 119 as being of a mandatory nature,[181] there are grounds for arguing that a national court should apply this Article of its own motion. The same may be true with respect to the prohibition of discrimination on grounds of nationality or Articles 85 and 86 EC, given their fundamental importance for the functioning of the common market.

In summary, if and in so far as national law obliges the courts to apply national provisions of their own motion, i.e. without the parties having relied on them, the same should also hold true for Community law provisions. Nevertheless, some Community law provisions must be applied *ex officio* in any case. For the time being it is uncertain which these provisions are.

It is to be expected that some light will be shed on these issues in the near future by the Court itself. In a reference for a preliminary ruling the *Hoge Raad* is seeking to ascertain whether it should apply Articles 3(f), 5 and 85 to 86 and/or 90 of the EEC Treaty even where a party to the proceedings which has an interest in the application of those provisions has not relied upon them.[182]

The same case also raises another crucial (and closely related) question: may a national procedural principle bar the application of Community law by national courts of their own motion? In other words, even if it is assumed that there is an obligation for the courts to proceed to an application of Community law of their own motion, can this obligation be limited by national procedural rules or principles? The main problem in this case is that according to a principle of Dutch civil procedural law the ambit of the legal dispute before the court is determined by the arguments brought in by the parties. This so-called principle

[179] Cf. Lenaerts 1993, p. 1106.
[180] Case 33/76 [1976] ECR 1989 and Case 45/76 [1976] ECR 2043. Cf. above, Subsection 8.2.1.
[181] Case 43/75, *Defrenne II*, [1976] ECR 455. For directives see e.g. Case 324/86 *Daddy's Dance Hall* [1988] ECR 739.
[182] Joined Cases C-430/93 and C-431/93, *Van Schijndel*, pending.

of passivity of the judge is intimately linked with the autonomy of parties in civil law.[183]

A similar problem was addressed by A-G Jacobs in another case currently pending before the Court of Justice.[184] According to the Belgian Income Tax Code, an argument based on Community law cannot be considered by the national court if the taxable person has not raised it within a certain prescribed period.

Obviously, these types of rules limit the possibilities for the national courts to give full effect to Community law and ensure protection of individuals. This seems to be incompatible with the Court of Justice dicta in cases like *Simmenthal* and *Factortame*.[185] On the other hand the line followed in *Rewe/Comet*, i.e. that rules of national procedural law apply under the two provisos of non-discrimination and effectiveness, does not necessarily entail that any national rule limiting the full effectiveness of Community law and the protection of individuals must be disapplied. As I contended in the last part of Subsection 8.2.1, the decisive difference could be whether the rules constitute an (almost) absolute bar for the application of Community law in general or whether they are justified procedural limitations of the exercise of the rights by the individuals concerned, which are to be considered as compatible with the Community legal order. Indeed, different considerations may serve as justification, such as legal certainty and the proper administration of justice.

A disturbing factor in the two cases discussed here, *Van Schijndel* and *Peterbroeck*, is that they in fact concern the failure of the parties to raise the arguments of Community law at the appropriate moment in the proceedings, rather than the impossibility for the courts to bring in the Community law issues of their own motion.

8.3.4 Remedies

The last category of cases relates to the question: "what can a court do in a concrete case?". To put it another way, provided that there is a court having jurisdiction, i.e. having the power to hear and decide the case, what can the content of its decision be? What type of remedy can the court grant and what can its substance be?

[183] Another interesting question submitted to the Court in this case relates to another rule of Dutch procedural law, namely that in an appeal for cassation, the court has no power to consider a point of Community law which is raised before it but was not raised before the courts hearing the case prior to cassation and which requires an investigation of facts.

[184] Case C-312/93, *Peterbroeck*, pending, opinion of 4 May 1994.

[185] Case 106/77 [1978] ECR 629 and Case C-213/89 [1990] ECR I-2433.

The Substance of Remedies and Sanctions

In Chapter 5, Subsection 5.2.4, where the Community law requirements as to the form and content of sanctions and remedies made available for contraventions of Community law were discussed, it was seen that in order to ensure real and effective judicial protection national courts had to disregard certain limitations, deriving from national rules, to the remedies and sanctions at issue.

Thus, for instance, contrary to that suggested by other case law,[186] in *Marshall II*[187] interest had to be paid to the applicant; and this was despite the fact that the national court had no power to award interest. Similarly, the statutory limitation of the damages to be given was found to be incompatible with Community law.

In *Steenhorst-Neerings*[188] the limitation of the award of social security benefit with only a restricted retrospective effect was at issue. In this case the Court accepted the limitation. It recalled that claims for the social security benefit at issue must be exercised in accordance with the conditions laid down in national law, subject to the two minimum requirements of non-discrimination and effectiveness. The latter were satisfied in this case. The submission that in accordance with the judgment in *Emmott*[189] the award of the benefits cannot be limited in time as long as the directive has not been properly implemented was dismissed for two reasons. In the first place, the rule laying down the limitation period did not affect the right of individuals to rely on Directive 79/7 (equal treatment in statutory schemes of social security)[190] against the defaulting Member State: it merely limited the retrospective effect of claims for the benefit. In the second place, the rule at issue met the requirement of good administration, in particular the need to control whether the person concerned satisfied the conditions for entitlement. Moreover, it was also necessary for safeguarding the financial equilibrium of the scheme at issue.

In brief, wherever Community law does not contain an explicit provision, it is common understanding that the Member States are, in principle, free to choose the sanctions and remedies which will apply for the enforcement of Community law in the national legal order. Once the choice has been made,[191] however, the *substance of the remedies and sanctions* chosen is not left entirely unaffected. Yet Community law goes further and influences the *type of remedy* to be made available to aggrieved parties. Consequently, it also interferes in this respect with the principle of procedural autonomy, according to which it is in principle a

[186] Cf. Case 130/79 *Express Dairy Foods* [1980] 1887, Case 54/81 *Fromme* [1982] ECR 1449: interest is a matter of national law.

[187] Case C-271/91 [1993] ECR I-4367.

[188] Case C-338/91 [1993] ECR I-5475.

[189] Case C-208/90 [1991] ECR I-4269. Cf. above, Subsection 8.2.3.

[190] OJ 1979, L 6/24.

[191] Often the "choice" may be more or less automatic since Community law is integrated into national law for which there already exists a system of enforcement.

matter of national law whether a certain type of action aiming at a particular remedy can be brought or not.[192]

Types of Remedies which Should be Available

In its case law the Court has so far defined a number of specific remedies to which individuals are entitled. From earlier case law it was already clear that private litigants should be entitled to repayment or restitution of sums of money (e.g. taxes or levies) paid contrary to Community rules. In *San Giorgio*,[193] for instance, the Court held that such a repayment is a consequence of, and an adjunct to, the rights conferred on individuals by the Community provisions prohibiting charges having an effect equivalent to customs duties or, as the case may be, the discriminatory application of internal taxes. On the other hand the Court accepted that an order for the recovery of charges improperly imposed should not necessarily be granted if this would amount to unjust enrichment of those entitled.[194] However, in the more recent case of *Cotter and McDermott II*[195] the Court seems to have overruled itself. The case did not concern repayment or restitution but the entitlement to social security benefits in pursuance of Directive 79/7 (equal treatment in statutory schemes of social security).[196]

The central question in this case was whether the national court could apply the principle prohibiting unjust enrichment, which under Irish law constitutes a ground for restricting or refusing relief in certain circumstances. Although the Irish government relied on the previous cases allowing the application of such a principle, the Court of Justice dismissed this argument. It found that if the national authorities could rely on the (national) principle prohibiting unjust enrichment, they would be able to use their own unlawful conduct as a ground for depriving the relevant provisions of the directive of their full effect.

The cases on repayment and restitution were as such not very revolutionary, in the sense that the existence or the availability of the remedies themselves was not at issue. Things were different in the more recent cases, such as *Heylens*, *Nimz*, *Factortame*, *Zuckerfabrik Süderdithmarschen* and *Francovich*.[197]

[192] Cf. the observations of the Member States in cases like *Factortame* (Case C-213/89 [1990] ECR I-2433) and *Francovich* (Joined Cases C-6/90 and C-9/90 [1991] ECR I- 5357).

[193] Case 199/82 [1983] ECR 3595.

[194] Cf. Case 68/79 *Just* [1980] ECR 501.

[195] Case C-377/89 [1991] ECR I-1155.

[196] OJ 1979, L 6/24.

[197] Case 222/86 [1987] ECR 4097, Case C-184/89 [1991] ECR I-279, Case C-213/89 [1990] ECR I-2433, Case C-143/88 [1991] ECR I-415 and Joined Cases C-6/90 and C-9/90 [1991] ECR I-5357.

The judgment in *Heylens* made clear that the individual concerned must be able to bring an action for judicial review even if no specific legal remedy is available against the decision in dispute under national law.

In *Nimz* the woman concerned applied to the Labour Court Hamburg for a declaration that her employer was under the duty to pay her a salary of a particular level. According to German law, the court could find that a provision of a collective agreement was incompatible with Article 119 of the Treaty and therefore void. However, the court had serious doubts as to whether it could fill the legal lacuna which resulted from the incompatibility. Under national law it followed from the autonomy of the parties to collective wage agreements, guaranteed by virtue of Article 21 of the Basic Law, that it was up to them and not the judge to find the proper solution to the problem. The Court dismissed the argument of autonomy of the parties to the collective agreement and the corresponding limitation of the power of the national court. It held that the latter must apply to the members of the group which is disadvantaged by the discrimination the same arrangements which are applied to other employees.

From *Factortame* it follows that an individual has the right to interim relief even if the injunction against the Crown sought by the applicants was unconstitutional in national law.

The action in damages against the State as construed in *Francovich* will undoubtedly alter considerably the system of State liability in several Member States.[198] The same can be said of the judgment in *Zuckerfabrik Süderdithmarschen*, which lays down in detail the conditions to be fulfilled for granting interim relief against a national administrative decision taken on the basis of a regulation which is alleged to be invalid.

Different grounds have been presented for this rather far-reaching – though not entirely unexpected[199] – interference by the Court of Justice with the national systems of remedies: in particular, the principle of effective judicial protection, the full effectiveness of Community law and the useful effect of Article 177. The Court did not stop here, however, indicating the appropriate remedies which have to be available.

In *Factortame*, notwithstanding the express question of the House of Lords, it side-stepped the issue of the circumstances under which a national court must give interim relief. In *Zuckerfabrik Süderdithmarschen*, however, for the sake of uniform application of Community law it defined uniform conditions under which interim relief must be given and which must be applied by the national courts instead of the conditions existing in national law. In this respect it must be pointed out that in contrast to *Factortame*, which concerned the compatibility of *national law* with the EEC Treaty, in *Zuckerfabrik Süderdithmarschen* the validity of secondary Community law itself was called into question. Furthermore, in *Factortame* the barrier against the measures which were applied for came from national law, while in *Zuckerfabrik Süderdithmarschen* it was a Community law barrier originating in the Court's earlier case law.[200] Moreover, since the judgment is tailored

[198] Cf. below, Chapter 12, in particular literature referred to in Section 12.2. Especially the immunity of the State in its capacity as a legislator cannot be raised as a valid argument.

[199] Cf. Case 106/77 *Simmenthal* [1978] ECR 629.

[200] Cf. Case 314/85 *Foto-Frost* [1987] ECR 4199: only the Court may declare a Community act invalid.

to the situation of the application of Community law (or, more precisely, a national decision based on it) having to be suspended, it is far from clear whether the conditions laid down in this judgment also apply to the "*Factortame-type*" situation.[201]

Be this as it may, that the Court is willing to lay down conditions to be fulfilled where national measures (or the absence of necessary measures) are at issue was clearly apparent in *Francovich*. In this case the Court defined three Community law conditions which – as soon as they are fulfilled – give rise to a right to compensation on the part of individuals for damage suffered as a result of non-implementation of a directive.

The foregoing clearly suggests that the initial assumption that the national legal systems provide sufficient means of redress for aggrieved parties has apparently been reconsidered by the Court of Justice. More recent cases have shown that the Court may deem it necessary to give strict instructions, with respect to both the types of remedies which should be available and the substantive conditions which must be fulfilled by the remedies applicable. Whether the Court's guidelines amount to an amendment of the existing remedies offered by national law or to a creation of new ones is a subject which has – until now – given rise to divergent views. In particular with respect to *Factortame* it has been argued that the judgment amounts to an obligation to create a new remedy.[202] *Factortame* can indeed be presented as a case where the national court had no power to grant interim relief against the Crown and therefore, after *Factortame*, there is a new remedy. Yet the problem can also be formulated in other terms – as the Court of Justice actually did – namely that the national court may in principle give an interim injunction, but a rule of national (constitutional) law curtails its power: it is prevented from doing this against the Crown.[203] From this perspective there is rather an expansion of an existing remedy.

Similarly, *Francovich* can be approached from both angles. It is arguable that it offers a new remedy in the sense that normally the national judiciary has no power to grant damages for breaches committed by the legislature.[204] On the other hand it is equally arguable that Francovich implies a (far-reaching) amendment of existing national rules on State liability.[205]

The divergence in approach may be due to conceptual differences between common law and the civil law tradition, and the double meaning of the term

[201] Cf. Oliver 1992, p. 360; see however also Curtin 1992, p. 42-43.

[202] Cf. Curtin 1992, p. 42, Boch and Lane 1992, p. 173, Toth 1990, p. 586, Barav 1994, p. 269.

[203] For a critical review of the Court's judgment cf. Barav 1994, p. 274 ff. His main objection is that the Court treated the matter as one of exercise of powers, whereas the crucial issue was the very existence of powers.

[204] Cf. Steiner 1993, p. 12, Craig 1993, p. 597-601.

[205] Cf. Schockweiler 1992, p. 48, Kapteyn 1993, p. 45. Obviously, in *Francovich* also the Court assumed as a premise that national rules on State liability exist in the Member States.

"remedy".[206] In so far as the term "remedy" is understood as a form of relief given by the court, the cases can indeed be considered as creating a new remedy. If, however, the term "remedy" is employed in the broad sense, i.e. as the means provided by law to obtain a certain form of relief, then it is conceivable that under common law it can still be said that a new remedy is created while in the civil law tradition there is not a new "*voie de recours*". The claimant seeks a new form of relief but he does so in an existing procedure which must, however, be adapted for this purpose.

In my view, it does not really matter whether the result of the requirements is called a new remedy or rather the adaptation of an existing system of national procedures and remedies. What *does* matter is the fact that the requirements imposed by the Court *broaden the powers of national courts*. This may be done either by removing restrictions of the existing powers or by giving the courts, in a *positive* way, the necessary powers to be able to do something which it is beyond their jurisdiction to do as a matter of national law alone.[207]

8.3.5 Direct Empowerment of the National Courts?

In the foregoing Sections it has been explained that national procedures and remedies which are used as vehicles for the enforcement of Community law and the protection of the rights which individuals derive from it must satisfy certain requirements. The next (and final) issue to be addressed in this context is *which organ*, within the Member State, is responsible for the appropriate measures being taken in order to guarantee the observance of these requirements.

For a long time it was assumed that it was for the national legislative bodies to secure access to the courts and to provide national courts with the necessary procedures, powers and remedies to enable them to afford adequate protection of individuals.[208] However, as early as *Simmenthal*[209] the Court had made clear that the national court should ignore national rules precluding it from giving full force and effect to Community law.

Despite the clear language of *Simmenthal*, for a while it was uncertain whether a national court, on its own authority, should disregard national rules on

[206] Cf. above, Subsection 8.3.1, n. 103 .

[207] This development did indeed not pass unnoted. Cf. recent literature on the changing position of national courts: Barav 1991, Grevisse and Bonichot 1991, Simon 1991, Schockweiler 1991, Barav 1994.

[208] Cf. Wyatt 1989, p. 205, Lauwaars and Timmermans 1994, p. 34, Kovar 1978, p. 248-250. Cf. also Case 98/79 *Pecastaing* [1980] ECR 691, in particular para. 10-11, which relate to the obligations of the Member States laid down in Article 8 of directive 64/221, OJ English Spec. Ed. 1963-1964, p. 117.

[209] Case 106/77 [1978] ECR 629.

procedures and remedies and, arguably, the rules defining their powers. Matters seem to be relatively uncomplicated in cases where the national court can rely on a written provision of Community law relating to procedural and remedial aspects, such as Article 6 of Directive 76/207 (equal treatment at work).[210] Using the technique of interpretation of national law in conformity with such a provision,[211] or by applying the doctrine of direct effect[212] the national court can reach the result desired by Community law. In contrast to these cases, in *Factortame* (and in fact earlier in *Simmenthal*) the Court found that it is a duty of the national court to depart, by disapplication, from the relevant rules defining its powers *without it being possible to indicate an explicit Community law provision* serving as the basis for the power of doing this. Since then, this assignment to the judiciary has been confirmed in an even more vigorous way in the *Francovich* and *Zuckerfabrik Süderdithmarschen* judgments.[213]

Arguably, these developments amount to a *direct empowerment* by Community law – whether written or unwritten – of the national courts to extend their existing powers or to assume, on the basis of Community law alone, new powers which do not exist under national law in order to fulfil effectively the task assigned to them by the Court of Justice.[214] However, firstly, an assignment of tasks to the national courts, entrusting them with a Community law mission or giving them a function in the enforcement of Community law, cannot as such create the necessary powers.[215] Secondly, the bases in Community law having such an investitive effect on which the Court relies, i.e. in particular the principle of effective judicial protection, the full force and effect of Community law and the

[210] OJ 1976, L 39/40.

[211] Cf. Case 14/83 *Von Colson* [1984] ECR 1891, Case C-177/88 *Dekker* [1990] ECR I-3941.

[212] Cf. Case 222/84 *Johnston* [1986] ECR 1651, Case C-271/91 *Marshall II* [1993] ECR I-4367; in relation to the EEX Treaty see Case 288/82 *Duijnstee* [1983] ECR 3663.

[213] Cf. also Case C-97/91 *Borelli* [1992] ECR I-6313.

[214] Cf. the opinion of A-G Mischo in *Francovich*, para 53 ("there can no longer be any doubt that in certain cases Community law may itself directly confer on national judicial authorities the necessary powers in order to ensure effective judicial protection of those rights, even where similar powers do not exist in national law") and Curtin 1990b, p. 736. For general (constitutional) implications of these developments cf. De Burca 1992, p. 239, Simon 1991, p. 491-492, Curtin and Mortelmans 1994, p. 457.

[215] Neither can eloquent catchwords, like "*juge national en sa qualité de juge communautaire*" (Simon 1991, p. 484), "*la fonction du juge de l'ordre juridique communautaire*" (Schockweiler 1991, p. 56) or the Community law mandate of the national judge (Louis 1990, p. 546, Curtin and Mortelmans 1994, p. 457) create the necessary powers. The first two merely describe the function of the national court. The second connotes the development brought about by the Court's case law which started to define the national courts' powers. However, the very problem is exactly that the basis for such a mandate is lacking. National courts, as organs of the State and not of the Community, still derive their authority from the State. Cf. also Dubouis 1992, p. 8-9.

useful effect of Article 177 respectively, are rather tenuous.[216] To this extent, the national courts' Community law mission is in urgent need of obtaining a more solid theoretical underpinning and, preferably, a legislative basis.

[216] Cf. with respect to *Zuckerfabrik Süderdithmarschen* Mortelmans 1991, p. 680, with respect to *Factortame* Lauwaars 1991, p. 480 and Simon and Barav 1990, p. 594. Cf. also above, Subsection 8.2.1, observations with respect to *Simmenthal.*

9

Conclusions Part II

In consequence of the conception of the new Community legal order expounded by the Court of Justice in the early sixties, directives are, like any other rule of Community law, integrated within the national legal orders of the Member States. As such they are law-creating. In the case of a conflict between a national rule and a directive the latter has precedence by virtue of the principle of supremacy of Community law.

A different question is whether a directive, or one or more of its provisions, creates or is intended to create individual rights and obligations. This is a matter of the *substance* of the directive and must be decided on the basis of the concrete text of the relevant directive provisions. Furthermore, a distinction must be made between situations in which a directive can be considered as a *direct* source of rights and obligations and those in which it is an *indirect* source. In principle, directives should be seen as indirect sources. As a rule, it is not until their implementation that actual rights for individuals are created. The same holds true for obligations. Under certain circumstances directives are direct sources of rights, i.e. they confer rights without the intercession of national implementing measures. They cannot, however, impose obligations upon individuals directly.

The question as to the creation of rights is a central issue in the case law of the Court of Justice. Firstly, the Court obliges the national judges to protect the rights which individuals derive from a directive (and from Community law in general). Secondly, the answer to the question whether a directive *intends* to confer rights on individuals is important for the modalities of implementation of directives. It is established case law that where the directive is intended to create rights for individuals, the implementing measures must be such as to enable the individuals to ascertain the full extent of their rights and, where appropriate, rely on them before the national courts. Thirdly, the question of rights is relevant for the application of the "*Emmott rule*":[1] national time limits for bringing proceedings do not apply so long as the directive has not been properly transposed.

When searching for the answer, one must realize that there are many pitfalls which should be carefully avoided.

Firstly, from the Court's judgments it is far from clear what it means by saying that a provision of Community law "creates rights" (or equivalent formulations). Very often the Court indicates in this way that the provision concerned has direct effect which, as such, does not necessarily mean that some substantive right has been created but merely a "*right to invoke*" the provision at

[1] Case C-208/90 [1991] ECR I-4269.

issue. As I have contended, whether a provision creates individual rights is a matter of its *content*. The question whether a provision has direct effect relates to its *quality*, i.e. whether it can be invoked by the individuals concerned. Direct effect of Community law provisions and the creation of substantive rights should therefore not be equated. They will often coincide, but they are not necessarily two sides of the same coin. For this reason the two issues must be considered separately.

Secondly, the classification of the legal effects resulting from a provision or set of provisions at national level cannot as such be decisive for the classification in Community law. There are considerable differences in approaches within the Member States and, moreover, they will also depend on the type of procedure in which the provisions are invoked.

The case law of the Court of Justice does not provide much guidance in this respect. This is not surprising since until now there has been no need for the Court to lay down parameters as to what is a substantive right in Community law. By stating that Community law creates rights which national courts must protect, the Court was merely indicating that the courts must offer protection, through application of directly effective provisions, to the individual's position, whatever the qualification of the effects of the Community law provision may be under national law. However, for the reasons mentioned above, it was submitted that the question can no longer be side-stepped.

For the purpose of establishing whether there is a Community law substantive right it may often suffice to look at the terms of the relevant provisions, coupled, if necessary, with the objective of, for instance, the directive of which they form a part. These may make it abundantly clear that the provisions intend to give rights to individuals. They do so either *expressis verbis* or as a correlative to an obligation imposed upon another subject of Community law. Wherever the terms are not conclusive in this respect, recourse should be taken to, at least, the following parameters.

Firstly, the (potential) parties to the legal relationships resulting from the provisions must be considered. It was submitted that the individual must be a party to one of the relationships to which the provision may give rise. Secondly, there is the (often notoriously difficult) question as to the interest which is protected. The relevant provisions must be there to protect the interest of the individual concerned. However, it is not clear whether the interest protected should be some *particular* interest of the individual or whether it suffices that the interest is *also* his interest. Thirdly, the content or subject matter of the right must be defined with sufficient precision. However, if it is not defined in sufficiently precise terms and its actual realization depends, for instance, on certain conditions first being fulfilled, this does not mean that the directive is not intended to create rights. Even then it may be possible to ascertain what the content of the right will be after another body (legislator or administration) has

STAFFS UNIVERSITY LIBRARY

intervened. The crucial aspect here is that the body is not left too much discretion. Finally, possible provisions as to the judicial protection to be organized may indicate that the provisions confer or intend to confer rights. However, the existence of such a provision should be considered merely as a pointer and not as a condition for the existence of a right.

As a rule, directives should be implemented in national law. Consequently, their effects will reach the individuals through the national implementing measures. All too often, however, things go wrong and directives are not implemented correctly or are not implemented in time. In such a situation, according to the Court of Justice, it is up to the national courts to protect the rights which directives confer upon individuals and to ensure the full force and effect of the directives' provisions. The basis for this task is Article 5 of the Treaty which presupposes that national courts, as organs of the Member State, are bound by the obligation laid down in this provision, like any other organ of the State. They must apply the rules of Community law, which is an integral part of the law valid in their Member State, just as any other legal rule in the disputes brought before them. Moreover, I have argued that the task similarly stems from the principle of the rule of law.

The national courts perform the task assigned to them within the context of national law. National procedures and remedies available under national law apply in the same manner as with respect to any other matter arising under national law. For some considerable time the choice as to the competent courts, appropriate remedies and procedures to be followed was left to the national legal systems of the Member States. This "*procedural autonomy*" was however not entirely unrestricted. The Member States had to ensure that *a* court would be competent to hear and decide cases involving Community law and that it would protect the Community law rights effectively. Furthermore, national procedural law had to satisfy two minimum requirements: the *principle of non-discrimination* and the *principle of effectiveness*. The first requires that the substantive and procedural conditions governing the actions for enforcement of Community law cannot be less favourable than those relating to similar actions of a domestic nature. The second principle requires that the conditions are not so framed as to render virtually impossible or excessively difficult the exercice of the rights conferred by Community law. However, in its early case law the Court did not fully develop the content and the potential implications of these requirements. Moreover, in so far as it did interpret them, this happened in only a limited field. Yet, the Court made clear that meeting the requirements imposed by the principle of non-discrimination was not a guarantee that the rules would be considered as satisfactory from the Community law point of view. In some cases they did not satisfy the requirements imposed by the principle of effectiveness.

Parallel to these general principles two other lines can be detected in the case law. One of these relates to judicial protection in the field of free movement of persons and concerns the interpretation of directive 64/221 (public policy and public health).[2] The other development took place along the line of direct effect and supremacy of Community law and culminated in the *Simmenthal*[3] judgment. From *Simmenthal* it clearly appeared that Community law may have considerable implications not only for substantive law but also for procedural law. In the ultimate analysis, *Simmenthal* resulted in empowering the national court to do something which it was not allowed to do as a matter of national law.

At first sight it appears difficult to reconcile the line followed in *Simmenthal* and the cases which impose merely minimum requirements. In both types of cases the effectiveness of Community law and the protection of individuals is compromised by national procedural rules. This apparent contradiction has continued to thrive in more recent cases and it has not yet been resolved in an entirely satisfactory way. One possible explanation could be that the Court differentiates between, on the one hand, national rules which form as such and in general an (almost absolute) obstacle to the effects which Community law should produce within the national legal order, and on the other hand, the rules which limit, often in a particular case, the exercise of the rights which individuals derive from Community law. In every single case it must then be considered whether the latter rules are compatible with Community law. In this context, an important feature seems to be the purposes served by the rules, such as, for instance, the protection of legal certainty, the prevention of unjust enrichment or the ensuring of good administration of justice. In any event, the latter type of case law clearly shows that full effectiveness and protection of individuals are not unqualified requirements to which any other – in themselves legitimate – rules must yield.

The *Johnston*[4] judgment marked a new era of more active interference by the Court of Justice in the field of judicial protection in national courts. The general *principle of effective judicial protection* expounded by the Court in this case serves as a ground for considerably curtailing the Member States' autonomy with respect to procedures and remedies to be made available for breaches of Community law or of national law which originates in Community law provisions. It has been suggested that the minimum requirement of effectiveness already present in earlier case law has been transformed in this way into a powerful device to improve the protection of rights which individuals derive from Community law. However, as I have contended, a difference still remains between the two

[2] OJ English Special Edition 1963-1964, p. 117.
[3] Case 106/77 [1978] ECR 629.
[4] Case 222/84 [1986] ECR 1651.

principles. The principle of effectiveness has a broader scope of application than the principle of effective judicial protection.

The more recent cases in which the principle of effective judicial protection in particular seems to be the main *Leitmotif*, along with the need to give full effect to Community law, strengthen considerably the Community law standards which national procedural and remedial rules must meet. In this respect, shortcomings have been turned into a virtue. These cases can be divided into three categories.

In the first category Community law lays down requirements for aspects relating to the *access to judicial process*. For instance, in order to enable the litigants to defend their rights under the best possible conditions, they must be given a reasoned decision; standing rules must be such as to safeguard effective judicial protection of those concerned and they should not make the exercise of the rights impossible in practice; appeals against acts which cannot be appealed under national law must nevertheless be declared admissible if so required for reasons of effective judicial protection. Another extremely important development in this context, with (potentially) far-reaching consequences is the *Emmott*[5] judgment. According to this judgment time limits for bringing action in the courts do not start to run until the moment the directive has been implemented in a proper way. The implications of *Emmott* for other types of limitation periods are as yet far from clear and so too are the conditions under which this rule applies. However, the first attempts to limit *Emmott* have already been made by the Court in *Steenhorst-Neerings*.[6]

The second category of cases concerns *rules applicable during the proceedings*. Firstly, Community law "effective protection requirements" play a crucial role in relation to evidential rules which, under certain circumstances, must be adjusted.

Secondly, there is the thorny question as to whether national courts are obliged to apply Community law of their own motion, i.e. without the parties to the dispute having relied on them. Furthermore, it is not yet clear whether a rule which limits the national court's powers to apply Community law of its own motion can be upheld in the light of Community law.

In relation to this issue I have argued that to impose an unqualified obligation upon the courts *as a matter of Community law* goes too far. In my opinion alliance should be sought with the rules applicable within the Member States with respect to application of national law by the courts of their own motion. However, in some cases the principles of effectiveness and effective judicial protection, coupled with the nature and importance of certain provisions, may entail the obligation for the courts to apply these provisions of their own motion, irrespective of what national law says. Provided that such an obligation is accepted, the application

[5] Case C-208/90 [1991] ECR I-4269.
[6] Case C-338/91 [1993] ECR I-5475.

of national rules limiting the court's powers to apply Community law *ex officio* may similarly be precluded, if they appear to be incompatible with the above-mentioned principles.

The last category of cases relates to *remedial aspects* of national law, and it is perhaps in this category that the developments have been the most revolutionary. A useful distinction can be made between the substance of the remedy and the type of remedy to be given.

As far as the substance is concerned, it was explained in Chapter 5, Subsection 5.2.4, that the requirement of effective judicial protection entails that the remedy available must meet certain requirements, for instance compensation must be full and adequate, and national courts must decide the case accordingly.

As far as the type of remedy is concerned, the Court has defined (in some cases in great detail) a number of remedies which must be available in cases of a breach of Community law. From the national point of view the interference might seem to be rather harsh, particularly where it runs against notions of constitutional law.

The development clearly results in broadening the powers of domestic courts under national law, either in a positive way, by requiring more ample powers for the domestic courts than they have under national law, or in a negative way, by requiring the disapplication of existing restrictions.

The orthodox understanding was that it was up to the legislature within the Member States to provide the courts with the necessary powers to enable them to safeguard rights deriving from Community law in an effective manner. However, after a prelude in *Simmenthal*, the recent cases suggest clearly that it is the national judiciary itself which is directly empowered by Community law to extend its own powers and where necessary to assume powers which do not exist as a matter of national law. In so far as such an empowerment follows from a written provision of Community law, even if the latter is broadly interpreted, one can be reconciled to it. However, where the basis is an unwritten principle or the mere necessity of full effectiveness of Community law, the juristic construction seems at odds with the principle of legality. Although I am not unsympathetic to the Court's case law on effective judicial protection in general, as far as the last aspect is concerned it is in need of a more solid theoretical and, preferably, a legislative basis. The national courts have been made an accomplice in the past. Today, they are perhaps asked too much.

STAFFS UNIVERSITY LIBRARY

Part III
Mechanisms for Enforcing Directives in National Courts

Introduction

Whenever a directive has not been correctly implemented or has not been implemented at all, an individual may find that although a provision exists which should be considered to be a part of the national legal order and which is intended to grant him rights or to allow him to benefit in other ways, his Member State's inadequate action or inaction means he appears to be left empty-handed. The actual situation is, however, less drastic. Apart from the fact that he can nevertheless rely on the directive before national authorities or other bodies which can be considered as an "emanation of the State",[1] an option which will not be elaborated further, he may have resort to a national court with a view to compelling observance of the directive at issue. In Chapter 8, Section 8.1, the obligation of national courts to give protection to the individual concerned was discussed in detail. It was also observed that by obliging the courts to do this the effective operation of directives is enhanced or, at least, the detrimental effects of incorrect transposition or non-transposition are toned down.

To enable the courts to fulfil this task, the Court of Justice has offered them three devices: the doctrine of direct effect, the interpretation of national law in conformity with the directive and, more recently, the principle of State liability for harm caused to individuals by breaches of Community law.

Despite the theories of the Court of Justice about integration of Community law into the national legal system of the Member States, for national courts Community law and in particular directives which, at first sight, may seem to be a type of instruction to the Member States, were and probably still are rules of external origin. From this point of view, their deployment in the courts is far from a foregone conclusion. The quintessence of the doctrine of direct effect is that it places Community law directly *before* the national courts, telling them that they must apply Community law in the same fashion as any other provision of national origin, provided that certain conditions are met.

Without wishing to deny the fundamental importance of direct effect for the development of Community law (it has been called one of the essential characteristics[2] and one of the twin pillars of the Community legal order[3]), in my view direct effect may be regarded as a mechanism put at the disposal of national courts for the effectuation of Community law. One may even go a step further and question whether direct effect might not be considered as a merely "transitional doctrine" which can be set aside at some time in the future.

[1] Cf. Chapter 4, in particular Section 4.4 and Subsection 4.5.2.

[2] Opinion 1/91 *EEA* [1991] ECR I-6079, para. 21.

[3] Wyatt and Dashwood 1993, p. 54.

The doctrine of direct effect does, however, have its limits. In respect of directives, one of the most important limits is the lack of horizontal direct effect. The Court of Justice, probably inspired by the existing practice in the courts in certain Member States, has designed another tool: the interpretation of national law in conformity with the directive. This technique constitutes, in general, a less drastic incursion into the national legal system than direct effect. In the ultimate analysis, it is then still national law which applies, although its content may be modified in the light of the directive. The effects should, in principle, be less radical than the application of a provision of a directive in lieu of national law. However, as will be demonstrated in Chapter 10, this does not always hold true, as the Court pushes this technique quite far.

The two mechanisms have in common that the legal consequences they entail are the consequences as determined by national law. In other words, the content of the national provision is modified in accordance with the directive but after such a modification it still applies as a rule of national law, or the directive provision is used directly, though in the same way as if it were a provision of national law. Basically, direct effect either amounts to application of the provision to the facts of the case or it is used as a standard for review of national measures. However the consequences, such as the remedies to be given, remain those as defined by national law.

The situation is different in the case of the third device, the State's liability. Whenever the Member State does not comply with its obligations under Article 189(3) and certain conditions formulated by the Court are satisfied, the consequence, i.e. the right to damages, is determined by Community law. Furthermore, it should be noted that this mechanism operates at a different level from the previous two. While the techniques of interpretation and direct effect operate at the primary level, in simple terms, the level of posing a rule of conduct, liability operates at the secondary level, i.e. the level of sanctions for the breach of a rule of conduct. Damages to be paid are, in this context, not based on the directive as such but are the consequence of the breach of a Community law obligation by a Member State. This does not, however, alter the fact that this last mechanism also serves to protect individuals.

In the next three Chapters I shall consider the different mechanisms in detail. Their content, the conditions for their operation, their effects and their limits will particularly be discussed. The order in which the mechanisms are presented is not fortuitous. In the *Johnston*[4] case the Court of Justice suggested that the national court should try first to reconcile the national provision and the provision of a directive through interpretation. Only when such an interpretation

[4] Case 224/84 [1986] ECR 1651. Cf. also Everling 1992b, p. 382.

is impossible should the court have recourse to direct effect.[5] In my opinion, this is a logical approach. Especially in the case of alleged inadequate transposition the court must interpret relevant provisions of national law first in any event, in order to determine whether inadequate transposition actually exists; and after all, why should a court seek a harsh confrontation with Community law if the matter can be settled in a "softer" fashion? Finally, by the nature of things, the liability of the State should come in the third position.[6]

[5] However, two more recent cases might be understood as indicating that direct effect is the first mechanism to be used and interpretation of national law comes in the second place. See Case C-334/92 *Miret* [1993] ECR I-6911 and Case C-91/92 *Faccini Dori* [1994] ECR I-3325. Cf. also Dal Farra (1992, p. 648), who suggests that interpretation of national law in conformity with the directive is of a subsidiary character.

[6] For a more detailed discussion see Chapter 12, Section 12.6.

10
Consistent Interpretation

10.1 INTRODUCTION: CONSISTENT INTERPRETATION IN GENERAL

In the *Von Colson* case the Court held that

"... the Member States' obligation arising from a directive to achieve the result envisaged by the directive and their duty under Article 5 of the Treaty to take all appropriate measures, whether general or particular, to ensure the fulfilment of that obligation, is binding on all authorities of Member States including, for matters within their jurisdiction, the courts. It follows that, in applying the national law and in particular the provisions of national law specifically introduced in order to implement Directive no. 76/207, national courts are required to interpret their national law in the light of the wording and the purpose of the directive in order to achieve the result referred to in the third paragraph of Article 189."[1]

The obligation for the national court laid down in this judgment and the subsequent developments of this new doctrine have been the subject of many comments and, similarly, many terms are used to denote this phenomenon. Indirect effect, concurring or concurrent interpretation, loyal interpretation, harmonious interpretation, benevolent interpretation, conciliatory interpretation, consistent interpretation, interpretative obligation, principle of purposive interpretation, *Von Colson* principle, uniform interpretation, "*invocabilité d'interprétation*",[2] they all indicate the requirement to interpret national law in conformity with the directive. Although the term "indirect effect" is most common in the English literature, I prefer to use the term "consistent interpretation" or simply the terms "interpretation in conformity with" or "in accordance with". In my view, the term "indirect effect" is not sufficiently clear and precise. It can, for instance, also be used to indicate the effects which an application of a directly effective provision might have *vis-à-vis* third parties[3] or any other effects produced by directives other than "direct effects". Furthermore, as will be explained later, some further differentiation of the concept could be necessary depending on the purpose for which the consistent interpretation is used.[4]

Some problems initially surrounding the requirement of consistent interpretation have now been resolved, but many old *and* new questions remain unanswe-

[1] Case 14/83 [1984] ECR 1891.

[2] Cf. Shaw 1991, p. 319, Betlem 1993, p. 204, Boch and Lane 1992, p. 181, Dal Farra 1992, p. 648, Plaza Martin 1994, p. 31, Curtin and Mortelmans 1994, p. 463.

[3] Cf. above, Chapter 4, Subsection 4.2.2.

[4] See Sections 10.4 and 10.5.

red. Before addressing the specific issues arising under this doctrine it is expedient to place it in its proper perspective. As will appear, the basic idea is less new than some might assume.

As far as traditional international law is concerned, in several Member States national courts attempt by means of interpretation to reconcile two – at first sight – conflicting rules. Often they will do so in order to evade an outright choice of one of the conflicting rules, in so far as such an option is possible,[5] or they will proceed to such an interpretation with a view to helping their State comply with its international law obligations and avoiding their State's liability.

In the Netherlands it is generally accepted that an interpretation of national law in conformity with a provision of an international treaty is one of the methods of resolving a conflict between the two.[6] In several cases the *Hoge Raad* has resorted to this interpretative technique, in particular in cases involving the ECHR.[7]

In the United Kingdom a similar method is applied by the courts, although in a more restrictive way. As Lord Diplock put it: "It is a principle of construction of United Kingdom statutes, now too well established to call for citation of authority, that the words of the statute passed after the treaty has been signed and dealing with the subject matter of the international obligation of the United Kingdom, are to be construed, if they are reasonably capable of bearing such meaning, as intended to carry out the obligation, and not to be inconsistent with it."[8] However, in principle the courts will construe a domestic statute in conformity with an international treaty only where the statute is ambiguous and from the context it clearly appears that the enactment of the statute was intended to meet the government's obligation resulting from the treaty.[9]

In France, if there is a conflict between a statute and a prior international treaty the courts will try to reconcile the two norms by an interpretation of the statute in accordance with the treaty concerned. This approach is based on the presumption that the legislator knows Article 55 of the Constitution[10] and that it wishes to respect the international obligations of the French Republic.[11] For a long time this was the only possibility available to the French courts for resolving a conflict between a statute and a prior treaty as they were not permitted to review the former in the light of the latter. Since the judgment of the *Cour de Cassation* in *Jacques Vabre*[12] and, more recently, the decision of

[5] In particular from a constitutional point of view.

[6] Cf. De Boer 1985a, p. 84, the opinion of A-G Moltmaker in HR 8 juli 1988, NJ 1990, 448, in particular point 4, De Lange 1991, p. 211.

[7] Cf. De Boer 1985b, p. 215.

[8] *Garland v. British Railway Engineering Ltd.* (1982) 2 All ER 402, at p. 415.

[9] Cf. De Burca 1992, p. 219-220, MacCormick and Summers 1991, p. 378.

[10] This Article provides as follows: "Treaties and agreements that have been regularly ratified have, from the date of their publication, an authority superior to that of statutes, provided that for every agreement or treaty, it is enforced by the other party."

[11] Cf. Abraham 1989, p. 107-108.

[12] *Cour de Cassation* 24 May 1975, CDE 1975, p. 631.

the *Conseil d'Etat* in *Nicolo*,[13] things have radically changed. Both decisions are understood as enabling the French courts to review statutes and to decide that a statute contrary to a prior treaty ought not to be enforced.[14] However, this does not necessarily mean that the courts will no longer have recourse to interpretation of statutes in conformity with a treaty. As the *commisaire du gouvernement* Laroque pointed out in the *Nicolo* case, the judge "always enjoys the very useful resource of interpretation, which enables him to empty applicable texts of their contradiction".[15]

In Germany, a current technique of construing national law similar to the interpretation in conformity with a treaty is the "*verfassungskonforme Auslegung*", i.e. interpretation in conformity with the Constitution. As a rule, if the wording of a norm, the genetic history, the coherence of the rules concerned and their sense and purpose allow several interpretations, the court has to follow that method of interpretation which brings the rule to be construed into conformity with the Constitution.[16] The "*verfassungskonforme*" interpretation is generally considered as a form of judicial self-restraint, a manner to respect, at least on the surface, the choice made by the legislature. It enables the courts to avoid a "hard clash" between the legal provision and the constitution which could ultimately result in a declaration of unconstitutionality, or any other consequence possible under German law.[17] However it has been pointed out that in some situations it may also be an instrument of judicial activism: the consequences, seen from the point of view of the legislature, may be more far-reaching than a declaration of unconstitutionality.[18]

With respect to interpretation in conformity with an international treaty in general, the same could also hold true. In some cases this interpretative technique will often be deployed with a view to giving effect to an international treaty, especially when other forms of application are excluded for constitutional reasons, such as maintaining the principle of separation of powers, as was the case in France. From this point of view, interpretation may be considered as a form of judicial activism. In other situations, particularly where review in the light of an international treaty is allowed, interpretation in conformity with the treaty may witness of judicial self-restraint.

In Community law, the approach of the Court of Justice is in principle no different. Provisions of secondary law must wherever possible be construed in conformity with the Treaty: "... when it is necessary to interpret a provision of secondary Community law, preference should as far as possible be given to the interpretation which renders the provision consistent with the Treaty".[19] Moreover, not only is the Treaty a standard for

[13] *Conseil d'Etat* 20 October 1989, RFDA 1989, p. 813.

[14] Cf. MacCormick and Summers 1991, p. 187-188.

[15] Quoted in MacCormick and Summers 1991, p. 188.

[16] Cf. MacCormick and Summers 1991, p. 101. Jarrass (1991a, p. 214) observes that the experience in Germany with "*verfassungskonforme Auslegung*" may be very useful for the doctrine of consistent interpretation. It is noteworthy that in German literature a parallel is drawn between consistent interpretation and interpretation in conformity with the Constitution rather than between the former and the *vertragskonforme Auslegugng* which does exist as a concept (cf. Bleckmann 1990, p. 335) but which is not well-established (cf. Ress 1985, p. 163).

[17] Cf. Zeidler 1988, p. 209-214.

[18] Cf. Jarass 1991a, p. 215, Heukels 1991, p. 128.

[19] Case 201/85 *Klensch* [1986] ECR 3477, para. 21.

interpretation, but so too are general principles of Community law: secondary Community law must be construed in conformity with those principles.[20]

In summary, the interpretation of a legal provision, be it of national or of secondary Community law, in conformity with a higher ranking (international) provision is as such nothing new. It is well known within the Member States and in the Community legal order. It can most appropriately be characterized as a judicial technique which is often applied in order to avoid an outright confrontation between the rules involved. Although the concept as such is therefore not unfamiliar, the conditions, modalities and scope of its application are considerably different. Some of the problems which may arise from these differences will be given further consideration in the Sections below.

10.2 Interpretation of National Law before Von Colson

The Court's approach described in the preceding Section obviously concerns the interpretation of a provision of secondary Community law in conformity with a provision of primary Community law. As far as the interpretation of *national law* in accordance with Community law and, in particular, with a directive is concerned, in the "pre-Von Colson era" a few cases were brought before the Court of Justice in which the interpretation of national law in conformity with a directive was touched upon in some way by the Court.

In *Haaga*[21] two *Oberlandesgerichte* disagreed about the interpretation of a provision of German company law. In order to avoid the risk of divergence within the case law the problem was referred to the *Bundesgerichtshof.* The latter found that the solution of the case depends on the interpretation of Article 10 (1) of the German law on limited liability companies, as amended to implement Directive 68/151 (first company law directive).[22] The *Bundesgerichtshof* was of the opinion that the interpretation of the national provision in its turn depended on the interpretation of Article 2 (1) (d) of the Directive. It accordingly referred a preliminary question to the Court of Justice. Apparently, both the Advocate General[23] and the Court were very pleased with this reference. The Court explained – somewhat proudly – in its judgment that:

"The *Bundesgerichtshof* ... considered it necessary to obtain an interpretation of the relevant provisions of the Directive of 9 March 1968 so as to ensure that the law adopted for the

[20] Cf. Joined Cases C-90 and 91/90 *Neu* [1991] ECR I-3617, para. 12.
[21] Case 32/74 [1974] ECR 1201.
[22] OJ English Spec. Ed. 1968 (I), p. 41.
[23] Opinion of A-G Mayras, in particular p. 1213.

implementation of that Directive by the Federal Republic of Germany should be applied in a manner which conformed to the requirements of Community law."[24]

Likewise, in *Bonsignore*[25] the Court mentioned that the national court, for purposes of application of certain national provisions, deemed it necessary to obtain from the Court of Justice the interpretation of the corresponding provisions of Directive 64/221 (public policy and public health)[26] "in order to ensure that national law is applied in accordance with the requirements of Community law."[27]

The Court's explanation had little meaning in the *Haaga* and *Bonsignore* cases. However, some one and a half years later the consideration was turned into an (additional) argument in the *Mazzalai* case.[28]

In *Mazzalai* the Italian Government argued that preliminary questions referred to the Court related to provisions of a directive which could not be considered as having direct effect. Therefore they were not relevant for the outcome of the case to be decided by the national court. The Court disagreed with this argument and pointed out that, firstly, its jurisdiction under Article 177 is not limited to those acts which are directly applicable and, secondly, that it is not within its jurisdiction to appraise the relevance of the questions referred to it under Article 177. To this the Court added that

"... regardless of the effects of the directive, in cases such as the present, an interpretation of the directive may be helpful to the national court so as to ensure that the law adopted for the implementaton of the directive is interpreted and applied in a manner which conforms to the requirements of Community law ...."[29]

In *Mazzalai* the Court in fact made plain *expressis verbis* what probably already happened to a certain extent in practice before that judgment and what certainly has happened since then: wherever a national court is confronted with a problem of interpretation of national law adopted with a view to implementing a directive, the court "will naturally be inclined"[30] to fall back upon the underlying directive. The relevant national provisions will then be construed in accordance with the directive, often following upon a preliminary ruling given by the Court of Justice at the request of the court concerned.[31]

[24] Para. 3 of the judgment.
[25] Case 67/74 [1975] ECR 297.
[26] OJ English Spec. Ed. 1963-1964, p. 117.
[27] Para. 4 of the judgment.
[28] Case 111/75 [1976] ECR 657.
[29] Cf. also Case 8/77 *Sagulo* [1977] ECR 1495, para. 12.
[30] Timmermans 1979, p. 535.
[31] Cf. also Case 270/81 *Rickmers* [1982] ECR 2771, para. 25.

Several authors have pointed out that, even where the directive is correctly transposed into national law it will remain relevant as a standard for interpretation of the implementing measures.[32] In fact, a national court will often first raise a question of interpretation of a directive in order to be able to examine whether the national implementing (or other) measures are compatible with it or with a view to ascertaining the meaning which should be given to the national provisions concerned. It is a "second-stage" issue, namely where the national court suspects that the national provisions and the directive are not compatible or cannot be made compatible through interpretation, the potential direct effect of the directive provision will be the subject of the reference to the Court of Justice. This is illustrated by numerous preliminary references to the Court of Justice concerning the interpretation of the substantive provisions of directives which do not raise the issue of their direct effect. In some cases there may actually already be established case law that the provisions at issue have direct effect. Consequently, the fact that the referring court does not ask questions concerning the direct effect does not always imply that the questions have been referred for purposes of interpretation of national law only. In other cases, however, this is indeed the case.[33]

Although the terms used by the Court in *Haaga* and *Mazzalai* were relatively non-committal, even before *Von Colson* it was suggested that the national courts are obliged to proceed to consistent interpretation of national implementing measures *and* of national law in general.[34] Since *Von Colson* there has been no doubt that the national courts are under a legal duty to interpret and apply national legislation adopted for the implementation of the directive in conformity with the latter.[35] The obligation is based on the binding nature of Article 189(3) and Article 5 of the Treaty. The national courts, like any other organ of the Member State, are bound by Article 189(3) and they are called upon to help to achieve the result of the directive at issue. The "appropriate measure" they have to take in this context is interpretation. However, many questions have arisen and continue to arise as to the scope of the obligation of consistent interpretation.

10.3 The Scope of Consistent Interpretation: the Resolved Issues

From the case law of the Court of Justice it appears that for the purposes of consistent intepretation it is immaterial whether the provisions which serve as

[32] Cf. Pescatore 1980, p. 172, Lutter 1992, p. 598.

[33] Cf. Pescatore 1980, p. 172 and 175, Everling 1989, p. 367.

[34] Cf. Timmermans 1979, p. 536.

[35] Cf. Case C-373/90 *X* [1992] ECR I-131, para. 7: consistent interpretation is labeled "a line of authority now well-established by the Court".

standard for interpretation are directly effective or not.[36] Thus in *Von Colson*,[37] for instance, the Court formulated the obligation of consistent interpretation of national law on sanctions although, according to the same judgment, the directive did not include any unconditional and sufficiently precise obligation as regards sanctions for discrimination on which individuals could rely directly.[38] In *Johnston*[39] the Court clearly indicated that the conflict at issue could be resolved either by means of consistent interpretation or by means of direct effect.

Likewise, the obligation applies irrespective of the legal relationship at issue in the main proceedings, i.e. whether there is a conflict between a private individual and the State or between two private individuals.[40] In the parallel cases of *Von Colson* and *Harz*, the former involved a State prison while the defendant in the latter was a private undertaking.[41]

Furthermore it must be pointed out that the duty of consistent interpretation is not confined to the wording of the directive. The national court must also construe national legal provisions in the light of the objective of the directive concerned. In other words, national courts are required to proceed to a *purposive interpretation* of national law, giving it a meaning which makes it suitable to achieve the objective of the directive. Thus not only the wording but also the purpose of the directive is an important element to be taken into account.[42]

A point of controversy in legal writing and in the opinions of some Advocates General,[43] discussed above in Chapter 2, Section 2.2, is the question whether the obligation of consistent interpretation already applies within the period between the entry into force and the deadline for implementation of the directive. In Chapter 2, I came to the conclusion that, in principle, there is no such

[36] Cf. the opinion of A-G Darmon in Case C-177/88 *Dekker* [1990] ECR I-3941, para. 15, Everling 1992b, p. 379. For another – "national" – view, based on Article 24 of the German Basic law, see Di Fabio 1990, p. 952-953. For a discussion of interpretation consistent with a directly effective directive on the one hand and a non-directly effective directive on the other see Bates 1986.

[37] Case 14/83 [1984] ECR 1891.

[38] See however also below, Chapter 11, Subsection 11.4.3.

[39] Case 222/84 [1986] ECR 1651, in particular para. 53-57.

[40] Cf. the opinion of A-G Darmon in Case C-177/88 *Dekker* [1990] ECR I-3941, para. 15.

[41] Case 14/83 [1984] ECR 1891 and Case 79/83 [1984] ECR 1921. Cf. also Case C-334/92 *Miret* [1993] ECR I-6911 and Case C-91/92 *Faccini Dori* [1994] ECR I-3325.

[42] Cf. Bleckmann 1992, p. 365.

[43] Cf. on the one hand the opinion of A-G Darmon in Case C-177/88 *Dekker* [1990] ECR I-3941, para. 11 and his opinion in Case C-236/92 *Comitato* [1994] ECR I-483, para. 27 (deadline is immaterial) and, on the other hand, the opinion of A-G Jacobs in C-156/91 *Mundt* [1992] ECR I-5567, para. 24 and 25 (obligation to consistent interpretation after expiry of the deadline). Cf. also Jarass 1991a, p. 221. Furthermore it must be noted that according to Hilf (1993, p. 15) the decisive moment is the actual transposition. It is understood that Hilf denies an obligation of consistent interpretation before transposition even if the transposition did not take place within the period prescribed.

obligation within the period provided for implementation but that, on the other hand, the national court has the possibility to proceed to consistent interpretation. An exception should be made, however, for implementing measures enacted *before* the time limit provided for implementation. In such a case of "premature" implementation, the national court not only has the faculty to proceed to consistent interpretation, which it will probably be inclined to do in any case, but on the basis of Article 5 of the Treaty it is also under the obligation to do so as a matter of Community law.[44]

The main issue to be addressed here concerns the *object* of the obligation of consistent interpretation. For some time disagreement existed with respect to the question of *what* had to be interpreted in conformity with the directive.

Von Colson was not entirely clear in this respect. While in one paragraph of the judgment the Court referred to "national law and in particular the provisions of a national law specifically introduced in order to implement Directive No 76/207", according to the operative part of the judgment it was solely the legislation adopted for the implementation of the directive that had to be interpreted in conformity with the directive.

In *Marshall I*, A-G Slynn underlined this discrepancy. Subsequently, he argued that the duty of consistent interpretation did not apply where the national legislation pre-dated the directive. The only exception the Advocate General was willing to make was a situation in which it was clear "that the legislation was adopted specifically with a proposed directive in mind."[45]

In *Kolpinghuis*,[46] A-G Mischo agreed with this point of view, but he formulated another exception. In his opinion the obligation of consistent interpretation also applied to national law which was deemed to satisfy the requirements of the directive even when, for that reason, the Member State considered it unnecessary to adopt implementing measures. In this respect it was cogently argued by Szyszczak that "it would be absurd to allow legislation predating the directive to be immune from the *Von Colson* principle ... simply because there was no need for amendment of existing legislation".[47]

[44] Cf. the opinion of A-G Jacobs Case C-156/91 *Mundt* [1992] ECR I-5567, para. 23 and Everling 1992b, p. 383. As to the effects of Article 5 before the implementation dealine has expired see supra Chapter 2, Section 2.2. Indeed if there were not such an obligation there would be a risk that the courts would interpret the relevant rules in a certain fashion, which could not, however, be considered as valid after the implementation deadline. This would of course not favour the correct application of the implementing measures after the deadline.

[45] Opinion of A-G Slynn in Case 152/84 [1986] ECR 723, at p. 732.

[46] Case 80/86 [1987] ECR 3969.

[47] Szyszczak 1990, p. 485. More recently the Court of Justice has stressed in Case C-334/92 *Miret* [1993] ECR I-6911 that consistent interpretation should in particular be followed in cases where the Member State believed that the already existing provisions of national law satisfied the requirements of the directive concerned (para. 21).

It is rather striking that neither A-G Mischo nor A-G Slynn gave any further explanation of their points of view. A-G Mischo simply agreed with the view expressed by A-G Slynn, and the latter was merely "not satisfied" that the obligation concerned the construction of pre-existing statutes as well. In his opinion it was a matter for national courts, and subject to the limits imposed on them by domestic rules, to decide whether a pre-existing national provision could be construed in accordance with a directive. His approach seems to start from and to accept fully (also for purposes of Community law) the British principle of statutory interpretation in the light of an *anterior* international treaty.[48] This rule of construction, which draws heavily on the presumption that Parliament intended to legislate in conformity with the treaty, reflects an attempt not to encroach upon the sovereignty of Parliament.[49] Yet it is by now quite clear that the theory of parliamentary sovereignty does not escape the influence of Community law and that it is less absolute than some would like to maintain. From this point of view, the rule of construction cannot validly be applied in a Community law context. Similarly, it cannot be accepted as an implicit rationale for restricting the duty of consistent interpretation only to legislation which is posterior to the directive. Several years after *Marshall I* the – by then former – Advocate General in fact gave another explanation. In his opinion it is still "quite impossible to lay down a rule of Community law that if a national judge is interpreting an act of 1870, he must interpret it in the light of a Community directive of 1992" because "judges should not have to twist and distort national legislation in order to give effect to Community directives, whatever article 5 of the Treaty says."[50] The point is, however, that the "age" of the statute does not *eo ipso* imply that its interpretation in accordance with a much younger directive amounts to a distortion. Much depends on other factors, like, for instance, the objective pursued by the statute. On the other hand, it is sustainable that the "older" the statute, the greater the chance that there will be considerable difficulties in construing it in conformity with the directive. However the appropriate question to be addressed should then relate to the *limits* of (the obligation of) consistent interpretation and not to its object, i.e. what has to be interpreted.

In *Kolpinghuis* the Court did not address this issue explicitly. It reiterated the famous paragraph from *Von Colson* and said that the duty of consistent interpretation relates to "national legislation" or to the "relevant rules of (its) national law" without any qualification whatsoever.[51] It should be noted that the rules to be interpreted in *Kolpinghuis* pre-dated the directive concerned and, furthermore, in no way were intended to implement the directive. According to

[48] Cf. above, Section 10.1.
[49] Cf. De Burca 1992, p. 220.
[50] Slynn 1993, p. 128.
[51] Case 80/86 [1987] ECR 3969, para. 13-14.

some authors, *Kolpinghuis* was already sufficiently clear on the issue as to whether the obligation of consistent interpretation also related to pre-existing law.[52]

In *Marleasing*, the Court put an end to all speculation and disagreement. It made explicitly clear that the obligation applies to national law irrespective of "whether the provisions in question were adopted before or after the directive".[53] The Court apparently proceeded from its theory that Community law is an integral part of the national legal systems: once this has been accepted and Community law must for that reason be taken into consideration by the national courts, it would be paradoxical to restrict the requirement of consistent interpretation only to implementing measures.[54]

Furthermore, it should be noted that the term "law" covers a broader category than legislation. It may, for instance, also include unwritten principles of law and judge-made law.

A number of problems having thus been resolved, the crucial question with respect to this doctrine now appears to investigate the limits of (the obligation of) consistent interpretation. These limits seem to lie, on the one hand, in general principles of law and, on the other hand, in the latitude for interpretation left to the national courts.

For a proper appreciation of these issues it is useful to make a distinction between cases where the directive as such has been correctly transposed into national law and cases where the directive has not been transposed correctly or not in due time. As will become apparent, in the former type of cases consistent interpretation is relatively unproblematic. It is notably in the latter type of cases that difficult questions as to the limits of the obligation may arise and the potential implications of the obligation of consistent interpretation within the national legal systems are thrown into high relief.

[52] Cf. Everling 1993, p. 212, Richter 1988, p. 396, Timmermans 1992, p. 818. Cf. also Morris 1989, p. 241 and Case 125/88 *Nijman* [1989] ECR 3533 where the terms "... and in particular ..." were deleted.

[53] Case C-106/89 [1990] ECR I-4135, para. 8.

[54] Cf. also the opinion of A-G Van Gerven in Case C-262/88 *Barber* [1990] ECR I-1889, para. 50. In *Marleasing* A-G Van Gerven argued that the legal basis of consistent interpretation followed not only from Article 189(3) combined with Article 5 of the Treaty but also from the principle of supremacy: directives, as part of Community law, take precedence over *all* provisions of national law (para. 9). Cf. also Lutter 1992, p. 604.

STAFFS UNIVERSITY LIBRARY

10.4 Consistent Interpretation within the Context of Judicial Implementation of Directives

Too often the obligation of the courts to interpret national law in accordance with a directive is discussed as a means to counteract inadequate transposition of a directive. This is fully understandable as the cases which have so far been decided by the Court of Justice, dealing with different aspects of the obligation, have concerned situations of directives which have not been (correctly) implemented.[55] Moreover, the developments in this area are the most interesting. However, in my view, this is too limited an approach. The famous paragraph from the *Von Colson* judgment[56] is worded in very general terms and clearly implies that the obligation exists irrespective of whether there is a deficiency in the implementing measures or whether implementation took place at all.[57]

As explained in Chapters 2 and 5, directives may be transposed in several ways.[58] Different modalities of transposition can be chosen, with verbatim transposition at one end of the spectrum and translation into national legal concepts and terminology at the other. Similarly, it has been observed that both methods have their advantages and disadvantages. From a Community law point of view, as a rule neither method is imperative, provided that the content of the measures adopted to transpose the directive is sufficiently clear and precise. Individuals must be able to ascertain their rights and duties and there must be no risk of the measures being misapplied in practice, judicial practice included. Where it appears that national courts systematically construe provisions of national law aimed at transposing a directive in a way which causes the provisions to be at variance with the directive, it could be an important indication that the directive has not been correctly transposed. If different wording had been chosen by the legislator the courts would probably also interpret the provision in another fashion, but this may not be so. It is conceivable that a directive as such has been transposed into national legislation in an adequate manner, satisfying the requirements developed by the Court of Justice. However, when construing the relevant provisions the courts choose one of the possible options for interpretation which, unfortunately, leads to a result inconsistent with the underlying directive. This would result in a sort of "de-

[55] Cf. Case 14/83 *Von Colson* [1984] ECR 1891, Case C-106/89 *Marleasing* [1990] ECR I-4135, Case 80/86 *Kolpinghuis* [1987] ECR 3969. In some cases the Court simply recalls the obligation with no further elaboration. Cf. Case C-373/90 *X* [1992] ECR I-131, Case 31/87 *Beentjes* [1988] ECR 4635, Case 125/88 *Nijman* [1989] ECR 3533.

[56] Quoted above, in Section 10.1.

[57] This distinction is also observed by e.g. Götz 1992, p. 1853-1854 and Betlem 1993, p. 212.

[58] See above, Section 2.3 and Subsection 5.2.2.

implementation", as one author called it: it is not the statute as such but its construction by the courts which fails to achieve the objective of the directive.[59] Today it is perhaps a truism to say that the application of any legal rule in a concrete case requires its interpretation.[60] However, it is important to realize that legislation, by the nature of things, is cast at a certain level of abstraction. This is equally true with respect to legislative measures transposing a directive. In other words, there will in principle always be a certain margin for national courts when they are applying and thus interpreting a legal rule.

The national courts have their own specific role in the process of implementation: they must apply the national provisions transposing the directive in a concrete case before them. Whenever the national court is called upon to apply a provision of national law intended to transpose a directive, it will necessarily come across the question of the meaning of the provision. Pursuant to the obligation laid down in *Von Colson*, this meaning must correspond with the meaning of the "counterpart – provision" of the directive. Obviously, considerable problems may arise in this respect. National legislation may literally just take over the terms of the directive, which could be unfamiliar to the national legal order. Similarly, the "translation" of the directive into national legal terminology is not necessarily a safeguard for proper interpretation and application by the courts. Neither of the methods of transposition is a watertight guarantee that the provisions will be understood and applied in perfect harmony with the underlying directive. Furthermore, the interpretation by the Court of Justice of the terms of the relevant directive may also evolve over time. Some examples may illustrate the (potential) problems.

In Case *C-373/90*[61] a "garagiste" in Bergerac, Mr. X, published advertisements with the exhortation: "Buy your new vehicle cheaper". Mr. Richard lodged a complaint before the *Juge d'Instruction* against X, together with a claim for civil indemnity, for untruthful and unlawful advertising, prohibited under Article 44 of Law No 73-1193. This Law transposed Directive 84/450 on misleading advertising.[62] The problem in this case was, *inter alia*, not an incorrect transposition of the Directive into national legislation, but rather the question of what constituted a "new car", since depending on this qualification the advertisement could be considered as misleading. There was a relatively recent judgment of the Criminal Division of the *Cour de Cassation* in which this court held, in a different but comparable context, that "to count as new, a vehicle must not only not have been driven, but must also not yet have been registered".[63] Both the Advocate General and

[59] Bates 1986, p. 185. Cf. also Everling 1992b, p. 380 who points out the danger of "de-harmonization" through interpretation.
[60] De Lange 1991, p. 188.
[61] [1992] ECR I-131.
[62] OJ 1984, L 250/17
[63] See Report for the Hearing, I-135.

the Court of Justice disagreed with the view that for the purposes of the Directive at issue and, moreover, within the broader context of protection which parallel imports enjoy to a certain extent under Community law, the cars should no longer be considered new because they had been registered (in Belgium) before importation into France. Therefore the directive had to be construed as meaning "that it does not preclude vehicles from being advertised as new ... when the vehicles concerned are registered solely for the purpose of importation [and] have never been on the road ...". Furthermore, the Court made plain to the national judge that he has to interpret national law in conformity with (this interpretation of) the Directive.[64]

Another example, taken from the area of sex discrimination, relates to dismissal. In three very similar cases[65] the Court of Justice drew a sharp distinction between age limits governing dismissal on the one hand and the pensionable age, i.e. the age at which a person is entitled to the payment of a retirement pension, on the other. With respect to the former type of age limits, discrimination between men and women, i.e. different age limits for men and women, was prohibited by virtue of Directive 76/207 (equal treatment at work).[66] On the other hand, differences in pensionable age were allowed, at least as far as statutory pensions were concerned, owing to an exception to that effect in Directive 79/7 (equal treatment statutory schemes of social security).[67]

Mrs *Beets-Proper* was dismissed at the age of 60 while her male colleagues were allowed to work until the age of 65. Her employer took the view that the employment relationship automatically ended, by virtue of an implied condition in the contract of employment, at the moment that she became entitled to an old age pension under a pension scheme of the employer's pension fund. For women this was the case at 60, for men at 65. The question in the national courts was whether such an implied condition was compatible with Article 1637ij of the Dutch Civil Code. This Article at the material time read as follows:

"(1) As regards the conclusion of a contract of employment, staff training, the terms of employment, promotion and the termination of the contract of employment, an employer may not make any distinction between men and women .... The terms of employment do not include benefits or entitlements under pension schemes. ...

[64] Another somewhat bizarre example to be mentioned briefly is the *Meilicke* case (C-83/91 [1992] ECR I-4871). The Second Company Law Directive (77/91, OJ 1977, L 26/1) was as such correctly transposed into German legislation, the *Aktiengesetz*, at least on the point at issue. Yet the interpretation given by the *Bundesgerichtshof* of the relevant provisions of the *Aktiengesetz* was, in the opinion of Dr. Meilicke, contrary to the directive, in particular its Article 11. Meilicke pointed out that the German courts were obliged to interpret the *Aktiengesetz* in accordance with the Directive. In this respect, A-G Tesauro fully agreed with him (para. 22 of the opinion). The Court, however, did not get down to the issue as, since the preliminary reference raised problems hypothetical in nature, there was "*pas lieu à statuer*".

[65] Case 152/84 *Marshall I* [1986] ECR 723, Case 262/84 *Beets-Proper* [1986] ECR 773 and Case 151/84 *Roberts* [1986] ECR 703.

[66] OJ 1976, L 39/40.

[67] OJ 1979, L 6/24.

(2) Any clause which is contrary to the first sentence of paragraph 1 shall be void."[68]

The *Gerechtshof Amsterdam*, which dealt with Beets-Proper's case on appeal, found that the exception referred to in paragraph 1 of Article 1637ij was applicable. It based its judgment on several factors which proved that there was a close connection between the termination of the contract of employment and the commencement of the pension. However, the *Hoge Raad* decided otherwise. Following an unequivocal preliminary ruling by the Court of Justice, the *Hoge Raad* considered that Article 1637ij of the Civil Code, which implements the Equal Treatment Directive, must be construed in such a manner that a condition in a contract of employment which makes this contract terminate on the date when the employee attains pensionable age, is covered by the first sentence of the first paragraph, which prohibits different treatment of men and women. The condition does not fall within the scope of the second sentence. Consequently, the disputed condition is, by virtue of the second paragraph of Article 1637ij, null and void.[69]

Obviously, it did not take much effort to decide the case in this way, in conformity with the directive at issue, as the terms of the provision to be construed lend themselves very well to such an interpretation. After all, dismissal can hardly be considered a benefit or entitlement under a pension scheme. It was rather the lower court which construed the provision in an artificial way, more or less departing from the "normal" meaning of the terms. Accordingly, Article 1637ij could be considered as an appropriate transposition of the Directive, even after the judgment of the Court of Justice and there was no need to subsequently amend the provision.

Two general conclusions can be drawn with respect to the interpretation by national courts of the measures intended to implement a directive. Firstly, case law will serve as a yardstick as to whether the implementing measures are sufficient or not. Secondly, national courts have a distinct role in the process of achieving the result prescribed by the directive. As explained in Chapter 3, Section 3.3, in this process it is not sufficient to transpose the directive into national legislative measures. The obligation goes further and involves the realization of the result in practice and *in concreto*. Viewed from this perspective, the national judge must be situated somewhere near the end of the "chain of implementation", as it is he who will often be called upon to apply the measures of transposition to a concrete case before him. In other words, the court is entrusted with the task of "*judicial implementation*". In this process the court must often interpret national law, in particular the provisions transposing the directive. That interpretation must be in conformity with the underlying directive.

[68] Case 262/84 *Beets-Proper* [1986] ECR 773, para.10.
[69] Judgment of 21 November 1986, NJ 1987 no. 351.

10.5 Consistent Interpretation and Inadequately Transposed Directives: Remedial Interpretation

Wherever a directive has been correctly transposed into national law, as a rule, consistent interpretation of the national provisions by the courts will not pose particular problems, provided that the courts are aware of the Community origins of the rules to be interpreted. Likewise, the courts will achieve the desired result by giving the provisions under consideration a certain meaning without resorting, from the national law point of view, to artificial and strained constructions.

Matters are somewhat different in the case of incorrect implementation.

In the United Kingdom a number of cases have concerned the same problem as in the *Beets-Proper*[70] case discussed in the previous Section, but the outcomes have been entirely different. The relevant national provision, Section 6 (2) (b) of the Sex Discrimination Act 1975, provided that "it is unlawful for a person, in the case of a woman employed by him at an establishment in Great Britain to discriminate against her". Furthermore, Section 6 (4) of the same Act provided that section 6 (2) (b), *inter alia*, "does not apply to provision in relation to death or retirement". This latter exception was interpreted by the courts as meaning "about retirement" with the consequence that dismissal of women at an earlier age than men was allowed since it fell within the scope of Section 6 (4). After the Court of Justice had made plain that age limits for dismissal and age at which pension becomes payable should be regarded as two separate matters, it was clear that the provision and certainly the construction of the provision by the UK courts was not compatible with Directive 76/207, as interpreted by the Court of Justice. Even then, however, the courts refused to construe the relevant Section in another way, although it was argued that another interpretation was not entirely impossible.[71] At the end of the day the Sex Discrimination Act had to be amended in order to bring it into line with the Directive.[72] It is submitted that when one compares the terms of the Dutch provision which had to be interpreted by the *Hoge Raad* and the terms of the provision of the Sex Discrimination Act, it cannot be denied that a consistent interpretation by the English courts would have required more effort and inventiveness and would probably be less obvious than in the Dutch case.[73] The next question to be answered in this respect is: does the obligation of consistent interpretation require such a *special effort*, going further than the national court would be inclined to do under the rules of construction usual in its Member State?

According to the Court's jurisprudence, consistent interpretation also has the function of *temporarily*[74] bridging the gap between national law and the directive

[70] Case 262/84 [1986] ECR 773.
[71] Cf. *Duke v. Reliance Systems Ltd.* [1987] 2 CMLR 24.
[72] Section 2 (1) of SDA 1986 repealed Section 6 (4) of SDA 1975.
[73] The reasons for refusing an interpretation consistent with the directive will not be considered here. For a discussion of the UK courts' approach see e.g. Scyczszak 1990, De Burca 1992.
[74] Cf. Case C-338/91 *Steenhorst-Neerings* [1993] ECR I-5375, para. 31-34.

which has not been adequately transposed. This function of consistent interpretation can probably best be labelled as "*remedial interpretation*", in order to distinguish it from the consistent interpretation in the context of judicial implementation. The next Sections will mainly concern this type of interpretation, which is only a palliative for inadequate implementation and will certainly *not cure* the Member State's non-compliance as such.[75]

Incorrect or inadequate transposition can take various forms. The most blatant is the situation in which the directive has not been transposed into national law at all, while it is plain, and is admitted by the Member State concerned that such a transposition is necessary in order to comply with Article 189(3). These "pathological" failures can be divided into situations where there is no national legislation covering the subject matter of the directive at all and situations where there is such legislation but it needs further adjustment.

The second type of inadequate transposition concerns a situation where no transposition measures have been adopted since the Member State is of the opinion that the result to be achieved under the directive is already fully realized within the national legal order; but upon further consideration this turns out not to be correct.

In the third type of situation the Member State has enacted the necessary measures but in fact it appears that these do not meet the requirements for correct transposition as developed by the Court of Justice.[76]

Finally, the directive may appear to have been transposed adequately at first sight, for instance by adoption of new legislation dealing fully and correctly with the subject matter of the directive, but the Member State has forgotten to "clear up" some other provisions which at the end of the day frustrate the application of the measures transposing the directive.[77]

There are of course several other forms of inadequate transposition, such as incorrect transposition of a part of a directive or a specific provision only. It is certainly not my intention to map them all. It is important in the context of the present Section to emphasize that the various categories of inadequate transposition are relevant for the question whether the national courts can proceed to remedial interpretation or not. Obviously, if there is no national law governing

[75] Cf. *ibid.*, the opinion of A-G Darmon, para. 47. See also Everling 1992b, p. 382-383 and Bleckmann (1984, p. 776) who points out that the *Von Colson* solution certainly did not amount to correct implementation. For another view see Jarass 1991, p. 218: "*soweit eine richtliniekonforme Auslegung des nationalen Rechts möglich ist kann der Mitgliedstaat in aller Regel auf eine gesonderte Umsetzung der Richtlinie verzichten*".

[76] Cf. above, Chapter 5.

[77] E.g. amended or newly introduced provisions which do not work within the broader context of the relevant legislation. This was for instance the basic problem in Case C-177/88 *Dekker* [1990] ECR I-3968.

the subject matter of the directive then there is also nothing to be interpreted. On the other hand, if national legal provisions exist but do not amount to adequate transposition, the chance that the national judge can temporarily remedy the defect will depend on the degree of variance between national law and the provisions of the directive. In some cases there can be an overt conflict; in other cases there may be merely a minor variance. Likewise, where it is plain that national law must be amended in order to satisfy the directive it will probably be more difficult to bridge the gap than where a directive has been transposed but the national provisions adopted for this purpose are not entirely satisfactory.

To put it differently, the possibility of giving provisions of national law an interpretation in conformity with the directive is closely linked to the terms of those provisions. The "closer" or the more "flexible" the terms, the more probable it is that consistent interpretation will be feasible. On the other hand, the greater the variance, the more difficult consistent interpretation will be. The degree of variance will in turn often depend on the type of inadequate transposition at issue.

This is not the end of the story. Whether a certain construction of national law is possible or not will, as already pointed out, equally depend on the limits of judicial interpretation. As will be illustrated below, from the point of view of national law, remedial interpretation may often result in an artificial or at least unusual construction. The question is indeed: "Where are the limits?". This question will, as a rule, not occur so often with respect to interpretation within the context of judicial implementation. It should however be noted that the distinction in practice between the latter type of interpretation and remedial interpretation, which seems to run alongside the difference between "usual" and "unusual" methods of interpretation, is not always easy to make.[78]

10.6 LIMITS TO CONSISTENT INTERPRETATION: NATIONAL RULES OF CONSTRUCTION

From the judgment in the *Von Colson* case it followed that, "for matters within their jurisdiction",[79] national courts are under a legal duty to interpret and apply national law in conformity with a directive. However, the national court

[78] Cf. Jans 1994, p. 250.
[79] As to the meaning of these terms see below, Subsection 10.8.4.

is obliged to do this "*in so far as it is given discretion ... under national law*".[80] This reference to discretion under national law can, within the context of the *Von Colson* judgment, be explained largely by the fact that the German government argued before the Court that the provision on compensation to be paid to a person discriminated against as regards access to employment (the provision was clearly incompatible with the requirements of Directive 76/207) did not necessarily exclude the application of the general rules of law regarding compensation. The Court of Justice held that "it is for the national court alone to rule on that question concerning the interpretation of its national law".[81] Nevertheless it went on to lay down the above-mentioned obligation of consistent interpretation.

The orthodox understanding of these references to national law was that it was up to the national court itself to decide whether it will be able to proceed to consistent interpretation or not. Likewise it was assumed that the obligation applied if several (alternative) interpretations were possible. In such a case the national judge had to choose the interpretation which would be in line with the directive. Whether this was the case was, however, again a matter for the national court to sort out.[82] Moreover, it was argued in legal writing that the Court in no way authorized the national judge to choose an interpretation *contra legem*.[83]

Obviously, as consistent interpretation is interpretation of *national* law, it is within the competence of the national courts and not within that of the Court of Justice. As such it fits entirely within the idea of the division of functions between the national courts and the Court of Justice as laid down in established jurisprudence.[84]

When searching for an answer to the question whether consistent interpretation is possible or not, and thus when addressing the issue of the discretion of the national courts under national law, the crucial factor is the approach, or methods or rules of interpretation or construction prevailing within the Member State concerned.[85] Quite naturally, the national judge will be inclined to hold that

[80] Case 14/83 [1984] ECR 1891, para. 28. In German version: "*unter voller Ausschöpfung des Beurteilungsspielraums den ihm das national Recht einräumt*"; in French version: "*dans toute la mesure où une marge d'appréciation lui est accordée par son droit national*", both of which seem more demanding than the English version.

[81] Para. 25 of the judgment.

[82] Cf. Galmot and Bonichot 1988, p. 22, Jarass 1991a, p. 218: national "*Auslegungsregeln*" are decisive.

[83] Cf. Galmot and Bonichot 1988, p. 22.

[84] Cf. in particular with respect to interpretation Case C-37/92 *Vanacker* [1995] ECR I-4947.

[85] Cf. Everling 1992b, p. 381. By all these terms I refer to the different principles, rules, canons etc. which may guide interpretation. In some legal systems they may have more a character of "real" rules while in others they are rather considered as guidelines. Cf. also Marsh 1973, p. 9.

consistent interpretation is impossible if it implies a departure from the usual rules of construction.

Soon after the judgment in *Von Colson* it became obvious, particularly from the UK experience, that the national rules of construction may form a very serious and perhaps too far-reaching restriction upon the doctrine of consistent interpretation.

In a number of cases the UK courts were not prepared to construe domestic legislation in accordance with a directive. One of the main arguments presented in this respect was that the legislation pre-dated the directive and, consequently, was not designed to transpose it.[86] These cases have been severely criticized in the UK in academic writing. According to one author they revealed "lack of understanding by the House of Lords of the principle of *indirect* effects".[87] In other cases the House of Lords was more responsive and applied a "purposive construction" of national legislation in order to bring it into line with the directives at issue[88]. However, the cases concerned interpretation of national legislation purported to transpose the directives. Moreover, it has been argued that the "purposive approach" of the UK courts does not correspond with the purposive interpretation desired by the Court of Justice when the latter refers to the purpose of the directive. The UK courts in fact did nothing more than base their interpretation on the (presumed) intent of the legislature behind the enactment of a piece of legislation. In other words, it was rather the purpose of the legislature than the purpose of the directive that played the central role in the UK courts' construction.[89]

Similarly in Germany, the aftermath of the *Von Colson* case illustrated vividly the kind of problems which the obligation of consistent interpretation may present at the national level.[90] The central issue in these cases was the limits of judicial law-making in pursuance of the obligations as formulated in *Von Colson*. Article 611a of the Civil Code, which was adopted to implement Directive 76/207, provided for damages as relief in the case of sex discrimination in respect of access to employment. The damages were limited to compensation for frustration of expectations ("*Vertrauensschaden*"), which would, as a rule, amount to indemnification of the costs incurred in relation to the application for a job, like stamps. In the view of the Court of Justice such compensation did not meet the

[86] Cf. *Duke v. Reliance System Ltd.* House of Lords [1988] 1 CMLR 719 (Sex Discrimination Act 1975 pre-dated Directive 76/207) and *Finnegan v. Clowney Youth Training Programme Ltd.* House of Lords [1990] 2 CMLR 859 (Sex Discrimination (Northern Ireland) Order 1976 had been enacted after the Directive 76/207, but in the view of the House of Lords the Order was also not adopted with the intention of complying with the Directive).

[87] Szyszczak 1990, p. 484. Cf. also De Burca 1992, p. 219 ff. and Mead 1991.

[88] *Ibid*.

[89] Cf. De Burca 1992, p. 222. For a similar approach in Germany see Spetzler 1991, p. 579. Interestingly, in Case C-334/92 *Miret* [1993] ECR I-6911 the Court introduced a similar fiction by stating that when national courts interpret and apply national law "*toute juridiction doit presumer que l'Etat a eu l'intention d'exécuter pleinement les obligations découlant de la directive concernée*" (para. 20).

[90] Cf. for a brief account Roth 1991, p. 141. For a more detailed discussion see Prechal and Burrows 1990, p. 255-259, on which the following description is partly based.

requirements of the Directive. It was, however, precisely the intention of the German legislature to limit the right to compensation to such a negligible amount. After *Von Colson*, the German courts had to face the problem whether they could override Article 611a by allowing damages on the basis of general principles of tort law.

The Labour Court of *Hamm*, which referred *Von Colson* to the Court of Justice, considered in this respect that according to the Federal Constitutional Court judges would be exceeding their judicial function if their interpretation contradicted the wording of the provisions at issue, the spirit of the measure and the intention of the legislature. The Labour Court recalled that, according to the intention of the legislature and the general rules of systemic interpretation, Article 611a of the Civil Code had to be interpreted as limiting the compensation to the very low amount payable in respect of "*Vertrauensschaden*" and as excluding the application of the general principles of tort law. In other words, the Labour Court did not have much discretion in this respect. However, it went on to consider that the interpretation required by the Court of Justice implied that the systemic and historical (i.e. focussing on the intention of the legislature) arguments of interpretation ought to be disregarded.[91] The compensation for "*Vertrauensschaden*" could then on the basis of its wording be construed as dealing with a specific ground for compensation *without* excluding the application of Article 823 of the Civil Code, the general provision governing compensation. On the one hand, this or a similar line of reasoning was also followed by several other courts. On the other hand, there were courts which were very hesistant. The Land Labour Court of *Niedersachsen*, for instance, expressed serious doubts as, in its view, it was a task for the legislature to bring national law into conformity with Community law. Another court refused to construe national provisions in accordance with the directive since two initiatives had been taken by the *Land of Hessen* and by the Socialist Party to amend the law. Under these circumstances, in the opinion of the court, there was no place for judicial intervention.[92]

The Supreme Labour Court finally settled the matter, giving the victims of discrimination higher compensation than that available for "*Vertrauensschaden*" only, but at the same time respecting the intention of the legislature.[93] In brief, on the one hand, it pointed out that the clear terms of Article 611a of the Civil Code cannot serve as a basis for a claim in damages in excess of those available for "*Vertrauensschaden*". It recalled that even interpretation of statutes in conformity with the Constitution reaches its limit at the point where it would conflict with the wording and the evident intention of the legislature. The position can be no different as regards the interpretation of national law in conformity with a directive. On the other hand, it held that the restriction of the liability to pay compensation to damages under Article 611a does not affect the right to compensation for non-pecuniary damage in respect of infringement of rights of personality under Article 823 (1) and 847 of the Civil Code. In particular, it referred to the fact that even before Article 611a was adopted, compensation for non-pecuniary damage under the two other articles of the Civil Code was recognized in cases of discrimination. Although the Supreme

[91] Cf. also Bleckmann 1984, p. 776.

[92] Cf. Roth 1991, p. 141 and Prechal and Burrows 1990, p. 255-259.

[93] Two judgments of 14 March 1989: *Re a rehabilitation centre* and *Re an animal house* [1992] 2 CMLR 21 and 29.

Court's construction may be in accordance with the requirements laid down by the Court of Justice in some cases, in others the result will be at variance with Directive 76/207. According to the Supreme Labour Court pecuniary damages only arise in the case of a serious infringement of the rights of personality. Whether this is the case depends in particular on the degree of *fault* on the part of the author of the discrimination. This approach seems to be at odds with the *Dekker* judgment.[94]

Be this as it may, in cases before the Court of Justice following on *Von Colson*, it was suggested, perhaps in reaction to the unfortunate UK experience, that national rules of construction should not apply without qualification.

In his opinion in the *Barber* case, A-G Van Gerven concluded from the manner in which Labour Court of *Hamm* interpreted national law, in pursuance of the obligation laid down in *Von Colson*, that "it would appear that Community law may set limits to certain methods of interpretation applied under a national legal system".[95] As explained above, this court decided to disregard the intention of the legislature which, in the opinion of the Supreme Labour Court, it was not allowed to do under national rules of interpretation.

Similarly, in *Marleasing* the Commission argued that since the Community legal system is an integral part of national law and the national court is also a Community court, the latter cannot be denied the possibility of interpreting national law in conformity with the directive. According to the Commission this type of interpretation should prevail over the rules of interpretation commonly recognized in the national legal order of the court concerned. In the Commission's view, it is the principle of supremacy of Community law which precludes the application of any rule of interpretation which might frustrate the result intended by the authors of the directive.[96]

The judgment in *Marleasing* suggests that the Court was not entirely insensitive to these arguments. Although it reiterated that according to *Von Colson* "the Member States' obligation arising from a directive to achieve the result envisaged by the directive and their duty under Article 5 of the treaty ... is binding on all authorities of the Member States including, for the matters within their jurisdiction, the courts", it held subsequently that "the national court called upon to interpret (national law) is required to do so, *as far as possible*, in the light of the wording and the purpose of the directive ...".[97] In summary, the reference to "discretion under national law" disappeared and was replaced by the terms "as far as possible". For the concrete problem at issue in *Marleasing* the Court found

[94] Cf. above, Chapter 5, Subsection 5.2.4 and below, Section 10.9.
[95] Case C-262/88 [1990] ECR I-1889, para. 50. Cf. also Everling 1992b, p. 381.
[96] Case C-106/89 [1990] ECR I-4135, Report for the Hearing, p. I-4142.
[97] *Ibid.*, para. 8 (emphasis added – SP).

that the requirement of consistent interpretation *precluded* the interpretation of national law in a different manner from that in conformity with the directive.[98]

What conclusions can be drawn from *Marleasing* as to the problem of applying national rules of construction? Several commentators have suggested that since *Marleasing* there has no longer been any scope for limitations resulting from the national methods of interpretation. Community law itself prescribes the methods to be used and that determines the limits of the obligation of consistent interpretation. The words "as far as possible" merely refer to the nature of the judicial function as such and no longer to the methods of construction under national law.[99] Similarly, this approach seems to imply that the question whether the national court is still within the boundaries of its judicial role or not would in the ultimate analysis be a matter of Community law as apposed to national (constitutional) law.[100]

The Court's far-reaching interference with the way national law had to be interpreted by the Spanish court in *Marleasing* militates in favour of this point of view. The Court specified in very concrete terms the manner in which the national court had to interpret the relevant provisions of national law in order to comply with the directive[101] and it prohibited the national court from choosing another interpretation. The latitude left to the national court was evidently reduced to zero. In my opinion, however, it would be an over-interpretation of *Marleasing* to conclude that the obligation of consistent interpretation is an *absolute* one, requiring national courts to give effect to directives, whatever the terms of the national provisions to be interpreted might be.[102] Such a conclusion would plainly be at odds with the "possibility for interpretation" put forward by the Court in *Marleasing* itself. This possibility depends at least upon the "flexibility" of the provision to be interpreted and, as will be explained in Section 10.7, it has its limits in general principles of law. The Court's strict wording must be seen within the context of the case. As the opinion of A-G Van Gerven makes clear the type of construction of national law desired by the Court of Justice was certainly possible.[103]

[98] *Ibid.*, para. 9 and 13.

[99] Cf. Curtin 1992, p. 40, Snijder 1993, p. 43, Prechal 1991, p. 1597. Tanney (1992, p. 1026) also suggests that national rules of interpretation are no longer relevant. "Wherever possible" should, in his view, be understood as "where there is no irreconcilable conflict as a matter of language".

[100] Cf. the discussion in German literature (Spetzler 1991, p. 579, Dänzer-Vanotti 1991, p. 754, Di Fabio 1990) as to the question whether consistent interpretation prevails over national methods of interpretation in which the limits of the judicial function play a part.

[101] Cf. Stuyck and Wytinck 1991, p. 210.

[102] Cf. De Burca 1992, p. 223. See also Case C-334/92 *Miret* [1993] ECR I-6911, para. 22, where the Court clearly accepts that consistent interpretation is not always possible.

[103] Cf. also Timmermans 1992, p. 819.

Spanish law lacked a specific rule as to the nullity applicable to limited companies. Instead, the general rule for the nullity of contracts applied by analogy. Under this rule, contracts lacking cause or having an unlawful cause have no legal effect. In pursuance of the obligation formulated by the Court of Justice the national judge had to interpret the concept of "unlawful cause" as including only the grounds of nullity listed in the directive at issue.

It is undoubtedly true that the Court's reasoning was not entirely satisfactory in this respect as it did not explain why in this concrete case the obligation of consistent interpretation was able to preclude any other interpretation. Similarly, it is arguable that the Court was at the boundaries of its own competence under Article 177, interfering perhaps too much with the construction of national law, when it prescribed how the national court must interpret the national provisions. However, if the judgment is placed within its proper context, *Marleasing* is much less revolutionary than would appear at first sight.

Be this as it may, it seems that national courts are no longer entirely free to determine the parameters of what is "possible" and what is not. The most obvious example in this respect can – again – be found in the *Marleasing* judgment. If, according to the Court, the obligation of consistent interpretation applies with respect to both national law predating the directive and national law enacted after the directive, the UK rule of "Community law consistent" construction which was restricted to posterior national provisions only, can obviously no longer apply. Before a more conclusive answer can be given as to the limits of the application of national rules of construction, it is necessary first to address the issue of general principles of law as limits of consistent interpretation.

10.7 Limits to Consistent Interpretation: General Principles of Law

To the three possible limits suggested in the literature, namely the flexibility of the terms, the methods of interpretation and the judicial function, the Court has added general principles of law. These principles were referred to in the *Kolpinghuis* judgment where the Court of Justice held that

> "(the) obligation on the national court to refer to the content of the directive when interpreting the relevant rules of its national law is limited by the general principles of law which form part of Community law and in particular the principles of legal certainty and non-retroactivity."[104]

[104] Case 80/86 [1987] ECR 3969, para. 13.

This quotation from the Court's judgment immediately gives rise to two questions: firstly, to what general principles of law is the Court referring, national or Community law principles? Secondly, which general principles of law function as limits to consistent interpretation in addition to the principle of legal certainty and the principle of non-retroactivity?

The answer to the first question is not entirely unproblematic. It has been argued that the principles to which the Court makes reference are Community law principles.[105] This would imply that their content and scope is entirely determined by Community law itself. An argument for this proposition could be that the obligation of consistent interpretation, being an obligation stemming directly from Community law, can only be limited by Community law principles.[106] However, in Chapter 2, Section 2.4, I observed that the reference to "general principles of law which form part of Community law" may likewise mean that Community law allows the application of national principles and it does so for the very reason that these principles must be considered as being a part of the Community legal order as well. The difference with the previous position is that these principles are national principles. But, as already argued in Chapter 2, Section 2.4, their content and application are not unlimited. They are subject to the control of the Court of Justice. I see no reason why this should be otherwise when the principles function as limits to the obligation of consistent interpretation. The difference between the application of Community law principles and national principles in their "curtailed" form may indeed seem mainly theoretical. However it also has some practical implications. In the first situation, i.e. the application of general principles of Community law, the national judge has to ascertain the existence of such a principle and, furthermore, how it is to be applied. In the second situation he can take the national principles as a point of departure and should subsequently discern whether the content given to the principle in national law and its way of application is permitted under Community law. The different approaches may often lead to subtle but nonetheless distinct results. For the time being no unequivocal answer can be given to the first question.

In relation to the second question, the Court's judgment in *Kolpinghuis* clearly suggests that principles other than those of legal certainty and non-retroactivity may also come into play.

It is not my intention to review all the principles now accepted by the Court of Justice as general principles of Community law[107] or all the possible candidates for consideration

[105] Cf. Timmermans 1988, p. 334.

[106] Cf. also below, Chapter 11, Subsection 11.5.2.

[107] For an overview of general principles of Community law see e.g. Schermers and Waelbroeck 1992, p. 27-94.

as principles which form part of Community law and which could serve as limits to consistent interpretation. By way of example, I shall mention unjust enrichment, equity and perhaps also proportionality. It should not be excluded *a priori* that consistent interpretation may, under certain circumstances, amount to unjust enrichment of a legal subject or to a result which can be considered as inequitable. Similarly, it is conceivable that the national court, when it proceeds to consistent interpretation, could achieve a result which on further consideration is disproportionate to the objective pursued by the directive or by the specific provision of a directive which serves as a standard for interpretation. Perhaps this case can best be labelled as a case of "consistent over-interpretation".

In the *Kolpinghuis* judgment itself two other principles were implicitly recognized as limiting the obligation of consistent interpretation, namely *nulla poena sine lege* and *nullum crimen sine lege*. Both principles can be regarded as underlying the prohibition of retroactivity of criminal law.[108] The proceedings against *Kolpinghuis* were criminal proceedings. It would be incompatible with both principles if consistent interpretation effectively "created" a new criminal offence or increased criminal liability.[109] Yet matters are different outside the sphere of criminal law. Although there too the rule is non-retroactivity, the principle is less absolute and under certain circumstances exceptions are allowed.[110]

Another principle of criminal law which could come into play as a limit to consistent interpretation is the presumption of innocence, the principle of *nulla poena sine culpa*.[111] In Chapter 5, Subsection 5.2.4, the case of Mrs *Dekker*[112] was briefly mentioned. In this case, the requirement of fault and absence of grounds of exemption applicable under the Dutch law on civil liability had to be disregarded as a direct consequence of the interpretation of Directive 76/207 (equal treatment at work)[113] given by the Court of Justice. Theoretically, in criminal proceedings the same may occur as well: the requirement of proof of fault on the part of the person concerned may, through the interpretation in conformity with a directive, turn into a system of strict criminal liability. Whether this is allowed or not will in the final analysis depend on the question as to how far certain restrictions of this principle are admitted.[114]

Returning to *Kolpinghuis*, the Court's explicit reference to legal certainty did not just appear out of the blue. On the one hand, to put it simply, interpretation is

[108] Cf. Case 63/83 *Kent Kirk* [1984] ECR 2689 and the opinion of A-G Jacobs in Joined Cases C-206/88 and C-207/88 *Vessoso and Zanetti* [1990] ECR I-1461, para. 25. Cf. also Article 7 of the ECHR.

[109] Cf. Case 80/86 [1987] ECR 3969, para. 13.

[110] Cf. Case C-331/88 *Fedesa* [1990] ECR I-4023. Moreover, not in every criminal case does the issue of "nulla poene / nullum crimen" arises. See for instance Case C-373/90 *X* [1992] ECR I-131, discussed briefly hereabove in Section 10.4, where consistent interpretation worked out more in favour of the suspect than to his disadvantage.

[111] Cf. Article 6 (2) ECHR.

[112] Case C-177/88 [1990] ECR I-3941.

[113] OJ 1976, L 39/40.

[114] Cf. Prechal 1991, p. 669. As to strict criminal liability see the opinion of A-G Van Gerven in Case C-326/88 *Hansen* [1990] ECR I-2911.

about giving a meaning to a legal provision which the judge applies to a particular situation.[115] On the other hand, the concept of legal certainty implies that the application of the law to a specific situation must be predictable.[116] This implies that, depending on the circumstances and, in particular, on its wording, a rule cannot be construed as bearing a meaning which would fly in the face of the meaning one may expect the rule to have.[117] This is perhaps somewhat over-simplified: firstly, because construction of rules may be a rather complicated operation; secondly, because the concept of legal certainty is very wide and encompasses various sub-concepts, such as non-retroactivity, vested rights and legitimate expectations. For these reasons, the search for an appropriate meaning of a provision which does not offend against legal certainty is anything but unproblematic. To gain a more precise impression as to the manner in which legal certainty could limit consistent interpretation would require a study of the application and interpretation of the concept in all its various manifestations. However, within the context of the present book I shall confine myself to offering only some general remarks.

In Chapter 5, Section 5.2 on the requirements laid down by the Court with respect to adequate transposition of directives, it appeared, *inter alia*, that the principle of legal certainty requires an unequivocal wording which gives the persons concerned a clear and precise understanding of their rights and obligations.[118] Similarly, it appeared that, in the Court's view, individuals are deemed to be unable to ascertain the full extent of their rights as long as a directive has not been properly transposed. It is only upon proper transposition that the state of legal certainty required by the Court is created.[119] In legal literature it has been submitted that if the Court proceeded in a comparable (restrictive) manner in matters relating to consistent interpretation, legal certainty as a limit to this interpretation would promptly be reached.[120] However this way of presenting things begs the question whether the two approaches can be compared. In my view, the principle of legal certainty then applies in different contexts which may call for different modalities of application. As far as implementation is concerned, legal certainty requires clear and

[115] Cf. Marsh 1973, p. 20.

[116] Cf. Schermers and Waelbroeck 1992, p. 52. Cf. also with respect to Community legislation Case 70/83 *Kloppenburg* [1984] ECR 1075: "Community legislation must be unequivocal and its application must be predictable for those who are subject to it" (para. 11).

[117] Cf. A-G Van Gerven who wondered in Joined Cases C-63/91 and C-64/91 *Jackson and Creswell* [1992] ECR I-4737, para. 29, whether the obligation of consistent interpretation also applies to a national rule which is clear and, as such, not susceptible of differing interpretation. However, in his opinion in Case C-271/91 *Marshall II* [1993] ECR I-4367, para. 10, he disapproved such an obligation as it would amount to an interpretation *contra legem* and, consequently, as I will argue below, infringe the principle of legal certainty.

[118] See e.g. Case 143/83 *Commission v. Denmark* [1985] ECR 427.

[119] Cf. Case C-208/90 *Emmott* [1991] ECR I-4269.

[120] Cf. Keus 1993, p. 65.

precise transposition in order to ensure a situation in national law which corresponds entirely with the directive at issue, enables those concerned to know their rights and obligations and safeguards its full effect. Where the directive prescribes "equal pay for work of equal value", the Member State cannot confine itself to prescribing "equal pay for equal work". With respect to consistent interpretation, the function of legal certainty is different. Here it is consistent interpretation which must ensure as far as possible the correspondence between the directive and the relevant national rules, while legal certainty functions as a restriction to this exercise. Where national legislation provides for "equal pay for equal work", while, according to the directive, it should be "equal pay for work of equal value", it should not be excluded *a priori* that, in order to bridge the discrepancy, equal work should be interpreted as including work of equal value. Whether such an interpretation will be possible, and thus whether it is still reasonable to give national terms a broader meaning of this kind, will depend on a number of other factors. It is, for instance, conceivable that in this sense a circular could be issued by labour inspectorates. Circulars do not amount to adequate implementation.[121] At the same time, however, they can serve as an element for accepting that the legal certainty on the part of – in this particular example – the employer has not (yet) been violated.

Another element could likewise be the very existence of the directive. In the case law on proper implementation of directives, in fact, there exists a fiction that individuals are not aware of their existence.[122] Yet in *Barber,*[123] for instance, the existence of two directives was considered to be an important element for accepting that the legal certainty of the parties concerned as to the scope of Article 119 deserved protection. In *Fedesa,*[124] although in a different context and in quite particular circumstances, the Court found that the probable knowledge of those concerned regarding the content of the directive at issue worked in the contrary direction: it blocked their argument drawing on the principle of protection of legitimate expectations.

Comparable inferences as to the relevance of the directive as an element to be taken into account when addressing the question of legal certainty can be drawn from the opinion of A-G VerLoren van Themaat in *Kloppenburg.*[125] In this case the Advocate General suggested that the individuals concerned could rely on the Sixth VAT Directive until the time when the Ninth VAT Directive (which postponed the implementation deadline of the Sixth Directive) was published.[126] He referred in this context to the "fundamental principle in the Community legal order (which) requires that a measure adopted by the public authorities shall not be applicable to those concerned before they have the opportunity to make themselves acquainted with it". Obviously, this suggests a deviation from the above-mentioned fiction that individuals are not aware of the existence of the directives.

[121] See above, Chapter 5, Subsection 5.2.3.
[122] Cf. Case C-208/90 *Emmott* [1991] ECR I-4269.
[123] Case C-262/88 [1990] ECR I-1889.
[124] Case C-331/88 [1990] ECR I-4023.
[125] Case 70/83 [1984] ECR 1075, at p. 1093.
[126] Directive 77/388, OJ 1977, L 145/1 and Directive 78/538, OJ 1978, L 194/16.

A recent example of such an approach has been discussed by Devloo: in a judgment of 20 May 1992 the Court of Appeal Brussels interpreted national law in conformity with Directive 86/653 (self-employed agents).[127] The court dismissed an argument drawing on legal certainty. In its view the parties concerned could have had knowledge of the changes to be introduced in national legislation, since the first draft of the Directive dated from 1977 and the final text was adopted in 1986.[128]

In summary, the application of the principle of legal certainty is very much dependent on the context. One must therefore be very careful about transposing the reasoning developed in one context to a different one.

Another implication of the principle of legal certainty is that no interpretation of national law in accordance with the directive can take place if the facts of the case at issue are situated within a period *before* the relevant directive was adopted.[129]

One of the limitations of consistent interpretation which is usually brought forward is the prohibition of interpreting national law *contra legem.*[130] Interpretation *contra legem* in this context seems to denote giving national provisions a meaning which clearly deviates from an initial (literal) reading of the provisions concerned. As a rule, in a case of this kind the wording as such cannot be stretched sufficiently far, but nevertheless the courts choose the deviating meaning. This prohibition can also be considered as deriving from the principle of legal certainty. Interpretation *contra legem* affects, almost by its very nature, legal certainty in the sense of predictability of the law, and from this point of view it is fully understandable that the prohibition should in principle apply as a limit in the field of consistent interpretation. Yet, in my view, the categoric manner in which this argument is generally presented is slightly surprising. Although within the national legal systems *contra legem* interpretation is certainly not a daily occurence, there are instances where the national courts arrive at such a result.[131] The prohibition is apparently not sacrosanct. Moreover, in the same line of argument, it should be observed that – in practice – legal certainty is a rather flexible principle which may, depending on the circumstances, allow various interpretations and which does not have to be safeguarded at all costs.

[127] OJ 1986, L 382/17.

[128] Devloo 1993-1994, p. 380. The judgment is criticized by the author since the presumption that everybody is supposed to know the law is extended to knowledge about initiatives *de lege ferenda.*

[129] Cf. Van Gerven 1993, p. 11. For this very reason the *Hoge Raad* refused to interpret the *Benelux Merkenwet* in conformity with Directive 89/104 (trade mark), OJ 1989, L 40/1, in *Michelin v. Michels*, 17 December 1993, Rechtspraak NJB 1994/2, p. 14. A case where a national court (*Rechtbank van Koophandel Namen*) did interpret the *Benelux Merkenwet* in accordance with the Directive is briefly discussed by Devloo (1993-1994, p. 380).

[130] Cf. Galmot and Bonichot 1988, p. 22, Van Gerven 1993, p. 10, Curtin 1992, p. 40.

[131] Cf. MacCormick and Summers 1991, p. 93, p. 181 and p. 191.

Therefore, in my opinion, the possibility that in certain (exceptional) circumstances consistent interpretation will amount to or will require interpretation of national law *contra legem* should not be excluded.

In academic writing the question has been raised whether the obligation of consistent interpretation as laid down by the Court of Justice in *Marleasing* in fact interferes with the principle of legal certainty or results in interpretation *contra legem*, as the case may be.[132] Indeed, as pointed out above, in this case the obligation was formulated by the Court in very strong terms. It is, however, submitted that such a reading again amounts to an over-interpretation of the judgment. In my opinion, a number of elements of the case must be taken into consideration. In this case, both the Commission and the Advocate General[133] pointed out that the construction of the Spanish Civil Code proposed by them is quite possible and does not amount to an interpretation *contra legem*. However, Marleasing's lawyer argued at the hearing that consistent interpretation as defended by the Commission would require the national judge to do something which is not allowed under national rules of construction laid down in the Spanish Civil Code[134] and, consequently, such a demarche would infringe the principle of legal certainty. In its judgment, the Court ignored both issues. It is indeed not very convincing to argue that the fact that the Court did not address this issue means that one has to deduce that it did not bother about legal certainty in the present case.[135] It is, however, important to realize that the Court was aware of both the *contra legem* argument and the argument of legal certainty but apparently found it unnecessary to address the problems.[136] Moreover, on more objective grounds it can be defended that legal certainty was not really at stake, as the interpretation prescribed in *Marleasing* resulted in an exclusion of certain grounds of nullity which previously existed under national law. In other words, it did not directly concern a situation in which an entirely unexpected obligation was imposed upon individuals. And it is notably in such a situation that concerns about legal certainty will come fully into focus.[137]

The final subject which I would like to address briefly in the present Section is the following: as a rule, general principles of law as limits to consistent interpretation are discussed in relation to the *obligation* of the domestic court.

[132] Cf. Betlem 1993, p. 250, Stuyck and Wytinck 1991, p. 211, Keus 1993, p. 65, De Burca 1992, p. 229.

[133] Case C-106/89 [1990] ECR I- 4135, Report for the Hearing, p. I-4141, opinion, para. 20.

[134] In particular, he referred to Article 1 of the Civil Code. He argued that, according to this provision, norms of international treaties are not directly applicable in Spain if they have not been integrated in the internal legal order by way of publication in the Spanish Official Journal and therefore they cannot be applied by the courts. Whatever the merits of such an argument might be from the Community law point of view, there is some force in them when considered from the point of view of legal certainty.

[135] Cf. Keus 1993, p. 62.

[136] Cf. Devloo 1993-1994, p. 379 and De Burca 1992, p. 231.

[137] Cf. below, Section 10.9.

Viewed from this perspective, they are a kind of "safety net" which should prevent the courts being forced to go to unacceptable lengths. A related question is whether the principles can also forbid the domestic courts to arrive at a certain interpretation which is still within the limits of their respective national legal systems and which they believe to be a consistent interpretation under Community law, but which, from a Community point of view, would not be acceptable. It is submitted that the answer to this question should be affirmative. The domestic courts are here operating within the context of Community law. For this very reason Community law, and especially Article 5 of the Treaty, may not only require them to do something positive but may also stop them if they should transcend the limits of what is considered as acceptable under Community law.

10.8 National Approaches to Interpretation, General Principles of Law and the Limits of the Judicial Function

10.8.1 Introduction

The national courts are required to construe national law in conformity with a directive "as far as possible". How this crucial qualification should be understood is unclear. If it is to be understood as referring to the *national methods of interpretation*, in Section 10.6 the somewhat tentative conclusion was that these methods cannot be applied without qualification. It was also suggested that the terms "as far as possible" refer to the *limits of the judicial function* rather than to the national methods of interpretation. In the same Section I argued that it amounts to an over-interpretation of the *Marleasing* judgment to hold that domestic courts enjoy no latitude in considering whether consistent interpretation is possible or not and that any interpretation of national law other than that in conformity with the directive is just bluntly prohibited. In my view, neither *Marleasing* nor any other case of the Court justifies such a conclusion. On the other hand, it must be assumed that national courts do not have a totally free hand as to the issue of "possibility"; the answer regarding possibility and impossibility seems to some extent to be brought under the control of the Court of Justice. The main questions are then in the Community law context: what are the margins for the application of national methods of interpretation and what are the boundaries of the judicial function of the national courts?

In Section 10.7 the *general principles of law* as limits to consistent interpretation were discussed. The construction chosen by the Court of Justice makes clear, in my opinion, that the Court wishes to anchor the possible restrictions of consistent

STAFFS UNIVERSITY LIBRARY

interpretation in Community law itself.[138] This again implies that national courts are curtailed in their freedom as to the manner of interpretation of national law. Viewed from this perspective, "as far as possible" should in any case be understood as "*within the limits of the general principles of law*". Whether these principles are general principles of Community law or national principles as circumscribed by Community law is, as observed in the preceding Section, not entirely clear.

In the present Section, I shall attempt to set out the interrelation between general principles of law, methods of interpretation and judicial function. I shall then discuss some conclusions which can be drawn as to the limits of consistent interpretation.

It is perhaps far too obvious to state that the obligation of consistent interpretation cannot be isolated from the context of interpretation of national law in general. It is not my intention to give an account here of all the issues arising within the context of interpretation of law by domestic courts, however interesting and instructive the subject might be when considered within one single country, and however fascinating in a comparative analysis. I shall confine myself to some very general remarks about interpretation and consider the way in which consistent interpretation, as a particular method of interpretation dictated by Community law, fits into this wider framework.

10.8.2 Interpretation of National Law in a Comparative Perspective

In their comparative analysis of judicial interpretation of statutes Summers and Taruffo[139] identify eleven basic types of arguments given by judges as reasons for their decision about the meaning of the text concerned. These constitute a "common core of good reasons for interpretative decisions" shared by different legal systems.[140] The authors describe how the different types of arguments operate in practice, how they may compete with each other and how the conflicts between arguments are solved. The most striking (though not very surprising)

[138] Cf. also Timmermans 1988, p. 334.

[139] In MacCormick and Summers 1991, p. 461 ff. The analysis is based on reports on statutory interpretations in 9 countries, including Germany, Italy, France and the UK.

[140] *Ibid*., p. 3. This typology of arguments runs partly parallel to what are in some countries known as canons of interpretation or principles of interpretational method, such as literal / grammatical / semiotic interpretation, historical interpretation, systemic / schematic intepretation, teleological interpretation on the one hand, and special types of legal arguments or techniques of interpretation, such as reasoning by analogy or *a contrario* on the other. The different distinctions and classifications are indeed a matter of legal methodology which varies between the countries concerned, and even within one single country often no consensus exists. Cf. MacCormick and Summers 1991, e.g. p. 77, p. 82, p. 89 and p. 179.

result of the analysis is the relative predominance of linguistic arguments.[141] The explanation for this is not very difficult: "A statutory text consists of a set of words, and we must resort to these words if we are to interpret the text at all."[142] The linguistic argument being thus, as a rule, a starting point for interpretation, it will often be either subsequently corroborated or completed or, on the contrary, confronted with other types of arguments. In other words, other types of arguments may reinforce a standard ordinary or technical meaning of words, they may clarify and thus determine the statutory meaning of words where linguistic arguments are indeterminate because of ambiguity, vagueness, evaluative openness etc. of the terms used, or they may support a contrary *special* meaning of the words at issue.[143] Moreover, the arguments may be used to *raise* issues of interpretation or to attack or undermine other arguments.[144]

The other types of arguments discerned by Summers and Taruffo are, *inter alia*, the following:

– contextual-harmonization arguments, referring to other elements of context, beyond the immediate context of use of the words of the section to be interpreted, such as other parts of the section, any related sections of the same statute and any other closely related statute;

– arguments from a precedent interpreting the statute, whether by virtue of the rule of *stare decisis* or by virtue of a persuasive or *de facto* effect common to civil law systems;

– arguments appealing to general legal principles. Under these arguments it is maintained that the chosen meaning coheres with a general principle of law applicable within the area of law in which the case falls. Principles under consideration here are for instance *nulla poena sine lege* in criminal law, "no liability without fault" in tort law, principle of fair hearing, freedom of speech, non-discrimination on racial and religious grounds or some other constitutionalized principle;

– arguments from statutory analogy, which are, however, not deployed to extend criminal prohibitions or a statute imposing a tax;

– arguments drawing on some special history of the adoption and evolution of the statute. In this respect consideration is given to the fact that the statute has come to stand for something different from that for which it was originally designed;

– teleological arguments according to which that interpretation must be chosen which best serves the ultimate purpose of the statute. Yet the construction of the purpose differs between the systems; in some cases it might be the actual historic purpose, in other cases "a purpose attributable to a rational or objective legislator";

[141] In this respect they distinguish arguments from a standard ordinary meaning of ordinary words and argument from a standard technical meaning of ordinary words or of technical words, legal or non-legal. *Ibid.*, p. 464.

[142] *Ibid.*, p. 466.

[143] *Ibid.*, p. 465.

[144] *Ibid.*, p. 464.

– arguments invoking the intention of the legislature. Arguments of this type are construed in different ways. Usually some consideration is given to the subjective intention of the legislator as it appears, in particular, from the *travaux préparatoires*. However, in the UK, where the use of *travaux préparatoires* is generally prohibited (or at least was until recently), the courts rely on a linguistically oriented concept of legislative intention, assuming that the ordinary or technical meaning of the text is the best indication of the intention. Moreover, appeal is often made to certain "presumptions" as to legislative intention: for instance, that the legislator does not intend violation of the constitution, fundamental human rights and international treaties, that it does not intend absurd or manifestly unjust outcomes, that it does not intend a statute to have retroactive effect, that the legislature is rational and strives for systemic coherence and unity etc.

It will hardly come as a surprise that there are certain types of arguments that seem to have more weight in one or more systems, but to be less important in other systems. Similarly, there are considerable variations between countries in the way the different types of arguments arise and operate.[145] Moreover, interpretation is equally affected by several other "*ad hoc*" factors, like the character of the statute, i.e. for instance, its age, the nature of the substantive field it covers (e.g. criminal or tax law), whether the statute is an isolated one or is inserted into an existing statutory framework, whether it breaks sharply from the past or should rather be regarded as a continuation of an existing regime, the way it is drafted etc.[146] Sometimes the addressees of the statute may also play a part. German and English courts tend to favour ordinary meaning where statutes are addressed directly to lay persons.[147] On the other hand, no such distinction according to the nature of the addressees is made in France.[148] Yet, apart from what has already been said about the overall decisiveness of linguistic arguments, other arguments which are quite extensively employed and highly influential in the different legal systems are systemic arguments (contextual-harmonization arguments), the intention of the legislature (in all the different forms) and arguments from coherence with general principles.

The relative weight of the arguments comes to light particularly where two or more arguments conflict. The courts may then deploy several modes of resolution: on further consideration one of the arguments may be deprived of its *prima facie* force and consequently be ignored, one of the arguments may be subordinated pursuant to a rule or maxim of priority, or it may be "outweighed". In general, there are no clearly formulated priority rules in the event of conflict between the different arguments.[149] However, the linguistic arguments in

[145] E.g. in Germany the "*verfassungskonforme Auslegung*" is quite systematically used while this is not necessarily the case in other countries. *Ibid.*, p. 464.

[146] *Ibid.*, p.474.

[147] *Ibid.*, p.107 and p. 394.

[148] *Ibid.*, p. 201.

[149] Cf. also Dänzer-Vanotti 1991 and Spetzler 1991. In some systems, however, there exist some legal norms which should discipline interpretation. Cf. Article 1 of the Spanish Civil Code (cf. above, n. 134) and the "preliminary provisions" of the Italian Civil Code (cf. MacCormick and Summers 1991, p. 231). Cf. also for international law Vienna Convention Art. 31-33.

particular seem to be relatively more difficult to set aside, or relatively less frequently subordinated by virtue of a rule of priority, or relatively more difficult to outweigh than other arguments.[150] MacCormick and Summers explain in this respect that

"there is every reason why statutes should be read simply in the context of an informed understanding of the natural language (or the technical language) in which they are written, and applied or not applied in that sense, unless some justificatory argument of the systemic or teleological-evaluative types can be shown to override an applicable linguistic argument rather than complement it."[151]

In their view, the values underpinning simple linguistic argumentation at the level of statutory interpretation, which function as a kind of second-level or priority criteria guiding the application of the first-level criteria, are democracy, the separation of powers and the rule of law.[152] One of the crucial aspects of the complex and many-facetted doctrine of the rule of law to which the authors refer is that it requires "reasonable generality, clarity and constancy in the law". A rational and reasonably well-informed citizen should be able to understand it.[153] These requirements can indeed be expressed in terms of legal certainty. In other words, legal certainty plays an important role in deciding to which type(s) of arguments priority should be given.

The maintenance of the principle of legal certainty is undoubtedly one of the major concerns of courts when interpreting the law and it will often militate in favour of a linguistic approach to the text.[154] Yet it has its limits. Firstly, the text may be unclear, ambiguous, abstract or "open-ended" so that linguistic arguments do not greatly assist the court. However, the question as to whether a text is ambiguous or not is already rather tricky. When answering it, much will depend on the attitude of the courts. If some courts are satisfied that a statutory provision is clear and unambiguous in the limited context of the statute the answer will certainly be different from that if they were to take into account

[150] MacCormick and Summers 1991, p. 481-482.

[151] *Ibid.*, p.533.

[152] For the sake of brevity, I confine myself to the values underlying linguistic arguments. However, as MacCormick and Summers observe, the justificatory force of other types of argument depends also on fundamental legal-constitutional values which have a special significance in the legal order concerned (p. 532-539). For instance, interpretation seeking to safeguard the coherence of the law can be brought back to the need to secure a relatively ordered and structured scheme of political, social and human values (p. 536).

[153] MacCormick and Summers 1991, p. 535.

[154] Cf. also Case 80/76 *Kerry Milk* [1977] ECR 425: "the elimination of linguistic discrepancies by way of interpretation may ... run counter the concern for legal certainty in as much as one or more texts involved may have to be interpreted in a manner at variance with the natural and usual meaning of the words" (para. 11).

matters outside the statute and thus give consideration to some "undermining" arguments.[155] In other words, the very first problem to be dealt with is often to recognize (or admit) the ambiguity of words.

Secondly, legal certainty may in certain circumstances compete with other values.

For instance as far as Germany is concerned, Alexy and Dreier[156] have explained that there is no general priority relation between formal (i.e. referring to legal certainty) and substantive reasons (i.e. concerned with the soundness of the decision with respect to its content). The absence of the priority rule is due to the point of view of the Constitutional Court that both elements are part of the rule of law. According to this Court "the principle of legal certainty and the principle of justice in individual cases have the status of constitutional principles; legal certainty and justice are both essential components of the rule of law, one of the leading ideas of the Basic Law".[157] Consequently, in Germany conflicts are "resolved by weighing the principles and working out concrete priority relations for individual cases or specific types of cases".[158]

Although Alexy and Dreier focus on the German situation the problem is a more general one: any court may find itself faced with competing values which must be resolved by a process of balancing. Depending upon the circumstances, the intelligibility of the interpretation by those concerned, in the sense that they consider it to be equitable and just, may prevail over a strictly linguistic approach which is then related to legal certainty in the strict sense of the term.[159]

Apart from legal certainty, another crucial factor which greatly influences the interpretative preference, i.e. the decision as to the arguments to which priority should be given, is the upholding of the separation of powers.[160] The relative roles which courts and legislatures play within the constitutional framework have a considerable impact on the outcome of the process of interpretation. While in

[155] Marsh (1973, p. 75), when comparing the attitude of English judges with that of their colleagues on the continent, said: "(the English judge) does not generally feel himself under the same obligation to search as deeply as possible for the most satisfactory meaning of the statute, if he has to hand an interpretation which accords with the normal usage of language as employed in the text of the statute, and with the more obvious and immediate implications of the text".

[156] In MacCormick and Summers 1991, p. 98.

[157] BVerfGE 7, 194 (196).

[158] MacCormick and Summers 1991, p.101.

[159] Cf. DeLange 1991, p. 197. However, it has also been argued that "... Parliament makes and unmakes the law; the judge's duty is to interpret and apply the law, not to change it to meet judge's idea of what justice requires". Lord Scarman in *Duport Steel Ltd. v. Sirs,* quoted by Frowein 1986, p. 555.

[160] MacCormick and Summers 1991, p. 534, De Lange 1991, Chapter 7.

some countries the courts are prepared to go quite a long way,[161] in other countries they may seek to "protect and preserve a constitutional balance of powers by generally taking a relatively restrictive approach to statutory interpretation".[162] It is no exception for the courts to admit in explicit terms that, in certain cases, the limits of their function within the legal system have been reached.[163]

10.8.3 The Broader Framework and Consistent Interpretation

In the previous Section I sketched a highly schematic picture of the main interpretative arguments and briefly addressed their interaction. Of course, this picture cannot match the complex realities of interpretation. It may, however, help in the understanding of some major problems raised by the doctrine of consistent interpretation. How does consistent interpretation then fit within this broader framework?

If the national court is under the obligation to proceed "as far as possible" to consistent interpretation, the minimum that should and certainly can be required is that judges *must under all circumstances take due account* of the relevant (provisions of the) directive.[164] In this way the directive becomes (at least) one of the arguments available for giving a certain meaning to the national text at issue. Likewise, the argument drawing on the directive can be deployed to raise an issue of interpretation or to undermine other arguments. Although this may in fact seem to be rather obvious, giving consideration to the directive is already an achievement when one realizes that, for instance in the UK, courts do not look beyond the statute unless the text is ambiguous. There is, in my view, an important difference between on the one hand looking to see whether national law is ambiguous and only in the case of an affirmative answer turning to the directive, and, on the other hand, giving proper consideration to the directive first and then seeking to interpret national law accordingly on the other.[165]

A related question is indeed what courts subsequently do with the "existence" of the directive. As a matter of principle, they are obliged to give effect to the directive through interpretation. As long as the – what I shall call, for the sake

[161] Although this does not always happen in an overt manner. For instance French judges disclaim any interpretative role, as in their view law-making is entirely an issue for the legislature which is the democratically elected organ of the people (MacCormick and Summers 1991, p. 503); that, however, does not mean that they do not interpret, sometimes even in a manner which may appear to be *contra legem* (*Ibid.*, p. 192).

[162] *Ibid.*, p. 396 (the quotation relates to the UK).

[163] De Lange 1991, p. 191-194, Bell and Engle 1987, p. 22-23.

[164] Cf. also Everling 1992b, p. 381.

[165] Cf. also Curtin 1990a, p. 222.

of convenience – "directive argument" reinforces or completes another argument,[166] so that the interpretation given is in conformity with the directive, no particular problems are to be expected. This situation will often occur where the directive has actually been implemented or where pre-existing legislation is deemed to satisfy the requirements posed by the directive. The directive argument may then be cumulated, for instance, with the intention of the legislature or at least with the presumption that the legislature intended to comply with the directive. Moreover, there will usually exist a national provision which, from the linguistic point of view, will not be too remote. Basically, this operation of the directive argument will occur in cases of consistent interpretation within the context of judicial implementation as discussed in Section 10.4.

Matters are different in a situation of conflict, i.e. where the directive argument has to compete with other types of argument. This may occur, for instance, if it appears from *travaux préparatoires* that the legislature's intention was different from the directive and, moreover, where this difference of view appears clearly from the words employed in the statute.[167]

In the preceding Section it was pointed out that in the resolution of the conflict certain types of arguments and especially linguistic arguments, have more justificatory force than others. Furthermore, the latitude enjoyed by courts with respect to the priority-setting of the arguments involved is strongly influenced by the two crucial values underlying the justificatory force, namely legal certainty and the maintenance of the separation of powers.[168] In my opinion, in the ultimate analysis, these two elements are decisive for the issue of "possibility" of interpreting national law in conformity with the directive. Or, to use more imaginative terms, legal certainty and separation of powers restrict the "fire-power"[169] of the directive argument, which by virtue of the supremacy of Community law is in principle very powerful.

10.8.4 The Priority Criteria within the Community Law Context

When considering the priority criteria of legal certainty and separation of powers within the context of consistent interpretation several observations can be made.

[166] Cf. also the opinion of A-G Mischo in Case 80/86 *Kolpinghuis* [1987] ECR 3969, para. 27.

[167] Cf. Galmot and Bonichot (1988, p. 22) who point out the paradox that incorrect but ambigous implementation can to a certain extent be corrected by the domestic court whereas in the case of a clear and unambiguous violation the court is powerless; indeed, as long as the deficiency cannot be remedied by direct effect.

[168] Although it should not be excluded that other principles or values might also have the role of priority criteria. Cf. above, Section 10.7. Yet I confine myself here to legal certainty and the separation of powers.

[169] MacCormick and Summers 1991, p 511.

In relation to *legal certainty*, it was already apparent in Section 10.7 that the concept is incorporated by the Court of Justice into the doctrine of consistent interpretation. Furthermore, it was submitted that the ultimate boundaries of the concept and its application are under the control of the Court of Justice. This implies, in my view, that the interpretative discretion of national courts as such is also within the control of the Court. At the same time, it implies something else as well. Legal certainty as an abstract concept has no reality. Its content must be attributed in every concrete case. In order to do this, on the one hand, the Court of Justice must give proper consideration to the issues arising under national law and on the other, the referring court should be required to explain meticulously the problems it is facing and all the factors involved. As it is national law which must be interpreted, the national court is in a better position than the Court of Justice to oversee the possibilities offered by the text. If, for instance, constraints are imposed by clear language, a statute cannot be interpreted in terms of a meaning which its words do not sustain. This factor must be respected by the Court if it wishes to uphold legal certainty.

Obviously, the need for safeguarding legal certainty will stand out wherever the terms of the national provision to be interpreted are clear. Linguistic arguments are then likely to take priority over directive arguments. However, even when the "sparkling clarity" is missing, other arguments, such as legislative intention (however conceived) and the legislative context, are elements which play a part with respect to the predictability of the law and which must therefore be taken into account when considering the question of legal certainty.

The *doctrine of separation of powers*, which includes the question of the limits of the judicial function referred to above,[170] is a much more unclear subject (and considerably more sensitive, particularly from a constitutional point of view[171]), than the issue of legal certainty. The key question can be put as follows: can the interpretative role assigned to the courts under the doctrine of consistent interpretation carry them beyond the judicial function as accepted under national law? The cases decided so far by the Court of Justice are not very helpful in this respect.

Indeed, "as far as possible" might be read as meaning "as long as the judge can do that *as judge*", i.e. without becoming a legislator or without usurping the powers of the executive.[172] However, it says nothing about the question as to the standards – national or Community – according to which this function must be considered and, moreover, it

[170] Cf. Section 10.6.

[171] Cf. De Burca 1992, p. 240.

[172] Cf. Curtin 1992, p. 40. As to the relationship between judicial function and interpretation see also Jarass 1991a, p. 218.

is common knowledge that the role of the judiciary differs from Member State to Member State.[173]

Another indication might be sought in the terms "for matters within their jurisdiction". The *Von Colson* formula, which was reiterated in other cases, holds that "for matters within their jurisdiction", the national courts are under the obligation of consistent interpretation. This formulation may suggest that reference is made to jurisdiction in the narrow sense, i.e. the competence of the court to hear and decide the case before it.[174] However, the term "jurisdiction" can also have a wider meaning, connoting the limits of the exercise of a court's power in general, including the fashion in which it is allowed to interpret the law. Furthermore, when one considers versions of *Von Colson* in other languages, the terminology is perhaps even more ambiguous. In German it says "*im Rahmen ihrer Züstandigkeiten*", in Dutch "*binnen het kader van hun bevoegdheden*", in French "*dans le cadre de leurs compétences*". A more appropriate English translation of these terms would be, in my view, "within the framework of their competence". In his opinion in *Faccini Dori* A-G Lenz argued that "*dans le cadre de leur compétences*" does indeed refer to the limits of interpretation and not merely to jurisdiction in the strict sense of the term.[175] Be this as it may, in my opinion, for the time being, neither the terminology employed nor the context indicate clearly the type of jurisdiction the Court had in mind.

Are there other reasons to believe that the qualification "as far as possible" does *not* require the national courts to disregard the limits of what is considered to be their judicial function within the national legal order?

The way in which Community law influences the position of national courts and seems to lead to a kind of "direct empowerment" was described in Chapter 8, Section 8.3. The advocates of this development tend to employ an argument which can be summarized, in somewhat over-simplified terms, as follows: the national judge in his function of Community law judge should be freed of all the constraints resulting from national law which prevent him from giving full effect to Community law. Whatever the merits of this position might be,[176] in my view it is not a matter of course that similar considerations, taking the courts beyond their powers under national law, should apply with respect to consistent interpretation.

Firstly, the fact remains that what is being interpreted is *still* national law. This is, in my opinion, a different matter from the application of directly effective Community norms, and where appropriate, the setting aside of provisions or

[173] Cf. Mead 1991, p. 500. See also MacCormick and Summers 1991, p. 496-508.

[174] As a rule this meaning of "jurisdiction" refers to four different aspects: authority to deal with the subject-matter of the dispute, authority over the persons, authority *ratione loci* and power to give the kind of relief sought. Cf. De Smith and Brazier 1989, p. 553 and Stroud's Judicial Dictionary 1986, p. 1379.

[175] Case C-92/91, opinion of 9 February 1994, nyr, para. 37 of the opinion. Cf. also already Richter 1988, p. 396 and Jarass 1991a, p. 216.

[176] Cf. above, Chapter 8, Subsection 8.3.5.

principles of national law, as was the issue in cases like *Simmenthal* and *Factortame*.[177]

Secondly, it is highly disputable what the basis of an enlargement of the judicial function should be. Neither Articles 189(3) and 5 of the Treaty, on which the obligation of consistent interpretation is based, nor the principle of supremacy of Community law can, in my view, serve as a basis for extending the interpretative powers of national courts and thus changing their judicial function.

Thirdly, even if one should accept that national courts are empowered on the basis of Community law to transcend the limits of their function, where should the new limits then lie? The answer seems to be simple: in Community law, as laid down by the Court of Justice. However, I wonder whether, in the final analysis, this would make much difference. The "common core of good reasons for interpretative decisions" is shared equally, for evident reasons, by the Court of Justice itself. Indeed, it is common understanding that the Court, in its interpretative role, often goes considerably further than the courts of the Member States. This is to be attributed to the very nature of Community law.[178] As a consequence the weight given to the distinct arguments differs from that which is usual in national legal systems and may cause a shift of priorities between them.[179] Consequently, it is not self-evident that the same "dynamic" approach will also hold true for interpretation of national law.

Yet, there are strong indications that the effect of the doctrine of consistent interpretation goes in the direction of requiring national courts to disregard the boundaries of their judicial function.[180] Where the limits lie is as yet far from clear.

10.9 Effects of Consistent Interpretation

The most obvious effect of consistent interpretation is that a provision of national law is given a meaning which it would not necessarily have had but for the directive.

In certain situations, which I have described as judicial implementation, the result achieved by consistent interpretation will be more or less "natural"; i.e. the domestic court's approach will follow the normal methods of construction accepted under its national law. Or, to put it in terms employed in Subsection 10.8.2, the directive argument will reinforce (an)other type(s) of argument already available. This process can perhaps be described as rendering explicit a meaning which was already implicit.

[177] Case 106/77 [1978] ECR 629 and Case C-213/89 [1990] ECR I-2433.
[178] Cf. Brown and Jacobs 1989, p.268-271.
[179] On "dynamic criteria" see Bengoetxea 1990, in particular p. 251-262.
[180] Cf. above, Section 10.6.

In cases of consistent interpretation in the sense of remedial interpretation, the interpretation must bridge the gap between national law and the directive. The very nature of this activity is more attributing a meaning to a provision of national law which it did not have before or which it certainly would not have had if only considerations of national law were taken into account. In the terminology of Subsection 10.8.2: the directive argument must compete with (an)other type(s) of argument. It is in this second type of situation in particular that the concerns for legal certainty and, where appropriate, separation of powers, will emerge most sharply. Where the limits *in a concrete case* will exactly lie is far from certain.

Furthermore, it must be stressed that consistent interpretation in the context of judicial implementation and remedial interpretation, when considered from the point of view of the interpretative efforts to be made by the domestic court, is not a matter of black and white. There is a large grey area in between.

Be this as it may, it is important to point out that in all situations it is *national law* that will be applied to the case concerned at the end of the day and not Community law. The latter merely gives direction to the meaning of national provisions.[181]

One of the major concerns which can be discerned in academic writing as to the effects produced by consistent interpretation relates to the question whether interpretation of a national provision in conformity with the directive can amount to a *de facto* (horizontal) direct effect of the directive.[182] In particular, the main issue is whether national law, interpreted in accordance with the directive, can impose obligations upon individuals. The considerations underlying this discussion are clearly prompted by the paradox that, on the one hand, according to the Court of Justice, directives cannot impose obligations upon private persons, while, on the other hand, this result would be reached through interpretation of national law. Some authors have suggested in this respect that if interpretation in conformity with the directive amounts to such a result, the limits of consistent interpretation have been reached.[183] The same idea can also be found in national case law.[184] Other authors, however, consider consistent interpretation as a judicial technique which can help to overcome the limitations of the Court's

[181] Cf. the opinion of A-G Van Gerven in Case C-106/89 *Marleasing* [1990] ECR I-4135. In this respect it seems that there is still a lot of misunderstanding. See e.g. Rodière (1991, p. 575) who argues on the basis of the Dekker judgment: "*L'employeur est consideré par la Cour de justice comme tenu de respecter les impératifs de la directive*" which was obviously not the case. The employer was bound by the provisions of the Civil Code. Cf. also Langenfeld 1991, p. 179.

[182] Cf. De Burca 1992, p. 231, Stuyck and Wytinck 1991, p. 210.

[183] Cf. Lauwaars 1993, p. 707, Keus 1993, p. 60.

[184] Cf. *Finnegan v. Clowney Youth Training Programme Ltd.*, House of Lords, [1990] 2 CMLR 859.

case law on (horizontal) direct effect of directives,[185] while yet others warn against considering consistent interpretation as a viable alternative for the absence of horizontal direct effect or inverse vertical direct effect of directives.[186]

Certainly, it cannot be denied that there is something rather hyprocritical about obliging a domestic court to secure by interpretation a result which cannot be achieved owing to the Court's own case law. However, this is not necessarily in itself a decisive argument against consistent interpretation of national law which amounts to imposing obligations upon individuals.

In Chapter 4, Subsection 4.2.2, it was postulated that it is not entirely clear what the Court means by stating that "a directive may not of itself impose obligations on an individual". One of the conclusions of that Subsection was that the Court seems to accept that a directive may affect the position of a private party, although the exact scope of such a "permitted" negative effect is far from plain.

Comparable considerations arise in the context of consistent interpretation. For instance, it has been pointed out that in *Marleasing*,[187] on the one hand, the directive did not impose any positive obligation on the company concerned, but, on the other hand, the judgment resulted in an indirect enforcement of the directive against it.[188] Thus, viewed from this perspective, it can be argued that the construction was permissible since it did not impose any obligation.[189] At the same time, however, it seems to be at odds with the Court's finding in *Marshall I* that "a directive may not be relied upon as such" against an individual.[190]

Attempts to redefine the effect of consistent interpretation in terms of direct effect and subsequently to see whether the limits of the doctrine of direct effect of directives have been transgressed pay insufficient attention to the fundamental difference between direct effect and consistent interpretation. While in the former case it is the provision of the directive that applies directly to the facts of the

[185] Cf. Curtin 1992, p. 40-41, Prechal 1990, p. 470. Moreover, I cannot resist mentioning another, highly paradoxical, advantage of consistent interpretation pointed out by *commissaire du gouvernement* Hagelsteen in the case of "*Cercle militaire mixte de la caserne Mortier*", 22 December 1989, AJDA 1990, p. 328. Mrs. Hagelsteen, in trying to convince the *Conseil d'Etat* to interpret Article 256 B of the *Code générale des Impôts* in accordance with the Sixth VAT Directive, referred to the notorious *Cohn-Bendit* case law and said: "*Mais, précisement, le fait que votre jurisprudence ne reconaisse pas un tel effet (i.e. direct effect – SP) aux directives constitue une raison de plus ... de faire l'effort d'interprétation ...*".

[186] Cf. Timmermans 1992, p. 820. For the two concepts see below, Chapter 11, Subsection 11.5.3.

[187] Case C-106/89 [1990] ECR I-4135.

[188] Cf. Stuyck and Wytinck 1991, p. 214. See also Curtin 1992, p. 40-41.

[189] See the opinion of A-G Van Gerven, para. 8: the problem in Marleasing concerned the exclusion of the grounds of nullity as they existed in national law and not an imposition of nullity.

[190] Case 152/84 [1986] ECR 723. Cf. also the opinion of A-G Mischo in Case 80/86 *Kolpinghuis* [1987] ECR 3969, para. 29.

case, in the latter it is the provision of national law which governs the situation concerned. In my view, national law interpreted in accordance with the directive can, as a matter of principle very well affect the legal position of an individual, as was the case in *Marleasing*, as well as impose an obligation upon him. The latter actually happened, for instance, in the *Harz*[191] case, once it had been decided by the competent Labour Court.[192]

This "position of principle" is however qualified: it should not imply that individuals will be confronted with different types of obligations for which they were in no way prepared.[193] A crucial safeguard is provided in this respect by the general principles of law which serve as a limit to consistent interpretation, and notably by the principle of legal certainty.

Thus the permissibility of the effects of consistent interpretation and, by implication, the permissibility of the theory itself depends on the interpretation and application of the general principles of law and not on the fact that consistent interpretation may come close to or amount to direct effect of directives. For the time being, the interpretation and application of these principles within the context of consistent interpretation are still at a formative stage. The only clear guidance provided so far by the Court concerns the limits of consistent interpretation in criminal proceedings: it may not result in the imposition or aggravation of criminal liability.[194] Similar considerations which militate in favour of restrictive interpretation, thus involving little space for consistent interpretation, will probably also apply in the field of tax law.[195]

In other branches of law, however, such as (general) administrative law and civil law, matters are different. No constraints similar to those in criminal or tax law apply here. As regards civil law, in *Zanetti* A-G Jacobs drew a distinction between criminal law and civil law.[196] In his view, consistent interpretation

[191] Case 79/83 [1984] ECR 1921.

[192] *Arbeitsgericht Hamburg,* 7 March 1985, DB 1985, p. 1402. Cf. also Jarass 1991a, p. 222, Langenfeld 1991, p. 183, and Case C-421/92 *Habermann-Bertelmann* [1994] ECR I-1657, in particular para. 8 and 9.

[193] To a large extent matters are not much different from overruling established case law by the courts. In these cases the courts may provide for some form of protection of legitimate expectations of the persons concerned who relied on a certain meaning of the provisions at issue. This, however, does not preclude that for the future the provisions will bear the "new" meaning. Cf. Everling 1992b, p. 384.

[194] Cf. above, Section 10.7.

[195] Cf. above, Subsection 10.8.2. See however *Conseil d'Etat,* 22 December 1989, AJDA 1990, p. 328 (*Cercle militaire mixte de la caserne Mortier*): the *Cercle militaire* had to pay VAT at the end of the day by virtue of the *Code générale des impôts* construed in accordance with the directive. Though in this case, the *Conseil d'Etat* did not need to do violence to the language. For a brief discussion see Dal Farra 1992, p. 665.

[196] Joined Cases C-206/88 and C-207/88 [1990] ECR I-1461, para. 24-26. Cf. also Betlem 1993, p. 222 ff.

"may have the result that obligations may arise and be enforceable in civil proceedings between private parties which would not result from an interpretation of the national legislation taken in isolation". He points out in particular that in civil law the *nulla poena* rule does not apply. This should, however, not be understood as implying that in civil law there are no safeguards. Legal certainty or the other principles, depending on the modalities of their interpretation and application, may indeed block consistent interpretation. In the opinion of A-G Van Gerven, for instance, consistent interpretation could not result in the imposition of a civil sanction such as nullity.[197]

A case which has been much discussed in this respect is *Dekker*.[198] It is undoubtedly true that *Dekker* produced a stricter liability for the private employer involved, which differed from liability under national law alone. Unfortunately, several authors read in *Dekker* things which did not come into play at all before the Court of Justice and, therefore, cannot be considered as decided by the Court. Some read in this case a confirmation of the fact that the Court requires an interpretation *contra legem*;[199] others deduce from *Dekker* that national courts are under the duty to "set aside national provisions incompatible with the directive also in litigations against a private employer and *irrespective of whether that national court is given discretion to do so under national law*";[200] yet others blame both the *Hoge Raad* (which referred the case to the Court) and the Court of Justice itself: the *Hoge Raad* for not having seen the problem (i.e. the question of how the directive could oblige the private employer to pay damages to the candidate for the job who was discriminated against), and the Court of Justice for evading the problem.[201]

The point is that *Dekker* illustrates sharply the far-reaching consequences which consistent interpretation can have. It is perhaps debatable whether the final national judgment is not beyond the limits set by the principle of legal certainty or the principle of equity.[202] However, neither this issue nor the discretion under national law was as such the subject of discussion before the Court. Apparently, the whole case was dealt with under the presumption that the *Hoge Raad* was able to resolve the issue of how to give effect to the directive on its own. Obviously, the Court is not obliged to resolve problems which have not been submitted to it. Whatever the merits of *Dekker* as decided by the *Hoge Raad* might be, I fail to see how the *judgment of the Court of Justice* can be considered as providing solutions to problems related to consistent interpretation.

The last issue to be addressed briefly here is the question as to whether a distinction should be made between, on the one hand, the situation in which an individual invokes the directive for the purposes of consistent interpretation in a

[197] Opinion in Case C-106/89 *Marleasing* [1990] ECR I-4135, para. 8.
[198] Case C-177/88 [1990] ECR I-3941.
[199] Cf. Betlem 1993, p. 249.
[200] Nielsen 1992, p. 169 (emphasis added – SP).
[201] Rodière 1991, p. 574-575.
[202] Cf. Keus 1993, p. 67.

dispute with another individual and, on the other hand, the situation in which it is the State that relies on the directive for the purposes of consistent interpretation against a private person. In both situations an obligation may be imposed by national law as the result of consistent interpretation. However, in the first situation it is an individual who seeks to compel obedience, while in the second situation it is the State.

It has been submitted in legal writing that the principle of estoppel which has been introduced by the Court of Justice as a rationale for direct effect of directives[203] should apply in this respect as well.[204] Thus, a State authority may wish to rely on the directive in order to have national law interpreted in a way which will result in affecting the legal position of an individual or imposing an (additional) obligation upon him. This possibility, however, should be blocked for the very reason that the Member State concerned cannot rely for any purposes whatsoever on the directive which it has failed to implement correctly or in time.

I have certain doubts about this line of reasoning. Obviously, in cases where consistent interpretation serves as a means of judicial implementation this argument can certainly not hold true. As a rule, in such a case the directive has been implemented correctly and in time. However, even in the case of incorrect implementation or total absence of implementation, some considerations may militate against this suggestion.

Firstly, it is not always obvious whether the measures adopted by the Member State amount to correct implementation or whether they must be dismissed as incorrect. It is, however, only in the latter situation that the Member State should not be allowed to rely on the directive for the purposes of consistent interpretation.

Secondly, the *Kolpinghuis* judgment is so ambigous in relation to this issue that it may be read as suggesting that such an interpretation of national law in conformity with the directive is allowed in principle, provided that the limits which lie in the general principles of law are observed.

Thirdly, this approach overlooks the fact that consistent interpretation means interpretation in the light of the wording and the purpose of the directive. Both the wording and, in particular, the purpose of the directive may intend to impose obligations upon individuals. It has already been noted[205] that Community law is not only concerned with the protection of the rights which individuals derive from it, but also with giving full effect to the rules in question.[206] Often, as has

[203] Cf. below, Chapter 11, Subsection 11.2.2.

[204] Cf. Betlem 1993, p. 227-229.

[205] Cf. above, Chapter 8, Section 8.1.

[206] Cf. also Langenfeld 1992, p. 964: *"richtliniekonforme Auslegung ... dient [...] in hohem Maße der Effektuierung der gemeinschaftlichen Vorgaben"*.

been the situation in the majority of cases decided up to now by the Court, the protection and full effect are two sides of the same coin. In some cases, however, the concern for protection of the individual and that for full effect of the rule at issue may lead in opposite directions.[207] In my view, it should not automatically be assumed that the choice made by the Court of Justice will always be to the advantage of the individual. If the terms of national law can bear the meaning construed with the aid of the directive and the general principles of law are observed, there are no grounds for denying an interpretation in conformity with the directive. Consistent interpretation should not *a priori* be excluded for the sole reason that it is public authorities which are relying on the directive for this purpose.

[207] For instance in the field of VAT.

11
Direct Effect of Directives

11.1 Introduction: A Glance at Past Discussions

Soon after the case law of the Court of Justice on direct effect of Treaty provisions started to develop, the question was raised as to the possible direct effect of directives. As is often the case in any doctrinal controversy, there were opponents of direct effect of directives, as well as its advocates and those taking an intermediate position, allowing some sort of "restricted direct effect" (particularly in order to maintain the distinction between regulations and directives) or, at least, not excluding such an effect *a priori*. Some authors who can be reckoned amongst the "third group" argued that directives could indeed contain directly effective provisions. In that case, however, the provisions concerned would be deprived of the character of a directive. Others were of the opinion that directives could under certain circumstances be relied upon as a shield but not as a sword. Yet others felt that the time was simply "not ripe" for accepting direct effect of directives.[1] Moreover, the discussion was complicated somewhat by the question whether there was a distinction between direct applicability and direct effect.[2] In the context of this discussion some denied direct applicability of directives but accepted direct effect.[3]

Indeed, it was cogently argued by Everling that nowadays it is often forgotten that the case law of the Court on direct effect of directives was preceded by an intensive controversy in academic writing which more or less "prepared the ground" for the Court's decisions.[4] The main arguments were as follows.[5]

The principal argument of those who denied the possibility of direct effect of directives was primarily based on the text of Article 189 of the Treaty. Firstly, they pointed out that according to paragraph 3 of this Article directives are only binding upon the Member States, which can thus be the only addressees of a directive. Moreover, directives are only binding in respect of the result to be achieved, leaving the choice of form and methods to national authorities. From these elements it would clearly follow that effects for individuals could only arise from the implementing measures. Secondly, they drew attention to the

[1] For overviews of the discussions see e.g. Lauwaars 1973, p. 32-35, Oldenbourg 1984, p. 215 ff., Oldenkop 1972, p. 100, De Ripaisel-Landy and Gérard 1976, p. 55 ff., Gilsdorf 1966, p. 163-169, Maresceau 1978, p. 137-140.

[2] See on this discussion below, Subsection 11.3.2.

[3] Cf. Lauwaars 1973, p. 33.

[4] Everling 1984, p. 97-98.

[5] Cf. also the observations of the Commission in Case 9/70 *Grad* [1970] ECR 825, at p. 831-833.

distinction, laid down in Article 189, between regulations and directives. Only the former are directly applicable in each Member State. A recognition of direct effect of directives would blur the distinction between regulations and directives, which would lead to legal uncertainty, affect the principle of special powers and upset the system of Community acts as laid down in the Treaty.[6]

An additional argument drew on the fact that directives do not have to be published. Direct effect would therefore depend on the chance of whether an individual wishing to invoke the directive was aware of the existence of the directive. This would have repercussions for equality before the law and, again, for legal certainty.

The advocates of direct effect of directives dismissed the above-mentioned arguments as formalistic. They referred to the Court's case law on direct effect of Treaty provisions and argued that it is the nature and the content of the provision concerned which is decisive and not the addressee of the act. They also argued that simply from the fact that Article 189 defines regulations as directly applicable it cannot be deduced that directives cannot have direct effect. Paragraph 3 of Article 189 does not say this explicitly. Moreover, acceptance of direct effect of directives would, in their view, both strengthen the legal protection of individuals and promote integration.

In 1970 the Court delivered judgment in the *Grad* case[7] which, seen in retrospect, decided the issue of direct effect of directives in a positive way. The reasoning given by the Court in favour of direct effect of decisions directed to Member States held equally true for the acceptance of direct effect of directives, as was confirmed some four years later in the *Van Duyn* case.[8] A few months after *Grad*, the approach seemed to be confirmed in *SACE*.[9] With respect to directives, however, neither *Grad* nor *SACE* clarified the problem entirely. Both cases related to the combined effect of directives and other provisions, namely a decision (*Grad*) and a Treaty provision together with the *Acceleration Decision 66/532*[10] (*SACE*). Moreover, the judgments concerned direct effect of a provision of a directive fixing a deadline. For these reasons they could be considered as special cases.

[6] According to some, direct effect of directives amounted to "*application abusive du traité de Rome au profit d'une quasi-législation communautaire*". Foyer, quoted by Everling 1984, at p. 96.

[7] Case 9/70 [1970] ECR 825.

[8] Case 41/74 [1974] ECR 1337.

[9] Case 33/70 [1970] ECR 1213.

[10] OJ 1966, p. 2971.

However, from the *Van Duyn* judgment it was deduced that both substantive provisions of directives and directives standing alone may also have direct effect.[11] In this case, the Court reasoned as follows:

"If ... by virtue of the provisions of Article 189 regulations are directly applicable and, consequently, may by their very nature have direct effects, it does not follow from this that other categories of acts mentioned in that Article can never have similar effects. It would be incompatible with the binding effect attributed to a directive by Article 189 to exclude, in principle, the possibility that the obligation which it imposes may be invoked by those concerned. In particular, where the Community authorities have, by directive, imposed on Member States the obligation to pursue a particular course of conduct, the useful effect of such an act would be weakened if individuals were prevented from relying on it before their national courts and if the latter were prevented from taking it into consideration as an element of Community law. Article 177, which empowers national courts to refer to the Court questions concerning the validity and interpretation of all acts of the Community institutions, without distinction, implies furthermore that these acts may be invoked by individuals in the national courts. It is necessary to examine, in every case, whether the nature, general scheme and wording of the provision in question are capable of having direct effects on the relations between Member States and individuals."[12]

The Court thus dismissed the *a contrario* argument and it gave three arguments in support of the thesis that directives may have direct effect: the binding effect attributed to directives in Article 189(3), the useful effect ("*effet utile*") of directives and an argument based on Article 177 of the Treaty. Not surprisingly, the soundness or otherwise of these arguments and, indeed, the further implications of this case law have been discussed at length in legal writing.[13] Whatever the merits of the discussions may have been, the binding nature of directives and *effet utile* remained the leading arguments for direct effect of directives.[14] Moreover, and leaving aside – for the moment – the discussion about the possible horizontal direct effects of directives,[15] ever since *Van Duyn* the question has been no longer whether directives *can* have direct effect but rather *under what circumstances* this may be the case.

In the next Sections four central issues of the doctrine of direct effect of directives will be discussed, including the developments which have taken place

[11] According to Bebr (1981, p. 586) this was the decisive case in this respect. Yet, in my opinion, it is arguable that also in *Van Duyn* there was still a link to Article 48 of the EEC Treaty. Cf. the opinion of A-G Mayras, p. 1355-1356.

[12] Case 41/74 [1974] ECR 1337, para. 12.

[13] Cf. Hartley 1994, p. 211-212, Dashwood 1978, p. 240-242, Grabitz 1971, p. 7-14 (on *Grad*), Bebr 1981, p. 586 ff., Easson 1979, 325 ff.

[14] See however below, Subsection 11.2.2. The not very convincing 177 argument disappeared quickly. See e.g. Case 51/76 *VNO* [1977] ECR 113.

[15] See below, Subsection 11.5.3 and 11.5.4.

since *Van Duyn*. However, a preliminary remark should be made as to the terms "direct effect of directives". The different types of provisions which a directive may contain will generally mean that a directive as a whole can hardly be considered as having direct effect. More properly, one should speak of "direct effect of a provision or a number of provisions of a directive". Whenever I use the term "direct effect of directives" it must be read with this qualification in mind.

11.2 Basis of Direct Effect of Directives

11.2.1 Binding Nature of Directives

Although the wording of Article 189 is in no way revealing as to the possible direct effect of directives, it is this provision which serves as the basis for such an effect. More particularly, the very fact that Article 189(3) provides that directives are binding made the Court decide to attribute direct effect to directives, provided that certain conditions are met.

Considered in isolation, it is not self-evident that the binding nature should entail the possibility of direct effect. After all, as pointed out by Hartley,[16] a measure can be fully binding at an interstate level without being enforceable in national courts by individuals. However, from the Court's conception of Community law as articulated in *Van Gend en Loos* it follows that directives are considered as an integral part of the legal systems of the Member States.[17] Seen against this background, the Court's position, according to which "the binding nature of a directive ... constitutes the basis for the possibility of relying on the directive before a national court ...",[18] is easier to understand.

Moreover, the Court added another important argument, namely the useful effect or effectiveness of directives.[19] Often, the – what is often called – "principle of useful effect" is considered as a basis of direct effect of directives. It must be noted however, that useful effect is not a substantive principle. It is merely a rule of interpretation which requires that "preference should be given to the construction which gives the rule its fullest effect and maximum practical value".[20] Seen against this background it is not useful effect as such which is the basis of direct effect of directives but rather Article 189(3) interpreted according to the interpretational rule of useful effect. As Grabitz put it, useful effect means

[16] Hartley 1994, p. 211.
[17] Cf. above, Chapter 7, Section 7.1.
[18] Cf. Case 152/84 *Marshall I* [1986] ECR 723, para. 47.
[19] Cf. Case 41/74 *Van Duyn* [1974] ECR 1337 and Case 148/78 *Ratti* [1979] ECR 1629.
[20] Kutscher 1976, p. 41. Cf. also Bengoetxea 1990, p. 254 (functional criterion for interpretation).

in this context "*das den Rechtsakten der Gemeinschaften derjenige Grad und derjenige Umfang an Rechtswirksamkeit beigemessen werden muss der den Zielen der Integration am besten gerecht wird*".[21]

In summary the *legal basis* of direct effect of directives is Article 189(3), since it provides that directives are binding. In 1988 the Court of Justice added another ground to the legal basis of direct effect, namely the obligation of co-operation laid down in Article 5 of the Treaty.[22]

Although the legal basis of direct effect of directives seems to be one of charming simplicity, the theoretical underpinning is more complex. Apart from the necessity of giving an interpretation to Article 189(3) such that it will secure as far as possible the practical and effective operation of the instrument, several other arguments have been put forward in this respect in legal writing. According to some, the principal motive for the Court's acceptance of direct effect of directives is the concern for judicial protection.[23] Another more practical consideration behind the Court's case law is the important role of citizens as vigilants who contribute in this way to the practical operation of Community directives[24] or to the need to combat inertia on the part of the Member States.[25]

There is a general consensus among scholars that all these arguments constitute very important elements of doctrine of direct effect of directives. Since the *Ratti* case,[26] however, many authors and Advocates General have argued that the quintessence of the Court's case law on direct effect of directives is an estoppel-like notion, according to which a Member State should not be able to rely on its own failure to implement the directive. This – what has been called – "*motif véritable*"[27] of the attitude of the Court with respect to direct effect of directives is far from uncontroversial and, moreover, if it is to be considered as the ultimate theoretical basis of the doctrine of direct effect of directives, it has far-reaching consequences.[28] It will therefore be discussed in detail in the next two Subsections.

[21] Grabitz 1971, p. 10.

[22] Case 190/87 *Moormann* [1988] ECR 4689. For a more detailed discussion of this case see below, Subsection 11.2.2.

[23] Cf. Everling 1984, p. 108, Jarrass 1990, p. 2422, Mertens de Wilmars 1991, p. 389.

[24] Cf. Curtin 1990a, p. 196.

[25] Cf. Galmot and Bonichot 1988, p. 13.

[26] Case 148/78 [1979] ECR 1629.

[27] Pescatore 1980, p. 175.

[28] In particular for the possibility of horizontal direct effect. See below, Subsection 11.5.3 and 11.5.4.

11.2.2 "Estoppel" Proposed as the Basis

Although the idea of estoppel did not appear in the Court's case law until the *Ratti* case, an early signal for the development of the "estoppel theory"[29] as the basis for direct effect of directives could be found in A-G Warner's opinion in the *Enka* case:

"A Member State that fails fully to give effect to a directive is in breach of the Treaty, so that to allow it (through its executive or administrative authorities) to rely upon that fact as against a private person in proceedings in its own Courts would be to allow it to plead its wrong."[30]

In the Advocate General's view this factor "makes a provision of a directive have direct effect".[31] There is undoubtedly a good deal of common sense in these considerations. However, I fail to see why this reasoning was necessary, as the main arguments for direct effect had already been formulated in previous case law. The Court of Justice did not take up the Advocate General's argument. It simply reiterated that the effectiveness of a directive would be weakened if individuals could not rely on it and domestic courts were prevented from taking it into consideration as an element of Community law.

In *Ratti* the Court, addressing "the general problem of the legal nature of the provisions of a directive adopted under Article 189 of the Treaty", simply recalled three arguments already mentioned in *Van Duyn*, namely the untenability of the *a contrario* argument about direct applicability of regulations, the binding effect which Article 189 ascribes to directives and the necessity of the effectiveness of directives. Thereupon the Court held:

"Consequently a Member State which has not adopted the implementing measures required by the directive in the prescribed period may not rely, as against individuals on its own failure to perform the obligations which the directive entails."[32]

Judgments rendered by the Court since *Ratti* present a varied picture as to the basis of direct effect of directives. In some cases the Court has recalled the "effectiveness argument" only,[33] in other cases the argument of the binding

[29] I use this term for reasons of convenience. It must be observed that the Court has never used the term "estoppel" nor "*nemo auditur*" nor "*venire contra factum proprium*". It simply says that the Member State may not rely on its own failure.

[30] Case 38/77 [1977] ECR 2203, at p. 2226. Cf. also (already) Dashwood 1978, p. 241 and 243.

[31] Cf. the opinion of A-G Warner in Case 131/79 *Santillo* [1980] ECR 11585, at p. 1609.

[32] Case 148/78 *Ratti* [1979] ECR 1629, para. 22.

[33] Cf. Case C-221/88 *Bussenni* [1990] ECR I-495, Case C-188/89 *Foster* [1990] ECR I-3313.

nature of directives,[34] and in yet other cases both arguments appear.[35] Similarly the Court frequently reiterates that a Member State may not plead its own wrong, sometimes as the sole argument,[36] sometimes in combination with one or both of the other arguments mentioned above.[37] It is difficult to decide on the basis of this case law how much importance the Court attaches to the "estoppel theory". Although some have observed that the principle of estoppel has displaced the requirement of "*effet utile*" which should be given to directives as the theoretical underpinning of their direct effect,[38] in other cases "*effet utile*" has reappeared.[39] Moreover, it would appear that the general tendency is to present this "estoppel-like notion" as a *consequence* of rather than as a basis for direct effect of directives.[40]

In the past, it was academic writing which especially raised this "consequence" to the rank of the ultimate rationale of direct effect of directives. The main proponent of this theory was the former Judge of the Court of Justice Pescatore who explained the idea as follows:

"According to the Court's analysis, directives may be relied upon in the Courts by individuals because they are binding on Member States and *as a reflection of their binding nature*. That is certainly much less than the direct applicability of regulations .... In short, the judgments of the Court on this question simply express the principle that is customarily described by the English legal term "estoppel", in the wide sense, and that lawyers of the Latin tradition like to identify with the maxim venire contra factum proprium, or nemo auditur ...."[41]

It is striking how many other authors adhered to this theory,[42] as did several Advocates General.[43] In Germany the "estoppel-doctrine" was generally

[34] Cf. Case 80/86 *Kolpinghuis* [1987] ECR 3969, Case 152/84 *Marshall I* [1986] ECR 723.

[35] Cf. Case 8/81 *Becker* [1982] ECR 53.

[36] Cf. Joined Cases C-6/90 and C-9/90 *Francovich* [1991] ECR I-5357, Case C-91/92 *Faccini Dori* [1994] ECR I-3325.

[37] Cf. Case 8/81 *Becker* [1982] ECR 53, Case 71/85 *FNV* [1986] ECR 3855.

[38] Cf. Curtin 1990, p. 196, Morris 1989, p. 310, 312 and 313, Schockweiler 1993c, p. 1205.

[39] Cf. Schockweiler 1993c, p. 1205.

[40] Cf. Case 152/84 *Marshall I* [1986] ECR 723, para. 47 ("... from that the Court deduced that ..."). Also according to Schockweiler (1993c, p. 1205) both in Ratti and Becker binding force and "*effet utile*" remained the basis of direct effect.

[41] Pescatore, 1980, p. 176. (English translation is taken from the opinion of A-G Mischo in Case 80/86 *Kolpinghuis* [1987] ECR 3969, para. 7).

[42] Cf. Easson, 1979, p. 342, Galmot and Bonichot 1988, p. 12, Leitao 1981, p. 437, Isaac 1992, p. 6, Oldenbourg 1984, p. 224-225, Hartley 1994, p. 212. Cf. also Emmert 1992, p. 64.

[43] E.g. A-G Slynn (Case 8/81 *Becker* [1982] ECR 53, Case 152/84 *Marshall I* [1986] ECR 723), A-G Mischo (Case 80/86 *Kolpinghuis* [1987] ECR 3969, Case C-221/88 *Busseni* [1990] ECR I-495) A-G Lenz (Case 103/88 *Costanzo* [1989] ECR 1839), A-G Darmon (Case 190/87 *Moormann* [1988] ECR

considered as a "*Ausprägung des Grundsatzes von Treu und Glauben*", an utterance of the principle of good faith.[44] It is not always clear whether the German authors refer in this context to the German principle or to the Community principle as laid down in Article 5 of the Treaty. However this might be, it was for them only a small step to consider, in this perspective, direct effect of directives as a sanction upon the failure of the Member State to comply with its obligation.[45] This same "sanction rationale" was ultimately also an important argument in a judgment of the German Constitutional Court which brought to an end domestic controversies about direct effect of directives.[46]

In the *Moormann* case[47] the Court expanded the legal basis of direct effect of directives by combining Article 189 with Article 5. This step was probably not entirely unrelated to the German reasoning that the principle of good faith was the basis of individuals' entitlement to rely before a court on a directive where the State has failed to meet its obligations. In this respect, the referring court indicated explicitly in its judgment the German principle of "*Treu und Glauben*" contained in the German Civil Code. In his opinion in *Moormann*, A-G Darmon first observed that the status and scope of Community rules cannot be derived from rules of national law. Subsequently, however, he sought an equivalent basis in Community law. In his view, the principle that a Member State may not plead its own failure constitutes a manifestation of the obligations contained in Article 5 of the Treaty. Allowing the Member State to rely on its own failure would amount to allowing it to disregard the principle of good faith and the duty not to adopt conflicting provisions as laid down in Article 5.

The reasoning of the Court of Justice in this case is less explicit. The Court recalled that according to Article 189(3) directives are binding and that Article 5 requires the Member States to take all appropriate measures to ensure the fulfilment of their obligations. Subsequently, the Court considered that

> "(i)t follows from the binding effect which the third paragraph of Article 189 ascribes to directives and the obligation of cooperation laid down in Article 5 that the Member State to which the directive is addressed cannot evade the obligations imposed by the directive in question."[48]

4689). Cf. also the opinion of A-G Van Gerven in Case C-188/89 (*Foster* [1990] ECR I-3313) who used this theory as basis for giving a broad interpretation of the concept of "the State".

[44] Cf. Nicolaysen 1984, p. 386, Oldenbourg 1984, p. 224.

[45] Cf. Jarass 1990, p. 2422, Winter 1991b, p. 659, Emmert 1992, p.57.

[46] Cf. Hilf 1988, p. 1.

[47] Case 190/87 [1988] ECR 4686.

[48] *Ibid.*, para. 22.

STAFFS UNIVERSITY LIBRARY

Furthermore the Court pointed out that whenever the provisions of an unimplemented directive are unconditional and sufficiently precise they may be relied upon as against the State and the national court must give precedence to the provisions of the directive. Accordingly, the right of an individual to rely on a directive "is based on the combined provisions of the third paragraph of Article 189 and Article 5 of the Treaty".[49]

The following observations can be made about these considerations. Firstly, Article 5 is deployed in order to *reinforce* the obligation which already follows from Article 189(3). The combination of Article 189 and Article 5 can, in a way comparable to cases on consistent interpretation, be understood as the basis for the obligation of the national court to give precedence to (and thus apply) the provisions of the directive to which the individual's right to rely on it corresponds. Secondly, the reference to Article 5 could also be understood as casting the "estoppel-principle" in a written Treaty provision, in accordance with the view of the Advocate General. However, it is striking that nowhere in the judgment does the Court refer to the "may not plead its own failure" prohibition. It simply says that the Member State "cannot evade the obligations imposed" which indeed necessarily follows from the concept of binding effect.

In some other cases, however, the Court has been more explicit. In the judgment in *McDermott and Cotter I* the Court held that the possibility for individuals to rely on a directive

> "is based on the fact that directives are binding on the Member States and on the principle that a Member State which has not taken measures to implement the directive within the prescribed period may not, as against individuals, plead its own failure to fulfil such obligations."[50]

In *Marshall I*[51] and, more recently, in *Faccini Dori*[52] the Court went a step further. In the latter case it held that the case law on direct effect of directives "seeks to prevent 'the State from taking advantage of its own failure to comply with Community law'".[53] It would seem that what was initially conceived as a consequence of direct effect of directives has become its purpose.

In summary, initially the Court merely said in the majority of cases that from the binding effect of the directive and the necessity of giving it useful effect it *followed* that a Member State may not rely, as against individuals, on its own

[49] *Ibid.*, para. 24. Cf. also, with respect to a decision, Case 249/85 *Albako* [1987] ECR 2345. In this case, however, no reference is made to Article 5.

[50] Case 286/85 [1987] ECR 1453.

[51] Case 152/84 [1986] ECR 723.

[52] Case C-91/92 [1994] ECR I-3325.

[53] *Ibid.*, para. 22.

failure to perform the obligations which the directive entails. Undoubtedly under the influence of doctrine and several opinions of Advocates General the desire to prevent the State from taking advantage of its own failure was transformed into the purpose of the Court's case law. Although a few cases may suggest that the concept of estoppel is the ultimate theoretical basis of direct effect of directives, in my opinion, the Court's case law in its totality does not justify such a conclusion.

11.2.3 Disqualifying the "Estoppel Theory"

In the previous Subsection it was argued that for some the principle of estoppel (or related notions) is the rationale of direct effect of directives. In the Court's case law the "estoppel theory" plays a prominent role. It is undoubtedly an important argument. However, it is not the sole and decisive one.[54]

The "estoppel theory" has never been entirely uncontroversial. However, it is striking that particularly in the last few years, despite the few cases which could be understood as favouring it, the theory has come increasingly under fire. This recent development must mainly be attributed to the fact that a theoretical underpinning by way of the principle of estoppel constitutes a serious obstacle to the recognition of horizontal direct effect of directives. In particular those who advocate such an effect question the "estoppel theory".[55]

It has been suggested by Pescatore[56] that the emergence of this theory, or what he calls "a clarification by the Court", must be placed against its proper historical background. Then, however, it appears that the real reasons for explaining direct effect of directives by the "may not plead its own wrong" prohibition were political rather than legal ones;[57] or, alternatively, the theory was at best an additional "*ex post facto* rationalisation designed to beg the question already resolved by the Court *sub silentio* on other grounds".[58]

A few years after the case law on direct effect of directives started to develop, two prominent courts of Member States openly showed their disagreement with the Court's approach. The French *Conseil d'Etat*,[59] basing itself on a strictly literal interpretation of Article 189(3), denied the possibility for an individual to invoke a directive with a view to challenging an administrative decision which is

[54] Cf. Schockweiler 1993c, p. 1205.

[55] Cf. Emmert 1992, Manin 1990, Van Gerven 1994b, Boch and Lane 1992. Cf. also the opinion of A-G Jacobs in Case C-316/93 *Vaneetveld* [1994] ECR I-763.

[56] Pescatore 1983, p. 169-171.

[57] Cf. also Nicolaysen 1984, p. 388.

[58] Wyatt 1983, p. 246.

[59] *Cohn-Bendit*, 22 December 1978, [1980] 1 CMLR 543.

addressed to him. Some three years later, the German *Bundesfinanzhof*[60] held, under explicit reference to the above-mentioned decision of the *Conseil d'Etat*, that there could be no reasonable doubt that a directive was incapable of creating legal rules directly applicable in a Member State.

These hostile attitudes of the two influential national courts certainly constituted a considerable danger to the Court's own "construction of Europe". However, in my opinion it is questionable whether the Court consciously deployed the "may not plead its own failure" prohibition as an argument to persuade the two national judiciaries.

The judgment in *Ratti* was rendered some three months after the decision of the *Conseil d'Etat*. Although the possibility cannot be excluded that this judgment was a very swift reaction to the *Conseil d'Etat*, it is equally arguable that the case would have been decided in the same way in any event; not least because the Court's conclusion that the Member State may not rely on its own failure as against individuals (who in this case complied of their own motion with the directive at issue) fitted perfectly with the circumstances of the case.

The judgment in *Becker*, where the Court reiterated its earlier "estoppel-finding" in Ratti, was indeed given "*en connaissance de cause*".[61] However, whether the Court really wanted to clarify the basis of direct effect of directives by reference to the principle of estoppel will remain a secret of the Court's deliberations.

In my view, with all respect to the eminent scholar, it should not be ruled out that Pescatore in his "*tentative de démythification*" and later in his famous article in the European Law Review[62] was making a personal attempt, by expounding a particular theory, to get the mutinous courts into line. It cannot be denied that, at the end of the day, his attempt was rather successful.[63]

The major objection against the "estoppel-theory" as a theoretical basis for direct effect of directives is that it does not fit within the conception of Community legal order which is integrated within the legal order of the Member States. If the principle that a Member State may not rely on its own failure to comply with the obligations imposed by the directive is considered as the basis of direct effect of directives, this direct effect is reduced to a sort of "side-effect", a "reflex" or a "corrollary" of the failure on the part of the Member State

[60] 16 July 1981, EuR 1981, p. 442.

[61] Pescatore 1983, p. 170.

[62] Pescatore 1980 and Pescatore 1983.

[63] As to the developments in Germany see Hilf 1988 (*Bundesverfassungsgericht* had accepted direct effect of directives). In France the situation remains unsatisfactory in that a review of an individual administrative decision in the light of a directive is not allowed if no implementing measures have been taken. Cf. Kovar 1992, and Simon 1992.

concerned.[64] In other words, the very existence of direct effect, which has been described as a capacity of the legal norm,[65] is made dependent on the failure of the Member State. This is in sharp contrast to the Court's conception of the Community legal order. In this view, as explained above,[66] Community law, of which directives are a part, is integrated in the national legal order from the moment of its entry into force. As a part of Community law, directives are considered as sources of law and, where appropriate, as sources of rights and duties of individuals who are subjects of the Community legal order.[67] Although directives are primarily conceived as indirect sources, this does not alter the fact that they are a part of a system of legal norms valid within a Member State and should accordingly be given practical effect, as this is the purpose of any legal rule.[68] Direct effect of directives as a reflex of a Member State's failure does not fit within this conception. It amounts to a misunderstanding of their legal nature as binding rules of Community law. As such, they are capable of producing direct effect in their own right, provided that certain conditions are satisfied.[69] In this respect, Manin[70] has pointed out that he fails to see how a principle like estoppel could determine the legal nature of a unilateral act. This nature can only be established by superior legal rules such as, within the E(E)C context, the Treaty.

In my opinion, the Member State's failure to comply with its obligations is at the utmost a condition for direct effect of directives. The possibility for the individual to rely on a directive and the corresponding duty of the courts to apply it presupposes that the directive has not been transposed in due time or has not been transposed correctly: whenever a directive has been adequately transposed there is no need to address the question of direct effect, as the effects of the directive will reach the individual through the implementing measures.[71] Such a condition of a practical nature cannot, however, amount to transforming the Member State's failure into the very basis of direct effect of directives. Moreover, the possibility should not be excluded in advance that even in the case of

[64] Cf. the opinion of A-G Reischl in Case 148/78 *Ratti* [1979] ECR 1629, p. 1650, Galmot and Bonichot 1988, p. 12-13, Pescatore 1980, p. 176, Leitao 1981, p. 433.

[65] Cf. Timmermans 1979, p. 538.

[66] See above, Chapter 7, Section 7.1.

[67] Cf. in this respect Green (1984b, p. 308), who remarks that under the "estoppel-theory" "it is unfortunate that individual rights exist as the fortuitous consequence and not the direct object of a legal rule".

[68] Cf. Everling (1984, p. 104), who denies the idea of "reflex" since "*Vielmehr treffen den Einzelnen die Wirkungen der Richtlinie ... direkt weil es sich bei der Richtlinie um eine Norm des Gemeinschaftsrecht handelt die Verwirklichung beansprucht.*" Cf. also Mertens de Wilmars 1991, p. 398.

[69] Cf. Curtin 1990a, p. 197.

[70] Manin 1990, p. 692.

[71] Cf. Case 8/81 *Becker* [1982] ECR 53, para. 19.

adequate transposition there may be a need for an individual to rely on the directive, for instance, wherever the implementing measures are not observed or enforced by national authorities.

Apart from these considerations which draw on the tension occasioned by, on the one hand, linking direct effect to the behaviour of the Member State and, on the other hand, considering directives as an integral part of the norms valid within the national order, there are other arguments which militate against the "estoppel theory" as the basis for direct effect of directives.

Several authors have submitted that this theory does not explain other instances of reliance by individuals upon Community law provisions, such as those of the Treaty.[72] In particular the reliance on Article 119 against private individuals where national legislation does not comply with this provision cannot be understood from the concept of estoppel. To this one may add that the "estoppel theory" seems to fail in cases where a public authority of the defaulting Member State is allowed to rely on a directive against another authority or the Member State itself.[73]

Another argument, based on the development of the doctrine of direct effect of directives over the last few years, is that the "estoppel theory" has outlived its usefulness.[74] In this respect it has been pointed out that owing to the extensive interpretation of the concept of "the State"[75] the theory has been "denatured and deprived of its substance". Individuals are now allowed to rely upon the failure of the State as against persons "exceedingly remote from and in all reasonableness not responsible for the failure".[76]

This contradiction was in fact present in the "estoppel-theory" from the very beginning. As has been pointed out,[77] the responsibility to implement the directive will usually lie with the legislature or the executive in its legislative capacity. The directive will not, however, actually be relied upon against the legislator, but against other bodies, such as tax authorities (*Becker*) and the public prosecutor (*Ratti*) which cannot, as such, be held responsible for the non-implementation and cannot be considered as the defaulting authority. In strict terms, therefore, the prohibition of "not pleading their own failure" already made little sense. Initially, however, several types of organs, owing to their close link, organic or otherwise, with the State, were obliged to bear the failure of those responsible for implementation. The Court of Justice has subsequently extended

[72] Wyatt 1983, p. 246.
[73] Cf. Winter 1991b, p. 663. See also below, Subsection 11.3.4.
[74] Cf. Boch and Lane 1992, p. 184.
[75] Cf. above, Chapter 4, Section 4.4 and Subsection 4.5.2.
[76] Boch and Lane 1992, p. 184.
[77] See above, Chapter 4, Subsection 4.4.1.

considerably the ambit of the estoppel principle, far beyond personal default and beyond any form of reasonable imputability; or, as A-G Jacobs has remarked:

"The well-known attempt at a rationale for assigning direct effect to a directive as against a Member State, namely that a Member State ought not to be allowed to rely upon its own failure to implement a directive, is singularly inapposite in relation to such a body, which has no responsibility for that failure."[78]

In a recent publication[79] A-G Van Gerven elaborated on the theme of effect given to directives "against authorities other than the defaulting authority", already evident in some of his opinions.[80] He has in fact redefined the problem and, moreover, he has given the principle of estoppel a content different from that which in this context was usually labelled as the application of estoppel. On the one hand, in his view, neither *nemo auditur* nor *venire contra factum proprium* can justify the (vertical) direct effect of directives since, generally, there is no negligence ("*turpitudine sua*" or "*factum proprium*") on the part of the authorities against which the directive is relied on. On the other hand, Van Gerven holds the opinion that the principle of estoppel can underpin direct effect. It must be observed, however, that in his view estoppel must be understood as a means of protecting legitimate reliance on the part of the plaintiff and not as a sanction against the Member State's failure.[81] The former can legitimately rely on the proper performance by the Member State of its obligations to implement the directive and it is for this reason that a course of action cannot be denied to him. In other words

"doctrine of direct effect of directives may be worded in terms of "legitimate expectations" (and thus estoppel[82]) rather than in terms of "faulty behaviour" (and thus nemo auditur)".[83]

Obviously, these practical and doctrinal developments show clearly the serious shortcomings of the "may not plead its own wrong" prohibition as a theoretical underpinning of direct effect of directives. In my opinion it can be submitted

[78] Opinion in Case C-316/93 *Vaneetveld* [1994] ECR I-763, para. 20.
[79] Van Gerven 1994b.
[80] Cf. Case C-188/89 *Foster* [1990] ECR I-3313, para. 5, and Case C-262/88 *Barber* [1990] ECR I-1889, para. 52.
[81] Cf. also his opinion in Barber, *ibid.*, in note 34, where he points out that "the "*nemo auditur*" principle is more clearly aimed at default whereas the doctrine of estoppel can, amongst other things, (also) refer to a contradiction in one's own conduct and the expectations thereby aroused in, and acted on by, another.
[82] As defined by Van Gerven.
[83] Van Gerven 1994b, p. 345, note 26.

without any exaggeration, and irrespective of the cases which may suggest otherwise, that the "estoppel theory" has lost all its explanatory force and should therefore be rejected as a (suggested) theoretical basis for direct effect of directives.

11.3 Content of the Concept of Direct Effect of Directives

11.3.1 Direct Effect versus Direct Applicability

It is no secret that there is no entirely uniform terminology in the literature, and to some extent in the case law of the Court of Justice as well, to denote the special character of Community law which is often called "direct effect". The matter is further complicated by the multilinguism of Community law.[84] Whatever the merits of the different terminological distinctions might be (and by saying this I am certainly not denying the need for a settled terminology, as it may at least help to avoid misunderstandings), there is one distinction which deserves particular attention since it has been argued that the distinction goes beyond the mere question of "labelling", and denotes two different conceptions in Community law. This distinction concerns the terms "direct effect" and "direct applicability". Moreover, it has played an important part in the discussions about direct effect of directives.

According to some authors, the terms direct effect and direct applicability can be used interchangeably, while according to others the terms must be carefully distinguished.[85] A third group admits that there is a distinction but the difference must not be dramatized.[86]

The origin of the confusion lies in Article 189(2), which provides with respect to regulations that they are *directly applicable* in the Member States. As mentioned in Section 11.1, the Court held in *Van Duyn* that regulations are directly applicable and, consequently, may by their very nature have direct effect. The Court's reasoning suggested that direct applicability is in this context not the same as direct effect: direct applicability *may lead to* direct effect. The central question is then: what is the difference between the two, particularly if one takes into consideration that with respect to Treaty provisions the Court uses the terms direct effect and direct applicability indiscriminately?[87]

[84] Cf. Kovar 1983, p. 137 and 1981, p. 151, Klein 1988, p. 3 ff., Easson 1979, p. 319-321, Oldenbourg 1984, p.14.

[85] Cf. Pescatore 1980, p. 155, Dashwood 1978, p. 229-230, Easson 1979, p. 319-321, Hartley 1994, p. 206-207.

[86] Cf. Bebr 1981, p. 560, Louis 1993, p. 494.

[87] Cf. e.g. Case 2/74 *Reyners* [1974] ECR 631, Case 43/75 *Defrenne* [1976] ECR 455.

In *Ratti*, when commenting on the formulation of the preliminary question of the referring judge, A-G Reischl found that "it is certainly not appropriate to speak of the direct applicability of a directive". He pointed out that this term is used only for regulations, "that is to say, for directly applicable Community legislation, which may also create legal relationships between individuals".[88] Directives, however, create obligations only for Member States and, in his view, they can produce at the most *similar* effects. The main point of the Advocate General's analysis seems to be that regulations can both confer rights and impose obligations upon individuals. However, since the Advocate General accepted that individuals can rely on the directive concerned against the defaulting Member State, some have observed that it follows from this analysis that direct effect is a residual concept.[89]

A further distinction is that expounded by Winter in his classic article in Common Market Law Review.[90] According to this theory "direct applicability", on the one hand, is used in Article 189(2) to make clear that, as far as regulations are concerned, the traditional requirement of incorporation by the Member States of legal rules stemming from an external (i.e. international) source into their national legal order is superseded. Incorporation is superflous and even forbidden.[91] Winter refers in this respect to the German version of the treaty which "seems to express this idea unambiguously". In this version a regulation "*gilt unmittelbar*" in the Member States (is a part of the law valid within the Member States) instead of "*ist unmittelbar anwendbar*" (which corresponds better with "is directly applicable"). Direct effect (in German often called "*unmittelbare Wirkung*"), on the other hand, should be reserved to indicate the capacity of a provision to create individual rights which must be enforced by the domestic courts.[92]

Those adhering to this theory correctly point out that regulations often contain provisions which are not meant to give private individuals enforceable rights or which are too vague and incomplete to make judicial application possible.[93] As "every provision of every regulation is directly applicable" by virtue of Article 189(2) "but not every provision of every regulation has direct effect, in the sense of conferring on private persons rights enforceable by them

[88] Case 148/78 [1979] ECR 1629, at p. 1650.

[89] Cf. Usher 1979, p. 272.

[90] Winter 1972. Cf. also (already) the observations of the Commission in Case 9/70 *Grad* [1970] ECR 825, at p. 832.

[91] Cf. Bebr 1981, p. 560. See also Case 34/73 *Variola* [1973] ECR 990 and Case 50/76 *Amsterdam Bulb* [1977] ECR 137.

[92] My own translations, making an effort to explain "the point" in English. See for terminological confusion Klein 1988, p. 3-7, Oldenbourg 1984, p. 14-18. Cf. also Winter 1972, p. 436.

[93] Cf. Winter 1972, p. 435, Easson 1979, p. 321, Hartley 1994, p. 207-208, Leitao 1981, p. 429.

in national courts",[94] the two concepts cannot be equated. A comparison is often drawn with a national statute, which is undoubtedly "directly applicable" in the sense of being part of the law valid within the national legal order but does not necessarily give rights to individuals, or is even entirely irrelevant for them.[95]

This theory certainly has the merit of solving the apparent contradiction between the direct applicability of regulations, as provided for in Article 189(2) and the assertion that provisions of regulations *may* have direct effect, which in turn is often also denoted by the term "directly applicable". Obviously to say that a regulation is directly applicable and may therefore have direct applicability does not make much sense.

Some writers hold a slightly different opinion. In their view, legal norms which are a part of the national legal system must in principle also have the capacity to be applied, since that is the normal state of the law.[96] The terms "directly applicable" must in their view be understood as embracing both concepts: being part of the law valid within the national legal order and having the capacity to be applied; the former is the condition for the latter and the latter is immanently linked with the former.[97] Yet the capacity to be applied must in turn be distiguished from the question whether the provisions concerned can *actually* be applied in a concrete case. The answer will depend on several other factors, like the precision of the drafting of the provision and its content. It is this actual application which they denote by the term "direct effect".

In summary, the subtle distinction between the two approaches lies in the more comprehensive understanding of "direct applicability" ("unmittelbare Geltung" and "unmittelbare Anwendbarkeit" are merged) by the second group of writers. Direct effect is in both approaches conceived as the creation of rights (and obligations, where appropriate) for individuals.

Other scholars have argued that direct effect and direct applicability coincide.[98] They point out that if direct effect is defined in terms of "invocability" of the provision at issue, i.e. the possibility of relying on the provision before a national court and the corresponding duty of the latter to apply the provision, there is no distinction between direct effect and direct applicability of regulations. Every provision of a regulation can be relied upon by an individual and the domestic court is obliged to apply it. Whether the court will be able to do this

[94] Opinion of A-G Warner in Case 131/79 *Santillo* [1980] ECR 1585, at p. 1608.

[95] Cf. the opinion of A-G Warner in Case 31/74 *Galli* [1975] ECR 47, at p. 71 and Easson 1979, p. 322.

[96] Cf. Klein 1988, p. 8 (*Anwendbarkeit, Anwendungsfähigkeit* of the norm), Pescatore 1980, p. 177.

[97] Cf. Klein 1988, p. 10-11.

[98] Cf. Lauwaars 1973, p. 14, Lauwaars and Timmermans 1994, p. 94.

in the concrete case before it is however dependent on the content of the relevant provision.[99]

This approach corresponds with the manner in which the Court of Justice handles regulations. The individual may as a rule rely on their provisions without further ado. A test as to whether the conditions of direct effect are satisfied is usually not applied.[100] In other words, regulations are presumed[101] to be directly effective because Article 189(2) says they are directly applicable in the Member States. However, this is not so for reasons of being directly applicable in the sense of being part of the national legal order. In my opinion, direct applicability should be understood as an indication as to their effects. The presumption is rather based on the fact that according to the legal definition of Article 189(2) regulations will be drafted in such a way as to have the actual capacity to be applied in a concrete case, as this is their primary purpose. The very fact that a regulation may and often will contain some provisions which are not suitable for such an application does not change the matter.[102]

What is the relevance of this excursion into problems related primarily to regulations for directives? Several points can be made in this respect.

Firstly, as I explained in Chapter 7, Section 7.1, in the Court's conception it is the whole body of Community law which is as such incorporated within the national legal system. Thus if the term "directly applicable" in Article 189(2) is understood as referring to the automatic incorporation of regulations into domestic legal order, directives are also directly applicable in this sense. In other words, what is provided in Article 189(2) for regulations *expressis verbis* also holds true for other provisions of Community law, including directives.[103] Several writers have pointed out that the Court has been careful never to say that directives are directly applicable.[104] This is undoubtedly true, but it seems to me that those authors must give a different meaning to direct applicability; for instance the meaning already mentioned, that direct applicability also means the direct creation of obligations for individuals.[105] Moreover, the Court's reticence from qualifying directives as directly applicable is probably prompted by the fear of blurring the distinction between regulations and directives, a danger which is not entirely imaginary, certainly as long as there is no clarity about the meaning of direct applicability. For this reason it is likewise to be expected that an explicit statement that directives are directly applicable would be a welcome argument

[99] Cf. Lauwaars and Timmermans 1994, p. 94, with further references.
[100] See however Case 9/73 *Schlüter* [1973] ECR 1135.
[101] Cf. Dashwood 1978, p. 241, Bebr 1981, p. 582.
[102] Cf. also Pescatore 1983, p. 164.
[103] Cf. Timmermans 1979, p. 534, Louis 1993, p. 503.
[104] Cf. Usher 1979, p. 269, Pescatore 1980, p. 174.
[105] Cf. also Hartley 1981, p. 214-215.

for those who still have difficulties with accepting direct effect of directives, and it could lead to a new wave of criticism.

Secondly, it was explained above that if direct effect is defined as "invocability" of the provision at issue, direct effect and direct applicability are the same thing. In principle, I see no reason why the same should not also hold true for directives. As will be discussed in more detail in Subsection 11.3.3, direct effect of directives also means two things: the right to rely on the relevant provision for the individual concerned, on the one hand, and the duty of national courts to apply the provision in the concrete case before it, on the other. From this point of view, a provision of a directive is also directly applicable. Yet in comparison to regulations a number of qualifications must be made. The orthodox understanding is that, unlike provisions of regulations, provisions of directives must first satisfy certain conditions, i.e. before being considered as directly effective. In other words, while regulations are presumed to be directly effective, directives are not. This again can be explained by the legal definition of directives in Article 189(3): they must be designed as acts which by definition need further implementation and therefore their capability of having direct effect is much less obvious (although it is no secret that in practice things are different). Moreover, in contrast to regulations, directives cannot impose obligations upon individuals. As mentioned above, this is for some an argument for denying direct applicability of directives.

Given the pitfalls which attend deploying the term "direct applicability" in connection with directives, I prefer to use the term "direct effect" of directives. Whenever in the forthcoming Sections I employ the term "apply directly", or similar terms, these terms have no special technical meaning but merely indicate the activity of the courts of doing what is part and parcel of their task: applying legal norms in the case before them.

11.3.2 "Direct Effect" and "Similar Effect"

In *Van Duyn* and subsequent cases the Court held that since regulations are directly applicable and "may by their very nature have direct effect, it does not follow from this that other categories of acts ... can never have similar effects".[106] Several authors have suggested that the Court uses the terms "similar effects" on purpose and consciously avoids the terms "direct effect".[107] Some have even argued that direct effect of directives would be an inappropriate term, since the real issue is the mere possibility that an individual may *rely on the*

[106] Case 41/74 [1974] ECR 1337, para. 12.
[107] Cf. Pescatore 1983, p. 167, Oldenbourg 1984, p. 151.

provision of the directive in question.[108] Thus for instance in *Becker* both the German government and the Commission argued that the case did not concern a question of examining the "direct applicability" or "direct effect" of the directive concerned. The crucial question was, in their view, whether an individual may rely on its provisions in proceedings before national courts.[109] These attempts to deny that directives do have direct effect (at least this is how I understand them) merit the following remarks.

Firstly, there could indeed be a problem of definition. If direct effect is defined as the creation of rights (and obligations, where appropriate) on the one hand, and the possibility for the individual to rely on the directive is considered merely as the corollary of the obligation of the Member States[110] on the other, then there is in fact an argument for saying that directives do not have direct effect. However, where direct effect is described as a matter of "invocability" and, moreover, one accepts that the "reflex idea" is a fallacious way to present matters,[111] then I see no reason for denying that directives are directly effective.

Secondly, it has been argued that by using the terms "similar effects" the Court was indicating that, in contrast to regulations which are directly applicable and will therefore as a rule have direct effect, directives do not have such direct effect "by their very nature" and an examination of certain conditions must first take place. With these carefully chosen words the Court wished to express that the result brought about by directives can be the same as that brought about by directly applicable provisions of a regulation. Its cautiousness could then be explained by its concern for maintaining the distinction between regulations and directives.[112]

The main objection to the position that directives do not have direct effect is, however, that it is just another of the myths surrounding them. In *Van Duyn* and in other cases, including the more recent ones,[113] the Court actually did use the

[108] Cf. Pescatore 1980, p. 174. According to some authors, however, this has to be considered as *a limited form of direct effect*. See e.g. Everling 1984, p. 106, Mertens de Wilmars, 1991, p. 389.

[109] Case 8/81 [1982] ECR 53, Report for the Hearing, at p. 59 and 65.

[110] Cf. above, Subsection 11.2.3.

[111] Cf. *ibid*.

[112] As to this concern cf. above, Section 11.1. It is no surprise that in particular those who equate direct effect and direct applicability, like Pescatore, have, from this point of view, some difficulty in saying that directives are directly effective.

[113] Cf. Galmot and Bonichot (1988, p. 13) and Schockweiler (1993c, p. 1205) who observe that the term "direct effect" disappeared at a certain point from the case law on directives. Yet it reappeared again in Case C-188/89 *Foster* [1990] ECR I-3313, in para. 20 ("directive capable of having direct effect"). Similarly several "titles" within judgments use the term. See e.g. Joined Cases C-19/90 and C-20/90 *Karella and Karrellas* [1991] ECR I-2691, Case 50/88 *Kühne* [1989] ECR 1925, Joined Cases 231/87 and 129/88 *Carpaneto I* [1989] ECR 3233.

STAFFS UNIVERSITY LIBRARY

term direct effect in its reasoning, although perhaps not in the *dictum.*[114] However, this last fact can hardly be considered as a convincing argument for the statement that direct effect of directives would be an inappropriate term and that there is a deeper purpose behind its absence from the *dicta.*

11.3.3 Creation of Rights and the Broader Concept of "Invocability"

The problem of whether direct effect should be regarded as the capacity to confer rights or rather as the capacity to be relied upon is an old one and concerns not only Community law and certainly not only directives. Illuminating in this respect is a publication by Bleckmann in 1978.[115] With respect to the content of the notion of direct effect,[116] i.e. the effects which norms of international law may produce within the national legal order without any interposition of national measures, Bleckmann distinguishes two basic approaches.[117] The first concentrates on the question whether the provisions concerned have to be applied by the domestic courts and by the administration. The second approach poses the question whether the provisions at issue create rights and obligations for individuals. Bleckmann prefers the first of these formulas. In his opinion, the notion of direct effect of a legal norm is much broader than the notion which refers only to creation of rights and obligations. In this respect he correctly points out that, in general, national judges do not solely apply norms which create rights and obligations for individuals. Whether or not the court has to apply rules which create rights and obligations depends, in his view, on the national rules governing the procedure.[118] In this case, however, it is a matter for national law to determine the conditions to be satisfied when addressing the question as to the creation of rights and obligations by the provision which is relied upon.

This "double-track" approach also clearly exists in Community law. In some cases the Court of Justice finds, when considering the direct effect of a provision, that the provision confers on individuals rights which are enforceable by them in the national courts and which the national courts must protect (or other

[114] Case 41/74 [1974] ECR 1337, para. 12. However, it must be noted that the French version uses the terms "*effets directs*" (thus plural) which are translated into, for instance, Dutch as "*directe gevolgen*". The usual term in Dutch for direct effect is "*directe werking*".

[115] Bleckmann 1978.

[116] He calls it "*applicabilité directe*", which suggests direct applicability, but Bleckmann apparently does not make the distinction discussed in Subsection 11.3.1. In general it should be noted that French authors are much less concerned about this distinction than, for instance, English and German authors.

[117] At p. 88 ("*formule de base*").

[118] Bleckmann points out, for instance, that the French administrative courts, in contrast to German courts, have to apply in a "*recours pour excès de pouvoir*" the relevant legal norms without taking into account whether they confer rights on the applicant.

equivalent terms).[119] In other cases it is said that the provision may be relied upon by individuals and must be applied by national courts.[120] The twinned terms "confer rights to be protected by the courts" are narrower than "provisions which can be relied upon and must be applied by the courts". The difference between the two formulas has already been discussed in detail in Chapter 7, Subsection 7.2.2. For this reason I shall here recall only the principal points.

The arguments of those who have contended that direct effect is a concept broader than the mere creation of rights correspond with those of Bleckmann. Actually, Bleckmann *is* one of the advocates of the broader approach of direct effect, also in Community law.[121]

As I pointed out in Subsection 7.2.2, provisions of Community law can be relied upon for several purposes and within the context of different types of proceedings. The way in which the Community law provision at issue will be deployed therefore depends on the character and subject matter of the proceedings in the national court. This implies that the classification of the effects produced by the provision will vary from procedure to procedure and, indeed, from Member State to Member State. Seen against this background, to say that direct effect means the creation of rights for the individual is an excessively limited way of presenting things, which does not do justice to the diversity of the effects which directly effective provisions may produce. It was therefore submitted that direct effect should be defined in more objective terms than those of creating rights, namely as the possibility for an individual to invoke provisions of Community law in order to protect his interests, or the capacity of a Community law provision "to be invoked by all persons concerned within the national legal system, particularly before a national court which is bound to apply the provision to the facts of the case".[122] In other words, it is the "invocability" which is at the heart of direct effect and not the creation of rights. The classification of the effects produced in the national legal order (e.g. whether as a "subjective" right or a legitimate interest, if these classification are necessary at all) is then a matter of national law.[123] Moreover, there is another argument for describing direct effect in terms of invocability: equating direct effect and creation of rights is likewise fallacious to the extent that Community law may create rights without being directly effective.

[119] Cf. (recently) Case C-236/92 *Comitato* [1994] ECR I-483, para. 14-15.

[120] Cf. Case 8/81 *Becker* [1982] ECR 53, para. 25 and 27.

[121] Cf. also Kovar 1983, p. 138.

[122] Timmermans 1979, p. 538.

[123] Cf. Case 13/68 *Salgoil* [ECR] 543. More recently the problem of classification was submitted to the Court in Case 380/87 *Enichem* [1989] ECR 2491 and Case C-236/92 *Comitato* [1994] ECR I-483 but it was not addressed as such by the Court.

As I have contended, a careful distinction must be made between creation of rights, which is a matter of the *content* of the provision, and direct effect, which concerns a certain *quality* of the norm. The creation of rights and direct effect may coincide, but this is not necessarily always the case.

For all these reasons it is in my view more appropriate and correct to describe direct effect in terms of "invocability", irrespective of whether or not the provisions at issue create rights. If one cannot refrain from describing direct effects in terms of rights, then the right created is at the utmost the "procedural" right to rely on Community law provisions.[124]

The latter expression is also occasionally used by the Court of Justice.[125] As long as the terms "right to rely" are explicitly employed, the situation seems fairly unambiguous. However, the Court usually finds that a Community law provision creates or confers rights without making clear the type of right it has in mind, whether "substantive" or "procedural", namely to rely on the directive. In some cases both notions even appear alongside each other.[126] Such an approach has the risk of blurring the necessary distinction to be made between direct effect and the creation of "substantive" rights.

11.3.4 Two Different Perspectives: the Individual and the Court

In the previous Subsection I rejected the description of direct effect in terms of creation of rights and gave preference to the definition of direct effect as the capacity of a provision to be invoked by individuals in national courts which are bound to apply it: thus *direct effect as invocability*. However, this concept is not entirely unproblematic and, as will be shown, the legal reality behind this concept is extremely varied.

The first point to be made concerns the terms "to invoke the directive" or "to rely on the directive".[127] These terms, used in the ordinary sense, could give rise to a good deal of confusion. An individual may rely on a directive in order to ask the national judge to interpret national law in conformity with the directive. Similarly, since the judgment in *Francovich*[128] it has been clear that an individual may invoke a directive when claiming damages for its non-implementation. However, these two situations are outside the scope of the doctrine of

[124] Cf. also above, Chapter 7, Subsection 7.2.2.

[125] Cf. Joined Cases C-87/90, C-88/90 and C-89/90 *Verholen* [1991] ECR I-3757, para. 15, Case C-338/91 *Steenhorst-Neerings* [1993] ECR I-5475, para. 21, Case 190/87 *Moormann* [1988] ECR 4689, para. 23.

[126] Cf. Case C-338/91 *Steenhorst-Neerings* [1993] ECR I-5475.

[127] As a rule the Court uses the term "rely". I will use the terms interchangeably.

[128] Joined Case C-6/90 and C-9/90 [1991] ECR I-5357.

direct effect. Thus "invocability" or "reliance on" used as the description of direct effect has a more specific meaning which must be carefully kept in mind.

This pitfall has in fact been observed in legal writing. Kovar,[129] for instance, distinguishes between two degrees of invocability. In the first place, invocability may be limited to a simple "taking into account". In this case, there is no requirement to fulfil any specific conditions. In the second place, invocability may involve application of the norm concerned by the national judge, provided that certain conditions are satisfied.[130] This "superior degree" of invocability is then direct effect and it means that an individual may rely on the provision as against a national legal rule or in order to derive rights from it.[131] Manin[132] makes a similar distinction, namely between "*invocabilité dans le cadre de l'effet direct*" and "*invocabilité au-delà de l'effet direct*". In his view the distinction has reached such a degree of sophistication that to make the system workable the "theory of invocability" should be unified, preferably by abolishing direct effect.

For a proper understanding of the content of the concept of direct effect of directives further analysis is necessary. The analysis will focus on two issues. Firstly, on the two "subjects" involved in the definition of direct effect; this will be analysed in the present Subsection. Secondly, in the next Subsection, the effects of direct effect will be discussed; in other words, the question will be addressed as to what it means *in concreto* that a provision of a directive is directly effective.

As a rule, two "subjects" are involved in the definition of direct effect: the individual who may rely on the provisions concerned and the court which is bound to apply them. First of all some brief remarks must be made regarding the question of "*who*" may actually be concerned by the definition, in addition to courts and individuals. First, as explained in Chapter 4, not only the courts are obliged to apply directly effective provisions but so too are all national authorities upon which the provisions are binding.

Second, there is common understanding that "individuals" in this context are not only natural persons but also legal persons.[133] However, the persons who may rely on a directive are a much broader category, namely "all those concerned".[134] Thus the ECSC or a body governed by public law, such as a

[129] Kovar 1988.

[130] On the conditions see below, Section 11.4.

[131] Cf. also case 8/81 *Becker* [1982] ECR 53, para. 25.

[132] Manin 1990.

[133] Cf. Case 31/87 *Beentjes* [1988] ECR 4635, Case 138/86 *Direct Cosmetics* [1988] ECR 3937.

[134] Cf. Case 41/74 *Van Duyn* [1974] ECR 1337, para. 12, Case 148/78 *Ratti* [1979] ECR 1629, para. 20.

municipality,[135] can also be considered as a person concerned for the purposes of direct effect. In *SACE*[136] it was even suggested that another Member State "concerned" in the performance of the Community law obligation may avail itself of the directly effective provision. For the time being it seems that any legal subject, whether private or public, may rely on a directive if it is "concerned" by its provisions.[137] It is with these remarks in mind that I shall continue the analysis.

As regards the reliance by individuals on the one hand and the application by the courts on the other, the Court's case law contains three basic modalities. In some cases the Court makes plain the meaning of direct effect if considered *from the point of view of the individual*: for instance, individuals may demand the application of the directive, they may rely on it before national courts etc.[138]

In other cases the Court's findings relate explicitly to both perspectives, i.e. the *implications both for the individual and the court concerned* are addressed: for instance, in the classic "*Van Duyn formula*" it was held that the relevant article "confers on individuals rights which are enforceable by them in the courts of a Member State and which the national courts must protect".[139]

Indeed, many more examples of both categories could be added. It is however striking that only rarely does the Court confine itself to stating the meaning of direct effect if considered *from the perspective of the court alone*. One of those rather exceptional cases is *Verholen*.[140] In this case the Court of Justice made clear that if the national court considers "either that Commuity law must be applied and, if necessary, national law disapplied, or that national law must be interpreted in a way that conforms with Community law" it may do so of its own motion, thus irrespective of whether or not (one of) the parties involved has relied on the directive. Provided that the conditions for direct effect are met, in such a situation the national court can also directly apply the directive or examine whether national rules are in conformity with its provisions.[141]

The Court's emphasis on direct effect as a matter of invocability can be explained by the way preliminary questions are posed, as their formulation may often determine the way in which the answer is phrased; or perhaps by the initial

[135] Cf. Case C-221/88 *Busseni* [1990] ECR I-495, Joined Cases 231/87 and 129/88 *Carpaneto I* [1989] ECR 3233. See also Winter 1991b, p. 663-664.

[136] Case 33/70 [1970] ECR 1213.

[137] As to the question whether somebody is concerned, see above, Chapter 8, Subsection 8.3.2.

[138] Cf. Case 222/84 *Johnston* [1986] ECR 1651, Case 31/87 *Beentjes* [1988] ECR 4635.

[139] Case 41/74 [1974] ECR 1337, para. 15. Cf. also Case 38/77 *Enka* [1977] ECR 2203, Case 126/82 *Smit* [1983] ECR 73.

[140] Joined Cases C-87/90, C-88/90 and C-89/90 [1991] ECR I-3757. Cf. also Case C-158/91 *Levy* [1993] ECR I-4287 and Case 36/75 *Rutili* [1975] ECR 1219, (in particular para. 16).

[141] As to the question whether national courts must apply Community law of their own motion see above, Chapter 8, Subsection 8.3.3.

formulation of direct effect, namely the creation of rights for individuals. Equally the Court often has recourse to a number of well-established formulas which are reiterated as magic spells on any occasion. The main point is, however, that in the ultimate analysis direct effect is, in my opinion, not so much concerned with the issue of what an individual can do with a provision of a directive but rather *whether the national court can apply it or not.*[142] In this respect I fully agree with Hilf, who has pointed out that the invocability of a directive is too narrow a concept since a directive may equally be applied by the domestic court of its own motion, as illustrated above by the *Verholen* case. In his view it is more appropriate to say that there is a "*Berücksichtigungspflicht zugunsten des einzelnen gegenüber allen nicht richtlinienkonformen nationalen Vorschriften*",[143] thus a duty to give consideration to directive provisions in favour of the individual and against any national rules which are not in conformity with the directive. Moreover, as mentioned above, the term "invocability" is as such misleading in that it may also refer to reliance on the directive for purposes other than direct effect. Indeed, it can be argued that there is no problem as long as it is kept in mind that invocability within the context of direct effect refers to the possibility for or the right of the individual to rely on the provision concerned, provided that the conditions of direct effect are fulfilled, and that there is a correlative duty of the national court to apply the provision. Yet it cannot be denied that such a definition does not entirely cover the reality of the situation and, furthermore, it does not make the system very transparent, either for the individual or for the national judge. Moreover, as will be explained in Section 11.4, the conditions for direct effect developed by the Court are intimately linked with the judicial function and its limits, which may be considered as a further indication that the important point is whether the court can apply the provision at issue.

In brief, for all these reasons and in contrast to the definitions presented above, the definition of direct effect would, in my opinion, be more appropriately phrased in terms of the obligation of the national court to apply the provisions concerned. The question is then, however, the meaning of application by the courts. This subject will be covered in the next Subsection.

11.3.5 Effects of Direct Effect of Directives

There is of course a multitude of effects produced by direct effect. According to Kovar, for instance, direct effect establishes a direct relationship between the individuals and the legal order of the Community.[144] Moreover, it changes the

[142] Cf. Timmermans 1979, p. 540-541, Pescatore 1983, p. 176.
[143] Hilf 1993, p. 9.
[144] Kovar 1988, p. 194.

function of national courts, which are obliged to set aside national rules that hamper the protection of the position individuals derive from Community law.[145] Other common and undoubtedly true assertions are that direct effect constitutes a sanction against non-compliance of the Member States and, consequently, it is a means to force the Member States to implement directives in time and to do so correctly; direct effect equally contributes to the enforcement of Community law, broadens the legal protection of individuals etc.[146] However, these "macro-effects" are not the effects at issue in this Section. As stated above, it will rather focus on the precise significance of direct effect in a concrete dispute before a domestic court.

On several occasions I have already stressed that directly effective provisions are invoked and applied within the framework of national procedures. The way in which the directive will be deployed is determined by the type of procedure as well as the subject matter of the action brought before the domestic court. In other words, one has to answer the question: for what purpose is the individual relying on the directive? In some cases the provisions will serve as a touchstone for reviewing the legality of national measures, for instance where an exception of illegality is raised in criminal or administrative proceedings. In other cases an individual may assert that he has a positive claim based on Community law, for instance, an amount of money as compensation by virtue of the product liability directive or the payment of arrears of wages under the Directive relating to the protection of employees in the event of the insolvency of their employer.[147] Both types of claims, the defensive and the offensive, are present in the central consideration of the *Becker* judgment, where the Court found that a directive may

> "be relied upon as against any national provision which is incompatible with the directive or in so far as the provisions define rights which individuals are able to assert against the State."[148]

Likewise, the manner of deploying the directive will depend on the state of national law. In some cases the examination of the compatibility of the provisions at issue with the directive and the subsequent disapplication of the national provisions concerned may suffice to achieve the situation aimed at by the

[145] *Ibid.*, p. 195. Cf. also Barav 1991, p. 2 ff.

[146] Cf. Curtin 1990, p. 718-722, Snijder 1993, p. 40-42.

[147] Directive 85/374, OJ 1985, L 210/29 and Directive 80/987, OJ 1980, 238/23. For a somewhat peculiar application of the doctrine see Case 96/84 *Slachtpluimvee* [1985] ECR 1157: the national court wanted to know whether a private party could rely on a directive against its Member State, in order to establish whether there was a case of "*force majeure*", relied upon in a civil procedure against another private party.

[148] Case 8/81 [1982] ECR 53, para. 25.

directive. In other cases it will be necessary for the provisions of the directive to be applied to the facts of the case in order to achieve the situation desired.

Some simple examples can perhaps illustrate the matter. A Law on Unemployment Benefit may provide that all unemployed workers are entitled to receive unemployment benefit for a period of two years after commencement of their unemployment. Yet married women are excluded. This amounts to sex discrimination under Directive 79/7 (equal treatment in statutory schemes of social security)[149] and is prohibited. According to this Directive, both men and women must be entitled to the benefit at issue. A national trade union may bring an action against the Member State concerned with the purpose of obtaining a finding that the State is acting unlawfully by maintaining in force and by applying such a provision. The task of the national court is then to examine the compatibility of the national provision at issue with the directive and to give the required declaration.[150] In another procedural setting a national court may deal with an appeal brought by an unemployed married woman against a decision of the competent national social security authorities refusing her the benefit. In such a case the national court may annul the decision because the exclusion of married women laid down in national law cannot apply since it is contrary to the directive. The national exclusionary provision is thus disapplied and the woman will consequently qualify as an unemployed worker for the benefit concerned. Depending on the national rules the domestic court can, for instance, merely annul the decision and leave the matter to the competent authorities. However, it is also conceivable that the national court could annul the decision and order the competent authorities to make a new decision in accordance with the judgment or, if empowered to do so, the national court itself could make the decision instead of the competent authorities.

In other situations such a "simple" disapplication is not sufficient. For example, on the one hand a national law on turnover tax may exempt from turnover tax the granting of credit. On the other hand, the Sixth VAT Directive obliges the Member States to exempt not only the granting of credit but also credit negotiation.[151] In a case where a credit negotiator requests to be exempted from VAT the answer is not the disapplication of national provisions, as there is nothing in national legislation to be set aside. On the contrary, there is a lacuna and then it is a matter of applying the exemption provided for in the directive to the facts of the case.

In summary, the way of using a directive in national proceedings may vary considerably and will depend on several factors such as the type of proceedings, the kind of claim made by the applicant, the scope of jurisdiction of the national court, the state of national provisions at issue etc. The judicial practice in which directives may play a part is in fact much more complex than the few examples I have just given. Yet in my view, at least as far as the use of a directive is

[149] OJ 1979, L 6/24.

[150] For a comparable situation cf. Case 71/85 *FNV* [1986] ECR 3855.

[151] Cf. Case 8/81 *Becker* [1982] ECR 53 (see in particular para. 33).

concerned, two basic formulas can be distinguished. On the one hand there is the *control of legality* of national rules or individual decisions made under national law. In *Rutili*, for instance, the Court held that the national court had the duty to review the compatibility of legislative measures with provisions of Community law and that "it is also for the national courts to examine whether individual decisions are compatible with the relevant provisions of Community law".[152] Here the directive serves as a touchstone, as a standard in the light of which the legality of the measures at stake must be reviewed. On the other hand, there is the possible *application of the provisions of the directive to the facts of the case*. In some cases the control of legality, often with the inapplicability of the contrary national rules as a sanction, may suffice to achieve the result prescribed by the directive in the concrete case.[153] In other cases it may be necessary for the domestic court to apply the provisions of the directive *instead of* the national provisions. This will be necessary in particular where the mere disapplication results in a lacuna or where there are no national legal provisions at all.

Seen against this background, direct application by the national court involves more than the basic Aristotelian syllogism of subsuming the facts under the general rule of the directive.[154] In my opinion, both forms of "application", in the broad sense of the term, fall within the concept of direct effect.

11.3.6 Direct Effect versus Legal Review

The distinction between direct effect in the sense of application of the provisions of a directive to the facts of the case on the one hand, and the review of the legality of national measures on the other, is not new.

This distinction has been made for instance by Timmermans. In his view, direct effect comprises two elements: the possibility of relying on the provision at issue in order to oppose the application of national law contrary to it *and* the

[152] Case 36/75 *Rutili* [1975] ECR 1219, para. 16 and 17.

[153] A further subtle distinction, based on the case law of the Dutch Council of State in environmental matters, has been introduced by Jans (1992). The result of the so- called "abstract-formal review" may be that a *piece of legislation* underlying a decision is held to be inapplicable, if it is contrary to the directive. The second type of review, the "concrete-substantive review", results in annulment or suspension of the individual decision where the *decision* is incompatible with the directive. The main difference in outcome is that in the first situation there is no national legal basis upon which the competent national authorities may act. In the second case there is a national legal basis but the national authorities are forced to act within the limits set by the directive even if their powers under the national provision are broader. According to Jans, the choice between the two methods of review should be determined by the result which the directive at issue wishes to achieve.

[154] However, according to Nicolaysen (1984, p. 391) and Langefeld (1992, p. 957) the Court of Justice considers direct effect as a matter of subsumption only.

direct application of the directive to the facts of the case.[155] On the other hand, legal review implies that the national courts are under the duty to review the lawfulness of national law with regard to the directive, without the possibility of the directive itself being directly applied instead. His analysis was based on the cases *VNO*, *Enka* and *Delkvist*,[156] where the Court found that national courts must determine whether the competent national authorities in adopting the disputed measures have observed the limits of their discretion as set out in the relevant directives. From the cases, in particular from the fact that there was discretion left to the Member States, it was clear that for the purposes of application of a rule to the facts of the case further implementation was needed first. Nevertheless, the national court was obliged to control the legality of the measures concerned in the light of the provisions of the directive.

In German legal writing[157] a similar distinction is made, namely between "*Wirkung als Maßstabsnorm*" (directive as a gauge for legal review) and "*unmittelbare subjectieve Wirkung*" (direct effect, used in the sense of creation of individuals rights). Often, "*Wirkung als Maßstabsnorm*" and "*Wirkung als Auslegungsnorm*" (directive as an aid to interpretation) are taken together under the heading "*objectieve Wirkung*".[158]

Galmot and Bonichot[159] also distinguish between the control of legality, which they call "*invocabilité d'exclusion*", and direct effect, which they indicate with the term "*invocabilité de substitution*".

Others, however, have argued that legal review is more a form of direct effect and not a distinct concept.[160] Even before the judgments in *VNO*, *Enka* and *Delkvist*, Bleckmann, for instance, argued that individuals should be able to rely on provisions of Community law limiting discretionary powers, in order to cause judicial review of national measures.[161]

I fully agree with this point of view. Cases like *VNO*, *Enka* and *Delkvist* have remained perhaps somewhat isolated on the Community level.[162] However, if one considers the way in which directly effective provisions are deployed at national level, it appears that quite often the method actually applied is the

[155] Timmermans 1979, p. 543-544.

[156] Case 51/76 [1977] ECR 133, Case 38/77 [1977] ECR 2203, Case 21/78 [1978] ECR 2327.

[157] Cf. Langenfeld 1992, Bach 1990.

[158] Others make a distinction in this respect between "direct effect in the broad sense" and "direct effect in the narrow sense". Cf. Winter 1991b.

[159] Galmot and Bonichot 1988.

[160] Cf. Maresceau 1980b, p. 665. Cf. also (already) Mertens de Wilmars 1969, p. 76, Lauwaars 1978, p. 837-838 and Lauwaars and Timmermans 1994, p. 32.

[161] Bleckmann 1978, p. 102 and 125.

[162] Cf. however the somewhat peculiar judgment in Case 126/82 *Smit* [1983] ECR 73 and, more recently, Case 222/84 *Johnston* [1986] ECR 1651 and Case C-156/91 *Mundt* [1992] ECR I-5567 (in particular the opinion of A-G Jacobs, para. 11).

control of legality of national rules, whatever might be the formulation adopted by the Court of Justice when answering the question whether a provision has direct effect or not. Moreover, if one takes into account the developments as to the conditions of direct effect to be discussed in Section 11.4, it seems that the distinction between direct effect and legal review as two different concepts is outdated. The review of legality of national measures is merely a form of judicial activity which takes place *within* the concept of direct effect.

11.3.7 Redefining Direct Effect?

In the foregoing Sections the concept of direct effect was scrutinized, to a large extent in the light of its practical operation. The definition of direct effect as the creation of rights for individuals which the national courts must protect was rejected as being too narrow. Subsequently it appeared that the other (and more appropriate) definition of direct effect, namely the capacity of the norm to be invoked by individuals in national courts which are bound to apply the provisions was not entirely satisfactory either. Firstly, I argued that the term "to invoke" is rather misleading since a directive may also be invoked for purposes other than direct effect. Moreover, even where the directive is not invoked as such, a national court may apply the relevant provisions of its own motion. Thus invocability as a central element of the definition is not entirely satisfactory. Secondly, I have argued that the term "to apply" is misleading to the extent that it suggests that what is at stake is the subsumption of the facts under the rules of the directive. I tried to make clear that the deployment of a directive in a national procedure amounts to something more, and will often also include the control of legality of the national measures. Thirdly, another argument can be added: the definition consists of the description of the consequences of direct effect for individuals (to invoke / to rely on) and for the courts (to apply). However, as pointed out in Subsection 11.3.4, national authorities other than the courts are equally obliged to apply the directive. Moreover, the category of subjects who may rely on a directive is very broad.

For these reasons it may be asked whether there is not a necessity to redefine the concept of "direct effect" in terms which take it a stage further than invocability by individuals and which correspond more closely to what is really important. In my view, a more appropriate definition would run as follows: *Direct effect is the obligation of a court or another authority to apply the relevant provision of Community law, either as a norm which governs the case or as a standard for legal review.*

Directly effective provisions are then provisions having the quality to be applied accordingly.[163]

11.4 Conditions for Direct Effect of Directives

11.4.1 Introduction

Whatever the most apt definition of direct effect might be, the central concern of this doctrine is that the provision at issue must lend itself to being applied (in the broad sense of the term) in a concrete case, by a court of law.[164] Perhaps it is more appropriate to say in *the* concrete case before the court since, as discussed above, the mode of application will depend on several factors and, it is submitted, so too will the content of the conditions to be met by the relevant provision.

The conditions for direct effect of directives as formulated by the Court of Justice have gone through a process of development which will be addressed here only briefly. Initially, the discussion focussed on the question as to whether the conditions laid down by the Court for direct effect of Treaty provisions also applied in the field of directives. These conditions were summarized by A-G Mayras in his opinion in the *Van Duyn* case as follows

"– the provision must impose a clear and precise obligation on Member States;
– it must be unconditional, in other words, subject to no limitation; if, however, a provision is subject to certain limitations, their nature and extent must be exactly defined;
– finally, the implementation of a Community rule must not be subject to the adoption of any subsequent rules or regulations on the part either of the Community institutions or of the Member States, so that, in particular, Member States must not be left any real discretion with regard to the application of the rule in question."[165]

The first few judgments of the Court were not entirely conclusive as to the question whether the same criteria applied and, moreover, there was some disagreement amongst the Advocates General as to this issue.[166] Similarly, in legal writing it was submitted that there are no compelling reasons to assume that

[163] As to the obligation for the courts to apply the provisions of their own motion see above, Chapter 8, Subsection 8.3.3.

[164] Cf. Case 158/80 *Butter-buying cruises* [1981] ECR 1805, para. 43. Furthermore it must be recalled that other authorities are also obliged to apply directly effective provisions of a directive. Cf. Case 103/88 *Costanzo* [1989] ECR 1839.

[165] Case 41/74 [1974] ECR 1337, at p. 1354. See for a discussion of these conditions Kapteyn and VerLoren van Themaat 1990, p. 333-338, Bebr 1981, p. 566-582, Hartley 1994, p. 200-206.

[166] Cf. Usher 1980, p. 472-473.

the test to be applied must be the same for Treaty provisions and provisions of regulations and of directives respectively.[167] According to others, however, the test for direct effect of directives is in essence the same as the one for direct effect of Treaty provisions, a view which is by now generally accepted.[168]

In *Van Duyn* the Court held that

> "it is necessary to examine, in every case, whether the nature, general scheme and wording of the provision in question are capable of having direct effects on the relations between Member States and individuals."[169]

The answer to this question was affirmative: the obligation of Article 3(1) of Directive 64/221 (public policy and public health)[170] was not subject to any exception or condition; it did not require the intervention of any act on the part of the Community institutions or of the Member States; since it concerned a derogation from one of the fundamental principles of the Treaty, legal certainty for those concerned required that they should be able to rely on the provision; the meaning and the scope of the provision was a matter of interpretation by the courts which could, if necessary, use the procedure under Article 177 of the Treaty. In other words, on the one hand the Court relied partly on the criteria laid down for direct effect of Treaty provisions. On the other, the test was more tailored to the specific provision at issue and therefore it did not provide clear guidelines as to the question of the more general circumstances under which the "nature, general scheme and wording" of a provision will bring about direct effect.

The next three cases decided by the Court in which the question as to the direct effect of a directive was again raised[171] did not illuminate the matter either. In fact the contrary was true. In *VNO*[172] the Court omitted a test of any kind for direct effect and it found that a national court before which the directive is invoked must determine whether the competent national authorities in adopting the disputed measure have kept within the limits of their discretion as set out in

[167] Cf. Easson 1981, p. 36.

[168] Cf. Pescatore 1983, p. 174, Kapteyn and VerLoren van Themaat 1990, p. 334 ("*mutatis mutandis*").

[169] Case 41/74 [1974] ECR 1337, para. 12.

[170] OJ English Spec. Ed. 1963-1964, p. 117.

[171] In a number of cases following upon *Van Duyn* and concerning equally free movement of persons, direct effect of directives as such was not explicitly considered by the Court. Though there was hardly any doubt that the relevant provisions were directly effective. Cf. Case 67/74 *Bonsignore* [1975] ECR 297, Case 36/75 *Rutili* [1975] ECR 1219, Case 118/75 *Watson and Belmann* [1976] ECR 1185.

[172] Case 51/76 [1977] ECR 133.

the directive. Similarly, in *Enka*[173] the relevant Article of Directive 69/74 (custom warehousing procedure)[174] could be relied upon "for the purposes of verifying whether the national measures adopted for its implementation (were) in accordance with (the provision)." If not, the national courts had to give the provision precedence over any national measures which were incompatible with its terms.[175] The approach of controlling the observance of the limits of discretion left to the Member States also appeared partly in *Delkvist*[176] where the Court itself decided that a Danish provision could not be regarded as exceeding the margin of discretion left to the Member State by Article 2(2) of Directive 74/562 (road passenger transport operators).[177]

These three cases caused some confusion in that, firstly, the Court did not examine whether the relevant provisions met the usual requirements for direct effect; nevertheless, it held that the national measures had to be reviewed in the light of the provisions in question. Secondly, such a review was held to be possible despite the clear margin of discretion in two of those three cases, while as regards direct effect, it was precisely the existence of discretion which usually blocked direct effect. Some authors have therefore argued that this "review of legality approach" is different from direct effect.[178]

Be this as it may, as far as the criteria for direct effect of provisions of directives are concerned, the Court's judgments following upon *Van Duyn* were particularly unhelpful. The two elements which, considered retrospectively, became the test for direct effect of directives appeared for the first time in *Ratti* where the Court found that

> "a national court requested by a person who has complied with the provisions of a directive not to apply a national provision incompatible with the directive ... must uphold that request if the obligation in question is unconditional and sufficiently precise."[179]

These requirements of being unconditional and sufficiently precise appeared again in *Grunert*.[180] However, in another judgment rendered in the same period the Court used yet different terminology: the provisions at issue were sufficiently well-defined and specific to enable them to be relied upon by any person

[173] Case 38/77 [1977] ECR 2203.

[174] OJ English Spec. Ed. 1969 (I), p. 82.

[175] It must be noted that, in contrast to *VNO*, it appeared from the judgment in *Enka* that the relevant provision of the Directive met the conditions for direct effect but the Court did not apply the usual test.

[176] Case 21/78 [1978] ECR 2327.

[177] OJ 1974, L 308/23.

[178] Cf. Timmermans 1979, Galmot and Bonichot 1988. See also above, Subsection 11.3.6.

[179] Case 148/78 [1979] ECR 1629, para. 23.

[180] Case 88/79 [1980] ECR 1827.

concerned and capable as such of being applied by any court.[181] It was not until *Becker* that the Court, in its famous "lecture" on the effects of directives in general, explained that provisions of directives are directly effective wherever they "*appear, as far as their subject-matter is concerned, to be unconditional and sufficiently precise*".[182] As a rule, since the *Becker* judgment the Court has referred to these conditions wherever the question of direct effect of directives arises.

In summary, in *Becker* the Court put an end to some uncertainties about the specific criteria to be applied for determining if a particular provision of a directive has direct effect or not. The next question is then: under what circumstances does a provision meet these criteria? I shall deal with this in the next Subsection. However, it is first necessary to point out that the question as to the direct effect of the provisions arises only if two other conditions are satisfied. Firstly, it must be established that the Member State concerned has not implemented the directive at all, or in time, or that it has done so incorrectly.[183] Secondly, the period for implementation must have expired. National courts are not allowed to apply the directive before the expiry of this period.[184]

11.4.2 The Meaning of "Unconditional and Sufficiently Precise"

Although since *Becker* the test for determining direct effect of directives focusses on the unconditional and sufficiently precise nature of the provisions involved, this does not mean that in every single case the Court scrutinizes explicitly and separately whether the two conditions are satisfied.

In some cases the Court confines itself to quoting or to describing the relevant provision and subsequently simply finds that the provision is precise and unconditional.[185] Similarly, in some cases a different formulation is chosen; such as in *Kühne*, where the Court held that the prohibition at issue is "complete, legally perfect and consequently capable of producing direct effects in the legal relations between Member States and persons within their jurisdiction."[186]

In other cases the Court examined more closely the relevant provisions, checking whether they are sufficiently precise and unconditional. The difference in approach may, first of all, be explained by the rather pragmatic way in which the Court deals with the question as to the direct effect of provisions at issue.

[181] Cf. Case 131/79 *Santillo* [1980] ECR 1585, para. 13.
[182] Case 8/81 [1982] ECR 53, para. 25.
[183] *Ibid*. Cf. also Case 270/81 *Rickmers* [1982] 2771.
[184] Cf. Case 148/78 *Ratti* [1979] 1629.
[185] Cf. Case C-38/88 *Siegen* [1990] ECR I-1447, Case 103/88 *Costanzo* [1989] ECR 1839, Case 96/84 *Slachtpluimvee* [1985] ECR 1157, Case 301/82 *Clin-Midy* [1984] 351.
[186] Case 50/88 [1984] ECR 1925, para. 26. Cf. also Case 271/82 *Auer II* [1983] ECR 2727 and Case 5/83 *Rienks* [1983] ECR 4233.

Moreover, it is not possible in every case to distinguish clearly between the two elements of the test, as the distinction is often rather fluid and both elements are interlinked by another condition of direct effect emerging from the Court's case law, namely the absence of discretion in the application of the provisions at issue. Finally, when addressing the question as to the meaning of "unconditional and sufficiently precise" one must keep in mind the purpose of these requirements, which is judicial application: provisions must be unconditional and sufficiently precise to enable them to be applied by a court of law, which is the quintessence of direct effect.[187]

Sufficiently Precise

The condition of a sufficient degree of precision is primarily concerned with the *wording* of the provision at issue. Several features are relevant in this respect. The Court may find that the provision is unequivocal and therefore sufficiently precise.[188] However, this does not imply that ambiguous or unclear provisions are incapable of being directly effective. Problems of ambiguity and lack of clarity can be resolved by interpretation by the courts and where necessary, by the Court of Justice in a preliminary procedure.[189] Similarly, the fact that a provision may require the evaluation of issues, economic or otherwise, does not preclude their direct effect, provided that the courts are able to make this evaluation themselves or to review the assessment required.[190]

The question of sufficient precision seems to correspond with justiciability: the national court must be able, equipped with the provision at issue, to deal with the problem before it. Specific, clearly defined or detailed provisions will satisfy this requirement.[191] On the other hand, when the provisions are so vague and general that for their application in a concrete case further measures must be adopted in order to "furnish workable indications for the national court",[192] they obviously cannot be applied by the court, as the latter would run up against the limits of its judicial function.[193]

The major difficulty with respect to the sufficient degree of precision lies in vaguely worded concepts. In some cases it will, after interpretation, appear that

[187] Several authors have pointed out in this respect that the same problem also occurs under national law: some legal norms may necessitate further elaboration by subordinate legislation before they can be applied by the courts. Cf. Louis 1993, p. 545, Abraham 1989, p. 21.

[188] Cf. Case 71/85 *FNV* [1986] ECR 3855, Case C-236/92 *Comitato* [1994] ECR I-483.

[189] See the clear reference in Case 41/74 *Van Duyn* [1974] ECR 1337, para. 14.

[190] Cf. Joined Cases 231/87 and 129/88 *Carpaneto I* [1989] ECR 3233.

[191] Cf. Case 131/79 *Santillo* [1980] ECR 1585, Case 103/88 *Costanzo* [1989] ECR 1839, Joined Cases 231/87 and 129/88 *Carpaneto I* [1989] ECR 3233.

[192] Cf. Pescatore 1983, p. 175. See also e.g. Joined Cases 372 to 374/85 *Traen* [1987] ECR 2141, Case 14/83 *Von Colson* [1984] ECR 1891 and Case 31/87 *Beentjes* [1988] ECR 4635.

[193] Cf. Bleckmann 1978, p. 99-100, Timmermans 1979, p. 541, Pescatore 1983, p. 176-177.

they are still capable of judicial adjudication.[194] In other cases, however, behind the vague terms will hide discretion, allowing several choices for the administration or the legislator, where appropriate. This will either make judicial application impossible or it will at least considerably restrict the possibilities of adjudication by the courts.[195]

Unconditional

According to Pescatore,[196] the determination of the unconditional character of the provisions involved is a relatively easy task. In his view, in every single case one has to consider whether there may be some reservation with a view to further implementing measures in respect of which discretion is left to the competent authorities. The reservation may be either inherent in the provision itself or in the system of which the provision is part. Whether such a reservation exists is a matter of legal analysis. Although this is undoubtedly true, in practice matters may be rather complicated. The requirement of unconditionality may relate to several issues.

Firstly, a provision will be conditional if its implementation is made dependent upon the *expiry of a certain period*. It was explained above that a directive can be directly effective only after the expiry of the period provided for its implementation. To this extent matters seem quite simple. However, directives may equally provide for deadlines other than those for their implementation. For instance, Article 12 of Directive 86/378 (equal treatment in occupational schemes of social security)[197] provides that the Member States must comply with the directive at the latest three years after the notification thereof, i.e. on 30 July 1989, but it follows from Article 8 that equal treatment in occupational schemes of social security must be a reality on 1 January 1993. This implies, in my opinion, that an individual can rely on the directive only after 1 January 1993.

Secondly, the application of a provision of a directive will usually depend upon the *fulfilment of certain (factual) conditions*, although as long as these are ascertainable by the judge the conditions do not preclude direct effect. Thus, for instance, under Directive 69/335 (taxes on the raising of capital)[198] Member States are prohibited from collecting capital duty when a contribution received by the company does not increase its assets. Whether a certain contribution does so or not can be verified by a court, which can, in the case of doubt, ask a

[194] E.g the so-called "indefinite legal concept" ("*unbestimte Rechtbegriffe*"). See also below in this Subsection.

[195] See further below in this Subsection.

[196] Pescatore 1983, p. 174-175.

[197] OJ 1986, L 225/40.

[198] OJ English Spec. Ed. 1969 (II), p. 412.

preliminary question for this purpose.[199] However, matters may be less clear. Article 4(5) of the Sixth VAT directive, for instance, requires certain activities to be treated as taxable if their treatment as non-taxable would lead to a significant distortion of competition. According to A-G Mischo,[200] this provision implied discretion for the Member States and could not be relied upon before a court. The Court of Justice admitted that the application of this provision involves an assessment of economic circumstances, but, nevertheless, it found that this assessment is not exempt from judicial review.[201]

Thirdly, the possible application of a provision of a directive may (seem to) be *made dependent on the adoption of certain further implementing measures*, such as the establishment of guarantee funds under Directive 80/987 (protection of workers – insolvency of employers),[202] the introduction of a certain, though unspecified, type of sanction under Directive 76/207 (equal treatment at work),[203] the definition of "building land" under Article 4(3)b of the Sixth VAT Directive,[204] the establishment of a system of supervision and control over waste-disposal activities under Directive 75/442 (waste)[205] or the adoption of any other measures explicitly provided for in the directive at issue.[206] Yet, whether or not provisions of this type will block direct effect will depend on a number of factors. For instance once the necessary measures have been adopted, the provision can no longer be regarded as conditional and a court may proceed to the application of its terms. Thus, for instance, once a Member State has made the choice as to the type of sanction to be imposed in the case of discrimination, the court may review whether the sanction is effective or not.[207] Similarly, not every provision prescribing further implementing measures will make the application of another provision conditional in the sense that without the measures the latter would be inoperative. As a rule this will only be the case when the competent authorities are left discretion with respect to the further implementing measures to be adopted and this discretion affects the result prescribed.[208] Moreover, it may happen that the further implementing measures

[199] Cf. Case C-38/88 *Siegen* [1990] ECR I-1447.

[200] Joined Cases 231/87 and 129/88 *Carpaneto I* [1989] ECR 3233 (opinion, para. 22-24).

[201] *Ibid*. Cf. also Case 27/67 *Fink-Frucht* [1968] ECR 223 for Treaty provisions.

[202] OJ 1980, L 283/23. Cf. Joined Cases C-6/90 and C-9/90 *Francovich* [1991] ECR I-5357.

[203] OJ 1976, L 39/40. Cf. Case 14/83 *Von Colson* [1984] ECR 1891. See however also Case C-271/91 *Marshall II* [1993] ECR I-4367, to be discussed below, in Subsection 11.4.3.

[204] OJ 1977, L 145/1. Cf. Case C-468/93 *Gemeente Emmen*, pending.

[205] OJ 1975, L 194/39. Cf. Joined Cases 372 to 374/85 *Traen* [1987] ECR 2141.

[206] Cf. Article 5 of Directive 79/7, OJ 1979, L 6/24 and Case 71/85 *FNV* [1986] ECR 3855.

[207] Cf. Case C-271/91 *Marshall II* [1993] ECR I-4367.

[208] Cf. Joined Cases C-6/90 and C-9/90 *Francovich* [1991] ECR I-5357 (discretion as to the organization of the guarantee funds), Case 71/85 *FNV* [1986] ECR 3855 (discretion as to the methods but not as to the result to be achieved).

are not relevant to the case at issue,[209] or that they are merely intended to facilitate the application of the provision concerned.[210]

Fourthly, where the issue of the possible conditionality of the relevant provision arises, the Court often looks into the *derogations, exceptions, reservations* etc. provided for in the directive to the rule invoked by the person concerned.[211] Derogations may take different forms. Sometimes they are laid down as an obligation for the Member States,[212] in other cases they take the form of an option.[213] Making use of the option is indeed a matter within Member States' discretion.[214] Once the choice has been made, matters may be different. As far as the content of derogations is concerned, they may be precisely drafted,[215] but they may also leave discretion to the Member States as to their material content.[216] Equally, a derogation may in turn be conditional.[217]

However, derogations as such do not necessarily amount to a condition, in the sense of rendering the provision to be applied conditional and, consequently, blocking its direct effect. It could be that the Member State did not make use of its faculty to derogate or that, for the case to be decided, the derogation is not relevant.[218] Indeed, if the derogation is relevant to the case, wherever it is precisely drafted the national court can verify whether and to what extent the derogation may apply. However, the matter is less unproblematic where the derogation as such applies, for instance because the Member State has made use of its option, but the derogatory provision leaves the Member States discretion as to its actual operationalization. Here again discretion may block or restrict

[209] Cf. Case C-221/88 *Busseni* [1990] ECR I-495 (adequate legal safeguard, by means of appropriate transitional provisions, for the rights of other creditors did not apply, as it referred to the protection of rights of creditors other than the two parties involved, namely the ECSC and the State), Case 8/81 *Becker* [1982] ECR 53 (discretion in other areas was not relevant for the application of Article 13 B).

[210] Case 8/81 *Becker* [1982] ECR 53.

[211] Conversely, an individual may of course also rely on a derogation.

[212] E.g. exemptions under the Sixth VAT Directive, OJ 1977, L 145/1.

[213] The Member States *may* do something (cf. Article 25 (2) of Directive 77/91 (second company law directive), OJ 1977, L 26/1) or the Directive will be "without prejudice to the right of the Member States to exclude ..." (cf. Article 2 (2) of Directive 76/207 (equal treatment at work), OJ 1976, L 39/40).

[214] Cf. Case 51/76 *VNO* [1977] ECR 133.

[215] See e.g. "precise, concrete derogations" in Joined Cases C-19/90 and C-20/90 *Karrella and Karellas* [1991] ECR I-2691, para. 22.

[216] Cf. Case 51/76 *VNO* [1977] ECR 133, Case 184/83 *Hofmann* [1984] ECR 3047, Case 222/84 *Johnston* [1986] ECR 1651.

[217] Cf. Article 9 of Directive 86/378, OJ 1986, L 225/40.

[218] Cf. the opinion of A-G Mischo in Joined Case 231/87 and 129/88 *Carpaneto I* [1989] ECR 3233, para. 15 ("obligation is unconditional in so far as a given activity can in no case come within the scope of the exception"). Cf. also Case 152/84 *Marshall I* [1986] ECR 723, para. 54.

direct effect. The scope of direct effect of the provision to be applied will then depend on the degree of judicial control which is possible.

Thus in *VNO*[219] the Court considered that the principle of deduction of VAT was subject to certain (optional) derogations and exceptions. Neither the exercise of the power regarding whether or not to make a derogation or exception, nor the use of the margin of discretion left to the Member States as to their material contents could as such be subject to legal review on the basis of the provisions of the directive. However, the national court was under the duty to determine whether the disputed national measures fell outside the margin of discretion and therefore could not be considered as a legitimate derogation from or exception to the principle of deduction.[220] Similarly, in *Johnston*[221] the Court decided that an individual may rely on Article 2(1) of Directive 76/207 (equal treatment at work),[222] i.e. the principle of equal treatment, in order to have a derogation from that principle under national legislation set aside *in so far as it exceeds the limits of the exceptions* permitted by Article 2(2). In my opinion, both cases illustrate that the national court must review whether the discretionary derogations are within the limits laid down in the relevant directives. If they are, the question of direct effect of the provisions laying down the respective principles is immaterial. If they exceed the limits, they are not legitimate derogations and the main provisions which were subject to the derogations apply, where appropriate.[223]

Discretion

In the foregoing discussion of the sufficient degree of precision of a provision and its unconditional character it was apparent that a constantly recurring question relates to the discretion on the part of the Member States. In legal writing it has been observed that the absence of discretion of the Member States with regard to the implementation of the directive provision is the common denominator of both conditions for direct effect or that it is the basic condition to which the other various criteria can be reduced.[224]

A crucial issue which must be kept in mind, particularly with respect to directives, is that the discretion must exist in respect of the content of the

[219] Case 51/76 [1977] ECR 133.

[220] See for a comparable although much less explicit approach by the Court Case 126/78 *Nederlandse Spoorwegen* [1979] ECR 2041, and the opinion of A-G Reischl, who proposed that the VNO-line be followed (para. 4).

[221] Case 222/84 [1986] ECR 1651.

[222] OJ 1976, L 39/40.

[223] In some cases it may also suffice to disapply the derogation which goes too far and apply the national rules giving effect to the main provision.

[224] Cf. Kapteyn and VerLoren van Themaat 1990, p. 336-338, Timmermans 1979, p. 539, Maresceau 1980a, p. 276, Lauwaars and Timmermans 1994, p. 32.

STAFFS UNIVERSITY LIBRARY

provision at issue.[225] The fact that the provision is an integral part of a directive which, taken in its entirety, reserves to the Member States a margin of discretion in various respects, is not an obstacle to direct effect of the provision. As long as the latter can be severed from the general body of provisions and applied separately it may, standing alone, be directly effective.[226]

As was already discussed in Chapter 5, Member States enjoy a degree of freedom as to the forms and methods of implementation of a directive. In some cases this freedom has been invoked to deny direct effect of a provision of a directive. In *FNV*,[227] for instance, the Dutch government argued that equal treatment of men and women in the legislation concerned could be achieved in at least four different ways and therefore the prohibition of discrimination laid down in Directive 79/7 (equal treatment in statutory schemes of social security)[228] could not be directly effective. In this respect, A-G Mancini perceptively observed that such argument confuses the issue of direct effect with that of the discretion available to Member States in transposing the directive into national law.[229] Equally, the Court of Justice held that the prohibition of discrimination was sufficiently precise and unconditional and a Member State could not invoke its discretion with regard to the choice of form and methods for implementing the principle of equal treatment in the field of social security in order to deny its direct effect.

The question as to whether or not discretion is left to the Member States is a matter of interpretation of the relevant provision or set of provisions. Sometimes matters may be quite straightforward. In other cases, however, things are less certain. In particular, provisions using vague concepts which have to be substantiated in the light of the facts of the case are notoriously difficult. A theoretical distinction often referred to in this respect is that between indefinite legal concepts and discretion. The former imply that there are several possible views as to their interpretation but only one is right; discretion means not only that a choice of different views is possible but also that it is lawful to follow any of them.[230] It is only the latter form, which some call "real discretion",[231] which seems to preclude direct effect. In practice, however, it is not always an easy task to decide whether such "real discretion" exists or not. This is witnessed,

[225] Cf. Case 8/81 *Becker* [1982] ECR 53, para. 25: "... as far as their subject-matter is concerned ...".

[226] *Ibid.*, para. 29.

[227] Case 71/85 [1986] ECR 3855.

[228] OJ 1979, L 6/24.

[229] At p. 3867.

[230] Definition by Kapteyn and VerLoren van Themaat 1990, p. 337.

[231] Cf. Timmermans 1979, p. 540.

for instance, by the different views of Advocates General on the one hand and the Court of Justice on the other with respect to the same provision.[232]

Originally the mere existence of discretion was generally considered to be an obstacle to direct effect.[233] However recent case law of the Court has altered this point of view. In *Francovich*[234] the Court admitted that several Articles of Directive 80/987 (protection of workers – insolvency of employers)[235] left the Member States discretion in determining the content of the guarantee to be paid to the employees concerned. Nevertheless it found that as it was possible to determine the minimum guarantee provided for on the basis of the terms of the directive as such, the provisions in question were unconditional and sufficiently precise.

The main argument relied on by the Court in arriving at its finding was rather peculiar and, it is submitted, was based on an incorrect reading of the relevant cases. The Court referred to its judgments in *FNV* and *McDermott and Cotter I*[236] and recalled in this respect that "the right of a State to choose among several possible means of achieving the result required by a directive does not preclude the possibility for individuals of enforcing before the national courts rights whose content can be determined sufficiently precisely on the basis of the provisions of the directive alone."[237] In my opinion, the Court here was caught in the pitfall of (the relative character of) the principle of equality. In *FNV* and *McDermott* the result to be achieved was clearly and unconditionally prescribed: equal treatment of men and women in social security. The argument of the respective governments, according to which equality could be achieved at several levels and by several different methods,[238] was dismissed as a matter of form and methods of implementation. In *Francovich*, however, it was the definition of the result itself which was at issue.[239] Whatever the merits of such faulty reasoning might be, the approach launched in *Francovich* was confirmed in a rather puzzling *obiter dictum* in *Marshall II* and more recently in *Faccini Dori*.[240]

[232] Cf. Joined Cases C-6/90 and C-9/90 *Francovich* [1991] ECR I-5357, Case C-221/88 *Busseni* [1990] ECR I-495, Joined Case 231/87 and 129/88 *Carpaneto I* [1989] ECR 3233.

[233] Cf. the judgment in *Kaefer and Procacci* (Joined Cases C-100/89 and C-101/89 [1990] ECR I-4647), where the Court held that "an unconditional provision is one which leaves no discretion to the Member States" (para. 26).

[234] Joined Cases C-6/90 and C-9/90 [1991] ECR I-5357.

[235] OJ 1980, L 283/23.

[236] Case 71/85 [1986] ECR 3855 and Case 286/85 [1987] ECR 1453.

[237] Joined Case C-6/90 and C-9/90 [1991] ECR I-5357, para. 17.

[238] By levelling-up, levelling-down, abolishing the benefits altogether etc., as long as men and women were treated equally.

[239] This difference was clearly pointed out by A-G Mischo, para. 22 and 23.

[240] Case C-271/91 [1993] ECR I-4367, para. 37 and Case C-91/92 [1994] ECR I-3325, para. 17.

Thus, in brief, discretion on the part of the Member States with respect to the content of the measures to be taken does not necessarily seem to be an obstacle to direct effect as long as the national court can itself construe the content of the provision to be applied on the basis of the terms of the directive. In *Francovich* it was still the "minimum default option" that had to be applied. It should however not be ruled out that the Court may go beyond such a minimum in the future.

Another important tendency in the Court's case law which implies that the mere existence of discretion does not necessarily prevent direct effect has already been discussed above.[241] In *VNO*[242] the Court recognized the possibility for the individual of invoking a provision of a directive to make the national court rule whether the competent national authorities have kept within the limits of their discretion as set out in the directive.

Indeed, conceptually it may seem difficult to reconcile the two approaches of the Court of Justice. The first, despite the concession made in *Francovich*, still focusses on the absence of discretion, while the second takes discretion as a starting point, and, subsequently, allows judicial control.[243] The crux of the matter is that direct effect must be considered within the context of the concrete case.

11.4.3 Direct Effect and the Context of the Case

The question whether the conditions for direct effect of a particular provision are satisfied cannot be separated from the concrete case to be decided and the answer will vary accordingly. The context of the case and, in particular, the way in which the national court deploys the directive will also determine the issue of direct effect.

The orthodox understanding of direct effect, which also explains the conditions of sufficient precision and unconditionality, was that Community law must provide an "*Alternativ-Normierung*", i.e. legal norms which can be applied by national courts, where appropriate, instead of national rules which are incompatible with Community law provisions.[244] The existence of discretion is hardly compatible with this idea, since the court is then unable to know what the applicable rules should be. Yet, as explained in Subsection 11.3.5, judicial activity is not limited to the positive application of the provisions of a directive to the

[241] See Subsection 11.3.6 and 11.4.1.

[242] Case 51/76 [1977] ECR 133. Cf. also the opinion of A-G Jacobs in Case C-164/90 *Muwi* [1991] ECR I-6049, para. 25.

[243] A kind of mixture of the "orthodox" approach to direct effect, i.e. taking unconditionality and sufficient degree of precision as a starting point, and the control of the observance of the limits laid down in a directive can be found in Case 126/82 *Smit* [1983] ECR 73.

[244] Cf. Kapteyn and VerLoren van Themaat 1990, p. 338, referring to Ipsen.

facts of the case. In several cases the court confines itself to reviewing the national law in the light of the directive and, where appropriate, disapplying the national provisions, without it being necessary to apply the directive instead. In such an event, the existence of discretion as such is not an obstacle to direct effect, provided that the limits of the discretion are sufficiently clear to serve as a touchstone.[245] Whatever a Member State does *within* those limits is as such not submitted to judicial review. However, once the limits are exceeded, it is up to the courts to intervene. The result may then indeed be that a provision has direct effect in some cases, but not in others.[246]

Further clarification of the subject under discussion here can be drawn from the trio of cases *Von Colson, Johnston* and *Marshall II.*[247] In all three cases the central provision at issue was Article 6 of Directive 76/207 (equal treatment at work).[248] This provision was interpreted by the Court of Justice as requiring effective judicial protection of the person discriminated against. This interpretation has two other implications, namely that the person concerned must have effective access to a court which will be able to review the disputed measures; and that the sanctions to be imposed in the event of discrimination must be such as to guarantee real and effective judicial protection.[249]

In *Von Colson* the Court was confronted with, *inter alia*, the following two questions: in the case of discrimination on grounds of sex in the matter of access to employment, is the employer required to conclude a contract of employment with the candidate discriminated against? If not, is it possible to infer from the directive any sanction other than the right to the conclusion of a contract of employment?[250] The Court of Justice found that the directive does not prescribe a specific sanction and that it leaves the Member States free to choose between the different solutions suitable for achieving its objective. In other words, the directive did not include any unconditional and sufficiently precise obligation as regards sanctions for discrimination which may be relied on by individuals in order to obtain specific compensation or a contract of employment under the directive. Consequently, the provision was not directly effective in this respect.

In *Johnston* one of the problems was whether, under application of Article 53(2) of the Sex Discrimination Order, the national court could be prevented from exercising judicial control. When considering the question of direct effect of Article 6, the Court recalled that the Article does not contain, as far as sanctions for discrimination are concerned, any unconditional and sufficiently precise obligation which may be relied upon by an individual. However, *in so far as it follows from that Article* that all (alleged) victims of

[245] Cf. Maresceau 1880a, p. 276.

[246] Cf. Kapteyn and VerLoren van Themaat 1990, p. 337, Lauwaars and Timmermans 1994, p. 31.

[247] Case 14/83 [1984] ECR 1891, Case 222/84 [1986] ECR 1651 and Case C-271/91 [1993] ECR I-4367.

[248] OJ 1976, L 39/40.vpl

[249] Cf. above, Chapter 8, Subsection 8.2.2.

[250] It should be noted that the plaintiffs required the conclusion of a contract of employment and, in the alternative, damages amounting to six months' salary.

discrimination must have an effective judicial remedy, that provision is sufficiently precise and unconditional to enable it to be relied upon.

The nature of the sanction and the possible direct effect of Article 6 were again under discussion in *Marshall II*. In this case the major issue was whether Ms Marshall could rely on Article 6 in order to have set aside a statutory limit on the amount of compensation to be paid to a victim of discrimination. In a cleverly constructed judgment the Court established first, drawing upon its earlier case law on effective sanctions, that in the particular case of discriminatory dismissal there were two options: either the victim is reinstated or she (or he) must be given financial compensation. Where financial compensation is the measure chosen, the compensation must be adequate, i.e. must make good in full the loss and the damage actually sustained. An upper limit applicable *a priori*, which could prevent full compensation being given to the victim, was not compatible with the requirements resulting from Article 6. As to the direct effect, the Court found that in this case Ms Marshall could rely on Article 6. The fact that this article left a choice among different sanctions to the Member States was immaterial, since a choice had already been made and the national authorities had no degree of discretion in applying the chosen solution, since the compensation had to be compensation "in full". Another implicit but important element in *Marshall II* was probably also the fact that the national court was perfectly able to ascertain, in accordance with the national rules, what the amount of full compensation should to be, but by virtue of the upper limit was prevented from granting it. The – quite simple – solution was then indeed to disapply the limitation.[251]

The most important lesson to be learned from these examples is that the question whether a provision will have direct effect depends on what the person relying on the directive is asking for, and whether the national court will be able to satisfy the claimant, while taking into account its judicial function. For a positive application of a directive the conditions of sufficient precision and unconditionality may often have a different content when compared to the degree of precision and unconditionality required for judicial review.[252] In the final analysis the ultimate test is to be found in the doctrine of separation of powers and the place attributed therein to the courts. Pescatore has pointed out in this respect that direct effect "depends less on the intrinsic quality of the rules concerned than on the *possumus* or *non possumus* of the judges".[253] The reality is that even the

[251] See for a more detailed discussion of *Marshall II* Moore 1993, Curtin 1994, Fitzpatrick and Szyszczak 1994b.

As other exaples of such a "variable approach" can be mentioned the Case 88/79 *Grunert* [1980] ECR 1827 and Case 108/80 *Kugelmann* [1981] ECR 433. While in the first case the transgression of the limits set by the directive enabled Mr Grumert to rely on it, this was not the case for Mr Kugelmann, since the national measures at issue remained within the limits of the directive.

[252] However, Galmot en Bonichot (1988, p. 17), for instance, argue that review of legality and direct effect in the sense of "substitution" are two different problems which have to be resolved in accordance with different criteria.

[253] Pescatore 1983, p. 177.

question of what the national court as a court of law can and cannot do is no longer entirely a matter of national law.

A final example may illustrate this point. The Dutch *Hoge Raad*[254] refused to apply Article 26 (prohibition of discrimination) of the International Covenant on Civil and Political Rights because the solution for the inequality at issue[255] was not a matter for a court but for the legislature. It is up to the latter to decide how equality must be realized in this respect.[256] Indeed, this is in sharp contrast to the finding of the Court of Justice in a number of cases, in particular, decided under Directive 79/7 (equal treatment in statutory schemes of social security)[257] that the choice of the form and methods for achieving the required result, i.e. equality, cannot constitute a ground for denying direct effect. According to the Court, in the absence of the implementing measures women are entitled to have the same rules applied to them as had been applied to men. Apparently, what seems to be a justiciable matter in the eyes of the Court of Justice is often, for reasons of judicial restraint, not necessarily considered to be jucticiable in the purely national context; or, as was pointed out by Mertens de Wilmars, "false" discretion may come into being through the powerlessness of the courts, which may fear the accusation of "*gouvernement des juges*".[258]

11.5 Limits of Direct Effect of Directives

11.5.1 Member States' Obligations under International Agreements

Although direct effect of Community law is considered to be one of the twin pillars of the Community legal system,[259] or one of its essential characteristics,[260] it is not sacrosanct. Direct effect of Community law and thus also direct effect of directives has its limits.

The first limitation I would like to discuss here in fact emerged relatively recently and is the result of the application of the conflict rule laid down in Article 234 of the EEC Treaty. According to the first paragraph of this Article

[254] HR 12 Oktober 1984, NJCM-Bulletin 1985, p.32.

[255] A woman could, upon marriage with a Dutch citizen, opt for Dutch citizenship while a man could not.

[256] Cf. the arguments against direct effect of Directive 79/7 put forward by the Dutch government in *FNV*; see above, Subsection 11.4.2.

[257] OJ 1979, L 6/24. Cf. e.g. Case 71/85 *FNV* [1986] ECR 3855 and Case 384/85 *Borrie Clarke* [1987] ECR 2865.

[258] Mertens de Wilmars 1969, p. 78.

[259] Cf. Wyatt and Dashwood 1993, p. 54.

[260] Opinion 1/91 *EEA* [1991] ECR I-6079, para. 21.

"the rights and obligations arising from agreements concluded before the entry into force of this Treaty between one or more Member States on the one hand, and one or more third countries on the other, shall not be affected by the provisions of this Treaty."

In two French cases[261] relating to the prohibition of nightwork of women the Court of Justice found that prohibition of nightwork of women where nightwork of men is not prohibited was contrary to the principle of equal treatment with regard to working conditions laid down in Article 5 of Directive 76/207(equal treatment at work).[262] Similarly, it was already established case law that this provision has direct effect. In principle, this implied that "the national court was under the duty to ensure the full effect of that rule by leaving unapplied any contrary provisions of national legislation".[263] However, the problem was that the contrary national provision at issue was enacted to give effect to ILO Convention No 89, prohibiting nightwork by women. France ratified that Convention by a law of 21 September 1953, thus before the entry into force of the EEC Treaty, and at the material time had not denounced it. In a carefully reasoned judgment[264] the Court came to the conclusion that the national court was not obliged to disapply the national provision which was contrary to the directive in so far as the application of the provision concerned was necessary to ensure the performance by the Member State concerned of obligations arising from an agreement anterior to the Treaty in the sense of Article 234. According to the Court of Justice it is for the national court to verify the concrete obligations under the agreement, in order to determine the extent to which these obligations constitute an obstacle to the application of Article 5 of the directive. Similarly, the national court must verify whether the national provisions in question are designed to implement the above-mentioned obligations.[265]

In summary, the application of Article 5 of the directive as a gauge for establishing the illegality of the relevant French provisions should normally lead to their disapplication. However, in the present case this effect was blocked by virtue of Article 234 of the EEC Treaty.

11.5.2 General Principles of Community Law

Establishing the direct effect of a provision is a matter of interpretation. As a rule, interpretation of a Community law provision by the Court of Justice has

[261] Case C-345/89 *Stoeckel* [1991] ECR I-4047 and Case C-158/91 *Levy* [1993] ECR I-4287, also discussed briefly in Chapter 2, Section 2.3.
[262] OJ 1976, L 39/40.
[263] Case C-158/91 *Levy* [1993] ECR I-4287, para. 9.
[264] Which was further elaborated in case C-13/93 *Minne* [1994] ECR I-371.
[265] *Ibid.*, para. 18.

retroactive effect, i.e. the provision *as interpreted by the Court* applies from its entry into force.[266] For direct effect of directives this implies, for reasons particular to directives,[267] that the provision which is declared to be directly effective produces this effect from the end of the period provided for its implementation, even if the judgment making this plain is rendered at a later stage. However, in exceptional cases the Court has been prepared to limit the general retrospective effect of its ruling. The basis for such a limitation is "important considerations of legal certainty".[268] One of the few cases in which the Court of Justice took this exceptional step concerned its finding that Article 119 EEC was directly effective in *Defrenne II*.[269] As yet, there are no reasons why the Court should not proceed in the same way where the provision at issue is a provision of a directive.

In my opinion, *Defrenne II* makes clear that the principle of legal certainty may under particular circumstances limit the direct effect of Community law provisions. It is however important to stress in this context that it is solely for the Court of Justice to determine whether the circumstances are such that the principle of legal certainty would be compromised. Moreover, for this very reason, the principle of legal certainty which applies in these types of situations is the *community principle*.[270] This is only logical, as to allow direct effect to be limited by a national principle of law would run against the rule of supremacy.[271]

Defrenne II was concerned with the limitation of direct effect as such. This situation must be carefully distinguished from the situation where the Court allows the application of national principles within the framework of national procedures used for the enforcement of Community law. As was already discussed in Chapter 8, in particular Subsection 8.2.1, in a number of cases the Court of Justice did not object to the application of the *national* principle of unjust enrichment[272] or the principle of legitimate expectations.[273] The difference lies, in my view, in the fact that *Defrenne II* restricts the direct effect itself, while the second type of cases limits the – what one may call – "effects of direct effect". Or, in different terms, national principles may not affect the (procedural)

[266] Cf. Case 61/79 *Denkavit Italiana* [1908] ECR 1205.

[267] Cf. Chapter 2, Section 2.2. As to entry into force of directive, see n. 20 in that Section.

[268] Cf. Case 43/75 *Defrenne II* [1976] ECR 455, Case 24/86 *Blaizot* [1988] ECR 379, Case C-262/88 *Barber* [1990] ECR I-1889.

[269] Case 43/75 [1976] ECR 455.

[270] As to the discussion on application of national principles or community principles see Chapter 2, Section 2.4. Cf. also Chapter 10, Section 10.7.

[271] Cf. the opinion of A-G Mischo in Case C-377/89 *Cotter and McDermott II* [1991] ECR I-1155, para. 34.

[272] See e.g. Case 68/79 *Just* [1980] ECR 501.

[273] See e.g. Case 265/78 *Ferwerda* [1980] ECR 617.

right of individuals to rely on Community law provisions; they may however limit the exercise of this right.

Indeed, this distinction is very subtle and may in some cases be extremely difficult to make. Illustrative in this respect is the *Cotter and McDermott II* case.[274]

At the origin of this case was the fact that direct effect of the prohibition of discrimination on grounds of sex laid down in Directive 79/7 (equal treatment in statutory schemes of social security)[275] resulted in some cases in payment to women of certain social security increases for dependent spouses and children even if there were no actual dependants and, moreover, it could result in double payments of these increases to one single household.[276] In this case it was argued that to allow such claims would offend against the principle prohibiting unjust enrichment, which under the national law at issue constitutes a ground for restricting or refusing relief in certain circumstances. The Court of Justice dismissed this argument, as it found that to allow the national authorities to rely on this national principle would enable them to use their own unlawful conduct[277] as a ground for depriving the directive of its full effect.

The link between direct effect of the relevant provision and the "effect of its direct effect" is so close that one may wonder whether the limitation of the immediate consequences does not amount to a limitation of the direct effect itself. However, as the Court's case law now stands, the distinction between direct effect as such and the effects of direct effect seems to remain the decisive criterion. Direct effect may only be limited by Community law principles, while the effects of direct effect may, under certain circumstances, be limited by the application of national principles of law. Yet the latter issue is a part of a broader problem, namely the extent to which national rules, both procedural and substantive, which serve as a vehicle for enforcement of Community law may limit the operation of the latter. I have already discussed this subject in Chapter 8.

[274] Case C-377/89 *Cotter and McDermott II* [1991] ECR I-1155.
[275] OJ 1979, L 6/24.
[276] This was the consequence of the combination of mainly two factors: the application of the "*FNV* rule" (see above, Subsection 11.4.3) and the fact that Irish legislation provided for "automatic" increases for male breadwinners.
[277] I.e. not having implemented the directive in due time.

11.5.3 Horizontal Direct Effect of Directives: the Debate before Marshall I

Introduction

The most important limitation of direct effect of directives is the absence of horizontal direct effect, as decided by the Court of Justice in the *Marshall I* case.[278] By the terms "horizontal direct effect" I understand that the relevant provision can be invoked and enforced by an individual *vis-à-vis* other individuals. For reasons to be explained later,[279] this concept must be distinguished from the concept of "inverse vertical direct effect"[280] which means that a Member State can rely on a provision against a private individual. As far as directives are concerned, such an effect has equally been denied by the Court of Justice.[281] Thus also in this situation direct effect is limited: the application of a directive may not amount to the State imposing an obligation upon private individuals and subsequently enforcing it against them.

The issue of horizontal direct effect has generated a considerable literature, both before and after the *Marshall I* judgment. For a long time, the main arguments in favour of and against horizontal direct effect of directives remained to a large extent basically the same. They can be summarized as follows.[282]

Arguments Pro and Contra

The *first argument* against horizontal direct effect of directives draws upon the definition of directives in Article 189(3). According to this definition directives are binding upon the Member States and therefore not upon private individuals. For this reason they cannot impose obligations on individuals but only on Member States. However, other scholars have drawn attention to the Court's case law with respect to direct effect of, notably, Treaty provisions. From this case law it appeared, firstly, that direct effect is not conditional upon the addressee of the relevant provision.[283] According to some, in particular the obligation to legal review, as laid down in *VNO* and *Enka*,[284] indicates that the nature of the legal

[278] Case 152/84 [1986] ECR 723.

[279] See below, Subsection 11.5.4.

[280] For the same distinction (which is, however, not made by everybody) cf. also Arnull 1988, p. 44, Langenfeld 1992, p. 958 Nicolaysen 1984, p. 390, Schilling 1988, p. 659.

[281] Cf. Case 80/86 *Kolpinghuis* [1987] ECR 3969.

[282] For the different arguments (and often further references) see e.g. Timmermans 1979, Easson 1979b, Wyatt 1983, Nicolaysen 1984, Schockweiler 1993c. Cf. also the opinion of A-G Jacobs in Case C-316/93 *Vaneetveld* [1994] ECR I-763 and the opinion of A-G Lenz in Case C-91/92 *Faccini Dori*, 9 February 1994, [1994] ECR I-3325.

[283] Cf. Barents, 1992 p. 98, Easson 1979b, p. 71.

[284] Case 51/76 [1977] ECR 113 and Case 38/77 [1977] ECR 2203.

relationship involved plays no part in the matter at all.[285] Another case which is often relied on in this respect is *Defrenne II.*[286] Despite the fact that, according to the letter of Article 119, the addressees are the Member States, the Court found in favour of horizontal direct effect. Yet those who oppose horizontal direct effect of directives pointed out that the definition within Article 189(3) is in this respect too explicit to allow an analogy.[287]

Further, the case law on direct effect of Treaty provisions has made clear that in determining the legal effects it is the content of the measure rather than its form which is decisive. Moreover, in the Court's case law on direct effect in general, thus including direct effect of directives, there has been no indication that direct effect is dependent on the legal character of the act in which the relevant provision has been laid down.[288]

More recently, A-G Jacobs expressed the view that the textual argument is neither convincing nor decisive.[289] In his opinion, the terms of Article 189 do not expressly exclude the possibility of derived obligations arising for persons other than Member States. A comparable point has been made by Richter[290] who argued that a distinction should be made between the obligation of the Member States, i.e. to implement the directive, and the obligations laid down in the substantive provisions of the directive itself. The mere fact that Member States are obliged to implement the directive does not as such decide the question as to the potential legal effects of the substantive provisions.

The *second argument* against horizontal direct effect of directives referred to the difference between regulations and directives. Only the former are, according to Article 189, directly applicable and may, for that reason, impose obligations on private individuals. Accepting horizontal direct effect of directives would amount to assimilating directives to regulations. This would deprive directives of their original character and, moreover, run counter to Article 189. Yet in this respect it has been observed that this argument is the same as that put forward against direct effect of directives in general, which has, however, been dismissed by the Court.[291] Moreover, allowing horizontal direct effect of directives would change nothing with respect to the obligation to implement them,[292] nor would it alter

[285] Barents 1982, p. 101.
[286] Case 43/75 [1976] ECR 455.
[287] Cf. Timmermans 1979, p. 541-542. Cf. also Langenveld 1992, p. 959.
[288] Cf. Barents 1982, p. 102.
[289] Opinion in Case C-316/93 *Vaneetveld* [1994] ECR I-763, para. 20. Cf. also Wyatt and Dashwood 1993, p. 74-75.
[290] Richter 1988, p. 397-398. Cf. also Winter 1991b, p. 665.
[291] Cf. Case 41/74 *Van Duyn* [1974] ECR 1337.
[292] Cf. the opinion of A-G Jacobs in Case C-316/93 *Vaneetveld* [1994] ECR I-763, para. 25.

the choice of form and methods left to the Member States.[293] According to Barents,[294] the concerns about the character of the directive which underlie this argument boil down, in fact, to the old problem of whether Community law provisions which may produce direct effect may be laid down in a directive at all. This is the question, which has already been resolved, as to the extent to which directives must leave room for Member States to implement them in their own way.[295] As such, it has nothing to do with horizontal direct effect. In the same line of reasoning there is also a recent remark of A-G Jacobs, who pointed out that the directive, as an instrument of Community law, has undergone an important development to which, however, Article 189 has not been adapted.[296]

The *third argument* relates to legal certainty. It comprises two distinct elements. Firstly, there is no legal requirement to publish directives in the Official Journal.[297] Some consider that to be a purely formal argument, having only a limited value, as in practice directives are published.[298] In their view, only in those – exceptional – cases where there has actually been no publication of the directive concerned, should individuals deserve protection.[299] Yet this argument is considered by certain other scholars to be an important one. A-G Lenz made a distinction in this respect between publication with a "constitutive" effect and a merely declaratory publication. In his opinion "*la condition élémentaire d'une charge imposée au citoyen par des actes législatifs est leur publication à charactère constitutif*".[300] The entry into force of directives is, under the "old" EEC Treaty, made dependent upon their notification and not their publication. This is now otherwise under Article 191 as amended by the Treaty of Maastricht.

Secondly, it was maintained that to allow directives to be pleaded against individuals would create a situation of considerable legal insecurity. In principle, certainly as far as obligations are concerned, individuals must be able to rely on national law. If horizontal direct effect were accepted, those concerned would then frequently be confronted with a conflict between requirements of national law which deviate from the obligations imposed by a directive. Moreover, in

[293] Cf. the opinion of A-G Lenz in Case C-91/92 *Faccini Dori*, 9 February 1994, [1994] ECR I-3325, para. 59. As to the textual arguments cf. also Emmert 1992, p. 64-65.

[294] Barents 1982, p. 103.

[295] Cf. above, Introduction to Part I.

[296] Opinion in Case C-316/93 *Vaneetveld* [1994] ECR I-763, para. 28. In contrast to what the terms of Article 189(3) suggest, the choice of form and methods has been curtailed, directives may be precise and exhaustive etc.

[297] According to Article 191 of the EEC Treaty, thus before its amendment by the EU Treaty.

[298] Cf. Timmermans 1979, p. 542, Barents 1982, p. 97 and Schilling 1988, p. 663. According to Richter (1988, p. 402), what really matters is that the law is accessible.

[299] Cf. Emmert 1992, p. 65 and the opinion of A-G Jacobs in Case C-316/93 *Vaneetveld* [1994] ECR I-763, para. 24.

[300] Opinion in Case C-91/92 *Faccini Dori*, 9 February 1994, [1994] ECR I-3325, para. 64.

order to discover the exact scope of their obligations, they would be required to scrutinize both national law and the relevant Community directives. This would indeed impose a heavy burden on private individuals. It has been countered that neither the situation under national law nor the situation with respect to regulations is much different.[301]

The *fourth argument* against horizontal direct effect of directives appeared in *Ratti*[302] where the Court held that a Member State which has not adopted the implementing measures required by the directive at issue may not rely, *vis-à-vis* individuals, on its own failure to perform the obligation which the directive entails. This so-called "principle of estoppel" has already been discussed at length in Subsection 11.2.2. Indeed, those who accept this notion as the conceptual foundation of direct effect of directives in general, cannot, it would appear at first sight, argue that directives *do* have horizontal direct effect. If direct effect is considered as arising, as a reflex, out of the obligation imposed on Member States which the latter have not met, there is scarcely room for horizontal direct effect. On the contrary, it was believed that an individual may very well plead the failure of the Member State to implement the directive as a ground for excusing him from compliance.[303] The most obvious counter-argument at this point is indeed that the Court of Justice has never attached much importance to the principle of estoppel as a conceptual basis. It was rather doctrine which declared this principle to be the ultimate rationale of direct effect of directives.[304]

From this brief discussion it follows that none of the arguments against horizontal direct effect of directives were really conclusive. Yet the arguments marshalled in favour of horizontal direct effect were not decisive either. Some scholars argued that the uniform application and the "effet utile" of Community law required such an effect. To allow horizontal direct effect of directives would undoubtedly increase their effectiveness, and would constitute a further incentive for the Member States to implement directives in time and safeguard as far as possible uniform application of Community law and the protection of rights which individuals derive from it.[305] The latter would be compromised not only by a denial of horizontal direct effect as such but also by fresh discriminations to which such a denial would lead.[306] It has even been submitted that to deny

[301] Cf. Emmert 1992, p. 65, Richter 1988, p. 402, Van Gerven 1994b, p. 352.
[302] Case 148/78 [1979] ECR 1629.
[303] Wyatt 1983, p. 245.
[304] Cf. above, Subsection 11.2.2 and 11.2.3. See also e.g. Emmert, 1992, p. 66.
[305] Cf. Emmert 1992, p. 63 ff., Curtin 1990, p. 197, Schockweiler 1993c, p. 1213 ff., Easson 1979b, p.75 and the opinion of A-G Jacobs in Case C-316/93 *Vaneetveld* [1994] ECR I-763.
[306] As to this argument see below, Subsection 11.5.4.

horizontal direct effect of directives would amount to a denial of supremacy of Community law.[307]

Mitigated Horizontal Direct Effect?

Some authors have suggested that at least a form of mitigated horizontal direct effect could be allowed. This mitigated horizontal direct effect would consist of a review of legality of national measures within the context of a dispute between two private parties. Thus without asking for the application of the provision of the directive to the facts of the case, the persons concerned could nevertheless invoke that provision in the national courts in order to oppose the application of national law which does not conform to it, even in a "horizontal" legal relationship.[308]

Timmermans, who – as was observed – made a distinction between direct effect and legal review as two different concepts, concluded that even a mitigated horizontal direct effect is hardly acceptable.[309] The outcome of such a construction would be that the national court could apply neither national law because of its incompatibility nor the relevant provision of the directive because the latter cannot have horizontal direct effect. In his view, legal certainty would then be seriously compromised. Moreover, the solution would also not result in uniform application of Community law. With respect to this point of view it may be observed that this author considered disapplicaton of national contrary provisions *and* the application of the provisions (not possible in this case) as one integral whole of the concept of direct effect.

According to Louis, on the other hand, such an effect is possible. In his view, what happens is to be considered as the "*jeu normal de l'exception de l'illegalité*" which should not be equated to imposing obligations upon individuals.[310]

In my view, this construction needs a balanced approach. Allowing without any further qualification the exception of illegality within a "horizontal" dispute is difficult to accept: the disapplication of certain national provisions may very

[307] Cf. Barents 1982, p 103, Boch and Lane 1992, p. 179-180, Manin 1990, p. 690.

[308] It should be noted that, although there are some common features, this situation differs from the one discussed in Chapter 4, Subsection 4.2.2. (multi-angular relationships). In the latter, a directive is relied upon against the State authority with possible negative consequences for a third (private) party; in the former the exception of illegality is raised in a case between two private parties.

[309] Timmermans 1979, p. 543 (with respect to direct effect). However, at p. 551 (with respect to the control of legality) the author takes a slightly different view.

[310] Louis 1993, p. 512. This possibility is apparently also accepted by Manin 1990, p. 690. A very similar approach has bee suggested by Stuyck and Wytinck (1991, p. 212) which they have termed "passive" horizontal direct effect: the application of a directive does not entail a "positive obligation" on an individual but only obliges him to respect the right which another individual derives from a directive.

well result in an obligation for an individual.[311] Whether this will be the case depends on the relevant provisions of national law and the concrete dispute at issue. These factors must also be taken into account. For instance, disapplication of a national prohibition which is contrary to the directive is quite different from the disapplication of a national rule permitting a private individual to do something. Therefore, it is submitted, the national court should in every single case examine what the actual effect would be if the exception of illegality were to be allowed.

11.5.4 Horizontal Direct Effect of Directives: Marshall I and Further

The Judgment in Marshall I

The judgment in *Marshall I*[312] laid the speculation to rest. In this case the Court found in favour of the textual argument, keeping closely to the terms of Article 189(3). Since, according to this paragraph, the binding nature exists only in relation to each Member State to which the directive is addressed, a directive may not of itself impose obligations on an individual. Consequently, a provision of a directive may not be relied upon as such against a private individual.[313]

The *Marshall I* judgment marked an important departure from the Court's usual approach to interpretation, which had often been inspired by "effet utile" (and thus the concern to make provisions of Community law as effective as possible) and concern with uniform application of Community law. According to some authors an argument of a political rather than a legal nature played an important part in this decision, namely the difficulty which some national courts had in accepting direct effect of directives at all.[314] The judgment gave rise to severe criticism on the part of some scholars.[315] Not surprisingly, in these commentaries many of the old arguments favouring or dismissing horizontal direct effect of directives were rehearsed and discussed again. One of these, namely the anomalies to which the denial of horizontal direct effect of directives would lead,[316] was particularly conspicuous after the *Marshall I* judgment: in this case the Court decided that an individual may rely on a directive against a State authority regardless of whether the latter is acting *qua* public authority or *qua*

[311] Furthermore, by analogy with what has been discussed in Chapter 4, Subsection 4.2.2, it may be asked under what circumstances should the effects be classified as imposing an obligation or merely (still acceptable) "negative" effects.

[312] Case 152/84 [1986] ECR 723.

[313] See for further implications and developments also above, Chapter 4, Section 4.2.

[314] Cf. Wyatt and Dashwood 1993, p. 74, Morris 1989, p. 314.

[315] See e.g. Nicolaysen 1986, Richter 1988, Curtin 1990, p. 196-197, Boch and Lane 1992, p. 179-180.

[316] Already pointed out before *Marshall* by e.g. Easson 1979b, p. 76.

employer. With the *Marshall I* judgment, the Court introduced an unfair distinction between, for instance, private employees and state employees: the latter may rely on a directive while the former may not. Similarly, the distinction may vary overtime, as in the case of privatization of nationally run businesses, and from Member State to Member State. Rather absurd situations may also occur when a person is, at the same time, employed partly in a private undertaking and partly by a public authority.[317] Obviously, this may result in discriminations and inequalities in conditions of competition, which can hardly be considered compatible with Community law as such.[318]

Re-opening the Discussion

Although it seemed at first that the criticism of the Court's denial of horizontal direct effect of directives would quieten down, certain developments in the Court's case law since then have caused the discussion to flare up again. This case law shows a number of tendencies.[319]

Firstly, the Court has stretched the concept of "the State" to all public authorities and equally to some public enterprises.[320] All these bodies, even if they could not be held responsible for the non-implementation of the directive at issue, have nevertheless been prevented from raising "their" Member State's failure as a defence. This development clearly undermined the principle of estoppel, in so far as the latter could be considered to be the basis of direct effect of directives.[321] Moreover, the determination of whether a body should be considered to be an emanation of the state or not is far from unproblematic.[322]

Secondly, the obligation of consistent interpretation[323] imposed upon national courts has placed considerable constraint upon the latter, forcing them to operate at the limits of their competences in order to give the fullest possible effect to Community law. In some cases, consistent interpretation comes very close to giving horizontal direct effect to directives. However, at the same time this doctrine cannot be considered to be a fully fledged alternative for the absence of horizontal direct effect, since it also has its limits.

[317] Cf. Prechal 1990, p. 456, Grabitz 1993, p. 68.

[318] Cf. e.g. the opinion of A-G Van Gerven in Case C-271/91 *Marshall II* [1993] ECR I-4367, para. 12.

[319] For discussion of these developments see e.g. Van Gerven 1994, Boch and Lane 1992, Emmert 1992, Grabitz 1993 and the opinion of A-G Jacobs in Case C-316/93 *Vaneetveld* [1994] ECR I-763.

[320] Cf. above, Chapter 4, in particular Section 4.5.

[321] See above, Subsection 11.2.3.

[322] See above, Chapter 4, Subsection 4.5.2.

[323] Discussed in extenso in Chapter 10. To this one may also add the disadvantageous effects which vertical direct effect may have for third parties. See above, Chapter 4, Subsection 4.2.2.

The third element to play a part in the issue is the Court's judgment in the *Francovich* case,[324] according to which the Member State is liable, under certain conditions, for damages incurred by an individual in the case of non-implementation of a directive. However, *Francovich* is only a second best solution. It cannot satisfactorily replace the direct application of a directive and, in particular, it does not remedy the unequal conditions under which the different legal subjects have to operate.[325]

Fourthly, the Court's more recent case law has been strongly influenced by the desire for national courts to give full and effective protection to the rights which individuals derive from Community law.[326] However, this full and effective protection is at the same time seriously compromised by the Court's refusal to give horizontal direct effect to directives.[327]

In summary, the Court's legal construction regarding the internal effects of directives is considered to be extremely complex, both for the national courts and the individual. It involves heavy burdens for national courts,[328] it may lead to considerable confusion[329] and there is the intrisic risk that, due to the case-to-case solutions, it could result in new inconsistencies and inequalities.[330] According to some, the system has become so extremely complicated and opaque,[331] that it is itself at odds with the principle of legal certainty.[332] It is against the background of these more general considerations that some scholars advocate the recognition of (some kind of) horizontal direct effect of directives. Such a recognition would, to a large extent, counter the disadvantages I have just described and would contribute to more complete, coherent and equal judicial protection of individuals.[333]

The Way Out

An acceptable solution, in particular for those who consider that the requirement of publication is a very fundamental one, would probably be horizontal direct

[324] Joined Cases C-6/90 and C-9/90 [1991] ECR I-5357.

[325] As to the shortcomings of *Francovich* in this context, see e.g. the opinion of A-G Van Gerven in Case C-271/91 *Marshall II* [1993] ECR I-4367, para. 12 and the opinion of A-G Jacobs in Case C-316/93 *Vaneetveld* [1994] ECR I-763, para. 30.

[326] Cf. above, Chapter 8, Section 8.3.

[327] Cf. Boch and Lane 1992, p. 172. Cf. also the opinion of A-G Jacobs in Case C-316/93 *Vaneetveld* [1994] ECR I-763, para. 29.

[328] Cf. Van Gerven 1994, p. 349.

[329] Cf. Boch and Lane 1992, p. 183.

[330] Cf. the opinion of A-G Van Gerven in Case C-271/91 *Marshall II* [1993] ECR I-4367, para. 12.

[331] Cf. Emmert and Pereira de Azevedo 1993, p. 517.

[332] Cf. the opinion of A-G Jacobs in Case C-316/93 *Vaneetveld* [1994] ECR I-763, para. 31.

[333] Cf. Van Gerven 1994 and Grabitz 1993. Grabitz (p. 71) takes the arguments even a stage further and argues that for reasons of "*Lastengleichheit*" inverse vertical direct effect should be accepted as well.

effect of those directives which will be published in pursuance of Article 191 as amended by the Treaty of Maastricht.[334] The problem with such a limited solution is that directives adopted (and published, although not obligatorily) under the "old" EEC Treaty may produce effects many years after their adoption, as was illustrated, for instance, by the case of *Ponente Carni*,[335] relating to a directive from 1969.

According to Boch and Lane[336] the Court can do two things: it should either return to the "effet utile" of directives and thus abandon the strict and literal interpretation of Article 189, or it should take the estoppel principle to its logical conclusion. As mentioned above,[337] these authors have argued that this principle has been deprived of its substance, owing in particular to the broad interpretation of the concept of "the State". The next logical and, in their view, not too disruptive step would then be to estop an individual from relying on the failure of the Member State to implement the directive in order to deprive another individual of a right which he has derived from the directive.

Similarly, A-G Jacobs has argued that the step from consistent interpretation, which *de facto* often amounts to horizontal direct effect, to the acceptance of horizontal direct effect of directives as such will not lead to an abrupt reversal of the case law.[338] Moreover, if necessary, the Court could give only prospective effect to the judgment.

Van Gerven[339] has opted for a limited solution in the sense that the Court should give horizontal direct effect to *some* provisions of a directive. As mentioned above,[340] Van Gerven has redefined the underlying thought of the Court's case law on direct effect of directives. In his view, the basic idea is that

> "someone, who would have been bound by an obligation imposed by a directive if that directive had been properly implemented by the member state concerned, can not take advantage of that member state's failure to do so, in order to deny a course of action brought against him by a person who would have obtained legal rights against him, if the member state's default had not occurred, *and who was entitled to act in reliance thereupon.*"[341]

[334] Cf. also the opinion of A-G Lenz in Case C-91/92 *Faccini Dori*, 9 Februari 1994, [1994] ECR I-3325, para. 65. The A-G, however, also seems to accept horizontal direct effect of "pre-Maastricht" directives, provided that this effect is limited to the future only.

[335] Joined Cases C-71/91 and C-178/91 [1993] ECR I-1915.

[336] Boch and Lane 1992, p. 184-185.

[337] See Subsection 11.2.3.

[338] Opinion in Case C-316/93 *Vaneetveld* [1994] ECR I-763, para. 32.

[339] Van Gerven 1994, p. 347-353.

[340] See Subsection 11.2.3.

[341] Van Gerven 1994b, p. 351.

This reasoning, which is in my view very close to that of Boch and Lane, is limited in three ways. Firstly, it is limited to those provisions which lay down specific rights for the individuals concerned. This implies that directives will not become binding "in their entirety" as regulations do. Secondly, individuals may rely on these provisions only against those persons who would have been bound by them. This seems to suggest that the directive will not have general application. Thirdly, the individuals concerned must be "entitled to act" in reliance upon the relevant provisions. In other words, in Van Gerven's view it seems to be the principle of legal certainty which protects the position of those who rely on the rights which the directive intends to give them.

It is very difficult to add anything new to this discussion on horizontal direct effect of directives. All the possible arguments seem to be on the table: some are more convincing than others, but not one of them is entirely decisive. In my opinion, it is the issue of legal certainty which lies at the heart of the entire discussion. On the one hand there is the legal certainty of those who are entitled to expect that their position as safeguarded by the directive will be protected. On the other hand there is the legal certainty of those who would be confronted with an obligation which is not laid down in national law. The ultimate question is: whose legal certainty deserves protection? This question cannot be answered once and for all, and in general terms. Depending on the context of the case the outcome may differ. As a rule, for the reasons already presented above, an individual should be able to rely on and enforce a provision of a directive against another individual.[342] The latter may raise in his defence that he was not and in all reasonableness could not have been acquainted with the obligations resulting from the directive at issue. Whether this defence will succeed depends on several factors, such as the publication of the directive, the experience and vigilance of the defendant etc.[343]

Does this approach also imply that under certain circumstances a Member State may rely on an obligation in a directive against a private individual? Arnull[344] has rightly remarked that the question whether a directive may ever impose obligations on private individuals is broader than the question whether they can produce horizontal direct effect. The Court answered the first question in the negative in *Marshall I* and it is this judgment which is often cited as an argument in cases concerning inverse vertical direct effect.[345] For both horizontal direct effect and inverse vertical direct effect the underlying principle, i.e. the

[342] Cf. however Langenfeld (1992, p. 960) who makes a choice in favour of the person who will be confronted with a new obligation.

[343] Cf. also Emmert 1992, p. 65, Wyatt 1983, p. 246, as well as the opinion of A-G Jacobs in Case C-316/93 *Vaneetveld* [1994] I-763, para. 34.

[344] Arnull 1988, p. 44.

[345] Cf. Case 80/86 *Kolpinghuis* [1987] ECR 3969.

binding nature of directives *vis-à-vis* the state, is the same. However, to allow horizontal direct effect of directives does not necessarily mean that inverse vertical direct effect is allowed as well. Reliance by a Member State on an unimplemented or not correctly implemented directive against a private individual may after all be precluded by the principle of estoppel,[346] brought down to its proper proportions, without making it the ratio of direct effect of directives.

Despite all the suggestions made by legal commentators and several Advocates General, in *Faccini Dori*[347] the Court maintained the position it took in *Marshall I*. After explaining that its case law on direct effect of directives seeks to prevent the State from taking advantage of its own failure to comply with Community law and from thus depriving the individuals of the benefit of the rights which directives may confer on them, the Court held:

"The effect of extending that case-law to the sphere of relations between individuals would be to recognize a power in the Community to enact obligations for individuals with immediate effect, whereas it has competence to do so only where it is empowered to adopt regulations."[348]

This position is in fact not much more than a recasting of an old argument used against direct effect of directives in general: the Community can create "direct" rights and obligations for individuals only by means of regulations.[349] In its case law the Court was prepared to make an exception in so far as rights to be asserted against the State are at issue. With respect to obligations to be imposed upon individuals such a step was apparently considered as being too adventurous.

[346] Or its equivalents (*nemo auditur / non venire*). Cf. Wyatt 1983, p. 247 and the opinion of A-G Jacobs in Case C-316/93 *Vaneetveld* [1994] ECR I-763, para. 33. Nicolaysen (1984, p. 389) and Langenfeld (1992, p. 959) would appear to see this rather as a consequence of the Court's case law in Article 169 proceedings: no excuses for non-implementation drawing upon direct effect.

[347] Case C-91/92 [1994] ECR I-3325. It should be noted that in this Case the Court invited the Member States to give their opinions as to the possible horizontal direct effect of directives. By many, this Case was considered as a test case.

[348] *Ibid.*, para. 24.

[349] Cf. Section 11.1.

12

Liability of the State in Cases of Inadequate Implementation of Directives

12.1 LIABILITY BEFORE FRANCOVICH

12.1.1 Introduction

Non-implementation or incorrect implementation of a directive amounts to a breach of Community law. In so far as this or any other breach of Community law causes loss and damage to individuals, they should be able to bring an action for damages against the Member State concerned in national courts.

The idea that infringement of Community law by a Member State should be actionable under national regimes of public non-contractual liability is as such not new. In 1975, in its suggestions on European Union, the Court of Justice proposed that persons affected by a failure of a Member State to fulfil an obligation under Community law should obtain redress before their national courts.[1] Moreover, as regards the infringement of Article 177 of the Treaty, the Court suggested as one of the remedies an action for damages against the Member State concerned at the suit of the party adversely affected.[2] More recently, although prior to the *Francovich* judgment, during the preparation of the Treaty on European Union the Commission proposed to insert into the Treaty a provision stipulating that the Member States should be obliged to make good the consequences of infringements of Community law; and furthermore, if necessary, the institutions should enact harmonizing or coordinating measures for that purpose.[3] Ultimately, however, such provisions were not included in the EU Treaty.

In earlier literature this option was similarly discussed and accepted as one of the remedies available for breaches of Community law.[4] Yet in general it was assumed that action for damages was entirely governed by national law.[5] Interestingly, in 1977 Millarg commented on some shortcomings of a German

[1] Bull. EC Supp. 9/75, p. 18. From other language versions it appears that the Court had in mind particularly damages.

[2] *Ibid*.

[3] Bull. EC 2/91, p. 152-153. Prieß (1993, p. 125) reports that the Court of Justice was also in favour of such a provision and stressed equally the need for harmonization.

[4] Cf. Karpenstein 1977, p. 65-68 (with further references), Pescatore 1972, p. 21, Kovar 1978, p. 271-275. Cf. also Fide Reports 1980.

[5] Cf. Karpenstein 1977, p. 65 ff.

draft Act on State Liability:[6] the draft in question excluded from State liability legislative action or inaction, *inter alia*, in so far as its illegality was rooted in a breach of directly effective provisions of Community law. With foresight, Millarg warned that the Court of Justice

"könnte geneigt sein, offensichtliche Lücken im Haftungssystem der Mitgliedstaaten, die zich zum Nachteil des "Marktbürgers" auswirken, durch Enwicklung einer gemeinschaftrechtlichen, mitgliedstaatlich anzuwenden Haftungsregel aus den allgemeinen Rechtsgrundsätzen der Mitgliedstaaten im Vorabentscheidungs-verfahren auszufüllen."[7]

In fact several cases involving breaches of Community law were decided by national courts in the "pre-Francovich" era under the relevant national rules of non-contractual liability, although with varying degrees of success for the applicants. Some of these cases have been discussed at length in legal writing, while others have been mentioned only in passing. It is not clear whether the cases discussed are merely the tip of the iceberg or whether simply very few cases have been brought under non-contractual liability within the Member States.[8]

In so far as the cases have been given attention, their discussion reveals divergence in approach and in outcome.[9] Obviously, the main reason for this is the differences in the rules governing public non-contractual liability of the Member States. The legal systems of all the Member States now recognize the principle of public non-contractual liability, which is apparently also presumed in Article 215 of the Treaty. At the same time, the conditions under which this liability gives rise to compensation and the types of acts (or activities) which give rise to liability differ considerably, despite some common tendencies.[10] Furthermore, a serious obstacle to employing the national systems of non-contractual liability lies in the impossibility of bringing an action for normative injustice, certainly as far as primary legislation is concerned.[11]

[6] *Staatshaftunggesetz*, which however never came into force as in 1982 the Federal Constitutional Court declared the Act unconstitutional for lack of competence. See Bell and Bradley 1991, p. 272.

[7] Millarg 1977, p. 225-226.

[8] Cf. Huglo 1993, p. 79, Schockweiler 1992, p. 38.

[9] Cf. e.g. for cases decided in different Member States Barav 1988, p. 156-165, Taylor 1985, p. 479-486; for a brief discussion of some French cases Simon 1992, Kovar 1992, Moreau 1991; for English cases cf. Oliver 1987, p. 899-906, Green 1984a, Ward 1990, Steiner 1986. Bok (1993, p. 48-50) discusses a number of Dutch cases. For an interesting effort to fit the problem of directives which have not been (adequately) implemented into the Dutch regime of non-contractual liability see Dekker 1991.

[10] Cf. for (relatively) recent comparisons of several national systems Schockweiler 1990, Bell and Bradley 1991, The liability of the State 1981.

[11] Cf. Schockweiler 1990, p. 73, Arts 1993, p. 504, Karl 1992, p. 440 and 442 as well as Fide Reports 1992.

Not surprisingly, both doctrine and legal practice searched for Community law arguments to overcome real or imaginary hurdles in national non-contractual liability law. The case law of the Court of Justice provided some elements which could be used for this purpose.[12] Firstly, there were indications as to the consequences which a judgment under Articles 169-171 has within the national legal order. Secondly, the requirement that national courts must give effective protection to rights which individuals derive from Community law was interpreted as implying that, where necessary, individuals should be entitled to damages. I will turn to these two approaches in the next Sections. In both perspectives, however, another, distinct problem remained: namely, what is the legal ground of State liability for breaches of Community law? Is the liability based in national law or in Community law?

12.1.2 Judgment under Article 169 as Argument for Liability

The effects of a judgment under Article 169 have been stated by the Court of Justice in strict terms. Such a judgment amounts to

> "a prohibition having the full force of law on the competent national authorities against applying a national rule recognized as incompatible with the Treaty and, if the circumstances so require, an obligation on them to take all appropriate measures to enable Community law to be fully applied."[13]

Similarly, "by reason solely of the judgment declaring the Member State to be in default, the State concerned is required to take the necessary measures to remedy its default."[14] These obligations concern all national authorities, including courts. In *Waterkeyn* it was held that

> "if the Court finds in proceedings under Articles 169 to 171 of the EEC Treaty that a Member State's legislation is incompatible with the obligations which it has under the Treaty the courts of that State are bound by virtue of Article 171 to draw the necessary inferences from that judgment", i.e. "to ensure, when performing their duties, that the Court's judgment is complied with."[15]

[12] Cf. Barav 1988, p. 150-156, Barav and Simon 1987, p. 166-167, Schockweiler 1992, p. 36-40. Cf. also the opinion of A-G Mischo in Joined Cases C-6/90 and C-9/90 *Francovich* [1991] ECR I-5357, para. 34-68.

[13] Case 48/71 *Commission v. Italy* [1972] ECR 527, para. 7.

[14] Joined Cases 24 and 97/80R *Commission v. France* [1980] ECR 1319, para. 16.

[15] Joined Cases 314 to 316/81 and 83/82 [1982] ECR 4337, para. 14. Cf. also Pescatore 1972, p. 15-16, and the judgment in Case C-101/91 *Commission v. Italy* [1993] ECR I-191.

The "necessary inferences" to be drawn or "appropriate measures" to be taken may indeed include making reparation for the damage which the Member State has caused to individuals by its unlawful conduct. Procedure under Article 169 is not only concerned with elimination of the infringement in the future but also in the past.[16] In particular, where it is no longer possible physically to comply retroactively with the obligations, reparation will often provide a partial remedy at least. Further authority for this may be drawn from the old *Humblet* case of 1960, where the Court ruled that

"if the Court rules in a judgment that a legislative or administrative measure adopted by the authorities of a Member State is contrary to Community law, that Member State is obliged, by virtue of Article 86 of the ECSC Treaty, to rescind the measures in question and to make reparation for any unlawful consequences which may have ensued."[17]

On the basis of these considerations it was already arguable that damages should be paid in the wake of a judgment under Article 169. Yet an even clearer indication that such a judgment may provide a basis for an action for damages by the individual concerned was given by the Court in Case *39/72* (*premiums for slaughtering cows I*). The Court held that the Commission may have interest in pursuing infringement proceedings, even though the national legislation complained of had been amended, because a judgment may be of interest

"as establishing the basis of a responsibility that a Member State can incur as a result of its default as regards other Member States, the Community or private parties."[18]

Since then, this finding has been reiterated in other cases, though sometimes in slightly different terms which do not, however, change the basic idea.[19] Some of the cases concerned the non-implementation of a directive.[20]

How liability *vis-à-vis* other Member States and the Community should take shape is not entirely clear.[21] As far as individuals are concerned, non-contractual liability as it exists under national law seemed the appropriate avenue. However the basis of this liability remained controversial. Essentially, two interpretations were possible. According to the first, the terms "can incur" made clear that the

[16] Cf. Case 70/72 *Commission v. Germany* [1973] ECR 813.

[17] Case 6/60 [1960] ECR 559 (Article 86 of the ECSC Treaty is equivalent to Article 5 E(E)C Treaty).

[18] *Commission v. Italy* [1973] 112, para. 11.

[19] Cf. e.g. Case 309/84 *Commission v. Italy* [1986] ECR 599, Case C-249/88 *Commission v. Belgium* [1991] ECR I-1275, Case C-287/87 *Commission v. Greece* [1990] ECR I-125.

[20] Case C-287/87 *Commission v. Greece* [1990] ECR I-125.

[21] Pescatore 1972, p. 17 suggested a sort of liability under international law *à la "L'usine de Chorzow"*. Cf. also White 1988, p. 302-311.

answer to the question whether such a judgment may be the basis of liability is a matter to be decided under national law. According to the second interpretation, the Court recognized the existence of non-contractual liability as a matter of Community law, but the terms "can incur" indicated that some other – as yet not established – conditions had to be satisfied first.[22]

12.1.3 Need for Effective Judicial Protection as Argument for Liability

The approach which takes the requirement of effective judicial protection as the point of departure[23] has one important merit: the action for damages is then not made dependent upon a judgment of the Court under Article 169. A national court is also entitled to find, whether or not in pursuance of a preliminary ruling of the Court of Justice, that its Member State is in breach of Community law. Furthermore, a judgment under Article 169 is declaratory in nature. The rights which individuals derive from Community law emanate from the provisions of Community law themselves.[24]

The development of the Court's case law as to the requirement of effective judicial protection was described in detail in Chapter 8. In that Chapter I also argued that, in general, the principle of effective judicial protection can be considered to be an expansion of the minimum requirement of effectiveness which was already present in earlier case law. Briefly summarized, this development took the following course: initially, the Court entrusted the national courts with the task of protecting the rights which individuals derive from Community law, although it was left for the national system of judicial protection to provide an appropriate remedy. Yet the protection had to be "direct and immediate"[25] and "effective".[26] Moreover, the exercise of the rights conferred upon individuals must not be made impossible in practice (the minimum requirement of effectiveness) and the applicable rules must be no less favourable than those relating to the same right of action on a internal matter (the requirement of non-discrimination). *Simmenthal*[27] added to the requirement of legal protection the principle of full effectiveness of Community law, which may not be impaired, and the judgment in *Johnston*[28] introduced the principle of effective judicial protection

[22] Cf. the opinion of A-G Mischo in Joined Cases C-6/90 and C-9/90 *Francovich* [1991] ECR I-5357, para. 57.
[23] Cf. e.g. Barav 1988, Barav and Simon 1987, Prechal 1990, Curtin 1990b.
[24] Cf. Joined Cases 314 to 316/81 and 83/82 *Waterkeyn* [1982] ECR 4337 (in theses cases still coupled with direct effect).
[25] Case 13/68 *Salgoil* [1968] ECR 453.
[26] Case 179/84 *Bozzetti* [1985] ECR 2301.
[27] Case 106/77 [1978] ECR 629.
[28] Case 222/84 [1986] ECR 1651.

as a general principle of law. Finally, *Factortame*[29] required the national court to grant interim relief; even where it was impossible as a matter of national law, in order to ensure the full effectiveness of Community law and to provide the necessary protection to the individuals affected.

As regards non-contractual liability, actions for damages in fact already existed in all the Member States. Yet the crucial question was whether a Member State can be held liable for breaches of Community law under the national rules of non-contractual liability and, if so, under what conditions. Not surprisingly, the more the Court substantiated *and* tightened the requirements as to the judicial protection to be afforded, the more compelling was the argument that effective judicial protection required the availability of an action for damages against the defaulting State wherever the payment of damages was the appropriate means to provide effective protection. If necessary, the national rules which would normally bar an action against the State or make such an action extremely difficult had to be set aside.

The only authority to deal explicitly with the question of damages was the judgment in *Russo*. The Court held that

> "[i]t is for the national court to decide on the basis of the facts of each case whether an individual ... has suffered ... damage. If [the] damage has been caused through an infringement of Community law the State is liable to the injured party [for] the consequences in the context of the provisions of national law on the liability of the State."[30]

Although this finding was – again – not entirely uncontroversial,[31] it was understood by some as an acceptance by the Court of a non-contractual liability based in Community law. The reference to the context of national liability law then merely meant that it governs the conditions of liability.[32]

Obviously, the main disadvantage of this construction remains that the divergent and, as far as State liability is concerned, often strict national conditions of non-contractual liability apply. Under certain circumstances, the conditions may be set aside or adapted in pursuance of the requirements of effectiveness or effective judicial protection, as the case may be. This involves, however, a case-to-case approach and, moreover, the exact scope of these principles is rather uncertain. Furthermore, it should be pointed out that the case law on which the principle of effective judicial protection drew was only concerned with breaches

[29] Case C-213/89 [1990] ECR I-2433.
[30] Case 60/75 [1976] ECR 45, para. 9.
[31] Cf. Bebr 1992, p. 572.
[32] Cf. Barav 1988, p. 156, Curtin 1990b, p. 732 as well as the opinion of A-G Mischo in Joined Cases C-6/90 and C-9/90 *Francovich* [1991] ECR I-5357, para. 44.

of directly effective provisions of Community law. The question whether damages as a remedy should be made available in the case of infringements of non-directly effective provisions was either not addressed at all or it was cautiously suggested that such a possibility was tenable.[33]

More recently, the judgment in *Foster*[34] has been relied upon as an authority for State liability for breaches of (directly effective) provisions of directives.[35] This argument is not very convincing. In Foster the Court *did* find that individuals concerned may rely on the provisions of the directive at issue "in a claim for damages". However, it is submitted that "damages" were *one of the statutory remedies for sex discrimination available under Sex Discrimination Act 1975.*[36] This is, in my opinion, a quite distinct issue from the question whether the State should be obliged, as a matter of Community law, to make good loss and damage caused by breaches of Community law in general.

12.2 THE PRINCIPLE OF STATE LIABILITY: THE CONSTRUCTION OF THE COURT OF JUSTICE IN FRANCOVICH

The judgment of the Court in *Francovich* ended the speculation as to the legal foundation of State liability. The judgment has correctly been described as one "of principle".[37] The Court did not limit itself to the concrete problem of that case, which related to a non-implemented directive, but addressed the question of State liability for breaches of Community law in general. It found that

> "it is a principle of Community law that the Member States are obliged to make good loss and damage caused to individuals by breaches of Community law for which they can be held responsible."[38]

The Court's main argument for this view was that such a liability is inherent in the system of the Treaty. The Court identified two grounds in this respect.

Firstly, there is the Community legal order's "own character", as defined in *Van Gend en Loos* and *Costa v. ENEL.*[39] Its main (and by now well known) characteristics are, in brief: the Community legal order is integrated into the legal

[33] Cf. Curtin 1990b, p. 739.

[34] Case C-188/89 [1990] ECR I-3313.

[35] Cf. Bebr 1992, p. 577, Van Gerven 1994a, p. 21, opinion of A-G Mischo in Joined Cases C-6/90 and C-9/90 *Francovich* [1991] ECR I-5357, para. 41.

[36] As appears from the Report for the Hearing, the question whether damages should be available or not was not at all under discussion. Cf. on this subject also Lewis 1990, p. 471.

[37] Cf. Gilliams 1991-1992, p. 877.

[38] Para. 37 of the judgment.

[39] Case 26/62 [1963] 1 and Case 6/64 [1964] 585.

systems of the Member States, the national courts are bound to apply its rules, it has as subjects not only the Member States but also their nationals and it is intended to give rise to rights (and obligations) of individuals, either expressly or as a correlative of clearly defined obligations of others.

Secondly, as the Court reiterated, referring to *Simmenthal* and *Factortame*,[40] national courts must ensure the full effectiveness of Community rules and the protection of the Community rights of individuals.

Up to this point there was in fact nothing new in the Court's judgment. However, the Court then took its reasoning a stage further, explaining the requirements of those principles if a Member State is in breach of Community law provisions. According to the Court, individuals must be in a position to obtain redress when their rights are infringed. Next, the Court stressed that the possibility of obtaining redress is in particular indispensable where the full effectiveness of Community rules depends on prior action of the Member States and where, consequently, in the absence of such action, individuals cannot enforce their Community rights.

An additional argument[41] was found in Article 5 of the Treaty, which requires, as had already been spelled out in *Humblet*,[42] that the Member States nullify the unlawful consequences of a breach of Community law. One of the means to achieve this is indeed making good loss and damage which individuals have incurred as a consequence of the breach.

Both the need to *protect individuals' rights* and to *ensure full effect* of Community law are at the basis of State liability as laid down in *Francovich*.[43] In this respect, the liability serves a dual purpose. In addition to this, in legal writing it has been pointed out that State liability for loss and damage caused to individuals is a fundamental principle inherent to the rule of law,[44] while according to Simon the *Francovich* liability must be considered as a direct consequence of the supremacy of Community law.[45]

It is striking that the Court did not refer in the judgment to its position in the infringement proceedings discussed above, namely that a judgment under Article 169 may establish the basis of liability of the defaulting Member State *vis-à-vis* private individuals. The Court apparently wished to avoid any suggestion that for the existence of State liability a judgment under this Article was necessary. In the *Francovich* judgment itself the Court merely observed that the breach of

[40] Case 106/77 [1978] ECR 629 and C-213/89 [1990] ECR I-2433.

[41] Many scholars consider this as reinforcing the former arguments. Cf. Bebr 1992, p. 573, Barav 1994, p. 286, Schockweiler 1992, p. 42, Simon 1993, p. 237.

[42] Case 6/60 [1960] ECR 559.

[43] Cf. Schockweiler 1992, p. 42.

[44] Cf. Karl 1992, p. 442 and, already before *Francovich*, Pieper 1990, p. 2457.

[45] Simon 1993, p. 237 and 240.

Community law by Italy "has been confirmed by a judgment of the Court",[46] without any suggestion that such a judgment should constitute a condition for State liability. In other words, for purposes of State liability it is sufficient that the national court finds that there is a breach of Community law. A judgment under Article 169 can support this finding, but it is not a prerequisite.[47] From the point of view of the individual this is extremely important as individuals have no possibility of compelling the Commission to start infringement proceedings.[48]

The interesting consequence of not making liability dependent on a judgment under Article 169 is, *inter alia*, that the national courts will be called upon to apply the requirements for proper implementation of directives developed by the Court of Justice in infringement proceedings.[49] It may be questioned whether the courts are adequately equipped to do this. In some cases the breach may be obvious. However, as experience in Article 169 proceedings shows, this is not always the case. In particular, the crucial role played by the Commission in infringement proceedings has to be played in national courts by private parties, which may draw heavily on their lawyer's knowledge and persuasiveness. Things of course change if the court refers the case to the Court of Justice under Article 177, when the Commission will submit its observations. However, ultimately it is still within the competence of the national court and not that of the Court of Justice to establish whether the Member State has infringed Community law or not. An alternative would perhaps be to allow the Commission to intervene in the proceedings at national level.

In brief, just as the Court found some three decades previously in *Van Gend en Loos*[50] that the Community autonomous legal system entailed that its provisions have, *as a matter of Community law*, direct effect, provided that certain conditions are satisfied, in a very similarly structured reasoning it found in *Francovich* that the existence of State liability in the case of breaches of Community law is based in Community law itself; or, in other words, a new right was added to the right to rely on Community law provisions, namely the right to reparation.

In general, the *Francovich* judgment has been warmly welcomed as the most important constitutional judgment since *Van Gend en Loos*, completing the system of judicial protection of individuals and strengthening considerably the possibilities of enforcement of Community law. On the other hand, critical comments have also been made, addressing in particular questions as to the limits of the law-

[46] Para. 44 of the judgment. The Case at issue was Case 22/87 *Commission v. Italy* [1989] ECR 143.
[47] Cf. also Bebr 1992, p. 580, Schockweiler 1993b, p. 115.
[48] Cf. Case 274/87 *Star Fruit* [1989] ECR 291.
[49] For a detailed discussion, see above, Chapter 5.
[50] Case 26/62 [1963] ECR 1.

making function of the Court of Justice.[51] Moreover, some have suggested that a narrower approach would have been preferable.[52] Indeed, the broad terms of the judgment give rise to many speculations, both on the Community law level and on the national level.[53] Many of the propositions made in *Francovich* are far from clear. Yet the main problem seems to lie not so much in what has been said but rather in what has not. It could almost be said that *Francovich* raises far more questions than it actually answers.[54] As in the case of any judgment which signifies – what seems to be – a new development, much remains to be clarified. What follows must be read with these considerations in mind.

12.3 LIABILITY FOR BREACH OF ARTICLE 189(3)

12.3.1 The Nature of the Breach

The very existence of the Community law principle of State liability is as such not sufficient to give rise to a right to reparation. For this purpose certain conditions must be satisfied. What these conditions are depends "on the nature of the breach".[55] In the *Francovich* judgment the Court gave only the conditions to be fulfilled in the case of a Member State's failure under Article 189(3) of the Treaty. The conditions with respect to other types of breaches have still to be decided.[56]

Equally, it is not yet entirely clear what the Court means by "the nature of the breach". Bebr, for instance, has wondered whether the Court is referring to the seriousness of the breach, drawing a parallel with the case law under Article 215 where the Court requires in the case of liability for Community legislative acts that the breach be sufficiently serious.[57] Another interpretation is that the

[51] Cf. Karl 1992, p. 441, Dänzer-Vanotti 1992, Schockweiler 1993b, p. 123.
[52] Cf. Ossenbühl 1992, p. 995.
[53] Cf. Steiner 1993, p. 10, Ross 1993, p. 58. For some discussion of the influence of *Francovich* on national systems of public non-contractual liability see e.g.: Karl 1992, p. 446-447, Schlemmer-Schulte and Ukrow 1992, p. 92-95, Geiger 1993, p. 471-473, Bok 1993, p. 50-56, Arts 1993, p. 503-510, Ross 1993, p. 69, Dubouis 1992, p. 6-7, Simon 1993 (for a combined discussion of Francovich and some recent French cases), Caranta 1993, p. 286-296 (for impact in Italy, France and the UK).
[54] Cf. in this respect also Case C-178/94 *Dillenkofer*, pending.
[55] Para. 38 of the judgment.
[56] The conditions with respect to breaches of "substantive" Treaty provisions (i.e. contrasted with the "definitional" provisions of Article 189(3)), will probably be dealt with by the Court in Case C-46/93 *Brasserie Le Pêcheur*, pending, and Case C48/93 *Factortame III*, pending. Cf. also the opinion of A-G Van Gerven in Case C-128/92 *Banks* [1994] ECR I-1173, and Van Gerven 1994a.
[57] Bebr 1992, p. 575. Cf. also Jarass 1994, p. 882-883.

Court is referring to the type of breach:[58] the infringement of a provision by certain conduct, such as breach of Article 189(3) by not having transposed a directive. In my opinion, given the context in which the "nature of the breach" is mentioned in Francovich, it is the latter interpretation which should be upheld. However, it is equally arguable, as was submitted by Bebr,[59] that a breach of Article 189(3) involves a breach of a fundamental provision of the Treaty, and such an infringement amounts *eo ipso* to a sufficiently serious breach.

12.3.2 Types of Breaches of Article 189(3)

The *Francovich* case was concerned with one particular kind of breach of Article 189(3), namely the non-transposition of a directive into national law. However, the terms "where a Member State fails to fulfil its obligations under the third paragraph of Article 189 of the Treaty to take all the measures necessary to achieve the result prescribed by a directive"[60] would suggest that the conditions laid down in the judgment relate to any possible breach of Article 189(3). As appears clearly from Chapters 3 and 5, the obligations of the Member States under Article 189(3) go far beyond the mere transposition of a directive into national law. Interestingly, in legal writing it is often more or less automatically assumed that the liability regime laid down in *Francovich* concerns only a breach of Article 189(3) by non-transposition or, at the most, by incomplete or incorrect transposition.[61]

In this respect it must be recalled that Article 189(3) requires not only that there is a transposition but also that the directive at issue is transposed properly. In its case law the Court of Justice has laid down certain requirements which must be satisfied. The *content* of the implementing measures must evidently correspond to the content of the directive to be implemented and they must meet a sufficient degree of clarity and precision. The latter requirements imply also the abolition of all conflicting legislation. Similarly, the *nature* of the implementing measures is not a matter for the Member States alone. As a rule, the implementing measures must be legally binding.

Furthermore, in Chapter 5, Subsection 5.2.4, it was explained that the implementing measures to be taken by the Member States must often obligatorily go beyond the actual text of the directive. As the Member States must ensure

[58] Cf. Barav 1994, p. 288-289. According to him it is the "type or kind of breach" by which, it is understood, he is referring to the rule breached.

[59] Bebr 1992, p. 575. Cf. also Jarass 1994, p. 883.

[60] Para. 39 of the judgment.

[61] Cf. Karl 1992, p. 441, Fischer 1992a, p. 42, Schockweiler 1992, p. 43, Barav 1994, p. 286 and 294, Arts 1993, p. 497.

"that the directive is fully effective in accordance with the objectives it pursues",[62] they may be required to provide for an appropriate system of sanctions, even if the directive is silent on this point. Moreover, the Court not only stipulates that there must be a sanction, it may also interfere with the form and content of the sanction.

In my opinion, there is little doubt that *Francovich* also applies to incorrect or incomplete transposition,[63] since the failure to transpose properly affects adversely the full effectiveness of Article 189(3) and may also affect the protection of individuals' rights, in exactly the same way as non-implementation. On the other hand, it should not be ruled out that the conditions then applicable may slightly differ.[64]

Matters are less clear in other respects, namely if one takes into consideration other obligations which result from Article 189(3). Firstly, transposition of a directive into national law, even if the transposition is as such correct, does not suffice. The obligation under Article 189(3) requires full application and enforcement of the directive concerned.[65] Thus the measures transposing the directive must be applied and enforced in practice. Wherever national authorities *and* national courts do not apply and enforce the directive, or, more properly speaking, the national measures implementing it, there is a violation of Article 189(3). Similarly, national courts and authorities are also under the obligation to construe national law in conformity with the directive, even in the case of correct implementation.[66]

Secondly, one has to consider the possible content of the obligation to be fulfilled. In Chapter 3 a distinction was made between the "hard core rules" of the directive, i.e. the rules relating to the legal and factual situation which the Member States are required to bring about in their legal orders, and the ancillary obligations for the Member States. The latter obligations are just as binding as the "hard core rules", although they are of a different character. However, since provisions relating, for instance, to notification of measures, informing and consulting with the Commission and/or other Member States or to periodical assessment of the operation of the directive's rules are part and parcel of the obligations resulting from Article 189(3), non-compliance with these provisions will as such amount to a breach of this Article.

Thirdly, where the Member State or the body primarily responsible for the implementation (i.e. as a rule, the legislator) has not transposed the directive or has not done so properly, by virtue of the Court's theory that the Member States'

[62] Case 14/83 *Von Colson* [1984] ECR 1891, para. 15.
[63] Cf. also Bebr 1992, p. 577, Gilliams 1991-1992, p. 879, Van Gerven 1994a, p. 17.
[64] In particular with respect to the requirement of "fault". Cf. below, Subsection 12.4.2.
[65] Cf. above, Chapter 3, Section 3.3 and Chapter 5, Subsection 5.2.4.
[66] Cf. above, Chapter 10, Section 10.4 and Chapter 4, Section 4.4. Cf also Pieper 1990, p. 2456.

STAFFS UNIVERSITY LIBRARY

obligation arising from a directive to achieve the result envisaged by the directive is binding on all authorities of the Member States, including the courts, the obligation under Article 189(3) entails that those authorities are called upon to apply – if possible – the directive in lieu of national law or to proceed to interpretation of national law in conformity with the directive, both by way of an "emergency measure".[67]

It is far from clear whether, and especially under what conditions, these types of breaches of Article 189(3) will give rise to the obligation on the part of the State to pay damages. Although it is very tempting to speculate about liability of Member States for these kinds of breaches and about the application or transferability of the conditions laid down in *Francovich* to them, the discussion which follows will mainly focus on situations of incorrect or non-transposition of directives only. In Section 12.6 I shall address briefly some problems to which the violation of Article 189(3), taken in the wider sense, may give rise.[68]

12.4 Community Law Conditions for Liability

12.4.1 Introduction

In *Francovich* the Court held that in the case of non-fulfilment of the obligations under Article 189(3) there should be a right of reparation if three conditions are fulfilled. Firstly, the result prescribed by the directive should entail the grant of rights to individuals. Secondly, it should be possible to identify the content of those rights on the basis of the provisions of the directive. Thirdly, there must be a causal link between the breach of the State's obligation and the loss and damage suffered by the injured parties. According to the Court "those conditions are sufficient to give rise to a right on the part of individuals to obtain reparation".[69]

The necessity to lay down Community law conditions which are as such sufficient to give rise to State liability is fully understandable if one takes into consideration the differences in State liability regimes as they exist in the Member States. In particular, the non-existence of public liability for legislative action and inaction in the majority of the Member States[70] would make illusory any right

[67] For bodies bound and the consequences of the Court's construction see in particular Chapter 4, Section 4.4.

[68] For "wider" speculations, concerning breaches of Community law in general, cf. Bebr 1992, p. 580 ff, Karl 1992, p. 447-448, Ross 1993, Craig 1993, p. 604 ff., Van Gerven 1994a and his opinion in Case C-128/92 *Banks* [1994] ECR I-1173.

[69] Para. 41 of the judgment.

[70] Cf. Schockweiler 1990, p. 73, Bell and Bradley 1991, p. 6.

to reparation if the conditions were left to the national legal systems. Although some other conditions are still left to the Member States,[71] once the above-mentioned conditions have been satisfied, the right to reparation can apparently not be denied. Another important aspect is that those conditions are Community law conditions. Questions as to their interpretation therefore ultimately have to be resolved by the Court of Justice and the scope of the conditions cannot be limited by national law.[72]

The most evident precedent for such far-reaching interference with the "procedural autonomy" of the Member States was undoubtedly the Court's judgment in *Zuckerfabrik Süderdithmarschen*.[73] In this case the Court held that, for the sake of coherence of the system of interim protection, national courts must order suspension of the enforcement of national measures based on a Community measure whose legality is contested, under the same conditions as those which are applied by the Court for the suspension of Community measures themselves. Yet in *Francovich* the Court did not go as far as was proposed by A-G Mischo. Following the solution found in *Zuckerfabrik Süderdithmarschen*, the Advocate General suggested that the liability of the Member States for breaches of Community law should be subject to the same conditions as those developed for the purposes of non-contractual liability of the Community under Article 215.

The choice of the Court not to follow the Advocate General in this respect is a fortunate one. The regime of Community non-contractual liability for, in particular, legislative acts is notorious for its low degree of success. Notably the requirement imposed by the Court for unlawful legislative acts involving choices of economic policy, namely that there be "a sufficiently serious breach of a superior rule of law"[74] makes it in practice almost impossible to obtain damages.[75] According to the Advocate General, the failure to implement a directive or to implement it correctly which has been confirmed by the Court of Justice in infringement proceedings amounts to a sufficiently serious breach of a superior rule of law. Yet this could be different in other types of breaches which, moreover, have not been confirmed in a judgment under Article 169.

It cannot be denied that there are some forceful arguments for the application of the Article 215 requirements. In the first place, these requirements are based on the principles in the legal systems of Member States governing public non-contractual liability. In the second place, it seems difficult to understand why a Member State should be held liable for breaches under conditions which are less severe than those applicable in the case of non-contractual liability of the Community itself.[76] In my opinion, however, the proper solution would be to mitigate the requirements for Community liability, rather than

[71] See below, Section 12.5.

[72] For instance, a Member State cannot impose stricter conditions for state liability.

[73] Case C-143/88 [1991] ECR I-415.

[74] The so-called "*Schöppenstedt-formula*". See Case 5/71 *Zuckerfabrik Schöppenstedt* [1971] ECR 975.

[75] Schockweiler (1993a, p. 23) has observed that an application of the 215-conditions would constitute a setback when compared to the national regimes of public liability of many Member States.

[76] Cf. also Court of Appeal in *Bourgoin* [1986] 1 CMLR 267.

transpose the severe standards to the liability of the Member States. After all, the former seem fairly questionable from the point of view of effective judicial protection at the Community level.[77]

12.4.2 The General Conditions for Non-Contractual Liability

As mentioned above, the Court formulated three specific conditions which must be satisfied in the case of a breach of Article 189(3) in order to give rise to a right to reparation. However, these conditions are not the only ones. In fact, before turning to the question as to whether they are satisfied, there are two or, arguably, three other conditions in the *Francovich* judgment which, logically, should be checked first.[78] The Court did not address them explicitly, perhaps because they are too obvious or because their fulfilment was presumed. Nevertheless, they merit further attention.

Unlawful Conduct

Firstly, for the purposes of non-contractual liability of the State there must be unlawful conduct of the Member State. A breach of a Community law provision undoubtedly amounts to unlawful conduct. In *Francovich* such a breach was clearly present. As yet, it is not entirely certain whether a breach *simpliciter* of Community law is sufficient to give rise to liability or whether the breach must be a serious one, amounting, for instance, to what the French call "*faute grave*" or a "sufficiently serious breach", as the Court requires for liability for normative acts under Article 215.[79] In Subsection 12.3.1 it was noted that, according to some authors, a breach of Article 189(3) can as such be considered a serious breach and consequently there is no need for the Court to qualify this requirement further.

Similarly other scholars, who in this context do not focus on the nature of the Article violated but rather on the nature of the breach itself, have pointed out that both in Community law and under certain non-contractual liability regimes of the Member States the illegality of an act as such is often not sufficient to give rise to liability. In particular where the public bodies concerned have to interpret complex legal rules or have to intervene in complex subject matters and, moreover, where they possess discretionary powers, not every misconstruction of the rules or other miscalculation (such as errors in the evaluation of a situation) automatically gives rise to liability in damages.[80] Often some form of further

[77] For another argument cf. Coppel (1993, p. 11-19); according to him the conditions for Community responsibility cannot apply since Article 215 functions within a specific context.

[78] See in particular para. 38 of the judgment. Cf. also Van Gerven 1994a, p. 16.

[79] Cf. Case C-63/89 *Assurance du Crédit* [1991] ECR I-1799, para. 12.

[80] Cf. Jarass 1994, p. 883, Craig 1993, p. 611, Bell and Bradley 1991, p. 8 and 12-13.

qualification of the breach is imposed in order to limit the potential scope of liability and (thus) leave the public authorities sufficient room for manoeuvre.

In the case of a "simple" non-transposition of a directive these considerations do not seem very relevant: as to the question whether a directive must be implemented, the Member States do not enjoy any discretion. The situation may, however, be different in the case of incorrect transposition, which may relate to a wide variety of issues, ranging from blatant disregard of the terms of the directive to minor (bona fide) misinterpretations of the provisions to be transposed. Although the latter also constitute a breach of Article 189(3), it is not a foregone conclusion that this type of breaches will *per se* give rise to liability in damages.[81]

In *Francovich* it was indisputable that what was at issue was the conduct of a Member State. Non-implementation or incorrect implementation of a directive is a matter for the Member State, as a rule for the legislator. In other cases, however, such as those concerning the non-application or erroneous application of the directive, the question may arise whether a commission or ommission is to be considered as conduct of the State or not. For the purposes of breaches of Article 189(3) the answer should be sought in case law relating to the problem of which bodies are actually bound by a directive. These are, as stated earlier, all national authorities, including the courts.[82] Furthermore, of particular relevance is the Court's case law on the concept of "the State". Although this case law is to be situated primarily within the context of direct effect, I see no reason why the approach should be different for the purposes of State liability.[83]

Damage

Secondly, non-contractual liability presupposes the existence of damage. The principle of non-contractual liability of the State as laid down in *Francovich* is after all a liability "for loss and damage caused to individuals".[84] In *Francovich* the existence of damage was – again and for obvious reasons – presumed. Nevertheless, the question may arise as to the kind of damage which will be taken into consideration for reparation. I shall return to this issue in Subsection 12.5.2.

[81] Cf. also below where the requirement of "fault" will be discussed. There may be a overlap between the further qualification of the breach and imposing the condition that the conduct must amount to a fault. Cf. Jarass 1994, p. 883. The main difference is that the first is objective in character (relating to the breach), while in the second a subjective element is introduced (relating to the author of the breach).

[82] Cf. above, Subsection 12.3.2.

[83] See Chapter 4, Section 4.5. Cf. also Schockweiler 1993a, p. 15. For a different view see Coppel 1993, p. 25-26, who argues that "*Foster*" is not an appropriate test in this context.

[84] Para. 35 and 37 of the judgment.

Fault

Thirdly, in legal writing it has been noted that, in contrast to what is common to most national regimes of non-contractual liability, the judgment does not contain any requirement of *fault*, in the sense that a certain degree of culpability on the part of the tortfeasor is required.[85]

The question as to whether the liability under Francovich is a strict liability[86] or not is one of the best examples of issues arising from the silence of the Court.

It has been suggested by some authors that as the judgment is silent on any requirement of fault, the liability under *Francovich* is a strict liability, allowing, in principle, no excuses whatsoever.[87] An important argument in this respect draws upon the Court's case law under Article 169,[88] which makes clear that any excuses, whatever their nature, offered by the Member States for their non-compliance with the obligations resulting from a directive are in principle not accepted by the Court of Justice. It is submitted that this argument should be approached with some caution. As I argued in Chapter 2, the Court's strict case law under Article 169 can be explained by the special nature of the procedure concerned. There it was stressed that the infringement procedure aims at an objective finding of a failure of the Member State. In such a procedure there is in principle no room for an element of culpability. However, it seems to me to be different when the procedure at issue concerns non-contractual liability. A simple transposition of the Article 169 case law is therefore not a self-evident matter.[89]

Moreover, when discussing the rigour of the obligation to implement the directive in time in Chapter 2, Section 2.3, I argued that one should not *a priori* exclude the possibility that in certain circumstances the Member States may be released, at least temporarily, from the obligation to implement the directive. In this context I mentioned a situation of serious internal disturbances or the application of the doctrine of *force majeure* in general. I also pointed out that obligations under an international agreement may in some circumstances validly block the implementation of the directive.

Problems may also arise if indications in the Court's case law make clear that the directive, or at least certain parts of it, are incompatible with primary

[85] Required degrees may in turn differ, e.g. from a deliberate act to mere negligence. Cf. Steiner 1993, Bell and Bradley 1991, p. 8-9.

[86] Or no-fault liability, liability based on risk.

[87] In this sense e.g. Bebr 1992, p. 579, Ossenbühl 1992, p.996, Nettesheim 1992, p.1003, Temple Lang 1992-1993, p.41, Schockweiler 1992, p. 46, Bok 1993, p. 39, Parker 1992, p. 184, Van Gerven 1993, p. 15 (at least in the case of non-implementation).

[88] Cf. Nettesheim 1992, p. 1002, Temple Lang 1992-1993, p. 41, Ross 1993, p. 57, Huglo 1993, p. 82, Coppel 1993, p. 23-24.

[89] For a different view see Coppel 1993, p. 31.

Community law but the directive has not been annulled or declared invalid.[90] In my opinion, it would be highly paradoxical to argue that the Member State is liable in damages for the simple reason that it is formally under the obligation to implement the directive at issue.[91]

An additional argument sometimes given in favour of strict liability is that under 215 there is also no requirement of fault.[92] Although this could be true, in the Article 215 regime there are other devices which already limit sufficiently the Community non-contractual responsibility. Moreover, it could be asked whether the requirement of "sufficiently serious breach" as interpreted and applied by the Court perhaps amounts to an introduction of the requirement of fault by the back door.[93]

On the other hand, some scholars have pointed out that a breach of Article 189(3) and certainly a breach consisting of non-implementation of a directive already amounts as such to a fault.[94] Consequently it is not surprising that the Court does not mention the requirement. However, it should not be deduced from this that there is no fault requirement at all.[95]

A system of strict liability in the case of non-implementation would, in my view, raise few objections. Matters are however different when it comes to incorrect implementation.

In Chapter 2, Section 2.5, I briefly discussed some problems related to the implementation of directives. The poor quality of Community legislation is no secret. Directives are often vague, open to various interpretations, and may be internally inconsistent or even incompatible with other instruments of Community law. In brief, the content of the obligation may be unclear both as to its meaning and as to its scope. Another relevant feature to be taken into account may be, in some cases, the conduct of the Commission. If the latter, after having scrutinized the implementing measures, indicates to the Member State concerned that in its view these are sufficient for implementing the directive, it is in my opinion not self-evident that the Member State will be held liable under all circumstances for incorrect implementation at a later stage.[96]

[90] See above, Chapter 2, Section 2.6.

[91] *Ibid.* Cf. also Jarass 1994, p. 882.

[92] Cf. Nettesheim 1992, p. 1003, Van Gerven 1994a, p. 28. Cf. also the opinion of A-G Mischo in Joined Cases C-6/90 and C-9/90 *Francovich* [1991] ECR I-5357, para. 74 and 75.

[93] E.g. "a manifest and grave disregard of the duties by the institution concerned" in Case C-63/89 *Assurances du Crédit* [1991] ECR I-1799, para 12, or "conduct verging to arbitrariness" in Case 116/77 *Amylum* [1979] ECR 3497, para. 19.

[94] Cf. Bebr 1992, 579, Oliver 1992, p. 358, Gilliams 1992-1993, p. 879, Huglo 1993, p.82, Coppel 1993, p. 23, Jarass 1994, p. 883.

[95] Cf. Jarass 1994, p. 882.

[96] Cf. e.g. Case 1251/79 *Italy v. Commission* [1981] ECR 205.

Similar concern, linked by some to the often unexpected interpretations by the Court, has been expressed by several authors,[97] who find, in brief, that Member States should not be held liable if an excusable error[98] has been made, in particular where a reasonable difference of opinion exists as to the meaning and scope of the provisions and the Member State believed in good faith that the directive had been properly implemented. According to Steiner "... the nature of Community law and principles of certainty and equity demand that States should not ... be liable in the absence of fault".[99] Consequently, in the opinion of several scholars, some element of culpability should be formulated as a condition for non-contractual liability of the Member State concerned.

Although, in principle, I am not entirely hostile to the introduction of a requirement of fault, as under certain circumstances it may be necessary to mitigate the harsh effects of strict liability, great care must be taken not to open the gates to all sorts of excuses for incorrect implementation. After all, the problems which arise can partly be imputed to the Member States themselves, since they participate in the elaboration and adoption of directives. For this reason in particular I argued in Chapter 2, Section 2.5, that in principle no excuses should be accepted. Another factor to be taken into account is that where unexpected interpretations by the Court really jeopardize the principle of legal certainty, the Court limits the effects of its judgment. Finally, the requirements of equity under certain circumstances should be taken into consideration: should the Member State bear the consequences of its unlawful conduct or should these be passed on to private individuals?[100]

Once it has been accepted that some sort of fault requirement ought to exist, the next question is how to fit it into the *Francovich* judgment. In this respect also, several solutions have been proposed. According to some, the requirement of fault is a part of the national conditions which the Member States are allowed to apply alongside the Community law requirements.[101] Others have, in my opinion rightly, rejected this possibility.[102] Accepting this proposition would, in my opinion, jeopardize the "sufficient" (*and Community*) character of the conditions laid down by the Court and open the gates to the vicissitudes of the different degrees of culpability required, as they exist within the Member States.

[97] Cf. Wyatt and Dashwood 1993, p. 86, Duffy 1992, p. 136, Barav 1994, p. 288 and p. 294 (quoting Lasok), Van Gerven 1993, p. 18-19, Steiner 1993.

[98] Cf. Van Gerven (1994a, p. 18) who suggests the application of the standard of "a normally diligent public authority".

[99] Steiner 1993, p. 22.

[100] As to this question see also Craig 1993, p. 618-619.

[101] Suggested by Lewis 1992, p. 454 and Lewis and Moore 1993, p. 167, Simon 1993, p. 243; submitted as a question by Barav 1994, p. 296.

[102] Cf. Karl 1992, p. 446, Parker 1992, p. 186, Schockweiler 1992, p. 46.

If a requirement of fault is to be imposed, then it should be defined by the Court of Justice.[103] In this respect it is conceivable that fault will be imposed in connection with the "nature of the breach", i.e the kind of conduct which occasioned the breach of Article 189(3).[104]

Another possible opening is the Court's statement that the Member States are liable for breaches of Community law *for which they can be held responsible.*[105] The matter depends on the interpretation of these terms.[106] Basically two different constructions are possible.

"For which they can be held responsible" may relate to the question of who is at the origin of the breach and whether the conduct of this body or person is attributable to the State: expressed in a different way, a sort of *objective* attributalibity.[107] In essence the problem relates to the question of which bodies come within the concept of "the State" under Community law.[108]

The second interpretation could involve a more subjective meaning of the terms, a *subjective* attributability: i.e. that the Member State cannot be held responsible for the breach if it has a valid excuse for its conduct.

12.4.3 The Specific Conditions Laid Down in Francovich

Where a Member State fails to meet its obligations under Article 189(3), it will be obliged to make good the loss and damage incurred by an individual, provided that at least the first two of the three above-mentioned general conditions are fulfilled. For any reparation it is crucial to know what has to be repaired. The mere breach of Article 189(3) is not sufficient for this purpose. This Article, which is the basis of the Member State's obligations,[109] in fact says nothing about the content of the Member State's obligations in a concrete case, i.e. about the result which the Member State was supposed to achieve. On the other hand, for the purposes of liability for loss and damage and, in particular, the assessment of the loss and damage caused, it is essential to know what the content of the obligation was. The Court has therefore linked the breach of

[103] A question as to the "fault-requirement" has been submitted to the Court in Case C-46/93 *Brasserie de Pêcheur*, pending.

[104] Cf. Wyatt and Dashwood 1993, p. 86; this implies further refinement of the concept of "nature of the breach". Cf. also Schockweiler 1993a, p. 17.

[105] Para. 35 and 37 of the judgment. Cf. Prechal 1992a, p. 12 and Van Gerven 1993, p. 18-19.

[106] Cf. Wattel 1992, p. 634, Van Gerven 1994a, p. 17-18.

[107] Cf. the Court's case law on admissibility of Article 215 actions: e.g. Case 175/84 *Krohn* [1986] ECR 753 and Case C-104/89 *Mulder* [1992] ECR I-3061.

[108] Cf. Chapter 4, in particular Section 4.5, for a detailed discussion of this problem. This is the interpretation given by Schockweiler 1992, p. 45 and 1993a, p. 15.

[109] See above, Chapter 2, Section 2.1.

Article 189(3) to the content of the directive at issue.[110] Thus since the specific conditions laid down in *Francovich* relate to the content of the directive, in every single case they require its analysis. Hereafter I shall discuss the separate conditions in turn. By the nature of things, however, the discussion cannot be other than general.

Granting Rights to Individuals

The first condition is that "the result prescribed by the directive should entail the grant of rights to individuals".

In my view this condition means that the directive as a whole, *or* some of its provisions, intends to confer rights to individuals which, if the directive had been (properly) transposed into national law, could have been enforced in national courts as a matter of national law, although of Community origin.[111]

In formulating the first condition the Court was apparently aiming to introduce the concept of "relative unlawfulness",[112] a *Schutznorm*, which is common to the non-contractual liability regimes of the Member States:[113] only a breach of a rule creating rights for individuals concerned or intended to create rights or, at least, protecting their interests can give rise to a right to reparation. Although, formally, the Member State commits a breach of Article 189(3) by not implementing a directive, *de facto* it is the violation of an individual right under the directive that really matters.

The quintessence of this requirement is to prevent excessive damages by demanding a connection between the infringement of the rule and the interest affected.[114] It is striking that, in contrast to its case law under Article 215 of the Treaty, the Court does not merely require that the provisions of the directive be given to protect the individual.[115] The first condition under *Francovich* seems to be more strict in that the Court requires that a (subjective) right be granted.[116]

It has been argued in legal writing, particularly by Barav,[117] that this condition must be understood as meaning that the purpose or objective of the

[110] Cf. Van Gerven 1994a, p. 25.

[111] Cf. Schockweiler 1992, p. 43.

[112] Cf. Van Gerven 1993, p. 19.

[113] Cf. Simon 1993, p. 237, Van Gerven 1994a, p. 16. Cf. also Ross (1993, p. 62) who points out that in English law the norm violated must impose a duty which is owed to the plaintiff. For a different opinion see Barav 1994, p. 291.

[114] Cf. Prieß 1993, p. 121. See also the opinion of A-G Darmon in Case C-282/90 *Vreugdenhil* [1992] ECR 1992, p. I-1937, para. 53-58.

[115] Cf. Bebr 1992, p. 575.

[116] Cf. Nettesheim 1992, p. 1002, Schockweiler 1992, p. 44.

[117] Barav 1994, p. 289-290. Less explicitly by Szyszczak 1992a, p. 696, Curtin 1992, p. 45, Schockweiler 1993b, p. 114. Cf. also Schockweiler 1992, p. 43.

directive must be the creation of rights.[118] I cannot agree with such a minimalist approach. Although in *Francovich* it was quite possible to construe the condition in such a narrow way, as there can be little doubt that Directive 80/987 (protection of workers – insolvency of employers)[119] aims at granting rights to employees concerned, the Court employed broader terms: the *result* should *entail* the grant of rights.

Firstly, the result prescribed refers, in this context, to the content of the directive and covers all its provisions. Equating the result with the purpose or the objective amounts to being caught in the same pitfall as German scholars in the past.[120]

Secondly, the term "entails" also suggests that it is erroneous to say that the purpose of the directive is to confer rights. In other words, it seems to be sufficient that the effect of the directive, upon proper implementation, is *inter alia* to confer rights. That is something quite different from the objective being to give rights.

Thirdly, it equally follows from the definition of the first condition that it is not the directive as a whole which must be taken into consideration,[121] as is suggested by the proposition that the purpose of the directive must be to grant rights. It suffices that some of its provisions intend to grant rights to individuals. This latter issue will be particularly relevant where there has been only a partially correct implementation. In such a case there must be an examination of whether the incorrectly or non-transposed provisions entail the grant of rights.

As a rule, directives contain a whole conglomerate of rights and duties for different legal subjects. The purpose of the Sixth VAT directive, for instance, is, on the whole, not immediately to create rights for individuals. Yet it contains several provisions which, once implemented, will give rights to individuals, such as exemption from taxation. Similarly, the purpose of Directive 76/491 on a Community procedure for information and consultation on prices of crude oil and petroleum products[122] is as such not to grant rights. Moreover, at first sight one may wonder whether this directive, which mainly regulates the relationship between the Member States and the Commission, could contain

[118] Which, in his view, seems to introduce a dichotomy in the category of directives; namely those which are designed to create right and those which are not.
[119] OJ 1980, L 283/23.
[120] Cf. Chapter 3, Section 3.1.
[121] Although the objective pursued by the directive may influence strongly the interpretation of its provisions.
[122] OJ 1976, L 140/4.

provisions granting rights to private parties. Nevertheless, it may be argued that Article 6 of this directive gives rise to rights of undertakings.[123]

The result prescribed by the directive which entails the grant of rights referred to in *Francovich* will primarily relate to the "hard core rules", which have to be transposed into national law.[124] This actually suggests that the non-compliance of a Member State with one of its "ancillary obligations"[125] cannot give rise to a right of reparation, although it amounts to a breach of Article 189(3). It is undoubtedly difficult to imagine how an obligation of, for instance, notification could give rise to a right of individuals.[126] However, it is not entirely self-evident that liability must be excluded *a priori* for this type of breaches. Whether or not there should be such a liability may depend on the legal consequences of such a notification and their objective.[127]

Although there are, in my opinion, good reasons for arguing that a broad interpretation must be given to the first condition laid down in *Francovich*, it is important to note that in the more recent judgment in *Faccini Dori* the Court suggests that it is indeed the "minimalist approach" which must be followed. In this judgment the Court reformulated the first condition by stating that "the purpose of the directive must be to grant rights to individuals".[128] If this is to be understood as an intentional amendment of the first condition, the scope of application of the liability regime laid down in *Francovich* will be seriously restricted. It is difficult to see how this limitation is to be reconciled with the broad statements about creation of rights for the benefit of individuals so forcefully stressed in the considerations about the principle of liability and the grounds on which this narrowing down of the first condition can be justified.

Be this as it may, the crucial question for the purposes of the first condition of liability is, obviously: in what circumstances does a right exist? In this respect, it is perhaps relevant to recall first that rights for individuals arise not only where they are expressly granted, but also by virtue of obligations imposed on others. Thus where directive provisions intend to create obligations for others, either private individuals or the Member State,[129] these provisions may also give rise to correlative rights for individuals.

[123] Article 6 provides: "All information communicated pursuant to Article 1 (1) ... shall be confidential. This provision shall not however prevent the distribution of general or summary information in terms which do not disclose details to individual undertakings ..."

[124] Cf. above, Chapter 3, Subsection 3.2.1.

[125] *Ibid.*, Subsection 3.2.2.

[126] Cf. Case 380/87 *Enichem* [1989] ECR 2491.

[127] Cf. Chapter 3, Subsection 3.2.2. Cf. also Chapter 7, Subsection 7.3.4.

[128] Case C-91/92 [1994] ECR I-3325, para. 27.

[129] For the sake of clarity: I refer here to the substantive obligations which should be distinguished from the obligation to implement the directive.

The issue of creation of rights as such has been discussed at length in Chapter 7, in particular in Section 7.3, where I tried to identify some parameters of the circumstances in which it can be said that a right has been created, or the intention is that a right is created in the implementation process. The actual impact of the first condition and therefore the scope of the State liability will indeed depend on the development of the Court's case law on this issue.

For the sake of clarity, it must be stressed again that the creation of rights and direct effect should not be equated. With respect to *Francovich*, legal writing seems to contain some confusion in this regard. Bebr,[130] for instance, suggests that the Community right at issue in the first condition is a right either formally granted or derived from Community rules having direct effect. Lewis and Moore[131] also seem to be of the opinion that the right infringed must be a directly effective right. Oliver[132] submits that the judgment, in so far as it relates to provisions having no direct effect, must be considered as exceptional. It appears that for some there is a difficulty in dissociating the issue of direct effect from liability as laid down in *Francovich*.[133]

Other scholars accept without difficulty that *Francovich* applies in cases where the relevant provisions do not have direct effect.[134] Interestingly, some writers have argued that liability under Francovich arises *only* in the absence of direct effect.[135] This latter problem seems to be closely related to the question concerning the relationship of direct effect and liability as a means of enforcement or protection of rights which individuals derive from a directive, in particular the question of which mechanism should be used first. I shall deal with this relationship in Section 12.6.

In my opinion, the question of liability as laid down in *Francovich* and the question as to the presence of direct effect of the directive concerned are two distinct issues. From Francovich itself it clearly appears that liability of the Member State is of particular importance where direct effect as the primary means of safeguarding individual rights fails. It should be recalled in this respect that the Court stressed that the possibility of obtaining redress is

"in particular indispensable where ... the full effectiveness of Community rules is subject to prior action on the part of the State and where, in the absence of such action,

[130] Bebr 1992, p. 577.
[131] Lewis and Moore 1993, p. 165.
[132] Oliver 1992, p. 358.
[133] See also the clever but nevertheless peculiar (and in my view otiose) construction of Van Gerven, (1994a, p. 21), who tries to reconcile the absence of direct effect in *Francovich* and the liability upheld by arguing, in fact, that the liability construed in *Francovich* is a matter of direct effect of Article 189(3), in combination with the directive.
[134] Cf. Ross 1993, p. 69, Schockweiler 1992, p. 43, Simon 1993, p. 238, Gilliams 1991-1992, p. 878.
[135] Cf. Lauwaars 1992, p. 709, Nettesheim 1992, p. 1002.

individuals cannot enforce before the national courts the rights conferred upon them by Community law."[136]

This will be the case where the conditions for direct effect are not satisfied by the relevant provisions. The same applies if the provisions do meet the required conditions but direct effect is denied because of the horizontal nature of the relationship within the framework of which they have to be relied upon.[137] Within the context of Francovich it seems to be immaterial who the addressees of the substantive provisions of the directive are, and thus who are under obligations by virtue of the directive once it has been implemented.[138]

The Content of the Rights

The second condition is that it must be possible to identify the content of the rights at issue on the basis of the provisions of the directive.[139] The need for this condition becomes clear if one takes into consideration that directives may intend to create rights for individuals but that further substantiation of the rights, the elaboration of their exact scope, is left to the Member States. Obviously, a right laid down in the directive in a rudimentary form will make it impossible to determine the loss and damage incurred by the individual.[140] A directive must therefore provide sufficient guidance in this respect.[141] If necessary, the national court may call upon the Court of Justice for this purpose.

In *Francovich*, the identification of the (minimum) content of the right was not a problem, as this had already been done by the Court when it examined the possible direct effect of the provisions at issue relating to the content of the right.[142] However, it is striking that the Court, when formulating the second condition, carefully avoided the terms that the provision must be "sufficiently precise and unconditional".[143] It probably chose different terminology in order

[136] Para. 34 of the judgment.

[137] Cf. Case C-91/92, *Faccini Dori* [1994] ECR I-3325. Also a combination of both may occur: no direct effect since the conditions are not fully met and since the situation the directive is aiming at is a "horizontal one". For another view see Geiger 1993, p. 471.

[138] Cf. Schlemmer-Schulte and Ukrow 1992, p. 85, Langefeld 1992, p. 961, Jarass 1994, p. 883. See also Wyatt and Dashwood 1993, p. 86 and the opinion A-G Mischo in *Francovich*, para. 67 and 68.

[139] According to Case C-91/92 (*Faccini Dori* [1994] ECR I-3325) minimum content is sufficient (para. 28).

[140] Cf. Karl 1992, p. 447.

[141] Cf. Schockweiler 1992, p. 44. Moreover, as was argued in Chapter 7, Subsection 7.3.5, one of the parameters of the existence of rights is their ascertainability.

[142] It must be noted that this is a different question from that relating to direct effect of the provisions in all their relevant aspects which I addressed hereabove.

[143] Cf. Gilliams 1991-1992, p. 879.

to avoid any confusion between the existence of rights and direct effect of the relevant provisions.

According to Barav[144] the second condition concerns the direct effect of the provisions concerned regarding the content of the right. In his view the content of the right should thus satisfy the requirements of direct effect. Indeed in *Francovich*[145] the ascertainability of the content of the right coincided with the ascertainability necessary for the purposes of direct effect of the provisions concerning the content of the right. However, in view of the different terminology employed by the Court, it is in my opinion premature to say that the conditions are identical. Sufficiently precise and unconditional terminology will undoubtedly make it possible to identify the content of the right.[146] On the other hand, the second condition seems to be less severe.

Although the second condition laid down in *Francovich* and the conditions for direct effect should therefore not be equated *a priori*, it could be asked whether, at the end of the day, there is in fact a difference between the two tests.[147] In particular, if one takes into consideration the development with respect to the conditions for direct effect described above, in Chapter 11, Subsection 11.4.2, i.e. that for purposes of direct effect it seems to suffice that a minimum guarantee can be construed on the basis of the provisions of the directive, it is submitted that the two tests may converge. However, it must be noted that there is an important difference: for the purposes of direct effect there may be more elements which must meet the test than for the purposes of liability. For instance, as was exemplified by *Francovich*, for both purposes the beneficiaries[148] and the content of the right had to be ascertainable. However, for the purposes of direct effect it was also necessary to ascertain *against whom* the provision can be relied upon. In the context of State liability this last element was irrelevant.

Causal Link

The third condition is the existence of a causal link between the breach of the State's obligation and the loss and damage suffered by the injured parties. The requirement of a causal link is, in contrast to the previous two conditions, not peculiar to breaches of Article 189(3). Any regime of non-contractual liability requires that the damage be caused by the unlawful conduct in question.[149] In

[144] Barav 1994, p. 290.

[145] Cf. also Case C-91/92 *Faccini Dori* [1994] ECR I-3325, para. 28.

[146] Cf. also above, Chapter 7, Subsection 7.3.5.

[147] Cf. also Boch and Lane 1992, p. 183 (there is no fundamental difference), Temple Lang 1992-1993, p. 29 (similar but not the same), Arts 1993, p. 500 (subtle difference), Schlemmer-Schulte and Ukrow 1992, p. 85 (parallel), Jarass 1994, p. 883 (*ganz ähnlich*).

[148] See below, Subsection 12.5.2 (*Who can sue?*).

[149] Cf. Van Gerven 1994a, p. 16.

Francovich the Court did not specify how remote the damage and the breach must be. Neither is it clear how much leeway is left to national courts to substantiate this condition.[150] As causation is largely a question of fact, i.e. it must be assessed in the light of the facts of the case, it is difficult to say in general terms what the exact content of the condition will be. The Court's case law under Article 215 teaches us that the damage incurred must be a sufficiently direct consequence of the unlawful conduct,[151] foreseeable for a prudent person,[152] and that, moreover, the chain of causation can be severed by conduct of the party claiming compensation.[153] Apart from this the case law is, for obvious reasons, characterized by a case-to-case approach.

In *Francovich* there was no need to address the condition of causation in further detail since the existence of the causal link was obvious. This will not always be the case. Particular problems are, for instance, likely to arise where a Member State has not (or not correctly) implemented a directive intended to impose obligations on private parties with the correlative of a right for another individual. It is not inconceivable that the Member State concerned could argue in defence that even if the directive had been (correctly) implemented, there would be no guarantee that the party under obligation would behave according to the terms of the implementing measures and that there is therefore no direct causal link between the breach of Article 189(3) and the injury suffered.

12.5 State Liability and the Context of National Law

12.5.1 Introduction

On the one hand, the fulfilment of the above-mentioned conditions was as such sufficient to give rise to a right to reparation for the individuals concerned. On the other hand, the action for damages is in other regards governed by the national rules on liability. The Court recalled in this respect that in the absence of Community legislation

[150] Van Gerven (1994a, p. 20 n. 61) points out that the national concepts of causation have considerable influence on the outcome of the case. According to Parker (1992, p. 184) causation can be used as an instrument of judicial policy to limit the extent of liability.

[151] Cf. Joined Cases 64 and 113/76, 167 and 239/78, 27, 28 and 145/79 *Dumortier* [1979] ECR 3091.

[152] Case 169/73, *Compagnie Continentale,* [1975] ECR 117, para. 23.

[153] Cf. Case 26/81 *Oleifici Mediterranei* [1982] ECR 3057.

"it is for the internal legal order of each Member State to designate the competent courts and lay down the detailed procedural rules for legal proceedings intended fully to safeguard the rights which individuals derive from Community law."[154]

Similarly, the Court recalled the two minimum requirements which national rules governing an action must observe.[155] In the case of non-contractual liability those requirements entail that

"the substantive and procedural conditions for reparation of loss and damage laid down by the national law ... must not be less favourable than those relating to similar domestic claims and must not be so framed as to make it virtually impossible or excessively difficult to obtain reparation."[156]

This reference to national rules merits some further attention. In particular it may seem somewhat difficult to identify the conditions which the Court is aiming at. Apparently, the conditions at issue are those which complement the conditions laid down in *Francovich* itself and which are necessary for the (further) settlement of the case. However, conditions which would interfere with those laid down in *Francovich*, such as, for instance, additional requirements wherever regulatory acts are at stake,[157] are obviously not allowed. As stated above, the fulfilment of the three conditions is as such *sufficient* to give rise to a right to reparation. In other words, conditions of national law which govern the *coming into being* of the right to reparation seem to be excluded.[158] This issue must be distinguished from questions relating to procedural conditions *stricto sensu*, from evidential rules and from substantive conditions such as rules concerning the content or form of the reparation to be given to the alleged victim. It is these latter issues which are governed by the relevant rules of national law.[159]

12.5.2 "Communautorization" of Other Conditions?

In so far as certain conditions and rules are left for the Member States, they also do not escape the influence of Community law. In Chapter 8 the expanding implications of, in particular, the principle of effectiveness and, to the extent that it can be separated from the former, the principle of effective judicial protection

[154] Para. 42 of the judgment.

[155] For a detailed discussion see above, Chapter 8, Subsection 8.2.1.

[156] Para. 43 of the judgment.

[157] E.g. a requirement that the rules must be *obviously unlawful* as it exists for certain remedies in Dutch law. Cf. Bok 1993, p. 54. According to Schockweiler (1993a, p. 19) the requirement of fault may not be imposed.

[158] Cf. also Karl 1992, p. 446, Schockweiler 1993a, p. 19.

[159] For other substantive conditions see Jarass 1994, p. 882 (e.g.*Mitverschulden, Verjahrungsfrist*).

were discussed. These principles also influence the remaining national procedural and substantive rules governing an action for damages. Thus rules relating to admissibility of an action, locus standi of the applicant, time limits for bringing action, evidential rules,[160] nature or categories of damage to be compensated, its assessment, the calculation of compensation to be paid, the form of redress, the award of interest or any other relevant matter may, under certain circumstances, be modified by virtue of the above-mentioned principles.[161] It is not my intention to discuss all the possible influences *in extenso*. Such a discussion would require a stock-taking of all the possible obstacles within the Member States, which is quite beyond the scope of this book. Nevertheless, some general – and perhaps somewhat speculative – remarks can be made here on the basis of some lessons which can be drawn from the Court's case law.

Damage and Amount of Compensation

In Subsection 12.4.2 it was submitted that the existence of damage is one of the conditions implicitly present in Francovich. Several questions emerge with respect to this condition and one must wait to find out how far the answers will be determined by Community law.

Firstly, there is the question of the form which the damage must take: does the damage have to be "actual and certain" or is it sufficient that there is a likelihood of damage in the future? In the Court's case law under Article 215 only claims for "actual and certain" or "imminent and sufficiently forseeable" damage are admitted.[162]

Secondly, what categories of damage are taken into consideration for compensation? In his opinion in *Marshall II*, A-G Van Gerven submitted that a national court, when considering the compensation to be awarded, must pay heed to each of the components of damage which are traditionally taken into account in rules governing non-contractual liability, namely loss of physical assets, loss of income or profit, moral damage like injury to feelings and damage on account of the effluxion of time.[163] The same or similar components can equally be found in the Court's case law under Article 215, where loss due to

[160] As far as rules of evidence are concerned, Bell and Bradley 1991, p. 14, point out that although, as a rule, the ordinary rules apply, it may be very difficult to obtain the necessary documentation as "in some countries traditions of official secrecy die hard".

[161] For Belgium, for instance, it has been argued that the requirements may imply doing away with the "execution immunity", i.e. that no forcible execution is possible against public authorities. Cf. Arts 1993, p. 509.

[162] Cf. e.g Joined Case 56-60/74 *Kampffmeyer* [1976] ECR 711. See also Toth 1988, p. 24-26.

[163] Case C-271/91 [1993] ECR I-4367, para. 18 of the opinion.

currency fluctuations is also taken into consideration for purposes of reparation.[164]

Thirdly, to what extent will the damage be compensated? Does fairly remote damage also come into consideration for compensation? The answer to this question is intimately related to the question concerning the causal link between the breach and the damage sustained. As has already been explained,[165] the existence of a causal link is a Community law condition which will need further elaboration in the future. In this way it will certainly also influence the extent of the damage to be compensated.

Once the nature and the extent of the damage considered for compensation have been established, the next question concerns the standards the compensation must satisfy. On the basis of the *Francovich* judgment it can be argued that full effectiveness of the directive[166] requires compensation in full.[167] Some further useful indications in this respect can be found in *Von Colson* and, in particular, in *Marshall II*.[168] In *Von Colson* the Court stipulated that the compensation awarded for the breach of the prohibition of discrimination "must in any event be adequate in relation to the damage sustained".[169] Indeed, it is disputable how the term "adequate" is to be interpreted. In *Marshall II*, in contrast to the Advocate General who argued that "adequate" does not necessarily mean "equal",[170] the Court found that in the particular circumstances of the case adequate reparation means that the loss and damage must be made good in full. An upper limit, restricting the amount of compensation *a priori* was not allowed.[171] Moreover, in the Court's view, the payment of interest must be considered as an essential component of compensation and, consequently, cannot be denied to the claimant.[172]

It is not my intention to assert that the same principles should apply automatically in cases of non-contractual liability. It must be borne in mind that the two above-mentioned cases were decided in the particular context of sex discrimination and the requirements laid down in those cases are the result of the

[164] Cf. Case 74/74 *CNTA* [1975] ECR 533.

[165] See above, Subsection 12.4.3.

[166] Cf. para. 39 of the judgment.

[167] Cf. Van Gerven 1994a, p. 17.

[168] Case 14/83 [1984] ECR 1891 and Case C-271/91 [1993] ECR I-4367. For a discussion of these aspects of the cases see Chapter 5, Subsection 5.2.4.

[169] Para. 23 of the judgment.

[170] Para. 17 of the opinion.

[171] Para. 30 of the judgment. For a different and more general approach to limitations of compensation see also the opinion of A-G Van Gerven in *Marshall II*, para. 14 ff.

[172] Para. 31 of the judgment. For a detailed discussion of different kinds of interest to be paid see again the opinion of A-G Van Gerven, para. 22 ff.

interpretation of Directive 76/207 (equal treatment at work).[173] An important element to be taken into account in this context is the objective aimed at by the directive concerned or the scope of protection the directive is intended to offer. It could therefore be argued that both the nature and the extent of the damage which should be taken into account for compensation and the standards the compensation must meet may differ from directive to directive.[174] However, it should not be ruled out that comparable requirements to those laid down in *Von Colson* and *Marshall II* may also be developed and applied in the field of the "*Francovich* liability". As the experience with sanctions has shown, the Court may decide to transpose certain requirements elaborated in one field of Community law to those in another.[175]

The Form of Redress

The Francovich case was concerned with pecuniary compensation for the loss and damage sustained. It could be asked, however, whether other forms of redress should also be made available to plaintiffs, in particular in cases where these seem more adequate and where the full effect of the directive is better safeguarded.[176] The least problematic seems to be a reparation in kind. Wherever a plaintiff prefers such a reparation, and a reparation in kind is physically possible, it is submitted that the principles developed in *Francovich* pose no obstacles. The same considerations apply when the plaintiff merely seeks a declaration. Much less certain is whether a court may, on the basis of *Francovich*, give an injunction, the content of which may, moreover, vary depending on the case. It may, for instance, contain a prohibition, an order to refrain from certain behaviour, possibly from the application of national rules, but it may equally contain a positive order, an order of specific performance. In particular in the case of an omission to implement a directive, the order could, theoretically, take the form of an order to legislate.[177] From a constitutional point of view this is indeed a very sensitive issue.[178]

[173] OJ 1976, L 39/40.

[174] Cf. Jarass 1994, p. 884.

[175] Cf. Case 68/88 *Commission v. Greece* [1989] ECR 2965, discussed in Chapter 5, Subsection 5.2.4. According to some, the nature and amount of damage to be compensated, as well as interest are matters to be decided ultimately by the Court of Justice. Cf. Temple Lang 1992-1993, p. 40. These issues are currently before the Court of Justice in Case C-46/93 *Brasserie de Pêcheur* and Case C-48/93 *Factortame III*.

[176] A positive reply is given by Temple Lang (1992-1993, p. 23 and 25), Bok (1993, p. 52) and Van Gerven (1993, p. 15).

[177] Not excluded by Langenfeld 1992, p. 961-962. Cf. also Trianfyllou 1992, p. 568 (*Normenersatzklage*) and Lewis and More 1993, p. 168.

[178] Cf. Lewis 1992, p. 451 and Lewis and Moore 1993, p. 169.

It is far from clear what, in this respect, the possible implications of *Francovich* are. The Court's judgment seems to concentrate on the reparation *a posteriori* of loss and damage already suffered. These must be "made good".[179] However it is conceivable that, in the future, the courts will be required to offer protection against any consequences of a breach of Community law, thus not only to give redress for breaches which have already occurred but also to prevent unlawful consequences which are likely to occur in the future.[180] Moreover, in some cases where damages *a posteriori* cannot fully make good the loss and damage sustained, a judicial order seems to be the most appropriate remedy, offering the best protection of the rights which individuals derive from Community law and safeguarding the full effectiveness of Community rules.[181]

Who Can Sue?

Like other matters under discussion here, *locus standi* in an action for damages under the liability regime established in *Francovich* is primarily a matter of national law. However, it follows from the *Francovich* judgment itself and, futhermore, from *Verholen*[182] that if the standing rules are, from the Community law point of view, such as to undermine the right to effective judicial protection and to render the exercise of the right to obtain reparation virtually impossible or excessively difficult, by virtue of these principles the national rules concerning *locus standi* cannot be decisive. This could imply that not only the – fairly obvious – category of persons to whom the directive intended to grant rights will be entitled to bring action, but also those who, for instance, incur damage as a consequence of the breach of Community law by the Member State concerned while themselves not being within the category of persons to whom the directive intends to confer rights.

In relation to the identity of plaintiffs, complications will arise if it seems impossible to identify, on the basis of the directive, the persons who are within the category of the potential beneficiaries. As Kapteyn[183] points out, the subjects must also be ascertainable on the basis of the directive. Whether or not the persons are ascertainable may indeed be ultimately resolved by the Court in a preliminary ruling. In *Francovich*, matters were straightforward.[184] Nevertheless,

[179] Cf. para. 37 of the judgment.
[180] Cf. Bok 1993, p. 52.
[181] Cf. Case C-213/89 *Factortame* [1990] ECR I-2433.
[182] Joined Cases C-87/90, C-88/90 and C-89/90 [1991] ECR I-3757, discussed above in Chapter 8, Subsection 8.3.2.
[183] Kapteyn and VerLoren van Themaat 1995, Chapter VI, Subsection 2.3.2. Cf. also Jarass 1994, p. 883 and Geiger 1993, p. 470.
[184] Cf. para. 13-14 and 45 of the judgment. Cf. also Case C-334/92 *Miret* [1993] ECR I-6911 and Case C-91/92 *Faccini Dori* [1994] ECR I-3325.

STAFFS UNIVERSITY LIBRARY

it is surprising that the Court did not formulate another condition, namely that the identity of the beneficiaries of the rights must also be ascertainable.[185] It could be that the Court considers the question to be part and parcel of the first condition, i.e. the right to be granted,[186] and since matters in *Francovich* were clear, it omitted to specify this in a way comparable to that in which it specified the requirements relating to the content of the right.

Who Can Be Sued?

Although according to the *Francovich* judgment it is the State which is liable for loss and damage caused by a breach of Community law, in my opinion it is not necessarily the State as such which should be sued in national courts. The question of which body of the State will be the appropriate defendant is again a matter of national law. At first sight, it seems logical that the body which is responsible *within the Member State* for the breach committed, is the one to be sued.[187]

In the case of an action brought for non-transposition or incorrect transposition it should be the body which was under the obligation of transposing the directive: as a rule, the State in its legislative capacity. In Member States where, in accordance with the principle of "institutional autonomy", other bodies are responsible for the transposition, such as "*Länder*" in Germany or regions in Belgium and Italy,[188] these bodies should in principle be the appropriate defendant. If, however, for some reason these bodies cannot be brought before the court, it should be the State, being the primarily responsible entity, against which the individual may claim.[189]

In cases of non-transposition or incorrect transposition matters seem to be relatively transparent. In contrast to this, it is to be expected that actions brought for other types of breaches of Community law, including Article 189(3), will pose considerable problems as to the question of who is the appropriate defendant. In this context the Court's case law concerning the legal subjects upon whom a directive is binding and who are to be considered as a part of the State becomes relevant.[190] At the same time it is also the Member State as such which is responsible for breaches committed by its bodies, even where it does not have the

[185] Cf. also Barav 1994, p. 290 and p. 291.

[186] One of the aspects of "relative unlawfulness" is that the provision infringed is meant to protect him or the group to which he belongs. Cf. Van Gerven 1994a, p. 16 and Jarass 1994, p. 883.

[187] Cf. Temple Lang 1992-1993, p. 37, Schockweiler 1993b, p. 117.

[188] Cf. above, Chapter 4, Section 4.3.

[189] Cf. Jarass 1994, p. 884.

[190] See above, Chapter 4, Section 4.3 and 4.5. Cf. also Bebr 1992, p. 578. For problems in federal type states see e.g. Arts 1993, p. 507-509.

necessary powers to control them.[191] It has been suggested, as a possible way out of this "institutional imbroglio",[192] that an individual should be able to claim against any plausible "emanation of the State" and that it is a matter for the State to sort out the internal allocation of responsibility.[193] Whether matters are so simple remains to be seen.

Limitation Periods

All the Member States have some type of limitation periods with respect to actions under the relevant non-contractual liability rules. The nature of these limitation periods may differ. They can be time limits for bringing action as they exist in administrative law. They can be periods after which the right of action or the substantive right itself is prescribed (prescription periods).[194]

One of the striking issues in *Francovich* is that the Court did not follow A-G Mischo, who proposed that the Court's judgment be limited in time.[195] The Court's choice could possibly be explained by the awareness that the actions for damages will in any event be time-barred under national law. In the light of the case law on time limits for bringing action, according to which a reasonable period is allowed by Community law, this would seem to be the correct position.[196] Matters are, however, less obvious if one takes into account the Court's judgment in *Emmott*.[197]

In brief, in *Emmott* the Court found, taking the "particular nature of directives" as the point of departure, that as long as a directive has not been properly transposed into national law, national time limits for bringing proceedings cannot apply. The transposition of the *Emmott* rule to the field of non-contractual liability gives rise to two major questions.

Firstly, there is the question whether *Emmott* applies to prescription periods, which are more common in civil law, or whether it is limited to the administrative law type of time limits, as was the case in *Emmott*. In Chapter 8, Subsection 8.3.2, I argued that from a Community law point of view a differentiation as to the nature of the periods, which is often historically determined, cannot be considered as relevant for the application of the *Emmott* rule. As soon as the application of a certain limitation period constitutes in effect a bar to obtaining

[191] Cf. Schockweiler 1993a, p. 15. See also above, Chapter 2, Section 2.3 and Chapter 4, Section 4.3.

[192] Term used in this context by Hessels and Mortelmans 1993, p. 929.

[193] Submitted by Ross 1993, p. 70.

[194] See on different types also above, Chapter 8, Subsection 8.3.2.

[195] Para 87 of the opinion.

[196] Cf. Schlemmer-Schulte and Ukrow 1992, p. 87, Ossenbühl 1992, p. 997, who also suggests that the 215 limitation could be applicable. This view is shared by Prieß (1993, p. 124) who finds such an application necessary in order to avoid divergences.

[197] Case C-208/90 [1991] ECR I-4269, discussed in detail in Chapter 8, Subsection 8.3.2 above.

a remedy, it should be treated as falling within *Emmott.* Moreover, the function of prescription periods in public non-contractual liability law is very similar to the function of time limits for bringing an action. Prescription periods also fulfil the need to prevent the activity of public authorities being called into question indefinitely. In other words, the major underlying concern is legal certainty.

Secondly, it is not entirely clear whether or not *Emmott* applies only in situations of direct effect, in other words in situations where an individual relies on directly effective provisions of a directive in order to enforce his rights.[198] Indeed, the *Emmott* case was concerned with precisely this type of situation. In my opinion, however, this point of view is too limited. The rationale underlying *Emmott* is that where directives are intended to create rights (directly and indirectly) for individuals the latter must be able to ascertain their full extent. This is only the case where the directive has been properly transposed into national law. Neither a judgment under Article 169 nor a Court's finding that the provisions concerned are directly effective brings the state of legal uncertainty to an end. In my view, the rights to which the Court refers in *Emmott* are the *substantive rights* under the directive and *not* the right to rely on the directive in judicial proceedings. Community law gives an individual different means for safeguarding the rights a non-implemented or incorrectly implemented directive intends to confer upon him. The person concerned may invoke the directive in order to ask the national court to proceed to consistent interpretation; he may rely on the directive for purposes of direct effect; and, finally, the individual may claim damages on the basis of the *Francovich* judgment. Whatever the individual does, the fact remains that "the legal certainty which must exist if individuals are to be required to assert their rights"[199] is not established as long as the directive has not been (correctly) transposed into national law, with the consequence that limitation periods, whether periods of appeal or prescription periods, cannot apply. On the basis of these considerations it is submitted that the *Emmott* rule also applies with respect to actions for damages and that, consequently, limitation periods of such actions begin to run only upon proper transposition of the directive.[200]

[198] Cf. Lauwaars 1993, p. 708, Wattel 1992, p. 633, Prechal 1992a, p. 8-9.

[199] Case C-208/90 *Emmott* [1991] ECR I-4269, para. 22.

[200] Cf. also Temple Lang 1992-1993, p. 44, Gilliams 1991-1992, p. 879, Van Gerven 1993, p. 21, Betlem and Rood 1992, p. 254, Curtin 1992, p. 47, Plaza Martin 1994, p. 52, Schockweiler 1993b, p. 120.

12.6 Liability of the State: A Tailpiece to Effective Judicial Protection

The *Francovich* judgment clearly illustrates the way of pushing the limits of remedies available in the case of failure of the Member States in their obligations under Article 189(3). Where only a few years ago direct effect of directives was considered to be the last resort,[201] today the non-contractual liability of the State for breaches of Article 189(3) has taken over, extending the possibilities of judicial protection a stage further, beyond what seemed for many years to be the ultimate limit.[202]

On the one hand, non-contractual liability of the State seems to be a safety net in cases where other devices designed by the Court fail. On the other, its exact scope has to be clarified in several respects and only future developments will show the real value of this safety net.

Compared with the instruments of direct effect or consistent interpretation, non-contractual liability as laid down in *Francovich* is, in my opinion, of a *subsidiary character*. Liability arises only if the injured party has been unable to safeguard his rights by means of direct effect or consistent interpretation.[203] To put this in a different way, liability is a supplement to direct effect and consistent interpretation, and not a substitute for them.[204] I therefore cannot agree with the suggestion made by Ross that the plaintiff has the choice of which avenue he will follow.[205] Neither can I agree with Steiner, who seems to prefer State liability to direct effect and consistent interpretation. In her opinion, liability is "more legitimate" than the other two instruments, as it lays the sanction directly at the door of the defaulting Member State. According to Steiner, direct effect and consistent interpretation "were simply expedients designed to secure the enforcement of Community law precisely because the State has failed to fulfill its obligations".[206] In my opinion, liability of the Member States is equally nothing more than another – and to my mind second-rank – "expedient". Community law is primarily interested in its application, for which, in the case of a Member State's failure, consistent interpretation and direct effect are the "second best" solutions, and not in the third best solution of "buying off" the failure. Similarly, an individual may be more favoured by the application of national law in

[201] Cf. the opinion of A-G Darmon in Case C-177/88 *Dekker* [1990] ECR I-3941, para. 10.

[202] Cf. the opinion of A-G Van Gerven in Case C-128/92 *Banks* [1994] ECR I-1173, para. 38.

[203] Cf. Ossenbühl 1992, p. 994, Schlemmer-Schulte and Ukrow 1992, p. 89, Schockweiler 1993b, p. 120.

[204] Cf. Duffy 1992, p. 135.

[205] Ross 1993, p. 59.

[206] Steiner 1993, p. 9.

conformity with the directive or by its direct application, than by a sum of money.

The subsidiary character of liability seems to be confirmed in the recent judgment of the Court in the *Miret* case and the *Faccini Dori* case,[207] which show that only where direct effect or consistent interpretation cannot bring sufficient relief does the State liability come into consideration. In *Miret*, which was concerned, like the *Francovich* case, with Directive 80/987 (protection of workers – insolvency of employers),[208] direct effect was of no help to the applicant, owing to the large margin of discretion left to the Member States as to the organization of the guarantee funds. Furthermore, from the national judge's reference to the Court it appeared that there was no possibility of interpreting the relevant national provisions in conformity with the directive. According to the Court, in such a situation, as follows from the *Francovich* judgment, the Member State is obliged to make good the damage incurred by individuals concerned as a consequence of the non-transposition of the directive. The judgment in *Miret* makes clear, in my view, that State liability is the last avenue to be followed. Obviously, if the national court had been able to apply the directive directly or to interpret national provisions in conformity with the directive no damage would have occurred. In other, more general terms, where direct effect or consistent interpretation are sufficient to safeguard the rights at stake, there is no room for liability.

On the other hand, the possibility should not be excluded that liability of the State as laid down in *Francovich* may function as a complement to the other two methods. It is conceivable that, under certain circumstances, direct effect or consistent interpretation as such do not suffice to achieve a situation which entirely corresponds with the result which had to be achieved *and* which would have been achieved if the directive had been correctly transposed (or transposed in due time, as the case may be) into national law. Thus the full effectiveness of the directive is also not necessarily always safeguarded by direct effect and consistent interpretation. From the point of view of the individual, neither of the devices guarantees that he will be put in the position in which he would have been had the breach not occurred. In particular, where the national court reviews the legality of national measures and subsequently disapplies them the result may be a lacuna.[209] The payment of damages to the persons affected may seem to be the appropriate complementary remedy.

[207] Case C-334/92 [1993] ECR I-6911; Case C-91/92 *Faccini Dori* confirms *Miret* in this respect.
[208] OJ 1980, L 283/23.
[209] See above, Chapter 11, Subsection 11.3.5 and 11.3.6. Cf. also Arts 1993, p. 501.

However, matters are more complicated than one might assume.[210] If an individual brings an action (not being a claim for damages, but, for instance, an action for judicial review of an administrative decision) relying on a directly effective provision or requires the court to proceed to consistent interpretation, it could be argued that damages for possible (additional) loss and damage incurred are a matter of national law. In other words, the "national" claim in damages is still part and parcel of the primary avenue of enforcement, based on the directive itself.[211] In my opinion, it should not, however, be ruled out that the "Francovich-type" claim for damages could come into consideration where the national regime for damages does not bring sufficient redress when considered from the Community law point of view and cannot be brought into line with Community law requirements by the use of the techniques of direct effect or consistent interpretation. In this respect too liability under *Francovich* has a subsidiary character.[212]

A further question is: with respect to which type of breaches of Article 189(3) will the principles laid down in *Francovich* apply? This question raises extremely complex issues which as yet are far from clear. In Subsection 12.3.2 I gave a short overview of the possible breaches. Should a breach of Article 189(3) by national courts or, where appropriate, national authorities through not giving national law consistent interpretation or through not applying a directly effective provision in a situation of non-implementation or inadequate implementation give rise to liability of the State? If the provisions at issue were directly effective or consistent interpretation was possible, is there still room for liability for non-implementation or incorrect implementation, which comes into consideration, as argued above, only in circumstances where no direct effect or consistent interpretation had been possible? Or should the individual rather sue the State or the administrative organ concerned for non-application of a directly effective provision or for not proceeding to consistent interpretation?

Equally, does *Francovich* give a right to damages for breaches by public authorities or courts if the directive as such has been correctly implemented, as in the case of a failure to enforce the implementing measures or to construe them in accordance with the underlying directive?[213] Last but not least, liability for

[210] Another complication, which I will not elaborate further here is the jurisdiction of the courts; e.g. for judicial review of administrative action often administrative courts, for actions in damages civil courts. Cf. Bell and Bradley 1991, p. 3-4 and 12.

[211] This is indeed nothing exceptional and happens where action in damages is the appropriate remedy under national law. Cf. e.g. Case C-177/88 *Dekker* [1990] ECR I-3941, which was brought under the Dutch rules of non-contractual liability.

[212] Indeed, where the national rules are more favourable to the plaintifs, there is no problem. Cf. Schockweiler 1992, p. 44.

[213] Temple Lang (1992-1993, p. 38 and 39), for instance, gives a positive answer. Cf. also Schockweiler 1992, p. 42.

this type of breaches raises the old and precarious constitutional issue of liability for loss and damage caused by judicial decisions.[214]

There is no doubt that these types of conduct also amount to a breach of Article 189(3) and, moreover, at first sight the specific conditions formulated in *Francovich* could apply here. Yet upon futher consideration, in particular in the light of the problems raised by liability of the State in this context, it could be asked whether the Court in *Francovich* was also aiming at this kind of breach. At least, one may wonder whether the conditions for liability to be satisfied will not be different, given the different nature of the breaches.[215]

The final potential problem which I would like to address briefly is State liability for breaches of Article 189(3), while the plaintiff is better off under (non-adjusted) national law. The *Francovich*, *Miret* and *Faccini Dori* cases related to a situation where (potential) direct effect, consistent interpretation and the right to damages concerned the protection of rights which the directive intended to grant to individuals. However, it could be that, while there has been no transposition or incorrect transposition of a directive, either direct effect or consistent interpretation is to the disadvantage of the individual. As discussed above,[216] the application of directly effective provisions may affect the position of a private individual, in particular in multi-angular relationships. Similarly, interpretation of national law in conformity with the directive may create or at least change obligations for a private party. If the directive did not exist, such effects would not occur.[217] The question is then indeed whether the individuals concerned may bring an action for damages against the Member State which has failed to meet its obligations under Article 189(3).

In the light of the conditions as laid down in *Francovich*, the answer seems to be negative. As explained above, in Subsection 12.4.3, the first condition especially links the breach of Article 189(3) to the content of the directive and, in particular, to the existence of a right which would have been granted to individuals concerned if the directive had been correctly transposed. Furthermore, it may be argued that the adversely affected individual would have been affected anyway if the directive had been implemented.[218] In other words, where the directive intends to create obligations for individuals, it is difficult at first sight to understand how they can incur damage by the non-implementation or incorrect

[214] Categorically denied by Steiner (1993, p. 11), not excluded by Szyszak (1992a, p. 696) and Pieper (1990, p. 2456). See for discussion of this issue within the framework of Article 169 proceedings Barav 1975, p. 379. Cf. also Nicolaysen 1985.

[215] For a discussion of some of these questions see Jarass 1994, p. 884-886.

[216] Chapter 4, Subsection 4.2.2.

[217] An obvious example of such a situation is Case C-177/88 *Dekker* [1990] ECR I-3941.

[218] Cf. the opinion of A-G Lenz in Case C-91/92 *Faccini Dori*, 9 February 1994, [1994] ECR I-3325, para. 62. Cf. also Prechal 1991, p. 602-603.

implementation. However, it is equally true that by not implementing the directive, the Member State did not enable the individuals to ascertain the full scope of the obligations upon which they would have been able to act. For the time being, the Court's case law does not provide a satisfactory answer to this problem. In my view, in the ultimate analysis, the problem boils down to the tension, already observed, which may occur between the desire to give full effect to Community rules and the need for effective judicial protection.[219]

[219] Cf. also above, Chapter 10, Section 10.9.

13
Conclusions Part III

The mechanisms designed by the Court of Justice which can be used to palliate the detrimental consequences of incorrect implementation of a directive or its non-implementation form a complex but relatively coherent system.

The first mechanism is *consistent interpretation* of national law with the directive at issue. From a chronological point of view, consistent interpretation as an obligation for national courts under Community law followed upon the elaboration by the Court of Justice of the doctrine of direct effect. From a practical point of view, however, as well as for considerations of judicial policy, consistent interpretation should precede the deployment of direct effect.

The obligation of consistent interpretation plays a part in two distinct contexts. Firstly, the national courts are obliged to proceed to consistent interpretation of national law in the context of judicial implementation of the directive: national courts have to apply the national rules transposing the directive. As any application of legal rules requires in principle its interpretation, in a case where the directive has been transposed the courts will also be called upon to interpret these national provisions. The interpretation given must be in conformity with the underlying directive.

Secondly, national courts are also obliged to proceed to consistent interpretation where the directive has not been transposed in due time or correctly. I have called consistent interpretation in this context "remedial interpretation": it helps to overcome the consequences resulting from the non-implementation or inadequate implementation in the concrete case before the court. It does not, however, release the Member State from its obligation to implement the directive and to do so correctly.

In practice it may be difficult to draw a borderline between consistent interpretation in the context of judicial implementation and "remedial interpretation". The main reason for this is that according to the Court of Justice the question whether a directive has been implemented correctly is also to be considered in the light of the interpretation and application of the implementing measures by the courts.

The obligation of consistent interpretation applies irrespective of whether the provisions of the directive meet the conditions of direct effect and irrespective of the relationship at issue, be it between private individuals or between individuals and the State. The national provisions to be interpreted in conformity with the directive are all provisions of national law; it makes no difference whether they are anterior or posterior to the directive and whether or not they have been enacted to implement it.

The most crucial question with respect to the obligation of consistent interpretation relates to its limits. This question occurs in particular in situations of "remedial interpretation", as the national court may then be asked to make an extraordinary effort in order to bridge the gap between the terms of national law and the terms and objectives of the relevant directive. At the heart of the problem lies the meaning of the terms "as far as possible": the national courts are required to interpret national law in conformity with the directive as far as such an interpretation is possible.

It has been suggested that the "possibility" or "impossibility" may refer to different issues. Firstly, there is the issue of the flexibility of the national provision: the terms of the provision must be such that the court is able to "stretch" its meaning.

Secondly, whether a certain interpretation is possible or not may depend on the methods of interpretation commonly used in the national legal system of the court concerned. However, it has been argued that consistent interpretation may entail a modification of or even a departure from certain rules of construction usually (or obligatorily) employed by the national court concerned. On the other hand, there seems to be a common understanding that the Court of Justice does not require the national courts to interpret their national law *contra legem*.

Thirdly, the Court of Justice has pointed out that the obligation of consistent interpretation has its limits in general principles of law, in particular the principle of legal certainty. Whether these principles are general principles of Community law or general principles of national law which are allowed to be applied in a Community law context is not entirely clear. The difference between the two is not fundamental. Nevertheless, their application in practice may lead to different results.

Fourthly, it has been suggested that "as far as possible" refers to the judicial function. In other words, the limits of consistent interpretation would be transgressed if the court exceeded its authority as a judicial body. The problem is, however: according to what standards – national or Community – are the limits of this judicial function to be appraised?

A brief and highly schematic discussion of the different types of arguments which play a part in interpretation of the law has revealed how consistent interpretation operates within the broader context of legal interpretation in general. The directive becomes one of the arguments which favour a certain interpretation.

Generally speaking, in a situation where different arguments for a certain interpretation come into conflict with each other, the conflict will be resolved by applying certain priority criteria. Two criteria play a crucial role in this respect: legal certainty and the separation of powers. As I have contended, it is these two priority criteria which determine in the ultimate analysis the content of the terms "as far as possible".

Legal certainty requires in this context that the law must be predictable. In this perspective it is also understandable why the provision to be interpreted must be sufficiently flexible to allow consistent interpretation. Similarly, it explains why so many scholars have stressed that consistent interpretation should not amount to an interpretation *contra legem*, since such an interpretation affects by its very nature legal certainty in the sense of predictability of the law.

The introduction of the principle of legal certainty by the Court of Justice as one of the limits to (the obligation of) consistent interpretation entirely fits into the scheme in which interpretative problems are resolved in the broader context. National courts are however no longer free to decide for themselves what legal certainty dictates in a particular case. The solution has to be found in co-operation with the Court of Justice, which, in turn, has to take into account the various factors playing a role in the national law context, in particular the wording of the provisions to be interpreted. In this process, it may occur that legal certainty as a limit to consistent interpretation may be pushed a little further than was customary under national law alone. To this extent national methods of interpretation will also be modified.

The second priority criterion, the separation of powers, is more complex. It is under this heading that the limits of the judicial function mentioned above must be situated.

The limits of the judicial function as conceived in national legal systems are reflected in the methods of interpretation. In so far as consistent interpretation entails a change in these methods of interpretation, pushing the limits a stage further, by implication this will amount to a modification of the position of the courts *vis-à-vis* other organs of the State, in particular the legislator. Similarly, consistent interpretation may lead to the (subjective) intention of the legislature having to be disregarded. Seen from this perspective, there is a "creeping" enlargement of the national court's function. It is however uncertain to what extent, and on what basis, national courts can be required to disregard the limits of their function as delineated under national law.

In legal writing it has also been argued that consistent interpretation is not allowed in so far as it results in imposing obligations upon individuals and amounts *de facto* to horizontal or inverse vertical direct effect. In my opinion this position does not take sufficiently into account the fundamental difference between direct effect and consistent interpretation: in the former case it is the directive itself that applies while in the latter it is still national law that applies. Furthermore, the general principles of law and especially the principle of legal certainty as limits to consistent interpretation provide sufficient safeguards against radically different interpretation of national law imposing entirely unexpected obligations upon individuals. Finally, the argument that consistent interpretation cannot amount to imposing obligations upon individuals ignores the fact that consistent interpretation is not a means solely to protect an individual's position but also to contribute to the full effectiveness of Community law. Where a directive intends to impose an obligation upon individuals, consistent interpretation may arguably also be deployed to achieve such an objective, provided that the limits as set out above are observed.

Where the mechanism of consistent interpretation leaves off, the doctrine of *direct effect* takes over.

The basis of direct effect of directives is the binding nature which Article 189(3) ascribes to directives, combined with Article 5 of the Treaty. Theoretically, direct effect of directives is underpinned by the necessity to give directives as much useful effect as possible. Article 189(3) is then interpreted accordingly. The discussion about the ultimate theoretical basis of direct effect of directives has been complicated by the introduction of the "estoppel theory": a Member State may not rely on its own failure to fulfil its obligations under the directive or, as reformulated in later case law, the Member State must be prevented from taking advantage of its own failure to comply with Community law.

Academic commentators and several Advocates General have accepted this theory with open arms. The Court's case law is less explicit in this respect. In any case, especially more recently, the idea of estoppel as a basis for direct effect of directives has come increasingly under fire and it has been suggested that as a theoretical basis it should be rejected. This does not, however, imply that estoppel cannot, where appropriate, serve as an additional argument in favour of direct effect, both in general and in respect of directives in particular.

Direct effect has been defined in several ways. One of the most common descriptions is that directly effective provisions create rights for individuals which national courts must protect. Some scholars have however pointed out that this definition is too narrow: direct effect is a broader concept than the mere creation of rights. They prefer to define direct effect in terms of "invocability". This means that directly effective provisions can be relied upon by individuals and they must be applied by the courts. If direct effect has to be defined in terms of rights then, at the most, a right to rely on the directive has been created. By choosing this broader definition, which is also often used by the Court of Justice, another conceptual complication can be circumvented: the distinction between direct effect and direct applicability. In this approach the two coincide.

Yet, the appropriateness of the definition of direct effect as "provisions which can be relied upon or can be invoked by individuals and which must be applied by the courts" can also be called into question. The term "rely upon" or "invoke" is misleading in that a directive can be relied upon or invoked for purposes other than direct effect, for instance, in order to ask the court to proceed to consistent interpretation of national law. Furthermore, the courts may also apply the directive of their own motion, thus without a party having relied upon it. Similarly, the term "to apply" suggests that the court is called upon to subsume the facts of the case under the rules of the directive. However, in individual proceedings procedure a directive will often serve as a yardstick for the legality of national provisions. From this point of view the term "apply" is less apt. Finally, a directive can be relied upon by a whole range of legal subjects and it has to be "applied" not only by the courts but also by other national authorities.

Indeed, one may stick to the above-mentioned definition, provided that all these nuances are carefully kept in mind. However, one may also decide to describe direct effect in other terms. In this respect I have proposed the following definition: direct effect is the obligation of a court or another authority to apply the relevant provision of Community law, either as a norm which governs the case or as a standard for legal review.

In order to be directly effective the provision must meet two conditions: it must be sufficiently precise and it must be unconditional. A sufficient degree of precision concerns primarily its wording. Unconditionality may relate to a whole range of issues which are difficult to grasp in more abstract terms. The way in which the two conditions are applied by the Court of Justice reveals that both can to a large extent be reduced to one common denominator: the absence of discretion.

For a long time it was generally understood that the existence of discretion will, as a rule, block direct effect. However, in particular more recent case law shows that some degree of discretion does not necessarily inhibit direct effect. As long as the court can use the directive for the purposes of the case in which the directive has been "brought in" and as long as it can do that as a court of law, without encroaching upon powers reserved to other bodies, the directive provisions are directly effective. In this context it is important to note that direct effect is a variable concept: in a certain case the provision concerned cannot be applied by the court, as in the particular respect required it does not provide judicially manageable standards by which to judge the matter; in another case, however, the same provision may give sufficient indications and thus enable the court to decide the case before it.

Like consistent interpretation, direct effect also has its limits. Apart from the conditions just discussed which must be satisfied by the provisions at issue, the most important limitation of direct effect of directives is the absence of horizontal direct effect or inverse vertical direct effect. Both forms can be reduced to the denial that directives may of themselves impose obligations upon individuals.

The arguments *pro* and *contra* horizontal direct effect have been regularly rehearsed in legal writing and also in a number of opinions of Advocates General. Although in the *Marshall I*[1] judgment the Court of Justice took the position that directives cannot impose obligations upon individuals and therefore

[1] Case 152/84 [1986] ECR 723.

cannot be relied upon against such a person since, according to Article 189(3), a directive is binding only in relation to the Member States concerned, several scholars and Advocates General have engaged in considerable efforts to make the Court change its mind. One of the important reasons for doing this was the Court's own case law in which it tried to find a way out of the impasse it had created for itself by the *Marshall I* judgment. However, in a recent judgment in the *Faccini Dori*[2] case the Court persisted in its initial position and introduced an additional argument against horizontal direct effect: the Community has the power to impose obligations upon individuals only by means of regulations.

Where the mechanism of direct effect can bring no relief, a device of (for the moment) last resort comes into consideration: *the liability of the State* for damages the individual incurs as a consequence of non-implementation or incorrect implemetation of the directive.

The Court's decision in *Francovich*[3] that the State is liable, as a matter of principle, for breaches of Community law, was not totally unexpected. It can rather be seen as an inevitable development of previous case law. In contrast with what had not been entirely undisputed in the past, in *Francovich* the Court made clear that the principle of State liability is a *Community law* principle which is inherent in the system of the Treaty and which also follows from Article 5. Two major considerations are at the basis of the Court's judgment: the need to protect rights which individuals derive from Community law and the necessity of ensuring full effect of Community law provisions.

Whether the principle of liability will give rise to a right to reparation in a concrete case depends on certain conditions which must be satisfied. The conditions, in turn, depend on the nature of the breach. The latter seems to refer to the type of breach committed by the Member State. The *Francovich* case was concerned with one particular type of breach, namely the breach of Article 189(3) by non-implementation of a directive. It would seem that the conditions given by the Court relate to this specific type of breach. There is, however, little doubt that, in principle, more or less the same conditions will apply in the case of incorrect implementation.

In *Francovich* the Court formulated three explicit conditions, but these are logically preceded by a number of general conditions of non-contractual liability which have to be fulfilled first.

Firstly, there must be unlawful conduct on the part of the Member State. From the *Francovich* judgment it cannot be deduced whether *any* breach of Community law will as such suffice to give rise to liability. Both Community law in a procedure under Article 215 and certain national regimes of public non-

[2] Case C-91/92 [1994] ECR I-3325.
[3] Joined Cases C-6/90 and C-9/90 [1991] ECR I-5357.

STAFFS UNIVERSITY LIBRARY

contractual liability require that the breach must be a serious one. With respect to the *Francovich* case it has been argued that a breach of Article 189(3) by non-implementation already amounts to a serious breach, which may explain why the Court did not formulate such a requirement explicitly. This could be otherwise, however, in other cases, for instance, where the Member States enjoy some discretion in implementation of the directive and the error in interpretation of the relevant provisions was merely a minor one.

Furthermore, whether the unlawful conduct can (still) be considered as conduct of a Member State is to be examined in the light of the Court's case law on the bodies which are supposed to be bound by a directive.

Secondly, there must be damage. The type of damage is not yet clear.

Thirdly, commentators have noted that the Court does not impose a requirement of fault, i.e. a certain degree of culpability on the part of the tortfeasor. While some scholars have argued that the liability under *Francovich* is a strict liability, according to others it cannot be deduced from the judgment that such a requirement does not apply. According to them, non-implementation of a directive already amounts to a fault. It was therefore not formulated *expressis verbis* by the Court. With respect to other types of breaches, like in the case of incorrect implementation, it is, in my opinion, quite conceivable or even necessary that some form of fault be required.

The specific conditions laid down in *Francovich* are as follows:

Firstly, "the result prescribed by the directive should entail the grant of rights to individuals". This condition raises many questions and is open to different interpretations. The possibility should not be excluded that in a more recent judgment in the *Faccini Dori*[4] case the Court has made an attempt to narrow down considerably this condition by reformulating it as follows: "the purpose of the directive must be to grant rights to individuals".

The second condition is that it should be possible to identify the content of the rights at issue on the basis of the provisions of the directive. Although in this respect the Court has used terminology different from the classical requirements for direct effect, i.e. that the provision must be sufficiently precise and unconditional, there are grounds for believing that the two tests are very close.

Furthermore, in legal writing it has been observed that the identification of the content of the right on the basis of the directive is not sufficient. It must also be possible to identify the potential right-bearers on the basis of the directive.

Thirdly, there must be a causal link between the breach by the Member State and the loss and damage suffered by the injured parties. For the time being it is difficult to say how this test should be fleshed out and how much leeway will be

[4] Case C-91/92 [1994] ECR I-3325.

left to the national courts in the appraisal of the question whether the causal link exists.

The fulfilment of these three conditions is, according to the Court, sufficient to give rise to a right to reparation. For the rest, the action for damages is governed by the provisions of national law. However, the substantive and procedural conditions applicable must not be less favourable than those relating to similar domestic claims and they must not be so framed as to make it virtually impossible or excessively difficult to obtain reparation. While the reference to procedural conditions is understandable, since for the action for damages the national procedure is used as a vehicle, there is less clarity concerning the extent to which the said substantive conditions apply. Since the three *Community law* conditions formulated by the Court are sufficient, it is not very likely that other national conditions may apply over and above these. It could be argued that the Court is referring to conditions which *complete* the above-mentioned three and which are necessary to bring the case to completion.

In Chapter 8 the influence of Community law, in particular the principle of effectiveness and the principle of effective judicial protection, upon the national procedures and remedies was discussed in detail. There is little doubt that the conditions of national law to be applied in the case of non-contractual liability in pursuance of the *Francovich* judgment will also not escape the "grip" of Community law. Matters such as the nature of damage to be compensated, the amount of compensation to be given, the form of redress which must be available, the questions of who should have standing in an action for damages, who can be sued and the limitation periods applicable are therefore inevitably matters which are also to be determined by requirements of Community law. In particular with respect to the limitation periods I have argued that, as follows from the *Emmott*[5] judgment, their non-application as long as the directive concerned has not been (correctly) implemented also holds true for non-contractual liability.

Liability of the State for non-implementation or incorrect implementation of a directive is a "tailpiece mechanism" in the hands of national courts, which are entrusted with the protection of rights which individuals derive from directives. By comparison with consistent interpretation or direct effect, it operates at a different level. While these two latter devices should as far as possible remedy the consequences of non-implementation or incorrect implementation at the level of the applicable norm itself, liability constitutes a "second rank device". To put this in terminology of rights: consistent interpretation and direct effect operate at the level of primary rights, while liability is a sanctioning right. It originates from the breach of a Community law obligation and not from the directive itself. Seen in

[5] Case C-208/90 [1991] ECR I-4269.

this perspective, liability comes into operation only if and in so far as the party concerned cannot safeguard its rights by means of consistent interpretation or direct effect. Whether the doctrine of liability of the State will be able to fill the lacuna due to the inherent limitations of these latter mechanisms remains to be seem. Much will depend on the development of the doctrine by the Court of Justice. The turning taken in *Faccini Dori*[6] does not give rise to much optimism.

[6] Case C-91/92 [1994] ECR I-3325.

14
Drawing the Lines Together

14.1 INTRODUCTION

In the foregoing Chapters a detailed account has been given of the main characteristics of directives, the main problems related to their implementation and the difficulties caused by their non-implementation or incorrect implementation. The role played by the national courts in enforcing directives and, in particular, in giving protection to rights which individuals may derive from directives has also been extensively discussed. Finally, the case law of the Court of Justice on consistent interpretation, direct effect of directives and the liability of the State in cases of breach of Article 189(3) has been analyzed and discussed in depth. An attempt has been made to elucidate the numerous questions which this complex subject raises and to bring together its many facets within one treatise. The main conclusion of the study has been presented in three stages: in Chapter 6, Chapter 9 and Chapter 13.

The purpose of the present Chapter is not simply to rehearse the conclusions once again. It will rather focus on a number of salient issues and, where possible, make connections between them.

14.2 ARTICLE 189(3): REINFORCING THE BINDING FORCE

The Court's case law relating to directives is characterized by, on the one hand, an exertion to maintain the limitations resulting from the definition of directives in Article 189(3), while, on the other hand, it tries to increase the effectiveness of directives and the protection of rights which individuals derive from them. In this process the Court has made a considerable effort to make the most of the binding obligations for the Member States resulting from Article 189(3) and, more concretely, from directives themselves.

Within the doctrine of direct effect it has merged the different types of obligations which a directive may contain for the State: the obligation to implement the directive and the obligations resulting for the Member States from the actual text and particularly from the substantive provisions of the directive. Similarly, it has stretched the concept of "the State" to entities which cannot, in all reasonableness, be held responsible for the failure to implement the directive and to do so correctly.

The doctrine of consistent interpretation has exemplified outstandingly that the binding effect of directives reaches further than the mere obligation of implementation: the obligation to achieve the result envisaged by the directive is binding on all national authorities, including the courts, and not only on those responsible for its implementation.

The consequences of the binding force of the directive were again brought a stage further in *Francovich*[1]: another dimension of the binding obligation is the liability for damages in the case of their non-fulfilment or incorrect fulfilment.

The case law on requirements which adequate transposition of directives must satisfy is marked by a strong emphasis on the binding elements within the definition of a directive. The preponderant concern with the result to be achieved has resulted in curtailing considerably what is left to the Member States: the choice of form and methods. This tendency has been further reinforced by the shift in attention from adequate transposition of directives into national law to their application and enforcement in practice. The requirement that directives are fully effective may entail additional obligations for the Member States which are beyond the actual text of the directive at issue.

14.3 The Pivotal Role of Protection of Rights

Most EC directives aim at the creation of rights and obligations for private individuals. These rights and obligations may exist *vis-à-vis* other individuals or *vis-à-vis* the State authorities. In contrast to what the definition of directives in Article 189(3) may suggest, there is nowadays little doubt that directives are to be considered as Community legislation. However, particularly when compared with regulations, their specific characteristics are that they provide for legislation in two stages: directive provisions lay down the norms which must be given full effect through the intercession of national law. The conception of the directive entails that only after they have undergone this process should the rights and obligations provided for by the directive become fully binding for the individuals within the Member States. Seen in this perspective, directives are indirect sources of rights and obligations for individuals, since the rights and obligations under national law have their origin in the directive.

The process of transforming the directive provisions into national law has proved, however, to be rather cumbersome. Many directives are not implemented in time or correctly (or both), with the consequence of a stalemate situation: although, at least in the philosophy of the Court of Justice, directives are, as any other provision of Community law, an integral part of the legal order of the Member States, the step required to give them full effect has not been taken, or has been wrongly executed.

[1] Joined Cases C-6/90 and C-9/90 [1991] ECR I-5357.

Concerned about both the full effectiveness of the norms laid down in directives and the protection of the rights which a directive may intend to give to individuals, the Court of Justice developed a strategy to break through the impasse as far as possible. It decided that individuals must be able to safeguard the rights they derive from a directive through proceedings brought before a national court, which is entrusted, in accordance with Article 5 of the Treaty, with the protection of Community law rights. The Court enabled the national courts to do this by using three mechanisms: consistent interpretation of national law, direct effect and liability of the State for damage caused by incorrect implementation or non-implementation of the directive concerned.

At this decentralized level of enforcement, the degree of emphasis given by the Court to the protection of rights is striking. Although this protection often goes hand in hand with the wish to ensure full effect of the directive, in so far as full effect would require the enforcement of obligations against individuals, the Court is extremely reticent. Only an indirect way of enforcing obligations would appear to find favour in its eyes: an individual may rely on directly effective provisions of a directive against public authorities even though this ultimately may have negative effects on the legal position of third (private) parties; similarly, consistent interpretation of national law may result in imposing obligations on or, at least, changing the obligations of private individuals. The extent to which such effects are allowed is, however, not entirely clear. A result of this may be that the protection of rights will also suffer, namely in so far as the enforcement of the right of one private individual would involve an obligation imposed directly upon another individual.

At the Community level of enforcement the concern about protection of rights does not come into play in the first stage. This is quite obvious since an action brought by the Commission in an Article 169 proceedings aims at the general and uniform observance of Community law and is, as such, not primarily intended to protect individual rights. However, in the second stage, namely where the Court examines whether a directive has been implemented in a satisfactory fashion, the possibility of effective protection of the rights the directive intends to create for the benefit of individuals serves as an important yardstick: the implementation must be such as to enable the persons concerned to rely on them before national courts.

14.4 The Mechanisms Operating at the Decentralized Level

The procedures in which direct effect and consistent interpretation are deployed and the outcomes to which they lead are governed by the requirements developed by the Court of Justice in the case law relating to effectiveness of national procedures and remedies in general and effective judicial protection in particular. In some cases these requirements follow from the directive concerned itself. In other cases the requirements are the consequence of the general character of this case law, and thus apply irrespective of whether the directive provides so or not. The requirements of effectiveness and effective judicial protection define the environment in which the mechanisms of direct effect and consistent interpretation are deployed. In other words, the requirements apply irrespective of whether the directive is effectuated by means of direct effect or consistent interpretation.

Matters are somewhat different in the case of the liability of the State. This liability itself is an extrapolation of the "effective judicial protection" case law. However, in so far as the Community law based liability has to be effected within the framework of national rules governing liability, the same "environment idea" applies as well.

With respect to the differences in use and effects of the three mechanisms, the following observations can be made.

Firstly, in contrast to consistent interpretation, direct effect and State liability can operate irrespective of the existence of provisions of national law which (should) apply to the case. Consistent interpretation presupposes that there are national provisions to be interpreted.

Secondly, while direct effect is limited to sufficiently precise and unconditional provisions of directives in the sense that the national court has at its disposal judicially manageable standards to decide the case before it, no such limitation exists in respect of consistent interpretation. For the purposes of liability, on the other hand, the ascertainability of the content of the right on the basis of the directive and, as was submitted, also of the identity of the potential beneficiaries, is a (logical) condition to be satisfied. The extent to which this condition differs from the requirements of sufficient degree of precision and unconditionality is not yet entirely clear.

Thirdly, the mechanisms of direct effect and, by its very nature, the liability of the State, can operate only against the State. This is not so in the case of consistent interpretation.

Fourthly, the mechanisms of direct effect and consistent interpretation have the effect of equating the situation for the individual concerned to that which would exist if the directive had been (correctly) implemented: consistent interpretation "modifies" the applicable national provisions; direct effect amounts to replacing the provisions of national law which govern the case but are incompatible with the directive or, when direct effect takes the shape of legal review, it renders the incompatible national provisions inapplicable. State liability, on the other hand, is not a substitute for incorrect implementation or non-implementation. It amounts rather to a cure in a strict sense of the term: the principle of liability has the effect of compensation for damage caused by the Member State.

Fifthly, all three mechanisms have their specific limits. In the case of consistent interpretation the most important limits lie in the principle of legal certainty and, arguably, the judicial function as such. In the case of direct effect the main limits lie in the justiciability of the case, i.e. whether the national court is able, equipped with the directive provisions, to deal with the problem before it, and, as already observed, in the possibility of using the directive solely against the State. The limits of State liability lie in the conditions to be satisfied in order to give rise to a right to damages.

These specific characteristics of the separate mechanisms allow them to operate in a complemetary fashion: one takes over where another leaves off. To a considerable extent they constitute a coherent system which comes into operation as a palliative or remedy wherever a directive has not been implemented or has not been implemeted correctly. How far the remaining lacunas will be filled will depend on the further development of the conditions governing State liability.

An important effect of the development of the separate mechanisms is the weakening of the "monopolistic position" of the doctrine of direct effect. For a long time the orthodox view was that only directly effective provisions can produce effects within the legal orders of the Member States without an intercession of national measures. However, consistent interpretation has shown that there are also other ways of giving effects to unimplemented or incorrectly implemented directives.

Subsequently, the *Francovich*[2] judgment suggested clearly that the breach of a Member State obligation under Article 189(3), irrespective of the direct effect of the provisions at issue, can give rise to damages to be claimed from the State. This was subsequently confirmed in the *Faccini Dori*[3] judgment where the directive at issue was not directly effective, in the sense that one individual could not rely on the relevant provisions against another individual. Nevertheless, the Court found that the party injured could in principle claim damages from the State which had not transposed the directive in due time. In particular these recent developments raise some intriguing questions as to the relationship of direct effect and the creation of rights.

[2] Joined Cases C-6/90 and C-9/90 [1991] ECR I-5357.
[3] Case C-91/92 [1994] ECR I-3325.

14.5 Once More: Direct Effect, Creation of Rights and their Protection in National Courts

At several points in this book I have stressed that direct effect and creation of (substantive)[4] rights must be distinguished. Direct effect relates to the quality ascribed to the provision in question, i.e. to be invoked by the persons concerned for different purposes and to be applied by the national courts. The creation of rights is a matter of its content. Upholding the distinction is especially important in two respects: equating them does not do justice to the concept of direct effect, which is broader than the creation of rights. On the other hand, it is a misconception to argue that only directly effective provisions can create rights. Often direct effect and creation of rights will coincide. This is however not necessarily always the case.

All this having been said, upon further consideration it must be observed that the two issues are closely linked. Firstly, in order to be able to say that a provision creates rights, it is necessary that its content is ascertainable. In *Francovich*[5] the Court in fact formulated this requirement by stating that it should be possible to identify the content of the right at issue on the basis of the provisions of the directive. This requirement corresponds closely with the conditions of sufficient degree of precision and unconditionality applied for the purposes of direct effect. The same is arguably true for establishing the beneficiaries of the rights.

Secondly, a crucial requirement in relation to rights is, as stated above in Section 14.1, that they are offered effective judicial protection. Part and parcel of direct effect is the obligation of the national courts to apply the relevant provisions satisfying the conditions of direct effect. This indeed amounts to giving protection to the rights at issue wherever direct effect and creation of rights coincide. However, where the mechanism of direct effect fails for some reason, the courts are nevertheless required to protect the rights in question by other means.

The main reason until now for direct effect and creation of rights not coinciding is that the addressees of the relevant substantive provisions of the directive, i.e. the persons on which the provision intends to impose obligations, are either not sufficiently determined in the directive itself or they are private individuals which, in pursuance of the limitations of the definition of the directive in Article 189(3), cannot be obliged on the basis of the directive alone. Wherever it is not possible to merge the obligations laid down in the substantive provisions of the directive and the obligation for the Member State to implement it with,

[4] As opposed to the "procedural" right to rely on the directive.

[5] Joined Cases C-6/90 and C-9/90 [1991] ECR I-5357.

as a result, a sort of curtailed right, i.e. a right which is as such not enforceable, the mechanisms of consistent interpretation or liability become important as means of safeguarding the protection of the rights the directive intends to create.

Apart from the relevance of the question of (intended) creation of rights in the context of protection to be given wherever the directive has not been implemented in due time or has not been implemented correctly, the issue of rights also plays a part in the context of criteria applicable with respect to the implementation of directives. Wherever a directive intends to create rights, the Court requires implementation such that the legal position of the individuals concerned is sufficiently precise and clear to enable them to ascertain fully the extent of their rights and, where appropriate, to rely on them before a court. Yet the grounds on which the Court decides that the directive intends to create rights are, with all respect, quite confusing. More in general, it may be asked whether the Court could simply be describing various legal positions in terms of rights in order to indicate that this position must be protected in law.

As long as direct effect was the central doctrine of Community law in relation to the protection of the position of the individual, there was perhaps no need to address questions as to the circumstances under which there is a right in Community law and the characteristics of this right. However, once "rights" start to play another role, namely denoting something distinct from direct effect, it is submitted that the Court will be forced in the course of time to develop certain parameters giving sufficient guidance as to the conditions under which a certain provision of Community law should be considered as conferring rights or as being intended to do so.

14.6 CENTRAL AND DECENTRALIZED LEVEL OF ENFORCEMENT: AN INTERACTION

As mentioned above, the Community level of enforcement focusses on the general and uniform observance of Community law rather than protection of rights or of the legal position of the individuals in general. In the past the Court has divorced the two levels of enforcement and found that no parallel may be drawn between them.[6] However, the Court merely wished to separate the two types of procedures. In fact there is interaction between the two levels.

The case law developed at the central level contains several elements which are also relevant within the context of decentralized enforcement and *vice versa*. Some of these can be mentioned briefly.

[6] Case 28/67 *Molkerei-Zentrale* [1968] ECR 211.

The first element, the (intended) creation of rights and the modalities of implementation resulting therefrom, was already touched upon in the previous Section. It seems logical that if the Court finds in an Article 169 proceedings that the unimplemented directive at issue aims at creating rights for the benefit of individuals, this finding will also hold true for the purposes of State liability.

Secondly, a good example of drawing consequences from the case law developed in infringement proceedings for the decentralized level can be found in the *Emmott*[7] judgment: the requirement that individuals must be able to become acquainted with the full extent of their rights from national measures transposing adequately the directive and the fact that direct effect does not release the Member State from its obligation of implementation resulted at the decentralized level in a prohibition of reliance on national time limits, in order to bar the initiation of proceedings by the individual concerned.

Thirdly, a judgment of the Court under Article 169 declaring that the Member State has not fulfilled its obligations resulting from Article 189(3) will be an important – although not necessary – indication that the Member State is in breach of this Article and the national court may be required to continue the examination in order to establish whether the State should be held liable in damages. In so far as a case of non-implementation is at issue, matters are quite straightforward. However, where the individual argues that the directive has not been implemented correctly, the national court should undertake an examination in this respect. Arguably, the criteria applied by the Court of Justice for this purpose will have to be applied by the national court as well.

Fourthly, the Court's case law on full effectiveness of directives, involving the requirement of an appropriate system for enforcement of the measures transposing the directive, which was developed mainly in the context of preliminary proceedings is, of course, also of importance in Article 169 proceedings where the adequate implementation of the directive is addressed.

On the other hand, judgments given by the Court in the framework of decentralized enforcement or in infringement proceedings do not necessarily always have consequences on the other level. An objective finding that the Member State has not implemented the directive (correctly) should not be transposed as a matter of course, as I have contended, to the level of decentralized enforcement. Due account must be taken of the nature of Article 169 proceedings which are in principle not concerned with the question of fault or the existence of grounds of justification on the part of the Member States.

Similarly, a finding of the Court that the directive is directly effective or the possibility that the national court can remedy inadequate implementation or non-implementation by means of consistent interpretation does not release the

[7] Case C-208/90 [1991] ECR I-4269.

Member State from its obligation of (correct) implementation. These are also not accepted as valid arguments of defence in infringement proceedings.

As has been noted, there exists some ambiguity with respect to consistent interpretation on the one hand and correct implementation, satisfying the requirements of precision and clarity in particular, on the other. According to the Court the question whether a directive has been implemented correctly has to be considered in the light of the interpretation and application of the implementing measures by the national courts. When the courts are under the obligation to interpret national (transposition) measures in conformity with the directive and they do so by giving the relevant provisions a somewhat strained meaning in order to meet their obligation, can it still be maintained that the directive has been implemented correctly? Differently expressed, there is a certain tension between the requirement of clear and precise implementation and the way in which the fulfilment of these requirements is assessed: this assessment takes into account the interpretation by the national courts while, at the same time, interpretation presupposes a certain degree of flexibility of the terms and must in any case be performed in conformity with the directive.

A final point to be addressed briefly relates to two lines in the case law which are, in my opinion, difficult to reconcile. According to the Court the finding in infringement proceedings that a Member State has failed to fulfil its obligations under Community law entails for both judicial and administrative authorities a prohibition having the full force of law against applying the national measures incompatible with Community law, as well as the obligation to take all appropriate measures to enable Community law to be fully applied.[8] This is the effect of the authority attaching to the judgment under Article 169. If this type of prohibitions and obligations is transposed to the national level of enforcement, in many cases the disapplication of contrary national rules may indeed suffice to decide the case in accordance with Community law. However, in other cases the disapplication will result in a lacuna: it may be that there are then no applicable rules at all if the relevant provisions of Community law lack the direct effect for this purpose and if there is also no possibility of filling the gap by means of consistent interpretation. Basically, the Court's approach poses the same problem as in the case of direct effect in the form of legal review: in some cases such a review will bring the relief required, depending on the particular context. In other cases, however, it will not suffice, as it may be necessary for the court to apply the provisions of the directive to the facts of the case. Furthermore, disapplication of national provisions may under certain circumstances result in imposing an obligation upon individuals, which has been however, with respect to directives, disallowed by the Court.

[8] Cf. Case C-101/91 *Commission v. Italy* [1993] ECR I-191.

The point is that when the problem of compatibility is raised at national level, the question as to the direct effect of the relevant provisions will be raised as well. However, no such question is under consideration in infringement proceedings. The Court merely examines whether the Member State has complied with its obligations resulting from a directive and may find that it has not. Moreover, the national court may still try, and is even so obliged by the Court, to interpret the national rules at issue in conformity with the directive and palliate temporarily the Member State's failure. In my view, therefore, these effects of a judgment under Article 169, as formulated by the Court of Justice, cannot in all circumstances be taken to their ultimate consequences, i.e. the absolute prohibition of applying provisions of national law which are incompatible with Community law.

In summary, if one is interested in the effects which directives may produce in the national legal orders and, in particular, in national courts, it is not sufficient to restrict attention to the case law on direct effect of directives, consistent interpretation and related matters. The case law relating to implementation of directives also contains several important elements.

14.7 JURISPRUDENTIAL EVERGREENS

Throughout this book a number of constantly recurring themes have appeared in different contexts. Apart from the full effectiveness of Community law and the requirement of judicial protection, which have already been rehearsed in this Chapter, the most striking are the principle of legal certainty, the incursion into the institutional autonomy of the Member States and the existence of discretion.

The paramount role played by the principle of legal certainty (in its various forms) in the Community legal system and, in particular, in the area of the different problems related to directives, is exemplified by the very broad scope of its application.

Although on the one hand Community law seems to require that a directive which has not been correctly implemented or a directive which has not been implemented in due time should be implemented by means of retroactive legislation, the admissibility of this legislation has its limits in the principle of legal certainty. Legal certainty is similarly one of the guiding principles underlying the requirements applied by the Court with respect to proper implementation of directives. Legal certainty also justifies the application of national time limits in some cases, while another case, where two different modalities of the principle competed with each other, was decided in a contrary sense.[9] In the context of consistent interpretation, legal certainty functions as a limit or, upon further

[9] Cf. Case C-208/90 *Emmott* [1991] ECR I-4269.

consideration, as a priority-rule used in order to resolve conflicts between different arguments favouring different interpretations. The principle can equally limit, in exceptional circumstances, direct effect of Community law and, furthermore, it was argued that legal certainty is one of the major concerns militating against horizontal direct effect of directives.

One of the major uncertainties relating to the principle of legal certainty is that it is not always clear whether the principle to be applied is the Community law principle or whether it is the national principle in its – what I have called – "curtailed form".

Another principle ostensibly maintained by the Court of Justice is the principle of institutional autonomy: it is a matter for the Member States to decide which bodies will be entrusted with the fulfilment of obligations resulting from Community law, including directives, and to give them the necessary powers for this purpose. The same also holds true for the courts: it is for the Member States to decide which court will have jurisdiction in matters involving Community law and to invest it with the necessary powers enabling it to provide effective judicial protection.

The central question remains: how much is left of this professed non-interference with the institutional structure of the Member States when it is considered in the light of recent developments?

Community law requirements relating to the nature of implementing measures also determine the body which has to implement the directive concerned. In order to compel national authorities, which are competent *ratione materiae* but independent from the central government, the Member States seem to be required to provide for a mechanism safeguarding that the authorities satisfy the obligations resulting from a directive. According to the Court *all* national authorities are bound by the obligation to achieve the result prescribed by a directive, not merely the legislature, which is primarily responsible for the implementation. Particularly for administrative authorities, this binding force entails that they are, where necessary, obliged to apply directly effective provisions of a directive and disapply national measures incompatible with it. This indeed amounts to a blow to the traditional subordination of the executive to the legislature. It may grant them powers they do not have as a matter of national law and, in such a case, it does not make the disapplication of national provisions dependent upon a decision of a court. This is the more remarkable if one takes into consideration the Court's case law according to which a Community measure must be held to be valid and applied accordingly as long as it has not been declared invalid by the Court. Apparently, the same standards do not apply at national level.

As regards the principle of institutional autonomy with respect to national courts, it would appear that the case law results in creation of autonomy for the courts instead of respecting the principle. While the norms to be enforced by the courts originate in a source other than the rules governing their enforcement, the articulation between the two is not always perfectly organized. Partly for this reason, and partly because the Community standards of judicial protection differ from the national standards, the Court of Justice poses certain requirements as to the quality of judicial enforcement which must be available, with the ultimate consequence of requiring national courts to do something they are not necessarily empowered to do as a matter of national law. This process brings about a change as to the place of the courts within the institutional structure of the State.

In fact, this change initially became visible in the wake of the doctrine of direct effect: national courts were required to disapply national law or to review it in the light of Community law and, where appropriate, to apply norms stemming, from a constitutional perspective, from an external source. What else does this amount to than changing the subordination of the judiciary to the legislature which was, in different degrees, the common model in many Member States? The tendency did not, however, stop at this point. Firstly, in particular the type of relief to be made available in order to safeguard effective judicial protection, culminating in the liability of the State for breaches of Community law, results in shifting the institutional balance existing in many Member States. Secondly, the same can be said of the ultimate effects of consistent interpretation: while under national law a court may refrain from giving the relevant provisions a certain meaning since it believes it is reaching the limits of its judicial function, Community law seems to require that these limits are pushed a stage further. In other words, the separation of powers as a priority-rule undergoes a modification.

The Court's case law is in both respects somewhat ambiguous. By referring, for instance, to the jurisdiction of national courts and thereby suggesting that they are still acting within their competence, the Court is concealing the real scope of its case law, while, for the time being, a solid basis is lacking. The latter is, however, perhaps symptomatic of any transitional stage.

Finally, the existence of discretion in the sense of latitude on the part of the Member States to act according to their own judgment, leaving them a certain degree of choice as to what they will do, appeared in several contexts as a crucial factor.

Although the Member States enjoy no freedom as to the question whether they will implement the directive, from its very definition given in Article 189(3) it follows that a directive as a whole must leave them some latitude with respect to the form and methods of implementation. However, this has not prevented directives from being very detailed, and neither has it prevented the Court of Justice from increasingly curtailing the freedom left to the Member States as regards implementation.

Similarly, the exercise of discretion given to Member States by a particular provision of a directive may be subjected to the supervision of a Community institution and, in the case of absence of such special supervision, there is always the possibility of control by the Court of Justice.

The existence of discretion is also highly relevant when addressing the question whether a provision gives rise to rights: existence of broad discretionary powers will not allow ascertainment of the content of the right. In different and oversimplified terms: discretion can be contrasted with duties; the latter in principle allow no choice as to what the duty-bearer has to do. Now, since rights are conceived as correlatives of a duty, where there is no duty there can be no right. This is also the quintessence of the requirement laid down in *Francovich*,[10] namely that the content of the rights must be identifiable on the basis of the provisions of the directive. Existence of (too much) discretion will make such an identification impossible. Since the Court found the provisions relating to the content of the right sufficiently precise and unconditional, in that case the right was therefore identifiable.

The step to direct effect seems then merely a matter of course: existence of (too much) discretion will also amount to denying direct effect. As has been observed, the absence of discretion is considered to be the basic condition for direct effect. However, it has equally been explained that, depending on the purposes for which the Community norm is deployed, existence of discretion does not necessarily block direct effect: the national court may be called upon to control whether the Member State or the national authority, as the case may be, has remained within the limits of the discretion which is left. Wherever the court is able to perform such a control using the directive as a standard for review, the directive has direct effect.

One may take the reasoning a stage further: if the Court of Justice is able to examine in infringement proceedings whether a Member State, in the exercise of its discretion as regards implementation, has remainded within the limits of the directive, without a problem of direct effect being raised, there are no fundamental reasons why a national court could not do the same. The characteristics which the two courts have in common is that they are courts of law.

Seen in this perspective, some control of the exercise of discretion, irrespective of how broad the latter may be, should always be possible. Today it is generally accepted that in a state governed by the rule of law no discretion is unfettered, and it should therefore be subjected to some degree of judicial control. That is, however, not exclusively a Community evergreen.[11]

[10] Joined Cases C-6/90 and C-9/90 [1991] ECR I-5357.

[11] Cf. Timmermans 1973, in particular p. 175-184.

Bibliographical References

Abraham 1989 – Abraham, *Droit international, droit communautaire et droit français*, Hachette, Paris 1989.

Adinolfi 1988 – Adinolfi, The Implementation of Social Policy Directives through Collective Agreements?, CMLRev. 1988, p. 291.

Alexy 1985 – Alexy, *Theorie der Grundrechte*, Nomos, Baden-Baden 1985.

Arnull 1988 – Arnull, Having your Cake and Eating it Ruled Out, ELR 1988, p. 42.

Arts 1993 – Arts, Het Francovich arrest en zijn toepassing in de Belgische rechtsorde, TBP 1993, p. 495.

Bach 1990 – Bach, Direkte Wirkungen von EG-Richtlinien, JZ 1990, p. 1108.

Barav 1975 – Barav, Failure of Member States to Fulfil Their Obligations under Community Law, CMLRev. 1975, p. 369.

Barav 1988 – Barav, Damages in the Domestic Courts for Breach of Community Law by National Public Authorities, in Schermers, Heukels, Mead (eds), *Non-Contractual Liability of the European Communities*, Nijhoff, Dordrecht 1988.

Barav 1989 – Barav, Enforcement of Community Rights in the National Courts: the Case for Jurisdiction to Grant Interim Relief, CMLRev. 1989, p. 369.

Barav 1991 – Barav, La plénitude de compétence du juge national en sa qualité de juge communautaire, in *L'Europe et le droit. Mélanges en hommage à Jean Boulouis*, Dalloz, Paris 1991.

Barav 1994 – Barav, Omnipotent Courts, in Curtin and Heukels (eds), *The Institutional Dynamics of European Integration. Liber Amicorum Henry G. Schermers*, Nijhoff, Dordrecht 1994.

Barents 1982 – Barents, Some Remarks on the "Horizontal" Effect of Directives, in O'Keeffe and Schermers (eds), *Essays in European Law and Integration*, Kluwer, Deventer 1982.

Barents 1994 – Barents, The Quality of Community Legislation, MJ 1994, p. 101.

Bates 1986 – Bates, The Impact of Directives on Statutory Interpretation: Using the Euro-meaning?, Statute Law Review 1986, p. 174.

Bebr 1981 – Bebr, *Development of Judicial Control of the European Communities*, Nijhoff, The Hague 1981.

Bebr 1992 – Bebr, Comment on Joined Cases C-6/90 and C-9/90 *Francovich*, CMLRev. 1992, p. 557.

Bell and Engle 1987 – Bell and Engle, *Cross Statutory Interpretation*, Second Edition, Butterworths, London 1987.

Bengoetxea 1990 – Bengoetxea, *The Justification of Decisions by the European Court of Justice*, Clarendon Press, Oxford 1990.

Bergamin 1991 – Bergamin, Publieke subjectieve rechten, in Holtermann (ed), *Algemene begrippen staatsrecht*, Third edition, Tjeenk Willink, Zwolle 1991.

Betlem 1993 – Betlem, *Civil Liability for Transfrontier Pollution*, Graham & Trotman, Nijhoff, London, Dordrecht 1993.

Betlem and Rood 1992 – Betlem and Rood, Francovich-aansprakelijkheid. Schadevergoeding wegens schending van het gemeenschapsrecht, NJB 1992, p. 250.

Beyerlin 1987 – Beyerlin, Umsetzung von EG-Richtlinien durch Verwaltungsvorschriften?, EuR 1987, p. 126.

Bijl 1986 – Bijl, Directe werking van EG-richtlijnen inzake omzetbelasting ten nadele van de burger?, WFR 1986, p. 285.

Bleckmann 1976 – Bleckmann, Art. 5 EWG-Vertrag und die Gemeinschaftstreue, DVBl. 1976, p. 483.

Bleckmann 1978 – Bleckmann, L'applicabilité directe du droit communautaire, in *Les recours des individus devant les instances nationales en cas de violation du droit européen*, Larcier, Bruxelles 1978.

Bleckmann 1984 – Bleckmann, Zur unmittelbaren Anwendbarkeit der EG-Richtlinien, RIW 1984, p. 774.

Bleckmann 1990 – Bleckmann, *Europarecht*, Carl Heymann, Köln 1990.

Bleckmann 1992 – Bleckmann, Probleme der Auslegung europäischer Richtlinien, ZGR 1992, p. 363.

Boch and Lane 1992 – Boch and Lane, European Community Law in National Courts: a Continuing Contradiction, LJIL 1992, p. 171.

De Boer 1985a – De Boer, Procederen wegens discriminatie, in *Staatkundig Jaarboek 1985*, Kobra, Amsterdam.

De Boer 1985b – De Boer, Omgangsrecht, omgaan met het EVRM, de HR gaat om, NJCM-Bulletin 1985, p. 211.

Bok 1992 – Bok, *Rechtsbescherming in Frankrijk en Duitsland*, Kluwer, Deventer 1992.

Bok 1993 – Bok, Het Francovich arrest en onrechtmatige wetgeving naar Nederlands recht, TPR 1993, p. 37.

Bonnes and Stoop 1991- Bonnes and Stoop, "Commentaar vanuit Brussel" en discussie, RegelMaat 1991, p. 57.

Boulouis 1975 – Boulouis, Sur une catégorie nouvelle d'actes juridiques: les "directives", in *Recueil d'études en hommage à Charles Eisenmann*, Cujas, Paris 1975.

Boulouis 1979 – Boulouis, L'applicabilité directe des directives. A propos d'un arrêt Cohn-Bendit du Conseil d'Etat, RMC 1979, p. 107.

Boulouis 1990 – Boulouis, *Le droit institutionnel des Communautés Européennes*, Second Edition, Montchrestien, Paris 1990.

Bridge 1984 – Bridge, Procedural Aspects of the Enforcement of European Community Law through the Legal System of the Member States, ELR 1984, p. 28.

Brown and Jacobs 1989 – Brown and Jacobs, *The Court of Justice of the European Communities*, Third Edition, Sweet & Maxwell, London 1989.

De Burca 1992 – De Burca, Giving Effect to European Community Directives, MLR 1992, p. 215.

Cane 1989 – Cane, *Administrative Law*, Clarendon Press, Oxford 1989.

Capotorti 1988 – Capotorti, Legal Problems of Directives, Regulations and their Implementation, in Siedentopf and Ziller (eds), *Making the European Policies Work: the Implementation of Community Legislation in the Member States*, (IEPA), Sage, London 1988.

Caranta 1993 – Caranta, Governmental Liability after Francovich, CLJ 1993, p. 272.

Classen 1993 – Classen, Zur Bedeutung von EWG-Richtlinien für Privatpersonen, EuZW 1993, p. 83.

Constantinesco 1977 – Constantinesco, *Das Recht der Europäischen Gemeinschaften*, Nomos, Baden-Baden 1977.

Constantinesco 1985 – Constantinesco, Division of Fields of Competence between the Union and the Member States in the Draft Treaty Establishing the European Union, in Bieber, Jacqué, Weiler (eds), *An Ever Closer Union*, Office for Official Publications of the EC, Luxemburg 1985.

Coppel 1993 – Coppel, *Individual Enforcement of Community Law: The Future of the Francovich Remedy*, EUI Working Paper No. 93/6, Badia Fiesolana 1993.

Craig 1993 – Craig, Francovich, Remedies and the Scope of Damage Liability, LQR 1993, p. 595.

Curtin 1990a – Curtin, The Province of Government: Delimiting the Direct Effect of Directives in the Common Law Context, ELR 1990, p. 195.

Curtin 1990b – Curtin, Directives: the Effectiveness of Judicial Protection of Individual Rights, CMLRev. 1990, p. 709.

Curtin 1992 – Curtin, The Decentralised Enforcement of Community Law Rights. Judicial Snakes and Ladders, in Curtin and O'Keeffe (eds), *Constitutional Adjudication in European Community and National Law*, Butterworth, Dublin 1992.

Curtin 1993 – Curtin, The Constitutional Structure of the Union: a Europe of Bits and Pieces, CMLRev. p. 17.

Curtin 1994 – Curtin, Comment on Case C-271/91 *Marshall*, CMLRev. 1994, p. 631.

Curtin and Mortelmans 1994 – Curtin and Mortelmans, Application and Enforcement of Community Law by the Member States: Actors in Search of a Third Generation Script, in Curtin and Heukels (eds), *The Institutional*

Dynamics of European Integration. Liber Amicorum Henry G. Schermers, Nijhoff, Dordrecht 1994.

Daig and Smidt 1991 – Daig and Smidt, Gemeinsame Vorschriften für mehrere Organe, in Von der Groeben, Thiesing, Ehlerman, *Kommentar zum EWG-Vertrag*, Fourth Edition, Vol. IV, Nomos, Baden-Baden 1991.

Dal Farra 1992 – Dal Farra, Les fondements de l'invocabilité de la directive devant le juge national: le malentendu conceptuel, RTDE 1992, p. 634.

Dänzer-Vanotti 1991 – Dänzer-Vanotti, Die Richtlinienkonforme Auslegung deutschen Rechts hat keinen rechtlichen Vorrang, RIW 1991, p. 754

Dänzer-Vanotti 1992 – Dänzer-Vanotti, Unzulässige Rechtsfortbildung des Europäischen Gerichtshof, RIW 1992, p. 733.

Dashwood 1978 – Dashwood, The Principle of Direct Effect in European Community Law, JCMS 1978, p. 229.

David 1984 – David, Sources of Law, *International Encyclopedia of Comparative Law* (II-3), Mohr, Nijhoff, Tübingen, The Hague 1984.

Dekker 1991 – Dekker, Diagonale werking van Europese richtlijnen?, SEW 1991, p. 782.

Devloo 1993 – Devloo, Richtlijnconforme interpretatie: een bron van recht?, RW 1993-1994, p. 377.

Dommering-van Rongen 1991 – Dommering-van Rongen, *Produktenaansprakelijkheid*, Kluwer, Deventer 1991.

Droit Communautaire et Droit National – *Droit Communautaire et Droit National*, Semaine de Bruges 1965, Collège d'Europe, Bruges 1965.

Dubouis 1988 – Dubouis, A propos de deux principes généraux du droit communautaire, RFDA 1988, p. 691.

Dubouis 1992 – Dubouis, La responsabilité de l'Etat pour les dommages causés aux particuliers par la violation du droit communautaire, RFDA 1992, p. 1.

Due 1992 – Due, Artikel 5 van het EEG-Verdrag. Een bepaling met een federaal karakter?, SEW 1992, p. 355.

Duffy 1992 – Duffy, Damages against the State: a New Remedy for Failure to Implement Community Obligations, ELR 1992, p. 133.

Durand 1987 – Durand, Enforceable Community Rights and National Remedies, The Denning Law Journal 1987, p. 43.

Easson 1979a – Easson, The "Direct Effect" of EEC Directives, ICLQ 1979, p. 319.

Easson 1979b – Easson, Can Directives Impose Obligations on Individuals?, ELR 1979, p. 67.

Easson 1981 – Easson, EEC Directives for the Harmonization of Laws: Some Problems of Validity, Implementation and Legal Effects, YEL 1981, p. 1.

Ehlermann 1987 – Ehlermann, Ein Pläydoyer für die dezentrale Kontrolle der Anwendung des Gemeinschaftsrechts durch die Mitgliedstaaten, in: Capotorti, Ehlermann et al. (eds), *Du droit international au droit de l'intégration. Liber Amicorum Pierre Pescatore*, Nomos, Baden-Baden 1987.

Emmert 1992 – Emmert, Horizontale Drittwirkung von Richtlinien?, EWS 1992, p. 56.

Emmert and Pereira de Avezedo 1993 – Emmert and Pereira de Avezedo, L'effet horizontal des directives. La jurisprudence de la CJCE: un bateau ivre?, RTDE 1993, p. 503.

Everling 1984 – Everling, Zur direkten innerstaatlichen Wirkung der EG-Richtlinien: Ein Beispiel richterlicher Rechtsfortbildung auf der Basis gemeinsamer Rechtsgrundsätze, in Börner et al. (eds), *Einigkeit und Recht und Freiheit. Festschrift für Karl Carstens*, Carl Heymann, Köln 1984.

Everling 1989 – Everling, Zur Funktion des Gerichtshofs bei der Rechtsangleichung in der Europäischen Gemeinschaft, in Lessman (ed), *Festschrift fur Rudolf Lukes*, Carl Heymann, Köln 1989.

Everling 1992a – Everling, Umsetzung von Umweltrichtlinien durch normkonkretisierende Verwaltungsanweisungen, RIW 1992, p. 379.

Everling 1992b – Everling, Zur Auslegung des durch EG-Richtlinien angeglichenen nationalen Rechts, ZGR 1992, p. 376.

Everling 1993 – Everling, Durchführung und Umsetzung des Europäischen Gemeinschaftsrechts im Bereich des Umweltschutzes unter Berücksichtigung der Rechtsprechung des EuGH, NVwZ 1993, p. 209.

Di Fabio 1990 – Di Fabio, Richtlinienkonformität als ranghöchstes Normauslegungsprinzip?, NJW 1990, p. 947.

Fide reports 1980 – *Remedies for Breach of Community Law*, Fide, Ninth Congress, London 1980.

Fide Reports 1992 – *La sanction des infractions au droit communautaire*, Fide, Fifteenth Congress, Lisbonne 1992.

Fischer 1991 – Fischer, Sind Vertragswidrig nicht umgesetzte Richtlinien innerstaatlich nur auf Antrag anwendbar?, EuZW 1991, p. 557.

Fischer 1992a – Fischer, Staatshaftung nach Gemeinschaftsrecht, EuZW 1992, p. 41.

Fischer 1992b – Fischer, Zur unmittelbaren Anwendung von EG-Richtlinien in der öffentlichen Verwaltung, NVwZ 1992, p. 635.

Fitzpatrick and Szyszczak 1994b – Fitzpatrick and Szyszczak, Remedies and Effective Judicial Protection in Community Law, MLR 1994, p. 434.

Frowein 1986 – Frowein, Randbemerkungen zu den Grenzen des Richterrechts in rechtsvergleichender Betrachtung, in Reinhart (ed), *Richterliche Rechtsfortbildung*, Müller, Heidelberg 1986.

Fuß 1965 – Fuß, Die Richtlinie des europäischen Gemeinschaftsrechts, DVBl. 1965, p. 378.

Fuß 1981 – Fuß, Die Verantwortung der nationalen Gerichte für die Wahrung des europäischen Gemeinschaftsrechts, in Bieber, Bleckmann, Capotorti et al. (eds), *Das Europa der zweiten Generation (I). Gedächtnisschrift für Christoph Sasse*, Nomos, Baden-Baden 1981.

Gaja, Hay and Rotunda 1986 – Gaja, Hay and Rotunda, Instruments for Legal Integration in the European Community, in Cappelletti, Seccombe and Weiler, *Integration Through Law*, Vol. 1: Methods, Tools and Institutions, Book 2, De Gruyter, Berlin/New York 1986.

Galmot 1990 – Galmot, Directives et règlements en droit communautaire, CJEG 1990, p. 73.

Galmot and Bonichot 1988 – Galmot and Bonichot, La Cour de Justice des Communautés européennes et la transposition des directives en droit national, RFDA 1988, p. 1.

Geddes 1992 – Geddes, Locus Standi and EEC Environmental Measures, Journal of Environmental Law 1992, p. 29.

Geiger 1993 – Geiger, Die Entwicklung eines Europäisches Staatshaftungsrechts, DVBl 1993, p. 465

Van Gerven 1993 – Van Gerven, Bescherming van individuele rechten op basis van normatieve aansprakelijkheid in het Europese Gemeenschapsrecht, TPR 1993, p. 6.

Van Gerven 1994a – Van Gerven, Non-Contractual Liability of Member States, Community Institutions and Individuals for Breaches of Community Law with a View to a Common Law of Europe, MJ 1994, p. 6.

Van Gerven 1994b – Van Gerven, The Horizontal Direct Effect of Directive Provisions Revisited: The Reality of Catchwords, in Curtin and Heukels (eds), *The Institutional Dynamics of European Integration. Liber Amicorum Henry G. Schermers*, Nijhoff, Dordrecht 1994.

Gilliams 1990-1991 – Gilliams, Het Hof van Justitie en de gelijke behandeling van man en vrouw 1988-1990, RW 1990-1991, p. 1355

Gilliams 1991-1992 – Gilliams, Overheidsaansprakelijkheid bij schending van Europees recht, RW 1991-1992, p. 877.

Gilsdorf 1966 – Gilsdorf, Rechtlicher Mittel zur Umsetzung von Gemeinschaftsrecht in nationales Recht durch Legislative und Executive der Mittgliedstaaten, EuR 1966, p. 162.

Götz 1992 – Götz, Europäische Gesetzgebung durch Richtlinien – Zusammenwirken von Gemeinschaft und Staat, NJW 1992, p. 1849.

Grabitz 1971 – Grabitz, Entscheidungen und Richtlinien als unmittelbar Wirksames Gemeinschaftsrecht, EuR 1971, p. 1.

STAFFS UNIVERSITY LIBRARY

Grabitz 1988 – Grabitz, Liability for Legislative Acts, in Schermers, Heukels, Mead (eds), *Non-Contractual Liability of the European Communities*, Nijhoff, Dordrecht 1988.

Grabitz Kommentar – Grabitz, *Kommentar zum EWG-Vertrag*, Gemeinsame Vorschriften fur mehrere Organe, Beck'sche Verlagsbuchhandlung, München (loose-leaf, version 1992).

Grabitz 1993 – Grabitz, Die Wirkungsweise von Richtlinien, in Everling (ed), *Europarecht, Kartellrecht, Wirtschaftsrecht: Festschrift für Arved Deringer*, Nomos, Baden-Baden 1993.

Green 1984a – Green, The Treaty of Rome, National Courts and English Common Law, RabelsZ 1984, p. 509.

Green 1984b – Green, Directives, Equity and the Protection of Individual Rights, ELR 1984, p. 295.

Grévisse and Bonichot 1991 – Grévisse and Bonichot, Les incidences du droit communautaire sur l'organisation et l'exercice de la fonction juridictionelle dans les Etats Membres, in *L'Europe et le droit. Mélanges en hommage à Jean Boulouis*, Dalloz, Paris 1991.

Haneklaus 1993 – Haneklaus, Direktwirkung von EG-Richtlinien zu Lasten einzelner?, DVBl 1993, p. 129.

Hartley 1981 – Hartley, *The Foundations of European Community Law*, Clarendon Press, Oxford 1981.

Hartley 1994 – Hartley, *The Foundations of European Community Law*, Third Edition, Clarendon Press, Oxford 1994.

Hecquard-Theron 1990 – Hecquard-Theron, La notion d'Etat en droit communautaire, RTDE 1990, p. 693.

Herbert 1993 – Herbert, L'accès au juge: qui peut agir?, in Verwilghen (ed), *Access to Equality between Men and Women in the European Community*, Presses Universitaires de Louvain, Louvain-la-Neuve 1993.

Hessel and Mortelmans 1993 – Hessel and Mortelmans, Decentralized Government and Community Law: Conflicting Institutional Developments?, CMLRev. 1993, p. 905.

Heukels 1988 – Heukels, The Prescription of an Action for Damages under Article 215(2) EEC, in Schermers, Heukels, Mead (eds), *Non-Contractual Liability of the European Communities*, Nijhoff, Dordrecht 1988.

Heukels 1991 – Heukels, *Intertemporales Gemeinschaftsrecht*, Nomos, Baden-Baden 1991.

Heukels 1993 – Heukels, Alternatieve implementatietechnieken en art. 189 lid 3 EEG: grondslagen en ontwikkelingen, NTB 1993, p. 59.

Hilf 1988 – Hilf, Der Justizkonflikt um EG-Richtlinien: gelöst, EuR 1988, p. 1.

Hilf 1993 – Hilf, Die Richtlinie der EG – ohne Richtung, ohne Linie?, EuR 1993, p. 1.

Holtmaat 1992 – Holtmaat, *Met zorg een recht?*, Tjeenk Willink, Zwolle 1992.

Huglo 1993 – Huglo, La responsabilité de l'Etat pour la violation de ses obligations communautaires: l'arrêt Francovich du 19 novembre 1991, in Pappas (ed), *Tendances actuelles et évolution de la jurisprudence de la Cour de Justice des Communautés européennes*, Vol. I, EIPA, Maastricht 1993.

Ipsen 1965 – Ipsen, Richtlinien-Ergebnisse, in Hallstein and Schlochauer (eds), *Zur Integration Europas. Feschrift für Carl Friedrich Ophüls*, Müller, Karlsruhe 1965.

Ipsen 1972 – Ipsen, *Europäisches Gemeinschaftsrecht*, Mohr, Tübingen 1972.

Isaac 1992 – Isaac, Effet direct du droit communautaire, in *Répertoire Dalloz de Droit Communautaire*, Dalloz, Paris 1992.

Jacobs 1993 – Jacobs, Remedies in National Courts for the Enforcement of Community Rights, in Perez Gonzalez et al. (eds), *Hacia un nuevo orden internacional y europeo. Estudios en homenaje al profesor Don Manuel Díez de Velasco*, Tecnos, Madrid 1993.

Jacqué 1985 – Jacqué, The Draft Treaty Establishing the European Union, CMLRev. 1985, p. 19.

Jans 1992 – Jans, *Over de grenzen van europees milieurecht*, Tjeenk Willink, Zwolle 1992.

Jans 1993a – Jans, Het belanghebbende-begrip in het licht van het europees recht, in Boxum et al. (eds), *Aantrekkelijke gedachten: beschouwingen over de algemene wet bestuursrecht*, Kluwer, Deventer 1993.

Jans 1993b – Jans, Legal Protection in Environmental Law, EELR 1993, p. 151.

Jans 1994 – Jans, Rechterlijke uitleg als implementatie-instrument van EG-richtlijnen: spanning tussen instrument en rechtszekerheid, in Hoogenboom and Damen (eds), *In de sfeer van administratief recht*, Lemma, Utrecht 1994.

Jarrass 1990 – Jarass, Voraussetzungen der innerstaatlichen Wirkung des EG-Rechts, NJW 1990, p. 2420.

Jarrass 1991a – Jarass, Richtlinienkonforme bzw. der EG-rechtskonformen Auslegung, EuR 1991, p. 211.

Jarrass 1991b – Jarass, Folgen der innerstaatlichen Wirkung von EWG-Richtlinien, NJW 1991. p. 2665

Jarass 1994 – Jarass, Haftung für die Verletzung von EU-Recht durch nationale Organe und Amtsträger, NJW 1994, p. 881.

Jeffreys 1991 – Jeffreys, The Role of Legislative Draftsmen in the UK in Making and Implementing EC Law, RegelMaat 1991, p. 39.

Kapteyn 1993 – Kapteyn, De organisatie van de rechtsbescherming van particulieren in de EG, NTB 1993, p. 38.

Kapteyn and VerLoren van Themaat 1990 – Kapteyn and VerLoren van Themaat, *Introduction to the Law of the European Communities*, Second Edition (edited by Gormley), Kluwer, Deventer 1990.

Kapteyn and VerLoren Van Themaat 1995 – Kapteyn and VerLoren van Themaat, *Inleiding in het recht van de Europese Gemeenschappen*, Fifth Edition (forthcoming), Kluwer, Deventer 1995.

Karl 1992 – Karl, Die Schadenersatzpflicht des Mitgliedstaaten bei Verletzungen des Gemeinschaftsrechts, RIW 1992, p. 440.

Karpenstein 1977 – Karpenstein, Zur Wiedergutmachung von Vertragsverstoßen der Mitgliedstaaten gegen Gemeinschaftsrecht, DVBl. 1977, p. 61.

Kellerman 1994 – Kelerman, The Quality of Community Legislation Drafting, in Curtin and Heukels (eds), *The Institutional Dynamics of European Integration. Liber Amicorum Henry G. Schermers*, Nijhoff, Dordrecht 1994.

Keus 1993 – Keus, Europees privaatrecht. Een bonte lappendeken, *Preadviezen voor de Vereniging voor Burgelijk Recht en de Nederlandse Vereniging voor Europees Recht*, Koninklijke Vermande, Lelystad 1993.

Klein 1988 – Klein, *Unmittelbare Geltung, Anwendbarkeit und Wirkung von Europäischen Gemeinschaftsrecht*, Vorträge, Reden und Berichte aus dem Europa Institut Nr. 119, Saarbrücken 1988.

Kooijmans 1967 – Kooijmans, De richtlijn van het Europese gemeenschapsrecht – karakter, functie en rechtsgevolg, SEW 1967, p. 122.

Kortenaar 1985 – Kortenaar, Een gemiste kans voor Europa, WFR 1985, p. 1272.

Kortmann 1991 – Kortmann, De vorm van implementatie van EEG-recht, RegelMaat 1991, p. 47.

Kovar 1978 – Kovar, Voies de droit ouvertes aux individus devant les instances nationales en cas de violation des normes et décisions du droit communautaire, in *Les recours des individus devant les instances nationales en cas de violation du droit européen*, Larcier, Bruxelles 1978.

Kovar 1981 – Kovar, L'intégrité de l'effet direct du droit communautaire selon la jurisprudence de la Cour de Justice de la Communauté, in Bieber, Bleckmann, Capotorti et al. (eds), *Das Europa der zweiten Generation (I). Gedächtnisschrift für Christoph Sasse*, Nomos, Baden-Baden 1981.

Kovar 1983 – Kovar, The relationship between Community law and national law, in *Thirty Years of Community Law*, Office for Official Publications of the European Communities, Luxemburg 1983.

Kovar 1987 – Kovar, Observations sur l'intensité normative des directives, in Capotorti, Ehlermann et al. (eds), *Du droit international au droit de l'intégration. Liber Amicorum Pierre Pescatore*, Nomos, Baden-Baden 1987.

Kovar 1988 – Kovar, L'invocabilité du droit communautaire devant les juridictions nationales, in *L'avocat et l'Europe des 12 et des 21*, Actes du XIIe congrès de l'Association française des centres de formation professionnelle du barreau, 1988.

Kovar 1992 – Kovar, Le Conseil d'Etat et le droit communautaire: des progrès mais peut mieux faire, Dalloz (Chronique) 1992, p. 207.

Kraemer 1992 – Kraemer, *Focus on European Environmental Law*, Sweet & Maxwell, London 1992.

Krislov, Ehlermann and Weiler 1986 – Krislov, Ehlermann and Weiler, The Political Organs and the Decision-making Process in the United States and the European Community, in Cappelletti, Seccombe and Weiler, *Integration Through Law*, Vol. 1: Methods, Tools and Institutions, Book 2, De Gruyter, Berlin/New York 1986.

Kutscher 1976 – Kutscher, Methods of Interpretation as Seen by a Judge at the Court of Justice, *Judicial and Academic Conference, 27-28 September 1976*, Luxemburg 1976.

De Lange 1991 – De Lange, *Publiekrechtelijke rechtsvinding*, Tjeenk Willink, Zwolle 1991.

Langenfeld 1991 – Langenfeld, Die dezentrale Kontrolle der Anwendung des europäisches Gemeinschaftsrechts im innerstaatlichen Rechtsraum – dargestelt am Beispiel der Richtlinie, in Siedentopf (ed), *Europäische Integration und nationalstaatliche Verwaltung*, Steiner, Stuttgart 1991.

Langenfeld 1992 – Langenfeld, Zur Direktwirkung von EG-Richtlinien, DöV 1992, p. 955.

Lasok and Bridge 1991 – Lasok and Bridge, *Law and Institutions of the European Communities*, Fifth Edition, Butterworths, London 1991.

Lauwaars 1973 – Lauwaars, *Lawfulness and Legal Force of Community Decisions*, Sijthoff, Leiden, 1973.

Lauwaars 1976 – Lauwaars, Comment on Case 41/74 *Van Duyn*, SEW 1976, p. 78.

Lauwaars 1978 – Lauwaars, Het voorbehoud voor de openbare orde als beperking van het vrije verkeer van personen in de EEG, SEW 1978, p. 329.

Lauwaars 1983 – Lauwaars, Implementation of Regulations by National Measures, LIEI 1983, p. 41.

Lauwaars 1991 – Lauwaars, Comment on Case C-213/89 *Factortame*, SEW 1991, p. 478.

Lauwaars 1993 – Lauwaars, "Voor elck wat wils" ofwel de vertraagde uitvoering van EEG-richtlijnen, FED 1993, p. 705.

Lauwaars and Maarleveld 1987 – Lauwaars and Maarleveld, *Harmonisatie van wetgeving in Europese organisaties*, Kluwer, Deventer 1987.

Lauwaars and Timmermans 1994 – Lauwaars and Timmermans, *Europees Gemeenschapsrecht in kort bestek*, Third Edition, Wolters-Noordhoff, Groningen 1994.

STAFFS UNIVERSITY LIBRARY

Leenen 1986 – Leenen, De derde richtlijn nader beschouwd, in Fase (ed), *Gelijke behandeling van man en vrouw in de sociale zekerheid*, Kluwer, Deventer, 1986.

Leitao 1981 – Leitao, L'effet direct des directives: une mythification?, RTDE 1981, p. 425.

Lenaerts 1992-1993 – Lenaerts, Rechtsbescherming en rechtsafdwinging: de functies van de rechter in het Europees Gemeenschapsrecht, RW 1992-1993, p. 1105.

Lenz 1990 – Lenz, Entwicklung und unmittelbare Geltung des Gemeinschaftsrechts, DVBl 1990, p. 908.

Lewis 1992 – Lewis, *Judicial Remedies in Public Law*, Sweet & Maxwell, London 1992.

Lewis and Moore 1993 – Lewis and Moore, Duties, Directives and Damages in European Community Law, Public Law 1993, p. 151.

The Liability of the State 1981 – *The Liability of the State*, Proceedings of the Ninth Colloquy on European Law, Madrid 1979, Council of Europe, Strasbourg 1981.

Louis 1976 – Louis, L'effet direct des directives, in *Mélanges en hommage au Professeur Jean Baugniet*, Bruxelles 1976.

Louis 1993 – Louis, Vandersanden, Waelbroeck and Waelbroeck, *Commentaire Megrèt*, Vol. 10, La Cour de justice. Les actes des institutions, Second Edition, Editions de l'Université de Bruxelles, Bruxelles 1993.

Lutter 1992 – Lutter, Die Auslegung angeglichenen Rechts, JZ 1992, p. 593.

MacCormick 1977 – MacCormick, Rights in Legislation, in Hacker and Raz (eds), *Law, Morality and Society: Essays in Honour of H.L.A. Hart*, Clarendon Press, Oxford 1977.

MacCormick 1982 – MacCormick, Rights, Claims and Remedies, Law and Philosophy 1982, p. 337.

MacCormick and Summers 1991 – MacCormick and Summers (eds), *Interpreting Statutes*, Darthmouth, Aldershot-Brookfield 1991.

Manin 1990 – Manin, L'invocabilité des directives: Quelques interrogations, RTDE 1990, p. 669.

Macrory 1992 – Macrory, The Enforcement of Community Environmental Laws: Some Critical Issues, CMLRev. 1992, p. 347.

Mortelmans 1991 – Mortelmans, Comment on Case C-143/88 *Zuckerfabrik Süderdithmarschen*, SEW 1991, p. 670.

Maresceau 1978 – Maresceau, *De directe werking van het Europese Gemeenschapsrecht*, Kluwer, Antwerpen, 1978.

Maresceau 1980a – Maresceau, De directe werking in het Europese gemeenschapsrecht, RBDI 1980, p. 265.

Maresceau 1980b – Maresceau, Het verbindend karakter van richtlijnen volgens de rechtspraak van het Hof van Justitie, SEW 1980, p. 655.

Marsh 1973 – Marsh, *Interpretation in a National and International Context*, UGA, Heule, Bruxelles, Namur 1973.

Mead 1991 – Mead, The Obligation to Apply European Law: Is Duke Dead?, ELR 1991, p. 490.

Mertens de Wilmars 1969 – Mertens de Wilmars, De directe werking van het Europese recht, SEW 1969, p. 62.

Mertens de Wilmars 1981 – Mertens de Wilmars, L'efficacité des différentes techniques nationales de protection juridique contre les violations du droit communautaire par les autorités nationales et les particuliers, CDE 1981, p. 377.

Mertens de Wilmars 1991 – Mertens de Wilmars, Réflexion sur le système d'articulation du droit communautaire et du droit national, in *L'Europe et le droit. Mélanges en hommage à Jean Boulouis*, Dalloz, Paris 1991.

Millarg 1977 – Millarg, Keine Staatshaftung für gemeinschaftswidrige Gesetzgebung?, ZRP 1977, p. 224.

Monaco 1987 – Monaco, Problèmes des directives communautaires dans l'ordre juridique italien, in Capotorti, Ehlermann et al. (eds), *Du droit international au droit de l'integration. Liber Amicorum Pierre Pescatore*, Nomos, Baden-Baden 1987.

Moore 1993 – Moore, Compensaton for discrimination?, ELR 1993, p. 533.

Moreau 1991 – Moreau, L'influence de développement de la construction européenne sur le droit français de la responsabilité de la puissance publique, in *L'Europe et le droit. Mélanges en hommage à Jean Boulouis*, Dalloz, Paris 1991.

Morris 1989 – Morris, The Direct Effect of Directives – Some Recent Developments in the European Court, JBL 1989, p. 233 and p. 309.

Nessler 1993 – Nessler, Richterrecht wandelt EG-Richtlinien, RIW 1993, p. 206.

Nettesheim 1992 – Nettesheim, Gemeinschaftsrechtliche Vorgaben für das deutsche Staatshaftungsrecht, DöV 1992, p. 999.

Nicolaysen 1984 – Nicolaysen, Richtlinienwirkung und Gleichbehandlung von Männer und Frauen beim Zugang zum Beruf, EuR 1984, p. 380.

Nicolaysen 1985 – Nicolaysen, Vertragsverletzung durch mitgliedstaatliche Gerichte, EuR 1985, p. 368.

Nicolaysen 1986 – Nicolaysen, Keine horizontale Wirkung von Richtlinien-Bestimmungen, EuR. 1986, p. 370.

Nielsen 1992 – Nielsen, Comment on Case C-177/88 *Dekker*, CMLRev. 1992, p. 160.

Oldenbourg 1984 – Oldenbourg, *Die unmittelbare Wirkung von EG-richtlinien im innerstaatlichen Bereich*, Florentz, München 1984.

Oldenkop 1972 – Oldenkop, Die Richtlinien der Europäischen Wirtschaftsgemeinschaft, JöR 1972, p. 55.

Oliver 1987 – Oliver, Enforcing Community rights in the English Courts, MLR 1987, p. 881.

Oliver 1992 – Oliver, Le droit communautaire et les voies de recours nationales, CDE 1992, p. 348.

Ophüls 1966 – Ophüls, Les règlements et les directives dans les Traités de Rome, CDE 1966, p. 3.

Ossenbühl 1992 – Ossenbühl, Der gemeinschaftsrechtliche Staatshaftungsanspruch, DVBl. 1992, p. 993.

Parker 1992 – Parker, Comment on Joined Cases C-6/90 and C-9/90 *Francovich*, LQR 1992, p. 184.

Perrott 1973 – Perrott, The Logic of Fundamental Rights, in Bridge et al. (eds), *Fundamental Rights*, Sweet & Maxwell, London 1973.

Pescatore 1971 – Pescatore, *L'ordre juridique des Communautés Européennes, Etude des sources du droit communautaire*, Les presses universitaires de Liège, Liège 1971.

Pescatore 1972 – Pescatore, Responsabilité des Etats membres en cas de manquement aux règles communautaires, Il Foro Padano 1972, p. 9.

Pescatore 1980 – Pescatore, L'effet des directives communautaires: une tentative de démythification, Dalloz (Chronique) 1980, p. 171.

Pescatore 1983 – Pescatore, The Doctrine of "Direct Effect": an Infant Disease of Community Law, ELR 1983, p. 155.

Pieper 1990 – Pieper, Die Direktwirkung von Richtlinien de Europäischen Gemeinschaft – Zum Stand der Entwicklung, DVBl. 1990, p. 684.

Plaza Martin 1994 – Plaza Martin, Furthering the Effectiveness of EC Directives and the Judicial Protection of Individual Rights Thereunder, ICLQ 1994, p. 26.

Prechal 1990 – Prechal, Remedies After Marshall, CMLRev. 1990, p. 451.

Prechal 1991 – Prechal, Richtlijnconforme uitleg: Alice in Wonderland, WFR 1991, p. 1596.

Prechal 1991 – Prechal, Comment on Case C-177/88 *Dekker*, SEW 1991, p. 665.

Prechal 1992a – Prechal, Comment on Joined Cases C-6/90 and C-9/90 *Francovich*, Aktualiteitenkatern Nemesis 1992, p. 10.

Prechal 1992b – Prechal, Comment on Case C-374/86 *Commission v. Belgium*, CMLRev. 1992, p. 371.

Prechal 1993 – Prechal, Comment on Joined Cases C-87/90, C-88/90 and C-89/90 *Verholen*, SEW 1993, p. 166.

Prechal and Burrows 1990 – Prechal and Burrows, *Gender Discrimination Law of the European Community*, Dartmouth, Aldershot 1990.

Prieß 1993 – Prieß, Die haftung der EG-Mitgliedstaaten bei Verstößen gegen das Gemeinschaftsrecht, NVwZ 1993, p. 118.

Ress 1985 – Ress, Die Kontrole internationaler Verträge und der Akte der Europäischen Gemeinschaften durch das Bundesverfassungsgericht, in Koening (ed), *Die Kontrolle der Verfassungsmäßigkeit in Frankreich und in der Bundesrepublik Deutschland*, Carl Heymann, Köln 1985.

Ress 1993 – Ress, Die Direktwirkung von Richtlinien: Der Wandel von der prozessrechtlichen zur materielrechtlichen Konzeption, in Leipold, Lüke, Yoshino (eds), *Gedächtnisschrift für Peter Ahrens*, Beck, München 1993.

Richter 1988 – Richter, Die unmittelbare Wirkung von EG-Richtlinien zu lasten einzelner, EuR 1988, p. 394.

De Ripaisel-Landy and Gérard 1976 – De Ripaisel-Landy and Gérard, La notion juridique de la directive utilisée comme instrument de raprochement des législations dans la CEE, in *Les instruments de raprochement des législations dans la Communauté Economique Européenne*, Editions de l'Université de Bruxelles, Bruxelles 1976.

Rodière 1991 – Rodière, Sur les effets directifs du droit (social) communautaire, RTDE 1991, p. 565.

Ross 1993 – Ross, Beyond Francovich, MLR 1993, p. 55.

Roth 1991 – Roth, The Application of Community Law in West Germany: 1980-1990, CMLRev. 1991, p. 137.

Salmond 1966 – Salmond on Jurisprudence, Twelfth Edition (by Fitzgerald), Sweet & Maxwell, London 1966.

Schermers and Waelbroeck 1992 – Schermers and Waelbroeck, *Judicial Protection in the European Communities*, Kluwer, Deventer 1992.

Scherzberg 1991 – Scherzberg, Verordnung – Richtlinie – Entscheidung, zum System der Handlungsformen im Gemeinschaftsrecht, in Siedentopf (ed), *Europäische Integration und nationalstaatliche Verwaltung*, Steiner, Stuttgart 1991.

Schilling 1988 – Schilling, Zur Wirkung von EG-Richtlinien. Versuch einer völkerrechtlichen Betrachtung, ZaoRV 1988, p. 637.

Schlemmer-Schulte and Ukrow 1992 – Schlemer-Schulte and Ukrow, Haftung des Staates gegenüber dem Marktburger für gemeinschaftsrechtswidriges Verhalten, EuR 1992, p. 82.

Schockweiler 1990 – Schockweiler, Le régime de la responsabilité extra-contractuelle du fait d'actes juridiques dans la Communauté européenne, RTDE 1990, p. 27.

Schockweiler 1991 – Schockweiler, L'emprise du droit communautaire sur les pouvoirs du juge national, Bulletin du Cercle Francois Laurent 1991/III, p. 51.

Schockweiler 1992 – Schockweiler, La responsabilité de l'autorité nationale en cas de violation du droit communautaire, RTDE 1992, p. 27.

Schockweiler 1993a – Schockweiler, *Die Haftung der Mitgliedstaaten bei vertragswidrigem Verhalten*, Zentrum für Europäisches Wirtschaftsrecht, Vorträge und Berichte Nr. 24, Bonn 1993.

Schockweiler 1993b – Schockweiler, Die Haftung der EG-Mitgliedstaaten gegenüber dem einzelnen bei Verletzung des Gemeinschaftsrechts, EuR 1993, p. 107.

Schockweiler 1993c – Schockweiler, Effets des directives non transposées en droit national à l'égard des particuliers, in Perez Gonzalez et al. (eds), *Hacia un nuevo orden internacional y europeo. Estudios en homenaje al profesor Don Manuel Díez de Velasco*, Tecnos, Madrid 1993.

Schwarz 1991 – Schwarz, Artikel 235 [Subsidiäre Rechtsetzungsbefugnis], in Von der Groeben, Thiesing, Ehlerman, *Kommentar zum EWG-Vertrag*, Fourth Edition, Vol. IV, Nomos, Baden-Baden 1991.

Seidel 1983 – Seidel, *Direktwirkung von Richtlinien*, Vorträge, Reden und Berichte aus dem Europa-Institut, nr. 14, Saarbrücken 1983.

Shaw 1991 – Shaw, Pregnancy Discrimination in Sex Discrimination, ELR 1991, p. 313-320.

Siedentopf and Ziller 1988 – Siedentopf and Ziller (eds), *Making the European Policies Work: the Implementation of Community Legislation in the Member States*, (IEPA), Sage, London 1988.

Simon 1991 – Simon, Les exigences de la primauté du droit communautaire: continuité ou métamorphoses?, in *L'Europe et le droit. Mélanges en hommage à Jean Boulouis*, Dalloz, Paris 1991.

Simon 1992 – Simon, Le Conseil d'Etat et les directives communautaires: du gallicisme à l'orthodoxie?, RTDE 1992, p. 265.

Simon 1993 – Simon, Droit communautaire et responsabilité de la puissance publique. Glissements progressifs ou révolution tranquille?, AJDA 1993, p. 235.

Simon and Barav 1987 – Simon and Barav, La responsabilité de l'administration nationale en cas de violation du droit communautaire, RMC 1987, p. 165.

Simon and Barav 1990 – Simon and Barav, Le droit communautaire et la suspension provisoire des mesures nationales, RMC 1990, p. 591.

Slynn 1993 – Slynn, Sanctions in Community Law: Overview, in Verwilghen (ed), *Access to Equality between Men and Women in the European Community*, Presses Universitaires de Louvain, Louvain-la-Neuve 1993.

Smit and Herzog – Smit and Herzog, *The Law of the European Economic Community*, Vol. 5, Bender, New York (loose-leaf, version 1993).

De Smith and Brazier 1989 – De Smith and Brazier, *Consitutional Law and Administrative Law*, Penguin Books, London 1989.

Snyder 1993 – Snyder, The Effectiveness of European Community Law: Institutions, Processes, Tools and Techniques, MLR 1993, p. 19.

Spetzler 1991 – Spetzler, Die richtlinienkonforme Auslegung als vorrangige Methode steuerjuristische Hermeneutik, RIW 1991, p. 579.

Steiner 1986 – Steiner, How to Make the Action Suit the Case, ELR 1986, p. 102.

Steiner 1993 – Steiner, From Direct Effects to Francovich: Shifting Means of Enforcement of Community Law, ELR 1993, p. 3.

Steyger 1991 – Steyger, De directe toepassing van EG-Richtlijnen door anderen dan de staat, RegelMaat 1991, p. 10.

Stuyck and Wytinck 1991 – Stuyck and Wytinck, Comment on case C-106/89 *Marleasing*, CMLRev. 1991, p. 205.

Szyszczak 1990 – Szyszczak, Sovereignty: Crisis, Compliance, Confusion, Complacency?, ELR 1990, p. 480.

Szyszczak 1992a – Szyszczak, Europaen Community Law: New Remedies, New Directions?, MLR 1992, p. 690.

Szyszczak 1992b – Szyszczak, Comment on Case C-208/90 *Emmott*, CMLRev 1992, p. 604.

Tanney 1992 – Tanney, Comment on *Webb* v. *EMO Air Cargo (UK), Ltd.* (Court of Appeal of England and Wales), CMLRev. 1992, p. 1021.

Taylor 1985 – Taylor, Damages as a Remedy for the Breach of Provisions of the EEC Treaty Having Direct Effect, in Jagenburg et al. (eds), *Festschrift für Walter Oppenhof*, München 1985, p. 475.

Temple Lang 1990 – Temple Lang, Community Constitutional Law: Article 5 EEC Treaty, CMLRev. 1990, p. 645.

Temple Lang 1991 – Temple Lang, The Sphere in which Member States are Obliged to Comply with the General Principles of Law and Community Fundamental Rights Principles, LIEI 1991/2, p. 23.

Temple Lang 1992-1993 – Temple Lang, New Legal Effects Resulting from the Failure of States to Fulfill Obligations under European Community Law: the Francovich Judgment, Fordham International Law Journal 1992-1993, p. 1.

Timmermans 1971 – Timmermans, De harmonisatie van nationale voorschriften op het gebied van het vennootschapsrecht, SEW 1971, p. 608.

Timmermans 1973 – Timmermans, *De administratieve rechter en de beoordelings-vrijheden van bestuursorganen*, Acco, Leuven 1973.

Timmermans 1979 – Timmermans, Directives: their Effect within the National Legal Systems, CMLRev. 1979, p. 533.

Timmermans 1988 – Timmermans, Comment on Case 80/86 *Kolpinghuis*, AA 1988, p. 330.

Timmermans 1992 – Timmermans, Comment on Case C-106/89 *Marleasing*, SEW 1992, p. 816.

Toth 1988 – Toth, The Concepts of Damage and Causality as Elements of Non-Contractual Liability, in Schermers, Heukels and Mead (eds), *Non-Contractual Liability of the European Community*, Nijhoff, Dordrecht, 1988.

Toth 1990 – Toth, Comment on case C-213/89 *Factortame*, CMLRev. 1990, p. 573.

Toth 1994 – Toth, A legal Analysis of Subsidiarity, in O'Keeffe and Twomey (eds), *Legal Issues of the Maastricht Treaty*, Chancery, London 1994.

Triantafyllou 1992 – Triantafyllou, Haftung der Mitgliedstaaten fur Nichtumsetzung von EG-Recht; zur Europäisierung des Staatshaftungsrecht, DöV 1992, p. 564.

Usher 1979 – Usher, The Direct Effect of Directives, ELR 1979, p. 268.

Usher 1980 – Usher, Direct Effect of Directives: Dotting the i's, ELR 1980, p. 470.

Waldron 1984 – Waldron, Introduction, in Waldron (ed), *Theories of Rights*, Oxford University Press, Oxford 1984.

Ward 1990 – Ward, Government Liability in the United Kingdom for Breach of Individual Rights in European Community Law, Anglo-Am L.Rev. 1990, p. 1.

Ward 1993 – Ward, The Right to a Effective Remedy in European Community Law and Environmental Protection, Journal of environmental law 1993, p. 221.

Wattel 1992 – Wattel, Het spectaculaire trio Emmott, Francovich & Bonifaci, WFR 1992, p. 626.

Weymüller 1991 – Weymüller, Der Anwendungsvorrang von EG-Richtlinien – Eine Diskussion ohne Ende?, RIW 1991, p. 501.

White 1984 – White, *Rights*, Clarendon Press, Oxford 1984.

White 1988 – White, State Responsibility in the Context of European Community Law, in Bin Cheng and Brown (eds), *Contemporary Problems of International Law: Essays in Honour of Georg Schwarzenberger on his Eightieth Birthday*, Stevens & Sons, London 1988.

Widdershoven and De Lange 1994 – Widdershoven and De Lange, *Tendencies towards European Standards in National Administrative Law, Dutch Report*, Utrecht / Amsterdam 1994.

Winter 1972 – Winter, Direct Applicability and Direct Effect. Two Distinct and Different Concepts in Community Law, CMLRev. 1972, p. 425.

Winter 1991a – Winter, Gevolgen van het Gemeenschapsrecht voor de lagere overheden in Nederland, RegelMaat 1991, p. 52.

Winter 1991b – Winter, Direktwirkung von EG-Richtlinien, DVBl 1991, p. 657.

Winter 1991c – Winter, Rechtschutz gegen Behörden, die Umweltrichtlinien der EG nicht beachten, NuR 1991, p. 453.

De Witte 1984 – De Witte, Retour à Costa. La primauté du droit communautaire à la lumière du droit international, RTDE 1984, p. 425.

Wyatt 1983 – Wyatt, The Direct Effect of Community Social Law -Not Forgetting Directives, ELR 1983, p. 241.

Wyatt 1989 – Wyatt, Enforcing EEC Social Rights in the United Kingdom, ILJ 1989, p. 197.

Wyatt and Dashwood 1993 – Wyatt and Dashwood, *European Community Law*, Third Edition, Sweet & Maxwell, London 1993.

Zeidler 1988 – Zeidler, Die Verfassungsrechtsprechung im Rahmen der Staatlichen Funktionen, Bundesrepublik Deutschland, EuGRZ 1988, p. 207.

Zuleeg 1993 – Zuleeg, Umweltschutz in der rechtsprechung des Europäischen Gerichtshofs, NJW 1993, p. 31.

Index

03354006

STAFFS UNIVERSITY LIBRARY